A BIOGRAPHICAL REGISTER OF THE FRANCISCANS IN THE CUSTODY OF YORK c.1229–1539

The officers of the Yorkshire Archaeological and Historical Society would like to thank the Trustees of the Elisabeth Exwood Memorial Trust for a grant towards this publication and their continuing support for the Record Series

THE YORKSHIRE
ARCHAEOLOGICAL AND HISTORICAL SOCIETY
FOUNDED 1863 *INCORPORATED* 1893

RECORD SERIES
VOLUME CLXV
FOR THE YEAR 2017

A BIOGRAPHICAL REGISTER OF THE FRANCISCANS IN THE CUSTODY OF YORK c.1229–1539

EDITED BY
MICHEL J.P. ROBSON

YORKSHIRE ARCHAEOLOGICAL AND HISTORICAL SOCIETY

THE BOYDELL PRESS

2019

First Published 2019

A publication of the Yorkshire Archaeological and Historical Society
in association with The Boydell Press
an imprint of Boydell & Brewer Ltd
PO Box 9, Woodbridge, Suffolk IP12 3DF, UK
and of Boydell & Brewer Inc.
668 Mt. Hope Avenue, Rochester, NY 14620-2731, USA
website: www.boydellandbrewer.com

ISBN 978-0-993238-39-0

A CIP catalogue record for this book is available
from the British Library

This publication is printed on acid-free paper

MIX
Paper from
responsible sources
FSC® C013056

Printed and bound in Great Britain by TJ International Ltd, Padstow, Cornwall

Contents

Acknowledgements

The seeds of this volume were sown when the Rt. Revd. John R.H. Moorman, bishop of Ripon (1959–75), the distinguished historian of the world of St Francis of Assisi and his followers, bequeathed his biographical register to the Franciscan Study Centre, Canterbury, where I was then lecturing.[1] Following the death of the scholarly prelate, I drove from Canterbury to Durham on a beautifully sunny Sunday morning in June 1990 to collect four trays of paper files on individual friars. The task of transcribing them began in earnest that summer in Canterbury, a labour that was brought to completion at St Edmund's College, Cambridge, about five years later. In its original form the material stored on the files was not yet ready for publication. It rapidly became clear that a great deal of work would be required to supply the bibliographical framework for the texts and to weed out a small number of duplicate entries. In the intervening quarter of a century editorial work has been carried out and additional names have been added, amounting to more than 9,600 entries. My focus on friars in the medieval custody of York was further stimulated by a lecture which I gave to the Church History seminar in the University of Cambridge on 4 December 1996 and a lecture in the Library of Lincoln cathedral on 15 September 2006 at the invitation of Dr Nicholas Bennett. This research was boosted by an Honorary Visiting Fellowship in the Borthwick Institute of Historical Research at the University of York for 1999–2000, an appointment which enabled me to explore the probate registers of the diocese and to amass materials for a series of articles on the friars' activities within the custody.

The development of my interest in the friars of the custody owes much to the kindness and erudition of the three exceptional scholars active in northern universities whom I shall name in alphabetical order. First, it was a privilege to know and consult Professor Barrie R. Dobson (†2013), the kindly doyen of historians of medieval York, who was unfailingly gracious and positive about my interests. Secondly, Professor David Smith was unfailingly generous in providing palaeographical assistance on my regular visits to the Borthwick Institute, then at Peasholme Green, York; he continues to supply information on friars from his research into the plea rolls at the National Archives; this material constitutes another significant source of friars' names and details. Thirdly, Professor John A. Watt, a scholar rightly proud of his Yorkshire roots, generously read drafts of my earlier research, proffering much sound and wholesome advice. Support and encouragement of a different sort were provided by my dear mother, Josephine (†2007).

A special debt of gratitude is owed to the staff of the Borthwick Institute and the Lincolnshire Archives Office for enabling me to consult episcopal and probate registers. Members of staff of the reading room at the National Archives, the British Library, Lambeth Palace Library, Cambridge University Library and the Bodleian Library at Oxford were continually helpful in permitting me to examine manuscripts

1 The Franciscan Study Centre at Giles Lane was built by the English provinces of the Friars Minor and the Friars Minor Conventual. I was among the first cohort of students admitted in the autumn of 1973. The formal opening took place on 10 September 1974. Bishop Moorman gave one of the lectures to commemorate the 750th anniversary of the friars' arrival in Canterbury. In recent years the institution suffered from depleted levels of staffing and dwindling registration of students, necessitating its closure in the summer of 2017.

and *incunabula*. Christopher C. Webb, the Director of the Borthwick Institute for Archives at the University of York and the Editor of the Yorkshire Archaeological Society, Record Series, has been a source of practical assistance throughout the gestation of this volume. Information about individual friars came from Dr Nicholas Bennett, Professor Christopher Brooke (†2015), Dr Joan Greatrex, Dr Bronach Kane, Dr Peter Murray Jones, Professor Hugh Lawrence (†2018), Professor Donald Logan, Dr John Robinson, Professor Bert Roest, Dr Jens Röhrkasten, Dr Patrick Zutshi and Dr Béatrice Sicouri, who prepared Michael Dawnay's family tree and the pie chart. My thanks to the copy-editor, Sarah Pearsall, for her expertise and valuable contributions to the preparation of the book, and also to Rebecca Cribb at Boydell & Brewer for her assistance.

The scene of St Francis preaching to the birds first caught my eye as a small boy at St Joseph's School, Pudsey, some six decades ago. In later years that interest matured and led me among the Friars Minor Conventual for four decades, prompting me to explore the impact of the saint's followers upon medieval England in general and the custody of York in particular.

Abbreviations

a.	Ordination as an acolyte
Acta Bonien.	*Acta Franciscana e Tabulariis Boniensibus deprompta*, ed. B. Giordani, AF, VII (Quaracchi, Florence, 1927)
Acta, Wells	*The Acta of Hugh of Wells bishop of Lincoln 1209–1235*, ed. D.M. Smith, LRS, LXXXVIII (2000)
AF	Analecta Franciscana
AFH	*Archivum Franciscanum Historicum*
AM	*Annales Monastici*, ed. H.R. Luard, 5 vols, RS, XXXVI (London, 1864–69)
Bale, *Index*	*John Bales's Index of British and Other Writers, Anecdota Oxoniensia* classical series, IX, ed. R.L. Poole and M. Bateson. Reprinted with an introduction by C. Brett and J.P. Carley (Oxford, 1902, Woodbridge, 1990)
Bartholomew of Pisa	*De conformitate vitae Beati Francisci ad vitam Domini Iesu auctore Fr. Bartholomaeo de Pisa edita a patribus Collegii S. Bonaventurae*, AF, IV (Quaracchi, Florence, 1906)
Bekynton's Correspondence	*Memorials of the reign of King Henry VI. Official correspondence of Thomas Bekynton, secretary to King Henry VI, and bishop of Bath and Wells*, ed. G. Williams, 2 vols, RS, LVI (1872)
BF	*Bullarium Franciscanum*, including *Bullarii Franciscani epitome*, ed. J.H. Sbaraleae and C. Eubel, 8 vols (Rome, 1759–1908)
BF, ns	*Bullarium Franciscanum, nova series*, ed. U. Hüntemann, J.M. Pou Y Marti and C. Cenci, 4 vols (Quaracchi, Florence and Grottaferrata, Rome, 1929–90)
BFAMA	Bibliotheca Franciscana Ascetica medii Aevi cura patrum Collegii Sancti Bonaventurae, Florence, Grottaferrata and Rome
BFSMA	Bibliotheca Franciscana Scholastica medii Aevi cura patrum Collegii Sancti Bonaventurae, Florence, Grottaferrata and Rome
BIA	Borthwick Institute Archives at the University of York
BL	British Library, London
Bonaventurae Opera Omnia	*Doctoris Seraphici S. Bonaventurae opera omnia ed. studio et cura PP. Collegii a S. Bonaventura ad plurimos codices mss. emendata, anecdotis aucta, prolegomenis scholiis notisque illustrata*, 11 vols (Quaracchi, Florence, 1882–1902)
BRUC	A.B. Emden, *A Biographical Register of the University of Cambridge to A.D. 1500* (Cambridge, 1963)
BRUO	A.B. Emden, *A Biographical Register of the University of Oxford to A.D. 1500*, 3 vols (Oxford, 1957–59)
BRUO, 1501–40	A.B. Emden, *A Biographical Register of the University of Oxford, A.D. 1501 to 1540* (Oxford, 1974)
BSFS	British Society of Franciscan Studies

BTS	Borthwick Texts and Studies
BTC	Borthwick Texts and Calendars
Cal. Inquisitions	*Calendar of Inquisitions post mortem and other analogous documents*, from 1904
Cart. St Leonard	*The Cartulary of St Leonard's Hospital, York Rawlinson Volume*, ed. David X. Carpenter, 2 vols, YAS, RS, CLXIII, Borthwick Texts and Studies, XLII (2015)
CBMLC	Corpus of British Medieval Library Catalogues
CCCM	Corpus Christianorum Continuatio mediaevalis
CCR	*Calendar of the Close Rolls preserved in the Public Record Office, 1272–1509* (London, from 1902)
Cenci, Documenta Vaticana	C. Cenci, '*Documenta Vaticana ad Franciscales spectantia ann. 1385–1492*', *AFH*, Part 1, XC (1997), pp. 85–135; Part 2, XCI (1998), pp. 65–131; Part 3, XCII (1999), pp. 143–98; Part 4, XCIII (2000), pp. 217–59; Part 5, XCIV (2001), pp. 85–145; Part 6, XCV (2002), pp. 351–97; Part 7, XCVI (2003), pp. 85–127; Part 8, XCVII (2004), pp. 133–57; Part 9, XCVII (2004), pp. 301–46
CF	*Collectanea Franciscana*
CFR	*Calendar of Fine Rolls, 1272–1509* (London, 1911–62)
Chantries, Guilds, Hospitals	*The Certificates of the Commissioners appointed to survey the Chantries, Guilds, Hospitals, etc. in the county of York*, ed. W. Page, 2 vols, SS, XCI, XCII (1894–95)
CLR	*Calendar of the Liberate Rolls preserved in the Public Record Office, 1216–60* (London, from 1916)
Constit. Fratrum Minorum, saec. XIII	*Constitutiones Generales Ordinis Fratrum Minorum, I (Saeculum XIII)*, ed. C. Cenci and R.G. Mailleux, AF, XIII, nova series, documenta et studia, I (Grottaferrata, Rome, 2007)
Constit. Fratrum Minorum, saec. XIV	*Constitutiones Generales Ordinis Fratrum Minorum, II (Saeculum XIV/1)*, ed. C. Cenci and R.G. Mailleux, AF, XVII, nova series, documenta et studia, V (Grottaferrata, Rome, 2010)
Convocation, York	*Records of Convocation, XIII: York, 1313–1461*, ed. G. Bray (Woodbridge, 2006)
Corpus Christi Guild	*The register of the guild of Corpus Christi in the city of York; with an appendix of illustrative documents, containing some account of the Hospital of St. Thomas of Canterbury, without Micklegate-bar, in the suburbs of the city*, ed. R.H. Skaife, SS, LVII (1872)
CPL	*Calendar of Entries in the Papal Registers relating to Great Britain and Ireland, 1198–1521*, ed. W.H. Bliss, C. Johnson, J.A. Tremlow et al., 20 vols (London, Dublin, 1901–2005)
CPR	*Calendar of the Patent Rolls preserved in the Public Record Office, 1216–1582* (London, from 1893)
Cross and Vickers, *MFN*	M.C. Cross and N. Vickers, *Monks, Friars and Nuns in Sixteenth Century Yorkshire*, YAS, RS, CL (1995)
CS	Camden Society
CUL, EDR	Cambridge University Library, Ely Diocesan Registry
CYS	The Canterbury and York Society

d.	Ordination to the diaconate
Davis, *London Clergy*	*Clergy in London in the late Middle Ages: a register of clergy ordained in the diocese of London, based on episcopal ordination lists, 1361–1539*, CD-ROM (London, 2000)
Eccleston	*Fratris Thomae vulgo dicti de Eccleston Tractatus de adventu Fratrum Minorum in Angliam*, ed. A.G. Little (Manchester, 1951)
EEA	*English Episcopal Acta*
EHR	*English Historical Review*
Faculty Office Registers 1534–1549	D.S. Chambers, *Faculty Office Registers 1534–1549: A Calendar of the first two Registers of the Archbishop of Canterbury's Faculty Office edited with an Introduction and Index* (Oxford, 1966)
Fasti Eboracenses	*Fasti Eboracenses. Lives of the archbishops of York*, ed. W.H. Dixon and J. Raine (London, 1863)
FF	*Fontes Francescani*, ed. E. Menestò, S. Brufani, G. Cremascoli, E. Paoli, L. Pellegrini and S. da Campagnola, Collana diretta da Enrico Menestò, Testi, II (Assisi, 1995)
Friars' Libraries	*The Friars' Libraries*, ed. K.W. Humphreys, CBMLC, I (London, 1990)
FS	*Franciscan Studies*, new series
GFC	J.R.H. Moorman, *The Grey Friars in Cambridge 1225–1538* (Cambridge, 1952)
GFCant	C. Cotton, *The Grey Friars of Canterbury 1224 to 1538*, BSFS, Extra Series, II (Manchester, 1924)
GFL	C.L. Kingsford, *The Grey Friars of London: their history with the register of their convent and an appendix of documents*, BSFS, VI (Aberdeen, 1915)
GFO	A.G. Little, *The Grey Friars in Oxford*, OHS, XX (Oxford, 1892)
GHL	the Guild Hall Library, London
Grosseteste as bishop of Lincoln	*Robert Grosseteste as Bishop of Lincoln: The Episcopal Rolls, 1235–1253*, ed. P. Hoskin (Woodbridge, 2015)
Heads, ii and iii	*The Heads of Religious Houses: England and Wales (1216–1540)*, ed. D.M. Smith and V.C.M. London, 2 vols (London, 2001–08)
Hierarchia catholica	*Hierarchia catholica medii et recentioris aevi: sive Summorum pontificum, S.R.E. cardinalium, ecclesiarum antistitum series: e documentis tabularii praesertim Vaticani collecta, digesta*, ed. C. Eubel et alii, 8 vols (Regensburg/Padua, 1913–78)
Historical Papers and Letters	*Historical Papers and Letters from the Northern Registers*, ed. J. Raine, RS, LXI (London, 1873)
Jean XXII, Lettres Communes	*Jean XXII (1316–1334) Lettres Communes: analysées d'après les registres dits d'Avignon et du Vatican*, ed. G. Mollat, Bibliothéque des Écoles Françaises d'Athènes et de Rome, 3e serie, 16 vols (Paris, 1904–46)
Jeayes, *White Vellum Book*	I.H. Jeayes, *Description of Documents contained in the White Vellum Book of the Scarborough Corporation* (Scarborough, 1914)

JEH	*Journal of Ecclesiastical History*
John Pecham, Letters	*Registrum epistolarum fratris Johannis Peckham archiepiscicopi Cantuariensis*, ed. C.T. Martin, 3 vols, RS, LXXVII (London, 1882–85)
LAO	Lincolnshire Archives Office, Lincoln
Leland, Itinerary	*The Itinerary of John Leland in or about the years 1535–1543*, ed, L. Toulmin-Smith, 5 vols (London, 1964)
Leland, De viris illustribus	*John Leland, De viris illustribus, On Famous Men*, ed. J.P. Carley with the assistance of C. Brett, PIMS, Studies and Texts, CLXXII (Toronto, 2010)
Le Neve, FEA, Lincoln	*John Le Neve, Fasti Ecclesiae Anglicanae 1066–1300, III. Lincoln*, ed. D.E. Greenway (London, 1977)
Le Neve, FEA, York	*John Le Neve, Fasti Ecclesiae Anglicanae 1066–1300, VI. York*, ed. D.E. Greenway (London, 1999)
Liber Albus, Worcester	*The Liber Albus of the priory of Worcester, parts 1 and 2, Priors John de Wyke, 1301–1317, and Wulfstan de Bransford, 1317–1339, folios 1 to 162. A short abstract of all the documents, with indices to the original*, ed. J.M. Wilson, WHS, XXXV (1919)
Libraries of Augustinian Canons	*The Libraries of the Augustinian Canons*, ed. T. Webber and A.G. Watson, CBMLC, VI (London, 1998)
Library of St Augustine's Abbey	*St Augustine's Abbey, Canterbury*, ed. B.C. Barker-Benfield, 3 vols, CBMLC, XIII (London, 2008)
Lincoln Wills, 1271–1532	*Lincoln Wills, A.D. 1271 to 1532*, ed. C.W. Foster, 3 vols, LRS, V, X, XXIV (1914–30)
Lincoln Wills, 1532–1534	*Lincoln Wills, 1532–1534*, ed. D. Hickman, LRS, LXXXIX (2001)
Little, 'The first 100 years'	Andrew G. Little, 'The first hundred years of the Franciscan School at Oxford', in *St Francis of Assisi: Essays in Commemoration 1226–1926* (London, 1926), pp. 165–90
LPFD	*Letters and Papers, foreign and domestic, of the reign of Henry VIII*, ed. J.S. Brewer, 23 vols, in 38 (London, 1862–1932)
LPL	Lambeth Palace Library
LRO	Lichfield Record Office, Lichfield
LRS	Lincolnshire Record Society
Materials, Ireland	Fitzmaurice, E.B. and A.G., *Materials for the history of the Franciscan province of Ireland A.D. 1230–1450*, BSFS, IX (Manchester, 1920)
Matthew Paris, HA	*Matthaei Parisiensis, monachi Sancti Albani, Historia Anglorum*, ed. F. Madden, 3 vols, RS XLIV (London, 1866–69)
MF	*Miscellanea Francescana*
MLGB, i	*Medieval Libraries of Great Britain. A List of Surviving Books*, ed. N.R. Ker, Royal Historical Society Guides and Handbooks, III, 2nd edn (London, 1964)
MLGB, ii	*Medieval Libraries of Great Britain. A List of Surviving Books, edited by N.R. Ker, supplement to the second edition*, ed. A.G. Watson, Royal Historical Society Guides and Handbooks, XV (London, 1987)

Monum. Franciscana	*Monumenta Franciscana*, ed. J.S. Brewer and R. Howlett, 2 vols, RS, IV (London, 1858–82)
NH	*Northern History: A Review of the History of the North of England and the Borders*
Nicholson, *Templars*	*The Proceedings Against the Templars in the British Isles*, ed. H.J. Nicholson, 2 vols (Aldershot, 2011)
North Country Wills	*North Country Wills being abstracts of wills relating to the counties of York, Nottingham, Northumberland, Cumberland and Westmorland at Somerset House and Lambeth Palace 1383 to 1558*, ed. J.W. Clay, 2 vols, SS, CXVI, CXXI (1908–12)
Notes on Religious Houses	*Notes on the Religious and Secular Houses of Yorkshire*, ed. W.P. Baildon, YAS, RS, XVII, LXXXI (1895–1931)
Obituary Roll, Durham	*The Obituary roll of William Ebchester and John Burnby, priors of Durham, with notices of similar records preserved at Durham, from the year 1233 downwards, letters of fraternity, etc.*, ed. J. Raine, SS, XXXI (1856)
OHS	Oxford Historical Society, 1st series, 2nd series
OMT	Oxford Medieval Texts
Orderic Vitalis	*The Ecclesiastical History of Orderic Vitalis*, ed. M. Chibnall, 6 vols, OMT (Oxford, 1969–80)
p.	Ordination to the priesthood
PIMS	The Pontifical Institute of Mediaeval Studies, Toronto
Poll Taxes, 1377, 1379, 1381	*The Poll Taxes of 1377, 1379 and 1381: Part three Wiltshire-Yorkshire*, ed. C.C. Fenwick, Records of Social and Economic History, new series, XXXVII (Oxford, 2005)
PThS	Publications of the Thoresby Society
'Records, Franciscan Province'	'Records of the Franciscan Province of England', in *Collectanea Franciscana*, I, ed. A.G. Little, M.R. James and H.M. Bannister, BSFS, V (Aberdeen, 1914), pp. 141–53
Reg. Appleby	*The Register of Thomas Appleby bishop of Carlisle 1363–1395*, ed. R.L. Storey CYS, XCVI (Woodbridge, 2006)
Reg. Antiq.	*The Registrum Antiquissimum of the Cathedral Church of Lincoln*, ed. C.W. Foster and K. Major, 10 vols, LRS, XXVII, XXVIII, XXIX, XXXII, XXXIV, XLI, XLVI, LI, LXII, LXII (1931–73)
Reg. Bainbridge	*Liber pontificalis Chr. Bainbridge archiepiscopi Eboracensis*, ed. W.G. Henderson, SS, LXI (1875)
Reg. Bothe	*Registrum Caroli Bothe, episcopi Herefordensis, A.D. MDXVI–MDXXXV*, ed. A.T. Bannister, CYS, XXVIII (1921)
Reg. Bubwith	*The Register of Nicholas Bubwith, bishop of Bath and Wells, 1407–1424*, ed. T.S. Holmes, 2 vols, Somerset Record Society, XXIX, XXX (1914)
Reg. Burghersh	*The Registers of Bishop Henry Burghersh 1320–1342*, ed. N. Bennett, 3 vols, LRS, LXXXVII, CX, CI (1999–2011)
Reg. Cancelarii, 1498–1506	*Registrum Cancelarii, 1498–1506*, ed. W.T. Mitchell, OHS, 2nd series, XXVII (1979–80)
Reg. Catterick	*The Register of John Catterick bishop of Coventry and Lichfield 1415–1419*, ed. R.N. Swanson, CYS, LXXVII (1990)

Reg. Chichele	*The Register of Henry Chichele archbishop of Canterbury 1414–1443*, ed. E.F. Jacob and H.C. Johnson, CYS, XLII, XLV, XLVI, XLVII (1938–57)
Reg. Cobham	*The register of Thomas de Cobham, bishop of Worcester, 1317–1327*, ed. E.H. Pearce, WHS, XL (1930)
Reg. Congreg, 1505–17	*Register of Congregations, 1505–1517*, ed. W.T. Mitchell, 2 vols, OHS, 2nd series, XXXVII, XXXVIII (1998)
Reg. Corbridge	*The Register of Thomas of Corbridge lord archbishop of York 1300–1304*, ed. W. Brown and A. Hamilton Thompson, 2 vols, SS, CXXXVIII, CXLI (1925–28)
Reg. Drokensford	*Calendar of the register of John de Drokensford, Bishop of Bath and Wells (A.D.1309–1329)*, ed. E. Hobhouse, Somerset Record Society, I (London, 1887)
Reg. Edington	*The Register of William Edington, Bishop of Winchester*, ed. S.F. Hockey, 2 vols, Hampshire Record Series, VII, VIII (1986–87)
Reg. Fleming	*The Register of Richard Fleming bishop of Lincoln 1420–1431*, ed. N.H. Bennett, 2 vols, CYS, LXXIII, XCIX (1984, 2009)
Reg. Fox	*The register of Richard Fox, lord bishop of Durham, 1494–1501*, ed. M.P. Howden, SS, CXLVII (Durham, 1932)
Reg. Gandavo	*Registrum Simonis de Gandavo, diocesis Saresberiensis, A.D.1297–1315*, ed. C.T. Fowler and M.C.B. Dawes, 2 vols, CYS, XL, XLI (Oxford, 1934)
Reg. Gilbert	*Registrum Johannis Gilbert, episcopi Herefordensis, A.D.MCCCLXXV–MCCCLXXXIX*, ed. J.H. Parry, CYS, XVIII (1915)
Reg. Godfrey Giffard	*Episcopal Registers, diocese of Worcester: register of Bishop Godfrey Giffard, September 23rd 1268 to August 15th 1301*, ed. J. Willis Bund, 2 vols, WHS, XV (1898–1902)
Reg. Gravesend	*Rotuli Ricardi Gravesend episcopi Lincolniensis A.D.MCCLVIII-M.CCLXXIX*, ed. F.N. Davis, LRS, XX (London, 1925)
Reg. Greenfield	*The register of William Greenfield, lord archbishop of York, 1306–1315*, ed. W. Brown and A. Hamilton Thompson, 5 vols, SS, CXLV, CXLIX, CLI, CLII, CLIII (1931–40)
Reg. Hallum	*The register of Robert Hallum, bishop of Salisbury, 1404–1417*, ed. J.M. Horne, CYS, LXXII (1982)
Reg. Halton	*The Register of John de Halton, bishop of Carlisle, A.D.1292–1324*, ed. W.N. Thompson, 2 vols, CYS, XII, XIII (1913)
Reg. Hethe	*Registrum Hamonis Hethe diocesis Roffensis A.D.1319–1352*, ed. C. Johnston, in 2 vols, CYS, XLVIII, XLIX (1948)
Reg. Kellaw	*Registrum Palatinum Dunelmense*, ed. T.D. Hardy, 4 vols, RS, LXII, London (1873–78)
Reg. King and Castello	*The Registers of Oliver King bishop of Bath and Wells 1496–1503 and Hadrian de Castello bishop of Bath and Wells 1503–1518*, ed. H. Maxwell-Lyte, Somerset Record Society, LIV (1939)
Reg. Kirkby	*The Register of John Kirkby, bishop of Carlisle 1332–1352, and the Register of John Ross, bishop of Carlisle, 1325–32*, ed. R.L. Storey, 2 vols, CYS, LXXIX, LXXXI (1993–95)

Reg. Lacy	*The Register of Edmund Lacy, bishop of Exeter, 1420–1455*, ed. G.R. Dunstan, 5 vols, CYS, LX, LXI, LXII, LXIII, LXVI (1963–72)
Reg. Langham	*Registrum Simonis Langham, Cantuariensis archiepiscopi*, ed. A.C. Wood, CYS, LIII (1956)
Reg. Langley	*The Register of Thomas Langley, bishop of Durham, 1406–1437*, ed. R.L. Storey, 6 vols, SS, CLXIV, CLXVI, CLXIX, CLXX, CLXXVII, CLXXXII (1956–70)
Reg. Langton	*The Register of Walter Langton bishop of Coventry and Lichfield, 1296–1321*, ed. J.B. Hughes, 2 vols, CYS, XCI, XCVII (2001–07)
Reg. Le Romeyn	*The Register of John Le Romeyn, lord archbishop of York, 1286 1296*, ed. W. Brown, 2 vols, SS, CXXIII, CXXVIII (1913–17)
Reg. Martival	*The registers of Roger Martival, 1315–1330*, ed. K. Edwards, C.R. Erlington, S. Reynolds and D.M. Owen, CYS, LV, LVI, LVII, LVIII, LIX, LXVIII (Torquay, 1959–75)
Reg. Mascall	*Registrum Roberti Mascall, episcopi Herefordensis, A.D. M.CCCCIV–MCCCCXVI*, ed. J.H. Parry and introduced by C. Johnson, Cantilupe Society, CYS, XXI (1917)
Reg. Mayew	*Registrum Ricardi Mayew, episcopi Herefordensis, A.D.MDIV–MDXVI*, ed. A.T. Bannister, CYS, XXVII (1919)
Reg. Melton	*The register of William Melton, archbishop of York, 1317–1340*, ed. R.M.T. Hill, R. Brocklesby, T.C. Timmins and D. Robinson, 6 vols, CYS, LXX, LXXI, LXXVI, LXXXV, XCIII, CI (1977–2011)
Reg. Morton	*The Register of John Morton Archbishop of Canterbury 1486–1500*, ed. C. Harper-Bill, 3 vols, CYS, LXXV, LXXVIII, LXXXIX (1987–2000)
Reg. Norbury	E. Hobhouse, 'The Register of Roger de Norbury, bishop of Lichfield and Coventry, from A.D.1322 to A.D.1358. An abstract of Contents and Remarks', *Collections for a History of Staffordshire*, William Salt Archaeological Society, old series, I (1880)
Reg. Pal. Dun	*Registrum Palatinum Dunelmense*, ed. T.D. Hardy, 4 vols, RS, LXII (London, 1873–78)
Reg. Pecham	*The register of John Pecham archbishop of Canterbury 1279–1292*, ed. F.N. Davis and D.L. Douie, 2 vols, CYS, LXIV, LXV (1968–69)
Reg. Poltone	*Registrum Thome Poltone, episcopi Herefordensis, A.D.MCCCCXX–MCCCCXXII*, ed. W.W. Capes, Cantilupe Society, CYS, XXII (1918)
Reg. Repingdon	*The Register of Bishop Philip Repingdon 1405–1419*, ed. M. Archer, 3 vols, LRS, LVII, LVIII, LXXIV (1963–82)
Reg. Reynolds	*The register of Walter Reynolds, bishop of Worcester, 1308–1313*, ed. R.A. Wilson, WHS, XXXIX and Dugdale Society, IX (London, 1927)
Reg. Rotherham	*The register of Thomas Rotherham, archbishop of York, 1480–1500*, ed. E.E. Barker, CYS, LXIX (1976)

Reg. Sandale and de Asserio	*The Registers of John de Sandale and Rigaud de Asserio, bishops of Winchester (A.D. 1316–1323) with an appendix of contemporaneous and other illustrative documents*, ed. F.J. Baigent, Hampshire Record Society (London, 1897)
Reg. Scrope	*A Calendar of the Register of Richard Scrope Archbishop of York, 1398–1405*, ed. R.N. Swanson, 2 vols, BTC, VIII, XI (1981–85)
Reg. Sede Vacante, Worcester, 1301–1435	*The Register of the diocese of Worcester during the vacancy of the see usually called registrum sede vacante, 1301–1435*, ed. J. Willis Bund, WHS, VIII (1897)
Reg. Sede Vacante, York, 1405–08	*The York Sede Vacante 1405–1408*, ed. J. Kirby, BTC, XXVIII (2002)
Reg. Sede Vacante, York, 1423–26	*The York Sede Vacante Register 1423–1426: a calendar*, ed. J. Kirby, BTS, XXXVIII (2009)
Reg. Spofford	*Registrum Thome Spofford, episcopi Herefordensis, A.D.MCCCCXXII–MCCCCXLVIII*, ed A.T. Bannister, CYS, XXIII (1919)
Reg. Stapeldon	*The Register of Walter de Stapeldon, Bishop of Exeter (A.D.1307–1326)*, ed. F.C. Hingeston-Randolph (London, 1892)
Reg. Stratford	*The register of John de Stratford, bishop of Winchester, 1323–1333*, ed. R.M. Haines, 2 vols, Surrey Record Society, XLII, XLIII (2010–11)
Reg. Stretton	*The registers or act books of the bishops of Coventry and Lichfield. Book 5, being the second register of Bishop Robert de Stretton, A.D.1360–1385: an abstract of the contents*, ed. R.A. Wilson, William Salt Archaeological Society, new series, VIII (London, 1905)
Reg. Sudbury	*Registrum Simonis de Sudbiria diocesis Londoniensis A.D.1362–1375*, ed. R.C. Fowler and C. Jenkins, 2 vols, CYS, XXXIV, XXXVIII (1927–38)
Reg. Sutton	*The Rolls and Register of Bishop Oliver Sutton, 1280–1299*, ed. R.M.T. Hill, 8 vols, LRS, XXXIX, XLIII, XLVIII, LII, LX, LXIV, LXIX. LXXVI (1948–86)
Reg. Swinfield	*Registrum Ricardi de Swinfield, episcopi Herefordensis, A.D.MCCLXXXIII–MCCCXVII*, ed. W.W. Capes, CYS, VI (London, 1909)
Reg. Trillek	*Registrum Johannis de Trillek, espiscopi Herefordensis, A.D. M.CCCXLIV–M.CCCLXI*, ed. J.H. Parry, CYS, VIII (1912)
Reg. Univ. Oxon.	*Register of the University of Oxford*, ed. C.W. Boase et al., 5 vols, OHS, I, X, XI, XII, XIV (1885–89)
Reg. Waldby	*A Calendar of the Register of Robert Waldby Archbishop of York, 1397*, ed. D.M. Smith, BTC, II (1974)
Reg. Walter Giffard	*The Register of Walter Giffard, lord archbishop of York, 1266–1279*, ed. W. Brown, SS, CIX (1904)
Reg. Walter Giffard and Henry Bowett	*The registers of Walter Giffard, bishop of Bath and Wells, 1265–6, and of Henry Bowett, bishop of Bath and Wells, 1401–7*, ed. T. S. Holmes, Somerset Record Society, XIII (1899)

Reg. Waltham	*The register of John Waltham bishop of Salisbury 1388–1395*, ed. T.C.B. Timmins, CYS, LXXX (1994)
Reg. Welton	*The Register of Gilbert Welton bishop of Carlisle 1353–1362*, ed. R.L. Storey, CYS, LXXXVIII (1999)
Reg. Wickwane	*The register of William Wickwane, lord archbishop of York, 1279–1285*, ed. W. Brown, SS, CXIV (1907)
Reg. Winchelsey	*Registrum Roberti Winchelsey Cantuariensis Archiepiscopi*, ed. R. Graham, 2 vols, CYS, LI, LII (London, 1952–56)
Reg. Woodlock	*Registrum Henrici Woodlock, diocesis Wintoniensis, A.D. 1305–1316*, ed. A.W. Goodman, 2 vols, CYS, XLIII, XLIV (1940–41)
Reg. Wykeham	*Wykeham's Register*, ed. T.F. Kirby, 2 vols, Hampshire Record Society (1896–99)
Rot. Gravesend	*Rotuli Ricardi Gravesend episcopi Lincolniensis A.D.MCCLVIII–MCCLXXIX*, ed. F.N. Davis, LRS, XX (1925)
Rot. Grosseteste	*Rotuli Roberti Grosseteste episcopi Lincolniensis A.D. MCCXXXV–MCCLIII necnon Rotulus Henrici de Lexington episcopi Lincolniensis A.D.MCCLIV–MCCLIX*, ed. F.N. Davis LRS, XI (1914)
Rot. Welles	*Rotuli Hugonis de Welles, episcopi Lincolniensis A.D.MCCIX–MCCXXXV*, ed. W.P.W. Phillimore and F.N. Davis, 3 vols, CYS, I, III, IV (1907–09)
RS	*Rerum Britannicarum Medii Aevi Scriptores*, Chronicles and Memorials of Great Britain and Ireland during the Middle Ages, published under the direction of the Master of the Rolls, 99 vols (London, 1858–96)
RTAM	*Recherches de Théologie ancienne et Médiévale*
Rymer, *Foedera*	*Foedera, conventiones, litterae, et cujuscunque generis acta publica, inter reges Angliae et alios quosvis imperatores, reges, pontifices vel communitates*, ed. T. Rymer, 4 vols in 7 parts (London, 1816–69)
Salimbene de Adam	*Salimbene de Adam, Cronica a.1168–1287*, ed. G. Scalia, 2 vols, CCCM, CXXV, CXXVa (Turnhout, 1998–99)
s.	Ordination as a subdeacon
SB	Spicilegium Bonaventurianum
Schneyer, *Repertorium*	*Repertorium der Lateinischen Sermones des Mittelalters für die Zeit von 1150–1350*, ed. J.B. Schneyer, vols 1–9 (Münster, 1969–74)
Scritti	*Francesco d'Assisi Scritti*, ed. C. Paolazzi, SB, XXXVI (Grottaferrata, Rome, 2009)
s. d.	Shillings and pence, the currency of medieval England along with the mark
Sharpe, *Handlist*	R. Sharpe, *A Handlist of the Latin Writers of Great Britain and Ireland before 1540*, Publications of the Journal Medieval Latin, I (Turnhout, 1997)
SS	Surtees Society
Stegmüller	*Repertorium Commentariorum in Sententias Petri Lombardi*, ed. F. Stegmüller, 2 vols (Würzburg, 1947)

Supplic. Apost. Penit.	*Supplications from England and Wales in the registers of the Apostolic Penitentiary 1410–1503*, ed. P.D. Clarke and P.N.R. Zutshi, 3 vols, CYS, CIII, CIV, CV (2012–15)
TE	*Testamenta Eboracensia; or wills registered at York illustrative of the history, manners, language, statistics, etc., of the province of York, from the year 1300 downwards*, ed. J. Raine and J.W. Clay, 6 vols, SS, IV, XXX, XLV, LIII, LXXIX, CVI (1836–1902)
Thomson, *Corpus Christi, Oxford*	R.M. Thomson, *A Descriptive Catalogue of the Medieval Manuscripts of Corpus Christi College, Oxford* (Cambridge, 2011)
Thomson, *Lincoln*	R.M. Thomson, *Catalogue of the Manuscripts of Lincoln Cathedral Chapter Library* (Cambridge, 1989)
Thomson, *Merton*	R.M. Thomson, *A Descriptive Catalogue of the Medieval Manuscripts of Merton College, Oxford* (Cambridge, 2009)
Thomson, *Peterhouse, Cambridge*	R.M. Thomson, *A Descriptive Catalogue of the Medieval Manuscripts in the Library of Peterhouse, Cambridge* (Cambridge, 2016)
Thomson, *Worcester*	R.M. Thomson, *A Descriptive Catalogue of the Medieval Manuscripts in Worcester Cathedral Library* (Cambridge, 2001)
TNA	The National Archives, at Kew Gardens, London, formerly known as the Public Record Office
UCLC	*The University and College Libraries of Cambridge*, ed. P.D. Clarke with an introduction by R. Lovatt, CBMLC, X (London, 2002)
UCLO	*The University and College Libraries of Oxford*, ed. R.M. Thomson with the assistance of J.G. Clark, 2 vols, CBMLC, XVI (London, 2015)
VCH, Beverley	*The Victoria History of the Counties of England, York East Riding*, vi, *The Borough and Liberties of Beverley*, ed. K.J. Allison (Oxford, 1989)
VCH, Lincs.	*The Victoria History of the Counties of England, Lincolnshire*, ii, ed. W. Page (London, 1906)
VCH, York	*The Victoria History of the Counties of England, Yorkshire: The City of York*, ed. P.M. Tillott (London, 1961)
VCH, Yorks.	*The Victoria History of the Counties of England, Yorkshire*, iii, ed. W. Page (London, 1913)
VCH, Yorks., East Riding	*The Victoria History of the Counties of England, York, East Riding*, iii, ed. K.J. Allison (Oxford, 1976)
WHO	Worcestershire Historical Society
Wilkins, *Concilia*	*Concilia magnae Britanniae et Hiberniae ab anno MCCLXVIII ad annum MCCCXLIX*, ed. D. Wilkins, 4 vols (London, 1737)
Wills and Inventories	*Wills and inventories illustrative of the history, manners, language, statistics, etc., of the northern counties of England from the eleventh century downwards*, ed. J. Raine, jnr, SS, II (1835)
Woodford, Respons.	Doyle, E., 'William Woodford, O.F.M.: His Life and Works together with a Study and Edition of his "*Responsiones contra Wiclevum et Lollardos*"', FS, XLIII (1983), pp. 17–187
YAJ	*Yorkshire Archaeological Journal*

YAS, RS	Yorkshire Archaeological Society, Record Series
York Civic Records	*York Civic Records*, ed. A. Raine and D. Sutton, 9 vols, YAS, RS, XCVIII, CIII, CVI, CVIII, CX, CXII, CXV, CXIX, CXXXVIII (1939–78)
York Clergy Wills, i and ii	*York Clergy Wills 1520–1600*, ed. C. Cross, 2 vols, BTC, X, XV (1984–89)
York Memorandum Book	*York Memorandum Book*, ed. M. Sellars and J.W. Percy, 3 vols, SS, CXX, CXXV, CLXXXVI (1912–73)
Yorks. Deeds	*Yorkshire Deeds*, ed. W. Brown, C.T. Clay, M.J. Hebditch and M.J. Stanley-Price, 10 vols, YAS, RS, XXXIX, L, LXIII, LXV, LXIX, LXXVI, LXXVI, LXXXIII, CII, CXI, CXX (1909–55)
Yorks. Inquisitions	*Yorkshire Inquisitions*, ed. W. Brown, 4 vols, YAS, RS, XII, XXIII, XXXI, XXXVII (1892–1906)
Yorks, Star Chamber	*Yorkshire Star Chamber Proceedings*, ed. H.B. McCall and W. Brown, YAS, RS, XLI, XLV, LI (1909–14)
Young, 'Religious Houses'	G.G. Young, 'Notices concerning religious houses in Yorkshire, with the names of their founders, and of persons buried therein', *Collectanea Topographica et Genealogica*, ed. F. Madden, B. Bandinel, and others, and afterwards by J.G. Nichols, 8 vols (London, 1834–43), iv, pp. 73–79

Explanatory Note

The term 'friars' denotes the Franciscans or Greyfriars, unless expressly applied to members of another mendicant order. Allusions to other orders of friars, Austin Friars, Blackfriars, and White Friars, also known as the Augustinians, Dominicans and the Carmelites, are made clear. The Friars of the Sack had friaries at York and Lincoln. A shortened version of the titles of monographs and articles has been used in the biographical register. Fuller bibliographical details are supplied in the table of abbreviations and the bibliography. References to Richmond concern the town in north Yorkshire unless otherwise stated. Dioceses in the former Crusading States (*in partibus infidelium*) without an English equivalent remain in their Latin form and are italicised, such as *Argos*, *Chrysopolis*, *Philippopolis* and *Soltaniensis*.

An introduction to the sources

St Francis of Assisi (1181/2–1226) was a figure ablaze with the love of God.[1] His penitential lifestyle and infectious virtue rejuvenated the medieval Church and inspired countless men to pursue the virtues enunciated in the sermon on the mount (Matthew 5.1–47). Men of all ages and backgrounds were drawn to his fraternity which rapidly blossomed into an international religious order whose tentacles reached throughout Christendom and into missionary territory as far afield as India and China. The Franciscans of England were known as Greyfriars, from the colour of their religious habit,[2] or Cordeliers in France and elsewhere.[3] They landed in Dover in the late summer of 1224 and quickly spread throughout the country, reaching northern Lincolnshire and Yorkshire within five or six years. They were the second of the four major mendicant orders to settle in England during the thirteenth century, along with the Dominicans, the Carmelites and the Austin Friars. The Franciscan custody of York consisted of friaries at Beverley,[4] Boston,[5] Doncaster,[6] Grimsby,[7] Lincoln,[8] Scarborough[9] and York.[10] Friars made a marked impact upon the region for over three centuries until 9 March 1539, when the friary at Scarborough was suppressed, the last surviving member of the custody of York.[11]

Friars were seemingly ubiquitous in medieval society and needed no introduction in the pages of William Langland's *Piers Plowman* and Geoffrey Chaucer's *Canterbury Tales*. They left their mark in various ways, such as the presence of their writings in monastic libraries, like the Cistercians of Meaux Abbey, whose catalogue of 1396

1 D.M. Knowles, *Saints and Sinners: Twenty-Five Medieval Portraits* (Cambridge, 1962), pp. 86–98.

2 *Matthew Paris, HA*, ii, p. 109: *tunicis griseis. Orderic Vitalis*, iv, pp. 310–13: *albedine in habitu suo precipue utuntur, qua singulares ab aliis notabilesque videantur. Nigrendo in plerisque locis sanctae Scripturae humilitatem designat. North Country Wills*, i, pp. 73, 90, where testators in the sixteenth century refer to the Carmelites, Dominicans and Franciscans by the colour of their religious habits, Whitefriars, Blackfriars and Greyfriars.

3 Cf. C.L. Kingsford, 'Defensio Fratrum Mendicantium', *Fratris Johannis Pecham quondam archiepiscopi Cantuariensis Tractatus tres de Paupertate*, ed. Kingsford, A.G. Little and F. Tocco, BSFS, II (Aberdeen, 1910), pp. 148–98, at 173, verse 301, where the friars are depicted as the *cordati* and the Dominicans as the *iacobite*. *Sir Thomas Gray Scalacronica 1272–1363*, ed. A. King, SS, CCIX (2005), pp. 14–15, refers to two friars as a *Cordeler* and a *Jacobyn*. Cf. *ibid.*, pp. 2–5, for further allusions to the *Cordelers*.

4 A.G. Little, 'The Grey Friars of Beverley', *VCH, Yorks.*, iii, pp. 264–66. Cf. R.E. Horrox, 'The Borough and Liberties of Beverley', *VCH, Beverley*, pp. 1–62.

5 A.G. Little, 'The Grey Friars of Boston', *VCH, Lincs.*, ii, pp. 215–16.

6 F.R. Fairbank, 'The House of Grey Friars, Doncaster', *YAJ*, XII (1892–93), pp. 481–86; A.G. Little, 'The Grey Friars of Doncaster', *VCH, Yorks.*, iii, pp. 266–67.

7 A.G. Little, 'The Grey Friars of Grimsby', in *VCH, Lincs.*, ii, p. 219.

8 A.G. Little, 'The Grey Friars of Lincoln', *VCH, Lincs.*, ii, pp. 222–24.

9 A.G. Little, 'The Grey Friars, Scarborough', *VCH, Yorks.*, iii, pp. 274–76.

10 A.G. Little, 'The Grey Friars of York', *VCH, Yorks.*, iii, pp. 287–91.

11 *LPFD*, xiv, pt. i, p. 188, no. 482. The surrender was announced on 9 March 1539, *ibid.*, xiv, pt. i, p. 194, no. 494, when Richard Yngworth, bishop of Dover, reported he had received *three poor houses of friars, Black, White and Grey, so poor that they have sold the stall and partclosys in the churche, so that nothing is left but stone and glass, yet there is meetly good lead.*

enumerates texts by theological luminaries of the school of the Cordeliers of Paris, such as Jean de la Rochelle, Bonaventure of Bagnoregio, Richard of Middleton and John Pecham.[12] Although the seven friaries of the custody of York left few traces on the local landscape,[13] the friars' footprints appear in multiple documentary sources: the hagiographical tradition, annals, sermons, theological debates, collections of *exempla* materials, inquisitions into proof of age, charters, binding agreements regarding suffrages, account books, registers of ecclesiastical guilds, correspondence concerning Parliament, manuscripts, *incunabula*, inventories of libraries, the *acta* of provincial councils, parish registers, urban archives, mortuary rolls, indulgences, deeds regarding the sale of land, the wardrobe accounts of several monarchs, the plea rolls, papal dispensations of numerous kinds, monastic cartularies and chronicles, papers pertaining to the Dissolution, registers of archdeaconries, the archives of the Universities of Bologna, Paris, Oxford and Cambridge, ecclesiastical and secular court cases, memoirs, letters of fraternity, contracts between the order and the municipal authorities, and the correspondence of friars, prelates and members of the royal family.

Dr A.B. Emden's comments on the 'ruthless suppression' of the Dominicans by the crown and the Parliament in 1538–39 and the survival of fragments of their archives apply equally to the Greyfriars.[14] There are tangible remains of the Greyfriars and their convents in several forms. A manuscript in Milan contains a fragment of an undated sermon preached to the clergy of Lincoln at the local Greyfriars by William de la Mare, regent master at Paris and the redoubtable adversary of Thomas Aquinas.[15] Echoes of the academic exercises followed by friars in the Faculty of Theology at Oxford between 1284 and 1300 appear in two manuscripts in Assisi: first, Biblioteca comunale, MS.158 transcribes questions debated by Philip of Bridlington and Adam of Howden;[16] MS.196 refers to the presence of Adam of Lincoln as *Lincolniensis* and Philip of Bridlington.[17] Balliol College Library at Oxford, MS.63, written in the fourteenth century, contains two long *quaestiones Beverley*: the first, folios 89r–93r, *Utrum Deus sit trinus et unus*, and the second, folios 93r–99v, *Utrum a quacumque creatura rationali solus Deus sit propter se finaliter diligendus*. Worcester Cathedral Library, MS.Q.99, contains a copy of Philip of Bridlington's *Vesperies* (fols. 63rb–vb) and two subsequent questions, *An essentia divina* (fols. 63vb–64va) and *An Deus intelligat* (fols.

[12] *The Libraries of the Cistercians, Gilbertines and Premonstratensians*, ed. D.N. Bell, CBMLC, III (London, 1992), pp. 34–82, at 49, 67, 78, 80, nn. 108, 109, 250, 321, 351.

[13] J. Burton, *Monasticon Eboracense: and the Ecclesiastical History of Yorkshire* (York, 1758), pp. 57, 58, 61, 63, 66; and T. Tanner, *Notitia Monastica; or, an account of all the abbies, priories, and houses of friers formerly in England and Wales, and also of all the colleges and hospitals founded before A.D.MDXL* (Cambridge, 1787), Yorkshire, nn. XII, XXVIII, CVI, CXXIX, where he reports that the friary was founded in the reign of King Henry III by that monarch and the city of York, citing BL, Harley MS.1408, fol. 66. *De fundatione domus fratrum minorum in civitate Ebor.*

[14] A.B. Emden, *A Survey of Dominicans in England based on the ordination lists in episcopal registers (1268 to 1538)*, Institutum Historicum FF. Praedicatorum Romae ad S. Sabinae, Dissertationes Historicae, XVIII (Rome, 1967), pp. 15, 16, 19.

[15] J.G. Bougerol, 'Sermons de maîtres franciscains du XIII siècle', *AFH*, LXXXI (1988), pp. 17–49, at 40.

[16] F.M. Henquinet, 'Descriptio codicis 158 Assisii in Bibliotheca Communali', *AFH*, XXIV (1931), pp. 91–108, 215–54, at 93, 98, 216, 234, 240–41; P. Glorieux, 'Le Manuscrit d'Assise, Bibl.comm.158: Date et mode de composition', *RTAM*, VIII (1936), pp. 282–95, at 289, 290, 294.

[17] D.H. Pouillon, 'Le manuscrit d'Assise, Bibl.comm.196. Description', *RTAM*, XII (1940), pp. 329–58, at 341, 352.

64va–65rb). New College Library, Oxford, MS.92, folio 82v, and Worcester Cathedral Library, MS.Q.46, folios 307r–08v, 246r–47v, 113v–16r, 259r–61v, contain copies of sermons preached by Adam of Howden at Oxford on 11 November 1290, 1 January 1291, 6 January 1293 and 25 March 1293.

One friar, John Holbeach, made a copy of Nicholas of Lyra's commentary on the books of the Old Testament (Peterhouse Library, Cambridge, MS.85), and a miscellany of medical texts (Trinity College Library, Cambridge, MS.1412 [O.9.10]). A gloss on the Pauline letters was donated to the friary in Lincoln through Master Ralph of Corbridge, who may have been the lector in the cathedral city after lecturing at Oxford (LPL, MS.56). Documentation regarding the friars' unsuccessful application to acquire an adjacent property in Scarborough in 1297 is conserved in the National Archives (TNA, SC 8/337/15934).[18] The seal of the guardian of York was appended to a receipt for a ton of wine provided by King Edward II through Stephen de Abyngdon in 1319 (TNA, E213/18). The guardian, and the Greyfriars of York granted an *obit* in their church on 12 January 1465 to William Butler in memory of his two deceased wives (YC/AT/G70/36).[19] An indulgence issued by the guardian of Doncaster in 1479 for Roger Alyn and his wife is conserved at the National Archives (C270/35/6). The pontifical purchased by William Duffield, friar and bishop of Ascalon, in London bears the inscription *Duffild, dom. Willelmus, S.T.P., O.F.M.C., Ascelenensis episcopus* (Colchester, Harsnett Library, H.h.14). It is unusual to have a date of death for a friar. An exception is provided by a heavily annotated copy of John Duns Scotus's *Commentary on the fourth book of the Sentences*, recording the death of John Kyngton in 1536 (Oxford, Bodleian Library, Bodleian, Auct.4.Q.4.9).

Folios from an account book at York for the autumn of 1537 and the following spring survive as reinforcements for the binding of an Act Book.[20] There are extant deeds of the surrender of the friaries at Grimsby on 9 October (TNA, E 322/94),[21] Doncaster on 20 November (E 322/73) and York on 27 November 1538 (E 322/276). Franciscans were depicted in two of the misericords at the parish church of St Mary at Beverley c.1445: first, a bare-footed and cowled friar with a knotted cord, denoting his three vows, reads from a scroll; secondly, a nun and a friar, replete with a cord, read

18 The Franciscans of Scarborough petitioned several people, including Cecily, duchess of York, and the king, to allow them to acquire a toft of land in Scarborough lately held by Adam le Gumer, who had been beheaded. An inquest into the matter had recently been held and had been returned to Chancery. The friars requested this property after Gumer's execution and the confiscation of his lands. The resultant inquisition dated 29 July 1297 denied their request. Cf. TNA, E143/26/13, *CPR, 1292–1301*, p. 416. On 18 May 1299 Gumer's son, Simon, granted the friars property adjacent to their church for the enlargement of their precinct and cemetery.

19 *York Memorandum Book*, ii, p. 231. The guardian and convent of the Greyfriars of York issued a bond in recognition of the fact that William Butler of Selby and his deceased wives, Cecily and Constance, had been the order's benefactors. The friars undertook to say a collect daily in the Mass of St Mary, namely *Omnipotens sempiterne Deus*, during the life of William and after his death the *Incliuna*. Their *obit* would be celebrated annually in the conventual church for the souls of the said William, Cecily and Constance with the *Placebo* and *Dirige* and requiem Mass at the high altar on 21 July. They bound themselves to 40s. to the lord mayor and commonalty for the celebration of the said suffrages for which the lord mayor and commonalty were to have the right of distraint of their goods, both spiritual and temporal.

20 J.S. Purvis, 'Four Antiquarian Notes', *YAJ*, XLII (1967–70), pp. 52–53.

21 Cf. H.S. Kingsford, 'The Seals of the Franciscans', *Franciscan History and Legend in English Medieval Art*, ed. A.G. Little, BSFS, XIX (Manchester, 1937), pp. 81–100, at 92, where he explains that this seal is from Grimsby rather than Lincoln.

from a scroll in the presence of two foxes. The wills of Bishop Warter, rector of St Mary at Castlegate, and Dr William Vavasour, the last guardian of the York Greyfriars and then a priest at St Mary, Bishophill Junior, were entered into the probate registers. The latter on 13 November 1544 enumerated his possessions and indicated a continuing bond with at least three of his former brethren, who ministered under the new ecclesiastical dispensation. Archaeological evidence forms another layer of information. Archaeologists may have located the friars' temporary house at Hatterboard, just outside Scarborough.[22] The results of more recent work on the Greyfriars of Lincoln[23] and Scarborough have been published by local societies.[24]

The custody of York has no equivalent to Jacques de' Tolomei de Sienne (1323–90) or Francesco da Lendinara, whose recollections spanned a shorter period (1382–1427). The first was a member of the Tuscan province, who preserved details of his admission to the order, ordination, his studies and his series of teaching and administrative posts prior to his appointment as bishop of Narni on 11 January 1378.[25] The second was a native of Lendinara in the province of Rovigo and a member of the Paduan custody, whose name occurs in various contemporary sources from the Veneto between 1378 and 1433. His memoir yields a mine of information regarding his reception into the order at Lendinara, his scholastic formation and the administrative and teaching positions that he filled in the different friaries over a period of 55 years.[26]

The one exception in the custody of York is Michael Dawnay, who testified in an ecclesiastical court case in 1425, when he was aged 49. His evidence sketches four generations of his family (see Figure 1) and illuminates his own movements as a friar. His family belonged to the minor gentry. In 1363 the Dawnay family held a manor in Escrick, a village equidistant from York and Selby, and acquired more than 100 acres.[27] They possessed land close to the city walls of York. Thomas Dawnay, Michael's father,

22 F.C. Rimington, *The Deserted Medieval Village of Hatterborard, near Scarborough*, Scarborough and District Archaeological Society, Research Report, 2 (Scarborough, 1961), pp. 11–12, 22.

23 J. Wilford, 'Lincoln Greyfriars: Retrospect and Prospect', *Lincoln Archaeology*, VI (1993–94), pp. 38–40.

24 T. Pearson, *The Archaeology of Medieval Scarborough: Excavation and Research 1987–2004*, Scarborough Archaeological and Historical Society, Research Report, XII (York, 2005), pp. 46–47.

25 P. Péano, 'Jacques de' Tolomei de Sienne, O.F.M. (1323–1390): éléments de biographie', *AFH*, LXVIII (1975), pp. 273–97. He was born on 25 March 1323 at Montalcino and entered the order on 30 May 1337 at the age of 14. He was ordained subdeacon on 19 September 1338, deacon on 22 May 1339 and priest on 21 December 1342. The second ceremony was conducted by the bishop of Arezzo and the third by the bishop of Massa. In 1346 he studied theology at Bologna. In that same year he was made *magister studi* at Siena. In 1347 he was a student *de debito* at Paris. In 1348 he became a bachelor at Treviso and filled the same office at Padua two years later. He was appointed as lector at Siena for two years. In 1352 he was appointed as custos of Siena for two years and attended the general chapter at Assisi. The following year he was elected as custos for the general chapter to be held in Assisi. In 1354 he was elected as definitor in the chapter at Santa Croce, Florence. In 1355 he was appointed as *discretus* at Siena and made visitator of the province of Genoa. In that year he was appointed as the lector of Assisi and served as vicar of the province of Assisi. In 1356 he was lector of Siena, where there was a *studium generale*. He remained there until 1357, when he was appointed as the visitator of all the monasteries in the Tuscan province, with the exception of the custody of Massa Maritima.

26 C. Cenci, '*Fra Francesco da Lendinara e la storia della Provincia di S. Antonio tra la fine del s. XIV e l'inizio del s. XV*', *AFH*, LV (1962), pp. 103–92.

27 K.J. Allison, 'Escrick', *VCH, Yorks., East Riding*, iii, pp. 17–28, at 21. By 1402 John Dawnay held Escrick Manor and a messuage called Grimsby's.

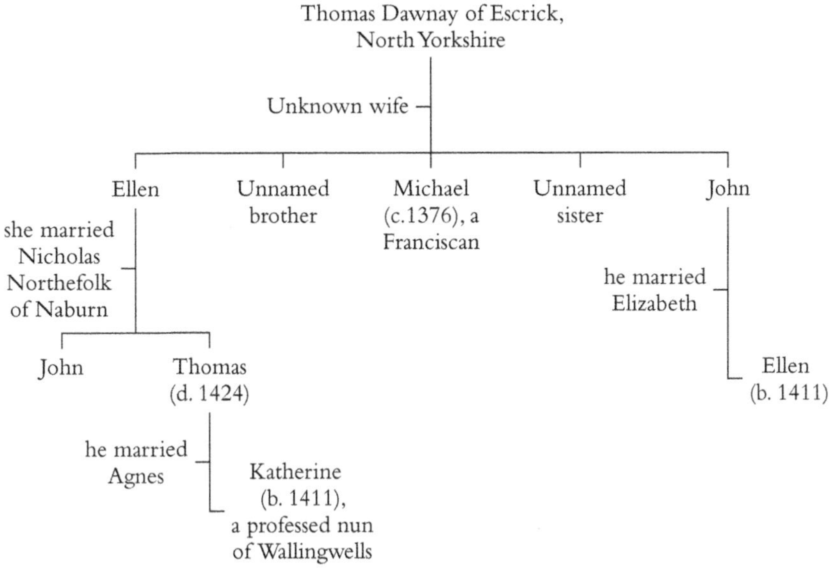

Figure 1. Four generations of Michael Dawnay's family

was among the 69 taxpayers of Escrick in 1381; his mother's name is not supplied. Michael had at least one unnamed brother and one unnamed sister, apart from Ellen and John.[28]

John Dawnay, Michael's brother, married Elizabeth and they lived not far from York. Their daughter, Ellen, was born in 1411. Michael's sister, Ellen Dawnay, married Nicholas Northefolk, whose father was a member of the minor gentry. Nicholas's father paid the princely sum of 5s., that is, more than double the amount contributed by his neighbours in 1381 for his lands at Naburn, a village approximately four miles south of York.[29] Ellen and Nicholas junior had two sons, John and Thomas. The matrimonial status of the first is unknown. Thomas Northefolk married Agnes, who gave birth to Katherine at Fulford in 1411, a village some two miles south of York. Thomas died in 1424 and his brother, John, became Katherine's guardian; she had entered the Cistercian nunnery priory of Wallingwells, Nottinghamshire, aged 13, she made her vows. In that year Katherine was abducted from the priory.

The plaintiffs included John Northefolk and the prioress against Katherine's mother, Agnes, and several companions, who allegedly orchestrated the assault on the nunnery. In 1426 the defendants presented an alternative account, complaining that, on the death of her father, Katherine was placed in the nunnery by her uncle in order to gain control of her lands in Naburn.

Michael Dawnay entered the order and was listed as a friar from the archdeaconry of Richmond, was ordained subdeacon at Holy Trinity Priory, Micklegate, York, on 22 September 1397 at the age of 21. He was probably also a friar of Richmond at the

28 *Poll Taxes, 1377, 1379, 1381*, p. 231. Thomas Downay and his wife, probably the friar's parents, were listed among the taxpayers of Escrick in 1381. Three other taxpayers in the village had the name of Downay.

29 *Poll Taxes, 1377, 1379, 1381*, p. 232.

time. He attested that from 1400 he had been a friar of Hartlepool, where he pursued the study of arithmetic, domification and the other sciences suitable for astronomy. His education in the sciences and theology honed his skills and groomed him for life at the University of Cambridge. Between 1411 and 1414 he was at Cambridge, where he became a professor of theology and then occupied the post of master of studies. Between 1414 and 1419 he was a friar of Richmond, probably as the lector.[30] From 1419 to 1425 he was the lector at Doncaster. From the beginning of his studies at Hartlepool Michael had taken a keen interest in recording the years, days, months and hours of the births of his nephews and nieces and their children.[31]

In several instances friars are represented by a single entry, such as William Scott', who was probably a friar of Scarborough at the time of his death. The breviator, the bearer of the mortuary roll of John Hemingborough, prior of Durham (†1416), was received at Scarborough. This deceased friar's name was entered on the roll and prayers for him were solicited. In contrast, more is known about his confrères in the schools, such as Adam of Howden, regent master in theology at Oxford University and then Cambridge, where he was embroiled in the dispute between the order and the university between 1303 and 1306. The life of his contemporary, William Gainsborough, is illuminated by the records of his ministry as minister provincial (1285–92), his sojourn in the schools as a student and regent master, his numerous commissions to act for King Edward I, his appointment as lector of the sacred palace at the papal court and finally his papal provision as bishop of Worcester on 22 October 1302. The commissions entrusted to friars in episcopal orders construct a good outline of their episcopal ministry. There are in excess of 200 references to Nicholas Warter, bishop of Dromore (1419–48).

This register brings together a complete spectrum of Franciscan life and experiences, ranging from the friars entrusted with menial tasks within their cloisters to the regent masters at the Universities of Oxford and Cambridge. The lives of friars who did not catch the eye of the chroniclers are contrasted with friars conversant with the ways of the papal court and others who enjoyed royal favour and patronage.

This introduction consists of ten short explanatory sections, beginning with a thumb-nail sketch of the structure of the Franciscan life at international, national and regional and local levels. Towards the end of the fourteenth century, Bartholomew of Pisa identified the friaries of the custody of York and noted that the administrative seat was at York,[32] the centre of the ecclesiastical and regional government. This is followed by a summary of the nine principal sources of information for this biographical register: the episcopal registers identify a large number of friars and yield a wealth of detail about the order's policies and the friars' lives. The probate registers teem with details about the economy of the friaries, the pastoral networks of individual friars, the movement of friars between different custodial houses and the organisation of the friary. The miscellaneous urban, ecclesiastical and royal sources constitute a vast quarry, preserving various witnesses to the place held by the friars in

[30] Friars of Richmond are not included in this register, unless they had a clear connection with the custody of York.

[31] Cf. B. Kane, 'Return of the Native: Franciscan Education and Astrological Practice in the Medieval North of England', *Franciscan Organisation in the Mendicant Context: Formal and informal structures of the friars' lives and ministry in the Middle Ages*, ed. M.J.P. Robson and J. Röhrkasten, Vita Regularis, XLIV (Münster, 2010), pp. 281–306, at 289–90.

[32] *BF*, v, pp. 580–602, at 580, enumerates each custody and its friaries. *De conformitate vitae Beati Francisci ad vitam Domini Iesu auctore Fr. Bartholomaeo de Pisa*, Analecta Franciscana, IV (Florence, 1906), p. 546.

the cities and major boroughs and the various roles played by the friars. The order's policy for the recruitment of friars and education are addressed in the section on the admission and training of friars for ordination. The order's educational policy was grounded in the threefold structure of schools at local and custodial levels as well as its schools in the Universities of Paris, Oxford and Cambridge. This educational endeavour was inextricably connected with the friars' ministry which forged strong bonds with their neighbours and this is demonstrated through their prayerful intercession: this dimension of the friars' ministry is explored within the context of the liturgical rhythm of the Greyfriars of York. Whereas the bibliographical sources vary, a *curriculum vitae* can be assembled for several friars. A sample of six friars demonstrates the comparative wealth of references. This is also true of the small cohort of friars elevated to the episcopate, especially those who provided long-term assistance as suffragans to the bishops of Lincoln and York. The closing section, on the accounts of the friars in regional histories, reflects on the order's impact upon the custody of York.

The constitution of the Franciscan order

There were four levels of authority within the order, which impinged upon the friars collectively and individually. First, the triennial general chapter which met alternately either side of the Alps. This body was attended by the ministers provincial and other officials, but it was remote from most friars, apart from the approval of the general constitutions and diverse decrees which were to be read in the refectory of each friary throughout the order. Secondly, the annual provincial chapter enacted legislation affecting all the friaries of England and Wales and appointed officials to each friary. Thirdly, the custodial chapters had a more direct impact upon the friars in their area, taking decisions about policies to be implemented in the regional friaries. Fourthly, each friar belonged to a specific friary and he had a voice in the domestic chapter, a body which regulated the life of the local community and the responsibilities of each member, made decisions regarding the profession and ordination of friars and struck formal agreements with benefactors and those who sought the friars' prayers.

Chapter eight of the Rule of St Francis required the friars to hold a general chapter at Pentecost every three years for the election of a minister general.[33] Following the death of the founder in 1226, the friars experienced a vacuum of authority. The general chapter of Assisi in 1230, for instance, was unable to resolve certain questions about the observance of the Rule of St Francis and accordingly appealed to Pope Gregory IX for authoritative guidance. This initiative gave rise to *Quo elongati* of 28 September 1230, the first papal judgement of how the Rule of St Francis should be applied. Initially the highest authority within the order was vested in St Francis and the ministers general who succeeded him.[34] Thus, the authority enjoyed by Elias of Cortona, minister general (1232–39), was the same as that exercised by St Francis and John Parenti, his predecessor.[35] This administrative pattern prevailed until the general chapter of 1239. What was new, however, was Elias's erratic behaviour, which was deemed to be both autocratic and despotic. It was alleged that he had set himself above the Rule of St Francis, whose teaching he flagrantly flouted. No general chapters were convened and the ministers provincial were treated harshly; perceived opponents were banished to remote provinces, such as Apulia, England and Spain.[36] This abuse of authority concentrated the friars' minds on the nature of leadership and provoked deliberation. Following Elias's defenestration, a multitude of constitutions was enacted in 1239[37] and it was agreed that thenceforth the highest authority within the order would reside in the general chapter rather than the minister general; this principle was reaffirmed by the earliest extant general constitutions.[38]

Policies regarding the establishment of new provinces and the suppression of others pertained to the general chapters. For instance, the general chapter of Rome in 1239 reduced the number of provinces from 72 to 36, with 18 either side of the Alps. One of the casualties of this decision was the relatively new province of Scotland, which

[33] *Francesco d'Assisi Scritti*, ed. C. Paolazzi, SB, XXXVI (Grottaferrata, Rome, 2009), pp. 332–33.

[34] *Francesco d'Assisi Scritti*, pp. 322–23.

[35] J. Schlageter, 'Die *Chronica* des Bruders Jordan von Giano. Einführung und kritische Edition nach den bisher bekannten Handschriften', *AFH*, CIV (2011), pp. 3–63, at 58–59, no. 61: *ipse enim habuit totum ordinem in sua potestate, sicut ipsum habuerant beatus Franciscus et frater Johannes Parens qui ante ipsum fuerant.*

[36] *Salimbene de Adam*, i, pp. 152–53.

[37] *Salimbene de Adam*, i, pp. 151, 245.

[38] *Constit. Fratrum Minorum, saec. XIII*, prol., no. 3, p. 69.

had been formed only three of four years earlier by Elias of Cortona.[39] Although Pope Innocent IV's *Ordinem vestrum* on 14 November 1245 offered further relaxations, the general chapter of Genoa in 1251 decreed that *Ordinem vestrum* should not prevail over the principles enshrined in Gregory IX's *Quo elongati*.[40] From the later thirteenth century the kings of England sent alms to the order to defray the costs of the general chapter. For example, King Edward II was at York on 24 January 1319 when he gave Thomas de Burton and John de la Lee, royal chaplains, a safe-conduct for one year to attend the general chapter of Marseille. Thomas Kingsbury, minister provincial, attended the general chapter of Padua and joined many of the ministers provincial in witnessing a document on 4 June 1382.

Each province of the order was divided into units along national or regional lines. Some countries established several provinces, such as France, which had eight.[41] In contrast, there was a single province in England and another one in Ireland. The minister general's writ ran in the English province, and, after the death of Agnellus of Pisa on 13 March 1236, Elias of Cortona reserved the right to appoint the next minister provincial, Albert of Pisa.[42] He also assigned Adam of York and Philip of Wales to teach theology to the friars at Lyon.[43] The minister provincial collaborated closely with the minister general. On his general visitation of England, John of Parma, minister general, was received with honour by King Henry III.[44] He presided over a provincial chapter held at Oxford in May 1248 and he recalled the friars to unity. Raymond Gaufredi, the minister general, visitated the English province in 1291, when he preached at Oxford on 28 October and 1 November.[45] During Passiontide in 1375 Leonard Rossi di Giffono, minister general, held a council of the masters and custodians of the province for three days at Bedford.[46] Antonio da Pereto, minister general, visited England from November 1411 until the summer of the following year. On behalf of Pope John XXIII he investigated the case for a matrimonial dispensation on behalf of Thomas, the son of King Henry IV. He was at London on 21 June 1412 when he granted a letter of fraternity to Sir John Pelham and his wife, Johanna.[47] The English province was, however, capable of some spirited independence, such as the leadership exercised by William of Nottingham at the general chapter of Genoa in 1251. Three years later English friars voted to re-elect William as minister provincial in defiance of the minister general, whose will prevailed.

Appointments to key posts and places in each custody were made by the provincial chapters, which laid down guidance for the training of novices and the teaching of theology at the provincial school and the selection of friars for study at Paris.[48] The provincial chapters selected the regent masters for the Universities of Oxford and

39 Eccleston, p. 42.

40 Eccleston, pp. 100–01. The general chapter of Genoa in 1251.

41 F.J. Mapelli, *L'amministrazione francescana di Inghilterra e Francia: Personale di governo e strutture dell'Ordine fino al Concilio di Vienne (1311)*, Medieovo, VII (Roma, 2003).

42 Eccleston, pp. 78–79.

43 Eccleston, p. 49.

44 *Salimbene de Adam*, i, p. 467. When John presided over the provincial chapter of Sens in 1248, he was kindly received by Louis's brothers.

45 Cf. A.G. Little, 'Two Sermons of Fr. Raymond Gaufredi, Minister General, Preached at Oxford in 1291', *CF*, IV (1934), pp. 161–74.

46 A. Gransden, 'A Fourteenth-Century Chronicle from the Grey Friars at Lynn', *EHR*, LXXII (1957), pp. 270–78, at 278.

47 C. Cenci, 'Antonio da Pereto, Ministro generale O.F.M. e i Capitoli generali di Roma (1411) e di Mantova (1418)', *AFH*, LV (1962), pp. 468–500, at 473. BL, MS. Add. Charters, 29260.

48 C. Cenci, 'Ordinazioni dei capitoli provinciali umbri dal 1300 al 1305', *CF*, LV (1985), pp.

Cambridge for two years in three, but in the third year the general chapter presented the regent masters, in accordance with Pope Benedict XII's *Redemptor noster*, bringing Italian and Spanish masters to lecture in England. Confessors and preachers were nominated by the provincial chapter and, after Pope Boniface VIII's *Super cathedram*, the names of these friars were submitted to the bishop for approval. William of Nottingham, junior, was at Leicester on 24 October 1320 when he wrote to Bishop Burghersh regarding licences for friars to hear confessions.[49] From the 1230s the ministers provincial found themselves employed by the crown on royal business, serving as messengers and envoys and diplomats.

The provinces of the order were subdivided into custodies which varied in number. Shortly after the first provincial chapter of London the province was split into four custodies,[50] a figure that was to increase to seven within a quarter of a century. Custodies were located at Bristol, Cambridge, London, Newcastle, Oxford, Worcester and York. Thomas of Eccleston attributes a particular virtue to each custody, noting that the zeal for evangelical poverty flourished under Martin Barton, the first custos of York, who was a witness to the beginnings of the order in distant Umbria. The variation in the geographical extent of the custodies is exemplified by the custody of Assisi in the province of that name with its constituent friaries at Assisi (the Sacro Convento, Santa Chiara, San Damiano, Portiuncula and the Carceri), Spello, Bettona, Bastia and Rocca Sant'Angelo.[51] The journey from Spello to Bastia is less than half the distance of that from Scarborough to York. The custody of Oxford, in contrast, covered a smaller and more densely populated geographical area than the custody of York, which stretched from Spalding in the south to Whitby in the north, totalling approximately 169 miles, and included parts of Nottinghamshire.[52] The borders between friaries, the *confinia locorum*, were arranged by the provincial chapters, lest friars from one convent intrude on the work of a neighbouring community.[53] The *limitationes* did not necessarily correspond to established boundaries, such as deaneries, archdeaconries, dioceses or even realms.[54] Adjacent provinces entered into agreements about their converging boundaries.[55] Friaries in the cathedral cities tended to attract testators from afar. The Greyfriars of York, for instance, received alms from testators at Ripon.[56]

The custos was responsible for these friaries and liaised with the minister provincial about the profession and ordination of friars; he notified the provincial chapter about

5–31, at 20, VI, no. 19. The provincial constitutions of Umbria in 1300 identified Perugia as the custodial school.

49 LAO, Register 5, fol. 265v.

50 Eccleston, p. 34.

51 L. Pellegrini, *Insediamenti Francescani nell'Italia del Duecento*, Storia e richerche, nuova serie (Rome, 1984), p. 300.

52 *Registrum Anglie de libris doctorum et auctorum veterum*, ed. R.A.B. Mynors, R.H. and M.A. Rouse, CBMLC, II (London, 1991), pp. 5–6.

53 E.g., J. Calamandrei, 'Constitutiones Fratrum Minorum Observantium Provinciae Thusciae ann. 1507 et 1523', *AFH*, VIII (1915), pp. 189–225, at 221–25.

54 *Reg. Hethe*, i, p. 368, admitted John de Witele, a friar of Winchelsea, to hear confessions *infra limitacionem [sic] fratrum minorum de Wynchelse* on 21 February 1326. There were no Franciscan friaries in the diocese of Rochester.

55 M. Bihl, 'Raymundus Gaufridi, Minister generalis, Parisiis 9 iunii 1292 confirmat conventionem initam inter Provincias Austriae et Alemaniae Superioris de terminis eleemosynarum conquirendarum in confiniis', *AFH*, XXXVI (1943), pp. 98–102.

56 *Memorials of the church of Ss. Peter and Wilfrid, Ripon*, ed. J.T. Fowler, SS, LXXIV, LXXVIII, LXXXI, CXV, 4 vols (1882–1908), e.g., i, pp. 331–32; iv, pp. 33–34.

the number of recently deceased friars. His duty was to oversee the way in which the Rule of St Francis and the constitutions of the order were observed. He was required to expound the Rule in the vernacular to the non-ordained members of the order and he collaborated with the crown, and the bishops of Lincoln and the archbishops of York about matters that pertained to the friars' public ministry. His approval was required for various agreements between the local bodies or individuals and the constituent friaries. Disciplinary cases were addressed to him and he presided over custodial chapters. In the vast majority of cases friars spent their whole lives within the custody, moving from one house to another, at the instigation of the custos, although there were some exceptions, as the register shows.[57] Some friars were given special duties outside the custody, such as the lecturers for the schools of Oxford and Cambridge as well as the provincial administration. In the later fifteenth and early sixteenth centuries custodial boundaries were more relaxed and there was more interaction, for instance, with the friaries of Richmond and Stamford in the custodies of Newcastle and Oxford respectively.

The custos was the senior friar in the custody. He was assisted by a vicar[58] and a team of advisors. One of his duties was to present friars to the bishop for a licence to preach and hear confessions. John, custos of York, was at the Old Temple, London, on 18 February 1330, when he presented certain friars for licences in the diocese of Lincoln. The seven friaries of the custody of York were independently constituted religious houses with their own group of officials under the jurisdiction of the custos. Unlike the monastic world with its network of priories dependent upon a founding abbey, there was no mother or filial house. The stature of the individual friary was linked to the city or town in which the friars lived. Friaries at Lincoln and York were the largest communities and they offered better amenities for education and the care of the infirm and the elderly. There were, nonetheless, distinctions between friaries. A *magnus conventus* and a *conventus solemnior* were acknowledged by the general constitutions.[59] The order's liturgical rubrics similarly made provision for a more solemn celebration of the daily Mass with a deacon and subdeacon in the large friaries. Alternative arrangements were to be made in the smaller friaries.[60] On 30 May 1267 Archbishop Giffard wrote to the unnamed custos to authorise the friars to hear confessions. The sheer size of the custody meant that the custos had to travel from Scarborough in the north to Boston in the south to conduct a canonical visitation; on occasion he excused himself from meetings with the bishop of Lincoln, deputing a friar in Lincolnshire to act for him. The boundary of the friary at York stretched as far northwards as Ripon. To the south-east, it reached the parochial borders between Leeds and Calverley, which was in *limitatio* of Doncaster.

An established friary consisted of 13 friars in continual residence; smaller institutions were known as 'non-conventuales' or *loca*.[61] Each community in the custody of York had more than the required 13 friars and it was led by a guardian. In some

[57] Emden, *A Survey of Dominicans in England based on the ordination lists in episcopal registers (1268 to 1538*), 21, where the Dominicans were seen to move generally within their 'visitation'.

[58] Cf. BL, Seal no. xxxvi. 243, the seal of the custos's vicar in the custody of Cambridge has been dated to c.1244.

[59] *Constit. Fratrum Minorum, saec. XIII*, no. 7a, p. 148.

[60] *Sources of the Modern Roman Liturgy: The Ordinals by Haymo of Faversham and Related Documents (1243–1307)*, ed. S.J.P. van Dijk, 2 vols, Studia et documenta Franciscana (Leiden, 1963), ii, p. 352, no. 60.

[61] *Constit. Fratrum Minorum, saec. XIII*, IX, nn. 20, 22, p. 94.

instances the guardian served more than a term[62] and, in others, he retained office for some years. William Vavasour, the guardian of York, was in the latter category. The guardian also corresponded with the local bishop about the friars' pastoral presence and conduct in the diocese. He was sometimes commissioned to act on behalf of the ordinary, such as on 6 May 1293, when the unnamed guardian of the Boston Greyfriars was licensed to absolve Peter de Cysters', a merchant, excommunicated because he seized John, the chaplain of Boston, by his hood.[63] On 7 August 1284 Archbishop William Wickwane authorised friars from each convent in the diocese to absolve the excommunicated.[64] Similarly, on 19 August 1286 Archbishop Le Romeyn authorised the friars in the diocese to absolve people excommunicated for laying violent hands on clerks. Friar John of Wodehalle was singled out in particular, whereas the other licensed friars went unnamed. In some instances the guardian and friary approached the crown about the acquisition of property adjacent to their precincts and this is exemplified by the friars of Scarborough in 1297. The guardian was frequently named in disputes concerning individual houses, such as the litigation involving the Doncaster Greyfriars in 1322 and 1372. Some friars served as guardian in more than one house. For instance, Richard Barton was the guardian at Beverley in the Michaelmas term of 1417 and at Lincoln in the Trinity term of 1425. The guardian was provided with a seal of office to be affixed to formal agreements.[65]

Each friary had its team of officials, such as archivist, bachelor or cursor of theology, bursar, chaplain, collectors of alms, infirmarian, lector, librarian, porters, sacristan and a vicar. Beyond the thirteenth century the vast majority of friars were ordained, with a small number of non-priests, who developed their own diverse talents. House chapters were held on Fridays and discharged business pertaining to the friary. Accounts were received and formal agreements with neighbours regarding land or the suffrages for Masses were approved. Rotas for the celebrants of Masses and the hearing of confessions were published and the arrangements for the absence of certain friars on preaching tours were recorded. Prayers for benefactors were recited in conjunction with such chapters, sometimes at tombs in the church. In addition, friars were sometimes authorised to undertake tasks outside the jurisdiction of their house. On 12 October 1301 Henry of Barton and his *socius* or companion received 60s. in expenses for travelling from York to London on the business of King Edward I. John Morton, the lector of Boston, made the journey to the episcopal manor of Buckden, Huntingdonshire, on 14 March 1319 to present friars to Bishop Dalderby for a licence to hear confessions. Some friars provided support for the London Greyfriars, the seat of the minister provincial.

For many friars, there were two focal points of their ministry. First, the apostolate to the local community, which was divided between the order's conventual church and different parishes in the city or major borough in which the friars dwelled. Friars built their own churches, where the liturgy was celebrated with dignity and devotion.

[62] Cenci, '*Fra Francesco da Lendinara e la storia della Provincia di S.Antonio tra la fine del s. XIV e l'inizio del s. XV*', pp. 121–27, 129–33, 135, 137–39, nn. 23, 26–31, 33, 36–37, 39–40, 44–46, 50–52. Between 1397 and 1426 Francesco served as the guardian of Lendinara, Venice, Vicenza, Rovighi, Piove di Sacco, Padua and Montagnana.

[63] *Reg. Sutton*, iv, p. 82.

[64] *Reg. Wickwane*, p. 317, no. 764.

[65] BL, Add. Charter 36070. Paul, the guardian at Ware, was attached to a formal agreement reached on 3 October 1525 regarding Masses to be celebrated for Thomas Hyde and his wife, Joan, at the friary in Ware. This text was attached to the seals of the local community and that of the minister provincial, Richard Brinkley.

Many were drawn to the order's churches on account of the fame of individual preachers, like William de la Mare, who preached to the clergy of Lincoln in the city's Greyfriars. William Melton, an exceptionally popular preacher, was invited to York in 1426 to preach during the festival of *Corpus Christi*. Following the example of their founder, friars expounded the Scriptures outside their friaries, as various miniatures of friars preaching in the open air attest. At Lincoln, for instance, the friars preached near the castle in the 1270s. They were guest preachers in the local churches on a regular basis, perhaps annually. Lincoln and York had an unusual number of parish churches in which the friars preached. In Boston, Doncaster and Scarborough there was a single parish church. Thomas Richmond delivered a homily to a large number of clergy and laity at the newly constructed church of St Anne on Foss Bridge, York, on 26 July 1426. Secondly, friars pursued an itinerant ministry in the towns and villages away from the friary, taking them as far as 25 or 30 miles from their convent. William White, a friar of Beverley and a limiter, was named by a testator of Little Wassand on 8 March 1527. The practice of the friars seeking alms (*for ther lyffyng*) within their territory was mentioned in the will of William Eyre of Saleby on 11 July 1531. Saleby, a village north of Alford, was closer to Boston than Grimsby or Lincoln.[66] Another example of the friars' outreach was in the letters of fraternity issued to individuals like Reginald Browne by Henry, the guardian of York, in 1479. Various aspects of the friars' conventual life emerge from a study of the episcopal registers.

[66] *Lincoln Wills, 1271–1532*, iii, pp. 146 47.

The episcopal registers, a source for the order's ministry

Dr Harold Richardson refers to the 'massive destruction' of the friars' libraries and archives at the Dissolution of the friaries in 1538–39, leaving historians to rely largely upon external sources.[67] The episcopal registers constitute 'a source of unique importance, as no similar records in such quantity have survived in any other country of western Europe', as Dr Emden observes.[68] In this context the registers assume a particular significance. The dioceses of Lincoln and York have an exceptionally good collection.[69] There is a full complement of registers from Hugh of Wells (1209–35) to John Longland (1521–47) in the diocese of Lincoln and from Walter de Gray (1215–55) to Edward Lee (1531–44) in the diocese of York. Individual registers for the two dioceses have been edited or calendared by the Surtees Society, the Lincoln Record Society and the Canterbury and York Society. There are also allusions to some lost archiepiscopal registers.[70] For instance, the register of Archbishop Thomas Arundel was consulted by William, vicar general, on 5 and 10 May 1397.[71] An insight into the contents of the register of the vicars-general of Archbishop Thoresby[72] and the *sede vacante* register for 1352–53 has been afforded by Professor Smith.[73] Two *sede vacante* registers in the diocese of York have been edited by Dr Joan Kirby and the registers of the archdeaconry of Richmond have been transcribed by Professor A. Hamilton Thompson.[74]

In addition to furnishing the names of ordinands, preachers and confessors, the registers occasionally yield details of the friars' parents or place of birth: first, Walter was styled as the son of John at his ordination as an acolyte; secondly, Robert Passelaw was described as *de Ledes* at his diaconal ordination. When Ralph Passelaw was ordained acolyte, he was styled as the son of Robert Passelaw, who does not appear among the taxpayers of Leeds in 1379.[75] Although the episcopal registers are a treasure-trove, there

[67] H. Richardson, 'The Mendicant Friars of Medieval York', *Annual Report of the Council of the Yorkshire Philosophical Society, for 1965* (1952–65), pp. 40–73, at 42.

[68] Emden, *A Survey of Dominicans in England based on the ordination lists in episcopal registers (1268 to 1538)*, p. 19.

[69] Cf. D.M. Smith, *Guide to Bishops' Registers of England and Wales: A Survey from the Middle Ages to the Abolition of Episcopacy in 1646*, Royal Historical Society Guides and Handbooks, XI (London, 1981).

[70] D.M. Smith, 'Lost Archiepiscopal Registers of York: The Evidence of Five Medieval Inventories', *Borthwick Institute Bulletin*, I (1975), pp. 31–37.

[71] BIA, Register 15, fol. 4rv, where the vicar general confirmed details of ordinations celebrated by the suffragan on 17 December 1390, 9 March 1392 and 5 June 1395 in the chapel of St Mary and All Angels, York, the parish church of St Michael-le-Belfrey and the conventual church of St Leonard.

[72] D.M. Smith, 'A Reconstruction of the Lost Register of the Vicars-General of Archbishop Thoresby of York', part 1, *Borthwick Institute Bulletin*, III, no. 1 (1983), pp. 29–61, and 'A Reconstruction of the Lost Register of the Vicars-General of Archbishop Thoresby of York', part 2, *Borthwick Institute Bulletin*, III, no. 2 (1984), pp. 102–13.

[73] D.M. Smith, 'A Reconstruction of the York *Sede Vacante* Register, 1352–3', *Borthwick Institute Bulletin*, 1 (1976), pp. 75–90.

[74] A. Hamilton Thompson, 'The Registers of the Archdeaconry of Richmond, 1361–1442', *YAJ*, XXV (1918–20), pp. 129–268, and 'The Register of the Archdeacons of Richmond, 1442–1477', *YAJ*, XXX (1930–31), pp. 1–132 and 'The Register of the Archdeacons of Richmond, 1442–1477', *YAJ*, XXXII (1934–36), pp. 111–45.

[75] D. Thornton, *Leeds: The Story of a City* (Ayr, 2002), pp. 49–50, provides examples of the members of this prosperous family in fourteenth-century Leeds. *Poll Taxes, 1377, 1379,*

are *lacunae*, particularly in the lists of ordinands. Only two ordinations were entered in the register of Archbishop Giffard and the next documented ceremony was on 21 December 1342. Similarly, there are no ordinations recorded in the diocese of Lincoln before 1290. Some extant registers, such as that of Archbishop Le Romeyn, survive, but without details of ordinations. The Lincoln registers of the fourteenth century contain few lists of ordinands and there are incomplete lists in the register of Bishop Thomas Bek from December 1345 to February 1347 and the *sede vacante* between February and May 1347. Although the registers of Bishops Henry Beaufort and Richard Fleming include some ordinations, gaps persist into the fifteenth century.

There are ample references to ordinations at the end of the thirteenth century and the beginning of the fourteenth. An anecdote regarding an ordination held at Huntingdon by Bishop Grosseteste was incorporated into *The Lanercost Chronicle*, on the testimony of an aged friar of Doncaster.[76] Bishop Dalderby engaged John Halton, bishop of Carlisle, to confer orders at Horncastle on 18 March and 1 April 1301[77] and Bishop Burghersh authorised John Kirkby, bishop of Carlisle, to hold an ordination at an unspecified location on 18 December 1333. Among the ordinands was Robert of Scaldeford, a friar of Lincoln and a subdeacon. Vestiges of the cycle of ordinations in the diocese of York are equally plentiful. On 4 February 1291 Archbishop Le Romeyn authorised Bishop Halton to hold an ordination.[78] The fact that William of Wynstede was ordained subdeacon on 7 April 1291 by Henry, bishop of Whithorn, at Beverley Minster was confirmed by letters testimonial on 23 September 1327. Archbishop Melton clearly had access to a list of ordinands that was not included in the register of Archbishop Le Romeyn.[79] On 21 December 1313 Bishop O'Tigernach was commissioned to ordain Robert de Holden, clerk of the household of the earl of Lancaster, in the Coventry and Lichfield diocese, to all minor orders.[80] Similarly, on 16 December 1318 John de Egglescliffe, bishop of Glasgow, was licensed to hold an ordination two days later.[81] Information about an ordination celebrated by Richard Kellaw, bishop of Durham, at Greyfriars, York, on 21 December 1336 was entered in his episcopal register.[82] Additional details of the round of ordinations in the diocese of York come from *The Chapter Act Book of Beverley Minster*, providing details of ceremonies held between Pentecost 1306 and September 1339.[83]

The registers are, on occasion, disappointingly imprecise. On 11 March 1318 Bishop Dalderby appointed ten Franciscans and the same number of Dominicans to hear confessions in the archdeaconry of Lincoln and four of each order for the archdeaconry of Stow. No friars' names were given.[84] Sometimes ordinands, especially

1381, p. 409, lists John Passelew, hostiler, and Ralph Passelow, barker, in the tax returns for 1379. The former paid 12d. and the latter 6d. Elinora and Johanna Passelew, who each paid 4d., may have been related to John and Ralph.

76 *Chronicon de Lanercost M.CC.I.–M.CCC.XLVI*, ed. J. Stevenson (Edinburgh, 1839), pp. 187–88.

77 *Reg. Halton*, i, p. 134.

78 *Reg. Le Romeyn*, ii, p. 95, no. 1359.

79 *Reg. Melton*, vi, p. 140, no. 432.

80 *Reg. Greenfield*, v, p. 135, no. 2576.

81 *Reg. Melton*, i, 73, no. 202.

82 *Reg. Kellaw*, iii, pp. 172–83.

83 *Memorials of Beverley Minster: The Chapter Act Book of the Collegiate Church of S. John of Beverley, A.D. 1286–1347*, ed. A.F. Leach, 2 vols, SS, XCVIII, CVIII (1898–1903), i, pp. 130–31, 173–74, 203, 253–54, 258, 367, 371–72, 383–84, 390; ii, pp. 8, 18, 25–26, 39, 48, 56, 77, 78, 82, 83, 85, 86, 90, 91, 98, 100, 101, 109, 116–17, 118, 128, 129, 133.

84 LAO, Register 3, fol. 382r.

acolytes, were styled as *fratres*. This omission is rectifiable through subsequent entries in some cases. Nicholas Burdette was, for instance, styled as *frater* at his diaconal ordination on 12 March 1351. His identity as a Franciscan is confirmed by the entries for his ordination as an acolyte, subdeacon and priest. The register of Bishop Kellaw does not unfailingly specify the mendicant order to which friars belonged. An ordination celebrated in Durham cathedral on 23 December 1335 lists three Franciscans ordained as acolytes. These names are immediately followed by eight subdeacons labelled as *ordinis mendicantium*. Nine deacons were portrayed as *religiosi* and one priest as a *frater*.[85] The quest for further identification is thwarted, unless these friars emerge from additional records as a member of one particular order. Some scribes indicated the friary to which an ordinand belonged and others were content to write *domus fratrum minorum*, as when William Welpdale was ordained deacon. During his visitation of the diocese of Lincoln, Thomas Arundel, archbishop of Canterbury, ordained 24 religious at Spalding Priory on 6 June 1411 without specifying the orders to which they belonged. Only two of the friars named appear in the registers from the custody of York. It is probable that more of these friars, bearing northern names, were followers of St Francis.[86] Scribal errors are not unknown. Two friars named Henry of Burton received the minor order of acolyte on 18 September 1334. The entries are separated by several lines.

It quickly becomes apparent that the extant registers do not unfailingly supply a complete account of the steps taken by individual friars towards the priesthood. The conspicuously high number of friars who make a solitary appearance in the registers inculcates caution. This pattern was not unique to the custody of York, as Professor Virginia Davis's analysis of the episcopal registers of London shows.[87] The register of the custody of York confirms the fragmentary nature of many of the entries for friars. William Atkinson was a friar of York ordained acolyte on 21 March 1523. He makes no further appearance in the registers of the two dioceses, but he was at York at the Dissolution on 27 November 1538. There is no extant documentation for the diaconal ordination of William Barnby, who was ordained priest on 19 September 1489. In some cases friars who were manifestly priests appear in other sources, as the pie chart below shows (Figure 2). One such was Thomas Effingham, the guardian of Lincoln, in the Easter term of 1384, when he was named in the plea rolls. This cumulative evidence points to another source besides the episcopal registers. Another explanation is that some friars received orders outside England, although this can only account for a relatively small number. Stephen *de Anglia*, for instance, was ordained deacon at an unspecified venue in Rome on 18 February 1486.[88] Dr Emden observes that some registrars did not trouble to enter the details of the ordination of religious, possibly because the religious did not enjoy a title affecting the ordinary.[89] There are instances of abbots commissioning suffragans, some of them Franciscans, to ordain monks and clerics within their jurisdiction.[90] Nonetheless, few friars surface in

85 *Reg. Kellaw*, iii, pp. 168–71.

86 Canterbury Registers: Thomas Arundel, volume two, fol. 88r–89r.

87 Cf. V. Davis, *Clergy in London in the Late Middle Ages: A Register of Clergy Ordained in the Diocese of London Based on Episcopal Ordination Lists 1361–1539* (London, 2000), p. 41, notes that most of the Dominicans and Franciscans ordained make no more than a single appearance in the register. She attributes this to the transient nature of the community.

88 Cenci, '*Documenta Vaticana*', part 8, p. 311.

89 Emden, *A Survey of Dominicans in England based on the ordination lists in episcopal registers (1268 to 1538)*, p. 20.

90 E.g., BL, MS.Add.14848, fol. 76r. On 1 June 1430 William Curteys, abbot of Bury St

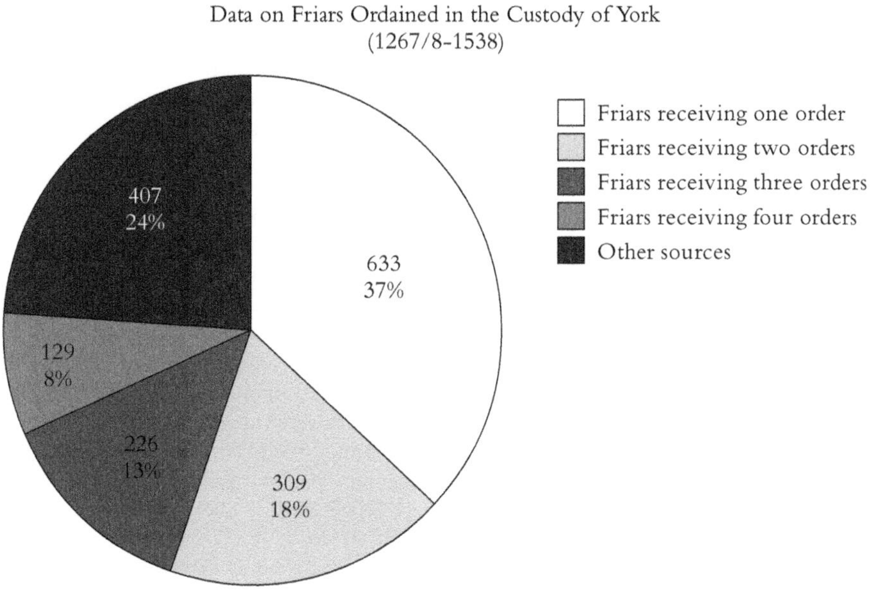

Figure 2. A pie chart and an accompanying table of recorded ordinations

monastic records of ordinations. It is clear that the episcopal registers do not contain a complete list of commissions by the ordinary for his suffragans to hold ordinations. One hypothesis is that friars enjoyed a privilege of arranging ordinations within their precincts, especially since there were so many members of the order serving as suffragans. Documentary support for this view may yet emerge.

The above chart, based on 1,704 entries in the biographical register of the custody of York, demonstrates that only 8 per cent of the friars were named four times in the registers for their ordination as acolyte, subdeacon, deacon and priest. Perhaps the most telling statistic is the 24 per cent of entries from diverse sources outside the registers of ordination, offering a pointer to the number of names lost from missing registers and rolls of ordinands.

The ramifications of the order's dealings with the secular clergy were incorporated into the episcopal registers, offering an insight into claims made by the friars and the level of distrust that had been engendered between the two groups from the middle of the thirteenth century. On 10 December 1293 Archbishop Le Romeyn distanced himself from the claims articulated by William of Hotham, the prior provincial of the Dominicans, that the people who had confessed their sins to a mendicant priest were not obliged to make their confession to their parish priest; this episcopal ruling was applied to the Greyfriars and Blackfriars of Scarborough.[91] For instance, on 15 April 1299 Bishop Sutton issued a mandate to the dean of Christianity in Lincoln to cause the clergy of the cathedral city to refrain from slandering the Dominicans

Edmund's, commissioned Robert Windell, the Franciscan bishop of Emly, to ordain clerics from his jurisdiction. The ordination was held on 3 June in the chapel of St Stephen inside the monastery and the names of the ordinands were supplied.

91 *Reg. Le Romeyn*, i, p. 40, no. 98; *Historical Papers and Letters*, pp. 102–03.

and Franciscans of the city. It was alleged that the friars had forged papal bulls; the clergy were also ordered to desist from threats to excommunicate any of their parishioners who wished to make their confession to such friars. The friars of the cathedral city were taken under episcopal protection. Nonetheless, Bishop Sutton counselled discretion and urged restraint, advising the friars to refrain from entering into polemics regarding the hearing of confessions. He undertook to deal with any cases of slanderous clergy through the dean of Christianity in Lincoln.[92] On occasion, the ordinary took the friars to task for their failings, such as their tardiness in re-interring bodies from the first friary in Scarborough in the early fourteenth century.[93]

Although the bishops of Lincoln and York licensed friars to hear confessions in their dioceses, there were tensions regarding the circumstances in which the latter functioned and this informed scholastic debates about the limited jurisdiction of the friars in the confessional. The increasing friction between the secular clergy and the friars culminated in the settlement formulated by Boniface VIII's *Super cathedram* which endeavoured to defuse the situation and to lay down principles for the future. Bishop Dalderby was one of the first English bishops to apply the principles of *Super cathedram* to his diocese. A copy of this papal decree reached Lincoln quickly where it was entered into the episcopal register on 18 April 1300.[94] The materials edited by Dr Little demonstrate that the bishop continually trimmed the lists of friars submitted by the minister provincial, Hugh of Hartlepool, from the early summer of 1300. For example, the minister provincial travelled to the episcopal manor of Dorchester on 26 July 1300 and submitted the names of 22 friars for a licence to hear confessions in the archdeaconry of Oxford. Among the nominated friars were members of the custody of York, who were resident in the university town for the purposes of lecturing and studying, Adam of Howden and Philip of Bridlington, William Shirburn and Thomas of Pontefract. The bishop baulked at the number of friars presented and concluded that four would be sufficient. However, in view of the population of Oxford and the stature of the university, he made an exception and approved six of the 22 names. After further representations from the minister provincial, the two doctors of theology were added.[95] An unsuccessful candidate was John Duns Scotus, the *doctor subtilis*, one of the greatest theologians of that era. In contrast, some friars selected secular priests as confessors. Robert Popley, probably a friar of Beverley, was styled as the spiritual son of Robert Halitreholme, rector of Biddenham in Bedfordshire, and was a beneficiary of his will.

Archbishop Giffard wrote to the Cistercian prioresses of Hampole and Nun Appleton on 17 February 1276 and other priories in the diocese, instructing them to draw their confessors from the ranks of the Dominicans and Franciscans, *qui in ecclesia Dei fulgent velud splendor firmamenti*; it seemed that the nuns were already engaging the services of friars for these duties.[96] On 5 February 1335 William of Alton and William of Barnby were licensed to hear the confessions of the Benedictine nuns of Stainfield, Lincolnshire. John Morton was appointed to hear the confessions of the Cistercian nuns of Legbourne, Lincolnshire, on 9 or 13 December 1339 together with Alan, vicar of Little Cawthorpe. Beyond this date the episcopal registers contain fewer entries for friars licensed as confessors in the custody. A later exception is John Wotton, a friar of Doncaster, who was appointed to hear the confessions of the nuns of the Cistercian

92 *Reg. Sutton*, vi, p. 160.
93 *Reg. Melton*, vi, pp. 86–87, no. 274.
94 LAO, Episcopal Register 3, fols. 3v–4v.
95 A.G. Little, *Franciscan Papers, Lists, and Documents*, Manchester University Press, CCLXXXIV, Historical Series, LXXXI (Manchester, 1943), p. 235.
96 *Reg. Walter Giffard*, p. 295, no. 892.

priory of Hampole on 10 September 1426. Artistic depictions of friars hearing the nuns' confessions survive in Bodleian Library, MS. Douce, MS.131, fol. 126r, and the British Library, MS.Add.42130, fol. 74r, a manuscript associated with the Luttrell family in the custody of York.

While there is minimal trace of the *acta* of the friars' annual provincial chapters, scattered materials survive in the form of petitions to the assembled friars.[97] Episcopal registers, too, preserve fragments of the decisions of the order's provincial chapters.[98] For instance, the provincial chapter of 1291 appointed 35 friars to preach the Crusade, that is, five friars for each of the seven custodies. Bishop Sutton's letter of 11 April 1292 confirmed this number of friars assigned to preach the Crusade. Friars were instructed to convene the people to meet *in loca ydonea* to humbly hear the proclamation of the Crusade entrusted to them by the apostolic see. Walter of Langele was, for example, assigned to the archdeaconries of Oxford and Buckingham. It is probable that two friars were assigned to the archdeaconries of Lincoln and Stow and three more across the river Humber.[99]

Registers of ordination offer a snapshot of the comparative health and appeal of the order in a particular custody in any period. Although only half of the ordinations were entered in the register of Bishop Sutton, that is, between 1290 and 1299, valuable statistics reveal, for instance, 201 Franciscans ordained between 27 May 1290 and 19 September 1299. About 40 per cent of these friars were probably from Boston, Grimsby and Lincoln; the remainder belonged to the custody of Oxford with its friaries of Bedford, Grantham, Leicester, Northampton, Nottingham, Oxford and Stamford. The number of Franciscans significantly exceeded that of their fellow mendicants, that is, 121 Dominicans, 114 Carmelites and 88 Austin Friars, and it easily surpassed the numbers for the larger monasteries in the diocese.[100] The 1290s probably represented the high-water mark for admissions to the Franciscan order. According to the registers of ordination in the diocese of York during the later fifteenth century, recruitment to the order was buoyant. In contrast, an analysis of the registers of ordination in the diocese of London between 1361 and 1539 reveals that the Dominicans at Ludgate were the largest order of friars, followed by the Carmelites and then the Franciscans at Newgate.[101] The paucity of Franciscans ordained between 1520 and 1538 in the custody of York equally presages the emergence of new ideas about the translation of the Bible into the vernacular and fierce debates about the source and exercise of authority in the Church during the 1520s and 1530s.[102]

The episcopal registers provide information on the emergence of the friars' new churches. By the middle of the 1250s the friars were beginning to accept burials in

[97] E.g., C. Cotton, 'Notes on the Documents in the Cathedral Library at Canterbury Relating to the Grey Friars', *Collectanea Franciscana*, ed. A.G. Little, C.L. Kingsford et al., BSFS, V, X (Manchester, 1922), ii, pp. 1–9, at 4–7.

[98] E.g., *Reg. Lacy*, iii, pp. 346–47, 386. Thomas Radnor, minister provincial, wrote to Edmund Lacy, bishop of Exeter, concerning the approval of the office of St Raphael by the provincial chapter of 15 August 1444 at Chichester.

[99] *Reg. Sutton*, iii, p. 195.

[100] *Reg. Sutton*, vii, pp. 124–27.

[101] M.J.P. Robson, 'The Grey Friars in York, c.1450–1530', *The Religious Orders in Pre-Reformation England*, ed. J.G. Clark, Studies in the History of Medieval Religion, XVIII (Woodbridge, 2002), pp. 109–19. Cf. Davis, *Clergy in London in the Late Middle Ages: A Register of Clergy Ordained in the Diocese of London Based on Episcopal Ordination Lists 1361–1539*, pp. 38–39.

[102] Emden, *A Survey of Dominicans in England based on the ordination lists in episcopal registers (1268 to 1538)*, 27, where a similar diminution in the number of Dominicans proceeding to ordination was pointed out.

their churches and cemeteries and this is mirrored in the will of Martin of St Cross, a member of the household of Nicholas Farnham, bishop of Durham (1241–49), master of Sherburn Hospital and prebendary of Holme in the East Riding.[103] The friars' church at Boston was constructed before 1268, when the theft of some wine was recorded.[104] Alice de Ros, whose date of death is unknown, was buried in the church of the Lincoln Greyfriars before 27 April 1286, when John Le Romeyn, archbishop of York, encouraged prayer for her soul.[105] Work on these churches was moving towards completion during the last quarter of the thirteenth century. Such activities in the custody of York were reflected in the indulgence granted by Pope Nicholas IV on 1 September 1290 to those who visited the friars' church at Doncaster on the feasts of Sts Francis, Anthony and Clare;[106] the same indulgence was also extended to the friars' churches at Scarborough on 15 October 1290[107] and York on 19 November 1290.[108] By 24 September 1303 the guardian and community at York were authorised to have their church and cemetery dedicated by any Catholic bishop,[109] a permission that enabled them to engage one of their own number in episcopal orders. The church and cemetery at Scarborough were completed by 20 March 1307, when the archbishop commissioned Bishop Gainsborough for the ceremony of dedication.[110] The friars of Doncaster, too, may have acted on the permission extended to them by Archbishop Melton on 14 October 1324 for the dedication of four portable altars.[111] On 3 June 1335 the metropolitan issued a licence for the dedication of altars and super altars (*superaltaria*) and ecclesiastical ornaments in the same friary. Both commissions were left open to be discharged by any Catholic bishop.[112]

The friars' churches in Beverley, Doncaster and York were spacious enough to accommodate the large number of clerics assembled for ordinations. An indication of the dimensions of the friars' church at Doncaster is that it was the venue for an ordination on 22 December 1347, when 194 acolytes, 101 subdeacons, 150 deacons and 151 priests were ordained. The church was clearly large enough for the 596 clerics and the officials of the diocese and the religious orders who accompanied and presented the ordinands.[113] Throughout the Middle Ages the Greyfriars of York was a regular venue for ordinations, frequently during Lent.[114] Many of these annual ceremonies were conducted by members of the order serving as suffragan bishops

[103] *John Le Neve, Fasti Ecclesiae Anglicanae 1066–1300, VI, York*, ed. D.E. Greenway (London, 1999), p. 79; *English Episcopal Acta 29, Durham 1241–1283*, ed. P.M. Hoskin (Oxford, 2005), no. 111, xxxvii–xxxviii, pp. 97–101. Writing between November 1259 and 9 August 1260, he requested burial in the nearest Franciscan cemetery, unless he should die at his church in York or Sherburn.

[104] *Placitorum in domo capitulari Westmonasteriensi asservatorum abbreviatio. temporibus regum Ric. I, Johann. Henr. III, Edw. I., Edw. II*, ed. W. Illingworth, Record Commission (London, 1811), p. 176.

[105] *Reg. Le Romeyn*, i, p. 13, no. 20.

[106] *BF*, iv, p. 171, no. 305.

[107] *BF*, iv, p. 181, no. 336.

[108] *BF*, iv, pp. 188, no. 356; *BF*, viii, p. 188, no. 1853.

[109] BL, Harley MS.6970, fol. 100v.

[110] *Reg. Greenfield*, iii, p. 127, no. 1409. Cf. BL, Harley MS.6970, fol. 138v.

[111] *Reg. Melton*, i, p. 80, no. 248.

[112] *Reg. Melton*, iii, p. 142, no. 244.

[113] BIA, Register 10A, fols. 19r–20r.

[114] Davis, *Clergy in London in the late Middle Ages: a register of clergy ordained in the diocese of London based on episcopal ordination lists 1361–1539*, p. 20, notes that, in contrast, six ordinations were held at the Greyfriars of London.

in the dioceses of Lincoln and York. Suffragans sometimes used the friars' churches as a matter of convenience. On 28 September 1425 John Kempe, archbishop of York, for instance, commissioned Bishop Warter to bless Peter de Snape as abbot of the Cistercian monastery of Jervaulx. The blessing took place at the high altar of the Greyfriars in York the next day. The suffragan witnessed the abbot's promise of obedience to the metropolitan.[115]

Among those who entered the friars' churches were fugitives, seeking sanctuary. On occasion this right was violated and the friars' privileges were trampled underfoot. This invariably led to their launching an appeal to one or more of their episcopal protectors, usually the bishops of London, Winchester and Worcester. For instance, responding to a letter from King Edward III, on 1 May 1363, Simon Sudbury, bishop of London, revoked the sentence of excommunication. William of Grimestone, rector of Goodmanham, and William of Grimestone, rector of Kilham, brought accusations against John of Lockington, who was found guilty and immediately fled to the friars' church in Beverley. His accusers pursued him there and tried to prevail upon him to leave and surrender himself to prison. When persuasion failed to achieve its end, they decided to drag him forcibly from the church in violation of the laws and the customs regarding sanctuary (*contra legem et consuetudinem*), thereby incurring the penalty of excommunication.[116] Such cases also occurred elsewhere in the custody.

Testamentary business occurs in several episcopal registers and at length in some places, such as the first register of Thomas Rotherham, archbishop of York, where it occupies folios 322 to 371. Such sources include numerous references to the order and its members. Walter, son of Thomas Orre de Drayton, requested burial in the cemetery of Drayton in his undated will, which was proved on 13 May 1346. He asked for Masses to be celebrated among the Greyfriars of York and Beverley, leaving 10s. for Thomas of Gard, a friar of York, and the same amount to Richard of Dalton, a friar of Beverley. Robert Scheffeld of West Butterwick, who was buried at St Martin's at Owston, made a bequest to the four orders of friars within their jurisdictions in his will of 4 December 1419 (*item lego quatuor ordinibus fratrum mendicantium limitantium 28s. 8d*). The nearest friary was at Doncaster, approximately 21 miles away.[117] The order's good relations with the regular clergy are reflected in two wills: first, William Alnwick, bishop of Lincoln, left 20s. to each mendicant house in Lincoln in his will of 12 October 1445;[118] secondly, the will of John Woodward, vicar of All Saints at Darfield upon Dearne, on 17 September 1537 gave 6s. 8d. to the unnamed doctor of the friary at Doncaster to preach to his parishioners either on the day of his burial or soon afterwards.[119] The bulk of the testamentary business, however, was recorded in the probate registers which include insights into the friars' domestic economy and various aspects of their lives and ministry.

115 *Reg. Sede Vacante, York, 1423–26*, pp. 77–78, nn. 496–98.
116 *Reg. Sudbury*, i, pp. 56–58.
117 *Reg. Fleming*, i, pp. 1–2, no. 5.
118 LPL, Register of John Stafford, archbishop of Canterbury, fols. 178v–79v.
119 BIA, Register 28, fol. 177rv. He also left 40d. to each of the four mendicant houses for a *placebo* and a requiem Mass.

The probate registers, a window on the friars' pastoral and social contacts

Although the episcopal registers identify a legion of friars, the gaps in such texts reflect the scale of the losses, the names which have perished, possibly as many as a third of the total number of friars, as Figure 2 confirms. The probate registers often amplify the biographical information culled from the registers of ordination and they offer a fount, furnishing supplementary information on friars whose ordinations were recorded and identifying friars, such as Friar William Dowson, who are known to posterity largely through wills. The number of extant testaments from the thirteenth century is small,[120] although the rate of survival from the fourteenth century is higher. The Dean and Chapter probate registers from 1321 to 1636 form the earliest registers at York.[121] The series of probate registers from 1389 to the Dissolution of the friaries is conserved at the Borthwick Institute at the University of York.[122] The *Testamenta Eboracensia*, edited by John Raine and James W. Clay in six volumes, provide a sample of a vast array of testamentary materials. Probate material in the diocese of Lincoln (1271–1534) has been edited by Charles W. Foster and David Hickman in four volumes for the Lincoln Record Society. Dr Alan Kissane cites testamentary materials from the Burwarmote Book, Lincoln Cathedral, MS.165, in his impressive monograph; this source contains 282 fragmentary wills recorded between 1315 and 1376.[123] In both dioceses some probate materials were contained in the early episcopal wills. The episcopal registers for the diocese of Canterbury transcribe some wills from the diocese of Lincoln. Registers from the two dioceses contain innumerable bequests to the friars from a wide spectrum of society. Merchants and tradesmen were conspicuous among the order's benefactors.

Testators from the thirteenth century reflect the early popularity of the friars and their need of material support. The second testament of Hugh of Wells, bishop of Lincoln, on 1 June 1233 gave a legacy to the poor religious houses in his diocese.[124] The will of Sir Alexander de St. Quintin on 30 April 1257 benefited the friaries of Beverley, Scarborough and York, leaving 20s. to the first community, a mark to the second and half a mark to the third. The testator referred to the friars *de scharheburg*,[125] although at that date the friars were still resident at Hatterboard in the parish of Scalby. Bishop Grosseteste bequeathed his theological books to the Greyfriars of Oxford on account of his friendship with Adam Marsh.[126] Hugh of Evesham, cardinal priest

[120] M. Sheehan, 'A List of Thirteenth-Century English Wills', *The Genealogist's Magazine*, XIII (1961), pp. 259–65.

[121] *Index of Wills, etc., from the Dean and Chapter's Court at York. A.D.1321 to 1636; with an appendix of original wills A.D.1524 to 1724*, YAS, RS, XXXVIII (1907). P.J.P. Goldberg, *Women, Work, and Life Cycle in a Medieval Economy: Women in York and Yorkshire c. 1300–1520* (Oxford, 1992), pp. 1–2, expatiates upon the abundant civic documents extant from medieval York.

[122] *Index of Wills in the York Registry 1389 to 1514*, YAS, RS, VI (1889) and *Index of Wills in the York Registry A.D. 1514 to 1553*, YAS, RS, XI (1891).

[123] E.g., A. Kissane, *Civic Community in Late Medieval Lincoln: Urban Society and Economy in the Age of the Black Death, 1289–1409* (Woodbridge, 2017), pp. 212–13.

[124] *Acta, Wells*, pp. 191–95, 192, no. 408.

[125] W. Brown, 'Old Wills from Harpham (preserved at Scampston)', *The Transactions of the East Riding Antiquarian Society*, XXI (1915), pp. 70–79, at 70–72. Earlier studies give the year 1267 as the first known reference to this friary.

[126] *F. Nicholai Triveti, de ordine Frat. Praedicatorum, Annales sex regum Angliae*, ed. T. Hog (London,

of San Lorenzo in Lucina, made bequests to several friaries in Rome and England, leaving five marks to the friary at York and 40s. to the friary at Grimsby in his will of 15 November 1286; the sum of £6 was to be divided among the Greyfriars and Blackfriars of Beverley.[127] Each custodial friary received a bequest from Oliver Wyth, a parishioner of St Nicholas at Great Yarmouth, whose will of 7 June 1291 requested burial in the friary at the town's Greyfriars and made an offering of half a mark to each friary in the English province.[128] Towards the close of the thirteenth century individual friars were named as beneficiaries. Christiana, widow of William of Long Bennington, bequeathed half a mark to the Greyfriars of Lincoln, at the disposition of Friar Geoffrey Sampson in 1283. Henry de Fillingham was probably a friar of Lincoln, when he received 6s. 8d. for a habit in the will of Master Jordan of Ingham, warden of the altar of St Peter in Lincoln cathedral and rector of East Torrington, on 24 April 1288.

Despite the order's profession of evangelical poverty, testators increasingly donated money to the friars. The will of Thomas Strey of Doncaster on 14 November 1530 gave 20s. to the friars of Doncaster and bequeathed 26s. 8d. to the Master Doctor of Doncaster Greyfriars *to bie hym a cotte*. Thomas Kirkham, a doctor of divinity and warden of the friary, witnessed the will.[129] Henry Lord Percy compiled his will at his manor of Spofford on 8 September 1349 and asked for burial in the church of St Mary at Sallay. He left the next provincial chapters of the Dominicans and Franciscans in England £20. The sum of 50s. was donated to the mendicant houses of York and £7 was to be equally divided between the friaries of Nottingham, Doncaster, Preston, Hartlepool, Richmond and Newcastle. The Greyfriars of Beverley and Scarborough were to share £4 in equal portions.[130] Richard Russell, citizen and merchant of York and parishioner of St John the Baptist in Hungate, compiled his will on 1 December 1435, leaving £10 to each mendicant house of York to celebrate Masses for himself and for the soul of his recently deceased wife, Petronilla, and the other souls specified.[131]

The agricultural economy of northern England is reflected in the donation of both livestock and crops. While two sheep were left to the friars of Beverley by Thomas Usher of Skipsea on 3 June 1524,[132] John Boswell of Epworth donated an ox to the friars of Doncaster on 20 December 1531.[133] The will of John Leek on 19 August 1527 left 5s. to each mendicant community in the town attending his funeral. For the ensuing decade this mercer of Boston undertook to provide a cow or a steer to be shared among the town's mendicant houses.[134] Dame Margaret Sutton, vowess of Burton by Lincoln, in her will of 1 October 1525 left three sheep or 20d. to each house of friars at Lincoln.[135] Roger Rockley of Rockley in the parish of

1845), p. 243: *ob cuius affectionem libros suos omnes conventui fratrum Minorum Oxoniae in testamento legavit.*

127 *I testamenti dei cardinali del duecento*, ed. A. Paravicini Bagliani, Miscellenea della società romana di storia patria, 25 (Rome, 1980), pp. 207–15, at 210, nn. 39–43.

128 P. Rutledge, 'The Will of Oliver Wyth, 1291', *A Miscellany*, Norfolk Record Society, LVI (1991), pp. 9–30, at 20.

129 *TE*, v, pp. 294–96.

130 *TE*, i, pp. 57–61.

131 *TE*, ii, pp. 52–57.

132 BIA, Probate Register 9, fol. 289r.

133 *Lincoln Wills, 1271–1532*, iii, p. 192.

134 *Lincoln Wills, 1271–1532*, ii, pp. 40–43

135 *Lincoln Wills, 1271–1532*, ii, pp. 17 18.

Worsborough, left 2d. to the Greyfriars of Doncaster for their dinner on each Friday for a term of 15 years in his will of 14 December 1522.[136]

Despite intermittent bouts of simmering tension with the secular clergy over canonical jurisdiction and parochial revenue, the friars' intercession was eagerly sought by numerous rectors and vicars. Adam de Lymbergh, rector of Algarkirk, Lincolnshire, left 6s. 8d. to each religious house in Lincoln on 18 March 1388.[137] Richard Ravenser, archdeacon of Lincoln and canon of York, Beverley and Westminster, gave 2s. to each chaplain in the friaries at Beverley and 12d. to the non-priests in his will of 15 May 1385. The same amount was donated to the chaplains and non-chaplains at York.[138] Robert Colle, alias Stevenson, a priest of Boston, gave his surplice to the local friary in his will of 2 April 1530. In return the friars should recite a *Pater Noster* and *Ave Maria* each Friday in honour of the passion and the joys of the Blessed Virgin Mary.[139] The will of William Cerff, rector of Rowley in the East Riding, shines a welcome light on the York Greyfriars on 26 February 1489. This former Cistercian of Meaux Abbey had family connections with York and he requested burial in the choir of the city's Greyfriars before the image on the high altar (*coram imagine in magno altari*). The sum of 12d. was given to the unnamed guardian and each member of the community. He donated 40s. towards the repair of the choir in the friars' church and eight members of the community were invited by name to celebrate Masses for the repose of his soul. Some canons gave money to a group of custodial friaries, such as Nicholas of Huggate, provost of Beverley and canon of Huggate, who provided alms for the friaries of Beverley, Doncaster, Scarborough and York in his will of 13 July 1338,[140] and William Waltham, canon of Lincoln and York, in his will of 8 September 1416 left 20s. to the friaries of Beverley, Boston, Grimsby, Lincoln and York.[141]

By the early fourteenth century individual friars were increasingly named as beneficiaries of wills. William of Garton, a friar of Beverley, was left 2s. in the will of Thomas, perpetual vicar of the prebendal church of South Cave, on 27 September 1326. On 16 May 1400, Thomas Dalby, archdeacon of Richmond, gave 66s. 8d. to each mendicant friary in Yorkshire within his jurisdiction to celebrate Masses for him. He also gave a mantle to Simon, a Franciscan. John Shirlowe, a friar of York, received 6s. 8d. and a pair of quartillets from the will of George Darrell on 3 October 1432. The will of Richard Russell on 1 December 1435 gave 40s. to Master John Riccall, a friar of York, and 6s. 8d. to Master William Neseham. A number of friars witnessed wills, including those made by clerics. Richard of Midelton, probably a friar at York, received five marks from John of Burton, rector of Huggate, in his will on 6–7 May 1373. The will of Peter Dalton, canon and treasurer of Lincoln cathedral, on 1 February 1402 left William Newbold 40s. for prayers for his soul, *si vivat*. John Harby was the guardian of Lincoln on 22 August 1493, when John Crokes, a parishioner of St John the Baptist at South Collingham, Nottinghamshire, gave him six marks to celebrate Masses daily for his wife and all the faithful in the friary for a year. He was Crokes's confessor and witnessed the will, which also donated ten sheep or the equivalent sum of money to each of the four orders of friars in Lincoln. Richard

[136] *TE*, v, pp. 159–61.

[137] A. Gibbons, *Early Lincoln Wills* (Lincoln, 1888), p. 6.

[138] LPL, Register of William Courtenay, archbishop of Canterbury, fols. 217v–18r.

[139] *Lincoln Wills, 1271–1532*, ii, pp. 174–75.

[140] *Memorials of Beverley Minster: The Chapter Act Book of the Collegiate Church of S. John of Beverley, A.D. 1286–1347*, ii, pp. 122–25.

[141] *Reg. Repingdon*, iii, pp. 128–30, no. 226.

Gosberkirke was the guardian at York on 1 August 1503, when he witnessed the will of Henry Atterton, a parishioner of St Mary's at Castlegate. On 2 July 1508 Henry de le See of Great Grimsby solicited the prayers of William Dowson and another unnamed friar of Grimsby for his soul and the souls of his parents and benefactors for the space of a year. John Smith was appointed an executor of the will of Nicholas Upton of Northolme by Wainfleet, Lincolnshire, on 9 January 1533.

Testamentary dispositions refer to the friaries of the custody and their place on the urban map, identifying parts of the conventual complex, such as the chapter house, the dormitory and the lector's study. On 1 October 1408 John del Bun (Bury) of York made a bequest of 13s. 4d. to the *fratribus minoribus ordinis sancti Francisci in Castelgate.*[142] The will of Thomas Carethorp of Scarborough on 11 November 1426 points to a portion in *Grayfrere Lane*, beside the house of St Leonard. The testator was the father of a friar of that name. John Kelk, a merchant, left 26s. 8d. to each house of friars in York, Hull and Scarborough on 4 February 1407, donating 40s. to the Beverley Greyfriars and an additional 95 marks to repair their church and dormitory. He also gave a cope and two chalices.[143] On 3 October 1482 Alice Baker, a widow of Kingston upon Hull, gave 20d. for the fabric of the friary *iuxta Westwod* at Beverley.[144] William Toy (Toyne), pictor and burgess of Beverley,left 10d to each mendicant house of the town (*lego fratribus ordinis Sancti Francisci manentibus in silva occidentalis Beverlac*).[145] The will of William Vasey, alderman of Doncaster, on 10 March 1515 mentioned Francisgate, where he owned property. He requested an annual *obit* at the *Freres Mynors*, leaving them 5s. He also made an offering of 6s. 8d. for the maintenance of *Freris Mynors*' bridge.[146]

The life of the friary, its conventions and some of the friars in residence are illuminated by some testators. On 1 June 1377 Sir John de Meux de Beswick, a soldier in Holderness, requested burial in the church of St Bartholomew in Aldbrough. He asked to be buried in the Franciscan habit, *quia eorum frater sum in eodem ordine.*[147] Robert of Howm, a parishioner of Holy Trinity, York, on 15 September 1396 left 40 marks to the Dominicans and Franciscans of York to enrol his name in their martyrologies; he bequeathed five marks to each mendicant house in Yorkshire to do the same.[148] One testator, Dame Katherine de Burgh, implies that there were financial distinctions among the friars, despite the vow of poverty taken by each friar. Her will of 29 December 1409 arranged that six yards of russet be placed on her body for burial in the church of St Augustine at Burgh and then given to a poor friar to pray for her.[149] The practice of inviting friars to celebrate Masses in the parish church of the testator is shown by Thomas Gra on 26 May 1417.[150] The will of Robert Manfield, provost of

142 BIA, Probate Register 2, fol. 586v.
143 BIA. Probate Register 3, fol. 263rv.
144 BIA, Probate Register 5, fol. 81v.
145 BIA, Probate Register 9, fol. 248r.
146 *TE*, v, p. 59.
147 *TE*, ii, pp. 100–01.
148 BIA, Probate Register 1, fols. 100v–01r.
149 J.W. Walker, 'The Burghs of Cambridgeshire and Yorkshire and the Watertons of Lincolnshire and Yorkshire', *YAJ*, XXX (1930–31), pp. 311–419, at 342.
150 *North Country Wills*, i, pp. 13–14: *item, volo quod immediate post decessum meum per quatuor dies quod tresdecim capellani de quatuor ordinibus Fratrum Mendicancium Ebor. in capella Sancti Johannis Baptiste, in ecclesia Beate Marie Virginis in Castelgate in Eboraco, cantent Placebo cum le Dirige et missam cum nota de Requiem in crastino, singulis diebus predictis, pro anima mea ......, et quod quilibet ordo dictorum quatuor ordinum habeat vjs.vid; et quod quilibet frater capellanus post missam suam celebratam iiid ......*

Beverley, on 12 April 1419 indicates that some ordained friars were known as *capellani* and asks that one might celebrate Masses for his soul for the period of five years.[151]

The friars' annual visits to preach in the parishes of the diocese of York are reflected in the wills of John Dale, vicar of All Saints at Batley, on 23 July 1435,[152] and William Darlay of Leeds on 27 July 1448.[153] The customary nature of these pastoral visits was portrayed as *ex consuetudine.*[154] The friaries of Doncaster and Beverley were dedicated to St Francis, according to Richard Cokson, vicar of Batley, on 1 December 1493,[155] and William Grymstone of Garton in Holderness on 12 January 1528 (*ordini sancti francisci beati Johannis Beverlac*).[156] The Beverley Greyfriars kept a *General Remembrance Book* which enumerated its benefactors' names for whom friars prayed perpetually, according to the will of Dame Joyce Percy, the widow of John Holme, on 3 August 1519. She gave them a damask cope, embroidered with lilies, so that each Friday in their chapter they would pray for her, her husband and the following six names, which should be inscribed in their martyrology: Norman Wasburne, and Elisabeth, Richard Serkeld, Sir Robert Percy, Eleanour Wyndame vel Crope and Dame Anne, the countess of Shrewsbury.[157] Testators who enjoyed a spiritual link with a friary are represented by John Arthyngton of Arthington, Yorkshire, who drew up his will on 10 June 1487 and left 3s. 4d. to each of the four orders of friars in York *cum litteris fraternitatis mee eisdem deliberandis.*[158] Reminders about anniversary Masses are reflected in the will of Robert Skyrley of Scarborough on 5 August 1522. The Greyfriars of Scarborough were required to celebrate a *Dirige* and a Mass for his and his wife's souls, *with the belman abowte the towne.* A house was left to the friars.[159] Formal contracts made between the friary and a benefactor are illustrated by the will of Walter Bradford of Houghton beside Pontefract, who left 6s. 8d. to the Greyfriars of Doncaster in his will of 28 May 1530. His executors were instructed to ensure that the guardian and convent of the Greyfriars of York celebrated a requiem Mass and a *Dirige* on the day of his funeral, in accordance with an agreement, in return for an annuity which he gave them in perpetuity.[160]

151 *North Country Wills*, i, p. 20: ... *Johanni Calere de Ordine Minorum, vel, ipso mortuo, alii capellano ydoneo et honesto, ut celebret per quinque annos pro animabus* ... He left 12d. to each priest at the friaries of Beverley, Doncaster, Lincoln and York to celebrate requiem Masses for him.

152 Cook, 'Wills of Leeds and District (Bardsey, Batley, Birstall, Bramham, Calverley, Castleford, Collingham, Featherstone, Fenton, Fryston, Garforth, Guiseley)', *Miscellanea*, PThS, XXII (1915), pp. 235–64, 238–39: *Item lego cuilibet ordini Fratrum mendicancium qui annuatim predicare solebant in ecclesia de Batley 3s. 4d.*

153 W. Brigg, '*Testamenta Leodiensia*', *Miscellanea*, PThS, II (1891), pp. 98–110, and 205–14, at 100–01: *et cuilibet ordini fratrum venientium ad predicandum apud Ledes xxd.*

154 E.g., BIA, Probate Register 5, fol. 132r. On 4 November 1478 John Smyth de Oremsby left 40s. to the mendicant orders collecting alms in his parish on an annual basis. *Ibid.*, fol. 137r: *item do et lego iiii ordinibus fratrum mendicancium elemosinas infra parochiam de Stoxelay predicte annuatim ex consuetudine colligen' ac pro missarum trentali pro anima mea dicenda et per eosdem fideliter celebrand' xxs.*

155 Cook, 'Wills of Leeds and District (Bardsey, Batley, Birstall, Bramham, Calverley, Castleford, Collingham, Featherstone, Fenton, Fryston, Garforth, Guiseley)', *Miscellanea*, p. 240: *item fratribus domus sancti Francisci apud Doncaster xiid.*

156 BIA, Probate Register 9, fol. 391r.

157 *North Country Wills*, i, pp. 104–06.

158 Cook, 'Wills of Leeds and District (Leeds, Aberford, Adel, Arthington, Allerton Bywater, Altofts, Ardsley, Austhorpe)', *Miscellanea*, PThS, XXII (1915), pp. 85–102, at 95.

159 *TE*, v, pp. 152–55, at 153.

160 *TE*, v, pp. 283–87, at 284.

The boundaries between neighbouring friaries were established by the provincial chapters and they are demonstrated by the licence issued on 10 August 1300 by Bishop Dalderby, who authorised four friars of Grimsby – Peter of Garton, Gilbert of Louth, Robert of Hale and William of Eltoft – to hear confessions *in limitacione [sic] fratrum de conventu de Grimesby*. Testators were well informed about the nearest mendicant houses of all four orders of friars[161] and their last wills facilitate the reconstruction of the territory assigned to an individual friary. Wills from northern Lincolnshire indicate the *limitatio* of the friary at Grimsby, that is, the area in which the friars preached, heard confessions and collected alms. In addition to the testators from the parish of St James in Grimsby, the friary attracted bequests from the Lincolnshire hamlets and villages of Barnetby, Burton Stather, Croxby, Donington on Bain, East Allington in the parish of Sedgebrook, Elsham, Garnthorpe, Great Cotes, Greenfield, Grimoldby, Irby on Humber next to Great Grimsby, Kirkby, Osgodby in Kirkby, Riby, Scunthorpe, Stain, Stenigot, Strubby, Tealby, Tetney, Thornton, Trusthorpe, Waltham, Westbarkworthe and Woldenewton, as it did occasional testators from the county town of Lincoln and from Beverley and Hull across the river Humber. John Waltham, bishop of Salisbury, in his will of 2 September 1395, gave 6s. 8d. to each friar of Grimsby to pray for his soul.[162]

The biographical register reveals the friars' social origins and their families.[163] John Freboys, a parishioner of St Mary's at Castlegate, left a friar of this name, possibly his cousin, an unspecified offering towards his habit and other necessities for his work on 7 January 1361. John Rillington was the son of Thomas of Rillington in the parish of Scampston and the brother of Robert. John de Kirkby was portrayed as *quondam famile mee* in the will of Cecilia de Yharom de Ebor, a parishioner of St Martin-le-Grand, Coney Street, on 16 February 1397. Adam de Acaster was the cousin of Robert Acaster of Riccall whose will of 12 June 1389 was extensive. Adam received 40s. and William Durem was given two marks in the will of William Durem, a merchant of York, on 24 June 1390; the latter was probably a relation. Robert Kirkby was the cousin (*cognatus*) of John Barker of Thirsk, who requested burial in the town's parish church of St Mary in his will of 12 November 1395. The testator left him £4 to pray for him for the space of one year. William Barker, John's brother, was a native of Whitby and asked for burial in the church of St Mary.

John Wayneman may have been a native of south Yorkshire. He was at York for his theological studies and was a member of that community when he passed from the subdiaconate to the priesthood between 21 September 1504 and 20 December of the following year. He was probably at Doncaster on 6 June 1527 when his sister, Agnes Kellome, compiled her will. She had been widowed twice and was a parishioner of St George's in Doncaster. Her will stipulated that if William Blenkynsope, the son of the first marriage, died without issue, her two houses would pass to John, her brother, for the support of the local friary. The residue of her estate was to be dispersed in alms on the Fridays before the feast of All Saints. She left 10s. to her curate, Sir John Drinkale, who was appointed as an executor along with her son. The fact that John's name does

161 *The Calverley Charters presented to the British Museum by Sir Walter Calverley Trevelyan, baronet*, vol. 1, ed. W.P. Baildon and S. Margerison, PThS, VI (1904), pp. 157–58, no. 209. The will of Elizabeth, widow of Thomas Poitevin of Headingley and a parishioner of St Wilfrid at Calverley, left 40s. each to the Greyfriars of Doncaster, the Blackfriars of Pontefract, the Whitefriars of York and the Austin Friars of Tickhill on 24 August 1342.

162 *Reg. Waltham*, p. 215.

163 Cf. N. Vickers, 'The Social Class of Yorkshire Medieval Nuns', *YAJ*, LXVII (1995), pp. 127–32, notes that the majority of the nuns of Swine were the daughters of influential county families.

not occur in lists of friars at the suppression of the friaries may indicate that he died in the decade after his sister's death.

Thomas Carethorp was the son of Thomas senior, who was resident in Scarborough. The testator, whose profession is not recorded, was nevertheless a man of substance, as his will demonstrates. His second wife, Margaret, bore him two more sons, William and John, who were described as *pueri nostri*. They were parishioners of St Mary's at Scarborough. Thomas's will, written on 11 November 1426, reveals the extent of his estate and properties, some of them in the vicinity of the local Greyfriars. He asked for burial in the chapel of *Corpus Christi* in his parish church and bequeathed various properties, including one opposite the chapel of St Sepulchre, to Margaret. He identified Robert, his son, as his heir, leaving him a portion in *Grayfrere Lane*, beside the house of St Leonard; this nomination might suggest that Thomas, who received 13s. 4d. for the purchase of a new habit, was the older son. Richard de Skipton was the son of John, a skinner, and Alice, parishioners of St Peter the Little in York. Alice's will of 18 October 1437 records that her husband had died before her and had been buried at Greyfriars. She requested burial beside him and her mortuary offering was left to the rector of her parish church. The only mendicants to benefit from her will were the Greyfriars. Alice asked Richard to administer the residue of her estate for the welfare of her soul.

While the episcopal and probate registers yield a vast amount of information on the order and the individual friars, these vital sources are supplemented by a miscellaneous collection of texts.

Municipal, ecclesiastical and royal sources, evidence of the friars' integration

These disparate sources preserve important information on the friars and their interaction with the community in which they lived, their ministry and their place on the local landscape. The ensuing texts are merely a sample of the varied materials which focus on the friars. The *White Vellum Book of Scarborough Corporation*, for instance, includes several documents pertaining to the friary, topographical allusions and contracts. Its contents include the undated charter of Reginald the miller, regarding the friars' move from nearby Hatterboard and their return to the coastal town of Scarborough in the last quarter of the thirteenth century. His charter is a unique text which describes the spatial dimensions of the friary. The English translation of the original reads:

The charter of foundation of the cloister of the Friars Minors

> 'Grant by Reginald Molendinarius (miller), of Scardburgh, to the commonalty of Scardburgh, to support the friars dwelling and serving God there, of all the undermentioned lands in the old borough of Scardburgh, viz, the land lying longwise from the cemetery of St Sepulchre's on the east to the king's way on the west, and broadways between the king's way on the south up to the gutter which is called Damyot on the north; and the land lying broadways between the said gutter in the south to the lands lately Adam Uthtred's and Walter de Collum's on the north, and longways from the king's way on the west to the land late John Nellingwycke's on the east; and also that land which lies broadways between the land late Adam Uthtred's on the west, and the land late John de Nellingwik's on the east, and longways from the land late Henry de Roston's on the south to the king's way on the north'.

The grant was witnessed by Thomas of Ebreston, John Bardh, Robert of Wyerne, William of Encrle, Geoffrey, son of Bartholomew, Lambert of Clechton, and William, the son of Ivo of the same. At the time of the Dissolution the friary occupied 3.25 acres.[164] Reginald, revered as a founder of the community, was interred before the high altar of the friars' church in Scarborough.[165]

Equally prominent in this collection of texts is *le conduit*, which is mentioned in a number of transactions.[166] As elsewhere, the friars were interested in bringing fresh water into their urban friaries.[167] For instance, the friars of York[168] and Lincoln piped

[164] I.H. Jeayes, *Description of Documents contained in the White Vellum Book of the Scarborough Corporation* (Scarborough, 1914), p. 28, no. 34b.

[165] C.G. Young, 'Notices Concerning Religious Houses in Yorkshire, with the Names of their Founders, and of Persons Buried Therein', *Collectanea Topographica et Genealogica*, ed. F. Madden et al., 8 vols (London, 1834–43), iv, pp. 73–79, 128–33, 132.

[166] E.g., Jeayes, *Description of Documents contained in the White Vellum Book of the Scarborough Corporation*, p. 28, no. 33b.

[167] Cf. J.S. Lee, 'Piped Water Supplies Managed by Civic Bodies in Medieval English Towns', *Urban History*, XLI (2014), pp. 369–93.

[168] Cf. *Cartularium abbathiae de Whiteby, ordinis S.Benedicti, fundatae anno MLXXVIII*, ed. J.C. Atkinson, 2 vols, SS, LXIX, LXXII (1879–81), i, pp. 234–35, no. 294. The undated deed, assigned to c.1270, was drawn up in the administration of Robert de Langtoft, abbot of

water into the two cathedral cities.[169] The 'goodly conduit' of the Boston Greyfriars was of great interest to the mayor of the town at the Dissolution.[170] The enthusiasm of the friars of Scarborough in arranging a source of water for their use is illustrated by a binding agreement with the borough. In or shortly before 1283 the burgesses of Scarborough gave a spring at Gilduscliff outside the town on Falsgrave Moor to Master Robert of Scarborough, dean of York, for him to make at his own expense a conduit for the use of the Greyfriars, on condition that the borough should have joint access to the water.[171] The source of the spring was about 3.2 km distant from the friary. King Edward II's licence of 12 July 1319 to the Greyfriars rehearsed the grant made earlier by the commonalty of the town.[172] The agreement reached on 7 March 1329 reiterated that the conduit was for the use of the town and the friary and that the cost was to be borne by the bailiffs, who would have the right to two-thirds of the water; the remaining third was for the benefit of the Greyfriars. The conduit was to be laid under the streets and lanes where it seemed appropriate for repair, when necessary. It was to be brought to the pavement between the new and the old borough of Scarborough and the friars were to have their own pipe; responsibility for its maintenance rested with the friars. The town's interests were to be represented by six deputed men. The charter was confirmed by King Edward III on 12 July 1339. Friars were permitted to place the conduit under roads and lanes and to prevent damage or inconvenience.[173] Part of the friars' conduit was discovered in 1975 at the junction of Stepney Road and Scalby Road. It consisted of a stone conduit bedded in clay, the base formed of solid rectangular sandstone blocks hollowed out to form a half-round channel and then capped with thin flags.[174]

The friars' presence left its mark upon local topography. There was a *venella versus Fratres Minores* at Beverley.[175] Records of that borough reflect the wider programme of building conventual complexes with large churches that was under way at numerous

Whitby (1265–78). If through any neglect on the part of the friars the property in Fishergate were damaged, the abbot and convent reserved the right (unless the friars, having been given a month's notice, made good the loss or the damage) of resuming possession of the spring and stopping up the conduit. Under no circumstances were the friars or Sir Wicher to be allowed to sell any rights pertaining to the spring or conduit.

169 *The Manuscripts of Lincoln, Bury St. Edmund's, and Great Grimsby Corporations: and of the Deans and Chapters of Worcester and Lichfield*, Historical Manuscripts Commission, Fourteenth Report, Appendix, Part VIII, XXXVII (London, 1895), p. 33. On 8 April 1535 permission was granted to the unnamed guardian of the Greyfriars to lay his conduit in the common ground of Lincoln where he deemed most convenient, and to have the licence under the common seal given to him out of charity.

170 *LPFD*, xiv, pt. i, p. 134, no. 348.

171 J. Binns, *The History of Scarborough from the Earliest Times to the Year 2000* (Pickering, 2001), pp. 27–28, explains that by this time the town had outgrown its original supply of water and that the borough well, that was fed mainly by the Damyot, was then both unclean and insufficient. He explains that for the following 500 years there was a plentiful supply of clean water.

172 *CPR, 1317–1321* pp. 376–77.
CPR, 1317–1321, p. 36.

173 Jeayes, *Description of Documents contained in the White Vellum Book of the Scarborough Corporation*, p. 42, nn. 47D and 47E.

174 L.E. Webster and J. Cherry, 'Medieval Britain in 1975', *Medieval Archaeology*, XX (1976), pp. 158–201, at 192.

175 *Beverley Town Documents*, ed. A.F. Leach, Selden Society, XIV (London, 1900), p. 27.

friaries in the second half of the thirteenth century and the first half of the next.[176] That building programme is reflected in the borough documents of Beverley on 1 December 1356, when John Butler, a friar, appeared before the town's keepers on behalf of the local Greyfriars and asked leave to take sand from Westwood to complete the friars' buildings. Permission was granted by way of exception. This friar also applied for permission to gather fallen timber in Westwood.[177] In 1520 the friars were given four tops of oaks for the fabric of their convent.[178] There is also some testamentary material preserved in borough archives along with the friary's relationship with the town's guilds. For instance, on 23 September 1398 John Ake requested burial in the parish church of St Mary, bequeathing 66s. 8d. to the local Greyfriars on condition that they provided a suitable chaplain to celebrate Masses for him for a year after his death. The friary also received 5s. in return for celebrating a trental of Masses for him.[179] In 1400 a deed of King Henry IV gave permission for a chantry to be established in the friars' church for the souls of Thomas of Kelk of Beverley and John, his son. The document was preserved in the common chest of the chapel of the Blessed Virgin Mary so that the twelve keepers of the town might inspect it at any time to ensure that the donor's wishes were being honoured with prayers for him, his family and all the faithful departed.[180]

The friars' dealings with the local guilds are echoed in a number of extant documents from the borough of Beverley. The butchers' guild held its meetings at the friary. The guild's ordinances required the aldermen to arrange an annual solemn sung Mass (*una solemnis Missa cum nota*) in the Greyfriars for deceased brothers and sisters of the guild on the Monday after the feast of *Corpus Christi*.[181] The guild of St Helen was accustomed to meet in the friars' church in the market town.[182] William of Doncaster received a stipend of 2s. for preaching at an *obit* for the guild of *Paternoster* at York in 1399/1400. William Barton, vicar of St Lawrence in the suburbs of York, admitted Dr Henry Sherwyn and Thomas Haswell to the guild of *Corpus Christi* at the county town in 1481. John Howe, a friar of Beverley, joined in 1497. Perhaps he had been a friar of York at an earlier stage and came to the attention of Thomas Topham, rector of St Gregory in York. Four of the friars admitted to the guild were masters of theology and one was a suffragan bishop. The register of the guild of *Corpus Christi* at Boston contains rubrics about *obits* to be celebrated annually at the Greyfriars.[183] Bishop Thomas Yngelby and John Bell,

176 A.G. Little, *Studies in English Franciscan History being the Ford Lectures delivered in the University of Oxford in 1916* (Manchester, 1917), pp. 72–73.

177 G. Poulson, *Beverlac; or, The antiquities and history of the town of Beverley, in the county of York; and of the provostry and collegiate establishment of St. Johns; with a minute description of the present minster and the church of St. Mary and other ancient and modern edifices*, 2 vols (London, 1829), ii, p. 771.

178 *Report on the Manuscripts of the Corporation of Beverley*, Historical Manuscripts Commission, LIV (London, 1900), p. 172.

179 *Report on the Manuscripts of the Corporation of Beverley*, pp. 145–46.

180 *Beverley Town Documents*, p. 43.

181 *Beverley Town Documents*, p. 123.

182 TNA, C47/46/446, which contains the *ordinacio* of the guild which were drawn upon on the feast of the Holy Cross on the first year of Richard II, that is, 14 September 1377.

183 BL, Harley MS.4795, fols. 81v–82r, 84r. The guild's register contains instructions regarding the celebration of the obituaries of a small number of its members, two of whose anniversaries were to be commemorated annually at the Greyfriars. On 3 July and 14 September Masses were to be celebrated for Richard Benyngton and Joan, and William Reede, a merchant of Boston, and his successive wives, Margaret and Anne. On the second of these

successive suffragan bishops in the diocese of Lincoln, were admitted to the same guild in 1479 and 1512 respectively; the latter served as its alderman six years later and admitted a former confrère, John Tynmouth, bishop of *Argos* and vicar of St Botolph's at Boston.[184]

There are plentiful references to the life of the friary at Lincoln in ecclesiastical and urban records. The friars' houses represented neutral ground in local disputes. The priory of Watton, a filial house of Sempringham, Lincolnshire, reached an agreement regarding the obedience owed to Robert de Chaury, bishop of Carlisle, for the church at Ravenstondale in Westmorland. This meeting occurred at the Greyfriars of Lincoln on 29 May 1276.[185] On 22 February 1330 King Edward III inspected one of his own earlier charters of 7 October 1327 referring to the buildings erected on the city wall close to the *mansum fratrum de ordine minorum*.[186] The parish of Holy Trinity below the hill was in Cleumarket *iuxta Fratres Minores*[187] or *ad fratres*.[188] The adjacent parish churches were Sts Edmund and Swithin. In the 1530s the urban authorities of Lincoln were faced with some dilapidated parish churches. In a series of decisions recorded between 12 September 1534 and 1 July 1535 the unnamed guardian of the Greyfriars was given leave to gather stones from the ruined churches of St Augustine and Holy Trinity 'at Grey Friars' and timber from the roof of St Bath's church for the maintenance of the friary.[189] A barometer of the changing perception of the order is the fact that cases of theft from friaries were reported with increasing frequency from the end of the thirteenth century. Thus, sessions of the justices of the peace for Lincoln confirm that John Elyot of Swaton and Edward of Wetherington were apprehended as felons and charged with stealing a maplewood bowl from the Greyfriars and four towels, worth 8s. and 4s. respectively, on 27 August 1352; they were arrested *in manso fratrum minorum Linc'* and tried before William of Skipwith and fellows at Lincoln on 6 April 1353.[190]

From the middle of the thirteenth century the friars were recruited by the bishops to assist in detecting theological error. They were drawn into the inquiries regarding the Knights Templar at the beginning of the fourteenth century. Investigations took place in the dioceses of Lincoln and York, where the friars interacted with the knights on a pastoral level. On 25 May 1310 Archbishop Greenfield directed his official to summon certain apostate Templars to appear before him and other papal

dates the bellman, accompanied by the guild's sacristan, was required to make a circuit of the town, exhorting people to pray for the merchant and his two deceased wives. The sum of 2s. was left for the friars attending the funeral and celebrating an annual Mass in their church, where they prepared a bier in their choir, with two candles burning during the Mass. They also received 3d. for their church.

184 BL, Harley MS.4795, fols. 48r, 56r, 57v–58r. The following year John Tynmouth served as alderman of the guild.

185 *Reg. Halton*, ii, pp. 211–12, refers to the *hospicium Fratrum Minorum*.

186 *The Manuscripts of Lincoln, Bury St. Edmund's, and Great Grimsby Corporations: and of the Deans and Chapters of Worcester and Lichfield*, p. 8.

187 *Records of Some Sessions of the Peace in the City of Lincoln 1351–1354 and the Borough of Stamford 1351*, ed. E.G. Kimball, LRS, LXV (1971), pp. 39–40, no. 116. Cf. *Reg. Antiq.*, x, pp. 293–94, no. 2956.

188 *Clerical Poll-Taxes of the Diocese of Lincoln 1377–1381*, ed. A.K. McHardy, LRS, LXXXI (1992), pp. 3, 99, 140, nn. 16, 1178, 1772.

189 *The Manuscripts of Lincoln, Bury St. Edmund's, and Great Grimsby Corporations: and of the Deans and Chapters of Worcester and Lichfield*, pp. 33–34.

190 *Records of Some Sessions of the Peace in the City of Lincoln 1351–1354 and the Borough of Stamford 1351*, pp. 37, 39, 43. nn. 104, 111, 123.

commissioners at Laneham on 2 July. In addition, the official was to question the parochial clergy, monks and friars (*secularibus quam religiosis*) who were accustomed to hear the Templars' confessions, clergy and laity, who were in the service of the military order throughout the diocese, along with household servants and friends.[191] On 20 June of the same year the official commissioned Roger of Mar and Richard of Wetherby, rectors of Whixley and Kirk Deighton respectively, to proceed to the area around the Templars' manors of Ribston, Wetherby and Temple Newsam in the West Riding and to summon those who had previously been in the Templars' service to testify what they had observed about the rites of admission. Replies were to be recorded under the seals of the two rectors and forwarded to the metropolitan by 29 September 1310.[192] The friars' testimony turns the spotlight on their ministry outside their own conventional complexes, and this is reflected in the presence of John Wederal at the table of Alan Malcake at Lockton in Blackmore, on the North Yorkshire moors, during the summer of the previous year. The friar, who may have been on a preaching tour, rehearsed the conversation that took place at table, adding that he had heard the confession of Richard of Hales, the commander of the preceptory of Foulbridge. The friar's evidence was communicated to Bishop Burghersh.[193] The friars visited various preceptories of the Knights Templar, perhaps to celebrate the sacraments, especially the Eucharist, and to hear confessions as well as to preach; it was not unusual for them to reside with the Templars. Dr Nicholson explains that the friars were among those who heard the confessions of their fellow religious, who had only one chaplain, Ralph of Ruston, in Yorkshire.[194] Robert of Ottringham senior recounted incidents at the preceptories of Ribston and Wetherby. The first occurred c.1290 and the second c.1303/4.[195] Thomas of Wintersham submitted written testimony regarding his visit to the preceptory of Temple Bruer, between Lincoln and Boston, on Christmas day about 1302/3 in the company of another friar, Simon of Geuertodes; the two friars made some observations about the liturgical practices followed by the Knights Templar.[196]

The royal records furnish a wealth of detail regarding benefactions to the order, taking many forms and shining a light upon the varied roles played by the friars in relation to their local communities and to the English province as an administrative unit. They highlight many of the friars' activities, providing a unique witness. One was the practice whereby the monarch on his journeys around the kingdom gave alms to the local friary. From the reign of King Edward I, the royal alms – *pro pitancia* or *pro putura* for a designated number of days – were paid in cash rather than in kind to the communities of friars. The sum of money earmarked was based on the assumption that each friar would receive 4d. for each day.[197] These accounts identify the friars who received the alms on behalf of their communities and indicate the

191 *Reg. Greenfield*, iv, pp. 285–86, no. 2271.

192 *Reg. Greenfield*, iv, pp. 334–35, no. 2301.

193 Nicholson, *Templars*, i, pp. 185, 200, 381.

194 Nicholson, *Templars*, ii, pp. xxiii, n. 81, pp. 192–93, n. 38.

195 Nicholson, *Templars*, i, pp. 184, 383.

196 Cf. Nicholson, *Templars*, i, pp. 185, 199–200. Thomas of Bokingham, described as *frater* rather than *de ordine minorum*, swore that he and his *socius* had spent Christmas Eve c.1305/06 at the preceptory of Faxfleet in the East Riding of Yorkshire and had celebrated Mass there. On a later occasion, when he preached to the Knights Templar, they grumbled about the length of the sermon.

197 Little, *Studies in English Franciscan History being the Ford Lectures delivered in the University of Oxford in 1916*, pp. 39, 68–72.

comparative size of particular communities within a custody. They offer a comparison of the number of friars living in different mendicant houses in a specific city or town. Tensions with Scotland over the succession to the throne at the end of the thirteenth century and the later incursions of Robert Bruce's army into Yorkshire brought the English monarchs into the custody of York on several occasions at the beginning of the fourteenth century. The period 1299/1300 shows King Edward I to have been a frequent visitor to Beverley, Boston, Doncaster, Lincoln and York; royal visits to Grimsby and Scarborough were not recorded in that period.

On 12 November 1299 the king gave alms to the 30 friars of Doncaster through Friar Edmund of Horburn for one day; payment was made at Wentbridge.[198] On 17 November he visited York and supplied alms to 52 friars for the three days through Friar John of Turbingthorpe.[199] On 24 November he visited Beverley Minster, where offerings were made at the tomb of St John, the church's high altar and the banner (*vexillum*) of the saint. The next day the monarch gave alms to 33 friars through Friar Richard de Warr'. On 20 January 1300 he was at Doncaster where he provided alms for 30 Greyfriars for two days, through the hand of Friar John de Potynden. An additional 6s. 8d. was paid to make good damage done to the friary on the occasion of the royal visit. On 22 May the king was in Boston and he gave alms to the 30 friars for two days through Friar Gilbert of Lonsdale. Two days later he reached Lincoln, where he gave alms for two days to the 30 friars through Friar Walter of Stokton. On 29 May he was back in Beverley, where he gave 38s. for three days through Friar Thomas Maynard. About 13/14 June he gave alms of 57s. for three days to the Greyfriars of York through Friar Henry of Shipton.

These figures indicate that the friary of York was the largest community in the custody, with 57 friars in 1300, followed by Lincoln with 52 and then Beverley, Boston and Doncaster with communities of 30 or more. The number of Franciscans exceeded that of their Dominican neighbours at York, Lincoln, Beverley and Boston. At York there were 33 Austin Friars, 25 Carmelites and three Friars of the Sack in 1300. The number of Dominicans resident on this occasion is obscured because they received the sum of 62s. 8d for the celebration of Masses in response to a report that the new queen, Margaret of France, had given birth. The previous year there were 52 Dominicans in the county town. In the same period there were 57 Franciscans, 47 Dominicans, 30 Austin Friars, 28 Carmelites and four Friars of the Sack at Lincoln. The king's son, probably Edward of Caernarfon, gave alms to some mendicant houses, including the Greyfriars of Lincoln which received 10s. on 3 June; the Greyfriars of Doncaster were left 10s. on 8 June.[200] On 29 November 1300 the royal alms of 19s. 4d. for the Greyfriars of Doncaster were received through Friar Ralph Trikyngeham. The following day the monarch gave an offering of 7s. to the friars' high altar.[201]

The wardrobe accounts also record alms sent to the general and provincial chapters and draw attention to the way in which friars were recruited by monarchs and queens of western Europe to serve as messengers. At an unspecified date in April 1300 King Edward I sent alms of 100s. to the general chapter which was to meet at St Liz [*sic*] in France, through Friar Henry Baynard. On 3 September of that year Friar Alan of York received the king's offering for the order's provincial chapter at Stamford. The

198 TNA, E101/356/7.

199 TNA, E101/356/7.

200 *Liber quotidianus contrarotulatoris garderobae. Anno regni regis Edwardi primi vicesimo octavo regni regis Edwardi primi vicesimo octavo. A.D.MCCXCIX & MCCC. Ex codice MS. in bibliotheca sua asservato typis edidit Soc. Antiq. Londinensis*, ed. J. Topham (London, 1787), pp. 25, 28, 36–40.

201 BL, MS.7966A, fols. 23r, 25v.

presence of the crown in York and its environs attracted friars from other parts of the order, such as Friar William Provost and his unnamed companion, who acted as messengers for the king of Cyprus. On 15 June King Edward I gave alms of £2 to Friar Peter de la Roqueigne and his *socius*, messengers of Alphonsus, king of Castile, on their return to Spain. On 10 December 1299 Friar James de Benfaunzon and his *socius* received £10 for their expenses in delivering a message to Queen Margaret from the king and queen of France.[202]

After laying the foundation of episcopal and probate registers with a disparate group of borough sources, attention turns to the admission to the order and the spiritual and intellectual formation of the friars.

[202] *Liber quotidianus contrarotulatoris garderobae. Anno regni regis Edwardi primi vicesimo octavo regni regis Edwardi primi vicesimo octavo. A.D.MCCXCIX & MCCC. Ex codice MS. in bibliotheca sua asservato typis edidit Soc. Antiq. Londinensis*, pp. 34, 44–45, 161, 181.

Admission of friars and their path to ordination

As the order spread throughout the country, it began to attract an increasing number of men from different strata of English society, especially the schools, the secular clergy, monks and the locality. First, recruitment from the schools and new universities is reflected in the admission of William of York, a solemn bachelor at Oxford, and Ralph of Corbridge, a regent master of theology at Paris. Thomas of Barnby was a fellow at Merton College, Oxford, before joining the order at an unknown date before 1288. Secondly, the order's appeal to members of the secular clergy is personified in Thomas of Geddington, the master of St Leonard's Hospital, York, Robert, the vicar of Horbling, Lincolnshire, and Nicholas de Turribus, rector of Kirkheaton. Thirdly, members of religious orders were drawn to the order, including Richard of Yarwell and John of Grimsby, successive priors of the Augustinian Canons of St Mary Magdalen at Nocton Park, Lincolnshire, between 1277 and 1292; the latter had previously been a canon of Thornton Curtis, Lincolnshire. It is more difficult to gauge the number of vocations from the unbeneficed clergy and the rank and file of the monasteries, whose transfers found no place in the episcopal registers. Little is known about the subsequent activities of the members of the second and third groups. Fourthly, Thomas of York typifies those who sought admission to the local friary and maintained a lifelong interest in it, despite his protracted sojourn at the nascent Universities of Oxford and Cambridge. Fifthly, the majority of friars were clerics by the end of the thirteenth century. There were, however, lay brothers, who rarely featured in ecclesiastical records and whose approximate number is difficult to calculate.

Although a great deal is known about the familial background of some friars, *lacunae* are plentiful. The order recruited from the ranks of the nobility and gentry. Thomas of Eccleston, for example, refers to the fact that the parents of Augustine and William of Nottingham were accustomed to dispense alms to poor children.[203] At the end of the fourteenth century William Woodford conceded that some vocations were drawn from the upper echelons of English society.[204] Whereas the order admitted the scions of the aristocracy and the gentry, such as William Vavasour of Copmanthorpe, their neighbours in the urban centres were largely tradesmen. The poll tax return for 1381 confirms that several tradesmen resided in the parish of St Mary at Castlegate, York, where the friars lived.[205] The available evidence indicates that some vocations came from the families of tradesmen. Richard of Skipton was the son of John, a skinner, and Alice, parishioners of St Peter the Little, York. Richard Warter was the son of Adam, a spurrier and a parishioner of St Martin-le-Grand, Coney Street, in the county town. John Leeming was the son of John, a cooper, and Joanne, parishioners of St Michael-le-Belfrey, York. John Harwood was the only son of Robert, a fletcher and parishioner of St Michael, Spurriergate. Henry Sherwyn's brothers, Robert and Thomas, a pewterer and a glazier, were parishioners of St Helen's parish, Stonegate, York. He survived them by at least a decade and may have been the youngest son. His brother-in-law, William Bukler, the husband of Joanne, was a tapiter. His other

[203] Eccleston, p. 102.

[204] *Woodford, Respons.*, p. 162, Q. 49: *aliqui etiam fratres sunt qui habent potentes amicos et divites de parentela sua vel aliunde.*

[205] E.g., *Poll Taxes, 1377, 1379, 1381*, p. 140, where the taxpaying members of the parish of St Mary, Castlegate, York, in 1381 were enumerated.

sister, Katherine, became a nun in the Augustinian house of Moxby.[206] Although little is known about Richard of Skipton, the other friars mastered their studies and progressed to ordination. Henry Sherwyn equipped himself for the priesthood and the more challenging intellectual environment of Cambridge. After his stint in the Fens, he returned to the city of his birth, where he held the office of lector for some years and was connected with some of the influential residents of the county town. These friars may have attended the grammar schools which were part of the local landscape[207] before entering the order's network of schools at local, custodial and university levels, as will be explained below.[208]

At the end of the thirteenth century it was still generally true that a man's name was derived from his birthplace or at least from his normal place of residence in youth. Several friars ordained in the time of Bishop Sutton bore the names of towns and villages in Yorkshire and northern Lincolnshire; parts of Nottinghamshire, such as Collingham and Retford, also lay in the custody. Such local names, however, are not necessarily a guarantee of the friars' geographical origins. The duplication of place names, sometimes within a few miles of each other, further bedevils the quest for fuller information on the friars' place of birth. Professor Barrie Dobson comments that toponymics have always been an erratic guide to the geographical origins of Englishmen.[209] Thus, John Spaldyng of York, a vintner, made bequests to Spalding in his will of 31 May 1394;[210] William Roderham of Beverley in the diocese of York was ordained to the diaconate on 30 May 1450;[211] and John Pudsey was a citizen of York and a weaver, when he drew up his will on 20 July 1442.[212] These local friars were joined by their confrères from more exotic locations in Ireland, Umbria, Tuscany or Denmark and Germany, reflecting the order's cosmopolitan character.[213] Fr Conrad Walmsley identified several Dutch friars from Arnham, Bosco, Deventer, Dordrecht, Harderwijk, Limburg, Middelburg, Roermond and Utrecht. John Leland asserted that Thomas of York was a native of the county town to which he retired late in his life and that William Gainsborough was born in the Lincolnshire town of that name. His information may have been gleaned from the *Catalogus de eruditis Franciscanis* at Oxford which he consulted as the shadow of the Dissolution was falling. From the fourteenth century, patronymics became more common, with some surnames denoting paternal profession,[214] such as Baker, Barker, Chapman, Draper, Fisher, Glover, Mason, Milner, Sadler, Slater, Smith and Taylor.

Although aspirants were accustomed to make their first contact with the nearest friary, they were clothed as friars at the custodial house, probably on one of the

206 Cf. M.J.P. Robson, 'A Prosopographical Study of the Greyfriars of York, ca.1230–1538', *Medieval Prosopography*, XXII (2001), pp. 1–29.

207 Cf. A.F. Leach, *Early Yorkshire Schools*, 2 vols, YAS, RS, XXVII, XXXIII (1899–1903); N. Orme, *English Schools in the Middle Ages* (London, 1973), and *Education and Society in Medieval and Renaissance England* (London, 1989).

208 Cf. B. Roest, *A History of Franciscan Education (c. 1210–1517)*, Education and Society in the Middle Ages and Renaissance, XI (Leiden, 2000).

209 *The Jewish Communities of Medieval England: The Collected Essays of R.B. Dobson*, ed. H. Birkett (York, 2010), p. 11.

210 BIA, Probate Register 1, fol. 67rv.

211 BIA, Episcopal Register 19, fol. 295rb

212 BIA, Probate Register 2, fol. 44r.

213 Cf. J.R.H. Moorman, 'The Foreign Element among the English Franciscans', *EHR*, LXII (1947), pp. 289–303.

214 Cf. J. Greatrex, *The English Benedictine Cathedral Priories: Rule and Practice c.1270–c.1420* (Oxford, 2011), pp. 48–49.

principal feasts in the liturgical calendar. William of York was admitted on the feast of the conversion of St Paul on 25 January 1229/30 at Oxford, and Richard Hanworth, the former abbot of Barlings, was clothed as a friar at York on the birthday of the Blessed Virgin Mary on 8 September 1285. The *Calendar of Inquisitions* offers two examples of friars entering the order at York: first, Robert, the son of Thomas de Rillington, a native of Rillington in the North Riding, was aged 56 when he confirmed the proof of age of William, the heir of William Latimer, a knight. He added that his brother, John, had been clothed as a friar at York around the feast of the Annunciation in 1330; secondly, John Proctour seems to have been a native of Bolton Percy in North Yorkshire. On 10 November 1382 his father, Robert, then aged 60, testified that Margaret, daughter of John, son of John, son of John Chaumont, knight, was born in the town of Colton and baptised in the church of All Saints, Bolton Percy, on 11 October 1367. Towards 1325 there were novices, such as Walter of Yarwelle, in York. There was diversity of practice within the order, with some custodies assigning the master of novices to another house rather than the custodial house.[215]

According to the general constitutions of 1260, a single friary was designated for the ascetical formation and instruction of novices. Where the numbers warranted it, a second house within a custody was to be opened.[216] The period of the novitiate was one of retreat' from society, a time of prayerful reflection and reorientation, when candidates were schooled in the teaching of the Scriptures and imbibed the customs and conventions of religious life, the special traditions and history of the order under the direction of an experienced and prudent friar. Instruction was proffered on the Divine Office and how to sing it and other liturgical activities. Novices also studied the penitential and mystical heritage of the fledgeling order. The Rule of St Francis and its application and the hagiographical tradition were also part of the syllabus. Manuals for the benefit of both masters and novices were compiled by friars such as David of Augsburg and Bonaventure of Bagnoregio. Novices were enjoined to avoid secular studies and any participation in the public life of the local Church; they were to play no part in the life of the school attached to the friary and restrictions were placed upon those novices who had already received some orders; they were not permitted to proceed towards the priesthood. Furthermore, novices who were already priests were not allowed to hear confessions in this period. In the early morning they probably served the Masses of the priests in the community before beginning their daily studies and embarking upon manual work. Testators of the fifteenth and early sixteenth centuries mentioned novices at different custodial friaries. There were, for instance, three novices at Doncaster and five at York at the Dissolution. In addition, there was, by the end of the fifteenth century, an expectation that novices would attend funerals within the city or town in which they resided. At the close of the novitiate year they were admitted to religious profession by declaring these words:

'I, Friar N. vow and promise to God, to the Blessed Virgin Mary, to St Francis, to all the saints, and to you, Father, to observe all the time of my life the Rule of the Friars Minor confirmed by the Lord Pope Honorius, by living in obedience, without anything of my own, and in chastity.'[217]

215 *Reg. Burghersh*, ii, pp. 69, 113, nn. 1709, 2062, indicates that the novitiate house for the custody of Oxford was Bedford in the early fourteenth century.

216 U. Nicolini, 'Le tavole dei capitoli provinciali dell'Umbria del 1408 e del 1431', *AFH*, LIX (1966), pp. 301–22, 307. The provincial chapter of Assisi at Perugia in 1408 appointed a *magister novitiorum et iuvenum* at both Spoleto and Foligno in the custody of Spoleto.

217 *Constit. Fratrum Minorum, saec. XIII*, I, nn. 7–11, p. 71.

Afterwards the newly professed friars were transferred from the care of the master of novices to the master of students. Robert Bewchampe was the *magister studentium* at York when he was licensed to preach anywhere in that diocese from 23 October 1483. The premium placed on continuing scholastic formation is reflected in the order's evolving constitutions that specified the stages whereby friars passed from the novitiate to the houses of study and to ordination, a theme to be explored more fully in the next section. The study of the liberal arts, consisting of the *trivium* (grammar, dialectic and rhetoric) and *quodrivium* (mathematics, geometry, astronomy and music), allied with physics, the natural sciences, logic and philosophy, provided the intellectual foundation for theological studies.[218] Ministers provincial were instructed to establish schools for the arts in their provinces.[219] The separation between the arts and theology was reflected in the general constitutions of Strasbourg in 1282 which ordained that law and philosophy should not be taught simultaneously by the same lector.[220] These schools imparted the necessary intellectual and theological information for ordination to the priesthood and the exercise of pastoral care.[221] Friars were among the scholars who explained the sciences for their contemporaries. John Pecham, for instance, was the author of treatises on perspective[222] and mathematics.[223] A century later John Somer was a distinguished astronomer at Oxford, when he compiled his much copied calendar.[224]

There was internal regulation of the friars' studies. Studies paved the way for the reception of the minor and then major orders. The clerical tonsure preceded the minor orders of porter, lector, exorcist and acolyte and the major orders of subdiaconate, diaconate and priesthood.[225] The six orders gradually leading to the priesthood resembled the steps leading to the throne of Solomon (1 Kings 10.18–19), according to Bonaventure of Bagnoregio.[226] The friars' reception of the minor orders, acolyte excepted, is not recorded in the episcopal registers of the dioceses of Lincoln and York, although elsewhere in the order it was. In the province of Bologna, for example, friars were ordained *ad titulum mensae conventus eiusdem [Bononiae]*.[227]

Evidence from the registers in the custody of York indicates that the majority of the friars moved from being acolytes to priests within the space of two years,

218 Cenci, '*Fra Francesco da Lendinara e la storia della Provincia di S.Antonio tra la fine del s. XIV e l'inizio del s. XV*', nn. 7–16, pp. 114–18, was ordained in 1391, nine years after being received into the order. Following his novitiate, he studied the arts, logic and philosophy at Lendinara, Treviso, Bologna, Ferrara and Piacenza. His theological studies came after ordination to the priesthood.

219 *Constit. Fratrum Minorum, saec. XIII*, X, no. 111, p. 58.

220 *Constit. Fratrum Minorum, saec. XIII*,VI, no. 11d, p. 181.

221 Cf. Roest, *A History of Franciscan Education (c.1210–1517)*.

222 *John Pecham, Tractatus de perspectiva*, ed. S.F. Brown, Franciscan Institute Publications, XVIII (St Bonaventure, New York, 1972).

223 B. Hughes, *De Numeris Misticis by John Pecham. A Critical Edition*, *AFH*, LXXVIII (1985), pp. 3–28, 333–83.

224 *The Kalendarium of John Somer*, ed. L.R. Mooney, Chaucer Library Series (Athens, GA, 1998).

225 *Magistri Petri Lombardi Parisiensis episcopi Sententiae in IV Libris distinctae*, ed. I.C. Brady, 2 vols, SB, IV,V (Grottaferrata, 1971–81), ii, lib. 4, dist. 24, cc. 4–11, pp. 395–405.

226 '*Breviloquium*',VI, c. 12, nn. 1 and 4, *Bonaventurae Opera Omnia*, v, pp. 277–78. The offices of tonsure and psalmodist were envisaged as a preparation for the seven orders.

227 E.g., C. Piana, 'Promozioni di religiosi francescani agli Ordini sacri a Bologna (an' 1349–1508), *AFH*, LVII (1964), pp. 3–89, at 15–16. Cf. C. Piana and C. Cenci, *Promozioni agli ordini sacri a Bologna e alle dignità ecclesiastiche nel Veneto nei secoli XIV XV*, SB, III (Florence, 1968).

although there were exceptions, such as Robert Cross, who was ordained an acolyte on 17 March 1492 and priest on 22 September of that year. Robert Ruston, ordained acolyte, subdeacon, deacon and priest between 3 March 1425 and 15 March 1432, represents the longer route to ordination; such delays may have been occasioned by illness. Notwithstanding the provisions of canon law, some friars received the minor order of acolyte and major order of subdiaconate during the same ceremony, particularly in the aftermath of the Black Death. Six friars were ordained as acolytes and subdeacons by Archbishop Thoresby at Greyfriars, York, on 26 May 1358. John Scarborough, a friar of Boston, received the same two orders in Lincoln cathedral on 20 September 1404.

There was a policy whereby a small group of friars in the custody progressed from the minor order of acolyte to the priesthood as members of the community in York and this principle was exemplified by Thomas Humlok, who received his orders between 21 December 1510 and 20 December 1511. He may, nonetheless, have been assigned to another friary in the custody before he became an acolyte. It is probable that there was a similar practice concerning the friary at Lincoln. John Wells was, for instance, a friar of Lincoln between 20 September 1404 and 14 March of the following year, when he received the orders of acolyte, subdeacon and deacon; details of his ordination to the priesthood remain unknown.

Policies regarding the friaries of York and Lincoln co-existed with a more general strategy of moving students for the priesthood from one custodial house to another, at the instigation of the custos, on the recommendation of the lectors of the different friaries. On occasion an ordinand sampled life in at least three friaries *en route* to the priesthood. William Barnby was at York when he was ordained acolyte on 13 March 1484, at Boston when he was ordained subdeacon on 5 April 1488, and at Oxford when he was ordained priest on 19 April 1489. Cornelius of Elmet was at Beverley on 2 April 1435, at Scarborough on 22 December 1436, and at York on 25 May 1437, when he was ordained subdeacon, deacon and priest. It was not uncommon for friars to receive all or most of their orders in a single county, apart from cases of higher studies. The special position of the custodial school of York in friaries north of the Humber is confirmed by the extant details of ordinations from the minor order of acolyte to that of the priesthood. In addition, the fact that few friars sampled life at both York and Lincoln *en route* to ordination implies that the latter school was second only to the former.

The movement of friars *en route* to ordination was not necessarily arranged neatly year by year, according to a blueprint devised by the custody. Instead, evidence points to the transfer of student friars once or twice during the academical year with relatively short sojourns at a particular friary. This seems to have been done on an *ad hoc* basis, but it was facilitated by a common *curriculum* of studies and set books for the custody or province. Thus, John of Doncaster was a friar of Lincoln on 19 September 1355, but was assigned to Boston before 19 December of that year. Robert Egrimond was at Lincoln on 14 February 1478 and at Grimsby on 7 March of that year. He was back at Lincoln by 21 March of the same year, progressing from being an acolyte to the diaconate. Richard Hansand was at York on 27 February 1496 and at Richmond on 28 May of that year, when he was ordained to the subdiaconate and diaconate respectively, returning to York for 17 December of that year, when he was ordained priest. It was not uncommon for friars from the same house to proceed towards the priesthood together. William Vavasour and John Ashton were friars of York when they were ordained as acolytes and subdeacons on 13 March 1484 and 18 December of that year. It is probable that they had entered the order at the same time and were fellow novices. John

Cade and Richard Cambridge were at York, where they were ordained as acolytes on 6 March 1501. Three weeks later they had been assigned to Lincoln, when they were ordained to the subdiaconate on 27 March. Appointments may have depended upon the particular theological strengths of a lector and his assistant or the bibliographical resources of a particular friary. It is equally conceivable that there was a custodial policy whereby friars combined time at some of the smaller friaries, such as Grimsby and Scarborough, with residence at one of the order's schools in the cathedral cities.

Friars were prepared for the minor orders of exorcist and acolyte as well as the major orders of subdiaconate, diaconate and priesthood. Domestic tests ensured that they were well equipped for their examinations by the diocesan officials in the days preceding the ordination. Bishops were accustomed to announce the venue and the day on which holy orders would be conferred, along with arrangements for clerics to check the candidates, two or three days prior to the ordination.[228] Evidence of dimissorial letters issued for the ordination of friars does not appear among the episcopal registers of Lincoln and York. There is, nonetheless, no hint that the friars were exempt from the episcopal investigation.[229] For instance, a group of four friars travelled from Beverley to Blyth, Nottinghamshire, for the assessment on 20 September 1274, two days before the ordination. The registers of Bishop Sutton identify the diocesan officials appointed to evaluate candidates for each of the orders. Thus, the bishop appointed Master Walter, archdeacon of Huntingdon, and Sir Robert of Warsop to inspect candidates for the priesthood on 22 September 1296; Master Jocelyn, archdeacon of Stow, for deacons; Master Nicholas of Whitchurch for subdeacons; and Sir John of Scalleby and Sir Richard of Toyton for acolytes. The examiners' names do not appear again in the registers until an ordination held at Lincoln cathedral on 21 September 1538, when John Cliffe, a friar of Lincoln, was scrutinised by Dr Robert Cliffe, chancellor of Lincoln. Such scrutinies were far from a formality, as clerics of Beverley Minster discovered. It was reported on 2 April 1337 that four of the seven sent for ordination, including two candidates for the priesthood, failed their inspection.[230] At least one diffident candidate resorted to impersonation during the appraisal of his levels of literacy.[231] In view of the large number of ordinands involved, it is difficult to take issue with Professor Logan's judgement that the diocesan officials had little time to spend for a 'comprehensive testing of each candidate' before the ceremony of ordination.[232]

The order's officials liaised with the ordinary for the ordination of friars on specific occasions.[233] Orders were conferred on the six customary days, that is, the Saturday of the first week of Lent; *Sitientes*, that is, the Saturday before Passion Sunday; the vigil of Easter; the eve of Holy Trinity Sunday; the Saturday following the feast of the exaltation of the Holy Cross and later St Matthew; and the Saturday

[228] Cf. CUL, EDR, G/1/1, De Lisle, fol. 85v.

[229] Cf. CUL, EDR, G/1/1, De Lisle, fol. 30r. On 27 November 1349 Master John de Oo, vicar general of the diocese of Ely, issued dimissorial letters to the prior of Ely cathedral for three monks of Ely, John of Walsingham, to be ordained to the priesthood, and Simon of Broughton and Thomas of Aldbrough to be ordained to the diaconate and priesthood.

[230] *Memorials of Beverley Minster: The Chapter Act Book of the Collegiate Church of S. John of Beverley, A.D. 1286–1347*, ii, p. 117.

[231] *Reg. Rotherham*, p. 192, no. 1547.

[232] Cf. F.D. Logan, *University Education of the Parochial Clergy in Medieval England: The Lincoln Diocese, c. 1300–c. 1350*, PIMS, Studies and Texts, CLXXXVIII (Toronto, 2014), p. 17.

[233] LPL, register of Walter Reynolds, archbishop of Canterbury, fols. 153v–54r.

following the feast of St Lucy. On 30 January 1349 an exception was made on account of the decimation of the priests' ranks by the Black Death (*propter ministrorum ecclesiasticorum per mortalitatis pestem nuper in provincia Ebor*). Pope Clement VI's letter of permission on 12 October 1349 was quoted by Archbishop Zouche in the preamble to the list of ordinands. On that occasion there was only one friar ordained.[234] Small groups of clerics were ordained at other times in order to meet pressing pastoral needs. Friars were generally presented for ordination by the guardian or another senior official of their community, as two examples from the diocese of Durham demonstrate: first, John Blok was presented by his guardian when he was ordained as a priest (*per gardianum suum debite presentatus*); secondly, Robert Todde bore letters from his guardian (*per litteras gardiani sui debite presentatus*) when he was ordained acolyte.

There are instances of friars undertaking lengthy journeys for ordination. As already mentioned, four friars of Beverley travelled to Blyth, Nottinghamshire, probably the priory church of Sts Mary and Martin, a journey of approximately 52 miles on 20 September 1274. Several friars were ordained on 18 December 1344 at Whitefriars, York. Among them were three deacons, Laurence of Copmanthorpe of Scarborough, John of Walton of Beverley and John of Dalton of Doncaster. The first had a journey of about 41 miles, the second about 32 miles and the third around 41 miles. Robert Grene and Godfrey of Saxonia, friars of York, received orders at St Katherine's Gilbertine priory in Lincoln on 6 June 1433. William Talbot, a friar of York, travelled even further afield and was ordained deacon at Ramsbury prebendal church, Wiltshire, in the diocese of Salisbury, on 23 September 1413. John Billam, a friar of York, was ordained subdeacon at the parish church of Oakham, Rutland, on 19 December 1360. Friars at Boston, Grimsby and Lincoln frequently had to travel to the far-flung episcopal manors for ordination. The journey from Grimsby to Buckden, Huntingdonshire, was approximately 115 miles. At the other end of the spectrum, many friars from York were ordained in their own church.

According to the order's general constitutions, friars were eligible for ordination to the priesthood from the age of 25.[235] The priesthood was primarily perceived in terms of the forgiveness of sins and the confection of the Eucharist.[236] Newly ordained friars probably assumed limited duties in the friary because they had no faculties to preach in the local diocese. They were probably restricted in their ministerial role and were described as *capellani*, attending funerals and celebrating Masses in local churches for the deceased. They were not yet deemed to be fully prepared for the preaching tours. This period may have been one of further theological and canonical study to prepare themselves for the position of confessor, an office open to suitable candidates who had attained the age of 30.[237] In addition to the theology of penance, friars preparing for the office of confessor were required to familiarise themselves with the canonical powers of the confessor and the sins which were reserved to the bishop. The qualities of the confessor were spelled out in the order's constitutions. Ministers provincial were

[234] BIA, Register 10A, fol. 38v. *Historical Papers and Letters*, pp. 401–02.

[235] *Constit. Fratrum Minorum, saec. XIII*, IX, no. 23b, p. 348: *precipit generalis minister cum generali capitulo universo, quod nullus frater de cetero promoveatur ad sacerdocium, nisi sue etatis completum habeat XXV annum.*

[236] E.g., *John Duns Scotus, The Report of the Paris Lecture, Reportatio IV–A*, 2 parts, ed. O.V. Bychkov and R. Trent Pomplun (St Bonaventure, New York, 2016), p. 62, no. 20: *absolvere enim peccatorem a peccatis per modum arbitrii et conficere corpus Christi verum sunt duo actus sacerdotis principales.*

[237] *Constit. Fratrum Minorum, saec. XIII*, IX, no. 23b, p. 348.

admonished to exercise discernment in nominating discreet and trustworthy friars for this office.[238] Those who promoted friars of unsuitable character to this office were to be disciplined.[239]

This consideration of the friars' preparation for the ministry paves the way for an account of the order's extensive network of theological schools.

[238] *Constit. Fratrum Minorum, saec. XIII*, no. 117, p. 58.
[239] *Constit. Fratrum Minorum, saec. XIII*, VI, no. 16, p. 83.

The friars' mission of evangelisation rested upon their firm commitment to the study of theology, largely through a detailed knowledge of the Bible and the scholastic method. For this reason Agnellus of Pisa, minister provincial, engaged Master Robert Grosseteste to teach the friars at Oxford from approximately 1229/30. The success of this scholastic venture was heralded by Thomas of Eccleston. Following Grosseteste's elevation to the diocese of Lincoln on 25 March 1235, three successive secular priests – Peter, who became a bishop in Scotland, Roger Weasenham, who became bishop of Coventry and Lichfield, and Thomas le Waleys, who became bishop of St David's – followed him. Adam Marsh became the first Franciscan regent master c.1242/43 and was succeeded by Ralph of Corbridge, a member of the custody of York. Graduates from the Oxonian school were appointed to the custodial schools and the local schools which were becoming an integral part of the local friary. The proliferation in the number of lectors was celebrated by Thomas of Eccleston, who attests that before 1254 there were 30 friars solemnly lecturing and another three or four who taught without disputations. In addition, friars were trained to serve as regent masters at Oxford and Cambridge.[240] Before the middle of the thirteenth century the friars had established major schools of theology in the seven custodies and lectors were appointed to several friaries.[241] The expansion of the local schools of theology conducted by the friars in the cities and boroughs between 1240 and 1270 was noted by Roger Bacon.[242] The number of lectors and their assistants increased steadily in the second half of the century until the point at which friars were engaged to teach theology to other religious communities, such as Christ Church cathedral priory in Canterbury from 1275 to 1314. The stature of the English province rose on account of its learning, and its lectors were appointed to teach theology in other provinces of the order from 1228, as the chronicles attest. In each community the lector, a friar who had been trained in the environment of the university, was responsible for the continuous theological education of the whole community.[243]

From the later 1220s a system of continuous education was devised for the order. Salimbene de Adam, the celebrated historian, was a witness to the lifelong nature of the friars' studies. Writing in 1284, he reflects that in the previous 45 years, he had never ceased to attend the lectures in the internal schools, beginning in the novitiate at Fano with lectures by Humile of Milan on Isaiah and Matthew.[244] The value of such a theological formation is reflected in the order's constitution and the statutes of its provincial chapters. Clerical friars, regardless of the offices occupied, were compelled to frequent the schools and to stay there until the end of the lectures.[245] The 1337 provincial statutes of the French province required the custos to ensure that all friars

[240] Eccleston, 50. Cf. A.G. Little, 'The Franciscan School at Oxford in the Thirteenth Century', *AFH*, XIX (1926), pp. 803–74.

[241] *Matthew Paris, HA*, ii, p. 110: *tandem scolas theologiae infra septa sua constituentes, legentes et disputantes ...*

[242] *Fr. Rogeri Bacon opera quaedam hactenus inedita*, pp. 398, 428–29.

[243] Cf. B. Roest, 'The role of lectors in the religious formation of Franciscan Friars, Nuns and Tertiaries', *Studio e Studia: Le scuole degli ordini mendicanti tra XIII e XIV secolo, Atti del XXIX Convegno internazionale, Assisi, 11–13 ottobre 2001, Società internazionale di studi francescani, centro interuniversitario di studi Francescani, nuova serie diretta da Enrico Menesto, 12* (Spoleto, 2002), pp. 83–115, 90, n. 10.

[244] *Salimbene de Adam*, i, p. 424.

[245] *Constit. Fratrum Minorum, saec. XIII*, VI, no. 11b, p. 125: *arcentur autem omnes fratres clerici ad*

attended the schools. The hours of hearing confessions were suspended during the principal lectures (*principalium lectionum*). No friar should absent himself from the lectures without the special permission of the vicar or the principal lector.[246] With the exception of the smallest friaries and the hermitages, each friary had its own school and its slate of lectures each morning. The order's schools operated on three levels: the local school; the custodial school; and the *studia generalia* or universities.

The first rung of the educational ladder was the local school over which the principal lector (*lector principalis*)[247] presided, sometimes with the assistance of a *lector secundarius*,[248] a bachelor or a cursor of theology.[249] In some cases the lectors' duties were divided between philosophy and theology. Thus, each friary in the custody of York had its own lector and team of theological assistants. In spite of earlier legislation, there was in some schools a *lector biblie* who also taught philosophy.[250] The scholastic year ran from the feast of St Francis until the end of the provincial chapter or Pentecost.[251] Lectures were given in the mornings and they were graded in terms of importance; the concept of the *lectio principalis* was established at a comparatively early stage.[252] The purpose of these schools was to educate friars for the apostolate. An early general chapter ordained that the ministers provincial should erect *schole artium* for the instruction of the younger friars.[253] The general constitutions of the order provided for instruction in law, philosophy and physics.[254] The quality of the teaching available in local schools is reflected in the experience of Michael Dawnay. After his ordination he studied at Hartlepool in the custody of Newcastle from 1400 to deepen his study of mathematics, domification and other subjects suitable for astronomy. From there he advanced to the University of Cambridge, where he lectured between 1411 and 1414 before returning to the custody of York.

The seven liberal arts and the sciences paved the way for the friars' study of theology. Lectors were instructed to teach the Bible cursorily (*de biblia cursorie*) and the text of the *Sentences of Master Peter Lombard*, the basic manual of theological questions.[255] John Linwod was styled as a professor of the theology of the *Sentences* (*theologiae Sententiarum professor*) of Peter Lombard on 10 July 1478. Once the scientific

ingressum scolarum, cum non fuerint circa iniuncta sibi officia occupati. Et qui otiositati dediti fuerint, gravi subiiciantur discipline vel de loco studii emittantur.

246 M. Bihl, 'Statuta provincialia provinciarum Aquitaniae et Franciae (saec. XIII–XIV)', *AFH*, VII (1914), pp. 466–501, at 493, VII, nn. 2–4.

247 Bihl, 'Statuta provincialia provinciarum Aquitaniae et Franciae (saec. XIII–XIV)', p. 493, VII, no. 4.

248 E.g., Cenci, '*Fra Francesco da Lendinara e la storia della Provincia di S. Antonio tra la fine del s. XIV e l'inizio del s. XV*', p. 173, no. 75. On 23 October 1409 there was a *lector Biblie* and a *lector philosophie* at Santa Maria Gloriosa dei Frari, Venice.

249 Cf. Roest, *A History of Franciscan Education (c. 1210–1517)*, pp. 81–87.

250 B. Bughetti, 'Tabulae Capitulares Provinciae Tusciae O.M. (saec. XIV–XVIII)', *AFH*, X (1917), pp. 413–97, 416, 418.

251 *Constit. Fratrum Minorum, saec. XIII*, VI, no. 11a, p. 125.

252 Bihl, 'Statuta provincialia provinciarum Aquitaniae et Franciae (saec. XIII–XIV)', p. 493, VII, no. 4.

253 *Constit. Fratrum Minorum, saec. XIII*, n. 111, p. 58: *quod ministri in suis provinciis ordinent studia in artibus pro iuvenibus provincie instruendis.*

254 *Constit. Fratrum Minorum, saec. XIII*, VI, no. 11d, pp. 181, 240, 315.

255 Bihl, 'Statuta provincialia provinciarum Aquitaniae et Franciae (saec. XIII–XIV)', *AFH*, VII (1914), p. 493, VII, nn. 2–4. In the province of France, with the exception of the principal schools (*exceptis principalibus studiis*), lectors were instructed to teach the Bible cursorily (*de biblia cursorie*) and the text of the *Sentences of Master Peter Lombard.*

foundation had been laid, friars had to be conversant with the Scriptures, the range of questions arising from the *Commentary on the Sentences* and the studies pertaining to moral theology and canon law for the confessional. A primary concern of these schools was the production of materials suitable for itinerant preachers, who required portable texts for their travels. The lectors and their assistants were engaged in the production of booklets designed to assist friars in the preparation of homilies for the Sundays and feasts of the liturgical year. Local schools offered expertise in a number of subjects connected with philosophy and theology as well as some degree of specialisation in the natural sciences. Numerous friars from these schools are encountered in the episcopal registers. Robert Simmonside was at Scarborough, for example, when he was ordained acolyte, deacon and priest between 13 June 1489 and 28 May 1491; he received the subdiaconate when he was assigned to the friary in York, where he spent no more than one term.

Information on lectors in the custody of York is rather fragmentary and the extant entries are sometimes succinct, such as a commission to hear confessions. John of Beverley was a friar at Oxford, who may have been attending the lectorate programme about 1256. The names of three lectors were associated with licences to hear confessions: first, J., the lector at Doncaster, was licensed to absolve on 20 March 1290; the permission was renewed a week later, on 27 March; secondly, Simon Jorz was the lector at Boston on 10 August 1300, when he was authorised to hear confessions in the *limitatio* of the friary at Boston; thirdly, John Morton, a native of Gainsborough, was the lector at Boston on 14 March 1319, when he was presented as the long-standing support of Bishop Dalderby, whom he may have known at Oxford at the end of the thirteenth century. Richard Leyton, a friar of Lincoln, was mentioned in a manuscript belonging to the friary in the cathedral city, where he may have been the lector. John Holbeach attained the rank of *magister* in his studies at Cambridge, where he transcribed texts on the Bible and medicine. Lectors studied in a university context, although they were not members of the universities. At the end of their stay at the *studia generalia* the newly qualified lectors returned to their own provinces, where they took up teaching positions in their native custody. The lectors' ranks, however, included many gifted theologians, some of whom had filled the office of regent master at Oxbridge.[256] Ralph of Corbridge, who was regent master at Oxford, in 1244/45, was later appointed to Lincoln, where he may have served as lector. Robert of Halifax, who had lectured at Oxford, Cambridge and Paris,[257] subsequently spent time at Doncaster, where he may have been the lector. Walter Percy, whose university is unknown and probably outside England, may have been the lector at Beverley. Most of the friars in the custody of York reflected the experience of the *fratres communes* among their Dominican neighbours. Fr Leonard Boyle explains that although such friars did not taste higher studies, they were the 'backbone of the order'. Daily study remained central to their ministry of inculcating the norms of the Gospel.[258] The theological education of most Franciscans, too, was confined to the local schools of the custody of York. The fact that the majority of the friars spent some time at York

[256] Cf. M.J.P. Robson, 'Franciscan Bachelors and Masters of Theology in the Custody of York (1250–1350)', *Revue d'histoire ecclésiastique*, CXI (2016), pp. 5–33.

[257] W.J. Courtenay, 'Some Notes on Robert of Halifax, O.F.M.', *FS*, XXXIII (1973), pp. 135–42.

[258] L. Boyle, 'Notes on the Education of the *Fratres communes* in the Dominican Order in the Thirteenth Century', *Xenia Medii Aevi Historiam Illustrantia oblata Thomae Kaeppeli O.P.*, ed. R. Creytens and P. Künzle, 2 vols, Storia e Letteratura raccolta di Studi e Testi, CXLI, CXLII (Rome, 1978), i, pp. 249–67, at 253–55, 256–57.

prior to ordination to the priesthood implies that the school in the county town played a twofold role, a local and a custodial school.

The custodial schools constituted the second tier of theological education.[259] They offered an advanced form of theological studies. One of their functions was to prepare friars for the lectorate programme at the universities and another was to groom a small knot of friars for the baccalaureate and doctorate in theology. The stature of the custodial school was reflected in its staffing levels.[260] Headed by a doctor of theology rather than a graduate of the lectorate programme, there was a division of the teaching duties between at least two lectors and possibly one or more bachelors or cursors of theology. The lector at York had already completed his term as regent master at the universities before returning to his own custody. One such was Adam of Lincoln, the twenty-fourth regent master at Oxford about 1292, who was one of the mendicant doctors of theology at York on 21 February 1311, when he was invited to participate in the provincial council. Thomas of Pontefract, the thirty-fifth regent master at Oxford, may have been either the second lector of York or a lector in another friary in the diocese. He, too, participated in at least one of the sessions of the council. A glimpse of the teaching staff of the custodial school of York is afforded by Archbishop Scrope's appointment of two lectors and three cursors of theology on 30 August 1398 to hear confessions in the diocese. The probate registers identify several of the lectors at the custodial house of York, such as John Riccall and William Neseham.

The custodial schools had a long history, reaching back to the 1240s, according to Matthew Paris. The school at York may have been responsible for the education in the liberal arts and cognate subjects, accounting for the fact that most friars spent some time there on their way to the priesthood. The attraction of these regional schools is reflected in the presence of friars from Germany, Holland, Ireland, Tuscany and Umbria in the custody, as the biographical register confirms. Contemporary practice in the custody and the lecture halls was codified by Pope Benedict XII's *Redemptor noster*, his constitution of 28 November 1336 for the order. The rubric regarding studies confirmed the stratification of the theological schools and named 21 approved *studia* including Coventry, Exeter, London, Newcastle, Norwich, Stamford and York, the custodial schools of England. The pope ordained that friars intending to complete their studies should first deliver lectures on the *Sentences* of Master Peter Lombard[261] and other approved texts of the doctors at these custodial schools before commenting on the same text at the Universities of Paris, Oxford or Cambridge.[262] Biblical texts and the *Sentences* of Master Peter Lombard, thus, formed the core of this education in theology.

259 Cf. Roest, *A History of Franciscan Education (c.1210–1517)*, pp. 65–81.

260 Nicolini, 'Le tavole dei capitoli provinciali dell'Umbria del 1408 e del 1431', p. 304. The provincial chapter of Assisi at Perugia in 1408 appointed a *lector*, a *lector biblie* and a bachelor to the Sacro Convento. Cenci, '*Fra Francesco da Lendinara e la storia della Provincia di S.Antonio tra la fine del s. XIV e l'inizio del s. XV*', pp. 117–18, no. 14, testifies that in 1389 Francesco was one of 28 students in logic at San Francesco, Ferrara, where he remained for two years before studying philosophy.

261 *Magistri Petri Lombardi Parisiensis episcopi Sententiae in IV Libris distinctae*; M.L. Colish, *Peter Lombard*, Brill's Studies in Intellectual History, XLI, XLII, 2 vols (Leiden, 1994); *Mediaeval commentaries on the Sentences of Peter Lombard: Current Research*, ed. G.R. Evans (Leiden, 2002); P.W. Rosemann, *Peter Lombard*, Great Medieval Thinkers (Oxford, 2002).

262 *Constit. Fratrum Minorum, saec. XIV*, p. 311, IX, no. 14. M. Bihl, 'Ordinationes a Benedicto XII pro Fratribus Minoribus promulgatae per bullam 28 Novembris 1336', *AFH*, XXX (1937), pp. 309–85.

Students at the custodial schools were educated in an environment that resembled life at the universities. Their teachers and tutors were friars who had already served as regent masters or the bachelors of theology who would form the next generation of masters at the universities. The quality of the teaching available in such a setting is emphasised by Professor William J. Courtenay, who points out that these schools were 'a place of importance only slightly less' than the *studia generalia*. These schools provided a more challenging syllabus of studies in the arts and theology and they scarcely differed from the educational programme available in the universities. In such a stimulating atmosphere some of the finest theologians of the English province cut their theological teeth and produced their best work.[263] After 1310 most *Commentaries on the Sentences* by friars were given in the form of a first draft before their lectures in the universities.[264] Examples of friars delivering one set of lectures on the *Sentences* in the custodial schools and another at Oxford come from Walter of Chatton and Adam Wodeham in the 1320s and 1330s respectively. Walter of Chatton probably delivered his *Reportatio super Sententias* at the custodial school of London between 1321 and 1323,[265] before going to Oxford where he prepared his *Lectura super Sententias* a few years later.[266] Adam Wodeham, a member of the custody of Cambridge, lectured on the *Sentences* first at London, then at Norwich and finally at Oxford. His *Lectura Norwicensis* was delivered between 1329 and 1332 and survives in a *reportatio*. It is conceivable that he was then awaiting an opportunity to teach at Oxford. In 1332 he lectured on the *Sentences* at Oxford,[267] where he was the sixty-first regent master.[268] Bachelors of theology from the custody of York delivered a *Lectura Eboracensis* in their native custody before their *Lectura Oxoniensis* or *Lectura Cantagbrigiensis*.

The role and competence of the custodial schools is illustrated by Thomas of York. His studies at York were completed by 1245, when he had joined the community at Oxford, where he was being nurtured to become the fourth regent master in theology. His proficiency in the arts was acknowledged by the university in the spring of 1253 *propter eminentiam moris, ingenii, litterature et experientie* and his appointment was endorsed. The fact that he had not lectured in the faculty of arts was waived because of his thorough preparation for that position. On the completion of his teaching at Oxford, he crossed to the Fens, where he became the sixth regent master at Cambridge. He produced scriptural commentaries and was the first English friar to join the fray of the polemical disputes regarding the friars at the University of Paris.[269] A copy of the treatise was among the books assigned to the warden's study at Merton College Library, Oxford, in 1483. Thomas proceeded to build a theological reputation for himself that passed beyond Dover through his *Manus, que contra Omnipotentem tenditur*, which he composed in the summer of 1256,[270] and his *Sapientiale*, a text

[263] Courtenay, *Schools and Scholars in Fourteenth-Century England* (Princeton, 1987), pp. 66–67.

[264] Courtenay, *Schools and Scholars in Fourteenth-Century England*, p. 68.

[265] *Walter Chatton, Reportatio super Sententias*, Libri III–IV, ed. J.C. Wey and G.J. Etzkorn, 2 vols, PIMS, Studies and Texts, CXLVIII, CXLIX (Toronto, 2004–05), ii, pp. ix–xiii.

[266] *Walter Chatton, Lectura super Sententias, Liber I, distinctiones 1–17*, ed. J.C. Wey and G.J. Etzkorn, 3 vols, PIMS, Studies and Texts, CLVI, CLVIII, CLXIV (Toronto, 2007–09).

[267] *Adam de Wodeham, Lectura Secunda in librum primum Sententiarum*, ed. R. Wood and G. Gál, 3 vols (The Franciscan Institute, St. Bonaventure University, New York, 1990), i, pp. 8*, 31*–33*.

[268] Eccleston, p. 57.

[269] *The Letters of Adam Marsh*, ed. C.H. Lawrence, 2 vols, OMT (Oxford, 2006–10), ii, pp. 450–51.

[270] *Bettelorden und Weltgeistlichkeit an der Universität Paris: Texte und Untersuchungen zum literarischen armuts-und exemtionsstreit des 13. Jahrhunderts (1255–1272)*, ed. M. Bierbaum, Franziskanische

which Fr Ephrem Longpré judged to be *la grande Somme philosophique du XIIIe siècle*, holding a very important place in scholastic history.[271] The *Sapientiale* was incomplete at Thomas's death about 1260, according to one manuscript, *explicit liber septimus quem non complevit morte praeventus* (Città del Vaticano, Biblioteca Apostolica Vaticana, Cod. Vat.lat 4301, fol. 194vb).[272] A small section of the treatise, I, 27–29, has been transcribed by Professor Fiorella Retucci, who is preparing an edition of the latter text.[273] Thomas's partial commentary on *Liber XXIV philosophorum*, which was incorporated in the *Sapientiale*, has been edited by Professor Françoise Hudry.[274] Some 70 years after Thomas's death, passages from the *Sapientiale* were reproduced verbatim by Berthold of Moosburg, the principal lector of the Dominican studium at Cologne, in his *Expositio super elementationem theologicam Procli*. His table of the doctors of theology on whose writings he had relied includes *Magister Thomas Anglicus minor*.

The third educational level consisted of the *studia generalia*. At the top of the scholastic pyramid was *le grand couvent des Cordeliers de Paris*, an institution that was unrivalled in the order during the thirteenth century. Promising candidates were required to spend two or three years of study in England before being appointed to Paris for a minimum of four years of theological study in the lectorate programme,[275] which drew friars from numerous provinces of the order. They probably heard the lectures on the customary texts by a bachelor of theology. Afterwards such newly qualified lectors returned to take up teaching posts in their own custodies, generally before the age of 30.[276] The general chapter of Paris in 1292 ordained that, on the completion of his lectorate programme, the new graduate was required to obtain a testimonial letter from the lector or guardian of the *studium generale*.[277] Some friars were ordained during their studies for the lectorate programme. One of them was William de Shirburn, who was ordained to the priesthood along with John Duns Scotus at St Andrew's at Northampton on 17 March 1291. On the completion of their studies they returned to their own province and custody, where, still in their third decade, they took up a teaching position.

The graduates of the lectorate programme subsequently selected for the degrees in theology at the University of Paris constituted a small minority of the student body,

Studien, 2 (Münster, 1920), pp. 37–168; A.G. Traver, 'Thomas of York's Role in the Conflict between Mendicants and Seculars at Paris', *FS*, 57 (1999), pp. 179–202.

271 E. Longpré, 'L'École Franciscaine. Histoire partiale. Histoire vraie', *La France Franciscaine*, 6 (1923), pp. 108–34, 112–13.

272 F. Retucci, 'The *Sapientiale* of Thomas of York, OFM: The Fortunes and Misfortunes of a Critical Edition', *Bulletin de Philosophie Médiévale*, LII (2010), pp. 133–55, at 140, 142.

273 F. Retucci, 'Tomasso di York, Eustrazio e la dottrina delle idee di Platone', *Per perscrutationem philosophicam Neue Perspektiven der mittelalterlichen Forshung*, ed. A. Beccarisi, R. Imbach and P. Porro, Corpus Philosophorum Teutonicorum medii aevi, IV (Hamburg, 2008), pp. 79–110, at 89–110.

274 *Liber viginti quattuor philosophorum*, ed. F. Hudry, CCCM, 143a (Turnhout, 1997).

275 *Constit. Fratrum Minorum, saec. XIII*, VI, nn. 12, 13, p. 83. Cf. Roest, *A History of Franciscan Education (c.1210–1517)*, pp. 87–97. Cf. Courtenay, 'The Instructional Programme of the Mendicant Convents at Paris in the Early Fourteenth Century', *The Medieval Church: Universities, Heresy, and the Religious Life. Essays in Honour of Gordon Leff*, ed. P. Biller and R.B. Dobson (Woodbridge, 1999), pp. 77–92.

276 W.J. Courtenay, 'Early Scotists at Paris. A Reconsideration', *FS*, LXIX (2011), pp. 175–229, at 176–77.

277 *Constit. Fratrum Minorum, saec. XIII*, VI, no. 20e, p. 318. Cf. C. Cenci, 'Constitutiones Provinciales Provinciae Umbriae anno 1316', *AFH*, LVI (1963), pp. 12–39, at 28, VI, no. 12.

that is, about 5 per cent, who were enrolled for the baccalaureate or the doctorate.[278] These friars had already gained experience as lectors in the local and custodial schools of their provinces and custodies. They were, according to Professor Courtenay, in their fourth decade or older when they were appointed to read the *Sentences*.[279] The friars' school had been incorporated into the University of Paris as a result of the vocation of Alexander of Hales, the former archdeacon of Coventry, who is known to posterity as the *doctor irrefragabilis*. The first masters of the Parisian school, including Alexander and his pupil, Bonaventure of Bagnoregio, shaped the theological vision of the nascent Franciscan school close to the banks of the river Seine, keeping it firmly within the Augustinian tradition with a discerning reception of the newly available Aristotelian materials.[280] The centrality of the Parisian *studium* in the life of the order is reflected in the order's early constitutions and in the flood of students from all parts of the Franciscan cosmos. Members of the English province crossed the Channel to study and then lecture there as bachelors (Richard Rufus of Cornwall, Roger Marston and William of Ware), or regent masters (William de la Mare, John Pecham and John of Wales).

By the later thirteenth century the Universities of Oxford and Cambridge were starting to draw students from other provinces of the order. Nicholas de Carbio, the confessor and biographer of Innocent IV before becoming bishop of Assisi, was one of the first students from other provinces to study in England in the later 1230s.[281] There were already at least two friars from the province of northern Germany studying in England by 1250.[282] The benefits of sending students to study theology at Oxford, Cambridge and London were explained to Geoffrey de Brie, minister provincial of France.[283] The unique range of academic resources in England was a further reason for dispatching students to the country, writes Adam Marsh.[284] One valuable resource was the system of indexing symbols that had been devised by Grosseteste with the help of Adam Marsh and continued by the friars.[285] *The Tabula septem custodiarum* and the inter-connected *Registrum Anglie de libris doctorum et auctorum veterum* perhaps grew out of that project; these twin texts frequently travelled in the same manuscripts (e.g., Cambridge, Peterhouse Library, MS.169); both tasks were completed by the Oxford Greyfriars between approximately 1309 and 1313/17.[286]

The friars' studies were nurtured by the formation of remarkably impressive libraries, whose administration and supervision were regulated by the order's general constitutions. The order's benefactors provided them with books to enrich their studies and their apostolate. One such donor was John, the vicar of Edlington, who gave the friary in Lincoln a copy of Peter Lombard's Commentary on the Psalter, which is now Lincoln Cathedral Library, MS.41 (A.2.10). Friars who augmented the

[278] Courtenay, 'Early Scotists at Paris. A Reconsideration', pp. 176–79, and 'Scotus at Paris: Some Reconsiderations', *Archa Verbi, Subsidia 4, The Opera Theologica of John Duns Scotus: Proceedings of 'The Quadruple Congress' on John Duns Scotus*, ii, ed. R. Cross, Franciscan Institute Publications (New York, 2012), 1–19, 13, n. 30. Cf. Roest, *A History of Franciscan Education (c.1210–1517)*, pp. 97–115.

[279] Courtenay, 'Early Scotists at Paris. A Reconsideration', p. 177.

[280] *John Pecham, Letters*, iii, p. 901.

[281] Eccleston, p. 88.

[282] *The Letters of Adam Marsh*, ii, pp. 410–11.

[283] *The Letters of Adam Marsh*, ii, pp. 414–17, 518–21.

[284] *The Letters of Adam Marsh*, ii, pp. 518–19.

[285] R.W. Hunt, 'Manuscripts Containing the Indexing Symbols of Robert Grosseteste', *Bodleian Library Record*, IV (1953–54), pp. 241–55.

[286] *Registrum Anglie de libris doctorum et auctorum veterum*, pp. xcviii–cxlviii, at cxxxiv.

conventual libraries are represented by Stephen of Lincoln, who donated Lincoln Cathedral Library, MS.208 (B.5.6). Some friars at the universities copied treatises or entire manuscripts, a practice which was exemplified by William Vavasour, who transcribed texts in two manuscripts at Oxford in 1490/91, notwithstanding the development of the printing presses.

Oxford's international appeal was reflected at the general chapter of Milan in 1285 which entitled the province of Aquitaine to send one student there.[287] It was becoming a major *studium* in the order.[288] Robert of Halifax had lectured there and then at Cambridge. By 1342 he was already known at Paris.[289] Several members of the custody of York held positions of prominence and influence at the Universities of Oxford and Cambridge and achieved distinction in their studies. The continuation of Thomas of Eccleston's roll-call of the regent masters at these schools includes many members of the custody, including Ralph of Corbridge, Thomas of York, Ralph of Toft, Thomas Barnby, William Gainsborough, Adam of Howden, Philip of Bridlington, Robert of Beverley, Thomas of Pontefract, William of Shirburn, John Wilton, John of Thornton, John of Ratford, John of Howden, Thomas Ratford, Robert of Cave, Robert of Halifax and William of Harleston. In the two centuries following 1350 the custody continued to be well represented at Oxbridge. Unfortunately there is no equivalent to the roll of honour for the regent masters for that period; information is fragmentary and this *lacuna* is compounded by the loss of the early records of the Universities of Oxford and Cambridge.

In the fourteenth century fewer English friars pursued their studies outside the country, as the list of friars at Paris in the summer of 1303 attests. One exception was Richard of Schelbruk, formerly guardian of Oxford. He became a master of theology at Bologna University on 3 February 1375. From the middle of the fourteenth century information on friars studying abroad becomes more fragmentary. Roger of Frisby was a doctor of divinity of Cambridge in 1382, when he condemned the teaching of John Wyclif. Some 20 years later he was drawn into polemics regarding the death of King Richard II and the accession of King Henry IV. Although he did not claim that Richard was still alive, he believed that, if it were the case, he would be the king. The king protested the legitimacy of his accession to the throne. Roger was imprisoned and then executed at Tyburn. Laurence Draper was at York when ordained subdeacon on 2 June 1515 at Blackfriars, York, and at Oxford when ordained deacon in March 1517. He was back at York when ordained priest on 18 June 1519 at Holy Trinity Priory, York. He was a friar of Cambridge at the Dissolution in 1538 and obtained parishes in the diocese of Ely in the new ecclesiastical dispensation. The friars' thorough grounding in theology equipped them for an effective ministry which was evident in the bond which they forged with their neighbours, who turned to them for prayers.

287 A. Callebaut, 'Acta Capituli Generalis Mediolani celebrati an.1285', *AFH*, XXII (1929), pp. 273–91, at 290, III, no. 7.

288 Cf. M.W. Sheehan, 'The Religious Orders 1220–1370', *The History of the University of Oxford*, vol. I, *The Early Oxford Schools*, ed. J.I. Catto (Oxford, 1984), pp. 193–223; and N. Şenocak, *The Poor and the Perfect: The Rise of Learning in the Franciscan Order, 1209–1310* (Ithaca, NY, 2012).

289 Courtenay, 'Some Notes on Robert of Halifax, O.F.M.', p. 135.

The friars' ministry to their neighbours in their church at York

The friars' fervent sermons and their devout celebration of the liturgy brought many to their churches, much to the displeasure of the local clergy, who protested that their pastoral influence was being eroded by the new religious order and that their revenues were being diverted from the parish to the friary.[290] The order's church in York brought a new architectural style with its focus on a large open nave, exemplified by Bologna's basilica di San Francesco or Siena's church of San Francesco. Such churches were designed to accommodate large numbers of the laity and the clergy assembled for sermons delivered by members of the local friary as well as by friars who were passing through York. In keeping with the practice of Francis of Assisi, the friars' sermons were delivered in the open air at the friary, a fact mentioned in a royal grant of 27 September 1268.[291] This aspect of the friars' ministry is illustrated by miniatures dating from the thirteenth century. For example, Lambeth Palace, MS.522, fol. 85r, depicts a Franciscan preaching and holding a processional cross. The order's church was attended by people from the adjacent parishes in the city as well as the lords and nobles from the countryside, as the friars pointed out in their protests to King Edward III early in 1372.[292] Whenever the rights and privileges of the friars' church were endangered, the order was not slow to seek redress from the crown.[293] The order's church in the county town also featured in agreements of various kinds and this is exemplified by an indenture between Thomas Seyntquintyn and Agnes, his wife, and Nicholas Gascoigne regarding the marriage to be contracted between Anthony St Quintin of Harpham and Elizabeth, the oldest daughter of Nicholas Gascoigne, in 1409/10. Nicholas undertook to pay the dowry of 260 marks in the friars' church at dates specified in the contract.[294]

The liturgical life of the friars' church benefited from the presence of the custodial school, with the masters and bachelors of theology taking their turn in the pulpit. The presence of visiting friars from other provinces of the order added an exotic note,

290 *Salimbene de Adam*, ii, pp. 637–38. Cf. *ibid.*, p. 634.

291 *CPR, 1266–1272*, pp. 260–61. TNA, C66/86, mem. 4. F. Drake, *Eboracum or the history and antiquities of the city of York from the original to the present times, together with the history of the cathedral church and the lives of archbishops of that see* (London, 1736), appendix, pp. xlvii–xlviii.

292 *CCR, 1369–1374*, p. 438. The friars complained that the stench from the offal dumped in the river Ouse by the butchers filled their church with unpleasant odours. The friars complained that this was driving people away from their church. Cf. E. Miller, 'Medieval York: The 12th and 13th Centuries', *VCH, York*, pp. 25–116, at 107.

293 *CPR, 1358–1361*, p. 255. The friars protested to the crown when the rights of sanctuary were flouted. Edward III notified the sheriff, the mayor and all other bailiffs and lieges on 28 July 1359 that he had learned that they or some of them and many acting on their authority had often ambushed felons fleeing for asylum at the friary and its church. Posting a watch on the friary, some of them had nefariously entered the friars' enclosure and seized the fugitives, dragging them forth in violation in contempt of the friars and ecclesiastical liberty. They had broken the friary walls and trodden down their gardens. The friars' liberty had been violated and their divine services disturbed; the friars dared not leave their close. The king then took the friars and their church, everything within their grounds, into his special protection. Heavy penalties were imposed upon those who interrupted the friars and their divine services. The men addressed by the king were required to observe the law of sanctuary and avoid ambushes and such things, doing violence to the friars, their households and their servants.

294 C.V. Collier, 'Documents at Scampston', *The Transactions of the East Riding Antiquarian Society*, XXI (1915), pp. 25–69, at 37.

as did friars from missionary territories. Homilies were delivered in either Anglo-Norman or the vernacular; Latin was reserved for sermons to the clergy. Sermons were framed to inculcate a penitential spirit which prompted the individual to acknowledge his or her failings in sacramental confession and to seek reconciliation with the Church, making satisfaction to wounded parties. The friars' church provided ample opportunities for sacramental confession. The extant provincial statutes attest that confessions were heard on a daily basis at an hour fixed by the provincial chapter.[295] Queues of penitents were conspicuously long during the penitential seasons of Advent and Lent. Towards the end of the fourteenth century William Woodford observed that penitents were especially numerous between Passiontide and Holy Saturday.[296] Friars were carefully trained for the office of confessor,[297] vetted and approved by the provincial chapter for this office.[298] Their popularity as confessors is reflected in the probate registers, which identify several friars who filled this office for citizens of York and its environs. The friars' new church was nearing completion in the 1290s. Among the visitors was Queen Isabella of France, the wife of King Edward II, who made an offering of a cloth of gold to the *magnum altare* on 8 March 1312.[299] At the beginning of the fourteenth century the kings of England were brought to York by the frequent tensions with Scotland. King Edward II attended Mass at the Greyfriars on 1 November 1319, and again on 29 November of that year for the feast of All Saints and the anniversary Mass for his mother, Queen Eleanor of Castile (†1290).[300]

Whereas many of the parishes of York were served by a rector, who was assisted by chaplains or chantry priests, the friary was the home of an army of priests who celebrated Mass at hours convenient for their neighbours. Masses were celebrated from 6.30 am. The daily Mass in honour of the Mother of God featured in the will of John Carre, a parishioner of St Sampson and a former mayor of York.[301] Sir John Roucliffe, knight of Cowthorpe, on 6 December 1531 requested that the 8.00 am Mass in the Greyfriars in honour of the Mother of God be celebrated for the repose of the souls of his wife, Margaret and their children, for his own father, Sir Brian, and for his father-in-law and his friends.[302] The daily Roucliffe Mass was mentioned by one testator.[303] The laity also frequented the order's churches for the daily celebration of the Divine Office, the public devotions to the Mother of God and the cults of the Franciscan saints, especially Sts Francis, Clare of Assisi and Anthony of Padua. A devout commemoration of the Passion flourished, especially on Fridays. The church was open daily and it was used for the private devotions of individuals. It was a place

[295] E.g., Bihl, 'Statuta provincialia provinciarum Aquitaniae et Franciae (saec. XIII–XIV)', pp. 495–96, VIII.

[296] *Woodford, Respons.*, p. 146, Q. 30.

[297] *Constit. Fratrum Minorum, saec. XIV*, c. 24, no. 5, p. 326: *qui autem ad huiusmodi confessionis officium assumentur, priusquam officium huiusmodi exequantur, sint sufficienter instructi de casibus sedi apostolice et diecesanis reservatis ac de prohibitionibus et penis, a iure statutis contra illos qui temeritate propria in casibus predictis absolvunt, vel in aliis in quibus absolvere non possunt.*

[298] *Constit. Fratrum Minorum, saec. XIV*, no. 4, p. 79: *minister vero nullos licentiet, nisi quos cum magna deliberatione discretos probaverit et securos; et hoc in provinciali capitulo diffinitiorum consilio tantum fiat.*

[299] *The Household Book of Queen Isabella of England for the fifth regnal year of Edward II, 8 July 1311 to 7 July 1312*, ed. F.D. Blackley and G. Hermansen (Alberta, Canada, 1971), pp. 236–37.

[300] BL, MS. Add.17362, fol. 3r.

[301] *TE*, iv, pp. 26–30, at 29.

[302] *TE*, v, pp. 319–23, at 321.

[303] *TE*, iv, p. 192.

of burial for many, and the relatives of the deceased often prayed at their forebears' graves, perhaps attending the friars' weekly prayers there. The church was often the venue for ordinations, generally held in Lent. For instance, the fraternity of St Mary was accustomed to meet in the friary (*in ecclesia conventuali fratrum minorum, Ebor*).[304] A guild of St Francis was mentioned by some testators and was associated with the church.[305]

Testators refer to the high altar,[306] the lady chapel[307] and the altars dedicated to St Francis,[308] St Katherine,[309] the resurrection,[310] the Holy Trinity on the north side of the church,[311] and the four altars in the centre of the church (*in ventre ecclesie*),[312] the crossway.[313] The rood in the middle of the church (*coram ymagine sanctae crucis in medio eiusdem ecclesie*) was mentioned by a testator on 4 May 1396.[314] There were also images of the Holy Trinity,[315] St Francis,[316] St Catherine,[317] the Blessed Virgin Mary[318] and Jesus.[319] John Carlisle's will of 21 September 1390 exhibits a good knowledge of the church and the distribution of its side altars. This parishioner of St Olave's, resident *in vico Sanctae Mariae* beside the gate of the monastery, gave precise instructions regarding Masses to be celebrated at specified altars in the womb of the friars' church.[320]

Although friars were pledged to the dovetailed apostolates of the pulpit and the confessional, they were religious whose intercession was highly prized by the laity and some clerics. An early expression of this comes from the order's acceptance of the mortuary rolls that passed from one religious house to another, soliciting prayers for the deceased monks, nuns and prelates.[321] There is ample evidence of the friars' intercessory role in York, whose citizens frequently turned to them for prayers, especially the celebration of Masses for the living and the dead. Archbishop Greenfield, for instance, left 40s. to the community on 20 February 1314 so that each

304 York Minster, Dean and Chapter Library, MS.L2/4, fol. 194rv.

305 D.J.F. Crouch, *Piety, Fraternity and Power: Religious Gilds in Late Medieval Yorkshire, 1389–1547* (York, 2000), pp. 129, 132–33.

306 *TE*, v, pp. 191–93.

307 BIA, Probate Register 3, fol. 316r (254v).

308 BIA, Probate Register 6, fol. 60v.

309 York Minster, Dean and Chapter Library, MS.Torre L1/8, fol. 873.

310 BIA, Probate Register 11, fols. 147v–48r.

311 *TE*, iv, pp. 102–07, 102. Cf. *ibid.*, v, pp. 319–23.

312 *TE*, i, pp. 140–41.

313 BIA, Register 3, fol. 536r; York Minster, Dean and Chapter Library, MS.Torre L1/8, fols. 874, 1436, On 2 November 1436 John Kirkely of York asked to be buried in the church of the Franciscans, where people are commonly accustomed to cross through the church, *ubi populi vulgarites solent maxime pertransire*.

314 BIA, Probate Register 1, fols. 95v, 100rv.

315 *TE*, v, p. 320.

316 BIA, Probate Register 2, fol. 431v.

317 BIA, Probate Register 6, fol. 60v.

318 *TE*, iv, pp. 116–17.

319 *TE*, iv, p. 105, n.

320 *TE*, i, pp. 140–41.

321 L. Rollason, 'Medieval Mortuary Rolls: Prayers for the Dead and Travel in Medieval England', *NH*, XLVIII (2011), pp. 187–223, 206, 208, 214; *Obituary Roll, Durham*, 52, no. 4. For instance, the obituary roll of Robert of Holy Island, bishop of Durham (†1283), was prepared that summer. Richard Claxton, prior of Durham, prepared the roll soliciting prayers for the deceased bishop. The notification was followed by an indulgence issued by Robert de Prebenda, bishop of Dunblane, for those who prayed for the deceased prelate. The *breviator* visited several religious houses of York, including the Greyfriars on 22 October.

priest in the community might offer Mass for the repose of the soul of his recently deceased brother, Robert.[322] Although extant evidence supplied by testators focuses on the friars' roles as intercessors, this has the effect of skewing the available evidence in favour of intercession. The will of Thomas del Abbay, clerk of York, on 14 August 1394 arranged that 13 Masses should be celebrated for his soul and the souls of departed brethren in the church of the Greyfriars in the city on the Friday of the first week of Lent annually.[323] On 6 November 1487 John Carre, former mayor of York and a parishioner of St Sampson's, left each mendicant house in the city a torch to burn at the high altar. Dr Henry Shirwyn was given 20s. The friars received 20s. for three trentals of Masses: one, *de nomine Jhesu*; two, *de Sancta Cruce*; and three, *de Spiritu Sancto*. A serge of wax was to be given to the friary to burn daily during the Lady Mass.[324] Dame Jane Strangways drew up her will on 28 October 1500 and left 10s. to each mendicant house in York to celebrate a trental of Masses for her with a *Placebo* and *Dirige* for her soul and all Christian souls. Each friary was to receive 10s for its maintenance. In addition, she asked for a daily Mass to be celebrated for her for the space of one year by members of the community for seven marks; she requested that the Masses might be celebrated by different members of the convent; each celebrant was to receive 2d.[325]

In his will of 28 December 1509 Sir John Gilliot, a knight and alderman of York, invited the four orders of friars with their processional crosses to escort his body to the parish church of St Saviour for the requiem Mass, leaving 10s. to each friary. The Greyfriars were asked to celebrate 30 Masses for his soul and those of his deceased friends: the first ten *de nomine Jhesu*; the second ten *de quinque vulneribus Jhesu Christi*; and the third *de Corpore Christi*.[326] A further insight into the rhythm of the liturgy in the Greyfriars comes from the will of John Besby of 23 July 1535 requesting burial between the altar of the resurrection and the grave of Sir Brian Roucliffe. This alderman and parishioner of St Michael, Spurriergate, gave 5s. to William Vavasour, the guardian, for his burial and instructed his wife, Margaret, to consult this friar about her role as executor of the will of which the friar was a supervisor; the friar received an additional 10s. for his labour. Besby requested Masses to be celebrated at the altar of resurrection at 6.30 am for his parents, his wife, his wife's parents and all Christians. The Sunday Mass was to be *De resurrectione domini*, *De corpore Christi* on Monday, *De omnibus sanctis* on Tuesday, *De requieme* on Wednesday, *De Trinitate* on Thursday, *De cinque vulneribus* on Friday and *De beata Maria virgine* on Saturday. The sum of 4d. was given to John Wikham, another friar, to celebrate Mass for him at the altar of *scala celi*.[327] The request for these seven types of Masses may have posed problems for the friars who were required to follow the order's liturgical calendar which bristled with so many saints' days.[328]

322 *Reg. Greenfield*, v, p. 33, no. 2443.
323 *York Memorandum Book*, iii, p. 48.
324 *TE*, iv, pp. 26–30, 29.
325 *TE*, iv, pp. 186–90, at 187. Cf. *TE*, v, pp. 321–22: *item I will that he that sayeth the sayde Messe one wooke shall not saye it agayne an odre weike, to his tourne and course come aboute ...*
326 *TE*, v, pp. 12–17.
327 BIA, Probate Register 11, fols. 147r–48r.
328 *TE*, v, p. 183. The will of Geoffrey Procter of Nether Bordley in Craven on 10 June 1524 specified Masses for the different days of the week in the church at Rilston in Craven: *De Trinitate* on Sunday, a requiem Mass on Monday, Tuesday *ad libitum*, Wednesday *De vulneribus Christi*, Thursday *ad libitum*, Friday Jhesu and Saturday Lady Mass, except when a double feast occurred.

The friars' churches provided an alternative place of burial for their urban neighbours, friends and benefactors.[329] Several testators requested burial close to or beside their parents, siblings or spouses. This practice is exemplified by Roger of Bolyngbrok who on 24 November 1361 asked for burial beside his mother, Agnes, in the Greyfriars of York.[330] Another was Sir Thomas Ughtred, a soldier and a member of a family well connected with the order. On 19 September 1398 he requested burial beside his wife, Katherine.[331] Alice Poumfreyt, a member of the guild of St Francis, asked for burial in the Greyfriars, next to her late husband, Roger, a skinner of York, in her will of 29 November 1429.[332] Legacies frequently named individual friars as beneficiaries along with gifts to the local friary. On 3 October 1432 George Darrell of Sessay sought burial at the friary and requested a friar to celebrate Masses for him in their conventual church for the space of one year. A solemn *obit* was requested for his soul at the end of that year; the sum of five marks was set aside for this. Each member of the community attending his funeral was given 12d. and each junior friar, that is, unordained, taking part in his exequies was to receive 6d. Four velvet cushions *de albo rubio et unum banquer* were left for the high altar. A bed was donated to the community and half of his *duodenam vasorum de pewter garenyst*. Friar John Belasys was left 6s. 8d. to pray for George's soul and Friar John Shirlowe received the same amount with a pair of sheets. A chair was to be given *cum duobus scamnis* for the office of the *Magister Fratrum Minorum*.[333] Henry Salvane, a soldier and citizen of York, wanted to be buried in the friars' choir of the church beside his brother, John, another soldier, in his will of 15 September 1464. Four marks were left to finance the carving of a stone bearing his name and that of his brother. Friar Snawhalle was left 5s. to celebrate a trental of Masses for the testator.[334] Dame Margery Salvin, widow of Sir John, a knight, requested burial in the friars' church on the north side *affore the ymage of our Blissed Lady*. She sought a good priest to celebrate Masses for her for the period of six years. A bone of St Ninian, a garment of white damask and a yard and a half of velvet for making vestments were among her bequests to the friary. Probate was granted on 24 June 1496.[335]

From the end of the thirteenth century, families assumed particular responsibility for chapels within Franciscan churches. The fact that chapels at Santa Croce in Florence were known primarily by the donors' names – Bardi, Peruzzi, Giugni and Tosinghi with the Spinelli – rather than by their patron saints offers an early example of this practice.[336] The ways in which families chose to be interred at the Greyfriars are reflected in the wills of Richard Burgh, a soldier, on 6 December 1407, his grandson, Sir Brian Roucliffe of Cowthorpe, and his son, Sir John Roucliffe, who invited the four orders of friars to meet his body at Holgate and escort it to the Greyfriars.[337]

329 Cf. C. Bruzelius, 'The Dead Come to Town: Preaching, Burying and Building in the Mendicant Orders', *The Year 1300 and the Creation of a New European Architecture*, ed. A. Gajewski and Z. Opacic (Turnhout, 2007), pp. 203–24, and *Preaching, Building, and Burying: Friars in the Medieval City* (New Haven, 2014).

330 *York Memorandum Book*, iii, pp. 22–23.

331 *TE*, i, pp. 241–45, at 242.

332 BIA, Probate Register 2, fol. 660v.

333 *TE*, ii, pp. 27–28.

334 *TE*, ii, pp. 263–64.

335 *TE*, iv, pp. 116–17.

336 Giorgio Vasari, *Le vite de' più eccellenti pittori, sculptori e architettori nelle redazioni del 1550 e 1568*, ed. R. Bettarini, 11 vols (Florence, 1966–87), ii, p. 98.

337 *TE*, i, pp. 347–48; iv, pp. 102–07; v, pp. 319–23.

Families arranged for Masses to be celebrated regularly, sometimes weekly or daily, for their deceased relatives. They enjoyed rights in relation to chapels and they were expected to furnish them with everything that pertained to the celebration of Mass.[338] In turn, such chapels provided the burial place for their forebears. The patrons of friaries displayed their coats of arms there.[339] The same pattern was repeated at the Greyfriars of York. The altar dedicated to the Holy Trinity was the burial place selected by members of the Roucliffe family on the edge of the county town. The family probably assumed some financial responsibility for the maintenance of the chapel and provision for the frequent – if not daily – celebration of Mass. On 12 March 1495 Sir Brian Roucliffe of Cowthorpe, one of the barons of the exchequer, compiled his will and requested burial beside the altar of Holy Trinity. His exequies, he insisted, should be conducted on a modest scale; pomposity was to be shunned. Prayers were requested for several ancestors, including Brian Roucliffe and Joanne, his wife; his parents, Guy Roucliffe and Joanne, his wife; John Burgh, his uncle, who had given him the manor of Cowthorpe; and Richard Burgh, the father of John; and Peter Arden, a soldier. The four orders of friars in York were invited to meet the funeral cortege and accompany it to the Greyfriars for the requiem Mass; each community was given 40d. The sum of 40s. was to be given to the Greyfriars; the other three mendicant communities were given half that amount. On the day of his funeral or the one following each priest at the Greyfriars was to receive 12d; novices would have half of that amount; novices in the other mendicant friaries were given 4d. The guardians or priors of the four houses of friars were to receive 20d. Secular priests and friars in the four mendicant houses were invited to celebrate a trental of Masses, receiving 6d. The Greyfriars of York were left three *quarteria frumenti*. Each of the other custodial houses in Yorkshire was left 13s. 4d. to celebrate on that day a *Placebo* and *Dirige* and a requiem Mass the following day.[340] The liturgy of the friars' church in York yields ample information about individual friars and provides references for a prosopographical study.

[338] L. Bourdua, '*Master* Plans of Devotion or Daily Pragmatism? The Dedication and Use of Chapels and Conventual Spaces by the Friars and the Laity at the Santo 1263–1310', *Il Santo: Rivista Francescana di storia dottrina arte*, LI (2011), pp. 491–510, at 498.

[339] B. Jennings, *The Grey Friars of Richmond* (Richmond, 1958), p. 9.

[340] *TE*, iv, pp. 102–07.

Some prosopographical studies

This biographical register of 1,704 friars in the custody of York draws together sufficient strands for a series of prosopographical studies of members of the custody, beginning with its first custos, and ending in the 1530s with the last generation of friars.[341] The early friars' warm commitment to evangelical poverty, one of the hallmarks of the order, is manifest in the policies promoted by Martin of Barton. The order's desire to foster close relations with the local bishop finds expression in the ministry of Ralph of Toft. He was a trusted member of Bishop Sutton's inner circle and witnessed clerical appointments, acting as the prelate's penitentiary. William Gainsborough was a friar with an exceptionally rich *curriculum vitae*, serving as minister provincial, regent master at Oxford, royal diplomat, lector at the papal court and finally as bishop of Worcester. The experience of Adam of Ludford demonstrates that some friars had a prolonged stay at a particular friary and had close ties with the crown and the local bishop. Richard Warter, the son of Adam Warter, was one of a number of friars whose family roots were among the tradesmen of York. His father's will illuminates the family's social status in the county town. The order's commitment to theological studies continued unbroken until the Dissolution. John Smith was one of the last generation of friars sent to the University of Oxford, where his name occurs in various academic exercises.[342] After his return to the custody, he became the guardian of the Greyfriars of Lincoln in the 1530s.

The mission to establish the Franciscan order in England was attributed to St Francis, whose proposal was ratified by the general chapter of 1224. Agnellus of Pisa was deputed to lead the band of nine friars who arrived in England during 1224. Careful preparations for the mission were made and it is probable that the friars, in the hope of attracting vocations in England, had already devised a list of suitable locations for foundations. Thomas of Eccleston emphasises the presence of the founder of the order in the beginnings of the mission and at crucial stages in its evolution in the 1230s and 1240s, a period of spectacular growth, evolution and development. The teaching of the saint and his appearances to friars in dreams were concerned with the preservation and consolidation of the order's mission among the English. The chronicler introduces a number of friars who had either met or known the founder and they played a key role in the oral tradition of the founder before the emergence of the hagiographical tradition at the end of the 1220s. Martin of Barton was one such friar. He was a native of Umbria and probably Assisi, who had firsthand knowledge of the birth of the order and its spectacular expansion after 1215. He belonged to the second wave of friars to cross the Channel in order to reinforce the group of friars who arrived in the summer of 1224. He was the first custos of York, and the man who encouraged its fidelity to evangelical poverty, according to the vision of *il poverello*.

One of the emphases that Martin conveyed to the friars was the founder's absolute determination to eschew all forms of ownership, especially at the Portiuncula, his spiritual home and the cradle of the fraternity, which would grow into an international religious order. The people of Assisi provided accommodation for some of the friars from different provinces travelling to the Umbrian town at a time when any member was welcome to attend the annual chapters. Some 5,000 friars attended the

[341] There is sufficient source material for comparable studies of Thomas of York, Adam of Howden, Adam of Lincoln, William of Doncaster, Henry Sherwyn and Thomas Kirkham.

[342] Cf. J.I. Catto, 'Franciscan Learning in England 1450–1540', *The Religious Orders in Pre-Reformation England*, pp. 97–104.

chapter. Seeing the stone building at a time when the majority of people lived in houses made of timber, Francis recoiled in horror and regarded it as a betrayal of his ideals at Santa Maria degli Angeli, the site of a crucial moment in his conversion; he wished the highest standards of religious observance to be enshrined there because it was the birth-place of the order, the friars' first home just outside Assisi. His instinct was to demolish the new building. Accordingly, he commanded that the edifice be destroyed and he clambered on to the roof to remove the tiles. Martin's brother, the seneschal (*senescallus*) of the chapter, and the knights of Assisi intervened on behalf of the city's commune to protect their building and to reassure Francis that the house belonged to the city rather than to the friars. At that point the saint withdrew. A fuller account of this episode is narrated in the *Compilatio Assisiensis*, whose authors may have consulted Martin about the event.

In keeping with this narrative, Martin schooled the friars in the principles of evangelical poverty and recounted the virtues of the saint. His impact upon the friars was noted by Thomas of Eccleston, who writes: 'in the custody of York over which Martin of Barton presided, the zeal of poverty flourished'.[343] Martin laid down the prudent rule of thumb that the number of friars assigned to a particular house should be regulated by almsgiving alone, with sufficient food without incurring any debts, the scourge of the first generation of friars. This principle was applied beyond the custody of York, where the potential flow of alms was assessed before decisions were taken about whether to open new friaries and how many friars might live there. This was the criterion invoked by the bishop of Coventry and Lichfield, when the order wished to make a foundation at Chester in the later 1230s. Thomas of Eccleston testifies that Martin held many offices in the English province, including that of vicar provincial. There were no further references to him in the chronicle, but his name occurs as the *custos Fratrum Minorum in Scotia* on 13 September 1235 in an agreement between the monks of Kelso and friars of Roxburgh. It is unknown whether he remained in the English province for long afterwards or whether he returned to his native Umbria.

From the outset, the friars fostered good relations with the bishops of England and Wales and assisted them in multiple ways. This collaboration is exemplified by Ralph of Toft, who also corroborates Professor Courtenay's hypothesis that masters in theology withdrew from the universities at the end of their regency and returned to their native custodies to fill a variety of roles, including teaching, pastoral care and administration.[344] Ralph was the fourteenth regent master at Oxford about 1285 and, at the end of his tenure, he went back to the custody of York where he worked hand-in-glove with Bishop Sutton. He was admitted to the prelate's inner circle on its progress around the largest diocese of medieval England. Among other things he witnessed clerical appointments and the institution of the parochial clergy. Walter of Lowthorpe, for instance, was appointed to the parish of Greetham, Lincolnshire, and was instituted at Edlesborough, Buckinghamshire, in the presence of Ralph and a canon of Lincoln on 6 June 1289. Ralph was in the bishop's chamber at Lincoln about the hour of vespers on 30 December 1291, when he headed the witnesses' list to the appointment of Jocelyn of Kirmington as archdeacon of Stow. He was at North Scarle, Lincolnshire, on 9 and 11 April 1291, when he witnessed a reading of the bishop's appeal to the pope against the action of the official of the archbishop of Canterbury, who had disregarded the bishop's appeal and renewed his demand that the

343 Eccleston, pp. 35–6.

344 Cf. Courtenay, 'Academic Formation and Careers of Mendicant Friars. A Regional Approach', *Studio e Studia: Le Scuole degli Ordini Mendicanti tra il XIII e XIV secolo. Atti del XXIX Convegno internazionale, Assisi, 11 13 ottobre 2001*, pp. 199–217.

abbots of Bourne and Notley should account for the custody and the revenues of the churches of Colsterworth and Quinton. Another Franciscan witness present on this occasion was John of Yarwell. Ralph was one of several witnesses at Stow Park, when the bishop drew up last will and testament on 18 May 1291; the document had been prepared the previous day.

Ralph's office as penitentiary presupposed a thorough knowledge of canonical procedures, forms of discipline, the investigation of allegations, the scale of penances to be imposed and condign satisfaction. His judgements and instructions were communicated to diocesan officials and entered in the episcopal registers. For example, on 20 June 1290 he was styled as the *penitenciarius episcopi*, when a note was made of the absolution granted to Hugh le Warenner, a servant of Lady Avis of Grele. The sentence of excommunication had been incurred because Hugh had assaulted Walter of Great Casterton, Rutland, stabbing him in the thigh. It was acknowledged that this crime had been preceded by a certain amount of provocation and the striking of the first blow. Hugh was instructed to make three penitential processions round the church at Great Casterton and the dean of Rutland was directed to supervise this penitential conduct. Similarly, absolution was granted to Richard Bishop of Fulstow, Lincolnshire, who had been excommunicated because of his consent to the forcible removal of a fugitive claiming sanctuary in Fulstow churchyard. On 30 August 1290 a punishment of five beatings was imposed upon the penitent on five Sundays in the same churchyard under the supervision of the rector. On 14 May 1291 absolution was granted to John of Craven, a servant of the Benedictine nuns of Stainfield, Lincolnshire, for striking a woman on the head with a stick in the parish churchyard. The penitent was ordered to make three penitential processions from the gate of the churchyard to the altar of the parish church on three Sundays, offering a candle on each occasion. A private penance was also imposed. Shortly afterwards Ralph's name disappears from the episcopal registers, perhaps on account of sickness or his transfer to a friary across the river Humber.

William Gainsborough's ministry is unusually well documented on account of the high-profile positions which he held. This graduate of the *studium* at York was earmarked for theological studies at Oxford, where he overlapped with some exceptional theologians in the later 1270s and early 1280s. He was elected as vicar provincial and, in that capacity, he wrote to the bishop of Worcester on 1 August 1285. Later that month the provincial chapter of Cambridge elected him as the twelfth minister provincial, an office which he held for seven years in the life of the order which was showing increasing signs of tension and some fragmentation over the interpretation of evangelical poverty. Since friars from other provinces of the order were drawn to study in Oxford from the 1230s, it is probable that William already knew confrères from diverse provinces. Furthermore, he attended the general chapters of Montpellier in 1287, Rieti in 1289, Paris in 1292, Assisi in 1295 and Lyon in 1299, making contacts with prominent friars from other parts of the order, including Matthew of Acquasparta, who was successively a regent master at Paris, an outstanding theologian, master of theology at the papal court, minister general of the order (1287–89), cardinal priest in 1288 and then cardinal bishop of Porto and San Rufino and papal penitentiary. During his last year in office as minister provincial William accompanied Raymond Gaufredi, the minister general, to Oxford where the latter preached on 28 October and 1 November. On 2 November 1291 William preached at Oxford, probably during a general visitation of the English province. His responsibilities as minister provincial were combined with various commissions from the crown. He was at Berwick in the king's council in June 1291 and again on 3 November 1291, when he was consulted about the succession to the Scottish throne.

At the end of his term as minister provincial in 1292, William completed his doctoral studies at Oxford and thereafter he was frequently in the diplomatic service of King Edward I, at a time of political ferment because of tensions with both Scotland and France. In 1294 he was sent by King Edward I with Hugh of Manchester, formerly prior provincial of the Dominicans, to King Philip IV of France to protest against the latter's seizure of Gascony. In August 1295 and September 1297 he participated in the parliaments at Westminster. He was instrumental in the negotiations leading to the marriage of King Edward I and Princess Margaret, the sister of King Philip IV of France, in 1299. He accompanied Hugh of Hartlepool, minister provincial, to the general chapter at Lyon in 1299. William's theological stature, his international network of contacts with the administration of the order and links with the papal court undoubtedly brought him to the attention of Pope Boniface VIII, who appointed him as lector in the Roman curia (*lector sacri palatii apostolici*). Royal records confirm the papal initiative (*ad mandatum pape ad legendum de theologia in palacio eiusdem pape*) and that by May 1300 he was in London to make preparations for his travel across the Alps. The king supplied him with expenses for the journey and entrusted him with further business of the crown. For two years William lectured on theology *cursorie et ordinarie* at the papal court and continued to act as one of the royal proctors and a special *nuncio* on important affairs at the papal court. On 24 October 1302 Pope Boniface VIII provided him to the diocese of Worcester. William was consecrated four days later at the papal court. On his arrival in England his brethren joined the first procession, which greeted him at the hospital of St Wulfstan before he entered his cathedral on 9 June 1303. He was one of the three bishops whom Pope Benedict XI appointed to protect the Franciscans' privileges in England. As a prelate he remained active in the service of the crown until his death on 17 September 1307 at Beauvais *en route* for England after an embassy to negotiate the marriage of Prince Edward of Caernarfon and Princess Isabella of France. He was buried among the Cordeliers at Beauvais.

Adam of Ludford may have been a native of Ludford, 23 miles north-east of Lincoln. All the extant references to him come from the diocese of Lincoln, although he did spend some time at friaries in Yorkshire, where he was admitted to the order at the custodial house. His novitiate may have been spent there or in another friary north of the river Humber. It is unknown where he received his orders, either in the diocese of York or in Lincoln before 1290, when the list of ordinands starts in the latter diocese. The scattered references to his presence in Lincoln indicate that he may have been in continual residence for more than two decades, a practice that was repeated by friars elsewhere in the custody. Bishop Dalderby was at the monastery of the Augustinian Canons of St James at Northampton on 10 August 1300, when he responded to the request of the custos of York and the guardian of Lincoln. Adam was one of the five friars licensed to hear confessions *in limitacione* [sic] *de conventu Linc'*. His authorisation was renewed on 12 October of that year, again at the request of the custos.

He was mentioned by King Edward II in a letter of 4 August 1317 to the guardian, or whoever supplied his place at the Lincoln Greyfriars. Certain writings, charters, covenants, fines and other muniments touching the inheritance of John, son and heir of Robert le Chaumberleyn, tenant in chief and a minor in the king's wardship, had been entrusted to Adam, a member of the community in the cathedral city, by Philip de Lyndeseye, who held certain lands of the aforesaid inheritance. The king issued an instruction that these documents were to be examined by Henry de Baiocis, kinsman of the heir, and William of Ayremynne, to whom the king had committed the lands, or William's deputy, to be kept by him for the use of the heir, as seemed best to Henry and William for his benefit. The king wished to provide for the heir's security now that Philip had defected to the Scottish rebels.

Adam was licensed on 20 June 1318 to hear confessions in the diocese of Lincoln. His name appears second in a long list of friars licensed by Bishop Dalderby; such a prominent position may indicate that he was already occupying a post of some seniority in the community, perhaps as vicar or lector. On occasion the guardian deputised for the custos of York. For instance, on 7 December 1321 Bishop Burghersh reported that Adam, guardian of the Lincoln Greyfriars, had travelled to the episcopal manor at Nettleham, a few miles north-east of the cathedral city, to present a letter of 20 November from John Thurgutthorp, the custos of York. The custos explained that the business of the order prevented him from travelling to meet the bishop in person and he submitted a list of eight friars nominated to hear confessions, in accordance with the terms of *Super cathedram*. Only one of the friars was licensed by the ordinary. By 26 March 1322 Adam had ceased to be the guardian, when he and Robert de Wynthorp, a Dominican, were commissioned by Bishop Burghersh to hear the confessions of the Benedictine nuns of Stainfield, ten miles to the east of Lincoln. The bishop noted the pastoral zeal of these two friars and their suitability as confessors. Adam was probably to be identified with Adam Lufdeford, priest and professed of Grimsby, whose death is recorded about 1334.

The social background of the friars has awakened curiosity among scholars in recent decades. There is some evidence that the order attracted men from across the spectrum of medieval society, including the sons of tradesmen who proceeded to the priesthood. Richard was the son of Adam Warter, a citizen and spurrier or spur maker of York. His mother's name remains unknown; she seems to have predeceased her husband. Richard and his sister, Agnes, were parishioners of St Martin-le-Grand, Coney Street, in the centre of the city's business life; their home was a short distance from the parish of St Michael, Spurriergate. Agnes married Walter Graystok, another parishioner of St Martin's; they had one son named John. Adam's will, which was written on 31 March 1430 and proved on 14 May of that year, asked for burial in the parish's cemetery. St Martin's parish was near the Greyfriars and on the same side of the river. Adam followed his trade as a spurrier in the county town. It remains unclear whether his origins lay in the East Riding or in York. His parents may have migrated from Warter to the prosperous centre of York in the wake of the Black Death. Adam left 5s. for the fabric of his parish church and 3s. 4d. for the fabric of York Minster. The chaplain of his parish church was given 12d. Adam donated 3s. 4d. to the Greyfriars, the only mendicant community mentioned in his will. The more handsome sum of 40s. was assigned to his son, Richard, listed as a member of that religious order. The bequest was not tied to a request for Masses because his son was not yet a priest. Richard was probably a friar at York when he was ordained acolyte on 21 May 1429 at Blackfriars, York, subdeacon on 22 September 1431 at Greyfriars, York, and deacon at the same venue on 7 March 1433. All three ceremonies were conducted by the suffragan, Bishop Warter, his confrère. Richard's ordination to the priesthood is not recorded in the registers of the bishops of Lincoln and York; he may have been ordained by another suffragan or in a neighbouring diocese. Along with his brother-in-law and John Arksay, another spurrier, Richard was an executor of his father's will. When probate was granted, Richard was appointed as administrator. The fact that Richard was named before Agnes in the will may indicate that he was the older of the two. Nothing further is known of his ministry as a friar and priest. He may have predeceased his brother-in-law, who does not mention him in his will on 18 March 1473. Graystok, a cellarer, requested prayers for his deceased wives and left 30s. 4d. to Thomas Graystok, chaplain and his son, and 20s. to Joanna Tesedale, his daughter. He nominated Canon John Graystok, another son, as one of his executors and left him 13s. 4d. It is probable that this friar was associated with the *Frater Richard Waretyr*, who was admitted to the *Corpus Christi* guild of York in 1453.

John Smith was one of several friars who studied at the Universities of Oxford and Cambridge in the first third of the sixteenth century, demonstrating that the order continued to invest in tertiary education. He received the orders of acolyte, subdeacon, deacon and priest between 14 March 1489 and 28 May 1491. On each occasion the ordination was held in York. He had undoubtedly given a good account of himself in his philosophical and theological studies and was selected for higher studies. He moved to Oxford in the first decade of the sixteenth century. He was a bachelor of theology on 30 June 1506, when he supplicated to incept. This was granted on condition that he did so before 2 February 1507. He was a still a bachelor of theology on 27 November 1506, when he made another supplication and this time he was granted a dispensation to do this before the feast of the Annunciation on condition that appropriate suffrages were offered for the regent house. On 26 January 1507 he supplicated for permission to incept in theology; he had studied theology for four years as a bachelor. He was dispensed from the *depositiones* on 3 July 1507. On 20 November 1507 he obtained a dispensation to preach his sermon before the feast of the conversion of St Paul. On 28 June 1508 he was dispensed from his sermon. On the completion of his studies he returned to the custody of York to take up a lecturing position, probably at one of the friaries in Lincolnshire. In that capacity he was appointed an executor of the will of Nicholas Upton of Northolme by Wainfleet, Lincolnshire, on 9 January 1533. He was dispensed to hold a benefice with a change of habit on 8 October 1539. Nothing is known about his activities in the aftermath of the Dissolution.

This small sample of studies shows that a great deal of information about individuals can be gleaned from the scattered records. The *curricula vitae* of friars raised to the episcopate provide even fuller accounts of the lives of some friars.

Franciscan suffragan bishops

Two friars were provided to the dioceses of England and Wales by Popes Nicholas III and Boniface VIII respectively, Archbishop John Pecham and Bishop William Gainsborough, both former regent masters at Oxford University, ministers provincial and then lectors at the sacred palace in Rome. From the middle of the thirteenth century some mendicants were appointed to bishoprics in the Crusading States. Augustine of Nottingham, bishop of Latakia (1254–60), was one. In later years Bishop Augustine returned to England, where he spent the remainder of his life at Windsor Castle. A second prelate was Hugh, bishop of Byblos, who was driven from his diocese after the fall of Tripoli in the spring of 1289. While Augustine was supported by King Henry III, Hugh was given hospitality for two years at the court of King Edward I. From the early fourteenth century, popes continued to appoint bishops, many of them friars, to dioceses in the former Christian territories. These prelates were effectively bishops *in partibus infidelium*, despite the fact that papal letters of provision instructed them to reside in their dioceses; such mandates were not infrequently followed by an acknowledgement that there was no episcopal *mensa* in that territory and a dispensation was granted to such bishops to exercise the episcopal office elsewhere.

Another factor behind a cluster of Franciscan bishops was the re-drawing of diocesan boundaries in Ireland with the suppression of small dioceses at the beginning of the fourteenth century. Casualties of this policy were the bishops of Annaghdown and Mayo, Bishops Gilbert ó Tigernaig and John Bell, who were effectively prevented from ministering in their dioceses by the metropolitan.[345] They both vigorously complained that the archbishop of Tuam had robbed them of their episcopal *mensa* and for that reason they found work in the dioceses of England and Wales. Some English friars appointed to Irish dioceses crossed the Irish Sea and took up residence. One of them was Richard Ledrede, bishop of Ossory (1317–60), although he did occasionally appear as a suffragan in the diocese of Rochester. From the end of the fourteenth century some English friars were routinely appointed to Irish sees with little expectation that they would reside there. Bishop Nicholas Warter, for instance, pointed to the political turmoil in the north of Ireland as a reason for failing to reside in his diocese. Bishop Bell was an exception in seeking to minister as the bishop of Mayo. Professor Watt wryly observes that there were simultaneously four bishops of Dromore active in English dioceses, two of them ministering in adjacent dioceses in the northern province, with one in Durham and another in York, in the later 1420s.[346]

Professor David Smith and Dr Lawrence Butler have published lists of the suffragans active in the dioceses of Lincoln and York; some of these prelates ministered in both dioceses. Many of them were Franciscans, whose confrères in episcopal orders were to be found in most of the dioceses of England and Wales. The first friar to assist as a

[345] Cf. J.A. Watt, *The Church and the Two Nations in Medieval Ireland*, Cambridge Studies in Medieval Life and Thought, 3rd series, 3 (Cambridge, 1970), pp. 78, 122, 142, 194–96, reflects that the diocese of Annaghdown was continually threatened by the metropolitan.

[346] Cf. Watt, 'The Papacy and Ireland in the Fifteenth Century', *The Church, Politics and Patronage in the Fifteenth Century*, ed. R.B. Dobson (Gloucester, 1984), pp. 133–45, at 136. At one stage there were two friars, one Dominican and the other Franciscan, who were bishops of *Soltaniensis* at the beginning of the fourteenth century.

suffragan in the diocese of York was Bishop Hugh.[347] In England he was frequently in the company of Thomas Bek, bishop of Durham. Walter of Guisborough attests that Bishop Hugh was living with Bishop Bek, who did not normally hold ordinations. Bishop Hugh was mentioned in conjunction with the bishop in the administration of the diocese of Durham in the first years of the fourteenth century. Bishop Bek made a concerted effort to alleviate the prelate's poverty by providing him with the revenues of the Durham cell of Coldingham Priory and he notified the pope that the exiled friar lacked material support. On 3 April 1304 Pope Benedict XI responded to the letter, approving the form of provision to Coldingham Priory. Bishop Hugh was authorised to retain the priory until such times as he might recover his diocese. There was a solitary reference to Bishop Hugh in the register of Archbishop Corbridge, who on 20 February 1302 commissioned him to reconcile the churchyard at Loftus in the North Riding.

Unlike Bishop Hugh, whose episcopal ministry in England was confined to the dioceses of York and Durham, Bishop ó Tigernaig became an itinerant suffragan bishop in several dioceses. He received the royal protection of King Edward II to remain in England for two years from 8 February 1308 and held four ordinations in the diocese of Coventry and Lichfield between 8 June 1308 and 23 December 1312. He acted as suffragan for Bishops Dalderby and Burghersh and for Archbishop Greenfield. His name first occurs in the Lincoln registers on 7 June 1308, when he received a licence to dedicate altars, fixed and portable, and to bless chalices and ecclesiastical ornaments during his journey through the diocese on his way from Lichfield to London. His letter of 3 December 1310 to the prior of Worcester confirmed that he had already exercised his episcopal office in different dioceses and offered his services for that diocese. He received suffragan commissions for the archdeaconries of Leicester and Oxford on 3 February 1312 and for the archdeaconries of Leicester and Northampton on 27 June 1312. He was not permitted to charge in excess of 28s. 8d. for consecrating or reconciling churches and churchyards. On 28 January 1313 Archbishop Greenfield commissioned Bishop ó Tigernaig to reconcile the church and churchyard of Rotherham and on 16 September 1313 he issued a similar commission for the churchyard of Preston. Similarly, on 27 December 1313 the archbishop authorised him to reconcile the churchyard of the chapel of Wentworth. On 11 February 1314 Archbishop Greenfield licensed him to reconcile the parish church of Skipton in Craven from the shedding of blood.

A different range of experiences brought Peter of Bologna, bishop of Corbavia in Croatia, to England, where he, too, became an itinerant suffragan. This native of Crespellano in the province of Bologna spent time at the friary in Bologna, where he witnessed several wills and duly served as lector at Modena before his episcopal provision about 1300. For a decade and a half he seems to have remained on the fringes of the papal court, first at Rome and then at Avignon; his name emerges from some collective indulgences. Pope John XXII sent him to England with two cardinals in the early summer of 1317 to negotiate a peace between King Edward II and Robert Bruce. At the end of this legation he decided to remain in England and was described as a suffragan of Archbishop Melton. Although there is more evidence of his ministry in the diocese of Lincoln, he was active in the dioceses of Canterbury and London. He died on 19 January 1332 and was buried at the London Greyfriars.

[347] Lists of suffragans active in the diocese of York frequently include Augustine of Nottingham and offer a date at the beginning of the fourteenth century. His death occurred in 1260. There are no corroborative texts to confirm that he assisted the archbishops of York.

An early suffragan from the custody of York was Thomas Salkeld, who was ordained acolyte on 29 May 1344 and priest on 10 June 1346 at Whitefriars, York. As the bishop of *Chrysopolis* he received a general suffragan commission issued on 11 July 1354. On 2 August 1356 Archbishop Thoresby authorised him to bless Robert of Beverley, the abbot elect of the Cistercian monastery of Meaux. His name appears in 1357 in an ecclesiastical court case in the diocese. Thereafter his name disappears from the diocesan registers of York. He was also active in the diocese of Carlisle, where he received two livings at Clifton and Crossthwaite, Cumberland. John Britt, bishop of Annaghdown, was a native of the custody of Newcastle. He served as a suffragan in a number of dioceses, including Bath and Wells, Hereford, Salisbury and Winchester as well as York and Durham. He was active in the diocese of York from 21 May 1414, when he witnessed Cuthbert de Rydemer's profession of obedience to the metropolitan. He celebrated ordinations at Cawood prebendal church on 13 June 1416, 10 April 1417, 1 April 1419, 23 March and 6 April 1420. On 17 December 1417 he was given a suffragan commission for the diocese of Durham. *Lacunae* in the registers are illustrated by the only reference to his ministry in the diocese of Durham. Letters patent confirm that he had ordained Robert Arnald as subdeacon, deacon and priest on 19 February, 26 March and 11 May 1418 respectively.[348]

By the turn of the fifteenth century suffragans were increasingly becoming more committed to a single diocese, and this is reflected in the custody, where between 1400 and 1426 six friars, John Greenlaw, Simon Brampton, Robert Foston, John Walcot, Nicholas Warter and Walter Forman, were elevated to the episcopate. Episcopal registers illuminate the lives and ministry of these friars *en route* to the priesthood. John Greenlaw was ordained acolyte on 7 June 1376, subdeacon on 23 May 1377 and deacon on 19 September 1377. He was provided to the diocese of *Soltaniensis* on 20 September 1400, that is, approximately 23 years after ordination to the priesthood. Simon Brampton was a friar at York when he was ordained acolyte and subdeacon on 13 March 1378 and deacon on 3 April of that year. He was probably ordained to the priesthood later in 1378 or 1379 and was provided to the diocese of Tripoli on 14 January 1414, that is, about 35 years after ordination to the priesthood. Robert Foston was ordained priest on 20 September 1393. His episcopal provision came on 16 February 1419, that is, 26 years after his ordination to the priesthood. John of Walcot was ordained subdeacon on 9 March 1381 and 33 years later, on 7 October 1414, Pope John XXIII provided him to the diocese of Nisch in Bulgaria, that is, 33 years after his ordination. He served fleetingly as a suffragan to the archbishop of York in 1414 and 1419. Nicholas Warter was ordained deacon in 1394 and was consecrated as a bishop some 25 years later, on 17 March 1419. Walter Forman was ordained priest on 22 September 1397 and provided to the diocese of Ross on 14 November 1418, some 21 years later. These friars were all at least in their later forties at the time of papal provision.

In normal circumstances the archbishop of York would have approached the custos of York and the minister provincial to discuss friars suitable to serve as suffragan bishops and to confirm their good character and reputation. He was well placed to know the pastoral qualities of some of those ministering in his diocese and may have presented some names to the order's officials. The metropolitan manifestly prized dedication to the apostolate, dependability, sharp pastoral antennae and a safe pair of hands in his suffragans. The members of the custody selected for this office did not generally have an academic profile. Robert Foston and Walter Forman were exceptions because

348 *Reg. Langley*, iii, p. 188, no. 862.

they were masters of theology at the time of their episcopal provision, as was Thomas Burton, bishop of Sodor and Man, a suffragan diocese of York. A later example was William Duffield, a doctor of theology from the University of Cambridge. Bishop Foston had served as a cursor of theology, when he was licensed to hear confessions in the diocese of York on 30 August 1398. He was also appointed as a confessor in the diocese of Durham on 30 December 1407.

One hypothesis is that the metropolitan nominated individuals to assist him as suffragans and, after due consultation with the custodial and provincial officials of the order, he dispatched these friars to the papal court in search of papal provision and consecration. Some of these friars were already at the papal court at the time of their provision to dioceses in Ireland or *in partibus infidelium*. Two members of the custody of York, for instance, were simultaneously at the papal court in Italy between papal provision and consecration. First, Robert Foston was at Constance on 16 February 1419, when Pope Martin V provided him to the diocese of Achonry. On 20 November 1419 the pope noted that Robert was still a bishop elect, when he acted as proctor at the papal court for Philip Repingdon, who resigned his diocese of Lincoln on 21 November 1419. On the same day the friar was dispensed from illegitimacy so that he might be consecrated. By 29 November of that year he had already been consecrated and was at Florence, when he personally made the payment of 66 gold florins for his diocese. His time in the dioceses of Durham and Lincoln introduced him to Bishops Thomas Langley and Philip Repingdon. Secondly, Nicholas Warter was provided to the diocese of Dromore on 17 March 1419. On 5 May of that year he was at the papal court in Florence, where he paid 33 gold florins for his diocese. In each case the newly consecrated bishops returned to the north of England, where they received multiple commissions from the archbishop of York and the bishop of Durham.

John Greenlaw, who had received a dispensation to hold a benefice six months earlier, was appointed as the bishop of *Soltaniensis* on 20 September 1400 and was consecrated on 8 September 1401 at London.[349] It is not known whether he spent time at the papal court, but the period between provision and consecration was unusually long. The case of John Kegill demonstrates that such bishops elect spent a considerable time at the papal court as they completed the formalities regarding their papal provision. Kegill was employed by King Henry VI in negotiations with the Holy See regarding the election of a prior for the Cluniac Priory of Pontefract. The king's letter of 26 June 1440 to Pope Eugene IV explained that the priory had been damaged by the administration of foreign priors and more recently its fortunes had improved at the hands of an English prior. The king sought papal approval for the free election of the next prior and commended his *nuncio*, John. It is not known when he reached the papal court, in Florence, where he clearly gave a good account of himself and impressed influential figures in the curia, including the elderly Cardinal Branda da Castiglione, the bishop of Piacenza, who seems to have recommended him to the pope. On 28 July 1441 the pope was in Florence, when he provided John to the diocese of *Philoppolensis*. John was instructed that, as soon as he had had the present letters expedited, he should settle in his diocese and not exercise pontifical offices elsewhere. On 6 August 1441 the pope addressed two letters to John acknowledging him as a bishop *in partibus infidelium*. *Cum nos pridem* issued a faculty for John to be consecrated by any Catholic bishop, who was to be assisted by two or three other

349 *Memorials of the church of Ss. Peter and Wilfrid, Ripon*, i, p. 71, records that the archbishop of York consecrated Thomas de Daltoun as bishop of Galloway at Ripon Minster on 15 August 1293.

prelates. The principal consecrator was instructed to receive and send to the pope John's oath of fealty as usual. *Sincerae devotionis* acknowledged that John's diocese was *in partibus infidelium* and authorised him to exercise his episcopal ministry in the diocese of York. On 20 December 1441 the pope, responding to petitions from John and Archbishop John Kempe, the newly created cardinal priest of St Balbina, conceded that the episcopal *mensa* in the diocese of *Philoppolensis* was deficient. Accordingly, John was authorised to receive *in commendam* a benefice. Two days later, 23 December, he was described as *episcopus Philippopolis*, when he made a payment of 10 florins through the hand of Andrew Oles, the procurator of King Henry VI. Following his episcopal consecration, he returned to England, where he became a suffragan bishop in the diocese of York from the spring of 1442 until the late summer of 1458. Robert Wells was provided to the diocese of Achonry on 14 July 1473, when letters were dispatched concurrently to the archbishop of Tuam, the chapter and clergy of the city and King Edward IV. On 24 July 1473 at his own petition and that of King Edward IV, Robert was granted permission to have, after consecration, and retain for life in *commendam*, the said church with two benefices and to resign or exchange them as he pleased. He was admitted to the confraternity of the English hospice in Rome on 29 December 1474. He was chaplain of the hospice in 1474, and he was an auditor of the hospital. He was consecrated on 4 June 1475 in the hospice chapel. On 8 May 1475 he paid the tax of 17 florins and 43 shillings for his diocese.

Details about the consecration of suffragan bishops are sparse. One exception was John Greenlaw, who was consecrated on 8 September 1401 in the great chapel within the Hospital of St Mary without Bishopsgate, London. This information was entered in the register of Henry Bowett, bishop of Bath and Wells, at a time when there was anxiety about the presence of bogus bishops masquerading as prelates in English dioceses. Bishop Greenlaw's consecrators were Thomas Butler, the Franciscan bishop of *Chrysopolis*, with John, bishop of *Sorensis*, and Thomas Ilshagh, Franciscan bishop of Coutances. It is significant that his consecrators were not bishops of dioceses in England and Wales. Some friars in episcopal orders received their consecration at the papal court. Thomas Yngleby was consecrated as bishop of Maghera on 23 April 1471 at the chapel of the English Hospital in Rome. Robert Wells was consecrated as bishop of Achonry in the same chapel on 4 June 1475.

A barometer of the value of such prelates is that between 19 September 1411 and 23 September 1452 all the recorded ordinations in the diocese of York were celebrated by five bishops of dioceses in Ireland or *in partibus infidelium*, with the exception of five ceremonies at which Archbishop Kempe presided. The five prelates, the bishops of *Soltaniensis*, Annaghdown, Nisch, Dromore and *Philippopolis*, were all Franciscans, Bishops Greenlaw, Britt, Walcot, Warter and Kegill. Whereas the first three were active in the diocese during the second decade of the fifteenth century, Bishops Warter and Kegill gave long-term service and monopolised the ordinations and other episcopal commissions between 15 February 1421 and 23 September 1452; they also held parishes in York, at St Mary, Castlegate, and Holy Trinity, Goodramgate. Although the latter continued to be active until shortly before his death in the summer of 1459, suffragans from other religious orders were also engaged by the metropolitans in this period. There was a similar pattern in the diocese of Lincoln, where Franciscan suffragans frequently assisted the ordinary of the diocese. By the fifteenth century at least one of the annual ordinations was held at the York Greyfriars; the same was true of the Blackfriars, Whitefriars and Austin Friars of York.

John Bell hailed from the custody of Worcester when he was ordained acolyte, subdeacon and deacon by Bishop Wells between 20 September 1477 and 14 February of the following year in Lichfield cathedral. He was provided to the diocese of

Mayo by Pope Alexander VI on 4 January 1493, received episcopal consecration in the Roman curia and proceeded to Ireland, where he strove to take possession of his diocese. In response to a series of difficulties experienced in the province of Tuam and acting on papal dispensation, he returned to England, where he carried out his ordination ceremony on 21 September 1499 at St Bartholomew's Hospital, Smithfield, in the diocese of London. He held several such ceremonies in the dioceses of London, Canterbury, Bath and Wells and Lincoln between 21 September 1499 and 11 June 1530. On 18 October 1501 Henry Deane, archbishop of Canterbury (1501–03), gave him a suffragan commission and mentioned him in his will as his suffragan. On 23 September 1503 he held an ordination at Lichfield cathedral. On 27 July 1504 he was appointed to the parish of St Andrew, Banwell, in the diocese of Bath and Wells, on the presentation of William, prior of Bruton, and the convent of the Augustinian Canons. Following an ordination at Buckden prebendal church on 27 February 1507, he settled in the diocese of Lincoln for the ensuing 23 years. Like many of his contemporaries, he was appointed to a parish in the diocese, becoming perpetual vicar of All Saints, Goxhill, in the archdeaconry of Lincoln, on 31 March 1507, on the presentation of the prior and convent of Bridlington. He received a suffragan commission for the archdeaconries of Northampton, Huntingdon and Leicester on 9 May 1521 and he held several ordinations each year in the diocese of Lincoln at Beckenfield, Buckden, Liddington, Lincoln, Northampton and Stamford. He returned to the diocese of Bath and Wells for two ordinations in the lady chapel of Bath and Wells cathedral on 22 September and 22 December 1515. On 22 March 1529 John Longland, bishop of Lincoln, at the Temple in London received John's voluntary resignation and granted him a pension. On 9 April 1529 Master Vincent Totoft, LLB, succeeded him as vicar of All Saints, Goxhill. Nothing else is known of the last decade of John Bell's life. He died in 1540.

The last Franciscan suffragan in the custody, William Duffield, the bishop of Ascalon, was active in both dioceses. John Longland, bishop of Lincoln, gave him a general commission on 12 November 1531 for the archdeaconries of Lincoln, Leicester, Northampton, Huntingdon and Bedford. This licence permitted him to bless and dedicate altars, belfries, vestments and altar vessels; he was licensed to bless chapels, oratories and cemeteries. In addition, he was authorised to ordain clerics to all major orders and to bless abbots, abbesses, widows, anchorites and hermits. He conferred orders in Lincoln cathedral on 30 March 1532 and 12 April 1533, holding a single ordination at Liddington prebendal church on 19 December 1532. His stay in the diocese of Lincoln was relatively brief because on 13 July 1535 Edward Lee, archbishop of York, gave him a suffragan commission. On 12 September 1536 William was licensed to consecrate the chapel of St Lawrence in the village of Elstronwick, in the parish of St Peter at Humbleton in Holderness. He celebrated ordinations at Greyfriars, York, on 11 March 1536 and at Blackfriars, York, on 1 April 1536. On 24 February 1537 he conferred orders at Whitefriars, York, the last ceremony in which friars of York and Richmond were ordained.

The last consideration is the way in which friars were seen through the historical lens.

The friars' activities reflected in northern chronicles

Whereas the Cistercians constructed monasteries in secluded and wooded areas,[350] the Franciscans, informed by an early thirteenth-century model of the *vita apostolica*, found their vocation in centres of population; their penitential lifestyle was dovetailed with pastoral engagement.[351] The friars based themselves in an urban setting.[352] Although the hermitage played a central role in the life of St Francis and was reflected in certain provinces of the order such as Umbria,[353] his disciples in England and Wales gravitated to the towns and cities, where they gave witness to the norms of the New Testament and successfully integrated themselves into the life and concerns of the local community. The friars' urban concentration attracted the attention of Matthew Paris, the chronicler of St Albans, who remarked that they lived *in urbibus et civitatibus*.[354] John Pecham maintained that his order's Rule required the friars to seek the salvation of souls in large centres of population,[355] a fact that is borne out by the cities and large towns in which the friars dwelled in the custody of York and the statistics concerning the most heavily populated centres, according to the taxable returns for 1334 and 1377.[356] One of the marks of a borough's perceived prosperity was, indeed, its maintenance of friaries.[357] The friars' engagement in English life is encapsulated by Sir Maurice Powicke's portrayal of Adam Marsh as a friar *who knew everybody*,[358] an interpretation confirmed by his voluminous correspondence with senior members of the royal family, the episcopate, rectors or vicars and young scholars in search of ecclesiastical patronage. He was the pupil, collaborator and then counsellor of Bishop Grosseteste and was buried beside him in Lincoln cathedral.[359] Among the young

[350] *The Ecclesiastical History of Orderic Vitalis*, ed. M. Chibnall, 6 vols, OMT (Oxford, 1969–80), iv, pp. 326–37.

[351] C.H. Lawrence, *The Friars: The Impact of the Early Mendicant Movement on Western Society*, The Medieval World (London, 1994), pp. 15–19.

[352] *Feet of Fines of the Tudor Period*, anonymous, 4 vols, YAS, RS, II, V, VII, VIII (1887–90), ii, p. 22. A grant of the Michaelmas term of 1572 referred to the site of the 'lesser brotherhood called the Grey Freers als. "le Freers minor"'.

[353] *I testamenti dei cardinali dei duecento*, pp. 236–37, no. 16. In June 1286 Cardinal Bentivegna Bentivegni left alms to each convent (*cuilbet conventui*) in the province of Assisi and to each hermitage (*cuilibet heremitario*).

[354] *Matthew Paris, HA*, ii, p. 109.

[355] John Pecham, 'Expositio super regulam Fratrum Minorum', c. 3, no. 13, *Bonaventurae Opera Omnia*, VIII, pp. 391–437, at 410; M. Cusato, 'Wall to Wall Ministry: Franciscan Ministry in the Cities of Thirteenth Century Italy', *Spirit and Life*, X (2000), pp. 31–61; D. Foote, 'Mendicants and the Italian Communes in Salimbene's Cronaca', *The Origin, Development and Refinement of Medieval Religious Mendicancies*, ed. D.S. Prudlo, Brill's Companions to the Christian Tradition, 24 (Leiden 2011), pp. 197–238.

[356] Cf. A. Dyer, 'Ranking Lists of English Medieval Towns', *The Cambridge Urban History of Britain, I, 600–1540*, ed. D.M. Palliser (Cambridge, 2000), pp. 747–70, at 755–60.

[357] *The Manuscripts of Lincoln, Bury St. Edmund's, and Great Grimsby Corporations: and of the Deans and Chapters of Worcester and Lichfield*, p. 272. A petition of the mayor, bailiffs and burgesses of Grimsby to the earl of Westmorland lamented the economic decline of the town that had once supported three parish churches, two houses of friars, an abbey and a house of nuns. Cf. R.B. Dobson, 'Yorkshire Towns in the Late Fourteenth Century', *Miscellany*, PThS, LIX (1983), pp. 1–21, at 6.

[358] F.M. Powicke, *The Thirteenth Century 1216–1307*, The Oxford History of England (Oxford, 1953), p. 73.

[359] *Chronicon de Lanercost M.CC.I.–M.CCC.XLVI*, p. 58. *Salimbene de Adam*, i, p. 353.

scholars whom he recommended were three future prelates, Walter Merton, Walter Giffard and Oliver Sutton. Another correspondent was Sewal de Bovill, chancellor of Oxford University, archdeacon and then dean of York before serving as archbishop (1255–58), for whom he wrote a lengthy reflection upon the episcopal office.[360]

St Francis was revered as an exceptional figure in the history of western Christendom. Chroniclers saluted his virtues and his refreshing effect upon the medieval Church. His followers brought a brand new form of religious life to England in general and the custody of York in particular, where the religious houses produced chronicles in the fourteenth century.[361] The novelty of the order is echoed in the chronicles and annals compiled in the custody of York. *The lives of the archbishops of York*, narrated by Thomas Stubbs, who flourished about 1373, records the appearance of the two principal mendicant orders during the administration of Archbishop de Gray.[362] The ideals of the two saints were incarnate in their followers' witness to the Gospel in the midst of the large centres of population. The Cistercian chronicle of Louth Park attests that the Rule of St Francis was confirmed in 1215,[363] a chronological error which also infects some Franciscan sources.[364] The Cistercian chronicler associates the approval of the friars' Rule with the Fourth Lateran Council of 1215 and its reforming canons, which the friars promoted and disseminated. Thomas Burton, the Cistercian abbot of Meaux (1396–99), devotes ample space to the circumstances of the conversion of the saint of Assisi, stating that his disciples reached England three years after the Dominicans.[365] Walter of Guisborough, the chronicler of the Augustinian priory in North Yorkshire, draws upon the early hagiographical tradition of the saint of Assisi and narrates his vocation, attesting that his followers reached England on 24 August 1224 and excelled in the ministry of mediation on the eve of the battle of Lewes and during the Scottish wars.[366] *Castleford's Chronicle* displays a sound knowledge of the religious reforms initiated by St Francis, detailing the friars' arrival in England (*Freers Menours into Englande*) and the formation of friaries at London and York (*Eborwik)*. Bonaventure of Bagnoregio, minister general of the Franciscan order, was appointed to the vacant diocese of York on 24 November 1265 by Pope Clement IV, but he successfully declined the nomination.[367] Pierre de Langtoft, the canon of Bridlington, reports that King Edward I sent William Gainsborough, *frère Cordiller*, and Hugh of

[360] *The Letters of Adam Marsh*, pp. 574–647.

[361] J. Taylor, 'Fourteenth-Century Chronicle Writing in the Diocese of York', *Proceedings of the Leeds Philosophical and Literary Society* (Literary and Historical Section), VIII, part 1, pp. 51–61, at 52, and *English Historical Literature in the Fourteenth Century* (Oxford, 1987).

[362] *The Historians of the Church of York and its Archbishops*, ed. J. Raine, 3 vols, RS, 71 (London, 1879–94), ii, p. 403; *Medieval Historical Writing in Yorkshire*, St Anthony's Hall Publications, XIX (York, 1961); and R.B. Dobson, 'Contrasting Chronicles: Historical Writing at York and Durham in the Later Middle Ages', *Church and Chronicles in the Middle Ages: Essays Presented to John Taylor*, ed. I. Wood and G.A. Loud (London, 1991), pp. 201–18.

[363] Cambridge University Library, MS.Ff.VI.15, fol. 239v: *confirmatio fratrum minorum*.

[364] E.g., *The Annals of Ireland by Friar John Clyn*, ed. B. Williams (Dublin, 2007), pp. 138–39.

[365] *Chronica monasterii de Melsa, a fundatione usque ad annum 1396, auctore Thoma de Burton, abate, accedit continuatio ad annum 1406 a monacho quodam ipsius domus*, ed. E.A. Bond, 3 vols, RS 43 (London, 1866–68), i, pp. 384–85, 403, 435, 442, adding that the Franciscans arrived three years after the Dominicans.

[366] *The chronicle of Walter of Guisborough previously edited as the chronicle of Walter of Hemingford or Heminburgh*, ed. H. Rothwell, CS, 3rd series, LXXXIX (London, 1957), pp. 150–51. *Ibid.*, pp. 196, 275.

[367] *Castleford's Chronicle or The Boke of Brut*, ed. C.D. Eckhardt, 2 vols, Early English Text Society, original series, CCCV, CCCVI (Oxford, 1996), ii, pp. 976, 987–88, 1014–15.

Manchester, *un Jacobyn*, to King Philip IV of France to protest against the seizure of Gascony. The two mendicant envoys who, *ke been seet sun mester*, were detained for a week at Calais in 1294 before proceeding to Paris, where they were received by the king.[368] In contrast, it fell to two historians from the Low Countries, Jean Froissart[369] and Jehan le Bel,[370] to give a report on the dinner for 60 ladies organised by Queen Isabella of France and Philippa of Hainault on Trinity Sunday in 1327 in the dormitory of the Greyfriars of York.

Information on the friars and some of the teething troubles of a religious order finding its niche on the ecclesiastical landscape are mirrored in various chronicles.[371] The friars' arrival in England was recorded by the anonymous historian of the Benedictine priory of Spalding, Lincolnshire, a dependency of Crowland Abbey.[372] The chronicler of St Mary's Abbey, York, notes the presence of the friars and their activities both within the custody and beyond it. The church of the Greyfriars at Dumfries was the scene of the shocking murder of John Comyn, one of the contenders for the Scottish crown in 1306.[373] The promulgation of Pope Boniface VIII's *Super cathedram* was noted by monastic historians on both sides of the river Humber. The chronicle of the Augustinian canons of Thornton-on-Humber announces the publication of the decree in neutral terms. Nonetheless, the papal bull was perceived to be particularly framed against the main mendicant orders, the Dominicans and Franciscans (*item in eodem anno constituit papa ne predicator[es] seu minores predicarent sine licencia, seu confessiones audirent*).[374] *The Hagnaby Chronicle* reproduces the papal constitution in its entirety and is more explicit in its declaration that it was written against the Dominicans and Franciscans (*littera domini pape contra ordines predicatorum et minorum*).[375] While the Austin Friars and the Carmelites seem to have been exculpated by these two monastic chroniclers, an entry in *The Coucher Book of Selby* refers to the decision of the provincial council of Canterbury against the mendicants.[376]

[368] *The Chronicle of Pierre de Langtoft, in French verse, from the earliest period to the death of King Edward I*, ed. T. Wright, 2 vols, RS, XLVII (London, 1866–68), ii, pp. 204–07. Cf. *Matthew Paris, HA*, ii, p. 298: *Fratres Praedicatores vel Jacobinos, a domo Sancti Jacobi, quae Parisius est …*

[369] *Chroniques de J. Froissart*, ed. S. Luce et al., 16 vols, Société de l'histoire de France, CXLVII, CXLVIII, CLIV, CLIX, CLXIX, CLXXX, CLXXXVIII, CCXXXVII, CCXXXVIII, CCLXIX, CCLXXXII, CCXCIV, CCCCXXV (Paris, 1869–1975), ii, pp. 44–45.

[370] *Les vrayes Chroniques de Messire Jehan le Bel*, ed. M.L. Polain, 2 vols, Académie Royale de Belgique (Brussels, 1863), i, p. 39.

[371] *Walter Map De nugis Curialium Courtiers' Trifles*, ed. M.R. James, C.N.L. Brooke and R.A.B. Mynors, OMT (Oxford, 1983), i, c. 25, pp. 84–113, for his extended critique of the Cistercians in England.

[372] Gonville and Caius College Library, Cambridge, MS.314/376, fol. 97r: *huius regis tempore anno M.CC. XXX. o dolor et plusquam dolor. O pestis triculenta fratres minores venerunt in Angliam.* This chronicler echoes the lament of the Peterborough chronicler on the arrival of the Franciscans, but does not offer any corroborative reasons for such a negative response to the friars' arrival.

[373] *The chronicle of St Mary's Abbey, York from Bodley MS. 39*, ed. H.H.E. Craster and M.E. Thornton, SS, CXLVIII (1934), p. 40. Cf. *Sir Thomas Gray Scalacronica 1272–1363*, pp. 50–53.

[374] BL, Campbell roll, xxi, 4. The short roll records that Pope Innocent IV consecrated Master Roger of Weasenham, dean of Lincoln, as bishop of Coventry and Lichfield in 1245 during the first council of Lyon (*in concilio Lugd.*). The accession of Nicholas IV, the first Franciscan pope, was recorded under the year 1288.

[375] BL, MS. Cotton Vespasian B.XI, fols. 49v–51r.

[376] *The Coucher Book of Selby*, ed. J.T. Fowler, vol 2, YAS, RS, X, XIII (1891, 1893), p. 398.

Some of these texts provide a unique witness to particular events. The annal attached to *The Anlaby Cartulary* cites the friars' practice of accepting burials in 1279.[377] *The Hagnaby Chronicle* reports that Archbishop Pecham carried out visitations in Lindsey and Holland in 1284. The following year Richard of Hanworth, abbot of the Premonstratensian monastery of Barlings, Lincolnshire, laid aside his abbatial mitre and pastoral staff to join the Greyfriars and was received into the order at York on 8 September 1285,[378] an event that was entered in the Cartulary of Barlings Abbey.[379] Although the will of Master Robert of Scarborough, archdeacon of the East Riding (from 1262) and then dean of York (1279–1290/91) is no longer extant, his bequest to the friars of Scarborough featured in the annals of the Cistercian monastery of Meaux in the East Riding. Sir John Ughtred, a soldier, a relative and an executor, demanded the settlement of the debt during the administration of Roger of Driffield, the thirteenth abbot (1286–1310). As a result the lead from the roof of the lay brothers' dormitory was removed and used for the roof of the friars' church in Scarborough.[380] Meaux was not the only Cistercian house of Yorkshire to face serious debts in this period.[381]

Many of the friaries were situated close to the main arteries of communication by road, boat and ferry. Visiting friars were part of the local landscape and they traversed the main routes on their journeys to or from York. The frequent presence of the crown in York in the first third of the fourteenth century increased the flow of friars who carried messages for the monarch. Parliament met both at York and Lincoln in this period; some of the meetings were held at the Greyfriars of York. The routine movement of friars around the custody, especially their preaching tours and along the routes to the numerous local shrines within the custody, gave them an extensive knowledge of local life; they were frequently the source of news at international, national, regional and local levels. Although friars were assigned to a specific community, they were forbidden to travel unnecessarily. Unnecessary and unauthorised travelling was censured by the order, which assigned each friar to a specified community living under obedience to the guardian. Legitimate journeys took them around the *limitatio* of their friary, along the roads to the schools of Oxford and Cambridge and the custodial, provincial and general chapters. The friars' mobility and dealings with confrères from other houses, custodies and provinces imparted an exotic air which is captured by vernacular literature of the later fourteenth century. On their preaching tours they brought news from one town or village to another and this made them keen observers of local events and thereby especially interesting to chroniclers.

One of the ways in which the friars contributed to their neighbourhood was through historical records. Their impact upon the compilation of national and

377 M.R. James, 'The Anlaby Chartulary', *YAJ*, XXXI (1932–34), pp. 337–47, at 341.

378 *The Medieval Lindsey Marsh: Select Documents*, ed. A.E.B. Owen, LRS, LXXXV (1996), pp. 68, 72, no. 31.

379 BL, MS. Cotton Faustina, B.I, fol. 110r: *Dominus Ricardus abbas de Barling ad ordinem fratrum Minorum apud Eborac' die nativitatis beate virginis Marie ...*

380 *Chronica monasterii de Melsa, a fundatione usque ad annum 1396, auctore Thoma de Burton, abate, accedit continuatio ad annum 1406 a monacho quodam ipsius domus*, ii, p. 237. Cf. *Memorials of the Abbey of St. Mary of Fountains*, ed. J.R. Walbran and J. Raine, 3 vols, SS, XLII, LXVII, CXXX (1863–1918), i, p. 98; Little, *Studies in English Franciscan History being the Ford Lectures delivered in the University of Oxford in 1916*, p. 15.

381 E.g., E.K. Clark, 'The Foundation of Kirkstall Abbey', *Miscellanea*, PThS, IV (1895), pp. 169–208, at 193–94, records the community's debts to Tockes, a Jew of London.

regional histories has already drawn the attention of Antonia Gransden.[382] Dr Andrew Little explains that the friars were more disposed to compile histories of the provinces than chronicles of particular houses. They were convinced that their order marked a new phase in the history of Christianity, a return to the zeal, vigour and edification of the primitive Church, the criterion of the halcyon days of Christianity.[383] Thus, there are no known Franciscan equivalents to the monastic accounts concerning the foundation and growth of particular communities, such as the Benedictine abbey of Selby[384] and the Cistercian monasteries of Kirkstall,[385] Byland and Jervaulx.[386] Although it is true that Thomas of Eccleston paints a portrait of the first four ministers provincial, he does not present histories of particular houses and rarely gives a date of foundation. He was more concerned with *exempla* materials than with a list of the guardians of a friary and their achievements. Moreover, many guardians were in office for no more than a single year and had little time to leave their mark in terms of building projects or other grandiose schemes.

Thomas of Eccleston celebrated the memory of the first friars in England and proudly trumpeted their virtues. One of those who circulated anecdotes about St Francis's was Martin Barton, who was perhaps the source of the extended account inserted into *The Compilatio Assisiensis*. Eccleston mentions Henry Misericord, the first guardian of Lincoln; Elias, a novice, who died in the odour of sanctity at York; and Eustace of Merc, who flourished at Oxford, and was later guardian and then custos of York. The relocation of the friary at York in the early 1240s was noted, along with the enlargement of the friary at Grimsby.[387] One of the three *Continuationes Chronici Martini Oppaviensis* was written by the friars of the English province between 1277 and 1316. The unnamed chronicler was well acquainted with the life of the papal court and its appointments. Among the nine cardinals created by Pope Nicholas III on 12 March 1278 were two friars, Jerome of Ascoli, formerly minister general, and Bentivegna Bentivegni, bishop of Todi. The papal provision of Archbishop Pecham, the author of a commentary on the Franciscan Rule, to the diocese of Canterbury was recorded, as was the election of Jerome of Ascoli as Nicholas IV, the first Franciscan pope, under the year 1288. Pope Boniface VIII provided William Gainsborough, master of theology at the sacred palace, to the diocese of Worcester on 22 October 1302. The following year Pope Benedict XI appointed the bishops of Winchester, London and Worcester as protectors of the order's privileges. Bishop Gainsborough undoubtedly knew the English author of the chronicle; he may have been the author of this short continuation of the chronicle.[388]

Thomas of Eccleston's focus on the south of England and the Midlands is complemented by *The Chronicon de Lanercost*'s concentration on events in Durham,

[382] A. Gransden, *Historical Writing in England*, 2 vols (London, 1974–82). A. Kehnel, 'The Narrative Tradition of the Medieval Franciscan Friars on the British Isles. Introduction to the Sources', *FS*, LXIII (2005), pp. 461–530.

[383] A.G. Little, 'Chronicles of the Mendicant Friars', *Franciscan Essays*, 2 vols, ed. P. Sabatier, F.C. Burkitt, H.E. Goad and A.G. Little (Manchester, 1912–32), ii, pp. 85–103, at 85–87.

[384] *Historia Selebiensis monasterii*, ed. J. Burton with L. Lockyer, OMT (Oxford, 2013).

[385] Clark, 'The Foundation of Kirkstall Abbey'.

[386] *The Foundation History of the Abbeys of Byland and Jervaulx*, ed. J. Burton, BTS, XXXV (York, 2006).

[387] Eccleston, pp. 10, 22, 32, 36, 40, 45, 64, 85, 88. Cf. *Compilatio Assisiensis*, no. 56, *FF*, pp. 1471–690, at 1540–42.

[388] L. Weiland, ed., *Continuationes chronici Martini Oppaviensis, iii, Continuationes Anglicae Fratrum Minorum*, in *Monumenta Germaniae historica*, scriptorum, XXIV, ed. G.H. Pertz (Hannover 1879), pp. 253–59.

Lincolnshire and Yorkshire. The latter is 'typically Franciscan' in its outlook on account of its compilers' strong interest in their neighbours' welfare and events concerning their own order.[389] It is more cosmopolitan in character and mixes local, national and international events, recounting the splendid translation of St Hugh of Lincoln and St William FitzHerbert. The first was celebrated on 6 October 1280 by Archbishop Pecham in the presence of King Edward I and Queen Eleanor of Castile, and the second on 9 January 1284 in the presence of the king and queen. Thomas Bek, prebendary of Caistor, was consecrated as bishop of St David's on the first occasion and Antony Bek, precentor of York, as the bishop of Durham on the second. The international nature of the Franciscan order is reflected in an eyewitness report of 1276 regarding the friars' unwillingness to extend Christian burial to a notorious usurer in Rome. Bulletins from English friars visiting Rome in 1285 and Padua in 1293 were inserted into the chronicle.[390] The chronicle contains a wealth of information regarding the Scottish wars, especially incursions into northern England at the beginning of the fourteenth century. In 1319 Thomas Randolf, earl of Moray, and James of Douglas crossed the border and invaded northern England, advancing as far as Boroughbridge. An assorted force, led by Archbishop Melton and Bishop Hotham, included many secular and regular clergy. The mendicants, no strangers to the battlefield, were among these forces. This company, inexperienced in military strategy, attacked the Scottish army at Myton-on-Swale, approximately 12 miles north-west of York, where they were easily routed and their troops were decimated. The Scottish invaders killed about 4,000 men, including the mayor of York, and many clerics; about 1,000 were drowned in the river Swale, where St Paulinus had once baptised converts to Christianity;[391] others were captured and held to ransom. The invading forces scorched Lancaster, exempting only the Benedictines and the Dominicans. The Lancashire town of Preston was burned, with the exception of the Greyfriars. Scottish troops entered the East Riding, laying waste to properties close to Beverley until they were bought off. The last entry of Franciscan interest concerns an unnamed friar in episcopal orders, who accompanied Archbishop Zouche and led troops into the battle of Neville's Cross on 17 October 1346, when David II, king of Scotland, was captured.[392]

Thomas of Otterburn, a Franciscan master of divinity, was active in the composition of chronicles of England.[393] Vestiges of lost Franciscan chronicles[394] have been traced in at least two texts compiled in the custody of York, *The Anonimalle Chronicle 1307 to 1334* and *The Kirkstall Chronicle*. The first of these narrates the severe flooding that afflicted northern England during 1315, when the river Ouse overflowed its banks and burst through the walls of the Greyfriars. Events from the London Greyfriars were reported, including the plight of a bishop who sought sanctuary there and a group of royal burials in London and Paris. The sequel to the order's disputes

[389] A.G. Little, 'The Authorship of the Lanercost Chronicle', *EHR*, XXXI (1916), pp. 269–79, and XXXII (1917), pp. 48–49; Gransden, *Historical Writing in England*, ii, p. 13.

[390] *Chronicon de Lanercost M.CC.I.–M.CCC.XLVI*, pp. 98–99, 105, 113, 121, 147–49; *The chronicle of St Mary's Abbey, York from Bodley MS. 39*, pp. 20–21.

[391] *Bede Ecclesiastical History of the English People*, ed. B. Colgrave and R.A.B. Mynors, OMT (Oxford, 1969), pp. 188–89.

[392] *Chronicon de Lanercost M.CC.I.–M.CCC.XLVI*, pp. 239, 246–48, 350–51.

[393] *Sir Thomas Gray Scalacronica 1272–1363*, pp. 6–7.

[394] Cf. H.S. Offler, 'A Note of the Northern Franciscan Chronicle', *Nottingham Medieval Studies*, XXVIII (1984), pp. 45–59.

regarding evangelical poverty at the court of Pope John XXII is chronicled.[395] The second of these commemorates St Anthony of Padua, Alexander of Hales, John Duns Scotus, Nicholas of Lyra and St Louis of Anjou, bishop of Toulouse, and the royal burials of Queen Isabella (†1358), the widow of the deposed King Edward II, and their daughter, Queen Joan (†1362), the wife of King David II of Scotland, and Joan of Kent (†1385), princess of Wales and duchess of Cornwall and countess of Chester and lady of Wake, the third wife of the Black Prince and the mother of King Richard II, at London and Stamford respectively. The *passio* of four friars from the provinces of Hungary, Genoa, Aquitaine and Provence was reproduced at some length under the year 1391. Entries of northern interest were the activities of King Richard II, the assassination of William of Appleton, the friar and surgeon of John of Gaunt, the duke of Lancaster, with Simon Sudbury, archbishop of Canterbury, on 14 June 1381 outside the Tower of London, and Lord Ralph Lumley's rebellion against King Henry IV in 1400. Lumley was beheaded at Cirencester and his head was exhibited on the south bridge of York; at the request of his wife, his body was buried at the Greyfriars of York.[396]

Another insurrection against King Henry IV, this time centring on Archbishop Scrope, in the early summer of 1405 is narrated in the continuation of the *Eulogium Historiarum* attributed to an unnamed friar, who received information from one or more confrères in York regarding the rebellion triggered by the prelate. The prelate had preached movingly in York Minster and fomented a rebellion. At Shipton Moor he was accompanied by members of all four orders of friars, including about 18 members of the Greyfriars, who joined the army led by Thomas Mowbray, the earl marshal, and Sir William Plumpton. The York chronicler reports that the metropolitan celebrated Mass at Shipton Moor.[397] After seemingly constructive discussions with the earl of Westmorland, the two armies agreed to disperse. The earl's ruse worked perfectly when he moved to arrest the archbishop, the earl marshal and Sir William Plumpton, conducting them to Pontefract castle, where they were tried and sentenced to death. The executions took place hurriedly in a field outside York on 8 June 1405.[398] Regarded as a martyr by Yorkshiremen, Mowbray was interred at the local Greyfriars, while his head was fixed on a stake on the city walls.[399] The veneration of his burial place is reflected on 6 December 1407, when Richard Burgh requested interment in

[395] *The Anonimalle Chronicle 1307 to 1334: From Brotherton Collection MS 29*, ed. W.R. Childs and J. Taylor, YAS, RS, CXLVII (Leeds, 1991), pp. 10, 12, 19, 38, 50, 86–87, 88–89, 92–93, 100–01, 116–17, 136–37, 144–45. Cf. *The chronicle of St Mary's Abbey, York from Bodley MS. 39*, p. 67: *et muros Fratrum Minorum asportavit Eboraci et Doncastrie et usque ad magnum altare eorum illa nocte et die fluere non cessavit.*

[396] *The Kirkstall Abbey Chronicles*, ed. J. Taylor, PThS, XLII (1952), pp. 25–26, 98, 99, 101–05, 107, 109, 110–11, 126–27.

[397] *The Historians of the Church of York and its Archbishops*, iii, p. 288.

[398] *Eulogium (Historiarum sive temporis): Chronicon ab orbe condito usque ad annum Domini M.CCC. LXVI., a monacho quodam Malmesburiensi exaratum*, ed. F.S. Haydon, 3 vols, RS, IX (London, 1858–63), iii, pp. 405–08. Cf. J.I. Catto, 'An Alleged Great Council of 1374', *EHR*, LXXXII (1967), pp. 764–71, at 765–66, where the Franciscan content of the continuation attracts comment. Cf. *An English Chronicle of the reigns of Richard II., Henry IV., Henry V. and Henry VI.* Written before the year 1471, ed. J.S. Davies, CS, Old Series, LXIV (London, 1856), pp. 31, 33. *The St Albans Chronicle, The Chronica Maiora of Thomas Walsingham, 1376–1422*, ed. J. Taylor, W.R. Childs and L. Watkiss, 2 vols, OMT (Oxford, 2003–11), ii, pp. 440–57.

[399] A.D.H. Leadman, 'The insurrection and death of Archbishop Scroope, and the Battle of Bramham Moor', *YAJ*, XI (1890–91), pp. 189–99. *The Historians of the Church of York and its Archbishops*, ii, pp. 431–33.

the friary *ad pedes Domini Marescall.*[400] William Gascoigne, the chief justice of England and a native of Yorkshire, had refused to play any part in the trial. His nephew, Thomas Gascoigne, a native of Hunslet and a visitor to the friars' libraries at Doncaster, York and Oxford, wrote an account of the slain archbishop of York.[401]

The last chronicler to mention the Greyfriars was Charles Wriothesley, Windsor herald, who reported that after Michaelmas 1538 friaries in various counties were suppressed and 'cleane put downe for ever'. For instance, the mendicant houses of London were dissolved on 12 November and 'the fryers clene put out'.[402] Hearing news of the progress of the royal suppression, the die was cast for the friaries of the custody of York, which fell one by one between 9 October 1538 and 9 March 1539. Wriothesley announced that Gilbert Berkeley, a relatively newly ordained priest, was said to be 'very loath to leave his ipochrytes coate till he was compelled for feare of punishment' at the suppression of the York Greyfriars on 27 November 1538.[403] Another perspective was provided on 15 December of that year, when Sir George Lawson and others notified Thomas Cromwell that they had 'quietly taken the surrenders and dissolved ... the friars at Tykhill, Doncaster, Pontefract and York'. They added that they had been 'thankfully received'.[404] Despite the royal suppression of the friaries, there is evidence that the bonds forged among the friars survived the great religious upheaval of the Dissolution, as the will of Dr William Vavasour demonstrates.[405]

Students of the history of the Greyfriars in the custody of York are indebted to a group of antiquarians, who preserved parts of their history and collected items of interest. The Library of the College of Arms in London, MS.L.8, includes notes on the religious orders of Yorkshire in the hands of John Wrythe, alias Wriothesley, garter (†1504), and his son, Sir Thomas Wriothesley, garter (†1534). This manuscript included information on the founders of the friaries of Beverley, Scarborough and York and a list of the distinguished people who were interred in their churches. On his visits to Lincolnshire and Yorkshire John Leland reported that the Easterlings were buried in the Greyfriars of Boston, as were the Mounteviles and the Withams.[406] Reginald Molendinarius, a merchant of Lincoln, was the founder of the city's Greyfriars. Henry Lacy and Nunny were great benefactors of the friary. Nunny was buried in the

400 *TE*, i, pp. 347–48, and iv, pp. 102–07, 105. Note how carefully a drinking cup given by him to the testator was entailed in the family of the latter as an heirloom.

401 *The Historians of the Church of York and its Archbishops*, iii, pp. 288–91. *Richard Scrope: Archbishop, Rebel, Martyr*, ed. P.J.P. Goldberg (Donington, 2007), R.M. Ball, *Thomas Gascoigne, Libraries and Scholarship*, Cambridge Bibliographical Society, XIV (Cambridge, 2006), p. 102, no. 50.

402 *A chronicle of England during the reigns of the Tudors, from A.D. 1485 to 1559, by Charles Wriothesley, Windsor herald*, ed. W.D. Hamilton, 2 vols, CS, New Series, XI, XX (London, 1875, 1877), i, pp. 87, 88.

403 *A chronicle of England during the reigns of the Tudors, from A.D. 1485 to 1559, by Charles Wriothesley, Windsor herald*, p. 82.

404 *LPFD*, xiii, pt. ii, p. 454, no. 1064.

405 Cf. J.L. Cruickshank, *Headingley-cum-Burley c. 1540–c. 1784*, PThS, 2nd series, XXII (2012), pp. 33–58, at 36–40, relates that the monks of Kirkstall read the signs of the ecclesiastical and political times after the failure of the Pilgrimage of Grace and began to seek ways of preserving the patrimony of their monastery. After the Dissolution some former monks maintained contact with each other. One of them succeeded in obtaining a substantial collection of the monastic library. Others preserved the vestments of the abbey.

406 *The Itinerary of John Leland in or about the years 1535–1543*, ed. L. Toulmin Smith (London, 1906–10), 5 vols, iv, pp. 114–15.

Greyfriars of York.[407] The Greyfriars of Beverley was founded by the Huthomes of Scorbrough by Lekingfield. Leland added that the last earl of Northumberland, save one, strove for the patronage of the friary.[408] The friars of Doncaster were at the north end of the bridge which was locally known as the 'Freres Bridge'.[409] The Greyfriars of York was described as being in the vicinity of the castle.[410] Francis Drake's *Eboracum*, written in 1736, shows an awareness of the importance of the city's Greyfriars and notes legacies and comments made about the friary by contemporary historians.[411]

[407] *The Itinerary of John Leland in or about the years 1535–1543*, i, pp. 31–32.
[408] *The Itinerary of John Leland in or about the years 1535–1543*, i, p. 46.
[409] *The Itinerary of John Leland in or about the years 1535–1543*, i, p. 35.
[410] *The Itinerary of John Leland in or about the years 1535–1543*, i, p. 55.
[411] Drake, *Eboracum or the history and antiquities of the city of York from the original to the present times, together with the history of the cathedral church and the lives of archbishops of that see*, pp. 282–83.

A glossary of terms

Acolyte: generally the first minor order to be recorded in the episcopal registers of Lincoln and York.

Cardinal protector: a senior prelate entrusted with business concerning the Franciscan order at the papal court.

Chapter: a friars' meeting at international, national, regional or domestic level.

Conventual friary: a house of at least 13 friars in continual residence.

Cursor: an academic grade in theology attained by a friar who assisted the lector.

Custodial chapter: meeting of representatives of each house within a specific region.

Custody: an administrative division of the English province of the Franciscan order. It generally denotes a geographical cluster of friaries.

Custos: the senior friar responsible for the level of religious observance within the custody and the friars' ministry within the administrative unit.

Deacon: a major order received by friars proceeding to the priesthood.

Friary or convent: the place in which the friars normally resided or from which they carried out their apostolate to the neighbouring towns and villages.

General chapter: the triennial meeting of friars representing every region of the order, the seat of the highest authority in the order.

Guardian: the friar responsible for the leadership of the community. He was sometimes known as the warden.

Lector: a theologian entrusted with the instruction of the members of a friary, especially candidates for ordination.

Lector of the sacred palace: the theologian appointed to teach theology at the papal court at Rome.

Letter of fraternity: a letter issued by the community of friars, generally in the name of the guardian, to those who were admitted to a share in the friars' prayers.

Limitatio: the designated area in which friars taught, preached, heard confessions and collected alms.

Martyrology or necrology: a book containing the names of the people for whom the friars agreed to pray, especially on their anniversaries.

Mendicants: friars (Austin Friars, Carmelites, and Dominicans) who derived material support from the collection of alms.

Minister provincial: the friar responsible for the governance of the province.

Novitiate: the year-long period of training for those who wished to become friars.

Observants: friars of the Observant reform, who reached England in 1482, and formed a community at Greenwich and then Canterbury, Newark, Newcastle, Richmond in Surrey and Southampton.

Province: a pastoral and administrative unit. There was one in England and Ireland, but eight in France.

Provincial chapter: the governing body of a province which met annually and represented the different custodies and communities.

Religious profession: the three vows of poverty, chastity and obedience taken at the end of the novitiate year.

The *Sentences*: the text compiled by Peter Lombard (†1160), a Parisian master of theology, in four books, that is, on God, the creation, the fall and the sacraments. From the 1220s bachelors and masters increasingly expounded this text.

Studium generale: the friars' schools at the Universities of Paris, Oxford and Cambridge.

Subdeacon: the first of the major orders leading to the priesthood.

Suffragan bishop: a non-resident bishop of a diocese in Ireland or *in partibus infidelium* who assisted the ordinary in the sacramental administration of his diocese.

Suffrages: prayers offered by the friars for benefactors.

Trental: a celebration of Masses for an individual on 30 successive days. Sometimes known as Gregorian Masses.

Vicar provincial: the designated deputy of the minister provincial.

Visitation: a canonical examination of the members of each friary conducted by the custos, the minister provincial and the minister general.

Chronology

1206: the conversion of St Francis.
1215, November: the Fourth ecumenical Council of the Lateran in Rome.
1223, 29 November: Pope Honorius III approved the *Rule* of St Francis.
1224, 24 August or 10 September: the Greyfriars or Franciscans reached England.
1226, 3/4 October: the death of St Francis at the Portiuncula, just outside Assisi.
1228, 16 July: Pope Gregory IX canonised St Francis.
c. 1229/30: friaries founded at Lincoln and York.
c. 1239: the friars reached Scarborough.
1243/44: Robert Grosseteste, bishop of Lincoln, heard the case brought by the Cistercians against the friars' foundation at Scarborough. As a result the friars were expelled from the town and settled at Hatterboard for some decades.
1244, 17 February: King Henry III donated 40 marks towards the building of the friary in York.
1244, Michaelmas: Ralph of Corbridge, former regent master in the University of Paris, was the second friar to lecture at the University of Oxford.
1251/52: Master William de Pocklington, a member of the household of Bishop Grosseteste, canon of Lincoln and prebendary of Langford Ecclesia from 1244, resigned his parish of Upton, Huntingdonshire, to become a friar in the custody of Oxford.
1253, 9 October: death of Bishop Grosseteste on his episcopal manor of Buckden, Huntingdonshire.
1258, 18 November: death of Adam Marsh, who was buried with his friend and collaborator, Bishop Grosseteste, in Lincoln cathedral.
1265, 24 November: Pope Clement IV provided Bonaventure da Bagnoregio, minister general of the Franciscans, as archbishop of York, an office which he declined.
–1276, 25 March: Thomas of Geddington, master of St Leonard's Hospital in York, entered the order. His successor, Roger of Malton, was elected by the canons in York Minster.
1278, 5 February 1278: Pope Nicholas III, who as a cardinal held a prebend at York Minster, commissioned Oliver Sutton, dean of Lincoln, John Le Romeyn, the chancellor of Lincoln, and Nicholas de Burser, custos of York, to confer it upon a suitable person.
1280, 6 October: John Pecham, archbishop of Canterbury, presided over the translation of the relics of St Hugh of Avalon in Lincoln cathedral. On the same occasion he consecrated Master Thomas Bek as bishop of St David's.
–1285, 8 September: Richard of Hanworth, abbot of the Premonstratensian Abbey of Barlings, Lincolnshire (1278/79–85), entered the order and was clothed as a friar at York.
1286, –10 May: Richard of Yarwell, prior of the Augustinian Canons of Nocton Park, Lincolnshire (1277–86), resigned to become a friar.
1289, 26 June: Nicholas, guardian of the Greyfriars of Lincoln, was one of the heads of local religious communities to petition Pope Nicholas IV for the canonisation of Bishop Grosseteste.
1290, 1 September: indulgence for those visiting the friars' church at Doncaster.
1290, 15 October: indulgence for those visiting the friars' church at Scarborough.
1290, 19 November: indulgence for those visiting the friars' church at York.

–1292, 26 July: Hugh of Grimsby, formerly a canon of Thornton Curtis, Lincolnshire, and prior of Nocton Park (1286–92), resigned to become a friar.
1293, –27 January: Nicholas de Turribus, rector of the church of Kirkheaton, resigned to join the order.
1295: the provincial chapter was held at Lincoln.
1300, 18 February: *Super cathedram* was promulgated by Pope Boniface VIII to regulate the friars' ministry of preaching and hearing confessions.
1300, 11 June: William de Tothale, prior of the Hospital of St John of Jerusalem, granted the friars of Scarborough a messuage of land abutting the town wall.
1300–02: Doctor William Gainsborough, formerly minister provincial and master at Oxford, lectured in theology at the papal court in Rome.
1302, 22 October: Pope Boniface VIII provided William Gainsborough to the diocese of Worcester. He was consecrated on 28 October in the papal curia and received the temporalities on 4 February.
1306, 22 November: John Dalderby, bishop of Lincoln, authorised the friars of Lincoln to preach in the cathedral.
1307, 3 August: in the church of the Greyfriars of Doncaster William Greenfield, archbishop of York, received the homage of John de Grey for lands held from him.
1307, 17 September: death of Bishop Gainsborough at Beauvais, where he was buried at the church of the Cordeliers.
1309: the provincial chapter was held at Lincoln.
1311, 1 July: Adam of Lincoln and Thomas de Pontefract, masters of theology, attended a provincial council at York, where the charges against the Knights Templar were heard.
1311, 10 August: a letter from Queen Isabella to William of Calverley.
1312, 24 February: King Edward II gave Margaret de Clare, the wife of Piers Gaveston, 40 marks to celebrate her churching. He held a feast at the Greyfriars of York.
1314: the provincial chapter was held at Lincoln.
1314, 20 February: Archbishop Greenfield granted the friars of York 40s. *de elemosina* and asked them to celebrate Mass for his recently deceased brother, Robert.
1314, 17 September: Gilbert Ó Tigernaig, bishop of Annaghdown, was commissioned to dedicate a newly built altar at the Greyfriars of York.
1315, 14 January: Archbishop Greenfield gave two marks *in subvencionem victus* to the friars.
1315, 18 November: Archbishop Greenfield donated five marks to the friars *propter excessivam temporis caristiam qua gravantur.*
1316, 13 February: Bishop Dalderby granted an indulgence of 30 days to those who contributed to the mendicants' needs during the time of scarcity.
1319, 1 November: King Edward II attended a high Mass at Greyfriars, York.
–15 November 1322: Parliament had recently been held at the Greyfriars of York.
1324, 14 October: the guardian and community of Doncaster were licensed to have four portable altars consecrated by any Catholic bishop.
1327, 15 August: the provincial chapter was held at Lincoln.
–1335, 9 June: King Edward III and Queen Philippa lodged at the Greyfriars of York, where Parliament was held.
1336, 28 November: Benedict XII's *Redemptor noster* lists York among the approved schools of theology, where masters might lecture before proceeding to teach at the Universities of Paris, Oxford and Cambridge.
1336, 21 December: ordination held at the Greyfriars, York, by Richard Bury, bishop of Durham.

1343, 29 March: Richard, bishop of Bisacien', held an ordination at Greyfriars, Beverley.

1343, 7 June: Richard, bishop of Bisacien', held an ordination at Greyfriars, York.

1347, 22 December: Hugh, archbishop of Damascus, held an ordination at the Greyfriars of Doncaster.

1349: the Black Death raged throughout the custody.

1360, 20 March: King John II of France gave 15 escuz in alms to each mendicant friary of Lincoln.

1361: the provincial chapter was held at York.

1380, 14 April: King Richard II took the friars of York under his special protection after a disturbance in the city.

1381: the Greyfriars of York was attacked during the peasants' revolt.

1381, 24 June: an assault on the Greyfriars of Scarborough to apprehend Robert le Aclom and many others.

1400, 20 September: John Greenlaw was provided to the diocese of *Soltaniensis*.

1405, June: 18 Greyfriars of York were arrested with Richard Scrope, archbishop of York, at Shipton Moor in his rebellion against King Henry IV.

1414, 28 January: Simon Brampton was provided to the diocese of Tripoli.

1414, 7 October: John Walcot was provided to the diocese of Nisch in Bulgaria.

1414, 24 November: John del Howe, lector at York, appeared before the cathedral chapter and was found guilty of making ill-considered comments about the clergy. He was accompanied by John Belaise, guardian of the friary.

1418, 14 November: Walter Forman was provided to the diocese of Ross.

1419, 16 February: Robert Foston was provided to the diocese of Elphin.

1419: 17 March: Nicholas Warter was provided to the diocese of Dromore.

1421, 1 July: Pope Martin V wrote to the bishops of Lincoln, London and Rochester, reporting the complaint of Master John Ixworth, rector of Boston, that a number of friars from all four orders were inflicting many injuries on him against the papal decision. The prelates were required to enforce the papal decree in defence of the rector.

1425, 29 September: Bishop Warter blessed Peter de Snape, abbot of Jervaulx, at the high altar of the Greyfriars, York, where he witnessed the abbatial promise of obedience to the metropolitan.

1426, 26 July: Thomas Richmond's vernacular sermon to the clergy and people in the newly constructed church of St Anne on Foss Bridge, York. He was accused of theological errors and was censured.

1438: the provincial chapter was held at York.

1441, 28 July: John Kegill was provided to the diocese of *Philippopolis.*

1481, 4 January: Pope Sixtus IV issued a faculty for the Observant Friars to make a foundation at Greenwich, at the request of King Edward IV.

1481, 24 September: Pope Sixtus IV granted Margaret, duchess of Burgundy, permission to build three friaries for the Friars of the Observance in England.

1486, 24 March: the newly crowned King Henry VII gave alms to the poor friars (*poore freres*) and prisoners of Lincoln on Good Friday.

1498, 26 February: William Cerff, rector of Rowley, requested burial in the York Greyfriars and named eight members of the community in his will.

1498/99: the friaries of Canterbury, Newcastle and Southampton were transferred to the Observant reform by the crown.

1534, 11 August: the Observants refused to accept the royal supremacy and were sent to the Tower of London by King Henry VIII, who suppressed the order. Some former Observants were assigned to the Greyfriars of Beverley, Lincoln,

Scarborough and York. William Ellel died at Doncaster, but it is unclear whether he had joined the community.

1536, 11 March: the last recorded ordination at the York Greyfriars was celebrated by William Duffield, a friar and bishop of Ascalon.

1536, autumn: there was some support for the Pilgrimage of Grace on the part of at least two friars.

1537, 24 February: the last recorded ordination of a friar, William Gibson, in the diocese of York.

1538, 21 September: the last recorded ordination of a friar, John Cliffe, in the diocese of Lincoln.

1538, 9 October: suppression of the Greyfriars of Grimsby.

1538, 20 November: suppression of the Greyfriars of Doncaster.

1538, 27 November: suppression of the Greyfriars of York.

1538, 15 December: the four commissioners of the north notified Thomas Cromwell that they had taken the surrender of the friaries of Doncaster and York by this date.

–1539, 22 February: suppression of the Greyfriars of Boston.

–1539, 22 February: suppression of the Greyfriars of Lincoln.

1539, 25 February: suppression of the Greyfriars of Beverley; there was no list of signatories to the surrender.

1539, 9 March: suppression of the Greyfriars of Scarborough; there was no list of signatories.

1539, 8 October: John Smythe, last guardian of Lincoln, was dispensed to hold a benefice with eleven former friars of Lincoln.

1544, 13 November: the will and testament of William Vavasour, the last guardian of the Greyfriars and then priest of St Mary, Bishophill Junior, York, was compiled.

The Biographical Register of the Custody of York

ABNEY, John: he was the guardian of Doncaster, when he was named in the plea rolls of the Hilary term of 1442 (TNA, CP40/724, mm. 24, 278).

ABRAHAM, William: he was ordained p. on 26 February 1401 at Bishop Burton church, near Beverley (*Reg. Scrope*, ii, pp. 55–56, 131).

ABY, Roger: he was ordained s. on 18 December 1372 at Whitefriars, York, and p. on 22 December 1375 at Cawood manor church (BIA, Register 11, fol. 389v, Register 12, fol. 123r).

ACASTER (Acastr') Adam de: he was ordained p. at an unknown date and location between September 1346 and the same month of the following year (BIA, Register 10A, fol. 18a). He was licensed in the diocese of York in place of Walter de Newton at an unspecified date between 1352 and 1373 (BIA, Register 11, fol. 396r). He was authorised to hear the confessions of the Cistercian nuns of Hampole for one year from 9 April 1375 (BIA, Register 12, fol. 18r). A friar of this name of no specified mendicant order was the cousin of Robert Acaster of Riccall in the diocese of York on 12 June 1389. The testator left 20s. to each of the mendicant houses in the county town and 40s. to Adam. The will was extensive (BIA, Probate Register 1, fol. 56rv).

ACASTER, Robert: he was the guardian of Doncaster in 1372, when he and Robert Benet were sued by Robert de Merbury. Benet had been in the plaintiff's service at Pontefract, but, leaving before his time had expired, had entered the service of the guardian (*Notes on Religious Houses*, i, p. 37). Robert's name occurs in the plea rolls of the Trinity term in 1372 as the guardian of Doncaster (TNA, CP40/446, m. 99).

ACLIFF, John: he was ordained a. and s. on 20 September 1410 and d. on 6 June 1411; both ceremonies took place at Cawood prebendal church. He was ordained p. on 17 December 1412 at Greyfriars, York (BIA, Register 18, fols. 392v, 394r, 395v).

ADAM of Lincoln: see Lincoln, Adam de.

ADAM of York: see York, Adam de.

ADEL (Addy), Henry: he was a friar of York when he was ordained a. on 6 April 1504 in the lady chapel of York Minster, d. on 2 June 1509 at Whitefriars, York, and p. on 16 March 1510 in the lady chapel of York Minster (BIA, Register 25, fol. 123v, Register 26, fols. 103r, 106v. Cf. Cross and Vickers, *MFN*, p. 441).

AGLIONBIE, Henry: he was a bachelor of divinity and guardian at Beverley in 1526, when he and the community accepted as their founder Thomas Lord Darcy Menell and Kaith, who intended to rebuild and maintain the friary (*Monastic Chancery Proceedings (Yorkshire)*, p. 10). Palmer claims this friar as the prior of the Dominicans in the town (Palmer, 'The Friars Preachers, or Black Friars of Beverley', pp. 38–40).

ALBERBURY, Walter de: he was a friar of Lincoln when he was ordained p. on 19 September 1355 in Lincoln cathedral (LAO, Register 9D, fol. 77r).

ALBERT: he was a friar of Lincoln when he was ordained s. on 1 June 1420 at the priory of St Katherine outside Lincoln (*Reg. Fleming*, ii, p. 63, no. 471).

ALBERTE (Alberti), Henry: he was a friar of York when he was ordained a. on 16 March 1499 at Whitefriars, York, s. on 25 May 1499 at Blackfriars, York, d. on 19 September 1500 at Whitefriars, York, and p. on 23 September 1503 at Greyfriars, York (BIA, Register 23, fols. 462v, 464r, Register 5A, fol. 528v, Register 25, fol. 120v. Cf. Cross and Vickers, *MFN*, p. 439).

ALDBOROUGH (Aldeburgh, Aldburgh), Thomas: he was a friar of York when he was ordained a. on 5 March 1463 at Blackfriars, York, s. on 26 March 1463 at Greyfriars, York, d. on 4 June 1463 at Whitefriars, York, and p. on 17 March 1464 at Greyfriars, York (BIA, Register 20, fols. 454r, 455r, 456r, 458v).

ALESBY, Richard: he was ordained p. on 19 May 1380 at Stillingfleet parish church (BIA, Register 12, fol. 137v). He was a friar of Beverley in receipt of a taxable stipend in 1406 (TNA, E179/66/411. Cf. Jurkowski, 'Were Friars Paid Salaries? Evidence from Clerical Taxation Records', p. 136, n. 28).

ALLANDES (Alandes), William: he was ordained a. on 20 December 1365 at York Minster, s. on 12 June 1367 and d. on 23 September 1368, both at Bishopthorpe manor chapel. He was ordained p. on 1 March 1371 at Whitefriars, York (BIA, Register 11, fols. 361r, 366r, 371r and 382r). He received 20d. from the will of Margaret, wife of William Palmer, a merchant of York and parishioner of St Peter the Little, on 17 August 1402; the Greyfriars of York received the same amount. William Palmer asked for burial beside his wife, Margaret, and left this friar 3s. 4d. in his will of 4 January 1406, when he also gave the same amount to each mendicant house at York (BIA, Probate Register 3, fols. 82v–83r, 247r).

ALLEMANIA, William de: he was ordained p. on 3 June 1368 at Bishopthorpe manor chapel (BIA, Register 11, fol. 370r).

ALLERBERY, John: he was a friar at Doncaster when he was ordained a. on 24 February 1442 at Greyfriars, York (BIA, Register 19, fol. 265v).

ALLERSTANE, John de: he was ordained s. at Durham cathedral on 19 April 1337 at Howden (*Reg. Kirkby*, i, p. 71, no. 369; *Reg. Kellaw*, iii, pp. 183–89). He was licensed to hear confessions in the diocese of York sometime before 6 January 1352, when he was replaced by Adam de Askham (BIA, Register 10, fol. 280r).

ALLERTON, William de: he was ordained p. on 20 September 1348 in Skipton parish church (BIA, Register 10A, fol. 25v).

ALLISTON, John de: he was licensed to hear confessions in the diocese of York at an unspecified date. About 6 January 1352 he was replaced by Adam de Askham (BIA, Register 10, fol. 280r).

ALTHORPE (Alythorp), William: he was a friar of Lincoln when he was ordained s. on 30 March 1532 at Lincoln cathedral (LAO, Register 26, fol. 30r).

ALTON, William de: he was one of the two friars licensed to hear the confessions of the Benedictine nuns of Stainfield, Lincolnshire, on 5 February 1335 (LAO, Register 5, fol. 490v).

ALVASTER, John: he was ordained a. on 11 March 1430 at Greyfriars, York (BIA, Register 19, fol. 236r).

ALWEN (Alwent), Adam: he was ordained a. on 19 September 1411 at St Michael-le-Belfrey, York, and s. on 28 May 1412 at Greyfriars, York (BIA, Register 18, fols. 39Cr, 39Dr).

AMESTON, John de: he was licensed to hear confessions in the diocese of Lincoln on 20 June 1318 (LAO, Register 3, fol. 390r).

AMYS, William: he was a friar at Nottingham when he was ordained a. on 21 December 1504. He was at York when ordained s. on 20 September 1505 at Bishopthorpe manor chapel, d. on 20 December 1505 and p. on 28 March 1506 at Greyfriars, York. The first and third ordinations were held at Austin Friars, York (BIA, Register 25, fols. 126r, 130r, 131r, 133r. Cf. Cross and Vickers, *MFN*, p. 441).

ANDERSON, William: he was a friar of York when he was ordained a. on 23 September 1486 at Whitefriars, York (BIA, Register 23, fol. 402v. Cf. Cross and Vickers, *MFN*, p. 436). He was a friar of Lichfield when he was ordained s. in March 1487 and d. on 31 May 1488 and at Nottingham when ordained p. on 22 December 1488 (LRO, B/A/1/12, fols. 222r, 238v, 241v).

ANDERSON, William: a novice, he was one of the ten friars of Doncaster who signed the deed of surrender on 20 November 1538 (*Eighth Report of the Deputy Keeper of the Public Records*, p. 19. Cf. Cross and Vickers, *MFN*, p. 447).

ANDREW (Andre, Andree, Andro), John: he was a friar of York when he was ordained a. on 18 September 1456 at Austin Friars, York, s. on 18 December 1456 at Greyfriars, York, d. on 12 March 1457 and p. on 10 March 1459; the last two ceremonies were held at Whitefriars, York (BIA, Register 20, fols. 426r, 427r, 428v, 438r). In the intervening period it is probable that he was assigned to other friaries in the custody. Within 18 years of his ordination he was deemed sufficiently senior to discharge the office of guardian at York, a position which he occupied when licensed to hear confessions on 31 March 1479 (BIA, Register 22, fol. 316r). It is not known how long he had already filled this position; one hypothesis is that he was the guardian of the large and talented community for only one year. Guardians were appointed at the annual provincial chapter by the minister provincial with the advice of the definitors and the custos. On 26 September 1479 Joanne Halifeld, a widow and parishioner of St Michael, Spurriergate, York, left 16d. to Friar Andrew, who was probably to be identified with the former guardian of the community (BIA, Probate Register 5, fol. 151r). Within months he had relinquished the office of guardian, perhaps at the next provincial chapter. He was succeeded by Henry, who issued a letter of fraternity to Reginald Browne at an unspecified date in that year (Wordsworth, 'On Some Pardons or Indulgences Preserved in Yorkshire, 1412–1527', p. 402). He may have remained at York after stepping down from the office of guardian and he was a member of the local Greyfriars, when he was licensed to hear confessions throughout the diocese on 14 March 1487 (*Reg. Rotherham*, p. 218, no. 1747). On 14 August 1488 Thomas Nelson, a parishioner of St Mary Bishophill, Junior, York, who requested burial at Holy Trinity, compiled his will in the presence of John Andre, described as a chaplain. Nelson left 5s. to each mendicant house of York and then bequeathed Friar John Andro 20s. to pray for his soul (BIA, Probate Register 5, fol. 381rv).

ANENELL, Richard de: he was ordained s. on 8 March 1365 at Bishopthorpe manor chapel (BIA, Register 11, fol. 359r).

APPLEBY (Appilby), John: he was ordained s. at St Mary's Abbey, York, on 19 September 1377 (BIA, Register 12, fol. 129v).

APPLEBY (Appilby, Appelby), John: he was a friar of Doncaster on 3 and 9 May 1425, when he was a witness in a case before the consistory court, giving a detailed report of the profession of Katherine Northefolk as a Cistercian nun of Wallingwells, Nottinghamshire (BIA, Cons.AB.2, fol. 59r, CP, fol. 156r; Kane, 'Return of the Native: Franciscan Education and Astrological Practice in the Medieval North of England', p. 288).

APPLETON (Apelton, Appelton), John de: he was ordained a. and s. on 26 May 1358 at Greyfriars, York, and d. on 15 June 1359 at the manor chapel of Cawood (BIA, Register 11, fols. 333rv, 338r).

APPLETON (Appilton), John de: he was at Boston when he was ordained d. on 13 March 1361 at Holbeach parish church (LAO, Register 9D, fol. 98v), and at York when he was ordained p. on 23 September 1363 at Bishopthrope manor chapel (BIA, Register 11, fol. 354r).

APPLETON (Apulton), John: he was ordained s. on 17 March 1397 at Greyfriars, York (BIA, Sede Vacante, 5A, fol. 229v; BL, MS. Cotton Galba, E.X, fol. 130r). He was a friar of Lincoln when he was ordained d. on 22 February 1399 and p. on 24 September 1401; both ceremonies were held at Stow prebendal church (LAO, Register 13, fols. 85r, 96r).

APPLETON (Appilton), Thomas: he was ordained s. on 17 March 1397 at Greyfriars, York (BIA, Sede Vacante, 5A, fol. 229v); another list of ordinands refers to him as John (BL, MS. Cotton Galba, E.X, fol. 130r). Cecilia de Yharom de Ebor, a parishioner of St Martin-le-Grand, Coney Street, York, left 6s. 8d. to a friar of this name in her will of 16 February 1397. She also names John de Kirkby, *quondam famile mee*, and Thomas of Scarborough, who each received the same sum (BIA, Probate Register 1, fols. 92v–93r).

APPLETON (Appilton, Appylton), William de: he was ordained a. on 3 March 1352 at Austin Friars, York (BIA, Register 10A, fol. 54r). He was a friar of Lincoln when he was ordained s. on 29 February 1360 in Lincoln cathedral (LAO, Register 9D, fol. 94r). He was ordained d. on 22 May 1361 and p. on 18 May 1364, both at York Minster (BIA, Register 11, fols. 344v, 356v).

APPLETON (Apilton, Appilton), William de: a knight and physician, he entered the order late in life (*GFL*, p. 19). As early as 15 March 1373 John of Gaunt, the duke of Lancaster and brother of King Edward III, described Appleton as a friar, physician and surgeon. His stipend was 40 marks per year for life from the issues of the manor of Pontefract with livery for four horses and salaries for two grooms (*John of Gaunt's Register*, p. 335, no. 836. Cf. *The Westminster Chronicle, 1381–1394*, p. 6; Little, *Studies in English Franciscan History*, p. 79). Appleton was styled as *grant justiciaire et surregene et grand maester ouecque le roy et duc de Lancester* (Trevelyan, 'An account of the rising of 1381', p. 517). His name is cited in connection with medical remedies in the *Tabula Medicine* (P. Murray Jones, 'Mediating Collective Experience: The *Tabula Medicine* [1416–1425] as a Handbook for Medical Practice', p. 299). John of Ardene, an army surgeon, complains about the friar as a rival specialist *in fistula in ano*. He reports that the friar had accompanied the prince of Wales in his campaign in Gascony. On new year's day 1381 he received £10 from the duke.

Knighton erroneously described him as *Iohannes de ordine minorum in armis bellicis strenuus in phsica peritissimus, domino Iohanni duci Lancastrie familiarissimus*, who had taken refuge in the Tower of London (*Knighton's Chronicle 1337–1396*, pp. 212–15). Along with the chancellor, Simon Sudbury, archbishop of Canterbury, he was dragged from the Tower and beheaded on some level ground nearby on 14 June 1381. The assassination angered the duke (*Chroniques de J. Froissart*, x, p. 111; Clarke and Denholm-Young, 'The Kirkstall Chronicle, 1355–1400', p. 125; *The Kirkstall Chronicles*, pp. 110–11). *The St Albans Chronicle* refers to the execution of a certain brother of the order of St Francis on account of his connection with the duke of Lancaster (*The St Albans Chronicle, The Chronica maiora of Thomas of Walsingham, i, 1376–1422*, ii, pp. 430–31). His murder was recorded by William Somer (Catto and Mooney, 'The Chronicle of John Somer, OFM', p. 241). He was buried in the lady chapel of the London Greyfriars (*GFL*, pp. 82, 134). On 20 June 1381 the guardian of London had licence to dispose of Appleton's possessions for the salvation of his soul (*CPR, 1381–1386*, p. 16; R.F. Green, 'Friar William Appleton and the Date of Langland's B Text', *The Yearbook of Langland Studies*, XI (1997), pp. 87–96).

ARDY, Robert: he was ordained d. on 21 December 1476 at Holy Trinity Priory, Micklegate, York (BIA, Register 22, fol. 363v).

ARMETHSTED, Christopher: he was ordained p. on 16 June 1481 at Blackfriars, York (BIA, Register 23, fol. 377r. Cf. Cross and Vickers, *MFN*, p. 435).

ARNHEM (Arnem), Arnold: he was a friar of Beverley when he was ordained d. on 23 December 1419 at Cawood prebendal church (BIA, Register 18, fol. 404v; Walmsley, 'Some Dutch Franciscans in England during the later Middle Ages', p. 248).

ASHBY (Assheby), John de: he was a friar of Lincoln when he was ordained d. on 21 September 1359. He was a friar of Northampton when he was ordained p. on 29 February 1360; both ceremonies took place at Lincoln cathedral (LAO, Register 9D, fols. 92v, 95r).

ASHTON (Eshton), John: he was a friar of York when he was ordained a. on 13 March 1484 at Holy Trinity Priory, Micklegate, York, s. on 18 December 1484 at Austin Friars, York, d. on 11 March 1486 at Holy Trinity Priory, Micklegate, and p. on 9 June 1487 at Blackfriars, York (BIA, Register 23, fols. 390r, 394r, 400v, 408r. Cf. Cross and Vickers, *MFN*, p. 435).

ASHTON (Ascheton), Laurence de: he was ordained d. on 17 December 1345 at Liddington prebendal church (LAO, Register 7B, fol. 2v).

ASHWELL (Aschewell), Robert de: he was ordained d. on 23 September 1346 at Austin Friars, Stamford (LAO, Episcopal Register 7B, fol. 8v).

ASKEBY, William: he was ordained s. on 15 March 1348 in York Minster (BIA, Register 10A, fol. 21r).

ASKHAM, Adam de: he was licensed in the diocese of York c.6 January 1352 (BIA, Register 10A, fol. 280r).

ASKHAM, John: he was ordained s. on 17 December 1379 at York Minster (BIA, Register 12, fol. 35v).

ASSENDEN (Assynden, Hasynden), John: he was ordained a. on 3 April 1400 at Blackfriars, York, s. on 12 June 1400 at Bishop Burton church and d. on 18 September 1400 at Cawood prebendal church (*Reg. Scrope*, ii, pp. 55, 57, 131).

ASSHEBY (Ascheby, Asseby), Hugh de: he was ordained a. on 20 September 1343 at Whitefriars, York (BIA, Register 10A, fol. 4v), s. on 20 December 1343 (*Reg. Kellaw*, iii, p. 131), d. on 21 May 1345 at Thirsk parish church and p. on 14 June 1348 at St Mary's monastery in York (BIA, Register 10A, fols. 11v, 25r).

ASSISI (Asisio, Assilio), John de: he was ordained d. on 16 June 1291 at Boston parish church. He may have been the John de Assilio ordained p. on 31 May 1292 in Lincoln cathedral (Reg. *Sutton*, vii, pp. 16, 30).

ASTERBY (Astreby), William de: he was probably a friar of Lincoln on 20 June 1318 when he was licensed to hear confessions in the diocese of Lincoln (LAO, Register 3, fol. 390r).

ASWELL (Ashwell, Hasswell, Hassewell), Thomas: he was a friar of York when he was ordained s. on 22 March 1466 at Whitefriars, York, d. on 5 April 1466 at the lady chapel of York Minster, and p. on 19 December 1467 at Austin Friars, York (BIA, Register 22, fols. 181v, 182v, 189v). He was at York when he received 6s. 8d. in the will of Thomas Roclyfe, gentleman of the county town, on 1 January 1504 (BIA, Probate Register 6, fol. 131r).

AT WODE, John: this son of unmarried parents entered the order and was ordained priest. He applied for a papal dispensation from *de defectu naturalium* on 14 June 1458 so that he might exercise the orders which he had received (*Supplic. Apost. Penit.*, i, p. 197, no. 938).

ATHELINGFLEET (Athelyngflete), Nicholas de: he was a friar of York who was probably treasurer of the provincial chapter held at Northampton on 29 July 1322. King Edward II paid him £7 10s. for the friars (BL, Stowe, MS.553, fol. 22v). The chapter was said to be about to take place at Northampton (TNA, E 403/199, mem. 2, E403/198, mem. 4). On 12 November 1327 he received the royal alms for the provincial chapter held at Lincoln (TNA, E403/234, mem. 4).

ATHRYN', John: he was a friar of York when he was ordained a. on 1 June 1420 at All Saints chapel, Cawood (BIA, Register 18, fol. 406r).

ATKINSON (Atkynson), James: he was a friar of Boston when he was ordained d. on 20 May 1497 at Sleaford prebendal church (LAO, Register 24, fol. 8v).

ATKINSON, John: he was ordained s. on 18 December 1479 at Whitefriars, York, and d. on 12 March 1481 at Austin Friars, York (BIA, Register 22, fol. 381v, Register 23, fol. 374r. Cf. Cross and Vickers, *MFN*, p. 435). He was a friar of Lincoln when he was ordained p. on 21 April 1481 at the church of St Lawrence, Lincoln (LAO, Register 22, fol. 4r).

ATKINSON (Atkynson), Thomas: he was a friar of York when he was ordained a. on 26 February 1480 at Greyfriars, York, s. on 21 December 1482 at Austin Friars, York, d. on 22 February 1483 at Holy Trinity Priory, Micklegate, York, and p. on 18 December 1484 at Austin Friars, York (BIA, Register 22, fol. 382r, Register 23, fols. 384v, 385v, 394v. Cf. Cross and Vickers, *MFN*, p. 435).

ATKINSON (Atkynson), Thomas: he was a friar of Lincoln when he was ordained s. on 3 April 1507 in the chapel of St Mary Magdalene in Lincoln cathedral (LAO, Register 24, fol. 65r) and at York when he was ordained d. on 23 September 1508 (York, Dean and Chapter Library, MS.H3/2, fol. 35r) and p. on 23 February 1510; these two ceremonies took place at Whitefriars, York (BIA, Register 26, fol. 106r. Cf. Cross and Vickers, *MFN,* p. 442). A friar of this name was at Babwell when he received his capacity on 10 March 1539 (Chambers, *Faculty Office Registers 1534–1549*, p. 180).

ATKINSON (Atkynson), William: he was a friar of York when he was ordained a. on 21 March 1523 at Whitefriars, York (BIA, Register 27, fol. 198v). He was at York at the Dissolution on 27 November 1538 (*Eighth Report of the Deputy Keeper of the Public Records*, p. 51). A priest of this name was the vicar of Wighill in 1562. There is a will of 6 April 1592, for a cleric of this name, who was then the parson of Hickling in Nottinghamshire. He disclosed that he had been born in Ripley in Yorkshire and made bequests to the poor of his birthplace, and to the poor of Hickling and Wighill. He does not seem to have been married and left most of his estate, which included three portions of £20 for each, to a nephew and two nieces in the Ripon area (BIA, Probate Register 17, pt. I, fol. 129r, Register 31, fols. 124v–25r. Cf. Cross and Vickers, *MFN*, pp. 445, 456).

AUCKLAND (Awkland), Richard: he was a friar of York when he was ordained d. on 23 February 1499 at Holy Trinity Priory, Micklegate, York, and p. on 25 May 1499 at Blackfriars, York (BIA, Register 23, fols. 462r, 464v. Cf. Cross and Vickers, *MFN*, p. 439).

AUDERNACO (Audernaco), Nicholas de: he was ordained d. on 22 March 1393 at Holy Trinity Priory, Micklegate, York (BIA, Register 14, fol. 66v).

AUSTIN (Austen), John: he was ordained s. on 26 February 1480 at Greyfriars, York (BIA, Register 22, fol. 382r).

AUSTIN (Auston), Robert: he was a friar of York when he was ordained s. on 23

September 1503 at Greyfriars, York (BIA, Register 25, fol. 120r. Cf. Cross and Vickers, *MFN*, p. 440).

AVOTE (Avott), Robert: he was ordained a. on 28 March 1433 at St Michael-le-Belfrey, York. He was a friar of York when he was ordained s. on 6 June 1433 at Blackfriars, York, and d. on 24 September 1435 at Holy Trinity Priory, Micklegate, York. On the third occasion his Christian name was given as John (BIA, Register 19, fols. 243v, 244v, 249v).

AWNE, William: a friar of York who spent many years at the friary in the county town both before and after ordination. He was there when he was ordained d. on 10 June 1419 and p. on 15 February 1421; both ceremonies took place at Cawood prebendal church (BIA, Register 18, fols. 403v, 408v). He was one of a number of friars in the custody to be licensed to hear confessions. Thomas Radnor, minister provincial, presented him, as a friar of York to Archbishop Kempe for a licence, which was granted on 5 January 1444 (BIA, Register 19, fol. 86v). He was described as a friar of York on 12 October 1448, when William Rok, a plumber and parishioner of Holy Cross, York, left him 20d. (BIA, Probate Register 2, fol. 381r). In 1449 he was admitted to the *Corpus Christi* guild at York (*Corpus Christi Guild*, p. 47). At an unknown date he moved to Beverley, where on 8 April 1457 he was commissioned to hear confessions within the archdeaconry of the East Riding (BIA, Register 20, fol. 130r).

AYNCOURT, J. de: he was a priest and professed friar of York, who died c.1334 (Little, '*Records, Franciscan Province*', p. 151).

AYNSHAM, Geoffrey de: the guardian of Lincoln presented him to the bishop of Lincoln for a licence on 7 December 1321, but he was rejected (LAO, Register 5, fols. 299v–300).

AYR (Aire), William: he was a friar of York when he was licensed to hear confessions in the diocese on 30 August 1398 (*Reg. Scrope*, ii, p. 12, no. 729).

BADBY, Simon: he was licensed in the diocese of York, but replaced by Robert Multon at an unspecified date in the administration of Archbishop Thoresby (BIA, Register 11, fol. 397r).

BADESWELL, John: he was ordained a. on 18 May 1371 at the church of St Mary, Nottingham (BIA, Register 11, fol. 384r).

BAKER (Bayker), John: he was a friar of York when he was ordained p. on 24 September 1496 at Austin Friars, York (BIA, Register 23, fol. 452r). He joined the Observant reform and was the guardian of Newcastle on 13 September 1532 (*LPFD*, v, p. 569, no. 1312). He was one of the three Observant friars detained at Richmond, Yorkshire, in 1534 (*LPFD*, vii, p. 601, no. 1607). He was given leave to change his habit and hold a benefice on 20 June 1536 (Chambers, *Faculty Office Registers 1534–1549*, p. 187), but probably remained at Richmond as a member of the Friars Minor Conventual until the Dissolution on 9 March 1539 (*Eighth Report of the Deputy Keeper of the Public Records*, p. 38). A priest of this name was the nuns' chaplain at Wykeham priory in 1539 and received 10s. for a quarter's wages when the house was dissolved, but any certain identification is impossible (Purvis, 'A Selection of Monastic Rentals and Dissolution Papers', p. 95; Cross and Vickers, *MFN*, pp. 438, 450).

BAKER, Nicholas: he was a friar of York when he was ordained s. on 26 March 1463 at Greyfriars, York (BIA, Register 20, fol. 455r).

BALDOK, William de: he was a friar of Grimsby when he was ordained d. on 21 December 1359 in Lincoln cathedral (LAO, Register 9D, fol. 93v).

BALSALE, Henry de: he was ordained a. on 7 June 1343 at Greyfriars, York (BIA, Register 10A, fol. 3v).

BAMPTON (Bompton), Richard de: he was ordained d. on 27 May 1290 at All Saints, Hertford, and p. on 31 May 1292 in Lincoln cathedral (*Reg. Sutton*, vii, pp. 2, 30).

BANDON, Hugh de: he was ordained p. on 23 December 1374 in the manor chapel at Thorpe (BIA, Register 12, fol. 118v).

BANKE, William: he was one of the six friars of Grimsby at the Dissolution on 9 October 1538, perhaps a lay brother (*Eighth Report of the Deputy Keeper of the Public Records*, p. 22).

BAPART (Bopart), John: he was a friar of Lincoln when he was ordained d. on 18 April 1489 in the chapel of St Mary Magdalene in Lincoln cathedral (LAO, Register 22, fol. 32r) and at York when he was ordained p. on 19 September 1489 at Whitefriars, York (BIA, Register 23, fol. 419r).

BARDNEY (Berdeney, Bardeney), Robert or Richard de: he was ordained s. on 23 September 1396 at Holy Trinity Priory, Micklegate, York (BIA, Register 14, fol. 73v), d. on 17 March 1397 at Greyfriars, York (BIA, Register 5A, fol. 230r) and p. on 20 September 1399 at Sherburn prebendal church (BIA, Register 16, fol. 169v; *Reg. Scrope*, ii, pp. 55, 58, 126, where the editor erroneously lists him as an Augustinian). The manuscript identifies him as *ordo minorum* (BIA, Register 16, fol. 169v).

BARDNEY (Bardenay), William: he was ordained p. on 15 February 1421 at Cawood prebendal chapel (BIA, Register 18, fol. 408v). He was guardian of York when he was mentioned in the plea rolls for Trinity term 1433 (TNA, CP40/690, mem. 404d). A friar of this name was admitted to the *Corpus Christi* guild at York in 1435/36 (*Corpus Christi Register*, p. 34).

BARHOLT, William de: he was the guardian of York, who died c.1334 (Little, '*Records, Franciscan Province*', p. 151).

BARKER, John: he was a friar of Lincoln when he was ordained s. on 7 March 1478 at Sleaford prebendal church and d. on 21 March 1478 in St Benedict's parish, Lincoln (LAO, Register 21, fol. 162rv).

BARKER, John: he was a friar of York when he was ordained a. on 19 March 1519 at Greyfriars, York (BIA, Register 27, fol. 183r. Cf. Cross and Vickers, *MFN*, p. 444).

BARLDAL, John: he was a friar of York when he was ordained p. on 21 December 1359 at Cawood manor chapel (BIA, Register 11, fol. 339v).

BARNARD (Bernard), John: he was a friar of Lincoln when he was ordained a.

on 12 June 1473 at Lincoln cathedral. He was at Grantham when ordained s. on 11 March 1475 at Sleaford prebendal church, d. on 20 May 1475 at Liddington prebendal church, and p. on 21 September 1476 at Banbury prebendal church (LAO, Register 21, fols. 139r, 148r, 150r, 156r).

BARNARD (Barnerd), William: he was a friar of York when he was ordained a. on 11 March 1486 at Holy Trinity Priory, Micklegate, York, s. on 9 June 1487 at Blackfriars, York, d. on 22 September 1487 at Whitefriars, York, and p. on 14 March 1489 at Holy Trinity Priory, Micklegate, York (BIA, Register 23, fols. 400r, 407v, 409r, 416r. Cf. Cross and Vickers, *MFN*, p. 436).

BARNBY (Barneby), Richard: he was ordained s. on 26 March 1418. He was at York when ordained d. on 11 March 1419 and p. on 15 April 1419. All three ceremonies took place at Cawood prebendal chapel (BIA, Register 18, fols. 400r, 402r, 403r).

BARNBY (Barneby, Banaby, Barnabe, Barnaby), Thomas de: he was probably a foundation fellow of Merton College, Oxford, appointed in 1274. He was still a fellow two years later, when Richard Kikwardby, archbishop of Canterbury, appointed him the first senior dean of the College (Garrod, *Injunctions of Archbishop Kilwardby 1276*, p. 12; Brodrick, *Memorials of Merton College with biographical notices of the wardens and fellows*, pp. 24, 185). He was an MA by 1276. He was already a friar when he received 25 marks for the friars of Oxford for the Easter term of 1288 (TNA, 403/57, m. 1, courtesy of Dr Jens Röhrkasten). He was doctor of theology by c.1292. He entered the Franciscan order and was the 23rd regent master of Oxford by 1291/92 (Eccleston, p. 54; *GFO*, p. 160; *BRUO*, p. 111). His name occurs in Merton College Library, Oxford, MS.55 (B.3.7), a late thirteenth-century copy of the writings of St Augustine. Folio 261v contains the inscription *memoriale fratris Thome de Barneby pro quatuor decem solidis*. This is probably a reference to a pledge. The volume seems to have belonged to the Greyfriars of Oxford in the first instance before passing to Merton College Library by c.1350 (Thomson, *Merton*, pp. 63–64; *Oxford Libraries*, ii, p. 819, no. 164). At the foot of folio 300v of another Merton manuscript, MS.266 (G.I.4), a copy of the works of John of Faenza, is a note headed *Barnbye* which might refer to this friar (Thomson, *Merton*, pp. 204–05). He is named in the margins of Città del Vaticano, Biblioteca Apostolica Vaticana, Vat. lat.MS. 869, fol. 60v, a collection of questions on Aristotle's *De anima* (Pelzer, *Bibliothecae Apostolicae Vaticanae, Codices Vaticani Latini, II, pars prior, Codices Vaticani Latini, II, pars prior, Codices 679–1134*, p. 245). He may have been the compiler and owner of MS.Assisi 158 (Glorieux, 'Le Manuscrit d'Assise, Bibl.comm.158: Date et mode de composition', p. 294). He was quoted by the Spanish Scotist Petrus Thomae (†1340) in his commentary on the first two books of Aristotle's *De anima* (Stella, '"Res generabilis simplex est": il radicalismo antilemorfico di Tomasso Barneby e di Giacomo di Carseto nella recensione di Pieto Tomás (Thomae)', pp. 757, 776, 782. Cf. Sharpe, *Handlist*, p. 640, no. 1696). He was probably custos of York on 12 October 1300 when he presented friars from the convents of Lincoln, Grimsby and Boston to Bishop Dalderby for licences to hear confessions (Little, *Franciscan Papers, Lists and Documents*, p. 238). A mutilated record of 20 March 1326 contains a reference to *fratri Barnabe magistro fratrum minorum* (TNA, 381/14, Q.R.Wardrobe 25/1; Little, 'The Franciscan School at Oxford in the Thirteenth Century', p. 860).

BARNBY (Barneby), Thomas de: he was licensed to hear confessions on the Isle of Axholme for one year from 23 September 1338 (*Reg. Burghersh*, iii, p. 361, no. 4713).

BARNBY (Barneby), William de: he was ordained s. on 22 March 1298 in Lincoln cathedral (*Reg. Sutton*, vii, p. 103). He was licensed to hear the confessions of the nuns of Stainfield, Lincolnshire, on 5 February 1335 (LAO, Register 5, fol. 490v).

BARNBY (Barnaby), William: a friar of York when he was ordained a. on 13 March 1484 at Holy Trinity Priory, Micklegate, York (BIA, Register 23, fol. 390r; Cross and Vickers, *MFN*, p. 435), at Boston when he was ordained s. on 5 April 1488 in Lincoln cathedral, and of Oxford when he was ordained p. on 19 September 1489 at All Saints, Northampton (LAO, Register 22, fols. 28r, 33r; *BRUO*, p. 110).

BARRINGTON (Baryngton), Richard de: he was licensed to hear confessions in the diocese of York in place of Robert de Lincoln during the administration of Archbishop Thoresby (BIA, Register 11, fol. 396r).

BARSWYK, John: he was a friar of York when he was ordained d. on 27 May 1396 at St Mary, Bishophill Senior, York (BIA, Register 14, fol. 72v).

BARTELBY (Bartelky), Richard: he was ordained s. on 10 March 1403 at York Minster (*Reg. Scrope*, ii, pp. 55, 59, 131).

BARTON, Henry de: a friar presented by the custos and the guardian of Lincoln for a licence in the *limitatio* of the friary of Lincoln on 10 August 1300 (Little, *Franciscan Papers, Lists, and Documents*, p. 237). On 31 October 1301 he was a friar of York when he and his *socius* received 40s. for travelling from York to London and back (BL, Add. MS.7966, fol. 26v).

BARTON, Hugh: a friar successfully presented by the minister provincial to the bishop at Boston on 16 May 1409, according to the terms of *Super cathedram* (*Reg. Repingdon*, i, pp. 149–50).

BARTON, John de: he was ordained d. on 1 March 1298 at an unspecified venue, and p. probably on 19 September 1299; the venue of the ordinations is unknown (*Reg. Halton*, i, pp. 109, 133). The custos of York nominated him for a licence to hear confessions in the diocese of Lincoln, but he was not approved on 7 December 1321 (LAO, Register 5, fols. 299v–300r). He was licensed as confessor to the Cistercian nuns of Legbourne, Lincolnshire, on 4 December 1338; his mandate included cases normally reserved for the bishop (*Reg. Burghersh*, iii, p. 363, no. 4722).

BARTON, John de: he was a friar of York when he was ordained a. and s. on 22 December 1375 in the manor chapel at Cawood and d. on 13 March 1378 at Holy Trinity Priory, Micklegate, York (BIA, Register 12, fols. 122rv, 131v). A friar of this name was at London in 1391 (*GFL*, p. 64; TNA, Chancery Warrants 1765/19).

BARTON, John: he was a friar of Lincoln when he was ordained a. on 12 June 1473 in Lincoln cathedral (LAO, Register 21, fol. 139r).

BARTON, Martin de: an Umbrian friar, probably a native of Assisi, who had frequently seen St Francis. He narrated that St Francis had ordered the destruction of a building that had been erected in Assisi for the 5,000 friars attending a chapter at the Portiuncula. His brother, the seneschal of the general chapter, defended the building on behalf of the community. He arrived in England c.1230 and was afterwards vicar provincial and filled other offices in his adopted province. He was the custos of York where he enforced the strictest poverty, ensuring that the number of friars assigned to a particular house should be regulated by the alms available. He also served as vicar provincial (Eccleston, pp. 32, 35–36). His jurisdiction included friaries in Scotland. He was styled as the *custos Fratrum Minorum in Scotia* as early as 13 September 1235 in a formal document (*Liber S.Marie de Calchou, Registrum cartarum abbacie Tironensis de Kelso*, ii, p. 321; Bryce, *The Scottish Grey Friars*, i, pp. 6–7, ii, pp. 1–2).

BARTON, Richard: he was ordained d. on 24 May 1404 and p. on 20 December 1404; both ceremonies were held at Cawood prebendal church (*Reg. Scrope*, ii, pp. 55, 59, 131). He was licensed in the diocese of Lincoln on 16 May 1409 (*Reg. Repingdon*, i, pp. 149–50) and was the guardian of Beverley in the Michaelmas term of 1417 (TNA, CP40/267, m. 245). He was the guardian of Lincoln in Trinity term 1425, when he was mentioned in the plea rolls (TNA, CP40/658, m. 435). A friar of this name attended a heresy trial at Norwich in 1429 (Tanner, *Heresy Trials in the Diocese of Norwich 1428–1431*, p. 79).

BARTON, Robert de: he was a friar of York when he was ordained s. on 22 December 1375 and d. on 8 March 1376; both ceremonies took place at Cawood manor chapel (BIA, Register 12, fols. 122rv, 123v).

BARTON, Robert: he was a friar of York when he was ordained d. on 16 March 1426 at St Martin-le-Grand, Coney Street, York (BIA, Register 5A, fol. 445v; *Reg. Sede Vacante, York, 1423–26*, pp. 99, 101, 125), and p. on 25 May 1426 at Holy Trinity Priory, Micklegate, York (BIA, Register 19, fol. 227v).

BARTON, William de: on 20 June 1318 he was licenced to hear confessions in the diocese of Lincoln (LAO, Register 3, fol. 390r). By 14 March 1319 he had been transferred from the diocese of Lincoln to a friary in the diocese of York (*ibid.*, fols. 411–12). He died before December 1321 when he was replaced by William de Ravensey (LAO, Register 5, fols. 299v–300r).

BARTRAM (Bertram), William: he was a friar of York when he was ordained d. on 28 February 1461 at Blackfriars, York, and p. on 30 May 1461 at Whitefriars, York (BIA, Register 20, fols. 446v, 448v).

BASE, William: he was a friar of York when he received 5s. in the will of Thomas Gryssop on 4 October 1446. This chapman of York and parishioner of St Michael-le-Belfrey, who was buried in York Minster, asked this friar to celebrate a trental of Masses for him (York, Dean and Chapter Library, MS.L.2/4, fol. 260r; *Probate Inventories of the York Diocese, 1350–1500*, pp. 569–73, 572).

BASILIA, James de: a friar of York when he was ordained d. on 4 June 1463 at Whitefriars, York (BIA, Register 20, fol. 456r).

BATEMANSON (Batemansey), Richard: he was a friar of York when he was ordained d. on 29 May 1507 at Blackfriars, York, and p. on 18 September 1507 at Whitefriars, York (BIA, Register 25, fol. 140v, Register 5A, fol. 580r. Cf. Cross and Vickers, *MFN*, p. 442).

BAUKEWELL, John de: he was ordained d. on 19 December 1360 in the manor chapel of Cawood (BIA, Register 11, fol. 343r).

BAWTRY (Bawtre), Robert: he was a friar of York when he was ordained s. on 19 February 1407 and at Beverley when he was ordained d. on 12 March 1407; both ceremonies took place at Blackfriars, York (BIA, Register 5A, fols. 323v, 324r; *Reg. Sede Vacante, York, 1405–08*, pp. 66, 68, 89).

BAYNE, William: he was a friar of York when he was ordained s. on 3 March 1436 and p. on 20 September 1438; both ceremonies took place at Greyfriars, York (BIA, Register 19, fols. 250v, 258r).

BAYNTON, John de: he was ordained a. and s. on 13 March 1367 at St Mary, Bishophill Senior, d. on 3 April 1367 at Bishopthorpe manor chapel and p. on 18 September 1372 at Greyfriars, York (BIA, Register 11, fols. 365rv, 389r).

BAYNTON, Walter de: he was a friar of York when he was ordained p. on 26 May 1358 at Greyfriars, York (BIA, Register 11, fol. 334r).

BAYOSE, William: he was a friar of York when he was ordained d. on 22 September 1436 at Greyfriars, York (BIA, Register 19, fol. 217v).

BECKINGHAM (Beckinham, Bekingham), John de: he was a friar of York accused of malpractice regarding property in Michaelmas 1298. The charge was later withdrawn (TNA, KB27/156, mem. 72, *Notes on Religious Houses*, i, pp. 243–44). On 14 June 1300 in the Franciscan house at Doncaster the will of Lady Eva de Tibetoft with the codicil was proved and administration was granted to Sir Roger de Wordham, rector of Arkeshey, and Adam de Radegrave, rector of Little Blakham, in the diocese of Norwich. This is followed by a memorandum that on 14 July of that year this friar had had this agreement confirmed by the archbishop's seal at Thorp (*Reg. Corbridge*, i, p. 24, no. 66).

BECKINGHAM (Bekingham), William de: a friar of Boston presented by the custos of York and the guardian of Lincoln for a licence to hear confessions. On 10 August 1300 he was licensed to hear confessions in the *limitatio* of Boston, and again on 12 October 1300 (Little, *Franciscan Papers, Lists, and Documents*, pp. 237, 238).

BECKINGTON, Henry de: he was licensed to hear confessions in the diocese of Lincoln on 20 June 1318 (LAO, Register 3, fol. 390rv). By 14 March 1319 this friar of Boston was too ill to discharge his office and his licence was revoked (*ibid.*, fols. 411v–12r).

BEGO [no Christian name]: he was ordained p. at Horncastle parish church on 21 December 1336 (*Reg. Kirkby*, i, p. 67, no. 346).

BEKARD, John: he was a friar of York when he was accused of malpractice regarding property in 1298. The charge was later withdrawn (*Notes on Religious Houses*, i, pp. 243–44).

BEKLES, Ralph: he was licensed to hear confessions in the diocese of Lincoln on 12 November 1401 (LAO, Register 13, fol. 38rv).

BELACYS (Belacyse, Belasys, Bellacis, Bellavyse), John: he was ordained s. on 19 September 1394 at Austin Friars, York (BIA, Register 14, fol. 70r) and p. on 22 September 1397 at Holy Trinity Priory, Micklegate (*Reg. Waldby*, p. 46). He was the guardian of York on 24 November 1414 when he accompanied John del Howe, doctor of divinity and lector of the friary, to appear before diocesan oficials in the chapter house of York Minster on the charge of having spoken injuriously about the clergy of the city (York, Dean and Chapter Library, MS.L2/3a, fol. 78rv). He was still the guardian, when Henry Lescrop, chivaler, accused him of seizing his wife Joan, at Faxfleet, and abducting and detaining her and certain goods and chattels in 1415 (*Notes on Religious Houses*, ii, p. 93). On 3 October 1432 he was left 6s. 8d. to pray for the soul of George Darell of Sessay, esquire, who was buried at the Greyfriars of York (*TE*, ii, pp. 27–28). A friar, John Bellacis, his confrère and the guardian of York, was mentioned in the plea rolls for Trinity term 1433 (TNA, CP40/690, mem. 404d).

BELARD, John: in Michaelmas 1298 he was a friar of York with Geoffrey of Retford, the guardian, and several others, including William of Pontefract, when John of Burton obtained a writ of novel disseisin against them, stating that he had been unjustly disseised of his free tenement in York. The writ was subsequently withdrawn (TNA, KB27/156, mem. 72; *Notes on Religious Houses*, i, pp. 243–44).

BELASISE, John: he was ordained a. and s. on 13 March 1367 at St Mary, Bishophill Senior, and d. on 3 April 1367 at Bishopthorpe manor chapel. The second entry gave his name as William (BIA, Register 11, fol. 365rv).

BELL, John: he was a friar of Lichfield when he was ordained a. on 20 September 1477 in Lichfield cathedral (LRO, B/A/1/12, fol. 261v) and s. 20 December 1477 (*ibid.*, fol. 263r). He was at Shrewsbury when he was ordained d. on 14 February 1478 in Lichfield (*ibid.*, fol. 264r). All three ceremonies took place in Lichfield cathedral and on each occasion he was ordained by Robert Wells, the Franciscan bishop of Achonry. There is no record of his priestly ministry in the custody of Worcester. On 4 November 1493 Pope Alexander VI provided John to the diocese of Mayo and granted him the temporalities of the diocese. John was consecrated in the Roman curia (*CPL*, xvi, p. 459). On 4 January 1497, responding to a petition from John, the pope wrote to the dean of the church of Annaghdown and Miler de Anglo and Miler Ochunamayn, canons of the church of Tuam, in John's favour. While John had obtained possession or almost of the rule and administration of the church, William Seoighe Joyce, archbishop of Tuam, claimed that the former diocese of Mayo by long tradition was part of the diocese of Tuam and protested that the papal provision and appointment were invalid. He occupied the church, receiving the fruits, etc. John complained that it was a matter of injustice that ecclesiastical benefices or cathedral churches were occupied without any canonical title, maintaining that the metropolitan enjoyed no canonical title to the church of Mayo. He petitioned the pope to correct this irregularity. Not having certain knowledge of this matter, the pope commanded the addressees of this letter or two of them to summon the archbishop and others concerned and to lawfully establish the papal provision. If they lawfully established the said provision, appointment and robbery, they were required to reinstate, replace and completely restore John to the possession or almost of his diocese. By the same token they were to appoint some suitable term for the archbishop within which he was bound to prove the canonical title by which he occupied the church of Mayo. If the archbishop had not adequately proved his title, they should impose upon him with regard to the church of Mayo. They were to assist John and not allow him to be molested in any way by the archbishop or by any others (*CPL*, xvi, pp. 459–60). In response to the continuing difficulties experienced by John in Mayo, Pope Alexander VI responded to the petition on 23 June 1498. John had explained to the pope that, having been consecrated bishop of Mayo five years earlier, he had been unable to obtain the rule and administration of the goods of his church on account of a persistent adversary, pointing out that he was in such straits that he was on the verge of being driven to beggary, to the shame of the episcopal office. Alexander granted him a dispensation to receive any two benefices, with or without cure, secular or regular of any order, and authorised him to retain them for life *in commendam* together with the church of Mayo. He was also permitted to resign them, at once or successively, simply or for exchange, as often as he pleased, and in their place to receive up to two other, similar or dissimilar, benefices (*CPL*, xvi, p. 581).

Perhaps in response to this series of obstacles placed in his path in the west of Ireland and acting on papal dispensation, John returned to England and began his ministry as a suffragan bishop in the diocese of London, where he held several ordinations between 21 September 1499 and 28 March 1506. On 18 October 1501 Henry Deane, archbishop of Canterbury, gave him a suffragan commission (Corpus Christi College Library, Cambridge, MS.170, 183, no. 136). Archbishop Deane made a bequest to John, whom he describes as his suffragan (*Sede Vacante Wills: A Calendar of Wills proved before the Commissary of the Prior and Chapter Christ's Church, Canterbury, during vacancies in the primacy*, p. 98). He was also active in the diocese of Bath and Wells before moving to the diocese of Lincoln. On 23 September 1503 he held an ordination at Lichfield cathedral (LRO, B/A/1/14ii, fol. 1rv). On 27 July 1504 he was appointed to the church of Banwell, vacant by the resignation of Master Thomas Bowden, on the presentation of William, prior of Bruton, Somerset, and the Augustinian Canons of that place (*Reg. King and Castello*, p. 99, no. 580). Shortly after his first ordination in the diocese of Lincoln he was appointed perpetual vicar of All Saints, Goxhill, in the archdeaconry of Lincoln, in succession to the late Master Edmund Percy MA on 31 March 1507. He was presented by the prior and convent of Bridlington (LAO, Register 23, fol. 123r). He returned to the diocese of Bath and Wells where he held two ordinations in the lady chapel of Bath and Wells cathedral on 22 September 1515 and 22 December 1515 (Somerset Record Office, D/D/B. Register 10, fol. 157rv). In 1512 he was admitted to the guild of Corpus Christi at Boston and was the alderman of the guild in 1518 (BL, Harley, MS.4795, fols. 56r, 57v). On 9 May 1521 John Longland, bishop of Lincoln, granted him a suffragan commission in the archdeaconries of Northampton, Huntingdon and Leicester in the same terms as that given to John, bishop of *Ariensis*, in the archdeaconries of Lincoln and Stow (LAO, Register 26, fol. 69r). As a rector he contributed £9 11s. to the subsidy collected in the diocese of Lincoln (*A Subsidy collected in the diocese of Lincoln in 1526*, p. 28). On 22 March 1529 Bishop Longland, at the Temple in London, received John's free resignation, granting him a pension (LAO, Register 26, fol. 166v). On 9 April 1529 Master Vincent Totoft, LLB, was appointed as vicar of All Saints, Goxhill in the diocese of Lincoln (LAO, Register 27, fol. 44v). John's name disappears from the registers and he died c.1541 (Smith, 'Suffragan Bishops in the Medieval Diocese of Lincoln', p. 26; *Handbook of British Chronology*, p. 367).

BELLEBOUCHE, William: he was ordained d. on 28 May 1401 at Bishop Burton chapel near Beverley (*Reg. Scrope*, ii, pp. 55, 60, 131).

BENNETT (Beneyt), John: on 6 March 1329 Pope John XXII wrote to Bishop Burghersh, instructing him to give permission to this friar, a priest, to enter the Cistercian abbey of Kirkstead (*BF*, v, p. 375, no. 770).

BENNETT (Beneyt), Robert: he was a friar of York when he was ordained s. on 2 June 1352 at St Mary's Abbey, York (BIA, Register 10A, fol. 55r).

BENTLEY, Anthony: he was a friar of York when he was ordained a. on 22 February 1494 at Whitefriars, York, s. on 15 March 1494, d. on 20 September 1494 and p. on 13 June 1495 at Blackfriars, York. The second and third ordinations took place at Greyfriars, York (BIA, Register 23, fols. 440r, 441r, 443r, 447r. Cf. Cross and Vickers, *MFN*, p. 438).

BENTLEY (Bentleye), John de: he was ordained s. on 18 December 1294 at Stow prebendal church (*Reg. Sutton*, vii, p. 60).

BENTLEY (Bentlay), Thomas: he was ordained a. on 18 September 1400 at Cawood prebendal church (*Reg. Scrope*, ii, pp. 55, 60, 131).

BENTON, John: he was ordained d. on 19 September 1394 at Austin Friars, York (BIA, Register 14, fol. 70r) and p. on 22 September 1397 at Holy Trinity Priory, Micklegate (*Reg. Waldby*, p. 46).

BENTON, John: he was ordained a. on 22 September 1403 at Blackfriars, York, s. on 24 May 1404 at All Saints at Cawood (*Reg. Scrope*, ii, pp. 55, 60, 131) and d. on 19 September 1405 at Greyfriars, York, and at Richmond when ordained p. on 21 May 1407 at Blackfriars, York (BIA, Register 5A, fols. 318r, 324v; *Reg. Sede Vacante, York, 1405–08*, pp. 66, 68, 89).

BERGEHAM, Peter: he was a friar of York when he was ordained d. on 18 December 1445 at Austin Friars, York (BIA, Register 19, fol. 283r).

BERGYS (Burgess), William de: he was a friar of Richmond when he was presented by the guardian of the friary and was ordained s. on 15 March 1432 in the manor chapel at Aukland *per gardianum ejusdem domus legitime presentatus* (*Reg. Langley*, iv, p. 44) and at Beverley when he was ordained d. on 20 September 1432 at St Leonard's Hospital chapel, York (BIA, Register 19, fol. 217r).

BERKELEY (Barclay, Barkley), Gilbert: he was a friar of Oxford when he was ordained s. on 28 February 1534 at All Saints, Oxford. He was a friar of Lincoln when he was ordained d. on 27 March 1535 in the cathedral, and at Northampton when he was ordained p. on 18 December 1535 at All Saints in that town. On the second occasion he was examined by the prior of St Katherine's and on the third occasion by Robert King, bishop of *Reonensis*, the suffragan, who also ordained him (LAO, Register 26, fols. 36v, 44r, 46v). He had studied theology for 24 years, receiving the degree of bachelor of divinity from Oxford in 1538. He was at York at the Dissolution on 27 November 1538 (*Eighth Report of the Deputy Keeper of the Public Records*, p. 51). He was said to be 'very loath to leave his ipochrytes coate till he was compelled for feare of punishment' (*A chronicle of England during the reigns of the Tudors, from A.D. 1485 to 1559, by Charles Wriothesley, Windsor herald*, i, p. 82).

He subsequently became a convinced Protestant, married and became rector at

Attleborough, Norfolk, in 1547, being deprived on this account soon after Queen Mary's accession. He went into exile at Frankfurt during her reign (Garrett, *The Marian Exiles: A Study in the Origins of Elizabethan Puritanism*, p. 87). On Elizabeth's accession, he returned to England and regained his Norfolk rectory, which he held until 1565. Regarded as an excellent and constant preacher, he was appointed bishop of Bath and Wells on 11 January 1560 and consecrated on 24 March of that year. He retained his see until his death on 2 November 1581 and was buried at Wells on the north side of the high altar. The fine altar tomb erected in his memory has been moved to St John's chapel (*BRUO, 1501–1540*, p. 45; Dickens, *Lollards and Protestants in the Diocese of York, 1509–1558*, pp. 147–48; Baskerville, *English Monks and the Suppression of the Monasteries*, p. 239, and 'Married Clergy and Pensioned Religious in Norwich Diocese, 1555', p. 201; Cross and Vickers, *MFN*, p. 456).

BERSPYK, Henry: he was a friar of York when he was ordained d. on 21 September 1426 at Blackfriars, York (BIA, Register 19, fol. 215r).

BERTEVILE (Berteuill, Bertonile), Laurence de: he was ordained s. on 24 September 1351 at St Mary's, Oxford, and p. on 7 June 1354 at Liddington prebendal church (LAO, Register 9D, fols. 53r, 72r).

BERWAYS, John de: he was ordained s. on 19 December 1349 at St Michael-le-Belfrey, York (BIA, Register 10A, fol. 35v).

BESWICK (Besewyk, Beswyk, Bosewyk), Thomas de: he was ordained a. on 13 March 1350 at Beverley Minster, s. on 12 March 1351 at Blackfriars, York, and d. on 2 June 1352 in St Mary's Abbey, York (BIA, Register 10A, fols. 44r, 51r, 55r).

BEVALL, William: he was a friar of York when he was ordained a. on 10 March 1498 at Greyfriars, York (BIA, Register 23, fol. 458r. Cf. Cross and Vickers, *MFN*, p. 439).

BEVERLEY, Geoffrey de: he was licensed in the diocese of Lincoln sometime before 18 February 1330 when he was replaced by William de Bondeby (LAO, Register 5, fol. 402v).

BEVERLEY, John de: this friar at Oxford was mentioned in Adam Marsh's letter to William of Nottingham, minister provincial. He may have been attending the lectorate programme. Thomas of York was described as having been kindly towards John's father (*Letters of Adam Marsh*, ii, pp. 416–17, 540–41; *GFO*, pp. 141, 186; *BRUO*, p. 183).

BEVERLEY, John de: he witnessed an act by Oliver Sutton, bishop of Lincoln, at Beadlow on 9 April 1285 (*Reg. Sutton*, viii, p. 100).

BEVERLEY (Beverlaco), John de: he was ordained d. on 21 December 1297 at an unspecified venue (*Reg. Halton*, i, p. 108). He may be identified with a John of Beverley, who was licensed in the diocese of Lincoln sometime before 5 October 1346, when he was replaced by William Filioll (LAO, Register 7, fol. 99r).

BEVERLEY (Beverlaco), Nicholas de: he was ordained d. on 19 May 1296 in Lincoln cathedral (*Reg. Sutton*, vii, p. 79).

BEVERLEY, Philip de: in Michaelmas 1298 he was a friar of York with Geoffrey de Retford, guardian of the friary at York, and several others, including William of Pontefract, when John of Burton obtained a writ of novel disseisin against them, stating that he had been unjustly disseised of his free tenement in York. The writ was subsequently withdrawn (TNA, KB27/156, mem. 72; *Notes on Religious Houses*, i, pp. 243–44).

BEVERLEY, Richard: he was a friar of York when he was ordained a. on 10 March 1498 at Greyfriars, York (BIA, Register 23, fol. 458r. Cf. Cross and Vickers, *MFN*, p. 439).

BEVERLEY, Robert de: he was the 33rd regent master at Oxford about 1305 (Eccleston, p. 54; *GFO*, p. 164; Little and Pelster, *Oxford Theology and Theologians*, p. 251; *BRUO*, p. 184). A Franciscan *Beverle* was mentioned among the disputants of 41 questions in Oxford at an unspecified stage between 1298 and 1302 (Glorieux, 'Jean de Saint-Germain maître de Paris et copiste de Worcester', pp. 527, 528). Robert may have been absent from the university, when his five predecessors as regent master were included on the list of names submitted to Bishop Dalderby on 26 July 1300 for a licence to hear confessions in the archdeaconry of Oxford (Little, *Franciscan Papers, Lists, and Documents*, p. 235). He appears among the named disputants in Worcester Cathedral Library, MS.Q.99, fols. 12r–27v, 60r–71r and 72–82v (Little and Pelster, *Oxford Theology and Theologians*, pp. 337, 358; Thomson, *Worcester*, p. 184). Worcester Cathedral Library, MS.F.139, fols. 24r, 105r, Richard of Bromwich's autograph text of the lectures on the *Sentences* given at Oxford cites the *opinio R. be.*, an allusion to Robert's lost commentary on the *Sentences* (Little and Pelster, *Oxford Theology and Theologians,* pp. 243–44; Thomson, *Worcester*, p. 97). There is a quotation from Beverley on the question *Utrum in Christo sunt duo nativitates reales* in the margin of Florence, Biblioteca Laurenziana MS. of William of Ware's *Commentary on the Sentences*, Plut. 33, Dext Cod.1, fol. 175r (Lechner, 'Beiträge zum mittelalterlichen Franziskanerschrifttum, vornehmlich der Oxforder Schule des 13./14. Jahrhunderts, auf Grund einer Florentiner Wilhelm von Ware-Hs', pp. 119–20; Little and Pelster, *Oxford Theology and Theologians,* p. 365). A copy of Robert's *Vesperies* was in the library of the Austin Friars at York by 1372 (Humphreys, *Friars' Libraries*, p. 58, no. 223b). Oxford, Balliol College MS. 63, fols. 89–99 contains two long *Questiones Beverlay*, fols. 89r–93r, *utrum Deus sit trinus et unus*, and fols. 89r–99v, *Utrum a quacumque creatura rationali solus Deus sit propter se finaliter diligendus* (Little and Pelster, *Oxford Theology and Theologians*, pp. 251–52; *UCLO*, i, p. 467, no. 79; Sharpe, *Handlist*, p. 525, no. 1430).

BEVERLEY (Beverlaco), Robert de: he was ordained a. on 13 March 1350 at Beverley Minster and p. on 4 March 1357 at Bishopthorpe manor chapel, near York (BIA, Register 10A, fol. 44r, Register 11, fol. 330r).

BEVERLEY, Robert de: he was a friar of York when he was ordained a. and s. on 3 April 1378 at Greyfriars, York (BIA, Register 12, fol. 132r).

BEVERLEY, Thomas: he was a friar of Beverley when he was ordained a. on 19 September 1495. He was a friar of York when he was ordained s. on 17 December 1496, d. on 18 February 1497, and at Beverley when he was ordained p. on 23 September 1497. The first, second and fourth ordinations took place at Whitefriars, York, and the third was held at Greyfriars, York (BIA, Register 23, fols. 447r, 452v, 454r, 457r. Cf. Cross and Vickers, *MFN*, p. 438).

BEVERLEY (Beverlaco), William de: he was ordained a. on 21 September 1364 at Bishopthorpe manor chapel (BIA, Register 11, fol. 357v). A friar of this name was ordained p. on 22 December 1375 in the manor chapel at Cawood (BIA, Register 12, fol. 123r).

BEVERTHORP, Richard de: he was ordained a. on 15 March 1348 at York Minster (BIA, Register 10A, fol. 21r).

BEWCHAMPE, Robert: he was the master of students at York when he was licensed to preach anywhere in that diocese on 23 October 1483 (*Reg. Rotherham*, p. 39, no. 304).

BIDENHAM, Thomas: he was licensed in place of the deceased John of Nottingham to hear confessions in the diocese of York at an unknown date during the administration of Archbishop Thoresby (BIA, Register 11, fol. 397r).

BILLAM, John de: he was a friar of York when he was ordained s. on 19 December 1360 at Oakham parish church (LAO, Register 9D, fol. 97v).

BILLINGSGATE (Billynsgate, Billingsgate, Byllyngsgate), Thomas: he was ordained d. on 22 September 1397 in Holy Trinity Priory, Micklegate, York (*Reg. Waldby*, p. 45). He was a friar of Lincoln when ordained d. on 21 December 1398 at Torksey Priory, Lincolnshire (LAO, Register 13, fol. 84r).

BILLOPP, Thomas: he was ordained p. on 6 March 1479 at Austin Friars, York (BIA, Register 22, fol. 377r).

BILLSBY (Blysby), Thomas: he was ordained a. on 20 March 1451 at Lincoln cathedral and at Lincoln when he was ordained s. on 18 September 1451; both ceremonies took place at St Margaret's in the close of Lincoln cathedral (LAO, Register 19, fols. 29v, 32v, 56r, 68r).

BILTON, John de: a friar of Doncaster who received the royal alms for the friary on 23 August 1328 (TNA, E.101/383/14).

BIRE, Richard: a friar of York when he was ordained a. on 18 September 1428 at York Minster (BIA, Register 19, fol. 216r).

BIRSTON (Burston), Robert: he was a friar of York when he was ordained d. on 24 September 1407 at Blackfriars, York (BIA, Register 5A, fol. 325r) and p. on 21 September 1409 at Cawood prebendal church (BIA, Register 18, fol. 391r; *Reg. Sede Vacante, York, 1405–08*, pp. 66, 68, 89).

BIRTON, John: he was a friar of York when he was ordained d. on 1 June 1420 at All Saints, Cawood prebendal chapel (BIA, Register 18, fol. 406r).

BITURBY, John: he was ordained s. on 15 February 1410 in St Martin's chapel, le charnel, Beverley (BIA, Register 18, fol. 39Av).

BLACBORNE (Blabourn), John: he was a friar of Lincoln when he was ordained s. on 25 March 1486 in Lincoln cathedral and d. on 14 April 1487 in the chapel of St Mary Magdalene, Lincoln cathedral (LAO, Register 22, fols. 21v, 25r).

BLACKBORNE, Bernard: an Observant friar sent to York after the suppression of his order in 1534 (*LPFD*, vii, p. 601, no. 1607. Cf. Cross and Vickers, *MFN*, p. 456).

BLAKE (Blaake), Matthew: he was a friar of York when he was ordained s. on 22 December 1459 at Austin Friars, York, and d. on 8 March 1460 at Greyfriars, York (BIA, Register 20, fols. 440v, 442r).

BLAKMAN, John: a friar of York when he was ordained p. on 24 September 1457 at Whitefriars, York (BIA, Register 20, fol. 431v). He went afterwards to London where he died on 31 July 1501 (*GFL,* pp. 65, 132).

BLAKWELL, Robert: he was a friar of York when he was ordained a. on 21 December 1392 at Holy Trinity Priory, Micklegate, York, s. on 1 March 1393 at St Michael-le-Belfrey, York, d. on 31 May 1393 at Holy Trinity Priory, Micklegate, and p. on 20 September 1393 at St Leonard's Hospital, York (BIA, Register 14, fols. 65rv, 67r, 68r).

BLAKYNBERY (Blakynbury), Walran: he was a friar of York when he was ordained a. on 18 September 1428 at York Minster, s. on 18 December 1428 at St Leonard's Hospital, York, and p. on 17 December 1429 at Austin Friars, York (BIA, Register 19, fols. 216r, 233r, 236r).

BLICON, Walter de Anglia: in an uncertain year, probably in the 1390s, this friar was given permission to visit the Roman curia with his *socius* regarding faculties for the friars to hear confessions in the cities and dioceses of Lincoln and York – *Quascumque personas utriusque sexus Eboracen. et Lincolnien. dioecesum et civitatum, sibi pro tempore sponte confiteri volentes, a peccatis earum, in illis casibus dumtaxat in quibus minores paenitentiarii papae in romana curia absolvere possunt, absolvendi et eis paenitentiam iniungendi facultatem papa ei concedit ac habendi unum fratrem socium necnon accedendi ad loca suprascripta, curiam romanam visitandi, licentia superiorum minime requisita* (Cenci, *Supplementum ad Bullarium Franciscanum*, i, p. 120, no. 144).

BLOK, John: he was ordained a. on 19 September 1433 at Whitefriars, York (BIA, Register 19, fol. 245r). He was a friar of Hartlepool when he was ordained d. in Durham cathedral on 17 December 1435 (*Reg. Langley*, vi, p. 24). He was a friar of Hartlepool when ordained p. at Durham cathedral on 22 September 1436 *per gardianum suum debite presentatus* (*Reg. Langley*, iv, p. 202).

BLOWN, William: he was a friar of York when he was ordained p. on 19 September 1489 at Whitefriars, York (BIA, Register 23, fol. 419r).

BLUNDEL (Blondel, Bloundelles), Nicholas: he was ordained a. on 17 December 1345 and s. on 11 March 1346; both ceremonies took place at Whitefriars, York. He was ordained d. at an unspecified venue and date between June 1346 and September 1347. He was ordained p. on 22 December 1347 at Greyfriars, Doncaster (BIA, Register 10A, fols. 13r, 14r, 18a, 20r).

BLYTON (Bliton), Henry: probably a native of Blyton, to the north of Gainsborough in Lincolnshire, he was at York when he was ordained a. on 20 September 1365 at Cawood manor chapel and s. on 20 December 1365 at York Minster. Shortly afterwards he was transferred to Beverley and was there when ordained d. on 28 February

1366 in St Mary, Bishophill Senior. He was back at York when ordained p. on 3 June 1368 at Bishopthorpe manor chapel (BIA, Register 11, fols. 360v, 361v, 362r, 370r). He received 6d. in the will of Richard Warter, a carpenter and parishioner of All Saints, Peasholme in-the-Marsh, York, on 21 November 1397 (BIA, Probate Register 2, fol. 9rv). In the last year of the century a yearning for greater stability moved him to join the queue of friars seeking papal dispensations, taking advantage of a more relaxed administration within the fraternity and a politically dependent pope at Rome during the Great Schism. Pope Boniface IX, recognised by the English crown, was prone to issue dispensations which would have displeased both St Francis and Pope Innocent III. On 15 March 1399 Blyton's petition was granted by Boniface, who described him as a professed member of the province for the past 40 years and then resident in the friary at York. He was granted permission to remain in that friary in perpetuity, regardless of any measures which might be taken by either the minister provincial or the custos of York. He was excused from filling any office in the friary which differed from that undertaken by the *antiqui fratres*. He was also permitted to proceed to the Roman curia with a *socius*. This dispensation was to be supervised by the archbishop of York, the bishop of Lincoln and abbot of St Mary's at York (*BF*, vii, p. 96, no. 278; *CPL*, v, p. 195).

BLYTON (Bliton), William: he was ordained d. on 31 May 1371 at Holy Trinity Priory, Micklegate, York (BIA, Register 11, fol. 382r).

BOALE (Boale), Cornelius: he was a friar of Lincoln when he was ordained s. on 22 April 1508 in Lincoln cathedral (LAO, Register 24, fol. 71r).

BOCTON, Simon de: he was licensed to hear confessions in the diocese of Lincoln on 20 June 1318 (LAO, Register 3, fol. 390rv).

BOKINGHAM (Buckingham), Richard de: he was ordained a. on 10 June 1346 at Whitefriars, York, and was a friar of Nottingham when he was ordained s. on 23 December 1346 in Newark parish church (BIA, Register 10A, fols. 15r, 17r). He was ordained d. on 26 May 1347 in Lincoln cathedral (LAO, Register 7B, fol. 14v).

BOLOGNA, Peter de: probably born about 1260, he was a native of Crespellano, a small town a few miles to the west of Bologna (*Acta Bonien*., pp. 125–26, no. 319). He witnessed wills in the friary at Bologna between 31 August 1284 and 3 October 1291 (*ibid*., pp. 114, 125–26, 211, 303, nn. 291, 319, 486, 632). He was transferred to Ravenna before 8 June 1289, where he witnessed another will in the friars' church, and was the lector at Modena on 5 July 1294, when he witnessed a will in the friars' church (*ibid*., pp. 175, 309–10, nn. 414, 643). He is described as a lector *de Mutina*, which may indicate that he filled that office there or that he was at the time a member of that community, having already exercised the office of lector elsewhere. He was consecrated bishop of Corbavia around 1300 and held the diocese until his death (*Hierarchia catholica*, i, p. 208). There is no evidence that he took up residence in his diocese. He entered the service of the papacy and was one of ten bishops who granted an indulgence to those visiting the little church of St Clare at Montefalco, Umbria, in 1313 (Nessi, 'S.Chiara da Montefalco e il Francescanesimo', p. 393). On 12 August 1308 Pope Clement V summoned the general council of Vienne with the bull *Regnans in caelis*, inviting all the metropolitans; the archbishop of Split and his suffragans, of which Peter was one, were called to the council (*Regestum Clementis papae V*, ii, edited by Benedictine monks, Rome, 1885–86, p. 394, no. 3629). The only known reference to his episcopal activity in the papal court comes in the *lettres communes* of Pope John XXII. On 4 December 1316 five papal letters were addressed to him on the subject of appointments to various churches in the dioceses of Terouane, Toulon, Toul, Tortona and Liege. In each case the letter of appointment was addressed to the cleric provided to the particular church, then Peter, and lastly a local official, such as an abbot, dean and archdeacon (*Jean XXII, Lettres Communes*, i, pp. 201, 202, 204, nn. 2141, 2145, 2146, 2157, 2174).

In the spring of 1317 King Edward II sent the bishops of Ely and Norwich, the earl of Pembroke and Bartholomew of Badlesmere to the papal court to ask for the sentence of excommunication to be promulgated against Robert Bruce and all his supporters, and for Scotland to be placed under interdict until reparations be made for acts committed against the king of England. Pope John XXII promised to send legates to inquire into relations between the two countries and put an end to all controversy (*Vita Edwardi secundi*, pp. 134–37). *Rex excelsus*, issued at Avignon on 17 March 1317, authorised Gaucelin d'Euse, cardinal priest of SS. Marcellino, and Luke dei Fieschi, cardinal deacon of Santa Maria in Via Lata and then SS. Cosma e Damiano, and Peter to negotiate a peace treaty between Edward and Bruce (*Reg. Stapeldon*, pp. 351–53). In May 1317 the cardinals were sent to England and were empowered to excommunicate all who infringed the truce (*CPL*, ii, p. 127; *CPR, 1317–1321*, pp. 2, 7, 9). The pope's *Crescit facile in immensum* of 29 May 1318 informed the cardinals that, on taking advice, he had appointed *ministri idonei*: his venerable brother, the bishop of Corbavia, and Master Aymeric of Gerard, archdeacon of Ely, as *familiares nostri et nuncii* (*Reg. Stapeldon*, pp. 354–56). The papal legation was in London by 1 July 1318. In late August it left York for Durham, where the prelates planned to take part in the consecration of Lewis de Beaumont as bishop of that city on the feast of the translation of St Cuthbert, 4 September. The cardinals, *cum famulis suis*, were intercepted at Ferryhill on 1 September, robbed, stripped of their clothing and then allowed to advance to Durham; Lewis de Beaumont, bishop elect of Durham, and his brother, Henry, were captured. Pope John XXII reports that the legation fell into the hands of Robert Gilbert de Milton, who seized their horses and wounded their servants. On their arrival in Durham the legates complained to the pope that the prior and monks of Durham refused to receive them (*CPL*, ii, p. 444). Another papal communication refers to the violent conduct of Bruce, who carried off the bishop elect of Durham, his brother, and one of the king's servants (*CPL*, ii, p. 431; *Chronicles of the Reigns of Edward I and Edward II*, p. 280). In early September Peter and Aymeric left Durham and travelled to Scotland to arrange a meeting with Bruce. They subsequently notified the cardinals that on their journeys they had been exposed to much hardship and danger. Eventually they reached the camp at Roxburgh where they received a licence and safe-conduct from Bruce who freely and graciously received them, listening attentively to their proposals. Bruce protested that he, too, wished for peace, replying, nonetheless, that he was obliged to consult his advisors and that this would not be possible before Michaelmas. He complained that the pope had refused to recognise him as a king and, on this account, he had excluded papal messengers bearing news of the election of Pope John XXII. The *nuncii* had taken the papal messenger with them to Bruce's court, where they were required to explain this aspect of papal policy towards Scotland. Eventually they decided that their objectives were not going to be met and Peter hurried back to Durham to inform the cardinals, who, in turn, explained the proceedings in a letter dated 7 September 1317 (*Reg. Melton*, iii, pp. 63–66, no. 141; Rymer, *Foedera*, ii, pars i, pp. 340–41). *Dudum, post nostrae promotionis auspicia*, written on 17 November 1319, explains that Bruce had refused to receive papal commands sent to him by the *nuncios* through the hands of Peter and Aymeric

(*Reg. Stapeldon*, pp. 354–56; Rymer, *Foedera*, ii, pars i, pp. 407–08). On the first of these dates the pope also wrote to the two cardinals, rehearsing the recent events and noting that Peter and the archdeacon of Perpignan had been sent to Bruce with papal letters telling him of their arrival and urging him to make peace. Bruce rejected the mission, tore up the pope's letters and took Berwick in breach of the truce (*CPL*, ii, p. 429). On 14 September 1318 at Dover the cardinals reported on their legation, describing the steps taken to conciliate Bruce, and specifically mentioning the role played by Peter and Aymeric (*Reg. Stapeldon*, pp. 356–66).

At the end of his legation Peter chose to remain in England, where he found work as a suffragan bishop in several dioceses. On 11 May 1318 he was one of the consecrators of Lewis de Beaumont as the bishop of Durham in London in the presence of the two cardinals (*Reg. Malton*, i, p. 68, no. 192). On 18 July 1319 he received 10 marks for his expenses from King Edward II (TNA, E403/188, mem. 3, E403/187, mem. 5; BL.MS. Add.17362, fols. 33r, 66r). He also assisted in the consecration of Roger Northburgh as bishop of Coventry and Lichfield on 27 June 1322 at the Premonstratensian Abbey of the Blessed Virgin Mary at Halesowen, Worcestershire (*Reg. Cobham*, pp. 128–29). Between 1321 and 1327 he was active in the diocese of Winchester, both during the *sede vacante* period and following the consecration of Bishop Rigaud of Assier. Afterwards his help was sought more intermittently by Bishop John Stratford (*Reg. Sandale and de Asserio*, pp. 412–13, 419, 420, 544–54; *Reg. Stratford*, i, pp. 19, 71, 151, 189, 210, 213, nn. 62, 227, 466, 590, 637, 644; ii, pp. 448–52, 452, 473–74, 475–77, nn. 1477, 1478, 1490, 1494). He held an ordination in the diocese of Exeter on 20 December 1326 (*Reg. Stapeldon*, pp. 351–53). As a bishop *in partibus* Peter himself reveals that he was dwelling at Greyfriars, London, on 10 October 1318, when he notified the abbot of Westminster that he had presided at the Mass of profession in the abbey (Pearce, *The Monks of Westminster being a register of the brethren of the convent from the time of the confessor to the dissolution with lists of the obedientiaries and an introduction*, pp. 78–79; Westminster Abbey, Muniments, no. 9325). His name is not mentioned in Gravesend's incomplete register and the only sources of information on his activity within the diocese come from incidental references in other documents, such as the *Annales Paulini*. He excommunicated those responsible for bloodshed in the choir of St Paul's cathedral early in 1328 and then reconciled the church. He consecrated a new bell for the cathedral in honour of St Mary around the feast of Pentecost in 1332 (*Chronicles of the reigns of Edward I. and Edward II.*, i, pp. xc–xcii, 340–41, 353). By May 1321 Peter was active in the diocese of Canterbury and he continued to be so until his death, assisting first Archbishop Walter Reynolds and then Archbishop Simon Meopham. On 14 May 1325 Archbishop Reynolds authorised him to bless the newly constructed Franciscan church and cemetery at Canterbury (LPL: The Register of Walter Reynolds, archbishop of Canterbury, fols. 102r, 126rv, 131r, 135v, 146v, 147r, 149r, 150r, 151r, 152v, 153v, 154r, 158v–59r, 184v–85r, Canterbury Cathedral Chapter Archives, MS.Q, fols. 122v, 130v, 176rv; Churchill, *Kent Records: Calendar of Institutions by the Chapter of Canterbury Sede Vacante*, pp. 147–51; Canterbury Cathedral Dean and Chapter Library, SVSB IV/3/1, SVSB, II/77/1; *Literae Cantuarienses. The letter books of the monastery of Christ Church, Canterbury*, i, pp. 300–01, no. 288). Peter received a stipend for consecrating altars in the cathedral priory in 1325, for reconciling the cemetery at Canterbury cathedral in 1329 (LPL, MS.242, fol. 352r, MS. 243, fol. 16r) and alms received from the monks on Christmas 1330 (Canterbury Cathedral Chapter Archives, Accounts of the Priory Almoner, Roll 40 (1329–30). He re-dedicated the high altar and the altar of St John the Baptist in the south transept of St Augustine's Abbey, Canterbury, in 1325 (*Library of St Augustine's Abbey*, ii, pp. 835, 836, nn. 786, 790).

Peter served as suffragan in the diocese of York, but the only extant reference to him in the register of Archbishop Melton concerns his activities outside the diocese in 1317–18 regarding the papal legation to Bruce and the episcopal consecration of the bishop of Durham. He is also mentioned among the York suffragans in connection with the consecration of Bishop Beaumont. The fact that Peter was described as a suffragan of York in March 1318 shows that his services were secured by the archbishop of York shortly after the collapse of the papal mission to Bruce. Peter appears intermittently as a suffragan in the diocese of Lincoln between 1322 and 1331. The episcopal register discloses that he was employed as frequently as the other four suffragans by Bishop Burghersh. He served intermittently in this diocese, receiving his first commission in December 1322 and his second in July 1325. On 16 November 1322 he received three commissions from Bishop Burghersh. One of them was for the blessing of some altars in the new Franciscan church in Northampton (LAO, Register 5, fol. 325r). Perhaps at this stage he spent much of his time in the diocese of Lincoln. His last recorded commission was issued by Bishop Burghersh from Liddington on Christmas day 1331 (LAO, Register 5, fols. 380r, 432r, 440v, 445v, 454r).

Peter's death is recorded in at least four places. An indication of his reputation is the fact that the sources external to the Franciscan order contain full tributes. First, his death is entered with a degree of considerable warmth and respect in the *Annales Paulini* which record that on the feast of St Wulfstan, Peter, bishop of Corbavia, died at the London Greyfriars. He was of their order, *vir excellentissimae vitae et omni bonitate repletus*, and exercised the episcopal office in many dioceses in ordaining clerics, dedicating or reconciling churches and other episcopal functions (*Chronicles of the reigns of Edward I and Edward II*, i, p. 356). Secondly, the *Registrum fratrum minorum Londonie* records that Peter died at Greyfriars, London, and was buried in their magnificent church: *Ad cuius dexteram* (i.e., Roger Conway) *in archu australi jacet venerabilis Pater et frater minor Petrus Bononiensis, quondam episcopus Corboniensis in Hungaria et suffraneus episcopi London: qui obiit ... die mensis Januarii Ao dni 1331* (*GFL*, p. 72). Thirdly, even though he died outside the diocese, Peter's reputation in Canterbury earned him a place rarely accorded to friars in the *Regestum prioratus sancte Trinitatis Cantuarie*, where his death was commemorated on 19 January, perhaps on the recommendation of the prior in gratitude for the various liturgical tasks which he had carried out in the cathedral and on the business of the priory; equally he may have been included in the necrology as a benefactor of the cathedral: *obierat bone memorie Petrus Corbaviensis episcopus de ordine fratrum minorum* (BL, MS.Arundel 68, fol. 13v.; and LPL, MS.20, fol. 159v). Fourthly, John XXII records the death of Peter *bonae memoriae in partibus Angliae* when appointing Boniface of Pisa to the vacant bishopric of Corbavia on 3 June 1332 (*Jean XXII, Lettres Communes*, xi, p. 205, no. 57374. Cf. Smith, 'Suffragan Bishops in the Medieval Diocese of Lincoln', p. 24; Robson, 'Peter of Bologna (c.1260–1332) Franciscan Bishop of Corbavia'; and Butler, 'Suffragan Bishops in the Medieval Diocese of York', pp. 50–51, 56).

BOLTON, Thomas: he was a friar of York when he was ordained a. on 20 March 1428 at Greyfriars, York, s. on 11 March 1430 at Greyfriars, York, and p. on 11 June 1435 at Blackfriars, York (BIA, Register 19, fols. 232r, 236v, 249v). A friar of this name received 3s. 4d. in the will of Thomas Chaumbre, a servant at Bolton Priory, on 12 September 1444 (BIA, Probate Register 2, fol. 92v). A friar of this name was admitted to the guild of *Corpus Christi* at York in 1451 (*Guild of Corpus Christi*, p. 51). He was a friar of London on 27 March 1460 when he witnessed an agreement with William Cantelowe regarding Masses (Kingsford, 'Additional Material for the History of the Grey Friars, London', pp. 74, 145–47). In this year he paid £5 6s.

8d. for his *cautio* at Cambridge (*Grace Book A*, p. 22). By the year 1471 he had taken his D.D. and had become guardian of Beverley. He had tried to gain security for his convent by granting the title of founder to Richard Neville, earl of Warwick, and he subsequently gave the patronage of the house to John Neville, Marquess Montagu. Both these noblemen fell at the feet of Barnet. He conferred the title and privilege of founder upon Henry Percy, earl of Northumberland (Young, 'Notices Concerning Religious Houses in Yorkshire, with the Names of their Founders, and of Persons Buried Therein', pp. 77–79, 129; Goldthorp, 'The Franciscans and Dominicans in Yorkshire', p. 294, *GFC*, pp. 153–54).

BONAVENTURE, Richard: he was a friar of York when he was ordained s. on 24 February 1526 at Whitefriars, York, d. on 7 March 1528 at Whitefriars, York, and p. on 28 March 1528 at Greyfriars, York (BIA, Register 27, fols. 209r, 215rv. Cf. Cross and Vickers, *MFN*, p. 445).

BONBEBY, William de: he was licensed in the diocese of Lincoln on 18 February 1330 in place of Geoffrey de Beverley (LAO, Register 5, fol. 402v).

BONBY, Thomas de: he was ordained a. on 29 May 1344 at Newark parish church (BIA, Register 10A, fol. 6r).

BOOTHAM (Bothom), John de: he was a friar ordained p. at Skipton parish church on 20 September 1348 (BIA, Register 10A, fol .25v).

BOOTHAM (Bothom), Robert de: he was ordained p. on 7 June 1343 at Greyfriars, York (BIA, Register 10A, fol. 4v).

BORWYKE (Borwyck), William: he was a friar of York when he was ordained d. on 24 September 1457 at Whitefriars, York (BIA, Register 20, fol. 431r).

BOSCO (Busco), Arnold de: he was ordained p. on 16 September 1391 at Holy Trinity Priory, Micklegate, York (BIA, Register 14, fol. 63r; Walmsley, 'Some Dutch Franciscans in England during the Later Middle Ages', p. 253).

BOSCO, John de: he was a friar of York when he was ordained a. on 7 March 1433 at Greyfriars, York. He was ordained s. on 22 May 1434 at Blackfriars, York (BIA, Register 19, fols. 243r, 247r; Walmsley, 'Some Dutch Franciscans in England during the Later Middle Ages', p. 253).

BOSCO, Romualdus de: he was a friar of York when he was ordained d. on 14 June 1432 at Blackfriars, York. He was a friar at Scarborough when he was ordained p. on 20 December 1432 at Austin Friars, York (BIA, Register 19, fols. 242v, 243r; Walmsley, 'Some Dutch Franciscans in England during the Later Middle Ages', p. 253).

BOSCO, Walter de: he was ordained p. on 15 March 1399 at Cawood prebendal church (*Reg. Scrope*, ii, pp. 55, 62, 131). The editor erroneously dates this ordination as 26 February 1401. The manuscript gives the earlier date (BIA, Register 16, fol. 153v).

BOSTON (S.Botolph), John de: he was ordained d. on 10 June 1346 at Whitefriars, York (BIA, Register 10A, fol. 16r) and p. on 26 May 1347 in Lincoln cathedral (LAO, Register 7B, fol. 15v).

BOSTON (S.Botulpho), John de: he was ordained a. on 22 September 1369 and s. on 8 June 1370; both ceremonies were at Bishopthorpe manor chapel. He was at Beverley when he was ordained d. on 21 December 1370 at Whitefriars, York (BIA, Register 11, fols. 375r, 378v, 380v). He was ordained p. on 23 December 1374 at the manor chapel of Thorpe (BIA, Register 12, fol. 118v).

BOSTON (S.Botolph), Laurence: he was ordained a. on 26 May 1347 in Lincoln cathedral (LAO, Register 7B, fol. 12v).

BOSTON (S.Botolph), Robert de: he was ordained s. on 18 December 1294 at Stow prebendal church and p. on 22 September 1296 at Lincoln cathedral (*Reg. Sutton*, vii, pp. 60, 85). He was the custos of York on 12 March 1319 and was at Boston when he wrote to Bishop Dalderby regarding friars who had moved elsewhere or were no longer fit to carry out their duties as confessors; he obtained licences for the three replacements (LAO, Register 3, fols. 411v–12r). He was still in office on 29 October 1319 when he presented a letter of the minister provincial and secured a licence for Simon de Caistor (Castre), probably a friar of Grimsby. He himself received a licence (LAO, Register 3, fol. 427rv).

BOSTON (St Botolph), Robert de: he was ordained a. on 21 December 1336 at Greyfriars, York (*Reg. Kellaw*, iii, p. 173).

BOSWORTH (Boseworth), Thomas de: he was ordained d. on 29 March 1343 at Greyfriars, Beverley. He was a friar of Doncaster when he was ordained p. on 24 September 1345 at Ripon Minster (BIA, Register 10A, fols. 3r, 13r).

BOTELER (Butler), Edmund: he was ordained a. in Darlington parish church in the diocese of Durham on 29 May 1344 (*Reg. Kellaw*, iii, p. 142). He was at York when he was ordained d. on 21 May 1345 at Thirsk parish church (BIA, Register 10A, fol. 11r).

BOTELER (Butler, Botiller), Robert: he was ordained d. on 29 May 1344 at Newark parish church (BIA, Register 10A, fol. 6v). A Robert Botiller was ordained p. on 22 December 1347 in Southwark manor chapel (*Reg. Edington*, ii, p. 127, no. 746).

BOTERALL, John: he was a friar of York when he was ordained s. on 24 March 1515 at Holy Trinity Priory, Micklegate, York (Register 27, fol. 167v. Cf. Cross and Vickers, *MFN*, p. 444).

BOTERALL, William: he was at York when he was ordained p. on 22 September 1515 at Austin Friars, York (BIA, Register 27, fol. 170r. Cf. Cross and Vickers, *MFN*, p. 444). This and the above entry may denote one rather than two friars in the event of scribal error.

BOTHEBY, Roger: he was ordained a. on 17 June 1413 at Greyfriars, York, and a friar of Beverley when he was ordained s. on 18 September 1417 at Cawood prebendal church (BIA, Register 18, fols. 39Fr, 398r).

BOTILESFORD (Bottlesford), Richard de: he was a friar of Lincoln when he was ordained s. on 19 December 1355 in Stow prebendal church (LAO, Register 9D, fol. 78r).

BOTILSTANE (Botilsham, Bottlestone), John de: he was ordained a. on 24 February 1369 at Bishopthorpe manor chapel and d. on 20 September 1371 at St Mary, Bishophill Senior (BIA, Register 11, fols. 372v, 384v).

BOTTEFORTH, Richard de: he was a friar of York when he was ordained p. on 26 May 1358 at Greyfriars, York (BIA, Register 11, fol. 334r).

BOTTESFORD, Geoffrey de: he was licensed to hear confessions in the diocese of Lincoln at an unspecified date in July 1300 (LAO, Register 3, fol. 13r).

BOWES, Gerard: he was a friar of Lincoln when he was ordained d. on 20 December 1432 at Liddington prebendal church (LAO, Register 17, fol. 209r).

BOWES, Philip: he was a friar of York when he was ordained a. on 3 April 1378 at Greyfriars, York (BIA, Register 12, fol. 132r).

BOWES (Baweg), William de/del: he was ordained a. on 20 September 1343 at Whitefriars, York (BIA, Register 10A, fol. 4v), s. on 20 December 1343 at Durham cathedral (*Reg. Kellaw*, iii, p. 131) and d. on 29 May 1344 at Newark parish church (BIA, Register 10A, fol. 6v). He was ordained p. on 18 December 1344 in Durham cathedral (*Reg. Kellaw*, iii, p. 148). He seems to have received some hospitality from the clergy and laity in Newcastle. In 1342 the bishop of London wrote to John Hirlaw, vicar of St Nicholas, Newcastle-on-Tyne, instructing him to excommunicate this friar of Newcastle, for apostasy. At the instigation of the guardian at Newcastle, the bishop of Durham, Richard de Bury, excommunicated him and had it published in all the churches of Newcastle (*Reg. Kellaw*, iii, pp. 513–14).

BOX, Thomas: he was a friar of Boston on 8 March 1347 when he was licensed in the diocese of Lincoln for one year. On 3 June 1347 he was commissioned to absolve Ralph, son of Roger de Sutterton, from the sentence of excommunication arising from a matrimonial irregularity (LAO, Register 7, fol. 100r).

BOXFORD, Geoffrey: he was ordained p. on 30 May 1366 at Bishopthorpe manor chapel (BIA, Register 11, 363v).

BOYNTON, Thomas: a friar of Beverley when he was ordained a. on 12 March 1407 and at York when he was ordained s. on 24 September 1407; both ceremonies took place at Blackfriars, York (BIA, Register 5A, fols. 324r, 325r). On 5 January 1444 Archbishop Kempe admitted him to hear confessions in the diocese of York. Thomas was presented by Thomas Radnor, the minister provincial, in accordance with the terms of *Dudum* (BIA, Register 19, fol. 86v). A friar of this name was guardian of Beverley in the Michaelmas term of 1448 (TNA, CP40/751, m. 459).

BOYS (Bois), Vincent: he was ordained a. on 20 December 1376 and s. on 18 February 1380; both ceremonies took place at Holy Trinity Priory, Micklegate. He was ordained p. on 19 December 1383 at All Saints, Cawood (BIA, Register 12, fols. 126v, 136r, 141r).

BRACEWELL, Richard: he was ordained a. on 22 March 1477 at Greyfriars, York (BIA, Register 22, fol. 365r).

BRADEHULL, Edward: he was a *scolar in sacra theologia* admitted to hear confessions in the archdeaconry of Richmond on 10 September 1444 (BIA, Register 19, fol. 214v. Cf. Hamilton Thompson, 'The Register of the Archdeacons of Richmond, 1442–1477', p. 84).

BRADFIELD (Bradfeld), William: he was a friar of York when he was ordained p. on 1 April 1419 in the prebendal chapel at Cawood (BIA, Register 18, fol. 402v).

BRADLEY (Bradlay), Henry: he was ordained a. on 20 December 1404 and s. on 14 March 1405 at Cawood prebendal church (*Reg. Scrope*, ii, pp. 55, 63, 131). He was ordained d. on 19 September 1405 at Greyfriars, York (BIA, Register 5A, fol. 318r; *Reg. Sede Vacante, York, 1405–08*, pp. 66, 69, 89).

BRADLEY, Richard: he was ordained d. on 28 May 1401 at Bishop Burton (*Reg. Scrope*, ii, pp. 55, 63, 131). He was a friar of Lincoln when ordained p. on 24 May 1404 at Liddington prebendal church (LAO, Register 13, fol. 115r).

BRADLEY, Thomas: he was a friar of Doncaster when he was ordained p. on 22 September 1487 (BIA, Register 23, fol. 409r. Cf. Cross and Vickers, *MFN*, p. 436).

BRADLEY, William: he was a friar of Lincoln when he was ordained p. on 12 June 1473 at Lincoln cathedral (LAO, Register 21, fol. 139v).

BRADLEY (Bradlay) [no Christian name]: he was ordained d. on 19 September 1472 at Holy Trinity Priory, Micklegate, York (BIA, Register 22, fol. 217r).

BRADMORE, William de: he was licensed in the diocese of Lincoln in January 1334 (LAO, Register 5, fol. 471r).

BRAKONHOLM, Alexander de: he was a friar of Grimsby on 8 March 1347 when he was licensed as a confessor in the diocese of Lincoln (LAO, Register 7, fol. 99v).

BRAMHAM, John de: he was ordained a. on 20 September 1371 at St Mary, Bishophill Senior, s. on 18 September 1372 at Greyfriars, York, d. on 18 December 1372 and p. on 11 June 1373; the third and fourth ceremonies took place at Whitefriars, York (BIA, Register 11, fols. 384r, 389r, 390r, 392r).

BRAMPTON, John: he was a friar of Lincoln when he was ordained d. on 14 March 1405 in Lincoln cathedral (LAO, Register 13, fol. 118v).

BRAMPTON, Simon: he was a friar at York when he was ordained a. on 13 March 1378 at Holy Trinity Priory, Micklegate, and s. on 3 April 1378 at Greyfriars, York (BIA, Register 12, fols. 131r, 132r). On 19 December 1392 he was left 20s. to pray for the soul of Richard Bridesall, a citizen, merchant of York and parishioner of St John the Evangelist, North Street, whose will was proved on 14 January 1393 (*TE*, i, pp. 174–75). Pope John XXIII was at Mantua on 28 January 1414 when he provided him to the see of Tripoli and three days later directed him to receive consecration from any Catholic bishop (*BF*, vii, p. 473, no. 1311, n. 6; *CPL*, vii, pp. 441–42, 453). On 20 December 1415, 13 March, 4 April, 18 April, 13 June and 19 September 1416 he held ordinations on behalf of John Catterick, bishop of Coventry and Lichfield. The venue for the first ordination is not recorded, but the second, third and fifth ceremonies took place in Lichfield cathedral, the fourth in the chapel of St Mary by the square, Lichfield, and the sixth in Coventry cathedral (*Reg. Catterick*, pp. 35–42, nn. 220–25).

BRANDON (Brand), Adrian: he was a friar of Grimsby when he was ordained d. on 11 April 1528 at Lincoln cathedral and he was a friar of Lincoln when he was ordained p. on 19 September 1528 in Liddington prebendal church (LAO, Register 26, fols. 21v, 22v).

BRANDON, Bernard: he was a friar of Oxford when he was ordained s. on 22 September 1526 at All Saints, Northampton (LAO, Register 26, fol. 15v). He was ordained d. on 15 June 1527 (Worcester Registers: Morton, fol. 164r). He was at York when ordained p. on 7 March 1528 at Whitefriars, York (BIA, Register 27, fol. 215r. Cf. Cross and Vickers, *MFN*, p. 445). He was at Lincoln on 8 October 1539 when he received his capacity (Chambers, *Faculty Office Registers 1534–1549*, p. 195).

BRANDON, William: he was ordained d. on 1 March 1393 at St Michael-le-Belfrey, York, and p. on 20 September 1393 at the hospital chapel of St Leonard's, York (BIA, Register 14, fols. 66r, 68r).

BRANTINGHAM, Adam de: he was appointed to hear the confessions of the Benedictine nuns of Wilberfoss in the East Riding on 2 July 1322; a Dominican was also licensed (*Reg. Melton*, vi, p. 86, no. 273). Adam died before 17 October 1347 when he was replaced by William de Filioll (BIA, Register 10A, fol. 278r).

BRENES (Brayne, Brayns, Breres), Robert: he was a friar of York when he was ordained a. on 8 March 1438 at Whitefriars, York, s. on 29 March 1438 at Greyfriars, York, d. on 7 June 1438 at Blackfriars, York, and p. on 17 December 1440 in St Mary's Castlegate, York (BIA, Register 19, fols. 256rv, 257v, 263r). He is perhaps to be identified with Robert Brayans, *magister noviciorum*, at London in 1492 (*GFL*, p. 65).

BRERELAY, Robert de: a friar of Doncaster when he was ordained a. on 21 September 1359 at the manor chapel of Cawood, and at Beverley when ordained d. on 12 March 1362 at the episcopal manor of Bishopthorpe (BIA, Register 11, fols. 338v, 348r).

BRID (Byrd, Bird), Thomas: he was ordained a. on 9 June 1403, s. on 22 December 1403, d. on 23 February 1404 and p. on 20 September 1404. The first three ceremonies were held at St Nicholas's chapel, Bawtry, and the fourth at Cawood prebendal church (*Reg. Scrope*, ii, pp. 55, 63, 131).

BRIDGEFORD, Robert: he was a friar of Lincoln when he was ordained p. on 7 April 1515 in Lincoln cathedral (LAO, Register 25, fol. 114r).

BRIDLINGTON (Bridelton, Bridilig, Bridilton, Bridillinton), Philip de: he was a bachelor of theology by 1290, when he responded to Master Richard de Heddrington or Herington on the question *An omnes beati equaliter participant beatitudine*, q. 79 (Little and Pelster, *Oxford Theology and Theologians*, pp. 255–56; Henquinet, 'Descriptio codicis 158 Assisii in Bibliotheca Communali', pp. 93, 98, 240–41; Glorieux, 'Le Manuscrit d'Assise, Bibl.comm.158: Date et mode de composition', p. 290). He seems to have remained in Oxford throughout the 1290s (Glorieux, 'Jean de Saint-Germain maître de Paris et copiste de Worcester', pp. 522, 524, 526, 527, 528, 532). He was the 29th regent master at Oxford c.1300–02 (Eccleston, p. 54; *BRUO*, p. 265). His *Commentary on the Sentences* was cited by William of Ware, William of Nottingham and Richard Bromwhich, a monk of Worcester cathedral priory (Stegmüller, *Repertorium*, i, pp. 339–40, no. 697). He appears among the named disputants in Worcester Cathedral Library, MS.Q.99, fols. 60r–71r, 72–82v and 83r–92r (Little and Pelster, *Oxford Theology and Theologians*, pp. 224, 232, 234, 235, 243–44, 248, 249, 255–56, 262, 274, 310, 365; Thomson, *Worcester*, p. 184). He became master in 1299 or 1300. His *Vesperies* probably took place in the first half of 1300 (Little and Pelster, *Oxford Theology and Theologians*, pp. 15, 35, 66, 68, 74, 87, 128, 365).

He is mentioned in the Biblioteca Laurenziana of Florence, MS. of Ware's Commentary on the *Sentences* (Plut.33, dext.1, fol. 75r), where references are given to his commentary on the *Sentences. Hoc argumentum fit apud Brdideligton lib1.d.28 secundum argumentum principale. Vide ibi solutionem.* He contested an opinion of Giles of Rome (Lechner, 'Beiträge zum mittelalterlichen Franziskanerschrifttum, vornehmlich der Oxforder Schule des 13./14. Jahrhunderts, auf Grund einer Florentiner Wilhelm von Ware-Hs', pp. 107–17, cited in Little and Pelster, *Oxford Theology and Theologians*, p. 365. Cf. Pouillon, 'Le manuscrit d'Assise, Bibl.comm.196. Description', p. 352). On 26 July 1300 he was one of the friars presented for a licence in the archdeaconry of Lincoln. He was one of the two doctors of theology licensed (Little, *Franciscan Papers, Lists, and Documents*, p. 235). In MS.Assisi 196, fol. 102v, he intervened in the question: *Utrum Deus videatur per speciem aliquam in patria* (Doucet, 'Bibliografia', p. 277). The *marginalia* on William of Nottingham's commentary on the *Sentences* mention him twice (Gonville and Caius College Library, Cambridge, MS.300/514, fols. 37vb, 54va). He was the regent master when John Duns Scotus was responding to questions (Longpré, 'Philip de Bridlington, O.F.M. et le Bx.Duns Scot', pp. 587–88; Little, 'The Franciscan School at Oxford in the Thirteenth Century', pp. 862–63; Sharpe, *Handlist*, p. 436, no. 1206).

BRIDLINGTON, Richard: in 1446 Robert Waltham, guardian at Grimsby, brought an action against this friar, a member of the community (Gillett, *A History of Grimsby*, p. 76).

BRIDLINGTON (Bridlyngton), William: he was a friar of York when he was ordained d. on 21 September 1426 at Blackfriars, York, and p. on 20 December 1427 at Austin Friars, York (BIA, Register 19, fols. 215r, 231r). On 11 November 1442 Alice Plastever, a widow of Scarborough, asked to be buried in the Greyfriars and appointed a friar of this name, probably resident in the local friary, as her executor (BIA, Probate Register 2, fol. 94v).

BRIDLINGTON (Bridlyngton), William: he was ordained a. on 20 September 1432 at St Leonard's Hospital, York, and s. on 20 December 1432 at Austin Friars, York. A friar of this name was at York when he was ordained p. on 24 February 1442 at Greyfriars, York (BIA, Register 19, fols. 217r, 242v, 266r).

BRITT (Bruyl, Bryt), John: a friar of this name was at the friary in Newcastle on 5 July 1396 when he was appointed a papal chaplain by Pope Boniface IX (*BF*, vii, pp. 59–60, no. 181; *CPL*, iv, p. 297). Little doubts whether this connection is correct (Oxford, Bodleian Library, MS. Eng. hist. d.440, 176). John was also for a time at Canterbury as lector. He annotated Bodleian Library, MS. Digby 153, fols. 102r–37r, signing the text in 1371 with an alphabetical table (*Library of St Augustine's Abbey*, ii, pp. 905–06; *GFCant.*, pp. 32–33). He was guardian of London on 1 March 1398

(*GFL*, pp. 56–57, 173–76) and held that office on 20 July 1398, when Edward Dee, the king's sergeant-at-arms, was appointed to arrest and deliver to him Walter Tolny, Thomas Knyght, John Camel and John Mynterne, apostate and vagabond friars (*CPR 1396–1399*, p. 433; Chancery Warrants, 1765/20).

On 25 January 1402 Pope Boniface IX provided him to the see of Annaghdown on the death of Henry Trillow, another Franciscan, and required him, as soon as his letters of provision had been expedited, to betake himself to his church and reside there, not exercising his episcopal office outside his city and diocese. This notwithstanding, he was authorised to work as a bishop elsewhere, at the direction of an ordinary (*BF*, vii, p. 139, no. 401, n. 6; *CPL*, v, pp. 503, 500). On 14 November 1402 a suffragan licence was issued to him in the diocese of Winchester (*Reg. Wykeham*, ii, p. 542). On 23 December 1402, 10 March 1403, 9 June 1403 and 22 September 1403 he held ordinations at Waltham chapel (*Reg. Wykeham*, i, pp. 354–57). On 22 September 1403 a suffragan commission was granted to him during the bishop's pleasure (*Reg. Wykeham*, ii, p. 550). On 27 September 1403 he was dwelling in London, when he received a mandate to investigate the petition of Richard Anstey, from the diocese of Lichfield. Anstey, when he was below his fourteenth year or thereabouts, was forced by the friends and kinsmen of Marion Ulger from the diocese of Lincoln to contract marriage with her; the marriage was not consummated. On reaching the years of discretion and heedless to threats, Anstey abandoned Marion and contracted marriage with Isabella Jonis from the diocese of Lichfield. His petition for the nullity of the former and the lawfulness of the latter marriage asserted that he did not dare to approach Henry Beaufort, bishop of Lincoln, who favoured Marion and was otherwise suspicious of him. In October 1403 he was instructed to collate a priest to a living in the diocese of York (*CPL*, v, pp. 532–53). He appears to have been deprived of his see in 1408 when Frater Johannes Wyn occurs as *electus in episcopum Enchdunsem* (*Materials, Ireland*, p. 171).

On 14 February 1413 John was commissioned to reconcile the churchyard of the parish church of Wedmor in the diocese of Bath and Wells (*Reg. Bubwith*, i, p. 139, no. 396). A memorandum was issued that on 21 May 1414 John was one of the ecclesiastical dignitaries, including the archdeacon of Cleveland, present in the church of the Augustinian friars at York, when Cuthbert de Rydemer, abbot elect of the Premonstratensian monastery of Coverham, made his profession of faith to the archbishop (BIA, Register 18, fol. 30v). He held five ordinations at Cawood prebendal church between 13 June 1416 and 6 April 1420 (BIA, Register 18, fols. 39Hv–Ir–406r). On 17 December 1417 Bishop Langley commissioned him to serve as a suffragan and penitentiary (*Reg. Langley*, v, p. 108, no. 1398). He held ordinations in the diocese of Durham between 19 February 1418 and 11 May of that year (*Reg. Langley*, iii, p. 188, no. 862, n. 2; v, p. 108, no. 1398). He held ordinations in the diocese of York between 1 April 1419 and April 1420 (BIA, Register 18, fols. 402v, 405v–6r). He held four ordinations in Hereford cathedral on 15 February, 8 March, 22 March and 17 May 1421 (*Reg. Poltone*, pp. 18–21). He held ordinations in the parish church of St Thomas the martyr in Salisbury on 7 March 1422, 19 September 1422, 27 March 1423, 18 March 1424, 23 September 1424 (Wiltshire Record Office, Reg. Chaundler, fols. 73rv–78r). Cf. Butler, 'Suffragan Bishops in the Medieval Diocese of York', p. 58).

BRNE (Burne, Browne ?), William: on 24 August 1398 Ralph de Wresill, rector of Howden, left this friar 20s. to pray for the repose of his soul. William may have been a friar of Beverley or York, the friaries asked to celebrate Masses for the rector. The will was proved on 5 September 1398 (BIA, Register 16, fol. 133r. Cf. *Reg. Scrope*, ii, p. 23). He was a friar of Beverley in receipt of a taxable stipend in 1406 (TNA, E179/66/411.

Cf. Jurkowski, 'Were Friars Paid Salaries? Evidence from Clerical Taxation Records', p. 136, n. 28).

BROMEN, Gerard: he was a friar of Boston when he was ordained d. on 18 December 1434 at Liddington prebendal church (LAO, Register 17, fol. 218v).

BROMPTON (Brumpton), John: he was ordained d. in St Martin's chapel (le charnel), Beverley on 15 February 1410 (BIA, Register 18, fol. 39Br) and p. on 17 May 1410 at Cawood prebendal church (BIA, Register 18, fol. 392v).

BROMPTON (Brumpton, Brunton), Thomas: he was ordained s. on 18 September 1400 at Cawood prebendal church and d. on 19 March 1401 at Blackfriars, York (*Reg. Scrope*, ii, pp. 55, 64, 131).

BROSANO, Nicholas de: he was a friar of York when he was ordained p. on 20 September 1449 at Holy Trinity Priory, Micklegate, York (BIA, Register 19, fol. 285v).

BROUGHTON (Brocton), John de: he was ordained d. on 19 May 1296 at Lincoln cathedral and p. on 21 December 1297 at Louth prebendal church (*Reg. Sutton*, vii, pp. 79, 101).

BROUWYKE (Broundyke), Richard: he was a friar of Lincoln when he was ordained s. on 27 March 1529 and d. on 16 April 1530; both ceremonies took place in Lincoln cathedral, the second of them in one of the chapels (LAO, Register 26, fols. 24r, 26r). He was at York at the Dissolution on 27 November 1538 (*Eighth Report of the Deputy Keeper of the Public Records*, p. 51; Cross and Vickers, *MFN*, p. 454).

BROWN (Browne), Hugh: he was a friar of Lincoln when he was ordained s. on 10 April 1512 in Lincoln cathedral (LAO, Register 24, fol. 88r) and a friar of Richmond when he was ordained d. on 5 June 1512 at Blackfriars, York (BIA, Register 26, fol. 119r. Cf. Cross and Vickers, *MFN*, p. 443). He was back at Lincoln when ordained p. at Buckden prebendal church on 18 December 1512 (LAO, Register 24, fol. 90v).

BROWN (Browne), James: he was a friar of York when he was ordained a. on 7 March 1433 at Greyfriars, York, and s. on 11 April 1433 at York Minster, lady chapel. He was ordained d. on 19 September 1433 at Whitefriars, York (BIA, Register 19, fols. 243r, 244r, 245r).

BROWN, Laurence: he was a friar of York when he was ordained s. on 22 February 1483 at Holy Trinity Priory, Micklegate, York, and p. on 24 Sepember 1485 at Rotherham parish church (BIA, Register 23, fols. 385v, 398v. Cf. Cross and Vickers, *MFN*, p. 435). Between these dates he was at Stamford and was ordained d. in April 1484 (London Registers: Rusell, fol. 14).

BROWN (Broune, Brum, Brunun), Robert: he was ordained a. on 2 June 1341 in Durham cathedral (*Reg. Kellaw*, iii, p. 109). He was the *cursor Sententiarum* at Newcastle when he was licensed for the diocese of York on 2 October 1350 (BIA, Register 10, fol. 279v).

BROWN, Robert: he was a friar of Lincoln when he was ordained d. on 23 September 1503 in Lincoln cathedral (LAO, Register 24, fol. 42r).

BROWN, Thomas: he was ordained s. on 19 September 1394 at Austin Friars, York (BIA, Register 14, fol. 70r).

BROWN (Broun), Thomas: he was a friar of Lincoln when he was ordained a. on 30 March 1510, d. on 19 April 1511 and p. on 10 April 1512; all three ceremonies took place in Lincoln cathedral. The first of these was in the chapel of St Mary Magdalene (LAO, Register 24, fols. 80, 84v, 88).

BROWN (Browne), Thomas: he was a friar of York when he was ordained d. on 24 February 1526 at Whitefriars, York, and p. on 26 May 1526 at Blackfriars, York (BIA, Register 27, fols. 209r, 210v). He was probably at Scarborough on 16 June 1539 when he received a dispensation to hold a living with a complete change of habit (Chambers, *Faculty Office Registers 1534–1549*, p. 187). There are wills of Thomas Browne, curate of Nether Poppleton, dated 18 April 1549, and Thomas Browne, curate of Bilton, dated 8 March 1553, and of Thomas Browne, curate of Walton, dated 2 January 1556. None of them can definitely be linked with the former friar of this name (BIA, Probate Register 13, pt. I, fol. 534v, pt. II, fol. 989r, 15, pt. II, fols. 85v–86r; Cross and Vickers, *MFN*, pp. 445, 452–53).

BROWN, Walter: he was a friar of York when he was ordained s. on 6 March 1490 at Holy Trinity Priory, Micklegate, York, d. on 27 March 1490 at Greyfriars, York, and p. on 5 June 1490 at Blackfriars, York (BIA, Register 23, fols. 420v, 421v, 423r. Cf. Cross and Vickers, *MFN*, p. 437).

BROWN (Bown, B[r]own, Broune), William: he was a friar of York when he was ordained d. on 16 March 1426 at St Martin-le-Grand, Coney Street, York (BIA, Register 5A, fol. 445v; *Reg. Sede Vacante, 1423–26*, pp. 99, 102, 125).

BROWN (Browne), William: he was ordained d. on 12 June 1400 at Bishop Burton (*Reg. Scrope*, ii, pp. 55, 64, 131).

BROWN, W: he was a friar of Lincoln when he was ordained d. on 12 April 1533 in Lincoln cathedral (LAO, Register 26, fol. 33v).

BRUG (Bridge), George: he was ordained a. on 1 March 1393 at St Michael-le-Belfrey, York (BIA, Register 14, fol. 65v).

BRUGES, Simon: he was ordained p. on 22 September 1375 at Whitefriars, York (BIA, Register 12, fol. 122r).

BRUGGEFORD, Hugh: he was licensed in the diocese of York in place of John Purchas who had died during the administration of Archbishop Thoresby (BIA, Register 11, fol. 397r).

BRUNBY, Thomas de: he was ordained d. on 17 December 1345 at Whitefriars, York (BIA, Register 10A, fol. 13v) and p. at Durham on 23 September 1346 in the church of St Oswald, Elvet, close to Durham (Durham Registers: Hatfield, fol. 94v).

BRUNNE, Philip de: he was ordained a. on 2 June 1352 at St Mary's Abbey, York (BIA, Register 10A, fol. 55r). He was a friar of Lincoln when ordained p. on 15 June 1359 at Liddington prebendal church (LAO, Register 9D, fol. 92r).

BRUNTON, John: he was ordained a. on 17 June 1413 at Greyfriars, York (BIA, Register 18, fol. 39Fr).

BRUON, Thomas: a friar successfully presented by the minister provincial to the bishop at Boston on 16 May 1409, according to the terms of *Super cathedram* (*Reg. Repingdon*, i, pp. 149–50).

BRUSSELS (Brokcella, Bruxelles), Anthony de: he was a friar of York when he was ordained s. on 3 April 1462 at Blackfriars, York, and d. on 18 September 1462 at Greyfriars, York (BIA, Register 20, fols. 451r, 452v).

BRUSSELS (Bruxselles), Arnaldus de: he was ordained s. on 13 March 1400 at Blackfriars, York (*Reg. Scrope*, ii, pp. 55, 64, 131).

BRUSSHYN, Geoffrey: on 13 July 1312 Bishop Dalderby wrote to this friar, at the request of John of Brittany, earl of Richmond, and authorised him to absolve the earl from excommunication incurred for an assault on a cleric, monk or canon of the diocese of Lincoln (LAO, Register 3, fol. 257r).

BRYNKHILL, Richard de: he was ordained p. on 26 May 1347 at Lincoln cathedral (LAO, Register 7B, fol. 15v).

BRYNSALE, John de: he was at Doncaster in 1332 when, together with the guardian and three other friars, he was sued by John de Malghum for false imprisonment. It looks as if he held some office in the friary at this time (*Notes on Religious Houses*, i, p. 37; TNA, CP40/292, m. 141, Michaelmas term 1332). He was still there in the Trinity term of the following year, when he was mentioned once again in the plea rolls (TNA, CP40/294, m. 272).

BUGTHORPE (Bughthorp), John de: he was ordained s. on 8 March 1365 at Bishopthorpe manor chapel (BIA, Register 11, fol. 359r).

BUK, Thomas: he was a friar of York when he was ordained a. on 18 September 1490 at Whitefriars, York. He was at Scarborough when he was ordained s. on 26 February 1491 at Greyfriars, York, but back again at York when he was ordained d. on 21 April 1492 at the lady chapel of York Minster, York, and p. on 1 June 1493 at Blackfriars, York (BIA, Register 23, fols. 423v, 425v, 432r, 438v. Cf. Cross and Vickers, *MFN*, p. 437).

BUNNAY, Tilman: he was ordained p. on 19 December 1467 at Austin Friars, York (BIA, Register 22, fol. 189v).

BURDETTE (Burdet, Burdeta, Burdett), Nicholas: he was a friar of York when he was ordained a. on 18 September 1350 at Whitefriars, York. He was ordained s. 18 December 1350 at Blackfriars, York, d. on 12 March 1351; both ceremonies took place at Blackfriars, York. He was at York when he was ordained p. on 11 June 1351 at St Mary's Abbey, York (BIA, Register 10A, fols. 49r, 50r, 51r, 52r).

BURELL (Burelli), John: he was a friar of York when he was ordained d. on 24 September 1496 at Austin Friars, York (BIA, Register 23, fol. 452r. Cf. Cross and Vickers, *MFN*, p. 438).

BURGH, John: he was ordained a. on 28 May 1412 at Greyfriars, York. He was a friar of York when he was ordained d. on 23 September 1419 and p. on 15 February 1421 at Cawood prebendal chapel (BIA, Register 18, fols. 39Dr, 404r, 408v).

BURGH (Burghe), Peter: he was a friar of Richmond when he was ordained a. on 15 February 1505 at Whitefriars. He was a friar of York when he was ordained s. on 29 May 1507 at Blackfriars, York (BIA, Register 25, fols. 127r, 140v). A Frater Peter Burghe was admitted to the *Corpus Christi* guild at York in 1511 (*Corpus Christi Guild*, p. 175). He was described as a subdeacon at the Dissolution of the friary of Richmond on 18 January1539 (*Eighth Report of the Deputy Keeper of the Public Records*, p. 38. Cf. Cross and Vickers, *MFN*, pp. 441, 450).

BURGH (Burgo), Richard de: he was ordained a. on 19 September 1366 at Rose chapel, s. on 16 September 1368 in Carlisle cathedral (*Reg. Appleby*, pp. 76, 80, nn. 347, 357) and d. on 21 December 1371 at St Mary, Bishophill, York (BIA, Register 11, fol. 386r). He was a friar of Carlisle on 17 February 1409, when Archbishop Bowett licensed him to hear confessions in the deaneries of Kendal and Cartmel for two years (BIA, Register 21, fol. 17v). A friar of this name was committed to the constable of the Tower of London or his lieutenant on 16 June 1412 to be held there until further notice (*CCR, 1409–1413*, p. 278).

BURGH, William: he was a friar of Boston when he was ordained a. on 23 March 1426 at Boston parish church (*Reg. Fleming*, ii, p. 121, no. 544) and at York when ordained s. on 14 June 1427 at Blackfriars, York (BIA, Register 19, fol. 230r).

BURGUNDY (Burgundia), William de: on 9 February 1332 he was licensed to hear confessions in the diocese of Lincoln (LAO, Register 5, fol. 455v).

BURN (Burne), Philip de: he was a friar of York, when he was ordained s. on 21 February 1377 in Whitefriars, York, d. on 23 May 1377 at York Minster and p. on 19 September 1377 in St Mary's Abbey, York (BIA, Register 12, fols. 127r, 128v, 130r).

BURN, William: he was a friar of Beverley on 12 August 1410, when he received £4 in the will of Master Thomas Walkington, rector of Houghton-le-Spring in the diocese of Durham and archdeacon of Cleveland, to celebrate Mass for his soul and the faithful departed for one year. He also witnessed the will (*Wills and inventories illustrative of the history, manners, language, statistics, etc., of the northern counties of England from the eleventh century downwards*, pp. 49–51; *Reg. Langley*, i, pp. 126–28, no. 161).

BURSER, Nicholas de: Pope Nicholas III wrote to him, when he was custos of York, on 5 February 1278 regarding an appointment to be made to a prebend at York vacated by the pope, who had held such a position (*BF*, iii, pp. 284–86, no. 6; *BF*, viii, p. 142, no. 1398; *Les Registres de Nicolas III (1277–1280)*, pp. 72–73, no. 215).

BURTON, Henry de: he was ordained a. on 18 September 1344 at St Mary's Abbey, York, and s. on 18 December 1344 at Whitefriars, York (BIA, Register 10A, fols. 7v, 8v). He was ordained d. on 17 December 1345 at Liddington prebendal church (LAO, Register 7B, fol. 2v).

BURTON, Hugh de: he was a friar at York when he was ordained s. on 22 December

1375 at Cawood manor chapel and d on 19 September 1377 in St Mary's Abbey, York (BIA, Register 12, fols. 122v, 130r).

BURTON, John de: he was ordained a. on 15 March 1348 at Blackfriars, Northampton. He was a friar of Leicester when he was ordained d. on 20 September 1348 at Blackfriars, Leicester. He was ordained p. on 6 June 1349 at Grantham parish church (LAO, Register 9D, fols. 1v, 7v 15v).

BURTON, John: he was a friar of Grantham when he was ordained a. on 20 May 1497 in the prebendal church of Sleaford, s. on 17 December 1502 in the prebendal church of Liddington, d. on 6 April 1504 in the prebendal church of Buckden. He was a friar of Lincoln when he was ordained p. on 21 September 1504 in the chapel of St Mary Magdalene at Lincoln cathedral (LAO, Register 24, fols. 8r, 37v, 44v, 46v).

BURTON, Robert de: he was at Leicester when he was ordained s. on 22 May 1372 at Sawley prebendal church and at Nottingham when he was ordained p. on 20 December 1376 at Colwich prebendal church (*Reg. Stretton*, pp. 259, 313). He is perhaps to be identified with a friar of this name, a cousin of Thomas Walkyngton, rector of Houghton-le-Spring and archdeacon of Cleveland, who left him £10, a breviary, a little Bible and a book of seven gifts in his will of 12 August 1412 (*Northern Wills & Inventories*, i, p. 50; *Reg. Langley*, i, pp. 125–26, no. 161). A friar Richard Burton received 20s. in the will of John Olney in 1420, but it is not certain to which order he belonged (Furnivall, *Fifty Earliest English Wills*, p. 48).

BURTON, Thomas de: he was ordained s. on 20 December 1298 in the prebendal church at Liddington (*Reg. Sutton*, vii, p. 112). On 24 January 1319 King Edward II was at York, when he gave this friar and John de la Lee, royal chaplains, a safe-conduct for one year to attend the general chapter of Marseille (*CPR, 1317–1321*, p. 268).

BURTON, Thomas: he was a friar of Worcester when he was ordained a. on 6 June 1411 (Worcester Registers: Peverel, fol. 188r) and at Bridgenorth when he was ordained s. and d. on 19 September and 19 December 1411 (LRO, B, A, 1/7, fol. 232rv). He was probably at Worcester when ordained p. in 1414 (*Reg. Mascall*, p. 160). He was licensed to hear confessions in the diocese of York on 5 January 1444, when he is described as *sacre theologie doctor* (BIA, Register 19, fol. 86v). He received 20s. for preaching before the king in March 1442 (TNA, E.161/409/9, fol. 33r). Under the year 1455 Luke Wadding describes him as a professor of sacred theology in the island and monastery of St Columba within the province of York (*Annales Minorum*, xii, p. 348, no. 300). On 25 September 1455 he was dispensed from defect of birth in order to receive the administration of the see of Sodor and Man or the Isles. Five days later he was provided to the diocese (*BF, ns*, ii, p. 44, nn. 83–84; *CPL*, xi, p. 233). Cenci reproduces a text to show that the papal provision took place in a secret consistory 'ad relationem d. cardinalis (Latini) de Ursinis'. On 15 October, Thomas, bishop of Sodor and Man, paid 30 gold florins. Ten days later he made a payment of 16 florins, 33s. 4d. (Cenci, 'Documenta Vaticana', part 4, p. 244; Brady, *The succession in England, Scotland and Ireland A.D. 1400 to 1875*, i, p. 107). His episcopal seal survives in the BL, an impression in red sealing wax, and another and sulphur caste (nn. xxxvi, 220, xliii, 182, D.C., G.68; Thompson, *Catalogue of Seals*, p. 420). In recording Burton's death the papal bull, dated 21 June 1458, states that the diocese of Sodor and Man was a suffragan diocese of York (*CPL*, xi, p. 359; *Monumenta de insula Manniae*, ed. J.R. Oliver, Manx Society, 3 vols, 4, 7, 9, Isle of Man, 1860–62, iii, pp. 21–22). Parkinson gives his name as Button (*Collectanea Anglo-minoritica: or, A collection of the antiquities of the English Franciscans, or Friers minors, commonly call'd Gray friers: in two part: with an appendix concerning the English nuns of the Order of Saint Clare*, p. 204). Burton's will was drawn up on 18 February 1458 (Stubbs, *Registrum Sacrum Anglicanum*, p. 212; *Le Neve*, iii, p. 326, quoting Booth's register). He was dead by 21 June 1458 (*CPL*, xi, p. 359).

BURY, Thomas: one of the three friars at York in 1415 when he was accused by Henry Lescrop, chivaler, of seizing his wife Joan, at Faxfleet, and abducting and detaining her and certain goods and chattels (*Notes on Religious Houses*, ii, p. 93).

BUSS (Bus, Busse), John: he was ordained s. on 18 December 1350 and d. on 12 March 1351; both ceremonies took place at Blackfriars, York. He was ordained p. on 17 December 1351 at Austin Friars, York (BIA, Register 10A, fols. 50r, 51r, 54r).

BUSSELL, John: he was at Boston when ordained p. on 17 December 1496 at All Saints, Northampton (LAO, Register 24, fol. 6r).

BUTLER (Boteler), John: he was ordained d. on 20 September 1343 at Whitefriars, York (BIA, Register 10A, fol. 5r) and p. on 20 December 1343 in Durham cathedral (*Reg. Kellaw*, iii, p. 136). He was at Beverley on 1 December 1356 when he asked leave of the town to take sand for the completion of the friars' building (*Beverley Town Documents*, p. 18; *Report on the Manuscripts of the Corporation of Beverley*, p. 64). On the same day he requested a licence from the same governors to gather fallen timber in Westwood (Poulson, *Beverlac; or, The antiquities and history of the town of Beverley, in the county of York*, ii, p. 771).

BYKHALL, John: he was ordained d. on 20 September 1393 at St Leonard's Hospital, in York (BIA, Register 14, fol. 68r).

BYKYNBY, William: he was at York when he was ordained d. on 13 March 1378 at Holy Trinity Priory, Micklegate, York (BIA, Register 12, fol. 131v).

BYRE, Thomas: he was the guardian of Doncaster in Trinity term 1425, when his name appeared in the plea rolls (TNA, CP40/658, m. 152d).

BYRLEY, John: on 25 August 1396 he received 100s. in the will of Robert Morton of Bawtry, who requested burial in the lady chapel of the conventual church of Worksop and gave alms to the friary in Doncaster (*TE*, i, pp. 210–14, at 213).

BYRS (Buse, Byrys), Robert: he was a friar of York when he was ordained a. on 18 December 1423, s. on 18 March 1424, both at York Minster, and d. on 22 April 1424 at St Michael-le-Belfrey, York (BIA, Register 5A, fols. 354r, 355v, 368v; *Reg. Sede Vacante, York, 1423–26*, pp. 99, 103, 125). He was a friar of Lincoln when he was ordained p. on 2 June 1425 in the prebendal church of Liddington, his name being then given as Byrys (*Reg. Fleming*, ii, pp. 114, 118, nn. 522, 542).

BYRY (Bury), Robert: he was ordained a. on 13 March 1378 at Holy Trinity Priory, Micklegate, York, d. on 12 June 1378 at York Minster and p. on 4 June 1379 at St Mary's Abbey, York (BIA, Register 12, fols. 131r, 133r, 134v).

CADE (Kade), John: he was a friar of York when he was ordained a. on 6 March

1501 at Greyfriars, York (BIA, Register 5A, fol. 530r; BL, MS. Cotton, Galba, E.X, fol. 145r). He was a friar of Lincoln when he was ordained s. on 27 March 1501 in the lady chapel of Lincoln cathedral, d. on 10 April 1501 in Lincoln cathedral, and p. on 21 September 1504 in the chapel of St Mary Magdalene in Lincoln cathedral (LAO, Register 24, fols. 27v, 28v, 46v).

CAISTOR (Castell, Castro), John de: he was ordained s. on 19 December 1366 at St Leonard's Hospital, York, and d. on 13 March 1367 at St Mary, Bishophill Senior, York (BIA, Register 11, fols. 364v, 365r).

CAISTOR (Castro), Simon de: he was licensed to hear confessions in the diocese of Lincoln on 29 October 1319 in place of the deceased William of Calverley (LAO, Register 3, fol. 427r).

CALERE, John: this friar was left 25 marks to celebrate Masses for the souls of Richard de Ravensere, Nicholas de Louth, John de Wendlyngburgh and Master Robert of Beverley, canon of Beverley, in the will of Robert Manfield, clerk and provost of Beverley, on 12 April 1419 (*North Country Wills*, i, pp. 20–25).

CALTHORN, Thomas de: he was ordained a. on 2 June 1352 at St Mary's Abbey, York (BIA, Register 10A, fol. 55r). He was a friar of Boston when he was ordained s. on 19 May 1353 in Stow prebendal church (LAO, Register 9D, fol. 66v).

CALVERLEY (Calverle), William de: he received a letter written on 10 August 1311 by Queen Isabella, wife of Edward II (*The household book of Queen Isabella of England for the fifth regnal year of Edward II, 8 July 1311 to 7 July 1312*, pp. 206–07). He was probably a friar of Doncaster on 19 March 1315 when he was licensed to hear the confessions of the Cistercian nuns of Hampole (*Reg. Greenfield*, ii, p. 210) and again on 31 January 1318 (BIA, Register 9, fol. 481r). Shortly afterwards he was transferred to one of the friaries in Lincolnshire, probably Grimsby, and on 20 June 1318 he was licensed for the diocese of Lincoln (LAO, Register 3, fol. 390r). He died about a year afterwards and was replaced by Simon de Caistor on 29 October 1319. He was then said to be in middle age (*ibid.*, fol. 427r; Robson, 'William de Calverley (c.1275–1319), a notable Franciscan friar active in the custody of York: some biographical notes').

CAMBRIDGE, Richard: he was a friar of York when he was ordained a. on 6 March 1501 at Greyfriars, York (BIA, Register 5A, fol. 530r; BL, MS. Cotton, Galba, E.X., fol. 145r). He was a friar of Lincoln when he was ordained s. on 27 March 1501 in the lady chapel of Lincoln cathedral, d. on 10 April 1501 and p. on 23 September 1503 in the cathedral (LAO, Register 24, fols. 27v, 28v, 42).

CAMPI, Otto: he was a friar of York when he was ordained d. on 2 March 1420 at Cawood prebendal chapel (BIA, Register 18, fol. 405r).

CAMYN (Camen), John: he was a friar of York when he was ordained a. on 22 September 1442 at York Minster and d. on 7 March 1444 at Whitefriars, York (BIA, Register 19, fols. 220v, 222v).

CAMPYS, Andrew: he was a friar of York when he was ordained d. on 23 September 1419 at Cawood prebendal chapel (BIA, Register 18, fols. 404r, 222v).

CANDISBY, Simon: he was ordained a. on 1 June 1398 in St Michael-le-Belfrey, York (BIA, Register 5A, fol. 255r; BL, MS. Cotton Galba, E.X, fol. 119v).

CAPELLA, John de: he was ordained d. on 21 September 1409 at Cawood prebendal church (BIA, Register 18, fol. 391r).

CAPELODE: see Whaplode.

CARBURTON (Kerbelston'), Robert de: he was ordained p. on 31 May 1292 in Lincoln cathedral (*Reg. Sutton*, vii, p. 30).

CARETHORP, Thomas: he was the son of Thomas Carethorp of Scarborough, whose profession is not recorded, and the brother of Robert. It seems that Thomas senior had married twice and that his second wife was named Margaret, who bore him two more sons, William and John, described as *pueri nostri*. They were parishioners of St Mary's at Scarborough. Thomas's will, written on 11 November 1426, reveals the extent of his estate and properties, some of them in the vicinity of the local Greyfriars. He asked for burial in the *Corpus Christi* chapel in the parish church of St Mary and made the customary mortuary offering to the rector of the parish. He bequeathed to Margaret various properties, including one opposite the chapel of St Sepulchre. He identified Robert, his son, as his heir, leaving him a portion in what is called Grayfrere Lane, beside the house of St Leonard. The friar received 13s. 4d. for the purchase of a new habit. Nothing further is known of this friar, who undoubtedly spent some time at the friary in York (BIA, Probate Register 2, fol. 500rv).

CARLISLE, Alexander de: the archbishop of York announced on 7 March 1320 that he had received papal bulls, which he had sent to the bishop of Durham. The latter announced that he had passed them to this friar, the guardian of Newcastle, for transmission to Robert Bruce (*Reg. Melton*, iii, pp. 32–33, 138, nn. 64, 231). He was guardian of Newcastle 1319–20 (*Papers and Letters from the Northern Registers*, p. 301).

CARLISLE (Karle, Karlo, Karlell), Robert de: he was ordained a. on 15 September 1369 and s. on 30 March 1370; both ceremonies were at Rose chapel (*Reg. Appleby*, pp. 81, 83, nn. 361, 364). On 23 September 1426 William Schroude, a chaplain of Richmond, asked for burial in the town's Greyfriars and left 3s. 4d. to a friar of this name, probably resident at Richmond (BIA, Probate Register 2, fol. 503r).

CARLISLE (Carlele, Karlele), Simon: he was a friar of Richmond when he was ordained s. on 22 September 1397 at Holy Trinity Priory, Micklegate, York (*Reg. Waldby*, p. 47) and p. on 22 February 1399 at Cawood prebendal church (*Reg. Scrope*, ii, pp. 38, 87, 131).

CARLISLE (Carlell, Carliol), Thomas de: he was ordained d. on 18 December 1372 in the Galilee chapel of Durham cathedral (Durham Registers: Hatfield, fol. 110v). He was a friar of Carlisle on 17 February 1409, when he was licensed to hear confessions in the deaneries of Copeland and Furness for two years (BIA, Register 21, fol. 18v).

CARLISLE (Karlo), William de: he was ordained s. on 17 February 1364 at Dalston (*Reg. Appleby*, p. 74, no. 339).

CARLISLE (Karliol), William de: he was a friar of York when he was licensed to hear confessions in the city and diocese of York on 27 October 1326 and again on 8 April 1327. On the second occasion he was presented in accordance with the terms of *Super cathedram* (BIA, Register 9, fols. 204v, 207r).

CARLISLE (Carlill), William: he was a friar of York when he was ordained a. on 19 September 1450 at Greyfriars, York, s. on 26 May 1453 at Blackfriars, York, d. on 22 December 1453 at Austin Friars, York, and p. on 21 September 1454 at Blackfriars, York (BIA, Register 19, fol. 295v, Register 20, fols. 415r, 416v, 418v).

CASSELDIA, Gerardus de: he was ordained p. on 22 December 1470 at Austin Friars, York (BIA, Register 22, fol. 208v).

CASTLE (Castell, Castro, Castle), Robert del: he was ordained a. on 22 September 1369 at the episcopal manor of Bishopthorpe, s. on 30 March 1370 at the episcopal manor of Bishopthorpe, and d. on 22 May 1372 at St Mary, Bishophill Senior (BIA, Register 11, fols. 375r, 377v, 388r).

CASTLE (Castle, Castr', Castro), Thomas de: he was ordained a. on 29 May 1344 at Newark parish church, s. on 18 December 1344 at Whitefriars, York, and d. on 24 September 1345 (BIA, Register 10A, fols. 6r, 8v, 13r).

CASUR (Caser), William: he was a friar of York when he was ordained d. on 18 December 1484 at Austin Friars, York, and p. on 11 March 1486 at Holy Trinity Priory, Micklegate, York (BIA, Register 23, fols. 394v, 400v. Cf. Cross and Vickers, *MFN*, p. 436).

CATHORP (Cathorpe, Catthorpe), Thomas de: he was a friar of Lincoln when he was licensed to hear confessions in that diocese on 10 August 1300. On 12 October of the same year he was licensed to hear confessions within the *limitatio* of the same house (Little, *Franciscan Papers, Lists, and Documents*, pp. 237–38).

CATTERICK (Ceteryk), Nicholas: he was a friar of York when he was ordained d. on 18 May 1448 at Holy Trinity Priory, Micklegate, York (BIA, Register 19, fol. 280rA).

CAUSBY, Simon: he was a friar of Boston, when he was ordained s. on 22 February 1399 at Stow prebendal church (LAO, Register 13, fol. 84v).

CAYSO, John: he was ordained p. on 22 September 1358 in the manor chapel at Bishop Burton near Beverley (BIA, Register 11, fol. 335r).

CAYTHORPE (Catthorpe), Richard de: he was ordained d. on 20 September 1292 in the parish church of St Giles, Northampton (*Reg. Sutton*, vii, p. 32).

CHABWORTH (Chaworth), Thomas: he was a friar of Boston when he was ordained a. and s. on 16 March 1426 and 25 May 1426; both ordinations were held in Boston parish church (*Reg. Fleming*, ii, pp. 121, 124, nn. 544, 546).

CHAMBERLAIN (Chamberleyn), Robert: he was ordained d. on 18 December 1350 and p. on 12 March 1351; both ceremonies took place at Blackfriars, York (BIA, Register 10A, fols. 50r, 51r). He was licensed in the diocese of York in place of Robert de Rymeswell (BIA, Register 11, fol. 396r).

CHAPMAN, Richard: he was a friar of York when he was ordained a. on 26 March 1502 in the lady chapel of York Minster, s. on 23 September 1503 at Greyfriars, York, and d. on 20 September 1505 in Bishopthorpe manor chapel (BIA, Register 25, fols. 111v, 120r, 130r). A petition to the crown from John Dobson, vicar of Muston, on 3 December 1537 described his meeting with this friar around the time of the Pilgrimage of Grace. He was shown certain prophecies by the prior of the Carmelites at Scarborough (*LPFD*, xii, pt. ii, pp. 427–28, no. 1212). Either this friar or the one of the same name was the guardian who surrendered the friary at Scarborough on 9 March 1539 (*Eighth Report of the Deputy Keeper of the Public Records*, p. 187. Cf. *LPFD*, xiv, pt. i, p. 188, no. 482; Goldthorp, 'The Franciscans and Dominicans in Yorkshire', 320, citing Conventual Leases, Yorks., nn. 898, 903, 904). He received a faculty to change his habit on 20 June 1539 (Chambers, *Faculty Office Registers 1534–1549*, p. 187). This former friar was unlikely to be identified with a priest of this name, who held a chantry dedicated to Our Lady in Scarborough parish church, which was worth 63s. 8d. a year in 1548, when he was 58 years old: he was of 'good condicions and qualities, and well lerened' (*Chantries, Guilds, Hospitals*, ii, p. 513). Margaret Harwod of Scarborough gave him a new sheet 'that is not sewed' in her will of August 1547 (BIA, Probate Register 13, pt. I, fol. 429v; Cross and Vickers, *MFN*, pp. 440, 451, 452).

CHAPMAN, Richard: he was a friar of York when he was ordained a. on 22 December 1509 at an unspecified venue and s. on 21 September 1510 at Holy Trinity Priory, Micklegate, York (BIA, Register 26, fol. 104v, 109r. Cross and Vickers, *MFN*, pp. 442, 452).

CHAPMAN, Thomas: he was a friar of Lincoln when he was ordained s. on 12 April 1533 in Lincoln cathedral and p. on 4 April 1534 in the lady chapel of Lincoln cathedral; he was examined by the prior of St Katherine's priory at Lincoln (LAO, Register 33, fols. 33v, 39r). He was one of the six friars of Grimsby at the Dissolution on 9 October 1538 (*Eighth Report of the Deputy Keeper of the Public Records*, p. 22).

CHEBWORTH, Thomas: he was a friar of York when he was ordained d. on 18 September 1428 at York Minster (BIA, Register 19, fol. 216v).

CHERYNG (Cheryng or Schyryng), John: he was a friar of Lincoln when he was ordained s. on 19 September 1355 in Lincoln cathedral. He was a friar of Nottingham when he was ordained d. on 9 April 1356 at Liddington prebendal church. He was a friar of Stamford when he was ordained p. on 30 May 1360 in Sleaford prebendal church (LAO, Register 9D, fols. 77r, 80r, 96r).

CHESTER (Cestria), John de: he was ordained a. on 10 June 1346 at Whitefriars, York (BIA, Register 10A, fol. 15r).

CHESTER, John: he was ordained a. on 8 March 1516 at All Saints, Northampton. He was a friar of Chester when he was ordained s. on 19 March 1519 at Greyfriars, York, and he was a friar of Grantham when ordained d. on 23 April 1519 in Lincoln cathedral (LAO, Register 25, fols. 117r, 129r). He was a friar of York when he was ordained p. on 20 December 1522 at Austin Friars, York (BIA, Register 27, fols. 183r, 197v). He was a friar of Nottingham at the Dissolution on 5 February 1538 (*Eighth Report of the Deputy Keeper of the Public Records*, p. 35; Cross and Vickers, *MFN*, p. 444).

CHESTER (Cestre), Roger de: he was licensed to hear confessions in the diocese of York, but died before 17 October 1347 (BIA, Register 10, fol. 278r).

CHESTER (Chestre), Thomas de: he was a friar of Richmond when he was ordained s. on 28 March 1444 at St Mary's, Castlegate, York. He was a friar of York when he was ordained d. on 20 February 1445 at Greyfriars, York, and at Richmond again when he was ordained p. on 18 September 1445 at Austin Friars, York (BIA, Register 19, fols. 223r, 280v, 282v).

CHINON (Chinone), Nicholas de: Friar Robert de Trikenham (Tregumham) heard an account from an unnamed lady, and he, in turn, communicated it to Nicholas that an unnamed Templar had a son who saw that the military order murdered an aspirant. Whereupon he told his father that he did not wish to join the order. He, too, was killed by his father. Nicholas's evidence was supplied in 1310 (Nicholson, *Templars*, i, pp. xxvi, 185, 381, 399, ii, pp. xxxiii–xxxiv, 194, 435, 456).

CLAPHAM, William de: he was ordained a. on 7 June 1343 at Greyfriars, York, s. on 10 June 1346 at Whitefriars, York, and d. on 15 March 1348 in York Minster (BIA, Register 10A, fols. 3v, 15v, 21v).

CLARKE (Clerk, Clerke), Robert: he was a friar of York when he was ordained a. on 18 September 1462 at Greyfriars, York, s. on 5 March 1463 at Blackfriars, York, d. on 4 June 1463 at Whitefriars, York, and p. on 17 December 1463 at Austin Friars, York (BIA, Register 20, fols. 452v, 454r, 456r, 457v).

CLARKE (Clark), Thomas: he was a friar of Lincoln when he was ordained a. on 2 September 1504 in the chapel of St Mary Magdalene, Lincoln cathedral (LAO, Register 24, fol. 46r).

CLARKE (Clerk), William: he was ordained s. on 18 September 1479 at Whitefriars, York, and d. on 7 April 1481 at Holy Trinity Priory, Micklegate, York (BIA, Register 22, fol. 380r, Register 23, fol. 375r. Cf. Cross and Vickers, *MFN*, p. 435). On 1 September 1488 he was licensed to hear confessions in the diocese of York (*Reg. Rotherham*, p. 226, no. 1784).

CLARKE (Clark), William: he was a friar of Lincoln when he was ordained s. on 26 March 1524 (LAO, Register 26, fol. 9r). A friar called William Clerke was at London on 6 September 1539 when he received his capacity (Chambers, *Faculty Office Registers 1534–1549*, p. 149).

CLAXEBY, Martin: he was a friar of Boston through whom the royal alms were paid on 12 September 1328 (TNA, E.101/383/14).

CLAXTON, Laurence: he was a friar of Newcastle when he was ordained a. in the chapel of the south aisle of Durham cathedral on 30 March 1499 (*Reg. Fox*, p. 85). He was a friar of York when he was ordained d. on 2 March 1504 at Whitefriars, York, and p. on 23 March 1504 at Greyfriars, York (BIA, Register 25, fols. 122r, 123r. Cf. Cross and Vickers, *MFN*, p. 441).

CLAY, John: he was a friar of York when he was ordained a. on 17 December 1446 at Whitefriars, York (BIA, Register 19, fol. 285v). He was a friar of Nottingham when he was ordained d. on 30 May 1450 in St Margaret in the close of Lincoln cathedral (LAO, Register 19, fol. 16r). He was back at York when he was ordained p. on 22 December 1453 at Austin Friars, York (BIA, Register 20, fol. 416v). A friar of this name was admitted to the *Corpus Christi* guild at York in 1463/64. The next entry is for John Clay and his wife, Margaret. Were they his parents? (*Corpus Christi Register*, p. 64).

CLAYTON (Claiton), Ralph: he was a friar of Oxford when he was ordained d. on 19 December 1528 in the prebendal church of Liddington (LAO, Register 26, fol. 23r). He was a friar of York when he was ordained p. on 25 March 1531 at Austin Friars, York (BIA, Register 5A, fol. 670v). He was then aged 22. He was at York at the Dissolution on 27 November 1538 (*Eighth Report of the Deputy Keeper of the Public Records*, p. 51). On 13 November 1544 William Vavasour, the last guardian, left him all the books in his study, apart from the 26 he had already bestowed, and appointed him one of the executors of his will (*York Clergy Wills 1520–1600: II. City Clergy*, ii, pp. 33–35). The former friar is likely to be associated with the priest of the same name who obtained a chantry in St Mary, Castlegate, York, worth £6 6s. 8d. a year. In 1548 he was said to be 39 years old and deemed to be a man 'of honest qualities and condicions, and well lerened' (*Chantries, Guilds, Hospitals*, ii, p. 466). He spoke Latin 'very often in his sickness, and most especially in his extreme sickness'.

Almost immediately after the Marian restoration, he lost his chantry and obtained the living of Hutton Buscel. About the feast of St Peter *ad vincula* in 1553 he married Emma Barnebie. Falling ill in the autumn of that year, when the Marian authorities were once more enforcing celibacy upon the clergy, he was particularly concerned about his wife's fate. Having made his will with Robert Cawdbeck and Nicholas Robinson, clerks, in attendance, a month before he died on Christmas eve, he had it read out several times in the presence of some of his parishioners. He urged John Horton, husbandman, to be 'good to the said Emme and not to fail her in any her business, if she should have any concerning his goods which he had given her'. Clayton's fears for Emma's inheritance proved to be well founded. In the court case over the will in 1554 the lawyers argued that Clayton, as a former friar, could not have contracted a valid marriage, while Emma, now regarded as no more than a priest's concubine, could not legally receive the goods which he had left her. The outcome of the case is not recorded, though Emma cannot have been left destitute because she had already married Lionel Birte before the suit began (Consistory Court Act Book, 18, fol. 317v; Chancery Court Act, 7, fols. 51v–55v, 63r, 76rv, 84r, 86v, 87r, 88rv, 89v, 91v, 93v; Cause Papers, G 3441; Cross and Vickers, *MFN*, pp. 445, 456–57).

CLEE, William: he was a friar of York when he was ordained s. on 10 June 1419 at Cawood prebendal chapel and p. on 6 June 1422 at Blackfriars, York (BIA, Register 18, fols. 403r, 413r).

CLEMETT, Hugh: he was a friar of York when he was ordained p. on 26 May 1442 at Blackfriars, York (BIA, Register 19, fol. 267r).

CLIFF (Clyff), Richard: he was ordained a. on 20 March 1451 in St Margaret's in the close of Lincoln cathedral (LAO, Register 19, fols. 29v, 56r).

CLIFF, William de: he was licensed to hear confessions in the diocese of York on 14 June 1350 (BIA, Register 10, fol. 279r).

CLIFFE (Cliffe), John: he was a friar of Lincoln when he was ordained s. on 20 April 1538 in Lincoln cathedral, having been examined by Doctor Cliff', the chancellor of the diocese (LAO, Register 26, fol. 57v).

CLIFTON (Clyffton), Robert de: he was a friar of York when he was ordained a. on 18 September 1350 at Whitefriars, York (BIA, Register 10A, fol. 49r). He was a friar of Boston when he was ordained d. on 22 December 1352 in Stow prebendal church (LAO, Register 9D, fol. 64r). He was back at York when ordained p. on 4 March 1357 at Bishopthorpe manor chapel (BIA, Register 11, fol. 330r).

CLIFTON (Clyfton), Thomas: he was a friar of York when ordained a. on 18 September 1428 at York Minster (BIA, Register 19, fol. 216r). He was a friar of Lincoln when ordained p. on 7 March 1433 at Sleaford prebendal church (LAO, Register 17, fol. 210v).

CLOUGH (Clowgh, Clugh), Richard: he was a friar of York when he was ordained s. on 17 December 1407 at Holy Trinity Priory, Micklegate, York (BIA, Register 5A, fol. 325v; *Reg. Sede Vacante, 1405–08*, pp. 66, 70, 89). He was ordained d. on 9 June 1408 at Blackfriars, York (BIA, Register 18, fol. 39r). He was ordained p. on 28 May 1412 at Greyfriars, York (BIA, Register 18, fol. 39Dv).

CLYNT, John: he was ordained d. on 18 September 1400 at All Saints, Cawood (*Reg. Scrope*, ii, pp. 55, 69, 131).

CLYNTON (Chynton), William: he was a friar of Boston when he was ordained p. on 24 May 1404 in the prebendal church of Liddington (LAO, Register 13, fol. 115r).

COBLENZ (Confluencia), Christianus de: he was ordained p. on 24 May 1404 at Cawood prebendal church (*Reg. Scrope*, ii, pp. 55, 70, 131).

COBUGHAM, John de: he was ordained s. on 17 December 1345 at Liddington prebendal church (LAO, Register 7B, fol. 2r).

COK (Cocq), Harman: he was a friar of Lincoln when he was ordained p. on 15 March 1432 in Sleaford prebendal church (LAO, Register 17, fol. 206r).

COKE (Cok), John: he was a friar of York when he was ordained s. on 24 February 1537 at Austin Friars, York (BIA, Register 28, fol. 197r). He may have been the priest of this name who witnessed a will in Beeford in 1543 (BIA, Probate Register 11, pt. II, fol. 691v; Cross and Vickers, *MFN*, pp. 445, 457).

COKERHAM, William: on 13 June 1404 John Hebbesson of Kerkgate in York asked for burial in the church of the York Greyfriars. He left 10s. to the friary, and Friar William Cokerham, probably a member of that community, was asked to celebrate for his soul and the souls of all the faithful departed for the period of two years after his death and was left the sum of £8 (BIA, Probate Register 3, fol. 110r).

COKSHILL, William de: he was ordained a. on 15 March 1348 at Northampton Blackfriars (LAO, Register 9D, fol. 1v).

COLEKERR, William: he was a friar of York when he was ordained d. on 6 June 1444 at Blackfriars, York (BIA, Register 19, fol. 280r).

COLLINGHAM (Colyngham), John: he was ordained d. on 18 September 1350 in Lincoln cathedral (LAO, Register 9D, fol. 45r).

COLMAN, Robert: he was a friar successfully presented by the minister provincial to the bishop at Boston on 16 May 1409, according to the terms of *Super cathedram* (*Reg. Repingdon*, i, pp. 149–50).

COLOGNE (Colonia), Adam de: he was ordained p. on 23 May 1472 at Blackfriars, York (BIA, Register 22, fol. 216r).

COLOGNE (Colonia), Alberdus de: he was a friar of York when he was ordained p. on 19 December 1461 at Austin Friars, York (BIA, Register 20, fol. 450r).

COLOGNE (Colonia), Anthony de: he was a friar of York when he was ordained p. on 26 May 1464 at Blackfriars, York (BIA, Register 20, fol. 460r).

COLOGNE (Colonia), Helpricus: he was ordained s. on 15 February 1410 in St Martin's chapel, le charnel, Beverley (BIA, Register 18, fol. 39Av).

COLOGNE (Colonia), James de: he was a friar of York when he was ordained a. on 26 March 1463 at Greyfriars, York (BIA, Register 20, fol. 454v).

COLOGNE (Colonia), John de: on 1 March 1408 the bishop of Lincoln granted a licence to John de Cologne, a friar of Cologne, to absolve German compatriots, religious and secular, living at or visiting Boston in reserved cases, with the usual exceptions (*Reg. Repingdon*, i, pp. 114–15).

COLOGNE (Colonia), John de: he was ordained d. on 20 December 1410 at Cawood prebendal church (BIA, Register 18, fol. 393r).

COLOGNE (Colonia), John de: he was a friar of Boston when he was ordained p. on 6 June 1422 at Liddington prebendal church (LAO, Register 16, fol. 180v).

COLOGNE (Colonia, Davendria), Martin de: he was ordained s. on 20 September 1410 at Cawood prebendal church (BIA, Register 18, fol. 392v; Walmsley, 'Some Dutch Franciscans in England during the Later Middle Ages', p. 250).

COLOGNE (Colonia), Michael de: he was ordained a. on 28 May 1412, s. on 24 September 1412 and d. on 17 December 1412. All three ceremonies occurred at Greyfriars, York (BIA, Register 18, fols. 39Drv, 395v).

COLOGNE (Colonia), Rumbald de: he was a friar of York when he was ordained d. on 24 February 1369 at Bishopthorpe manor chapel and p. on 21 December 1370 at Whitefriars, York (BIA, Register 11, fols. 373r, 381r).

COLOGNE (Colonia), Walrannus de: he was ordained d. on 21 May 1429 at Blackfriars, York (BIA, Register 19, fol. 235r).

COLOGNE (Colonia), William de: he was a friar of Leicester when he was ordained d. on 13 June 1394 at Eccleshall prebendal church (LRO, B/A/1/6, fol. 152r). He was ordained p. on 1 June 1398 in St Michael-le-Belfrey, York (BIA, Register 5A, fol. 256v; BL, MS. Cotton Galba, E.X, fol. 120v).

COLSUL (Colsull), William: he was ordained s. on 6 June 1349 at Grantham parish church (LAO, Register 9D, fol. 13r).

COLT, John: he was a friar of York when he was ordained p. on 10 March 1498 at Greyfriars, York (BIA, Register 23, fol. 458v. Cf. Cross and Vickers, *MFN*, p. 439).

COLTHORP, William de: on 5 October 1331 he received the royal alms for the Cambridge friars (TNA, E403/259, m. 1, TNA, E403/261, mem. 1, TNA, E403/260, mem. 2). He also seems to have received the alms for the Oxford friary on 22 October 1331 (TNA, E403/259, m. 3, TNA, E403/261, mem. 5, TNA, E403/260, mem. 4). He was licensed to hear confessions in the archdeaconry of Stow on 23 November 1335 (LAO, Register 5, fol. 517v).

COLYN (Gollyn), William: he was a friar of York when he was ordained a. on 19 September 1506 in Tadcaster parish church, s. on 20 March 1507 at Greyfriars, York, d. on 3 March 1509 at Greyfriars, York, and p. on 24 March 1509 at Blackfriars, York (BIA, Register 25, fols. 135r, 138r, Register 26, fols. 100r, 101r. Cf. Cross and Vickers, *MFN*, p. 442).

CONSTANTIA, John de: he was ordained p. on 1 March 1393 at the parish church of St Michael-le-Belfrey, York (BIA, Register 14, fol. 66r).

COPMANTHORPE (Copmanford, Coupmanthorp), Laurence: he was a friar of Scarborough when he was ordained d. on 18 December 1344 at Whitefriars, York (BIA, Register 10A, fol. 9r). He was ordained p. on 6 June 1349 in the prebendal church of Grantham (LAO, Register 9D, fol. 15r).

CORBITT (Corbett), John: he was a friar of York when he was ordained a. on 17 December 1468 at Austin Friars, York, s. on 27 May 1469 at Blackfriars, York, and d. on 16 June 1470 at Blackfriars, York (BIA, Register 22, fols. 197r, 201r, 206r). He was probably at York on 26 February 1489 when William Cerff, rector of the church of Rowley in the East Riding, asked him to celebrate a trental of Masses for him (BIA, Probate Register 5, fols. 357v–58r). A Frater John Corbett was admitted to the *Corpus Christi* guild at York in 1492 (*Corpus Christi Register*, p. 133).

CORBRIDGE (Colebruge), Ralph de: according to Mariano of Florence, Ralph expounded the greater part of the Bible and commented on the four books of the *Sentences* (Anonymus, Directio Periodici, 'Compendium Chronicarum Fratrum Minorum scriptum a Patre Mariano de Florentia', p. 102). He was a regent master of theology at the University of Paris, when he informed Alexander of Hales about a dream in which the devil tried to rub his face in excrement as he slept. Shortly afterwards a messenger arrived from England with news that he had been offered a prebend worth 300 marks. The interpretation of this dream led him to the order. After a short time he was sent to England (Oliger, 'Liber exemplorum fratrum minorum saeculi XIII', pp. 264–65). There is another version of this event in Bernard of Bessa's 'Liber de laudibus beati Francisci', p. 1275. As a novice he was sent to Oxford by the minister general, Crescentius da Iesi, and became the second Franciscan regent master there in 1244/45 (Eccleston, p. 50; *GFO*, p. 139; *BRUO*, p. 484; *Letters of Adam Marsh*, i, p. xvi). He and Adam Marsh received a letter from Bishop Grosseteste about the appointment to benefices (*Letters of Adam Marsh*, i, pp. 40–41). LPL, MS.57, a glossed copy of the Pauline epistles, folio 1 recto, contains this inscription: *iste liber est de communitate fratrum minorum Lincoln ex legato fr.Radulfi de corbrige*. Bartholomew of Pisa refers to him and Ralph of Maidstone as *orbi scientia praelucentes, ordinem ingrediendo, scientia et vita Anglicos imbuerunt* (*Bartholomew de Pisa*, p. 339). Leland attests that Ralph lectured with verve and aplomb at Oxford to the great gain of his audience (*Leland, De viris illustribus*, pp. 456–57, no. 250; Little, 'The Franciscan School at Oxford in the Thirteenth Century', pp. 837–38).

COOTS (Cotes), Thomas: he was a friar of York when he was ordained a. on 21 December 1510 at Austin Friars, York, s. on 15 March 1511 at Whitefriars, York, d. on 5 April 1511 at Greyfriars, York, and p. on 20 September 1511 at Holy Trinity Priory, Micklegate, York (BIA, Register 26, fols. 110r, 111r, 112v, 115v). A Thomas Cottis was asked to celebrate a trental of Masses for John Serlle, a parishioner of St Cuthbert's at Sessay, whose will was written on 26 November 1532, and refers to this friar as *our lemyto*'; he was probably a friar of York at the time (BIA, Probate Register 11, fol. 34r). He was at Scarborough when he received his capacity on 20 June 1539 (Chambers, *Faculty Office Registers 1534–1549*, p. 187. Cf. Cross and Vickers, *MFN*, pp. 443, 453).

CORKBY (Korkeby), John: he was a friar of Carlisle when he was ordained a. on 31 May 1382 at Rose chapel (*Reg. Apple*by, p. 103, no. 420). He was ordained d. on 20 December 1382 at an unspecified venue (BIA, Register 12, fol. 140v).

CORNELIUS, son of John: he was ordained s. on 6 June 1444 at Blackfriars, York (BIA, Register 19, fol. 280r).

CORNELL, William: he was a *cursor* of theology at York on 30 August 1398, when he was licensed to hear confessions (*Reg. Scrope*, ii, p. 12, no. 729).

CORNHILL (Cornell), Richard: he was ordained a. on 1 June 1398 in St Michael-le-Belfrey, York (BIA, Register 5A, fol. 255r; BL, MS. Cotton Galba, E.X, fol. 119v) and d. on 24 May 1399 at the chapel in Cawood Castle (*Reg. Scrope*, ii, pp. 55, 70, 131).

COSTON, Reginald de: he was a friar of Nottingham when he was licensed to hear confessions in the diocese of York on 29 October 1351 (BIA, Register 10A, fol. 280).

COTES, J.: he was a friar of Scarborough, priest and professed. He died shortly before 1327 (Little, '*Records, Franciscan Province*', p. 149). A friar called John de Cotes was licensed by the bishop of Salisbury in December 1322 or May 1323 (*Reg. Martival*, v, pp. 505–06).

COTTELL (Cotterell), Thomas: he was a friar of Grantham when he was ordained d. on 27 March 1512 in Liddington prebendal church. He was a friar of Lincoln when he was ordained p. on 10 April 1512 in Lincoln cathedral (LAO, Register 24, fols. 87v, 88r).

COTTINGHAM (Continham), Hugh: this friar in the diocese of Lincoln was appointed a papal chaplain by Pope Boniface IX on 25 May 1393 (*BF*, vii, p. 33, no. 103; *CPL*, iv, p. 286).

COTTINGHAM (Cotyngham), Nicholas de: he was ordained s. on 29 May 1344 at Darlington parish church (*Reg. Kellaw*, iii, p. 142) and was a friar of York when he was ordained d. on 18 September 1344 at St Mary's Abbey, York. He was ordained p. on 20 December 1348 at York Minster (BIA, Register 10A, fols. 8r, 26r).

COTTINGHAM (Cotyngham, Kotyngham), Robert de: he was ordained a. on 26 May 1347 at Lincoln cathedral (LAO, Register 7B, fol. 12v), d. on 19 September 1349 at York Minster (BIA, Register 10A, fol. 33v) and p. on 11 June 1351 in Boston parish church (LAO, Register 9D, fol. 50). A friar of this name, probably at York, received five marks in the will of John de Burton, rector of Huggate, near York, in his will on 6–7 May 1373 (York Minster, Dean and Chapter Library, MS.L 2/4, fol. 56v).

COTTINGHAM (Cotyngham), Roger de: he was ordained d. on 26 May 1347 at Lincoln cathedral (LAO, Register 7B, fol. 14v).

COTYS (Coytes, Cotys, Oates), William: he was a friar of York when he was ordained a. on 23 December 1424 at Whitefriars, York. He was ordained s. on 3 March 1425 at Greyfriars, York (BIA, Register 5A, fols. 394r, 398v; *Reg. Sede Vacante, York, 1423–26*, pp. 99, 104, 125), and d. on 25 May 1426 at Holy Trinity Priory, Micklegate (BIA, Register 19, fol. 227r). Joan Kirby treats these as two friars.

COUMBRE, William de: he was ordained a. and s. on 26 May 1358 at Greyfriars, York (BIA, Register 11, fol. 333rv).

COUTON', John de: on 8 January 1307 this friar was mentioned as the confessor of Richard Oysel, who was sick (*Reg. Greenfield*, iv, p. 202, no. 2083).

COUTON, William de: he was ordained d. on 29 March 1343 at Beverley Greyfriars (BIA, Register 10A, fol. 3r).

COVELE, Robert de: he was ordained s. on 24 September 1351 at St Mary's church, Oxford (LAO, Register 9D, v, fol. 53r).

COVERHAM, John: he was ordained a. on 20 September 1432 at St Leonard's Hospital, York (BIA, Register 19, fol. 217r).

COWTON, Robert: he was a friar of York when he was ordained a. on 19 March 1491 at Blackfriars, York. He was a friar of Scarborough when he was ordained s. on 28 May 1491 at Holy Trinity Priory, Micklegate, York. He then returned to York and was there when ordained d. on 7 April 1492, and p. on 21 September 1493. The third and fourth ordinations took place at Whitefriars, York (BIA, Register 23, fols. 425v, 427v, 431v, 439r. Cf. Cross and Vickers, *MFN*, p. 437).

COWYN, John: he was a friar of York when he was ordained p. on 20 September 1460 at Greyfriars, York (BIA, Register 20, fol. 445v).

COWYS, John: he was ordained s. on 22 May 1361 at Cawood manor chapel (BIA, Register 11, fol. 344v).

CRAUNCEWYK, Robert de: he was a friar of York when he was ordained p. on 26 May 1358 at Greyfriars, York (BIA, Register 11, fol. 334r).

CRAWLEY, William de: he was licensed to hear confessions in the diocese of York in place of John Kirkeby at an unspecified date during the administration of Archbishop Thoresby (BIA, Register 11, fol. 397r).

CREDLEY, John de: he was ordained s. on 3 June 1357 at Cawood manor chapel (BIA, Register 11, fol. 330v).

CREMONA (Cremonia), John de: he was a friar of Lincoln, when he was ordained s. on 20 September 1404 in Lincoln cathedral (LAO, Register 13, fol. 115v).

CREMONA (Cremonia), Tilman de: he was a friar of Lincoln when he was ordained s. on 20 December 1404 at Lincoln cathedral (LAO, Register 13, fol. 117r).

CRESSOP, John: he was a friar of York when he was licensed to hear confessions in the diocese of York on 30 August 1398 (*Reg. Scrope*, ii, p. 12, no. 729).

CRETLYING', John: he was a friar of Boston when he was ordained d. on 3 March 1352 at Sleaford prebendal church (LAO, Register 9D, fol. 57v).

CREYTE, Michael: he was a friar of Boston when he was ordained a. and s. on 20 September 1404 and d. on 14 March 1405; both ceremonies took place in Lincoln cathedral (LAO, Register 13, fols. 115v, 118v).

CROFT, Michael: he was a friar of York when he was ordained a. on 19 March 1519 at Greyfriars, York, and at Richmond when he was ordained s. on 17 December 1519 at Austin Friars, York (BIA, Register 27, fols. 183r, 186r. Cf. Cross and Vickers, *MFN,* p. 444).

CROFT, William: he was ordained p. on 9 March 1476 at Greyfriars, York (BIA, Register 22, fol. 237v).

CRONALL, William: he was a friar of Beverley when he was ordained d. on 11 June 1362 at Cawood manor chapel (BIA, Register 11, fol. 349v).

CROSS (Cruce), John de: he was ordained p. on 20 September 1343 at Whitefriars, York (BIA, Register 10A, fol. 5r).

CROSS (Crosse), Robert: he was a friar of York when he was ordained a. on 17 March 1492 at Greyfriars, York, s. on 7 April 1492 at Austin Friars, York, d. on 16 June 1492 at Blackfriars, York, and p. on 22 September 1492 at Whitefriars, York. On the third occasion the name Roger was given (BIA, Register 23, fols. 430r, 431r, 433r, 434v. Cf. Cross and Vickers, *MFN*, p. 438).

CROSS (Crasse), Stephen: he was ordained a. on 13 March 1400, s. on 12 June 1400 at Bishop Burton, d. on 19 March 1401 and p. on 23 September 1402. The first, third and fourth ceremonies were held at Blackfriars, York (*Reg. Scrope*, ii, pp. 55, 71, 131).

CROSS (Crossby, Crosse), Thomas: he was a friar of York when he was ordained d. on

20 September 1460 at Greyfriars, York, and p. on 19 December 1461 at Austin Friars, York (BIA, Register 20, fols. 445v, 450r).

CROSSTHWAITE (Crosthwayt), Thomas: he was ordained s. on 13 March 1378 and d. on 18 February 1380 at Holy Trinity Priory, Micklegate, York (BIA, Register 12, fols. 131v, 136r).

CROWLAND, John de: he was a friar of Boston when he was ordained a. on 20 September 1399 at Stow prebendal church and s. on 12 June 1400 in the manor chapel at Little Stow (LAO, Register 13, fols. 88v, 93).

CROXELL, John de: he was ordained p. on 24 September 1373 at St Mary, Bishophill Senior (BIA, Register 11, fol. 393r).

CROXTON, John: he was a friar of Lincoln, when he was ordained s. on 18 September 1451 at St Margaret's parish in Lincoln cathedral close (LAO, Register 19, fols. 32v, 68r).

CROXTON, William: he was a friar of Richmond when he was ordained d. on 1 April 1430 at Blackfriars, York, and at York when he was ordained p. on 5 April 1432 at Whitefriars, York (BIA, Register 19, fols. 237r, 242r).

CRUMPTOM, John de: he was ordained p. on 23 September 1357 at Thirsk parish church (BIA, Register 11, fol. 331v).

CUDBERT, Richard: he was a friar of York when he was ordained p. on 21 December 1443 at Austin Friars, York (BIA, Register 19, fol. 222r).

CUNNYNGES (Connynge), John: he was ordained a. on 20 September 1371 at St Mary, Bishophill Senior, York, and s. on 11 June 1373 at Whitefriars, York (BIA, Register 11, fols. 384r, 391v).

CURIA, Giles de: he was ordained p. on 22 September 1397 at Holy Trinity Priory, Micklegate (*Reg. Waldby*, p. 46).

DALDERBY, William: he was ordained a. on 20 December 1432 at Austin Friars, York (BIA, Register 19, fol. 242v).

DALE, Thomas: he was ordained s. on 21 September 1476 at Whitefriars, York, and d. on 21 December 1476 at Holy Trinity Priory, Micklegate, York (BIA, Register 22, fols. 362r, 363v).

DALE, William: he was a friar of Doncaster when he was ordained d. on 19 September 1461 at Blackfriars, York (BIA, Register 20, fol. 449r) and p. on 22 December 1464 at Whitefriars, York. Details of this ordination are entered twice in the register (BIA, Register 5A, fols. 466r, 491v).

DALTON, Gilbert: he was a friar of York when he was ordained s. on 22 December 1442 at Austin Friars, York (BIA, Register 19, fol. 267v).

DALTON, John de: he was ordained s. on 29 March 1343 at Greyfriars, Beverley.

He was a friar of Doncaster when he was ordained d. on 18 December 1344 at Whitefriars, York (BIA, Register 10A, fols. 3r, 8r). He was licensed to preach in the diocese of Carlisle at an unspecified date. He was replaced by a friar of Carlisle c.1355 (*Reg. Welton*, p. 105, no. 568).

DALTON, John de: he was ordained s. on 20 September 1348 in Skipton parish church and p. on 20 December 1348 at York Minster (BIA, Register 10A, fols. 25r, 26r).

DALTON, Peter: he was a friar of York when he was ordained d. on 18 December 1456 at Greyfriars, York (BIA, Register 20, fol. 427v).

DALTON, Richard de: Walter Orre of Drayton, whose will was proved on 13 May 1346, left this friar 10s. to celebrate Masses for him at the friary in Beverley. The same instructions were issued to Thomas Garde of the York Greyfriars (BIA, Register 10, fols. 302v–03r). The former was guardian at Beverley when he was licensed to preach and hear confessions in the diocese of York for one year on 2 October 1350 (BIA, Register 10, fol. 279v).

DALTON, William de: he was ordained a. on 15 March 1348 at York Minster (BIA, Register 10A, fol. 21r). He was a friar of Lincoln in the Michaelmas term of 1368, when he was named in the plea rolls with the guardian of Lincoln (TNA, CP40/432, m. 14d, 475). He was still at Lincoln the following Easter when he was again mentioned with the guardian in the plea rolls (TNA, CP40/434, m. 262d).

DALTON: see North Dalton

DAM, Peter de: he was described as *ordinis Sancti Francisci* when he was ordained p. on 16 September 1391 at Holy Trinity Priory, Micklegate, York (BIA, Register 14, fol. 63r).

DANBY, George: he was the guardian of Scarborough in 1476 when he and a merchant of York were sued for a trespass brought by Thomas Sage. On 26 October 1476 John Thomson, merchant, failed to appear when sued with Danby (*CPR, 1467–1477*, p. 578). He was at Doncaster on 8 April 1480 when he received a general pardon (*CPR, 1476–1485*, p. 193).

DANIEL (Daynell, Danyel), Thomas: he was ordained s. on 26 May 1358 at Greyfriars, York. He was a friar of York when he was ordained d. on 21 December 1359 at the manor chapel in Cawood and p. on 23 September 1363 at Bishopthorpe manor chapel (BIA, Register 11, fols. 333v, 339v, 354r).

DARELL, Ralph: he was ordained a. on 17 December 1468 at Austin Friars, York. He was at York when he was ordained s. on 27 May 1469 at Blackfriars, York. He was ordained d. on 16 June 1470 at Blackfriars, York, and p. on 21 September 1471 at Whitefriars, York (BIA, Register 22, fols. 197r, 201r, 206r, 212v). A John Darell left 20s. to his brother, Ralph, a friar of Canterbury, in 1496 (*GFCant*, pp. 48–49).

DARLINGTON (Darlinton), John: he was ordained s. on 5 June 1395 at the conventual church of St Leonard, York (BIA, Register 14, fol. 71v).

DARLINGTON (Derlyngton), John de: he was a friar of Boston on 28 January 1348, when he was licensed to hear confessions within the convent's *limitatio* (LAO, Register 9C, fol. 41r).

DARNSEY, William: he was a friar of York when he was ordained d. on 18 December 1456 at Greyfriars, York (BIA, Register 20, fol. 427v).

DAVISE, John: he was a friar of York when he was ordained s. on 2 June 1515 at Blackfriars, York (BIA, Register 27, fol. 169r. Cf. Cross and Vickers, *MFN*, p. 444).

DAWELL (Dawel), Thomas: he was a friar of York when he was ordained s. on 26 March 1463 at Greyfriars, York (BIA, Register 20, fol. 455r).

DAWNAY (Daunay), Michael: born about 1376, he was the son of Thomas Dawnay of Escrick. He had a brother named John and a sister called Ellen as well as at least one unnamed brother and sister. He was ordained s. on 22 September 1397 at Holy Trinity Priory, Micklegate, when he was described as from the archdeaconry of Richmond; he was probably a friar of Richmond (*Reg. Waldby*, p. 47). In 1425, then aged 49, he testified that he had formerly been a friar of Hartlepool, where he had pursued the study of the liberal arts about 1400. Between 1411 and 1414 he was at Cambridge, where he became a professor of theology and then occupied the post of master of studies. From 1414 to 1419 he was at Richmond and from 1419 to 1425 he was at Doncaster. He carefully recorded details of the births and subsequent lives of the children of his nephews and nieces (BIA, Cause Papers, CP.F.89 [1425]. Cf. Kane, 'Return of the Native: Franciscan Education and Astrological Practice in the Medieval North of England'). Thomas Wykerslay, rector of Derfield, left 20s. to one *Magistro Dawnay de Doncastre* on 10 July 1434 (*TE*, v, p. 247). He was not mentioned in the will of Margaret Dawnay (Daunay), whose husband, John, died in 1424. She left money to the Greyfriars of Doncaster in her will of 12 May 1454 and may have been a relative of this friar (*TE*, ii, pp. 193–95).

DAX (Aquis), Simon de: he was ordained d. on 1 March 1393 at St Michael-le-Belfrey, York (BIA, Register 14, fol. 66r).

DAYVILL (Dayvill), Robert: he was probably a friar of Lincoln on 20 June 1318 when he was licensed to hear confessions (LAO, Register 3, fol. 390rv).

DEIGHTON (Drayton), John de: he was ordained p. on 30 May 1366 at Bishopthorpre manor chapel (BIA, Register 11, fol. 363v).

DEIGHTON (Dighton, Ditton, Dyghton), Nicholas de: in 1332 he and four friars of Doncaster were accused of seizing and imprisoning John de Malghum (*Notes on Religious Houses*, i, p. 37; TNA, CP40/292, m. 141 for the Michaelmas term). He was still at Doncaster when his name appears in the plea rolls of the Trinity term 1333 (TNA, CP40/294, m. 272). In 1334 he acted as treasurer when the king paid £15 towards the expenses of the provincial chapter at Cambridge on 8 September (Little, *Franciscan Papers, Lists, and Documents*, p. 214).

DEIGHTON (Dighton), Roger de: he was licensed in the diocese of Lincoln on 20 June 1318 (LAO, Register 3, fol. 390r). By 14 March 1319 he had been transferred from the friary at Grimsby to a friary across the river Humber (*ibid.*, fols. 411–12).

DEODRICUS, Nicholas: see Dordrecht.

DERAM (Dereham), Robert: he was a friar of York when he was ordained a. on 24 February 1453 at Blackfriars, York (BIA, Register 20, fol. 412v).

DERBY, Hugh de: he received 6d. in the will of Richard Warter, a carpenter and parishioner of All Saints, Peasholme-in-the-Marsh, York, on 21 November 1397 (BIA, Probate Register 2, fol. 9rv).

DEREM, John: he was ordained s. on 19 May 1380 at Stillingfleet parish church (BIA, Register 12, fol. 137r).

DEREM (Deram, Durram, Durham), William de: he was ordained a. on 13 March 1378 and s. on 18 February 1380; both ceremonies were held at Holy Trinity Priory, Micklegate, York (BIA, Register 12, fols. 131r, 136r). A William Durem received two marks in the will of William Durem, a merchant and parishioner of Holy Cross, York, drawn up on 24 June 1390 and proved on 10 February 1391 (BIA, Probate Register 1, fol. 20r). The two wills drawn up by Alice, his widow, on 24 June and 25 October 1390, name this friar. The first describes him as a friar of York, leaving him 40s. The second reduces the amount to 20s. and three *uluas de blankett*. This name also appears among the executors, but is not prefixed by *Frater*. Her will was proved on 10 February the following year (*ibid.*, fols. 20v–21v).

DEVENTER (Dawntre), Simon: he was a friar of York when he was ordained s. on 18 March 1508 at Greyfriars, York (BIA, Register 5A, fol. 587r, H3/2, fol. 29v). He was a friar of Northampton when he was ordained d. on 23 September 1508 in the prebendal church of Liddington and p. on 3 March 1509 (LAO, Register 24, fols. 72v, 74r; Walmsley, 'Some Dutch Franciscans in England during the Later Middle Ages', p. 250).

DEYN, Stephen: he was a friar of Beverley when he was ordained p. on 18 September 1490 at Whitefriars, York (BIA, Register 24, fol. 424r. Cf. Cross and Vickers, *MFN*, p. 437).

DEYVILL (Daynill), John: he was ordained a. on 20 December 1348 at York Minster (BIA, Register 10A, fol. 26r).

DEYVILL (Deynill), Robert: he was a friar of York when he was ordained p. on 18 December 1344 at Whitefriars, York (BIA, Register 10A, fol. 9r).

DICKSON (Dicson), Robert: he was a friar of York when he was ordained a. on 23 September 1503 at Greyfriars, York (BIA, Register 25, fol. 120r. Cf. Cross and Vickers, *MFN*, p. 440).

DICKSON (Dicson), William: he was a friar at Richmond when he was ordained a. on 5 June 1512 at Blackfriars, York, and s. on 18 September 1512 at Holy Trinity Priory, Micklegate, York. He was a friar of York when he was ordained d. on 18 December 1512 at Austin Friars, York, and p. on 12 March 1513 at Whitefriars, York (BIA, Register 26, fols. 119r, 120r, 121v, 123r. Cf. Cross and Vickers, *MFN*, pp. 443, 444).

DICKSON (Dycson), William: he was a novice at York at the Dissolution on 27 November 1538 (*Eighth Report of the Deputy Keeper of the Public Records*, p. 51).

DIKMAN (Dikemans), Richard: he was a friar of York when he was ordained s. on 20 September 1516, and d. on 19 December 1517; both ceremonies were held at Greyfriars, York. He was still at York when he was ordained p. on 18 December 1518 at Austin Friars, York (BIA, Register 27, fols. 174r, 179r, 182v. Cf. Cross and Vickers, *MFN*, p. 444).

DISNEY, Edmund de: on 6 September 1328 this friar received the alms for the friary of Lincoln (TNA, E101/383/14).

DITTON, Nicholas de: he was licensed to hear confessions in the diocese of Lincoln for one year on 9 February 1332 (LAO, Register 5, fol. 455v). On 24 August 1338 he was described as a Dominican, when he was licensed as a confessor to an anchoress at Stockfold (LAO, Register 5, fol. 151v).

DOCYGTON, John de: this guardian of Grimsby died c.1304 (Little, '*Records, Franciscan Province*', p. 153).

DODENHAM (Dodenhaben), Henry: he was a friar of York when he was ordained p. on 18 September 1484 at Whitefriars, York (BIA, Register 23, fol. 394r. Cf. Cross and Vickers, *MFN*, p. 436).

DODINGTON (Dodyngton), William: he was a friar of York when he was ordained d. on 21 February 1456 at Greyfriars, York (BIA, Register 20, fol. 424r).

DOFMAN (Doffman), Godfrey: he was a friar of York when he was ordained d. on 23 December 1424 at Whitefriars, York (BIA, Register 5A, fol. 394r; *Reg. Sede Vacante, York, 1423–26*, pp. 99, 105, 125).

DONCASTER (Donecastre), Adam de: he was ordained p. at Whitefriars, York, on 10 June 1346 (BIA, Register 10A, fol. 16r).

DONCASTER (Doncastr), John de: he was a friar of Lincoln when he was ordained s. on 19 September 1355 at Lincoln cathedral, and at Boston when he was ordained d. on 19 December 1355 in Stow prebendal church (LAO, Register 9D, fols. 77r, 78r).

DONCASTER (Doncastr, Doncastre), John: he was a friar of York when he was ordained a. on 19 September 1422 at Holy Trinity Priory, Micklegate, York. He was ordained s. on 19 December 1422 at Cawood prebendal chapel. He was at York when he was ordained d. on 18 December 1423 at York Minister (BIA, Register 18, fols. 413v, 414r, Register 5A, fol. 354v; *Reg. Sede Vacante, York, 1423–26*, pp. 99, 105, 125). He was at Lincoln when he was ordained p. on 18 March 1424 at the prebendal church of Liddington (*Reg. Fleming*, ii, p. 99, no. 495).

DONCASTER (Doncastr), Richard: he was a friar of Doncaster when he was ordained a. on 24 September 1440 at York Minster (BIA, Register 19, fol. 219r).

DONCASTER (Doncastre), William de: he was licensed to hear confessions in the diocese of Lincoln on 20 June 1318, when he was probably a friar of Lincoln (LAO, Register, 3 fol. 390r).

DONCASTER (Doncastre), William de: he was a friar of York when he was ordained

a. on 27 May 1363 at Bishopthorpe manor chapel, s. on 21 December 1364 at Greyfriars, York, and d. on 7 June 1365 also at Bishopthorpe manor chapel. He was duly ordained p. on 20 September 1365 at Cawood prebendal church (BIA, Register 11, fols. 352v, 358v, 360v, 361r). He emerges as a beneficiary of four wills, which implies a lengthy association with the friary at York. These testators were among the wealthier citizens of York and left substantial wills. First, on 15 October 1391 Master Richard de Thorner, prebendary canon of York, left him five marks to celebrate Masses for him (BIA, Register 14, fol. 28v). Secondly, on 3 September 1400 he received a small piece of silver in the will of Isabell Persay, who was buried in the choir of St Mary's at Castlegate. She bequeathed 3s. 4d. to each house of friars in the city and left the Greyfriars a dish for washing the friars' feet (BIA, Probate Register 3, fol. 63v; *TE*, i, pp. 270–72). Thirdly, on 6 November 1400 he was mentioned in the will of Thomas de Syke, senior, and tapiter of York, who was buried in the cemetery of St Mary, Bishophill Senior. John de Wakefield of the local Greyfriars was given four marks to pray for Syke, his deceased wife, and the souls of all the faithful departed for the space of a year. In the event of this friar being unable to fulfil this request, the testator nominated Doncaster as a replacement (BIA, Probate Register 3, fol. 49v). Fourthly, on 10 March 1405 Beatrix, wife of Thomas Santon, draper and citizen of York, who was buried at All Saints, Pavement, left 6s. 8d. to each community of friars in the city and singled out Doncaster, to whom she bequeathed 6s. 8d. (*ibid.*, fol. 246v). A friar of this name was paid 2s. for preaching at an *obit* for the guild of Paternoster at York in 1399/1400 (Hoskin, 'The Accounts of the Medieval Paternoster Gild of York', p. 22).

DONINGTON (Donington), Thomas de: he was licensed in the diocese of Lincoln on 20 June 1318 (LAO, Register 3, fol. 390r).

DONINGTON (Donyngton), William: he was a friar of Lichfield when he was ordained d. on 30 May 1461 and p. in September 1462 (LRO, B/1/12, fols. 183r, 188r). A friar of this name was at Nottingham on 31 March 1479, when he was licensed to hear confessions in the diocese of York (BIA, Register 22, fol. 316r).

DONMOWE (Dunmow, Dunmaw), Nicholas: he was a friar of York when he was ordained s. on 22 September 1453 at Greyfriars, York, and d. on 21 September 1454 at Blackfriars, York (BIA, Register 20, fols. 415v, 418r).

DORCHESTER, John de: he was ordained a. on 2 June 1352 at St Mary's Abbey, York (BIA, Register 10A, fol. 55r), and p. on 23 December 1357 in the manor chapel at Cawood (BIA, Register 11, fol. 332r).

DORDRECHT (Dordraco), John de: he was a friar of York when he was ordained d. on 22 December 1442 at Austin Friars, York (BIA, Register 19, fol. 267v; Walmsley, 'Some Dutch Franciscans in England during the Later Middle Ages', p. 251).

DORDRECHT (Deodricus), Nicholas: he was a friar of Boston when he was ordained p. on 6 March 1479 in the prebendal church of Louth (LAO, Register 21, fol. 165v).

DORDRECHT (Dordraco), Peter de: he was a friar of Boston when he was ordained s. on 21 September 1420 at the parish church of Deeping St James and d. on 20 September 1421 at the prebendal church of Sleaford (*Reg. Fleming*, ii, pp. 65, 77, nn. 472, 480).

DORDRECHT (Dordraco), Walter de: he was ordained d. on 20 December 1432 at Austin Friars, York (BIA, Register 19, fol. 243r; Walmsley, 'Some Dutch Franciscans in England during the Later Middle Ages', p. 251).

DORTHETLAYE, John de: on 7 November 1303 he was at York when he received the royal alms for the 49 friars there (TNA, E101/366/14).

DOUTON, John: on 3 July 1411 the archbishop of York licensed this friar *iuxta constitutionem Dudum* (BIA, Register 18, fol. 303v).

DOWSON (Doweson), William: he was at Oxford when he was ordained p. on 27 May 1480 at All Saints, Northampton (LAO, Register 21, fol. 171v). On 2 July 1508 he was a friar of Grimsby who was asked to pray for the soul of Henry de le See of Great Grimsby and the souls of his parents and benefactors for a year in the church of St James at Grimsby. He and another friar were asked to pray for him, his parents and all the faithful departed in the friars' church for the space of four years and more, provided his estate could support this. This friar was also a witness to the will (*Lincoln Wills, 1271–1532*, i, pp. 35–36). He was at Grimsby when he received 10s. in the will of Richard Burgh in 1513 (*VCH, Lincs.*, ii, p. 219, citing P.C.C., Rous, fol. 32, P.C.C., Fetilplace, fol. 18). A Friar Dowson, probably a friar of Beverley, received 10d. in the will of John Hicson on 24 March 1526 (BIA, Probate Register 9, fol. 341v). Friar Dowson received 3s. 4d. in the will of Dame Jane Hiliard de Winestead, who made bequests to the friaries of Grimsby and Beverley, on 20 July 1527 (*TE*, v, p. 230; BIA, Probate Register 9, fol. 390v). The friar may be the Sir William Dowson who received 6s. 8d. for prayers in the will of Robert Jordan on 6 March 1529. He was probably at Scarborough. The entry follows a bequest of barley to the friary of Scarborough (*ibid.*, fol. 438r).

DOWSYNK, Martin: he was a friar of York when he was ordained p. on 17 December 1485 at Austin Friars, York (BIA, Register 23, fol. 399r. Cf. Cross and Vickers, *MFN*, p. 436).

DRAPER, Laurence: he was a friar of York when he was ordained s. on 2 June 1515 at Blackfriars, York, and at Oxford when he was ordained d. on 7 March 1517 (Salisbury Registers: Audley). He was back at York when he was ordained p. on 18 June 1519 at Holy Trinity, Micklegate, York (BIA, Register 27, fols. 169r, 185r. Cf. Cross and Vickers, *MFN*, p. 444). He was a friar of Cambridge at the Dissolution of the friary at an unspecified date in 1538 (*Eighth Report of the Deputy Keeper of the Public Records*, p. 14). On 26 February 1546 he was presented by King Edward VI to the living of Hartley in Cambridgeshire (CUL, EDR, G/1/8, fol. 176r). In November 1556 he was collated to the vicarage of Gamlingay, but he died before September 1557 (*ibid.*, Thirsby, fols. 32r, 35v; *GFC*, p. 171).

DRAPER, William: he was a friar at York when he was ordained s. on 30 May 1523 at Holy Trinity Priory, Micklegate, York, and at Scarborough when he was ordained d. on 10 June 1525 at Blackfriars, York. He was back at York when ordained p. on 26 May 1526 at Blackfriars, York (BIA, Register 27, fols. 200r, 207r, 210v. Cf. Cross and Vickers, *MFN*, p. 445).

DREWHIT, Thomas: he was ordained s. on 24 September 1468 at Greyfriars, York (BIA, Register 22, fols. 193r, 216r).

DUFFIELD (Doffeld), William: there were two friars of this name simultaneously active in the northern custodies in the early sixteenth century: one was a friar of Newcastle when he was ordained a. in the chapel of the south aisle of Durham cathedral on 30 March 1499 (*Reg. Fox*, p. 85). The other was a friar of York when he was ordained s. on 18 September 1501 and at Hartlepool when he was ordained d. on 26 March 1502 in the lady chapel of York Minster (BIA, York, Register 25, fols. 109v, 112r. Cf. Cross and Vickers, *MFN*, p. 439). One of them proceeded to Cambridge where he took his D.D. in 1521–22 (*Grace Book B*, ii, p. 98, i, p. 203). On 20 December 1525 a friar of this name was licensed to preach in the diocese of Hereford (*Reg. Bothe*, p. 175). He was provided to the diocese of Ascalon about 1531. In London he purchased a pontifical, which is now Colchester, Harsnett Library, H.h.14, with the inscription *Duffild, dom. Willelmus, S.T.P., O.F.M.C., Ascelenensis episcopus*. The manuscript later passed to the friars of Coventry. Duffield was already a bishop when he was admitted to membership of the guild of St Katherine at Stamford in 1532; this may indicate that he was spending some time in the locality, if not the town (BL, Add.MS.4938, fol. 117r). He acted as suffragan in the dioceses of York, Canterbury and Lincoln.

John Longland, bishop of Lincoln, gave him a general commission on 12 November 1531 for the archdeaconries of Lincoln, Leicester, Northampton, Huntingdon and Bedford. This permitted him to bless and dedicate altars, belfries, vestments and altar vessels; he was permitted to bless chapels, oratories and cemeteries. In addition, he was authorised to ordain clerics to all major orders and to bless abbots, abbesses, widows, anchorites and hermits (LAO, Register 26, fol. 214r). He conferred orders on 30 March 1532 in Lincoln cathedral, on 19 December 1532 at Liddington prebendal church, and in Lincoln cathedral on 12 April 1533 (LAO, Register 26, fols. 30rv, 32r–34r). In 1533 he acted as suffragan for Henry Standish, bishop of St Asaph. On 13 July 1535 Edward Lee, archbishop of York, gave him a suffragan commission (BIA, Register 28, fol. 101r). On 12 September 1536 he was licensed to consecrate the chapel of St Lawrence in the village of Elstronwick in the parish of St Peter at Humbleton in Holderness. He held ordinations at Greyfriars, York, on 11 March 1536 and 1 April 1536, at Blackfriars, York, and on 24 February 1537 at Whitefriars, York, the last ceremony in which friars of York and Richmond were ordained (BIA, Register 28, fols. 194–97v; Cf. *GFC*, pp. 172–73; Smith, 'Suffragan Bishops in the Medieval Diocese of Lincoln', p. 27; Butler, 'Suffragan Bishops in the Medieval Diocese of York', p. 60; Robson, 'William Duffield, bishop of Ascalon'.

DUNNING (Dunnyng), John: this friar of Boston apostatised. On 21 October 1391 King Richard II sought aid in apprehending this vagabond friar. He appointed Robert Rokeley, Richard Dane and John Barton to escort the friar who had been caught and delivered to Robert, the guardian of the London Greyfriars. These men were to accompany the apostate friar back to the care of the guardian of Boston (*CPR, 1388–1392,* p. 522; Logan, *Runaway Religious in Medieval England, c.1240–1540*, p. 244).

DUNSTAPLE, William: he was a friar of Lincoln when he was ordained d. on 25 March 1486 in Lincoln cathedral and p. on 24 April 1486 in Sleaford prebendal church (LAO, Register 22, fols. 21v, 22r).

DUVALL, Giles: he was a friar of York when he was ordained a. on 11 March 1486 at Holy Trinity Priory, York (BIA, Register 23, fol. 400r. Cf. Cross and Vickers, *MFN*, p. 436).

DYNLAY, William: one of the three friars at York accused by Henry Lescrop, chivaler, of seizing his wife Joan, at Faxfleet in the East Riding, and abducting and detaining her and certain goods and chattels in 1415 (*Notes on Religious Houses*, ii, p. 93).

DYRAM, John: a friar of Lincoln who received half a quarter of barley for the friary in the will of James de Kyneton, rector of Hedon, on 6 March 1398 (BIA, Probate Register 2, fol. 12v).

DYST (Dyste), John: he was a friar of Lincoln when he was ordained d. on 22 February 1399 in Stow prebendal church (LAO, Register 13, fol. 85r).

DYST, Rayner de: he was a friar of Boston when he was ordained p. on 14 March 1405 in Lincoln cathedral (LAO, Register 13, fol. 118v).

EASBY (Eseby), John: he was a friar of York when he was ordained s. on 22 December 1498 at Rotherham parish church, d. on 23 February 1499 at Holy Trinity Priory, Micklegate, York (BIA, Register 23, fols. 461v, 462r. Cf. Cross and Vickers, *MFN*, p. 439), and at Cambridge when he was ordained p. on 13 March 1500 (CUL, EDR, G/1/6; *GFC*, p. 175; *BRUC*, p. 214).

EASINGWOLD (Esingwold), John de: he was a friar of Lincoln when he was ordained s. on 21 September 1359 and at Grimsby when he was ordained d. on 21 December 1359 and p. on 17 December 1362; all three ceremonies took place in Lincoln cathedral (LAO, Register 9D, fols. 92v, 93v, 108v). He may have been the John Essewold, a friar of Lincoln, named in the plea rolls of the Michaelmas term of 1366 (TNA, CP40/425, m. 340d).

EASINGWOLD (Esyngwald), Thomas: he was ordained s. at Blackfriars, York, on 22 September 1414 (BIA, Register 18, fol. 39Gr).

EASINGWOLD (Esyngwald), William: he was a friar of York when he was ordained a. on 26 May 1453 at Blackfriars, York (BIA, Register 20, fol. 415r).

EASINGWOLD (Esyngwald), William: he was a friar of York when he was ordained a. on 31 May 1488 at Blackfriars, York, and s. on 4 April 1489 at Greyfriars, York. He was ordained d. on 18 September 1490, and p. on 7 April 1492. The third and fourth ceremonies were held at Whitefriars, York (BIA, Register 23, fols. 412v, 416r, 423v, 431v. Cf. Cross and Vickers, *MFN*, p. 436).

EBOR: see York

EBRESTON (Ebirston), Robert: he was ordained d. on 31 May 1393, and p. on 27 May 1396; both ceremonies took place at St Mary, Bishophill Senior, York (BIA, Register 14, fols. 67r, 73r).

EBRON, John: erroneously described as a Franciscan at Pontefract when he was ordained a. on 2 April 1468 at Austin Friars, York. The previous entry was for a Richard Barton, a Dominican, at Pontefract. On the three subsequent ordinations Ebron was named as a Franciscan. He was a friar of York when he was ordained s. at an unspecified place and date, probably Whitsuntide 1468. He was ordained d. on

24 September 1468 at Whitefriars, York. He was ordained p. on 22 September 1470 at Greyfriars, York (BIA, Register 22, fols. 191r, 195r, 196r, 207v).

ECCLESTON, John: he was ordained a. on 2 June 1352 at St Mary's Abbey, York (BIA, Register 10A, fol. 55r).

ECCLESTON (Ecliston), Thomas de: he was a friar of York when he was ordained s. on 10 June 1346 at Whitefriars, York (BIA, Register 10A, fol. 15v).

ECOP, John: he was a friar of York when he was ordained s. on 19 September 1506 in Tadcaster parish church, d. on 19 December 1506 at Austin Friars, York, and p. on 27 February 1507 at Whitefriars, York (BIA, Register 25, fols. 135v, 136r, 137v. Cf. Cross and Vickers, *MFN*, p. 442).

EDLINGTON (Edlyngton), Thomas: he was a friar of York when he was ordained a. on 23 March 1504 at Greyfriars, York (BIA, Register 25, fol. 122v. Cf. Cross and Vickers, *MFN*, p. 441). Either he or the friar immediately below was one of the six who signed the surrender of the friary at Grimsby on 9 October 1539 (*Eighth Report of the Deputy Keeper of the Public Records*, p. 22).

EDLINGTON (Edlyngton), Thomas: he was a friar of York when he was ordained a. and s. on 7 March 1506 at Whitefriars, York, and d. on 19 September 1506 in Tadcaster parish church (BIA, Register 25, fols. 131v, 135v. Cf. Cross and Vickers, *MFN*, p. 441). He or the friar above was at Grimsby at the Dissolution on 9 October 1538 (*Eighth Report of the Deputy Keeper of the Public Records*, p. 22).

EDMUNDSON (Edmondson), Hugh: he was a friar of York when he was ordained a. on 7 March 1506 at Whitefriars, York, s. on 29 May 1507 at Blackfriars, York, d. on 18 March 1508 at Greyfriars, York, and p. on 23 December 1508 at Whitefriars, York (BIA, Register 25, fols. 131v, 140v, Register 5A, fol. 588v, Register 26, fol. 100r. Cf. Cross and Vickers, *MFN*, p. 441).

EFFINGHAM (Effyngham), Thomas: he was the guardian of Lincoln when he was named in the plea rolls of the Trinity term 1384 (TNA, CP40/493, m. 144).

EGRIMOND, Robert: he was a friar of Lincoln when he was ordained a. on 14 February 1478 in the prebendal church of Liddington. He was a friar of Grimsby when he was ordained s. on 7 March 1478 in the prebendal church of Sleaford. He was back at Lincoln when he was ordained d. on 21 March 1478 at St Benedict's church, Lincoln (LAO, Register 21, fols. 161r, 162rv).

EGTON (Egthon), Thomas de: he was a friar of Boston when he was licensed in the *limitatio* of the house on 10 August and again on 12 October 1300 (Little, *Franciscan Papers, Lists, and Documents*, pp. 237, 238).

ELIAS (Helias): he was a lame novice who had to be carried into the newly built domestic oratory at Cambridge c.1225/30. He died later at York and appeared to William de Esseby, one of the other two friars then present at Cambridge (Eccleston, p. 22; *GFC*, pp. 9, 173; *BRUC*, p. 297).

ELLAND (Elland), Thomas: he was ordained a. and s. on 22 September 1414 at

Blackfriars, York (BIA, Register 18, fol. 39Gr), and p. on 13 June 1416 at an unspecified location in the diocese of Durham (*Reg. Langley*, v, p. 86, no. 1356).

ELLEBRANT (Hellerbrand), Hugh: he was ordained a. on 22 December 1431 at Austin Friars, York. He was a friar of Beverley when he was ordained d. on 20 September 1432 at St Leonard's Hospital, York (BIA, Register 19, fols. 217r, 240v).

ELLEL, William: this former Observant died at Doncaster. It is unclear whether he had joined the community there (*LPFD*, vii, p. 601, no. 1607).

ELLERTON, John de: a friar who received a honey-coloured robe in the will of Lucy, wife of Lord Bartholomew Fanacourt, who was buried in the conventual church of St Mary at Gisburn, on 6 January 1347 (BIA, Register 10, fol. 310v; *TE*, i, pp. 32–33).

ELLESLAY (Ellisley), Henry de: he was ordained p. on 14 June 1348 at St Mary's Abbey, York (BIA, Register 10A, fol. 25r).

ELLIS (Elles, Ellys), Matthew: he was a friar of York when he was ordained s. on 18 September 1507 at Whitefriars, York, d. on 23 December 1508 at Austin Friars, York, and p. on 24 March 1509 at Blackfriars, York (BIA, Register 5A, fol. 579r, Register 26, fols. 99v, 101r. Cf. Cross and Vickers, *MFN*, p. 442).

ELLITHORPE, William: he was a friar of Lincoln when he was ordained a. on 8 April 1531 in Lincoln cathedral (LAO, Register 26, fol. 27v).

ELIPHAT: see Halifax.

ELMET, Cornelius de: he was a friar of Beverley when he was ordained s. on 2 April 1435 at Whitefriars, York. He was at Scarborough when he was ordained d. at Austin Friars, York, on 22 December 1436, and at York when he was ordained p. on 25 May 1437 at Blackfriars, York (BIA, Register 19, fols. 248v, 252v, 254v).

ELTOFT, William de: a friar of Grimsby who was licensed to hear confessions within the *limitatio* of that house on 10 August and 12 October 1300 (*Franciscan Papers, Lists, and Documents*, pp. 237, 238).

ELYNSALE, William de: he was ordained p. on 3 June 1368 at Bishopthorpe manor chapel (BIA, Register 11, fol. 370r).

EMER, Walter: he was ordained d. on 24 May 1399 in the chapel of Cawood Castle and p. on 12 June 1400 at Bishop Burton, although the register lists him as a deacon for the second time (*Reg. Scrope*, ii, pp. 55, 74, 131).

EMPINGHAM (Empyngham), William de: he was ordained a. and s. on 26 May 1358 at Greyfriars, York, (BIA, Register 11, fol. 333rv).

EMPINGHAM (Empyngham), William de: he was ordained s. on 19 December 1360 at Cawood manor chapel and d. on 24 September 1362 at Bishopthorpe manor chapel (BIA, Register 11, fols. 343r, 350v).

ERKENDEN (Arkender), John: he was ordained s. on 26 May 1358 at Greyfriars,

York. He was ordained d. at 30 May 1360 and p. on 11 June 1362. The second and third ceremonies took place at Cawood manor chapel (BIA, Register 11, fols. 333v, 341r, 349v).

ESCRICK (Esryk), Nicholas de: he was a friar of Beverley when he was ordained a. on 21 December 1359 and d. on 19 December 1360; both ceremonies took place at Cawood manor chapel (BIA, Register 11, fols. 339r, 343r). He was at Lincoln when he was ordained p. on 17 December 1362 in the cathedral (Register 9D, fol. 108v).

ESTERBY, William de: he was licensed to hear confessions in the archdeaconry of Lincoln on 23 November 1335 for one year (LAO, Register 5, fol. 517v).

ESTFELD, Robert: he was ordained p. on 21 December 1342 at Doncaster parish church (BIA, Register 10A, fol. 2v; *Reg. Kirkby*, i, p. 154, no. 733). He was licensed for the diocese of York on 14 June 1350 (BIA, Register 10, fol. 279r).

ESTHETEE, Thomas: he was a friar of York when he was ordained d. on 26 May 1453 at Blackfriars, York (BIA, Register 20, fol. 415r).

ETTYRBYE, John: he was a friar of York when he was ordained a. on 19 September 1405 at Greyfriars, York (BIA, Register 5A, fol. 317v).

EUSTACE (Ewstace), John: he was ordained d. on 18 September 1367 at Bishopthorpe manor chapel (BIA, Register 11, fol. 367r).

EUSTACE, Philip: a friar of York when he was ordained p. on 21 December 1370 at Whitefriars, York (BIA, Register 11, fol. 381r).

EVIN'ME, William: born of unmarried parents, this friar in the diocese of Lincoln applied for a dispensation to hold any conventual office in the order, including that of guardian, on 3 April 1456 (*Supplic. Apost. Penit.*, i, p. 194, no. 913).

EWELL, William de: he was ordained s. on 21 December 1297 at Louth prebendal church (*Reg. Sutton*, vii, p. 100).

EXTHORP, Robert: he was a friar of York when he was ordained p. on 18 September 1406 at Blackfriars, York (BIA, Register 5A, fol. 323r; *Reg. Sede Vacante, York, 1405–08*, pp. 66, 72, 89).

EXTON, Thomas de: he was ordained d. at Lincoln cathedral on 26 May 1347 (LAO, Episcopal Register 7B, fol. 14v).

EYNSAM, John de: he was a friar of York when he was ordained a. on 19 September 1377 at St Mary's Abbey, York, s. on 13 March 1378 at Holy Trinity Priory, Micklegate, and d. on 3 April 1378 at Greyfriars, York (BIA, Register 12, fols. 129r, 131v, 132r).

EYVILLE, Robert de: he was ordained d. on 3 April 1294 at Spaldwick (*Reg. Sutton*, vii, p. 51).

FAIRCLOUGH (Fairclogh), Richard: he was a friar of York when he was ordained s. on 21 May 1345 in Thirsk parish church (BIA, Register 10A, fol. 11r).

FARNAKYNS, Gilbert: he was a friar of York when he was ordained p. on 22 May 1350 at Blackfriars, York (BIA, Register 10A, fol. 48r).

FASSET, William: he was ordained a. on 6 June 1433 at Blackfriars, York. He was a friar of York when he was ordained p. on 26 May 1442 at Blackfriars, York (BIA, Register 19, fols. 244v, 267r).

FAULRHILL, Philip: he was ordained d. on 18 March 1413 at Austin Friars, York, and p. on 17 June 1413 at Greyfriars, York (BIA, Register 18, fols. 39Ev, 39Fv).

FAWDONER, John: he was custos of York on 28 August 1398 when he was one of the friars licensed to preach and hear confessions in the diocese of York (*Reg. Scrope*, ii, p. 12, no. 729).

FAWLEY (Fallesley), Robert de: he was probably a friar of Grimsby licensed to hear confessions in the diocese of Lincoln on 20 June 1318 (LAO, Register 3, fol. 390).

FAYRHILL, Philip: he was ordained s. on 24 September 1412 at Greyfriars, York (BIA, Register 18, fol. 39Dv).

FEAN (Fene), Adrian de: he was a friar of Beverley when he was ordained d. on 31 March 1408 at Austin Friars, York (BIA, Register 5A, fol. 326v; *Reg. Sede Vacante, York, 1405–08*, pp. 66, 72, 89).

FERRIBY (Feriby), William de: he was ordained s. on 22 May 1350 at Blackfriars, York (BIA, Register 10A, fol. 47r), d. on 18 September 1350 in Lincoln cathedral and p. on 17 December 1351 in Sleaford prebendal church (LAO, Register 9D, fols. 45rv, 56r). He was licensed in the diocese of York at an unknown date, but he was later replaced during the administration of Archbishop Thoresby (BIA, Register 11, fol. 396r).

FEYG (Feyg, Fyge), William: he was a friar of York when he was ordained a. on 18 September 1428 at York Minster and s. on 23 September 1430 at Holy Trinity Priory, Micklegate, York (BIA, Register 19, fols. 216r, 238r).

FFONEA, Albert de: he was ordained d. on 2 June 1414 at St Michael-le-Belfrey, York (BIA, Register 18, fol. 39Gr).

FILIOL (Filiol, Filioll), William: he was ordained d. on 21 December 1336 at Greyfriars, York (*Reg. Kellaw*, iii, p. 178). He was licensed in the diocese of Lincoln on 7 October 1346, replacing the deceased John of Beverley (LAO, Register 7, fol. 99r). He was then licensed in the diocese of York on 17 October 1347 in place of Adam de Brantingham, another deceased friar (BIA, Register 10, fol. 278).

FILLINGHAM (Filingham, Fylingham), Henry de: he was probably a friar of Lincoln when he received a legacy of 6s. 8d. for a habit in the will of Master Jordan of Ingham, warden of the altar of St Peter in Lincoln cathedral and rector of East Torrington, on 24 April 1288. The *inspeximus* and probate were granted by the sub-dean and chapter of Lincoln on 7 November 1292 (*Reg. Antiq.*, x, no. 2877, pp. 207–10, at 209). He was a friar of Lincoln when he was licensed in the *limitatio* of the friary on 10 August and 12 October 1300 (Little, *Franciscan Papers, Lists, and Documents*, pp. 237, 238).

FIRTH, Richard: a friar of York when he was ordained s. on 23 September 1503 at Greyfriars, York, d. on 19 December 1506 at Austin Friars, York, and at Doncaster when ordained p. on 27 February 1507 at Whitefriars, York (BIA, Register 25, fols. 120r, 136v, 137v. Cf. Cross and Vickers, *MFN*, p. 440).

FISH (Fyshe), Anthony: he was a friar of Lincoln when he was ordained p. on 8 April 1531 in Lincoln cathedral (LAO, Register 26, fol. 28r). This former friar of Lincoln obtained his capacity on 8 October 1539 (Chambers, *Faculty Office Registers 1534–1549*, p. 195).

FISHER (Fyssher), Peter: he was a friar of York when he was ordained d. on 19 December 1467 at Austin Friars, York, and when ordained p. The venue and date were not entered in the register. The ceremony probably occurred on 11 June 1468 (BIA, Register 22, fols. 189v, 195v).

FISHLAKE (Fishlakey), Thomas de: he was a friar of York when he was ordained d. on 21 December 1359 in the manor chapel at Cawood (BIA, Register 11, fol. 339v).

FLEMING (Flemyng), William: he was a friar of York when he was ordained a. on 23 September 1368 at the manor chapel of Bishopthorpe (BIA, Register 11, fol. 370v). A friar of this name was ordained p. on 12 June 1378 at York Minster (BIA, Register 12, fol. 133v).

FONKE, Henry: he was ordained p. on 19 December 1478 at Holy Trinity Priory, Micklegate, York (BIA, Register 22, fol. 375r).

FORDE, John: on 31 March 1479 this friar of Nottingham was licensed to hear confessions in the diocese of York (BIA, Register 22, fol. 316r).

FOREST, John: he was ordained a. on 7 April 1481 at Holy Trinity Priory, Micklegate, York. He was at York when ordained s. on 21 September 1482 at Whitefriars, York (BIA, Register 23, fols. 374v, 383v. Cf. Cross and Vickers, *MFN*, p. 435).

FORMAN (Formay), Walter: he was ordained p. on 22 September 1397 at Holy Trinity Priory, Micklegate, York (*Reg. Waldby*, p. 46). A friar of this name, a master of theology, was provided to the see of Ross on 14 November 1418 (*BF*, vii, p. 512, no. 1395). He died before 19 August 1426, when his successor was appointed (Cenci, 'Documenta Vaticana', Part 2, pp. 73, 107, *Materials, Ireland*, pp. 178, 182).

FORTE, Richard: he was a friar of York when he was ordained a. on 16 March 1510 at Greyfriars, York, s. on 25 May 1510, d. on 14 June 1511, and p. on 20 September 1511 at Holy Trinity Priory, Micklegate, York. The second and third ordinations took place at Blackfriars, York (BIA, Register 26, fols. 106v, 108r, 114r, 115r; *Reg. Bainbridge*, p. 364. Cf. Cross and Vickers, *MFN*, p. 443).

FOSCETON, W. de: a friar of Beverley, priest and professed. Died c.1327 (Little, '*Records, Franciscan Province*', p. 149).

FOSTER, William: he was a friar of York when he was ordained s. on 24 September 1457 and d. on 22 September 1459. Both ceremonies took place at Whitefriars, York (BIA, Register 20, fols. 431r, 439v).

FOSTON (Sosten), Robert: there are two Fostons, one north-east of York and the other north-west of Grantham. This friar was probably at one of the friaries in Lincolnshire when he was ordained acolyte, subdeacon and deacon; there are no ordination records for the diocese of Lincoln in this period. He was ordained p. on 20 September 1393 in St Leonard's Hospital, York (BIA, Register 14, fol. 68r). He was the *cursor* to the friars when licensed to preach and hear confessions in the diocese of York on 30 August 1398 (*Reg. Scrope*, ii, p. 12, no. 729), and he became a professor of theology. On 30 December 1407 he was a friar of Hartlepool when he was admitted to hear confessions *juxta formam Clementine Dudum* (*Reg. Langley*, i, p. 39, no. 42). At Constance on 16 February 1419 Pope Martin V appointed him as bishop of Elphin (*BF*, vii, p. 501, no. 1373; *Materials, Ireland*, p. 178; *Reg. Langley*, ii, pp. 180–81, no. 530). A letter of 20 November 1419 from the same pope stated that Robert had acted as proctor at the papal court for Philip Repingdon, who resigned his diocese of Lincoln on 21 November 1419. Robert had communicated this decision to Branda da Castiglione, cardinal priest of San Clemente, Rome (*CPL*, vii, p. 134; *Reg. Chichele*, iii, p. 62). On the same day he received a dispensation as a son of a priest and an unmarried woman to be consecrated as a bishop (*CPL*, vii, p. 68). The pope wrote to King Henry V, requesting him to show favour to Foston and the diocese of Elphin (*Reg. Langley*, ii, p. 182, no. 531). Robert was then at the curia. He seems to have remained in Italy throughout the following year. By 29 November 1419 he had already been consecrated and was at Florence when he personally made the payment of 66 gold florins for his diocese (Cenci, 'Documenta Vaticana', Part 2, p. 68). A subsequent letter on this matter, written on 10 October 1422, by Pope Martin V at Santa Maria Maggiore in Rome, reiterates that Repington's resignation was made by his proctor at the papal court, Robert Foston, bishop of Elphin (*CPL*, vii, p. 213).

By the end of 1419 Robert seems to have been on his way back to the north of England, where he may already have renewed contact with Bishop Langley. He was appointed as suffragan bishop and penitentiary in the diocese of Durham on 6 February 1420 at the ordinary's good pleasure (*Reg. Langley*, ii, p. 182, no. 532, v, p. 137, no. 1444), and on 21 March 1420 he was authorised to hold ordinations, to consecrate the chrism, to reconcile altars, to bless cemeteries, chalices and ecclesiastical ornaments, and to confirm (*Reg. Langley*, v, p. 137, no. 1443). He conferred holy orders on numerous occasions between 2 March 1420 (*Reg. Langley*, v, pp. 141–42, no. 1455, n.) and 18 December 1434 (*Reg. Langley*, v, pp. 144–46, no. 1126). Many of the ceremonies were conducted in Durham cathedral and its chapel of St Cuthbert, Tynmouth, St Nicholas's, Newcastle, St Nicholas at Durham, St Oswald's, Durham, the collegiate church of St Andrew at Auckland and the chapel of Randolph, count of Westmorland, in the castle at Raby. On 16 January 1429 a mandate to execute Cardinal Beaufort's commission to further the progress of the Crusade against the heretics of Bohemia was addressed to Robert and others for the city and archdeaconry of Durham (*Reg. Langley*, iii, pp. 128–46, nos. 794–800). On 12 February 1430 Pope Martin V wrote to Robert, whom he styled as bishop in the universal church (*in universali ecclesia episcopus*), recounting the circumstances of his election to Elphin and his removal from that see. Bishop Langley's petition to the holy see to permit Robert to hold a benefice was granted by the pope (*Reg. Langley*, iii, pp. 200–01, no. 884; *BF*, vii, p. 732, no. 1881; *CPL*, viii, p. 175). Robert was presented by John, the prior, and the convent of Durham, to the church of Kimblesworth on 1 September 1430 (*Reg. Langley*, iii, p. 201, no. 885). He appears to have held the parish until his death (*Reg. Langley*, iii, p. 201, no. 885; *Fasti Dunelmenses*, pp. 47, 174). On 2 and 3 September 1430 Robert was admitted to the living and given the appropriate dispensations. An order for induction was issued to the archdeacon (*Reg. Langley*, iii, pp. 201–02, no.

886). On 12 December 1431 Robert, now described as *nuper* bishop of Elphin, was commissioned to consecrate the chapel and churchyard of St Margaret in the Old Burgh of Durham because St Oswald's, the parish church, was inconveniently distant (*Reg. Langley*, vi, pp. 12–13, no. 1563). Bishop Langley obtained benefices for two of his suffragans, Oswald, bishop of Galloway, and Foston. An annual salary of £13 6s. 8d. was paid to each suffragan from the bishop's palatine exchequer (Storey, *Thomas Langley and the Bishopric of Durham 1406–1437*, pp. 89, 175–76). Three of the extant accounts record payments for this amount to Foston for the years 1424–25, 1427–28 and 1434–35 (Durham University Library, Archives and Special Collections, Church Commission Durham Bishopric, receiver-general's accounts, CC 189810, 190184, 188686). The last date shows that Foston's stipend continued to be paid after his appointment to the parish of Kimblesworth; in this case the income from the parish was not deemed to be sufficient to discontinue the annual stipend. On 6 March 1435 Thomas Ryall was presented to the church of Kimblesworth, vacant by the death of Foston. The order for the induction was issued on 23 May 1435 (*Reg. Langley*, vi, pp. 20–21, no. 1587).

FOX, John de Lee by Gainsborough: in 1350 he was a friar of Lincoln who was involved in the abduction of Margaret Everingham, a nun from Broadholme Priory, a Premonstratensian house in Nottinghamshire; also involved were Thomas de Longesdon, another friar of the same house, and William Fox, priest of Lea in Lincolnshire (Cole, 'The Priory of Broadholme', pp. 66–67; Power, *Medieval English Nunneries c.1275–1535*, pp. 449–50; Logan, *Runaway Religious in Medieval England*, p. 89). John was described as a friar of Lincoln in Michaelmas 1351, when he was mentioned in conjunction with the guardian, Richard de Skyrbek (TNA, CP40/367, mm. 173d, attorneys, 8). On 10 February 1352 he received a royal pardon from King Edward III and was described as a friar of Lincoln. He may have been the parson's brother (*CPR, 1350–1354*, p. 225).

FOX, Thomas: he received one mark from John Melton, formerly a soldier of Aston, York, whose will was drawn up on 1 April 1455 (BIA, Probate Register 2, fol. 319v).

FRANCIS (no surname was given): he was a friar of York when he was ordained s. on 19 September 1377 at St Mary's Abbey, York (BIA, Register 12, fol. 129v).

FRANCIS (Frances, Fraunce, Fraunch), John: a Friar Fraunch of Richmond was left 40s. in the will of Dame Jane Strangways, a widow, on 28 October 1500 (*TE*, iv, pp. 186–90). He was a friar of Richmond when he was ordained a. on 27 March 1501 in the parish church of Barnard Castle (*Reg. Fox*, p. 152). He was at York when he was ordained s. on 18 September 1501 at Greyfriars, York, and back at Richmond when he was ordained d. on 18 December 1501 (BIA, Register 25, fols. 109v, 111r). In an ecclesiastical court case concerning the profession of Elizabeth Lutton, a nun of the Benedictine priory of Yedingham, heard at York on 31 April 1532, the prioress, Agnes Brayderick, confirmed that Francis, a friar of Scarborough, was the convent's confessor (BIA, CP, G216). A John Fraunce obtained a dispensation to hold a benefice with a complete change of habit on 20 June 1539 (Chambers, *Faculty Office Registers 1534–1549*, p. 187. Cf. Cross and Vickers, *MFN*, pp. 439, 453).

FREBOYS, John: he was a friar of Boston when he was ordained s. on 13 March 1361 in Holbeach parish church (LAO, Register 9D, fol. 98v) and at York when he was ordained d. on 18 December 1361 at York Minster (BIA, Register 11, fol. 346v). John

Freboys, a parishioner of St Mary's at Castlegate, left a friar of this name, who may have been his cousin, an unspecified offering towards his habit and other necessities appropriate for his work on 7 January 1361 (*York Memorandum Book*, iii, pp. 146–47). He was ordained p. on 20 September 1365 in the manor chapel at Cawood (BIA, Register 11, fol. 361r).

FRESTON, John de: a friar of Lincoln licensed for that house on 12 October 1300 (Little, *Franciscan Papers, Lists, and Documents*, p. 238).

FRESTON, Thomas de: he had been licensed in the diocese of York but died before 17 October 1347, when he was replaced by John of St Martin (BIA, Register 10, fol. 278r).

FRISBY (Frysby), Roger de: he was a friar of Boston when he was ordained s. on 7 June 1354. He was a friar of Stamford when he was ordained d. on 19 March 1356; both ceremonies occurred at Liddington prebendal church. He was a friar of Grantham when he was ordained p. on 4 March 1357 at Oakham parish church (LAO, Register 9D, fols. 71v, 79v, 83v). He was by 1363 a doctor of theology of Cambridge and among those who attended the council convened at Blackfriars, London, to examine some opinions of John Wyclif in 1382 (*Fasciculi zizaniorum magistri Johannis Wyclif cum tritico*, pp. 287, 499). He was one of the doctors of theology before whom William Swinderby, a priest of the diocese of Lincoln, appeared and recanted in Lincoln cathedral on 11 July 1382. He was probably a friar of Leicester at that time; an Austin Friar and a Dominican, probably friars of Leicester, accompanied him (*Knighton's Chronicle 1337–1396*, pp. 316–19n). He was already an old man when he became guardian of Leicester. In 1402 he was arrested with his brother, Richard, on the grounds of subscribing to prophecies of John of Bridlington. Although he did not claim that King Richard was still alive, he believed that, if it were the case, he would be the king. The king maintained the legitimacy of his accession to the throne. He was committed to the Tower and hanged at Tyburn in 1402 (*Eulogium Historiarum*, iii, pp. 391–93; *An English Chronicle of the Reigns of Richard II, Henry IV, V and VI*, pp. 23–26; *BRUC*, pp. 244–45; *GFC*, pp. 177–78).

FRYSTON, John: a friar of Lincoln when he received the royal alms of 14s. 8d. on 21 December 1304 (BL, MS.Add.35292, fol. 62v).

FRYSTON (Fryston), Simon: he was the younger son of Beatrix of Selby from York and the younger brother of Robert de Lyndsay. The family lived in the parish of All Saints, Pavement, at York. His mother's will, completed on 5 November 1398, does not mention her husband, who had probably predeceased her. She requested burial in her parish church and made the customary mortuary offering to the rector of the parish along with money for forgotten tithes; there were payments associated with her funeral arrangements. The sum of 3s. 4d. was left for the fabric of York Minster. Varied amounts were bequeathed to the local mendicant communities: 20d. to the Blackfriars, 3s. 4d., to the Greyfriars, 6s. 8d., to the Whitefriars for the construction of their church, and 20d. to the Austin Friars. Beatrix seems to have been on good terms with the local Whitefriars and made bequests to three friars of York, William Fynche, William Hovedon and Andrew Stoketon. Her older son, Robert de Lyndsay, was left household valuables. Simon de Fryston, identified as the testator's son, received 12d. although there is no indication of whether he was then resident at the local friary (BIA, Probate Register 3, fol. 18v).

FULBERY (Folbery, Fulbery), Richard: he was ordained s. on 23 September 1402 at Blackfriars, York, and d. on 24 May 1404 at All Saints, Cawood (*Reg. Scrope*, ii, pp. 55, 78, 131).

FURNESS (Furneys), John de: he was ordained s. on 20 September 1348 in Skipton parish church (BIA, Register 10A, fol. 25r).

FURNESS (Fournays, Fourneys, Furnas), Thomas: he was ordained a. on 14 March 1405 and s. on 4 April 1405 at All Saints, Cawood (*Reg. Scrope*, ii, pp. 55, 77, 131), d. on 19 September 1405 at Greyfriars, York. He was a friar of York when he was ordained p. on 24 September 1407 at Blackfriars, York (BIA, Register 5A, fols. 318r, 325v; *Reg. Sede Vacante, York, 1405–08*, pp. 66, 73, 89).

G.: at the request of Master Peter de Ros, precentor, and Master Robert de la Forde, prebendary of Osbaldwick, on 14 March 1300 the goods of Henry Newark, archbishop of York (†1299), were sequestered on account of something due to the diocese and deposited in the York Greyfriars. The following day two friars, G., chamberlain of the friary, and H. de Newark, delivered nine large and four small chests containing the late prelate's goods to the cathedral chapter house (*Fasti Eboracenses*, i, p. 353n, citing *Acta Capit.*, fol. 9b).

GAINSBOROUGH (Geynesburg), John de: he was ordained s. on 23 September 1290 at St Leonard's at Stamford (*Reg. Sutton*, vii, p. 6). Adam de Ludford, guardian of Lincoln, unsuccessfully presented a friar of this name to the bishop of Lincoln for a licence on 7 December 1321 (LAO, Register 5, fols. 299v–300r).

GAINSBOROUGH (Gaynesburgh), John de: he was a friar of York when he was ordained a. on 19 September 1377 at St Mary's Abbey, York (BIA, Register 12, fol. 129r).

GAINSBOROUGH, William de: Leland believed that William was a native of Gainsborough in northern Lincolnshire. William studied at Oxford prior to his election as the vicar of the English province on 1 August 1285 (*Reg. Godfrey Giffard*, p. 263). He was elected minister provincial at the provincial chapter held in Cambridge on 15 August 1285 (TNA, Chanc. Misc.4/2) and was addressed as such by Archbishop Pecham on 31 October of that year (*Letters of John Pecham*, iii, pp. 909–10). He appears as minister again in 1287 (TNA, Chancery Warrants, I, 1792, no. 12). About June of the following year he received expenses for travelling from Bordeaux to England (TNA, E36/201, fol. 31r). Between 1286 and 1289 he recieved 66s. 8d. from the king's treasurer for a journey to Boulogne (*Records of the Wardrobe and Household 1286–1289*, p. 106, no. 961). On 2 May 1289 the king gave William's *garcio* 2s. for carrying royal letters to him at Paris (*ibid.*, p. 314, no. 2705). He appointed Adam de Preston as his vicar during his absence at the general chapter of Assisi in 1288 (Chancery Warrants, I, 1792, no. 13). He was still minister provincial during Raymund Gaufredi's visitation of the English province, when he preached at Oxford on 2 November 1291 (Worcester Cathedral Library, MS.Q.46, fol. 298v; Thomson, *Worcester*, p. 147; Little and Pelster, *Oxford Theology and Theologians*, p. 157; Schneyer, *Repertorium*, ii, p. 459). He may have been absolved at the general chapter of Paris on 25 May 1292 or more probably at the provincial chapter at Cambridge in August or September 1292. He was the 25th regent master at Oxford c.1292 to c.1294 (Eccleston, p. 54; Little, 'The Franciscan School at Oxford in the Thirteenth Century', pp. 861–62).

On 24 October 1292 he was among the prelates and clerics invited to give their judgement on the succession to the Scottish throne (*Edward I and the Throne of Scotland 1290–1296*, ii, pp. 212–13). In 1294 he was sent to France by Edward I on a royal mission and was mentioned by St Thomas Gray in conjunction with Hugh of Manchester, prior provincial of the Dominicans (*Sir Thomas Gray Scalacronica 1272–1363*, pp. 14–15). On 1 March 1295 King Edward I sent letters of credence on behalf of William, a member of the royal council, and John de Wilton to the minister general and chapter of Assisi. The two English friars were to act on the king's behalf and would explain the royal business to the minister general (*CCR, 1288–1296*, p. 440). On 26 March 1295 William and his unnaned *socius* received £30 *euntibus in nuncium regis ad capitulum suum generale in Alemann' apud Argentinum pro expensis suis* (TNA, E403/90, m. 3, courtesy of Dr Jens Röhrkasten). On 1 August 1295 he received a royal payment for travelling to London at the king's command to the Parliament of August (Sayles, *The Functions of the Medieval Parliament of England*, p. 22, n. 1). On 1 September 1295 he received 20s. in expenses for travelling to London for Parliament in August. He went to Lincoln for the provincial chapter and then returned to the king's curia (TNA, E36/202, fol. 44v). He was associated with the bishop of Ponteys in negotiations with King Philip IV in 1295–98, which led to the treaty of Chartres and marriage of King Edward I and Queen Margaret, the king's sister, in 1299 (Rymer, *Foedera*, i, part ii, p. 766). On 5 February 1298 the king wrote to the treasurer and barons of the exchequer on behalf of the friar and John Lovel (*Documents Illustrating the Crisis of 1298–98 in England*, pp. 183–84). On 4 April 1299 he and Hugh of Hartlepool, minister provincial, were given 10 marks in alms for going to the general chapter at Lyons (TNA, E101/356/8). King Edward I was at St Albans on 15 April 1300 when he wrote to Pope Boniface VIII about negotiations for peace with France ... *fideles nostros venerabilem in Christo patrem Ioannem Wynton episcopum, Fratrem Willelmum de Geynesburgh de ordine minorum, Gerardum archidiaconatum Richmond ... procuratores nostros ...* (TNA, C.76/8; Rymer, *Foedera*, i, pars ii, pp. 920–21). In May 1300 he was summoned by Pope Boniface VIII to lecture in theology at the sacred palace in Rome, where he also acted for King Edward I, who provided William and his unnamed *socius* with alms to purchase horses for the journey (BL, MS.Add.35291, fol. 71v; *Liber quotidianus contrarotulatoris garderobae*, pp. 164–65). Two letters of King Edward I to Pope Boniface VIII on 9 September 1302 name W. de Geinesburgh and H. de Hertepole *de ordine minorum*, among the *procuratores et nuncii* to the Holy See in search of the crown's measures to make peace with France (Rymer, *Foedera*, i, pars ii, pp. 943–44). On 26 September 1300 Edward I named him among the *procuratores nostros et nuncios speciales* to effect peace with France (Rymer, *Foedera*, i, pars ii, pp. 922–23).

William was still lecturing in Rome when Pope Boniface VIII provided him to the see of Worcester on 24 October 1302 (Bodleian Library, Digby, MS.168, fol. 210v; *BF*, iv, no. 244, pp. 562–63, gives the date of 29 October). The following day the pope announced that he had appointed the friar to the see of Worcester and asked King Edward I to receive him into his favour (*Original Papal Documents in England and Wales from the accession of Pope Innocent III to the Death of Pope Benedict XI (1198–1304)*, p. 478, no. 1047). William was consecrated in the curia on 28 October 1302 and made his profession before the high altar in Canterbury in the absence of Robert Winchelsey, archbishop of Canterrbury, at an unknown date (*Canterbury Professions*, p. 89). The Franciscans of Worcester processed to meet him when he entered his episcopal city on 8 June 1303 for enthronement the following day. They took part in his installation and on the day following the ceremony they were present in the chapter house of the cathedral priory where Gainsborough preached; on 10 June he confirmed boys in the Franciscan church (*Reg. Sede Vacante, Worcester, 1301–1435*, pp. 52–55). He witnessed charters on 8 October and 20 October 1305 (TNA, c.53/91). On 20 March 1307 he was given a licence to dedicate the Franciscan church and cemetery at Scarborough (BL, Harl.MS.6970, fol. 138v). He was sent to France to negotiate the marriage of Edward, prince of Wales, and Isabella of France. On his return journey he died at Beauvais on 17 September 1307 and was buried among the friars there (Eccleston, p. 54; *GFO*, pp. 160–62; *Franciscan Papers, Lists, and Documents*, 193–94). He was the author of a collection of *questions subtiles* (*Leland, De viris illustribus*, pp. 714–15, no. 507), a copy of which was at the Cistercian monastery of Buckfast (*Libraries of the Cistercians, Gilbertines and Premonstratensians*, p. 11, no. 7; *BRUO*, pp. 750–51; Sharpe, *Handlist*, p. 771, no. 2059; Little and Pelster, *Oxford Theology and Theologians*, p. 157).

GAMBLE, John: he was a friar of Lincoln when he was ordained s. on 12 April 1533 in Lincoln cathedral (LAO, Register 26, fol. 33v). A friar of this name was at Norwich when he was ordained p. in December 1533 (Norwich Registers).

GAMELL, John: he was ordained a. on 8 June 1476 at Blackfriars, York (BIA, Register 22, fol. 239v).

GARDE, Thomas: the will of Walter Orre of Drayton, proved on 13 May 1346, left him 10s. to celebrate Masses for him at the friary in York (BIA, Register 10, fols. 302v–03r). He was licensed to hear confessions in the diocese of York, but had been transferred elsewhere and was replaced by William de Herlaston on 17 October 1347 (BIA, Register 10, fol. 278r).

GARGRAVE, Lawrence: he was ordained a. on 22 September 1403. The editor states that the friar was ordained s. on this occasion (*Reg. Scrope*, ii, pp. 55, 78, 131).

GARNER (Garnar), Thomas: he was a friar at York when he was ordained a. on 5 April 1511 at Greyfriars, York, and s. on 14 June 1511 at Blackfriars, York (BIA, Register 26, fols. 112r, 114r. Cf. Cross and Vickers, *MFN*, p. 443).

GARTON, Peter de: he was a friar of Grimsby when he was licensed for the *limitatio* of that house on 10 August and 12 October 1300 (Little, *Franciscan Papers, Lists, and Documents*, pp. 237, 238) and on 20 June 1318 (LAO, Register 3, fol. 390rv). A friar of this name, probably at York, had a copy by Peter Comester (Durham Cathedral Library, MS.B.11.36, fol. 3r).

GARTON, William de: on 4 November 1304 he was a friar of York who received £10 for the next provincial chapter to be held at Nottingham on 8 September of that year (TNA, E403, 122, mem. 3). A friar of this name was at Beverley when he was left 2s. in the will of Thomas, perpetual vicar of the prebendal church of South Cave, on 27 September 1326 (York Minster, Dean and Chapter Library, MS.L 2/4, fol. 6r).

GEDDINGTON (Gaytinton, Geytington), Thomas de: from 1263 or 1265 he was master of St Leonard's Hospital, York, but resigned on or before 25 March 1276 to become a friar. His successor, Roger of Malton, was elected as master on 16 May of that year (*Reg. Walter Giffard*, pp. 257–58, no. 798). On 11 October 1280 he was a witness to the extent of the hospital (*Cart. St Leonard*, ii, pp. 909–11, 937).

GEFFRAY, Thomas: he was a friar of York when he was ordained p. on 2 June 1509 at Whitefriars, York (BIA, Register 26, fol. 103r. Cf. Cross and Vickers, *MFN*, p. 442).

GENE (Gent), Patrick: he was a friar of York when he was ordained s. on 15 June 1443 at Blackfriars, York, and d. on 24 September 1446 at Austin Friars, York (BIA, Register 19, fols. 269v, 225r).

GERARD, Michael: he was a friar of Lincoln when he was ordained p. on 15 March 1432 at Sleaford prebendal church (LAO, Register 17, fol. 206r).

GERARD, Peter: he was a friar of Lincoln when he was ordained p. on 17 June 1473 in Lincoln cathedral (LAO, Register 21, fol. 139v).

GERM, William: on 18 April 1393 John Parys de York, a goldsmith and parishioner of St Helen in Stonegate, York, left money to be distributed to the poor on the day of his burial and left this friar 12d. (York, Dean and Chapter Library, MS.L 2/4, fol. 106rv).

GERNANS, John: he was ordained p. on 22 May 1350 at Blackfriars, York (BIA, Register 10A, fol. 48r).

GERNOUN' (Gernem, Gernounn), William: he was ordained a. on 20 December 1348 at York Minster and s. on 7 March 1349 at St Michael-le-Belfrey, York. He was a friar of Beverley when ordained p. on 19 September 1349. The first and third ceremonies took place at York Minster (BIA, Register 10A, fols. 26rv, 29v, 34r).

GEYTINGTON, Thomas de: Arundel Castle, MS.25, a copy of Richard Rolle's *The Prick of Conscience*, a later fourteenth-century manuscript, has the inscription on a loose flyleaf to the effect that Thomas de Geytington, when he was a secular, left this book to the Greyfriars of York (*istum librum legavit frater Thomas de Geytington dummodo fuit secularis post vitam suam et fratris sui* ...). The manuscript seems to have been donated to the friars in the early fifteenth century (Arundel Castle, Biblioteca Norfolciana). (The information and a photocopy were kindly supplied by Dr John Martin Robinson, Librarian of Arundel Castle, in a letter of 4 September 1996.)

GHENT (Gandavo), John de: he was ordained a. on 3 April 1400 at Blackfriars, Beverley (*Reg. Scrope*, ii, pp. 55, 78, 131).

GHENT (Gandavo), Peter de: he was ordained p. on 8 March 1376 at Cawood manor chapel (BIA, Register 12, fol. 123v).

GIBSON, Thomas: he was a friar of Richmond when he was ordained a. on 18 September 1512, and at York when ordained s. on 18 December 1512 at Austin Friars, York, d. on 12 March 1513 at Whitefriars, York, and p. on 24 September 1513. The first and fourth ceremonies took place at Holy Trinity Priory, Micklegate, York (BIA, Register 26, fols. 120r, 121r, 123r, 125r). A Sir Thomas Gybson, a priest, was appointed as an executor of the will of John Leek, a mercer of Boston, whose will was compiled on 19 August 1527 (*Lincoln Wills, 1271–1532*, ii, pp. 40–43). On 16 January 1528 this priest was appointed as an executor of the will of Robert Lound, a butcher of Boston (*Lincoln Wills, 1271–1532*, ii, p. 60). On 27 February 1538 Bishop Tunstall and John Uvedale reported to the king that, when the previous Sunday a friar named Thomas Gibson had been helping the wife of Sir William Bulmer of county Durham to go through her evidence for signs of embezzlement, she came across a letter to her husband by the late rebel, Sir John Bulmer (*LPFD*, xiii, pt. i, p. 125, no. 365). Thomas Gibson was instituted to the rectory of All Saints, Peasholme-in-the-Marsh, York, on

23 April 1551, but only held it for a few months (BIA, Register 29, fols. 43v, 44r; Cross and Vickers, *MFN*, pp. 443, 457–58).

GIBSON, Thomas: he was a friar of York when he was ordained p. on 26 May 1526 at Blackfriars, York (BIA, Register 27, fol. 210v. Cf. Cross and Vickers, *MFN*, p. 445).

GIBSON, William: he was a friar of York when he was ordained p. on 24 February 1537 at Austin Friars, York (BIA, Register 28, fol. 197v). A cleric of this name witnessed a will at Ruston early in 1547. A priest of this name, rector of Brantingham, died in 1559. A different William Gibson was said not to reside in his benefice of Kinoulton in 1567 and at a subsequent visitation of 1571 to be 'given to drinking and to idle life'. A will dated 6 June 1582 survives for William Gibson, clerk of Birkin, but contains nothing to link him positively with the former friar (BIA, Probate Register 13, pt. i, fol. 295v, Caveat Book, i, fol. 123rv, v.1567–8 CB i, fol. 28r, v.1571, Court Book, i, fol. 168v; BIA, Probate Register 22, pt. I, fol. 289r; Cross and Vickers, *MFN*, pp. 446, 458).

GILLOW (Gilles), William: he was a friar of York when he was ordained a. on 24 February 1442, d. on 21 September 1443, both ceremonies at Greyfriars, York. He was a friar of Richmond when he was ordained p. on 28 March 1444 at St Mary, Castlegate, York (BIA, Register 19, fols. 265v, 221r, 223).

GINGE (Gignes, Gynges), Richard de: he was ordained s. on 19 September 1293 in Lincoln cathedral, d. on 3 April 1294 at Spaldwick parish church and p. on 18 December 1294 at Stow prebendal church (*Reg. Sutton*, vii, pp. 40, 51, 61).

GIPTON (Guypton), John de: he was ordained d. on 29 May 1344 at Newark parish church (BIA, Register 10A, fol. 7r).

GLEST, Robert: he was a friar of York when he was ordained a. on 18 February 1497, d. on 5 June 1501 at Blackfriars, York, and p. on 18 September 1501. The first and third ordinations took place at Greyfriars, York (BIA, Register 23, fol. 453v, Register 25, fols. 108Bv, 110v. Cf. Cross and Vickers, *MFN*, p. 438).

GLEST (Gleste), Thomas: he was a friar of York when he was ordained a. on 18 February 1497 at Greyfriars, York (BIA, Register 23, fol. 453v). A friar of this name was ordained s. in March 1498 at St Bartholomew's priory, London (London Registers: Savage; Davis, *London Clergy*, no. 9547). He was at Oxford when ordained d. on 22 September 1498 (Salisbury Registers: Blyth, fol. 115r) and was back at York when ordained p. on 6 March 1501 at Greyfriars, York (BIA, Register 5A, fol. 531r; BL, MS. Cotton, Galba, E.X, fol. 146r).

GOCLALCHO: he was a friar of Stamford who was licensed to hear confessions of all Germans in the diocese of Lincoln on 9 March 1366 (LAO, Register 12, fol. 28v).

GODFREY (Godfray, Godray), Richard: he was a friar of York when he was ordained a. on 14 March 1500, s. on 4 April 1500 at Holy Trinity Priory, Micklegate, York, d. on 19 December 1500 at Austin Friars, York, and p. on 6 March 1501. The first and fourth ordinations took place at Greyfriars, York (BIA, Register 23, fols. 466v, 467v, Register 5A, fols. 529v, 531r; BL, MS. Cotton Galba, E.X, fols. 144v, 146r. Cf. Cross and Vickers, *MFN*, p. 439).

GODYSKALL, Henry: he was a friar of York when he was ordained d. on 26 May 1464 at Blackfriars, York (BIA, Register 20, fol. 460r).

GOESSWINI, Nicholas: he was a friar of York when he was ordained d. on 14 June 1432 at Blackfriars, York (BIA, Register 19, fol. 242v).

GOMERSALL (Comersal, Gomersal), John: he was a friar at York when he was ordained a. on 18 February 1497 at Greyfriars, York, s. on 19 December 1500 at Austin Friars, York, d. on 6 March 1501 at Greyfriars, York, and p. on 27 March 1501 at Whitefriars, York (BIA, Register 23, fol. 453v, Register 5A, fols. 529v, 531r, 532r; BL, MS. Cotton Galba, E.X, fols. 144r, 146r. Cf. Cross and Vickers, *MFN*, p. 438).

GONNESSE (Gounesse, Gunnesse), John de: on 25 January 1304 King Edward I sent a pittance of 40s. 4d. for two days to the next general chapter of the order in Assisi and 25s. 4d. to the friary at Oxford through him, guardian of York (TNA, E403/118, mem. 4, E403/117, mem. 3, where the scribe describes Assisi as part of Tuscany; BL, Add.MS.8835, fol. 5v; Goldthorp, 'The Franciscans and Dominicans in Yorkshire', p. 319). On 11 May of the same year the same friar received £25 *ad opus* for the friary of York and the alms for the friaries at Oxford and Cambridge. The former received 12 marks and the latter 25 marks (TNA, E403/122, mem. 2; TNA, E403/121, mem. 1).

GONSOUL, John: he was ordained p. on 6 June 1349 in the prebendal church of Grantham (LAO, Register 9D, fol. 15v).

GOSBERKIRK (Gosberkirke, Gosberkyrke), John de: he was ordained a. on 21 September 1364. He was a friar of Doncaster when he was ordained s. on 3 June 1368; both ceremonies took place at the manor chapel of Bishopthorpe (BIA, Register 11, fols. 357v, 369v).

GOSBERKIRK (Gosberkyrk, Gosbirkirk), Richard de: he was ordained d. on 22 September 1397 in Holy Trinity Priory, York (*Reg. Waldby*, p. 45). He was a friar of Lincoln when he was ordained p. on 21 December 1398 in Torksey Priory (LAO, Register 13, fol. 84r).

GOSBERKIRK (Gosberkyrk), Richard: he was the guardian of Doncaster when he was licensed to hear confessions on 31 March 1479 (BIA, Register 22, fol. 316r). He was at York on 26 February 1489 when William Cerff requested him to celebrate a trental of Masses (BIA, Probate Register 5, fols. 357v–58r). He was the guardian at York on 1 August 1503 when he witnessed the will of Henry Atterton, who asked for burial in the cemetery of St Mary at Castlegate, York (BIA, Probate Register 6, fol. 74r).

GOSBERKIRK (Gosberkirke), William de: he was a friar of Boston when he was ordained s. on 7 June 1354 at Liddington prebendal church (LAO, Register 9D, fol. 71v).

GOSBERKIRK (Gosburkirk), William: he was ordained p. on 19 December 1467 at Austin Friars, York (BIA, Register 22, fol. 189v).

GOSBERKLEY, Richard: he was ordained a. on 16 June 1470 at Blackfriars, York (BIA, Register 22, fol. 205v).

GRAA (Gra), John: he was ordained s. on 19 September 1366 at Bishopthorpe manor chapel. He was at York when ordained d. on 23 December 1368 at Cawood manor chapel and p. on 20 December 1371 at St Mary, Bishophill Senior (BIA, Register 11, fols. 363v, 371v, 386r).

GRAHANNA, Thomas de: he was ordained s. at Horncastle parish church on 21 December 1336 (*Reg. Kirkby*, i, p. 65, no. 346).

GRAITON, William de: he was ordained a. in the parish church of Burton by Lincoln on 17 March 1347 (LAO, Register 7B, fol. 10v).

GRANGER, Gawin: he was a friar of Boston when he was ordained s. on 27 March 1529 and d. on 12 April 1533; both ceremonies took place in Lincoln cathedral (LAO, Register 26, fols. 24r, 33v).

GRANTHAM, Hugh de: he was ordained s. on 10 June 1346 at Whitefriars, York (BIA, Register 10A, fol. 15v) and d. on 26 May 1347 at Lincoln cathedral (LAO, Register 7B, fol. 14v).

GRASBY (Grosseby, Gressby), Thomas de: he was a friar of Lincoln when he was licensed to hear confessions in the diocese on 20 June 1318. He was replaced on 18 February 1330 (LAO, Register 3, fol. 390rv, Register 5, fol. 402v).

GRAUNFORD, Richard de: he was ordained a. on 15 March 1348 at Blackfriars, Northampton (LAO, Register 9D, fol. 1v).

GRAUNT, John: he was ordained a. on 21 December 1392 (BIA, Register 14, fol. 65r) and p. on 22 September 1397; both ceremonies took place at Holy Trinity Priory, Micklegate (*Reg. Waldby*, p. 46).

GREEN (Grene), James: he was ordained p. on 18 December 1479 at Austin Friars, York (BIA, Register 22, fol. 381v).

GREEN (Grene), John: he was ordained a. on 27 May 1363 at Bishopthorpe manor chapel (BIA, Register 11, fol. 352v).

GREEN (Grene), John: he was ordained a. at Bishopthorpe manor chapel on 12 June 1367 (BIA, Register 11, fol. 366r).

GREEN (Grene), John: he was a friar of York when he was ordained d. on 22 September 1442 at York Minster (BIA, Register 19, fol. 220v).

GREEN (Grene), Robert: he was a friar of York when he was ordained s. on 6 June 1433 at St Katherine's Priory, Lincoln, and at Boston when he was ordained d. on 20 February 1434 at Buckden prebendal church (LAO, Register 17, fols. 211r, 214r). He was back at York when he was ordained p. on 20 September 1438 at Greyfriars, York (BIA, Register 19, fol. 258r).

GREENLAW (Grenehowe), John: he was ordained a. on 7 June 1376 at Whitefriars, York. He was a friar of York when he was ordained s. on. 23 May 1377 in York Minster and d. on 19 September 1377 at St Mary's Abbey, York (BIA, Register 12, fols. 124v, 128v, 130r). On 21 January 1400 Pope Boniface IX at Rome dispensed him to hold a benefice with or without cure (*BF*, vii, p. 101, no. 297; *CPL*, v, p. 329). On 20 September 1400 the same pope provided him to the see of *Soltaniensis* and instructed him that, as soon as he had the present letters expedited, he should reside in his diocese (*BF*, vii, p. 109, no. 320; *CPL*, v, p. 288). He was consecrated bishop on 8 September 1401 in the great chapel within the hospital of St Mary without Bishopsgate, London, by Thomas Butler, the Franciscan bishop of *Chrysopolis*, with John, bishop of *Sorensis*, and Thomas Ilshagh, Franciscan bishop of Coutances, assisting (*Reg. Walter Giffard and Henry Bowett*, pp. 17–19). On 9 December 1401 Bishop Bowett explained that he could not personally carry out all the duties committed to him because he was occupied with diverse arduous affairs concerning his diocese and the kingdom. Accordingly, he authorised John to hold confirmations, reconcile churches and cemeteries, consecrate churches and the principal altars, bless chalices and vestments and hold ordinations (*Walter Giffard and Henry Bowett*, p. 17, no. 16). Seeing that John had in his diocese no Catholics and that he could not exercise his ponitifical office there, on 31 December 1401 the pope authorised him to pursue his episcopal ministry in other cities and dioceses, as required by the diocesans (*CPL*, v, p. 480). And at the same time, on 31 December 1401, he had a dispensation to hold a benefice (*CPL*, v, p. 329). He served as suffragan bishop of Bath and Wells between 1401 and 1408 and Exeter in 1402. On 9 December 1401 he was given a suffragan commission by Henry Bowett, bishop of Bath and Wells (*Reg. Walter Giffard and Henry Bowett*, p. 17, no. 16). He assisted in the diocese of Salisbury and held an ordination in the Franciscan church at Salisbury on 21 September 1409 (*Reg. Hallum*, pp. 163–64, no. 1032).

After Henry Bowett's translation to the diocese of York, John followed him to Yorkshire and became his principal suffragan bishop. On 24 June 1411, he was commissioned to visitate the archdeaconry of Richmond (BIA, Register 18, fol. 265v). He received an undated suffragan commission for the diocese of York (BIA, Register 18, fol. 285r). He held regular ordinations in the diocese between 19 September 1411 and 21 December 1420 (BIA, Register 18, fols. 39Crv–39Grv–Hrv, 397r–407rv). Eight of these ceremonies were held in the Greyfriars of York between 19 December 1411 and 17 June 1413. The prebendal church of Cawood was the venue for his recorded ordinations between 14 March 1416 and 21 December 1420. The sacrament of holy orders was also celebrated at St Michael-le-Belfrey, York, Austin Friars, York, and Blackfriars, York. On 10 June 1411 he was appointed to the mediety of Cotgrave in the archdeaconry of Nottingham (BIA, Register 18, fol. 219r). On 10 November 1421 he had swapped his benefice for that of Long Whatton in the diocese of Lincoln (BIA, Register 18, fol. 258v; *Reg. Fleming*, ii, 5, no. 49). He held six ordinations in the prebendal church of Liddington between 27 February 1423 and 18 March 1424 (*Reg. Fleming*, ii, pp. 90–99, nn. 489–93, 495. Cf. Smith, 'Suffragan Bishops in the Medieval Diocese of Lincoln', p. 26; Butler, 'Suffragan Bishops in the Medieval Diocese of York', p. 58).

GRENEGAR, Christopher: he was ordained a. on 18 September 1406 at Blackfriars, York (BIA, Register 5A, fol. 322v; *Reg. Sede Vacante, York, 1405–08*, pp. 66, 74, 89).

GRENELOW (Grouegar), John: he was a friar of Doncaster when he was ordained d. on 19 December 1444 at Austin Friars, York (BIA, Register 19, fol. 224r).

GRIMSBY (Grymseby, Grymmseby), Gilbert de: he was a friar of York when he was ordained a. on 18 September 1350 at Whitefriars, York (BIA, Register 10A, fol. 49r).

He was ordained d. on 19 September 1360 at St Mary's church, Gateshead (Durham Registers: Hatfield, fol. 103r). Lincoln Cathedral Library MS.41 (A.2.10), a copy of Peter Lombard's *Commentary on the Psalter*, was donated to the friars of Lincoln by Master John, vicar of Edlington. The lower margin of folio 1 contains a request in a late fourteenth-century hand: *orate pro anima fratris Gilberti de Grymmesby qui omnes psalmos huius libri ac etiam eorum versus a primo usque ad finem ceriose cotauit* (Thomson, *Lincoln*, p. 29; *MLGB, i*, p. 65).

GRIMSBY (Grimesby), Hugh de: this Augustinian Canon of Thornton Abbey was appointed prior of Nocton Park, Lincolnshire, by Bishop Sutton in succession to Richard of Yarwell on 19 June 1286. He resigned to join the Franciscans and his successor was confirmed on 26 July 1292 (*Reg. Sutton*, i, pp. 83–85, 168–69; *Heads*, ii, p. 434).

GRIMSBY (Grymesby, Grymsby), John: he was the guardian of York when he was licensed to hear confessions in the diocese of York on 30 August 1398 (*Reg. Scrope*, ii, p. 12, no. 729). Dame Constantia, lady of Skelton in Cleveland, asked for burial in the choir of the Augustinian Canons of Gisborough and disposed that 100 marks should be left for priests to celebrate for her soul; one of these was a friar of this name, who was also appointed to superintend or assist her will of 1 May 1402. On this second occasion he may have been a friar of Hartlepool, which was left 40s. (*TE*, i, pp. 292–94; BIA, Probate Register 3, fol. 78rv).

GRIMSBY (Grymesby), Peter de: he was ordained a. on 18 September 1344 at St Mary's Abbey, York, and s. on 18 December 1344 at Whitefriars, York (BIA, Register 10A, fols. 7v, 8v).

GRIMSBY (Grimesby, Grimmesby), Robert de: he was ordained s. on 18 December 1350 at Blackfriars, York (BIA, Register 10A, fol. 50r).

GRIMSBY (Grymesby), Simon de: he was ordained a. on 19 December 1366 at St Leonard's Hospital, York, s. on 23 September 1368, and d. on 22 September 1369; the second and third ceremonies were held at Bishopthorpe manor chapel (BIA, Register 11, fols. 364r, 370v, 375v).

GRIMSBY (Grymsby), Thomas: he was ordained s. on 18 December 1344 at Whitefriars, York (BIA, Register 10A, fol. 8v).

GRIMSBY (Grymesby), William de: he was ordained a. on 18 September 1344 at St Mary's Abbey, York (BIA, Register 10A, fol. 7v). He and the above friar may be one and the same, despite the different Christian names.

GRIMSBY (Grymesby), William: he was ordained s. on 19 September 1394 at Austin Friars, York (BIA, Register 14, fol. 70r).

GRISSINGTON, John: he was a friar of York when he was ordained a. on 19 March 1519 at Greyfriars, York. He was a friar of Richmond when he was ordained s. on 17 December 1519 at Austin Friars (BIA, Register 27, fols. 183r, 186r. Cf. Cross and Vickers, *MFN*, p. 444).

GROUALE (Gronale), Thomas de: he was ordained a. on 13 March 1350 at Beverley

Minster. He was ordained s. on 18 December 1350 and d. on 12 March 1351; the second and third ceremonies took place at Blackfriars, York (BIA, Register 10A, fols. 44r, 50r, 51r). He was a friar of Lincoln when he was ordained p. on 29 March 1354 in Daventry priory (LAO, Register 9D, fol. 71r).

GRUHERDE, George: he was a friar of York when he was ordained d. on 10 June 1503 at Blackfriars, York, and p. on 23 September 1503 at Greyfriars, York (BIA, Register 25, fols. 119v, 120v. Cf. Cross and Vickers, *MFN*, p. 440).

GUERETODES, Simon de: Thomas of Wintersham submitted written testimony regarding a visit to the Templars at the preceptory of Temple Bruer, between Lincoln and Boston, on Christmas day about 1302/03 in the company of this friar. The two friars made observations about the Templars' liturgical practices (Nicholson, *Templars*, i, pp. 185, 387, ii, pp. 193–94, 442).

GUNNY (Gunby), Thomas: he was a friar of Lincoln when he was ordained a. on 17 December 1351 in Sleaford prebendal church. He was a friar of Boston when he was ordained d. on 3 March 1352 in Sleaford prebendal church and p. on 19 May 1353 in Stow prebendal church (LAO, Register 9D, fols. 55r, 57r, 59r, 67r).

GUS, Cornelius de: he was ordained d. at St Michael-le-Belfrey, York, on 2 June 1414 (BIA, Register 18, fol. 39Gr).

GWENT: see Went.

GWYNBORNE: see Swynborn.

GYMBER, John: he was a friar of York when he was ordained a. on 22 September 1515 at Austin Friars, York (BIA, Register 27, fol. 169v. Cf. Cross and Vickers, *MFN*, p. 444). He was a friar of Northampton when he was ordained d. on 19 March 1519 at Liddington prebendal church (LAO, Register 25, fol. 128r).

GYNEL, Thomas: he was ordained p. on 22 September 1352 in Stow prebendal church (LAO, Register 9D, fol. 62v).

GYNESHAM, John de: he was ordained s. on 19 December 1360 at Cawood Manor chapel (BIA, Register 11, fol. 343r).

HADDON, John de: he was ordained s. on 4 June 1379 at St Mary's Abbey, York (BIA, Register 12, fol. 134r).

HADVYN, John: he was ordained p. on 18 September 1423 at All Saints, Cawood (BIA Register 18, fol. 416v).

HALADAND, Richard: he was a friar of Boston when he was ordained p. on 11 April 1517 in Lincoln cathedral (LAO, Register 25, fol. 121v).

HALE, Robert de: he was licensed by the bishop of Lincoln for the *limitatio* of Grimbsy on 10 August and again on 12 October 1300 (Little, *Franciscan Papers, Lists, and Documents*, p. 238).

HALHAM, Alan: he was licensed to hear confessions in the diocese of York on 30 August 1398 (*Reg. Scrope*, ii, p. 12, no. 729).

HALIDAY (Halyday), Richard: he was a friar of Lincoln when he was ordained s. on 23 September 1514 in Lincoln cathedral (LAO, Register 25, fol. 10v).

HALIDEN (Halyden), William de: he was a friar of Richmond when he was ordained s. on 27 May 1396 at St Mary, Bishophill Senior (BIA, Register 14, fol. 72v), d. on 16 June 1397 in St Leonard's Hospital, York (*Reg. Waldby*, p. 41) and p. on 24 May 1399 in the chapel of Cawood Castle (*Reg. Scrope*, ii, pp. 55, 81, 131).

HALIFAX (Alifax, Eliphat), Robert: a scholar of considerable importance who achieved distinction at Paris, Oxford and Cambridge. He had lectured on the *Sentences* by 1332, when he was quoted by Adam Wodeham. He was a doctor of theology, possibly at Paris. An abridgement of the first book of the *Commentary on the Sentences* is extant (Edwards, 'Themes and Personalities in *Sentence* Commentaries at Oxford in the 1330s', p. 382; Stegmüller, i, pp. 359–60, no. 736). He was the 55th regent master at Cambridge c.1336 (Eccleston, p. 61; *BRUO*, pp. 850–51; *GFC*, p. 146). He was probably a friar of Doncaster when he received 20s. in the will of Nicholas de Launeyr, rector of the church of Briseley in the diocese of Norwich, on 28 May 1348; this was proved on 18 June of that year (BIA, Register 10, fol. 326r). He was still there when he was licensed for one year to hear confessions in the diocese of York on 27 February 1349 and 2 October 1350 (BIA, Register 10, fols. 278v, 279v). He enjoyed a high profile in scholastic circles and was described as one of the celebrated masters of theology. He and other English friars were described as: *opera in sacra pagina condentes, in orbe clara eorum memoria patet* (*Bartholomew de Pisa*, pp. 339, 547; Courtenay, 'Some Notes on Robert of Halifax, O.F.M.', pp. 135–42; *GFO*, pp. 222n, 238. Cf. Sharpe, *Handlist*, p. 552, no. 1470).

HALL (Halle), John: he was a friar of York when he was ordained s. on 22 September 1492 at Whitefriars, York (BIA, Register 23, fol. 434r. Cf. Cross and Vickers, *MFN*, p. 438), and at Nottingham when he was ordained d. on 23 March 1493 at Liddington prebendal church and p. on 15 March 1494 in the church of St Mary *ad pontem* at Stamford (LAO, Register 22, fols. 48v, 52v).

HALL, William: he was ordained a. and s. on 20 September 1410 and d. on 6 June 1411; both ceremonies took place at All Saints, Cawood (BIA, Register 18, fols. 392v, 394r). A friar of this name and a member of the community at York was given 6s. 8d. in the will of Isabell Langwath on 16 December 1426 (BIA, Probate Register 2, fol. 604r).

HALL (Halle), William: he was a friar of Lincoln when he was ordained s. on 11 April 1528 in Lincoln cathedral (LAO, Register 26, fol. 21r). He was one of the ten friars of Doncaster who signed the deed of surrender on 20 November 1538 (*Eighth Report of the Deputy Keeper of the Public Records*, p. 19). A cleric of this name, then aged 40, was one of three chantry priests in Sheffield parish church in 1548 (*Chantries, Guilds, Hospitals*, ii, p. 400). After losing his chantry he seems to have remained in the area. On 8 June 1554 the burgesses and commonalty of Sheffield agreed to discharge the crown of several pensions among which was that of £5 to William Halle (*CPR, 1553–1554*, p. 172; Cross and Vickers, *MFN*, pp. 447–48).

HALSALE (Halsal), Henry de: he was a friar of York when he was ordained s. on 24 September 1345 at Ripon Minster and d. on 11 March 1346 at Whitefriars, York (BIA, Register 10A, fols. 12v, 14R).

HALTON, Alexander de: he was ordained a. on 18 September 1350 (LAO, Register 9D, fol. 44r), s. on 18 December 1350 at Blackfriars, York, and d. on 2 June 1352 at St Mary's Abbey, York (BIA, Register 10A, fols. 50r, 55r). He was for a time licensed in the diocese of York. After his death he was replaced by John de Wisbeche at an unspecified date during the administration of Archbishop John Thoresby (BIA, Register 11, fol. 396r).

HALTON, William de: he was ordained s. on 19 September 1293 at Lincoln cathedral (*Reg. Sutton*, vii, p. 40). He was at Oxford on 9 February 1329 when he received the royal alms on behalf of his friary (TNA, E403/241, m. 8; *BRUO*, p. 859). He was at Doncaster during the Michaelmas term in 1332 when, together with the guardian and three other friars, he was sued by John de Malghum for false imprisonment. He probably held an office in the friary at that time (*Notes on Religious Houses*, i, p. 37, TNA, CP40/292, m. 141). He was still there when his name appears in the plea rolls of the Trinity term 1333 (CP40/294, m. 272).

HALYSBY (Alysby), Richard de: he was a friar of York when he was ordained s. on 23 May 1377 in York Minster and d. on 19 September 1377 at St Mary's Abbey, York (BIA, Register 12, fols. 128v, 130r).

HAMBURGH, Henry: he was a friar of Boston when he was ordained d. on 18 December 1434 at Liddington prebendal church (LAO, Register 17, fol. 218v).

HAMPSTHWAITE (Hamsthwaite, Hamswayt, Hamsthwayt), John: he was ordained s. on 13 June 1416 in the prebendal chapel at Cawood (BIA, Register 18, fol. 39Ir). He was one of three friars of York who accompanied Thomas Richmond of York when he preached at the chapel of St Anne on Foss bridge on 26 June 1426. On 13 August of that year John attended the chapter house of York Minster with Richmond and, in the presence of the bishop of Durham, confirmed the content of the friar's vernacular sermon; no attempt was made to excuse the views attributed to Richmond (*Convocation, York*, p. 390; *Records of the Northern Convocation*, p. 151; Wilkins, *Concilia*, iii, p. 488). On 29 November 1429, Alice Poumfreyt, who asked for burial in York Greyfriars, left him a *mappa* (BIA, Probate Register 2, fol. 660v). On 2 May 1443 he was described as a professor and a friar at York when he received 13s. 4d. in the will of Nicholas Usflete, merchant and alderman of York (BIA, Probate Register 2, fol. 59r).

HAMPTON, William de: he was ordained s. on 24 September 1351 in St Mary's parish church, Oxford (LAO, Register 9D, fol. 53). A William de Hamptone was ordained d. on 24 March 1352 in the parish church of Cheltenham (*Reg. Trillek*, p. 578).

HAMPTON, William: he was ordained d. on 18 September 1395 (Worcester Registers: Winchcombe, fol. 126). He was ordained p. in March 1399 and licensed to hear confessions in the diocese of Coventry and Lichfield in October 1405 (LRO, B/A/1/7, fols. 213v, 157). A friar of this name was licensed to hear confessions in the diocese of York on 12 April 1400 (*Reg. Scrope*, ii, p. 12, no. 734).

HAMSWYK, Thomas: he was a friar of York on 1 June 1491 when he witnessed the will of Richard Baynbrig, chaplain of York Minster (York Minster, Dean and Chapter Library, MS.L 2/4, fol. 377r).

HANDEN (Handey), Nicholas: he was ordained a. on 1 June 1398 in St Michael-le-Belfrey, York (BIA, Register 5A, fol. 255r; BL, MS. Cotton, Galba, E.X, fol. 119v).

HANWORTH (Haneworth), Richard: his surname appears in BL, MS. Cotton Faustina B.I. fol. 104r. He occurs between Michaelmas 1278 and Michaelmas 1279 as abbot of the Premonstratensian monastery of Barlings, Lincolnshire (TNA, E159/52, m. 15d). He was named on 17 October 1281 (BL, MS. Cotton Faustina, B.I, fol. 108v), 8 July 1281 and 20 January 1282 (TNA, Lincs. F. CP25/1/132/53, no. 32; TNA, 133/54, no. 11). He resigned the abbacy and was clothed in the Franciscan habit at York on 8 September 1285 (*The Medieval Lindsey Marsh*, pp. 68, 72, no. 31; BL, MS. Cotton Faustina, B.I, fol. 110r; *Heads*, ii, p. 492).

HARALD, Hugh: he was ordained p. on 23 September 1402 at Blackfriars, York (*Reg. Scrope*, ii, pp. 55, 81, 131).

HARANDON, Thomas de: he was licensed to hear confessions in the diocese of York on 10 October 1348 in place of John de Shefeld (BIA, Register 10, fol. 278v).

HARBERGH, Roger de: he was a friar of Nottingham licensed in the diocese of York on 29 October 1351 (BIA, Register 10, fol. 280r).

HARBY (Harvy), John: he was a friar of Oxford when he was ordained d. on 18 September 1484 at Osney Abbey (LAO, Register 22, fol. 15v) and at York when he was ordained p. on 24 September 1485 at Rotherham parish church (BIA, Register 23, fol. 398v. Cf. Cross and Vickers, *MFN*, p. 436). He was the guardian of the friary of Lincoln on 22 August 1493 when John Crokes, a parishioner of St John the Baptist at South Collingham, Nottinghamshire, left him six marks to celebrate Masses daily for his wife and all the faithful in the Greyfriars for a year (*ad celebrandum pro salute anime mei uxoris meae et omnium amicorum meorum in ecclsia predicta per unum annum*). He was Crokes's confessor and witnessed the will, which also left ten sheep or the price of them to each of the four orders of friars in Lincoln (BIA, Probate Register 5, fol. 437rv).

HARCOERT, Nicholas: he was ordained a. in the parish church of Newark, Nottinghamshire, on 29 May 1344 (BIA, Register 10A, fol. 6r).

HARDING (Hardyng), John: he was ordained s. on 3 April 1400 at Blackfriars, Beverley, and ordained d. on 18 September 1400 at All Saints, Cawood (*Reg. Scrope*, ii, pp. 55, 81, 131).

HARDING, Richard: he was a friar of York when he was ordained s. on 20 September 1516 at Greyfriars, York, d. on 11 April 1517 at York Minster and p. on 18 December 1518 at Austin Friars, York (BIA, Register 27, fols. 174r, 177r, 182v. Cf. Cross and Vickers, *MFN*, p. 444).

HARDWICK (Harderwijk, Hardwich), Lambert: he was a friar of York when he was ordained p. on 31 May 1488 at Blackfriars, York (BIA, Register 23, fol. 413v. Cf. Cross and Vickers, *MFN*, p. 436; and Walmsley, 'Some Dutch Franciscans in England during the Later Middle Ages', p. 253).

HARDWICK (Hardwik), Simon de: he was licensed to hear confessions in the diocese of Lincoln in July 1338 (LAO, Register 5, fol. 151v).

HAREHOGH, William: he was ordained d. on 19 May 1380 in Stillingfleet parish church (BIA, Register 12, fol. 137r).

HAREWINE, John: he was ordained a. on 10 June 1346 at Whitefriars, York (BIA, Register 10A, fol. 15r).

HAREWOOD (Arewode, Harewod, Harwod, Harwode), Adam de: he was ordained a. on 21 May 1345 at Thirsk parish church. He was a friar of York when he was ordained s. on 24 September 1345 at Ripon Minster, d. on 1 April 1346 at Whitefriars, York, and p. at an unspecified venue and date between 23 September 1346 and 22 September 1347 (BIA, Register 10A, fols. 10v, 12v, 14v, 18a).

HAREWOOD (Harwod, Harwode), John: he was ordained a. on 7 June 1343 at Greyfriars, York, s. on 17 December 1345 at Liddington prebendal church, d. on 26 May 1347 at Lincoln cathedral and p. on 20 December 1348 at York Minster (BIA, Register 10A, fol. 3v; LAO, Register 7B, fols. 2r, 14v; BIA, Register 10A, fol. 26r).

HARKEY (Herka), Richard: he was a friar of York when he was ordained s. on 4 April 1495 at Holy Trinity Priory, Micklegate, York, and p. on 13 June 1495 at Blackfriars, York (BIA, Register 23, fols. 445v, 447r. Cf. Cross and Vickers, *MFN*, p. 438).

HARLESAY, Thomas: he was a friar of Lincoln when he was ordained p. on 18 September 1507 in the chapel of St Mary Magdalene, Lincoln cathedral (LAO, Register 24, fol. 68r).

HARLESTON (Harlestone), William de: he was a friar of York when he was licensed to hear confessions in the diocese on 16 October 1347 (BIA, Episcopal Register 10, fol. 278r). He was the 71st regent master at Cambridge c.1352 (Eccleston, p. 61). He was licensed in the diocese of Ely on 24 February 1352 (CUL, EDR, G/1/1, De Lisle, fol. 89r; BL, Add.MS.5824, fol. 121r; *BRUC*, p. 287; *GFC*, pp. 100, 145, 182).

HARLETON (Harltone), Roger: after the suppression of the Observants in 1534, he was sent to Scarborough (*LPFD*, vii, p. 601, no. 1607). There is a report of this friar inveighing against John Forest in 1537 (BL, MS. Cotton Cleopatra, E, IV, fol. 133r. Cf. Cross and Vickers, *MFN*, p. 453).

HARLOW (Hirlawe), William de: he was ordained p. on 19 March 1295 at Stow prebendal church (*Reg. Sutton*, vii, p. 66).

HARN, John de: he was ordained s. at an unknown date and venue beween 23 September 1346 and 22 September 1347 (BIA, Register 10A, fol. 18a).

HAROM, William: he was a friar of York when he was ordained a. on 24 April 1350 at Greyfriars, York. He was ordained s. on 18 December 1350 at Blackfriars, York (BIA, Register 10A, fols. 45v, 50r).

HARPHAM, Thomas: he was a friar of York when he was ordained p. on 4 March 1452 at Austin Friars, York (BIA, Register 19, fol. 301v).

HARRISON (Herrison), Henry: he was a friar at York when he was ordained a. on 25 May 1510 at Blackfriars, York, and s. on 5 April 1511 at Greyfriars, York (BIA, Registers 26, fols. 108r, 112r).

HARRISON (Herrison), John: he was a friar of York when he was ordained a. on 20 December 1427 at Austin Friars, York (BIA, Register 19, fol. 230v).

HARTLEPOOL (Hertilpole), William: he was a friar of York when he was ordained p. at Greyfriars, York, on 21 September 1443 (BIA, Register 19, fol. 221v).

HARUM, William: he was the guardian of Lincoln when he was named in the plea rolls of the Michaelmas term of 1366 (TNA, CP40/425, m. 340d).

HARWE, Richard: on 20 May 1531 William Bucknall of Canwick, near Lincoln, left the Greyfriars in Lincoln half a quarter of malt and one *styke* of barley. He gave 10s. to Sir Richard Harwe, his confessor, to celebrate a trental of Masses for him and all Christian souls in the parish church at Canwick. He was one of the witnesses to the will, which was proved on 23 February 1532, and was undoubtedly a friar of Lincoln (*Lincoln Wills, 1530 to 1532*, iii, p. 137).

HARWOOD (Harwod, Harwode), John: he was born out of wedlock and was the son of Robert Harwood, citizen of York and a fletcher, who requested burial in the choir of St Nicholas in the parish church of St Michael Spurriergate. His will was compiled on 28 January 1475. A friar of this name was admitted to the *Corpus Christi* guild at York in 1455 (*Corpus Christi Guild*, p. 56). John was already a priest at York when he made overtures to Dominic de Capranaica, cardinal priest of Santa Croce in Jerusalem, for a dispensation to proceed to major orders; he may have aspired to fill other offices in the fraternity. The cardinal, the vicar in spiritual matters, wrote to the archbishop of York and on 14 June 1458 issued the letter of dispensation, which was copied into the episcopal register. Archbishop Booth wrote to Harwood, quoting the letter which he had recently received from Rome. The letters of dispensation from defect of birth were inspected at Cawood Castle on 26 August 1458 (BIA, Register 20, fol. 200rv). John's approach to the Roman curia was probably made not long after the completion of his studies and may have been associated with his arrival in the diocese of York as a comparatively junior priest in the community. In his father's will of 28 January 1475 he was appointed an executor (BIA, Register 4, fol. 223r). He was on good terms with Robert Shirwyn, the brother of Henry, another member of the local Greyfriars. On 24 July 1475 Robert Shirwyn appointed his brother, Henry, to supervise his will. In the event of Shirwyn being absent, Harwood was to be appointed to supervise the will (BIA, Probate Register 5, fol. 336rv). On 21 May 1488 Harwood was left 40s. in the will of John Gaunte, a merchant of York who asked for burial in St Mary's at Castlegate. He was requested to celebrate Masses for Gaunte and the souls of all the faithful departed in the Greyfriars for the period of a year following his death (BIA, Probate Register 5, fol. 336rv). On 26 February 1489 William Cerff, rector of Rowley, compiled his will at York and asked John to celebrate a trental of Masses for him and appointed him as a witness to the will (BIA, Probate Register 5, fols. 357v–58r).

HASSIA, Conrad de: he was ordained d. on 19 September 1411 at St Michael-le-Belfrey, York (BIA, Register 18, fol. 39Cr).

HASWELL, Roger de: he was ordained p. on 23 September 1290 at St Leonard's, Stamford (*Reg. Sutton*, vii, p. 7).

HASWELL (Hawswell), Thomas: he was admitted to the guild of *Corpus Christi* at York in 1481 (*Corpus Christi Guild*, p. 109). He was at York on 26 February 1489 when William Cerff asked him to celebrate a trental of Masses for him (BIA, Probate Register 5, fols. 357v–58r). He was a friar of York when he witnessed the will of Richard Baynbrig, chaplain of York Minster, on 1 June 1491 (York Minster, Dean and Chapter Library, MS.L 2/4, fol. 377r).

HATCLIFFE (Hatclyff), Nicholas: he was ordained a. on 19 September 1433 at Whitefriars, York. He was a friar of York when he was ordained s. on 2 June 1436 at Blackfriars, York (BIA, Register 19, fols. 245r, 252r).

HAUKESWELL, John de: he was a friar of Richmond when he was licensed to hear confessions in the diocese of York in 1349, being presented to the archbishop by Richard, custos of Newcastle (BIA, Register 10, fol. 278v).

HAUKSWELL, Thomas: on 23 September 1426 William Schroude, a chaplain of Richmond, asked for burial in the town's Greyfriars and left this friar, the master at the friary in Richmond, 100s. to celebrate for his soul for the period of one year (BIA, Probate Register 2, fol. 503r).

HAUSAND (Hansand), Richard: he was a friar of York when he was ordained s. on 27 February 1496 at Greyfriars, York. He was a friar of Richmond when he was ordained d. on 28 May 1496 at Holy Trinity Priory, Micklegate, York. He was at York again when he was ordained p. on 17 December 1496 at Whitefriars, York (BIA, Register 23, fols. 449r, 451r, 453r. Cf. Cross and Vickers, *MFN*, p. 438).

HAWARD, Richard: he was guardian of the friary at Carlisle on 2 October 1350 when he was licensed to hear confessions in the diocese of York (BIA, Register 10, fol. 279v).

HAWE, John de: he was ordained a. on 16 June 1375, s. on 8 March 1376 and p. on 22 December 1380; all three ceremonies took place at Cawood manor chapel (BIA, Register 12, fols. 120r, 123r, 138v).

HAWE, Thomas de: he was licensed to hear the confessions of the members of the household of Thomas Wake for one year from 17 December 1338 (LAO, Register 5, fol. 152r).

HAWELEY, William: he was the guardian of Grimsby in the Easter term of 1384. He brought an action against John Thomsson of Beswick, a chaplain who was detained in York castle (TNA, CP40/493, m. 334).

HAWKE (Hawk), Robert: he was a friar at Lincoln when he was ordained a. on 27 March 1535 at Lincoln cathedral, s. on 15 April 1536 in the chapel of St Mary Magdalene in Lincoln cathedral, d. on 10 June 1536 at the prebendal church of

Buckden and p. on 31 March 1537 in the chapel of St Mary Magdalene in Lincoln cathedral (LAO, Register 26, fols. 43r, 52rv, 54v). He was one of the ten friars of Doncaster who signed the deed of surrender on 20 November 1538 (*Eighth Report of the Deputy Keeper of the Public Records*, p. 19. Cf. Cross and Vickers, *MFN*, p. 447).

HAWKSWORD (Haukesword), Richard de: on 7 December 1321 the guardian of Lincoln unsuccessfully presented this friar for a licence to hear confessions in the diocese of Lincoln (LAO, Register 5, fols. 299v–300r).

HAWKYSWELL, Thomas de: he was ordained s. on 7 June 1366 at St Mary's, Gateshead, and p. on 2 April 1373 in St Mary's, Newcastle (Durham Registers: Hatfield, fols. 107v, 110v). He is described as *cursor* of York when licensed in the diocese of York on 30 August 1398 (*Reg. Scrope*, ii, p. 12, no. 729). He was a doctor of theology of Oxford when he was mentioned as an opponent of John de la Zouche, minister provincial, in 1405 (Bodleian Library, MS.Arch.Selden, B.23, fol. 56; Whitfield, 'Conflicts of Personality and Principle: The Political and Religious Crisis in the English Franciscan Province, 1400–1409'; *BRUO*, p. 886).

HAWKYSWYK, Thomas: he was a friar of York when licensed to hear confessions in the diocese on 30 August 1398 (*Reg. Scrope*, ii, p. 12, no. 729).

HAWLAY (Haweley, Hauley), William de: he was ordained a. and s. on 22 December 1358 and d. on 15 June 1359 and p. on 11 June 1362; all three ceremonies took place at the manor chapel of Cawood (BIA, Register 11, fols. 335v, 338r, 349v). He was the guardian at Grimsby when named in the plea rolls of Trinity term 1384 (TNA, CP40/493, m. 334).

HAWTE, Richard: he was a friar of York when ordained p. on 1 April 1441 at Austin Friars, York (BIA, Register 19, fol. 264v).

HAWYK, John: on 1 March 1335 he received the royal alms for the friars of York (TNA, E101/387/9).

HAXAY (Haxay), John or William de: he was a friar of Doncaster when he was ordained s. on 3 June 1368 at Bishopthorpe manor chapel. He was ordained d. on 18 September 1372 at Greyfriars, York (BIA, Register 11, fols. 369v, 389r).

HAXEY (Haxay), John: he was a friar of Doncaster when he was ordained a. on 2 March 1420 at Cawood prebendal chapel (BIA, Register 18, fol. 405r). A friar of this name was permitted to hold a benefice on 11 July 1442 (*BF, ns*, i, p. 283, no. 601).

HAYDO', Richard: he was ordained a. on 19 September 1405 and p. on 22 April 1413; both ceremonies took place at Greyfriars, York (BIA, Register 5A, fol. 317v, Register 18, fol. 395v). A Friar Haydo whose first name was not entered was resident at York when he was left 6s. 8d. to pray for the soul of Thomas Bardolsse, a woolman and parishioner of St Sampson, whose will was drawn up on 4 April 1432 (BIA, Probate Register 2, fol. 604v).

HAYDOK, Henry de: he was ordained p. on 24 September 1351 in York Minster (BIA, Register 10A, fol. 53r).

HAYLAND, Hugh: he was a friar of Boston when he was ordained s. on 19 May 1353 at Stow prebendal church (LAO, Register 9D, fol. 66v).

HAYNE, Robert de: he was a friar of York when he was ordained d. on 24 September 1496 at Austin Friars, York (BIA, Register 23, fol. 452r). He was a friar of Boston when he was ordained p. on 17 December 1496 at All Saints church, Northampton (LAO, Register 24, fol. 6r. Cf. Cross and Vickers, *MFN*, p. 438).

HAYTEFELD, Thomas: he was a friar of York when he was ordained d. on 23 September 1419 at Cawood prebendal chapel (BIA, Register 18, fol. 404r).

HEDYN, Simon: he was a friar of York when he was ordained d. on 25 May 1426 at Holy Trinity Priory, Micklegate, York (BIA, Register 19, fol. 227r).

HEKILFELD (Hekylsale), Thomas: he was ordained s. on 3 April 1400 at Blackfriars, Beverley, and d. on 17 December 1401 at St Mary's Abbey, York (*Reg. Scrope*, ii, pp. 55, 82, 131).

HELMSLEY (Helmeselay), William de: he was ordained d. on 12 June 1367 in Bishopthorpe manor chapel (BIA, Register 11, fol. 366v).

HELWYK, John: on 4 March 1336 he received the royal alms for the friars of York (TNA, E101/387/9).

HEMINGHAM (Hemyngham), Richard de: he was ordained a. on 20 December 1348 at York Minster (BIA, Register 10A, fol. 26r).

HEMMYSLEY (Hemmysley), John: after the suppression of the Observants in 1534, he was sent to the Greyfriars of Scarborough (*LPFD*, vii, p. 601, no. 1607. Cf. Cross and Vickers, *MFN*, p. 453).

HEMPINGHAM, William: he was a friar of Boston when he was ordained p. on 16 March 1359 at Liddington prebendal church (LAO, Register 9D, fol. 91v).

HENCLE, Nicholas de: he was ordained s. at Horncastle parish church on 21 December 1336 (*Reg. Kirkby*, i, p. 65, no. 346).

HENRY: he was the guardian of York in the Hilary term of 1378 and the Trinity term of the same year when he was mentioned in the plea rolls (TNA, CP40/469, mm. 24d and attorneys, m. 4 and CP40/471, m. 19d).

HENRY: he issued a letter of fraternity to Reginald Browne at an unspecified date in 1479 (Wordsworth, 'On Some Pardons or Indulgences Preserved in Yorkshire, 1412–1527', pp. 369, 402, 416–17).

HEPHAM, William de: a friar who received the royal alms for the friary at Boston on 7 July 1312 (BL, MS. Cotton Nero C.VIII. fol. 52r).

HERICE (Heris, Heriz), Richard de: on 20 June 1318 he was licensed to hear confessions in the diocese of Lincoln (LAO, Register 3, fol. 390). By 17 November 1320 he had moved to York (LAO, Register 5, fols. 265v–66; *BRUO*, p. 917).

HERLE, William de: he was ordained s. on 20 December 1343 at Durham cathedral (*Reg. Kellaw*, iii, p. 131). He was a friar of Richmond when he was ordained d. on 23 December 1345 in Auckland collegiate church (Durham Registers: Hatfield, fol. 93r), and p. on 20 December 1348 at York Minster (BIA, Register 10A, fol. 26r).

HERTLINBURG (Hertilburgh), Ralph de: he was licensed to hear confessions in the diocese of York on 17 October 1347 in place of John de Newark, who had died (BIA, Register 10, fol. 278r). He was the guardian of Scarborough on 2 October 1350 when he was licensed to hear confessions (BIA, Register 10, fol. 279v).

HERVY, Robert: he was ordained p. on 22 September 1478 at Holy Trinity Priory, Micklegate, York (BIA, Register 22, fol. 375r).

HESAM (Hesham), John: he was ordained s. on 6 June 1411 at Cawood prebendal chapel, d. on 19 December 1411 and p. on 17 December 1412. The second and third ceremonies took place at Greyfriars, York (BIA, Register 18, fols. 394r, 39Cv, 395v).

HESHAM, William: he was a friar of York when he was ordained a. on 27 May 1469 at Blackfriars, York, and d. on 21 April 1470 in the lady chapel of York Minster (BIA, Register 20, fols. 200v, 205r).

HESILDEN (Hasylden), John: he was ordained a. on 14 March 1394 at All Saints, Pavement, York, d. on 27 March 1395 at Holy Trinity Priory, Micklegate, York, and p. on 1 June 1398 in the parish church of St Michael-le-Belfrey, York (BIA, Register 14, fols. 69r, 71r, Register 5A, fol. 256v; BL, MS. Cotton Galba, E.X, fol. 120v).

HESILDEN (Hasleden), Robert de: he was a friar of Richmond when he was ordained s. on 27 May 1396 at St Mary, Bishophill Senior (BIA, Register 14, fol. 72v), d. on 16 June 1397 in St Leonard's Hospital, York (*Reg. Waldby*, p. 41) and p. on 24 May 1399 in the chapel at Cawood Castle (*Reg. Scrope*, ii, pp. 55, 83, 131). He was at Hartlepool when he was licensed as a penitentiary on 30 December 1407 (*Reg. Langley*, i, p. 39).

HESKYN, Robert: he was ordained s. on 11 June 1351 at St Mary's Abbey, York (BIA, Register 10A, fol. 52r) and p. on 20 December 1354 in the diocese of Coventry and Lichfield (LRO, B/1/1, fol. 210v).

HESLINGTON (Heslyngton), Richard de: he was ordained a. on 5 June 1406 at Austin Friars, York (BIA, Register 5A, fol. 321v; *Reg. Sede Vacante, York, 1405–08*, pp. 66, 75, 89), d. on 9 June 1408 at Blackfriars, York (BIA, Register 18, fol. 39r), and p. on 6 June 1411 at Spalding conventual church (Canterbury Registers: Thomas Arundel, ii, fol. 89r). He was guardian at Doncaster on 3 May 1425 when he was a witness in the investigation concerning the abduction of Katherine Northefolk (BIA, Cause Papers, CP, fol. 156).

HESSAY, John: he was ordained a. on 13 March 1367 at St Mary, Bishophill Senior, York. He was a friar of Doncaster when ordained s. on 3 June 1368. He was ordained d. on 24 February 1369; the second and third ceremonies took place at Bishopthorpe manor chapel (BIA, Register 11, fols. 365r, 369v, 373r).

HESSAY (Hessey), Thomas de: he was a friar at Doncaster when he was licensed to hear confessions in the diocese of York on 14 June 1350 in place of a deceased friar (BIA, Register 10, fol. 279r).

HEWE, John: he was a friar of York who received 13s. 9d. in 1485 for repairing the Minster organs at the altar of the Blessed Virgin Mary, and for carrying them to and from the convent (*The Fabric Rolls of York Minster*, p. 88).

HEXHAM (Hextildesham), John de: he was ordained a. on 28 February 1344 in Durham cathedral (*Reg. Kellaw*, iii, p. 149). He was a friar of Carlisle when he was ordained s. on 17 December 1345 in Auckland collegiate church, and he was ordained d. on 23 September 1346 in Elvet parish church (Durham Registers: Hatfield, fols. 93r, 94r). He was ordained p. on 15 March 1348 at York Minster (BIA, Register 10A, fol. 21v).

HEXHAM, Thomas de: he was ordained p. on 2 June 1352 in St Mary's Abbey, York (BIA, Register 10A, fol. 55v).

HEXTHORPE (Exthorp, Hoxthorp), Robert: he was a friar of Lincoln when he was ordained a. on 24 May 1404 in Liddington prebendal church, s. on 20 September 1404 in Lincoln cathedral and d. on 20 December 1404 in Lincoln cathedral (LAO, Register 13, fols. 114r, 115v, 117r).

HEXTHORPE (Hexthorp), William de: he was ordained d. on 21 December 1364 at Greyfriars, York, and p. on 12 June 1367 at Bishopthorpe manor chapel (BIA, Register 11, fols. 358v, 366v).

HEY, Stephen: he was a friar of York when he was ordained d. on 23 September 1419 at Cawood prebendal chapel (BIA, Register 18, fol. 404r).

HEYSAM, Hugh: he was a friar of Lincoln when he was ordained p. on 29 March 1354 in Daventry priory church (LAO, Register 9D, fol. 71r).

HIGHBURGH, John de: he was ordained s. on 10 June 1346 at Whitefriars, York (BIA, Register 10A, fol. 15v).

HIKAM (Hikham), William: he was the guardian of Lincoln when he was mentioned in the plea rolls in the Trinity terms of 1468 and 1473. John Preston, probably a friar of Lincoln, was named on both occasions. The same two friars were cited again in the Trinity term of 1481 with Hikam still in office, but did not appear (TNA, KB27/829, rex mm. 11d, 14d, KB27/848, rex m. 35, KB27/878, rex m. 12d).

HILDENSEM, Thomas: he was a friar of York when he was ordained p. on 4 March 1452 at Austin Friars, York (BIA, Register 19, fol. 301v).

HILDEYERD (Hildyard), Arnald: he was ordained p. on 15 June 1359 at Cawood manor chapel (BIA, Register 11, fol. 338r). He was licensed in the diocese of York at an unknown date. After his death he was replaced by Richard de Multon (BIA, Register 11, fol. 396r).

HILDYRWELL, Thomas de: he was a friar of Richmond when he was ordained s. on 22 September 1397 in Holy Trinity Priory, Micklegate, York, and d. on 22 December 1397 in Ripon Minster (*Reg. Waldby*, pp. 47, 49).

HILL, William: he was ordained p. on 20 September 1393 at St Leonard's Hospital, York (BIA, Register 14, fol. 68r).

HILLINGTON (Hyllington), Thomas: he was a friar of Stamford when he was ordained d. on 23 February 1404. He was a friar of Boston when he was ordained p. on 24 May 1404; both ceremonies were held at Liddington prebendal church (LAO, Register 13, fols. 113v, 115r).

HILTON (Hylton), John: he was a friar of York when he was ordained s. on 5 June 1501 at Blackfriars, York (BIA, Register 26, fol. 108Bv. Cf. Cross and Vickers, *MFN*, p. 439). A friar of this name was a member of the community at Northampton during the Dissolution on 30 October 1538 (*Eighth Report of the Deputy Keeper of the Public Records*, p. 34).

HILTON, William de: he was ordained a. at an unspecified date between 23 September 1346 and 22 September 1347 (BIA, Register 10A, fol. 18a).

HILTON, William: he was a friar of York when he was ordained s. on 2 June 1509 at Whitefriars, York (BIA, Register 26, fol. 103r).

HINKLEY (Hynkele), Roger de: he was ordained p. on 26 May 1347 at Lincoln cathedral (LAO, Register 7B, fol. 15v).

HIRST, Richard: he was a friar of York when he was ordained a. on 24 September 1502 at Blackfriars, York (BIA, Register 25, fol. 113v. Cf. Cross and Vickers, *MFN*, p. 440).

HODGESON (Hogeson), John: he was a friar of Lincoln when he was ordained s. on 3 April 1507 in the chapel of St Mary Magdalene in Lincoln cathedral (LAO, Register 24, fol. 65). He was a friar of York when he was ordained d. on 18 December 1507 at Austin Friars, York, and p. on 24 March 1509 at Blackfriars, York (BIA, Register 5A, fol. 584r, Register 26, fol. 101r).

HOGHARD, Richard: he was a friar of York when he was ordained a. on 14 June 1511 at Blackfriars, York (BIA, Register 26, fol. 113v. Cf. Cross and Vickers, *MFN*, p. 443).

HOLBEACH (Holbeche), John: he transcribed two books written by his confrères: first, *Tractatus de medicinis fratris Willelmi Holm de ordine minorum*, an English friar, in Trinity College Library, Cambridge, MS.1422. O.9.10, folios 114rb–19rb. He copied the whole manuscript, with the exception of the *Remedium contra pestilenciam* (fols iii, ra-iv, rb). The *Tabula super Avicennam* has the *explicit Tabula Avicenne Fen. super interpretaciones dictionum Ebro Ebraicarum, Grecarum et eciam Persidarum script[a] per Fr. Iohannem Holbeche m[agistrum]. ordinis minorum* (Cambridge, Trinity College Library, MS.O.9.10, fols. 114r–19r, 66v; James, *The Western Manuscripts in the Library of Trinity College, Cambridge: A Descriptive Catalogue*, iii, p. 449, no. 1422; and Mooney, *The Index of Middle English Prose. Handlist 11: Manuscripts in the Library of Trinity College, Cambridge*, p. 138). Secondly, Nicholas of Lyra's commentary on the books of the Old Testament. His name occurs at the end of almost each book as the scribe. There is an exhortation that those who read the manuscript after his death should recite a *Pater Noster* or *Ave Maria* for the repose of his soul. The commentary on the book of Deuteronomy, for instance, concludes with this note: '... written by Friar John Holbeche of the order of Friars Minor. If anyone should use this book after his death, he should faithfully and devoutly pray a *Pater Noster* and *Ave Maria* for his soul'. Similarly, there is a comparable exhortation to recite the same prayers for John's soul at the end of the second book of Maccabees (Peterhouse Library, Cambridge, MS.85, fols. 27va, 54ra, 68va, 85ra, 101vb, 112vb, 125vb, 144rb, 158rb, 187vb, 200va, 211va, 223vb, 235va). The last entry, the second book of Maccabees, has an inscription: *unde istum librum scripsit Frater Iohannes Holbeche et ideo si quis habuerit vel respexerit intuitu caritatis oret devota mente pro eius anima dicendo pater noster et ave maria* (fol. 235va). It is probable that he was either enrolled for the lectorate programme at Cambridge or was a member of the university registered for the baccalaureate or doctorate A friar of this name was licensed to hear confessions in the diocese of Ely on 25 May 1411 (CUL, EDR, G/1/3, fol. 260r).

HOLBEACH (Holbech), Thomas de: he was a friar of Boston when he was licensed to hear confessions in the diocese of Lincoln on 14 March 1319 until the next provincial chapter (LAO, Register 3, fols. 411v–12).

HOLBEK (Holbek), Thomas: he was ordained a. on 6 March 1406 at Holy Trinity Priory, Micklegate, York (BIA, Register 5A, fol. 319v; *Reg. Sede Vacante, York, 1405–08*, pp. 66, 75, 89).

HOLCOTE, Simon: a friar successfully presented by the minister provincial to the bishop at Boston on 16 May 1409 according to the terms of *Super cathedram* (*Reg. Repingdon*, i, pp. 149–50).

HOLE, Henry: he was ordained a. in the chapel of St Martin, called the charnel chapel, Beverley, on 15 February 1410 (BIA, Register 18, fol. 39Av).

HOLLAND (Hoyland'), John de: he was ordained s. on 22 September 1291 at Grantham parish church, d. on 19 September 1293 at Lincoln cathedral and p. on 17 December 1295 at St James's Priory, Huntingdon (*Reg. Sutton*, vii, pp. 18, 42, 73).

HOLLAND (Hollandia), John de: he was a friar of York when he was ordained s. on 19 December 1433 at Austin Friars, York (BIA, Register 19, fol. 245v; Walmsley, 'Some Dutch Franciscans in England during the Later Middle Ages', p. 251).

HOLLAND (Holand), Thomas: he was ordained p. on 21 September 1409 at Cawood prebendal chapel (BIA, Register 18, fol. 391r; Walmsley, 'Some Dutch Franciscans in England during the Later Middle Ages', p. 254).

HOLME (Holm), John: he was ordained d. on 1 March 1393 at St Michael-le-Belfrey, York, and p. on 19 September 1394 at Austin Friars, York (BIA, Register 14, fols. 66r, 70v).

HOLME (Howm), John de: he was a friar of Beverley when he was ordained p. in 1274 (*Reg. Walter Giffard*, p. 198, no. 697).

HOLME, Richard: he was a friar of York when he was ordained s. on 19 September 1489 at Whitefriars, York (BIA, Register 23, fol. 418v. Cf. Cross and Vickers, *MFN*, p. 437). He was a friar of Stamford when he was ordained d. on 27 March 1490 at

Liddington prebendal church, and at Lincoln when he was ordained p. on 11 April 1490 (LAO, Register 22, fols. 35r, 36r). A Richard Holmes of Leicester received his capacity on 20 May 1540 (Chambers, *Faculty Office Registers 1534–1549*, p. 216).

HOLME (Holm, Holne), Robert: he was ordained a. on 28 May 1401 at Bishop Burton, s. on 23 September 1402 at Blackfriars, York (*Reg. Scrope*, ii, pp. 55, 84), d. on 19 December 1405 at the same venue (BIA, Register 5A, fol. 319r; *Reg. Sede Vacante, York, 1405–08*, pp. 66, 75, 89) and p. on 9 June 1408. All the other ceremonies took place at Blackfriars, York (BIA, Register 18, fol. 39r).

HOLNLOKE (Humlocke), George: on 24 July 1534 he was licensed to preach and hear confessions in the city and diocese of York (BIA, Register 28, fol. 85v). He was one of the ten friars of Doncaster who signed the deed of surrender on 20 November 1538 (*Eighth Report of the Deputy Keeper of the Public Records*, p. 19. Cf. Cross and Vickers, *MFN*, pp. 447, 448).

HONDAN, Nicholas: he was ordained a. on 1 June 1398 at St Michael-le-Belfrey, York (BIA, Register 5A, fol. 255r).

HONYNGHAM, Thomas de: he was a friar of York when he was ordained d. on 26 May 1358 at Greyfriars, York. He was ordained p. on 18 September 1361 at Cawood manor chapel (BIA, Register 11, fols. 333v, 346r).

HOODE (Hood), Anthony: at the suppression of the Observant province he was sent to Lincoln in 1534 (*LPFD*, vii, p. 601, no. 1607).

HORBURN, Edmund de: on 12 November 1299 he received the royal alms for the friars of Doncaster. Payment was made at Wentbridge (TNA, E101/356/7).

HORNCASTLE (Horncaster'), William de: he was ordained s. on 15 March 1348 at York Minster (BIA, Register 10A, fol. 21r). He was a friar of Boston when he was ordained p. on 20 September 1348 at Leicester Blackfriars (LAO, Register 9D, fol. 8v).

HORNCASTLE (Horncaster, Horncastre), William de: he was ordained p. on 16 June 1375 at Cawood manor chapel (BIA, Register 12, fol. 121r).

HOSEHAM, John: he was ordained a. on 15 February 1410 in St Martin's chapel (le charnel), Beverley (BIA, Register 18, fol. 39Av).

HOSYLL (Hesyll), Richard de: he was ordained p. on 30 May 1366 at Bishopthorpe manor chapel (BIA, Register 11, fol. 363v).

HOTHAM (Hothum), Giles de: he was a friar of York when he was ordained d. on 18 December 1344 at Whitefriars, York. He was ordained p. on 22 December 1347 at Greyfriars, Doncaster (BIA, Register 10A, fols. 9r, 20r).

HOTHAM (Hothom), Robert: he was ordained a. on 18 September 1406 at Blackfriars, York. He was a friar of York when ordained p. on 17 December 1407 at Holy Trinity Priory, Micklegate, York (BIA, Register 5A, fols. 322v, 326r; *Reg. Sede Vacante, York, 1405–08*, pp. 66, 75, 89).

HOTHAM (Hothom), Thomas de: he was ordained a. on 22 September 1369 at Bishopthorpe manor chapel (BIA, Register 11, fol. 375r).

HOTHENS, Thomas de: he was ordained a. on 20 December 1376 at Holy Trinity Priory, Micklegate (BIA, Register 12, fol. 126v). A friar of this name was ordained d. on 20 December 1376 in the same ceremony, unless it is a mistake for s. (BIA, Register 12, fol. 127r).

HOTHORP, Hugh de: on 20 June 1318 he was licensed to hear confessions in the diocese of Lincoln (LAO, Register 3, fol. 390rv; *BRUO*, p. 971). He had been transferred to a friary in Yorkshire by 18 November 1320 (LAO, Register 5, fols. 265v–66r).

HOTON (Howetun, Howton, Houghton), Adam: he was a friar of York when he was ordained a. on 25 May 1499 at Blackfriars, York, and when he was ordained d. on 18 September 1501 at Greyfriars, York (BIA, Register 23, fol. 464r, Register 25, fol. 110r; Cross and Vickers, *MFN*, p. 439). He was guardian of Grimsby at the Dissolution on 9 October 1538 (*Eighth Report of the Deputy Keeper of the Public Records*, p. 22; *LPFD*, xiii, pt. ii, p. 223, no. 572; *VCH, Lincs.*, ii, p. 219). On 8 October John Freman informed Cromwell that he had taken the surrender of the friary (*LPFD*, xiii, pt. ii, p. 220, no. 567).

HOTON (Hotton), John de: he was ordained p. on 20 December 1365 in York Minster (BIA, Register 11, fol. 361r).

HOTON (Hotom, Howeton, Huton), Thomas: he was a friar of York when ordained a. on 26 May 1464 at Blackfriars, York (BIA, Register 20, fol. 459v), and when he was ordained s. on 5 April 1466 at the lady chapel of York Minister, and d. on 23 May 1467 at Blackfriars, York. He was ordained p. on 19 September 1467 at Greyfriars, York (BIA, Register 22, fols. 182v, 186v, 188r).

HOTON, William: he was a friar of Richmond when he was ordained s. on 22 September 1397 at Holy Trinity Priory, Micklegate, York (*Reg. Waldby*, p. 47), d. on 1 June 1398 at St Michael-le-Belfrey, York (BIA, Register 5A, fol. 256r; BL, MS. Cotton Galba, E.X, fol. 119v), and p. on 18 September 1400 at All Saints, Cawood (*Reg. Scrope*, ii, pp. 55, 85, 131).

HOUGHTON (Houton), Reginald de: he was ordained s. on 31 May 1292 in Lincoln cathedral (*Reg. Sutton*, vii, p. 26).

HOUGHTON (Houton, Houchton), Walter de: he was ordained p. on 23 September 1290 in St Leonard's, Stamford (*Reg. Sutton*, vii, p. 7). He was at Lincoln when he was licensed to hear confessions for that house on 12 October 1300 (Little, *Franciscan Papers, Lists, and Documents*, p. 238).

HOUSON (Housom), John de: he was ordained s. on 26 May 1347 at Lincoln cathedral (LAO, Register 7B, fol. 13r). He was at York when he was ordained p. on 18 September 1350 at Whitefriars, York (BIA, Register 10A, fol. 49v).

HOWDEN (Hovedon, Haudene, Hofdene), Adam de: he preached at Oxford on 11 November 1290, 1 January 1291 and 6 January and 25 March 1293. His opinion concerning original sin is cited in Assisi, MS.158, fol. 235c as *Hofdene*, on the nature of evil as the *privacio boni* (Henquinet, 'Descriptio codicis 158 Assisii in Bibliotheca Communali', p. 234). Four of his sermons at Oxford have survived in *reportationes*: first, Worcester Cathedral Priory Library, MS.Q.46, fols. 113v–16r (*Invenerunt puerum cum Maria matre eius*), a homily for the feast of the Epiphany; secondly, fols. 246r–47v (*Consummati sunt dies octo*) preached on 1 January 1291; thirdly, fols. 259r–61v (*Ave gratia plena*) preached on 25 March 1293; and fourthly, fol. 307r–08v (*Esto vir fortis et preliare bella Domini*), a sermon for 11 November, the feast of St Martin of Tours. There is also a copy of the first sermon in New College Library, Oxford, MS.92, fol. 82v; Little and Pelster, *Oxford Theology and Theologians*, pp. 155, 156, 163, 178, 187; Schneyer, *Repertorium*, i, pp. 45–46; Thomson, *Worcester*, pp. 145–47). He was among the disputants named in Worcester Cathedral Library, MS.Q.99, between c.1298 and c.1302, MS.99, fols. 12r–27v and 72r–82v (Glorieux, 'Jean de Saint-Germain maître de Paris et copiste de Worcester', p. 527; Thomson, *Worcester*, pp. 183–84; Little and Pelster, *Oxford Theology and Theologians*, pp. 66, 88, 123, 183, 185, 187, 224, 232, 235, 256, 261, 264, 266, 269, 277, 292, 314, 335, 336, 359). He was already a doctor of theology on 26 July 1300 when he was licensed to hear confessions in the archdeanery of Oxford (Little, *Franciscan Papers, Lists, and Documents*, p. 235). He was 28th master there about 1298/1300 (*BRUO*, p. 976), and became the 29th master at Cambridge c.1303, having incepted at Oxford (Eccleston, pp. 54, 59). While at Cambridge he was involved in a protracted dispute with the University, beginning on 15 November 1303. He and the Dominican master, Nicholas de Dale, refused to swear to some new statutes (Little, 'The Friars v. the University of Cambridge', pp. 686–96, 687, 694). He was mentioned as a procurator of his convent on 2 May and 10 May 1304 along with Nicholas de Dale. The dispute was finally resolved in 1306, when Adam seems to have completed his term of office (Little, 'The Franciscan School at Oxford in the Thirteenth Century', p. 862; *GFC*, pp. 33, 36–38, 144, 184, 230; *BRUC*, p. 317; Sharpe, *Handlist*, pp. 16–17, no. 25).

HOWDEN (Hoveden), John: He was the 57th regent master at Oxford c.1330 (Eccleston, p. 57; *GFO*, p. 172; *BRUO*, p. 976). On 19 February 1348 the archbishop of York gave permission to this friar of York to hear confessions in the diocese, especially in the archdeaconry of Richmond, for one year. He was the archbishop's penitentiary. The licence of this friar of York, *sacre pagine professor*, was renewed on 22 February 1349 (BIA, Register 10, fol. 278rv). A Friar John of Hoveden' was ordained p. at Greyfriars, York, on 21 December 1336 (*Reg. Kellaw*, iii, p. 180).

HOWDEN (Hovedon), Robert de: he was ordained a. and s. on 26 May 1369 at Bishopthorpe manor chapel (BIA, Register 11, fols. 373v, 374r).

HOWE, John del: on 24 November 1414 this doctor of theology at York appeared before diocesan oficials in the chapter house of York Minster and was accompanied by his guardian, John Belasise, for the hearing. The lector was accused of having spoken ill of the clergy of the city in his sermons. On the third Sunday of Advent (1413), John, the guardian, had preached in the chapter house (York, Dean and Chapter Library, MS.L 2/3a, fol. 78rv).

HOWE, John: he was a friar at Beverley in 1497 when he was admitted to the guild of *Corpus Christi* at York (*Corpus Christi Guild*, p. 145).

HOWLYN, Thomas: he was ordained s. on 26 May 1431 at Blackfriars, York, and d. on 19 December 1433 at Austin Friars, York. He was at York when ordained p. on 12 March 1435 at Greyfriars, York (BIA, Register 19, fols. 240r, 245v, 248r).

HOWTHAM, Thomas de: he was ordained s. on 17 March 1375 at Cawood manor chapel (BIA, Register 12, fol. 119r).

HOWTHORPE (Hanthorpe, Huthorpe), Hugh de: he was ordained s. on 22 December 1296 in Huntingdon priory church, d. on 22 March 1298 in Lincoln cathedral, and p. on 20 December 1298 in Liddington prebendal church (*Reg. Sutton*, vii, pp. 87, 104, 112).

HUDSON (Hudsey), William: he was a friar of Newcastle when he was ordained s. on 9 June 1498. He was a friar of York when ordained p. on 25 May 1499; both ceremonies took place at Blackfriars, York (BIA, Register 23, fols. 460v, 464v. Cf. Cross and Vickers, *MFN*, p. 439).

HUGATE (Hugat), Robert de: he was ordained s. on 17 March 1375 at Cawood manor chapel and d. on 22 September 1375 at Whitefriars, York (BIA, Register 12, fols. 119r, 121v).

HUGH: this English friar was consecrated as bishop of Byblus c.1282 (Golubovich, *Biblioteca Bio-Bibligrafica della Terra Santa*, ii, pp. 428–29). His diocese was overrun by the Muslims in the spring of 1289, when he was an eyewitness to the fall of Tripoli. He reported the martyrdom of an English friar, the former guardian of Oxford, who had valiantly encouraged the Christians in the face of death. Similarly, he produced a lengthy account of the martyrdom of Luceta, the abbess of the Poor Clares of Tripoli, whose body he buried. Exiled from the Crusading States, he returned to England, where he spent two years at the court of King Edward I (*Chronicon de Lanercost*, pp. 128–31, 138–40). His name occurs in certain royal documents, such as the arbitration of the claims to the throne of Scotland. The members of the king's council met on 3 November 1291 to consider the competing claims. Among those to be consulted by the king was Hugh, who was once again among the prelates attending a Parliament held at Berwick on 14 October 1292; present were the bishops of Bath and Wells, Durham, Winchester, Ely, Carlisle and the archbishop of Dublin, along with other prelates and clerics from England. With the exception of the archbishop of Dublin, Hugh was the sole prelate from a diocese outside England. On 24 October 1292 the prelates and clerics were invited to give their judgement. Hugh's advice was that the king should proceed in accordance with the laws by which he judged subjects and determine accordingly in this case (*Edward I and the Throne of Scotland 1290–1296*, ii, pp. 212–13, 216–17). Hugh and Antony Bek, bishop of Durham, dined with Edward of Caernarfon, prince of Wales, on 7 March 1293 and 17 May 1293 (TNA, E101/353/18, m. 3d, E101/353/18, m. 5d).

Hugh travelled to the north and was active as a suffragan bishop in the dioceses of York and Durham. His solitary commission in the York registers was issued by Archbishop Corbridge on 20 February 1302 to reconcile the churchyard of Loftus, in the North Riding, from the shedding of blood (*Reg. Corbridge*, i, p. 30, no. 342). Hugh's accounts of the fall of Tripoli and his reminiscences and anecdotes about pilgrims to the Holy Land were incorporated into *The Lanercost Chronicle*. Walter of Guisborough attests that Hugh, exiled from his diocese, was living with Bek, who did not normally hold ordinations (*The Chronicle of Walter of Guisborough*, p. 346). He was with Bishop Bek for the visitation of Durham cathedral priory on 20 May 1300; on that occasion mendicants were present ('Gesta Dunelmensia, A.D. M.CCC', pp. 5, 50). Although Bishop Bek's register is no longer extant, there are traces of Hugh's ministry in the diocese. He was in the chapter house of Durham cathedral on 26 May 1300 when he witnessed the instrument regarding the process of the visitation by the ordinary (*Records of Antony Bek*, pp. 59–67, no. 67). On 2 October 1300 he fixed his seal to the document recording the resignation of Richard Hoton, prior of Durham. His seal is described in some detail (*Records of Antony Bek*, pp. 76–78, no. 73). On 20 June 1303 he witnessed the notarial authentication of Greatham Hospital to Greatham church (*Records of Antony Bek*, pp. 87–90, no. 84). Bishop Bek informed Pope Benedict XI that because the diocese of Byblos had been overrun, Bishop Hugh had no means of material support. The pope was petitioned to provide assistance for Hugh in the form of provision to Coldingham priory, a dependency of Durham cathedral priory, for life. The pope responded on 3 April 1304 by authorising Bishop Bek to proceed (*Records of Antony Bek*, pp. 100–01, no. 92). On 4 October Bishop Hugh was granted the priory of Coldingham in the diocese of St Andrews. The papal provision was, however, vigorously opposed. On 20 March 1305 King Edward I found in favour of the monks of Durham. On 5 April 1305 Hugh was summoned to a meeting of Parliament. He appeared before the king and numerous prelates. The apostolic letters of papal provision were examined. It was decided that the papal provision should be nullified and that Hugh should surrender the priory (*Records of the parliament holdfen at Westminster on the twenty-eighth day of February, in the thirty-third year of the reign of King Edward the First, A.D. 1305*, xlii–iii, pp. 297–301, no. 464; *Priory of Coldingham. The correspondence, inventories, account rolls, and law proceedings, of the priory of Coldingham*, pp. 3–7; *CPL*, i, p. 613; Rymer, *Foedera*, i, pars ii, pp. 969–70). Bek, now the titular patriarch of Jerusalem, made further provision for Hugh, who was appointed as keeper of the diocese of Oristano in Sardinia during a *sede vacante* period on 26 February 1306. On 21 July 1307 Hugh was appointed as archbishop of that diocese. On 19 March 1308 he was translated to the diocese of Pola, where he remained until his death in the late summer of 1325 (Robson, 'Hugh, the Exiled Bishop of Byblos (c.1245/50–1325)'.)

HULL, Henry: he was ordained d. on 22 September 1414 at Blackfriars, York (BIA, Register 18, fol. 39Gv).

HUMBERSTON (Humbreston, Humberstan), John: he was ordained p. on 31 May 1393 at Holy Trinity Priory, Micklegate, York (BIA, Register 14, fol. 67v). He was the guardian of Oxford when on 26 February 1421 he had a licence to preach in the archdeaconry of Oxford (LAO, Register 16, fol. 215r; *BRUO*, p. 983).

HUMBERSTON (Humbirston), William: he was a friar of York on 18 September 1426 when he witnessed the public revocation by Thomas Richmond (*Convocation, York*, pp. 399–400; *Records of Northern Convocation*, p. 167).

HUMLOK (Hummyloks), Thomas: he was a friar of York when ordained a. on 21 December 1510, s. on 15 March 1511 at Whitefriars, York, d. on 5 April 1511 at Greyfriars, York, and p. on 20 December 1511. The first and fourth ceremonies took place at Austin Friars, York (BIA, Register 26, fols. 110r, 111r, 112v, 116r. Cf. Cross and Vickers, *MFN*, p. 443).

HUNTE (Hunt), Robert: he was a friar of Grimsby on 9 October 1538 when he signed the deed of surrender with five others (*Eighth Report of the Deputy Keeper of the Public Records*, p. 22).

HUNTER, William: he was a friar of York when he was ordained a. on 5 April 1511 at Greyfriars, York, and s. on 14 June 1511 at Blackfriars, York (BIA, Register 26, fols. 112r, 114r; *Reg. Bainbridge*, p. 363. Cf. Cross and Vickers, *MFN,* p. 443).

HUSE, Henry de la: he was ordained s. on 20 September 1292 in St Giles's, Northampton, and d. on 18 September 1294 at Dunstable (*Reg. Sutton*, vii, pp. 31, 56).

HUSON, John: he was a friar of York when he was ordained p. on 23 September 1396 at Holy Trinity Priory, Micklegate, York (BIA, Register 14, fol. 74r).

HUSTHWAYT', Thomas de: on 12 August 1314 he was appointed as confessor to the nuns of Moxby (*Reg. Greenfield*, iii, p. 85, no. 1326).

HYCHON, Robert: at the suppression of the Observant province he was sent to Lincoln in 1534 (*LPFD*, vii, p. 601, no. 1607).

HYLLESAY, Henry de: he was ordained s. at an unknown venue and date between September 1346 and September 1347 (BIA, Register 10A, fol. 18a).

HYRM, Thomas: this former friar of Lincoln obtained his capacity on 8 October 1539 (Chambers, *Faculty Office Registers 1534–1549*, p. 195).

ILKETON, William de: he was ordained d on 7 March 1349 at St Michael-le-Belfrey, York (BIA, Register 10A fol. 27r).

IRBY (Yrby) John de: he was the guardian of Newcastle in 1342 when he received a mandate for the excommunication of William Bows, an apostate friar (*Reg. Kellaw*, iii, p. 513). On 2 October 1350 he was licensed to hear confessions in the diocese of York, being then custos of the Newcastle custody (BIA, Register 10, fol. 279v), and on 7 August 1351 his licence was renewed for a year (*ibid.*, fol. 280r).

IRELAND (Hibernia), Donatus de: he was ordained a. on 20 September 1399 at Stow prebendal church. He was a friar of Boston when ordained s. on 12 June 1400 at the manor chapel at Little Stow (LAO, Register 13, fols. 88v, 93r).

IRENAM (Irenham), John: he was guardian of Doncaster in the Michaelmas term of 1429 (TNA, CP40/675, m. 500) and in the Trinity term of 1430 when he was mentioned in the plea rolls (TNA, CP40/678, mm. 260d, 408d).

IRFORD, John de: he was licensed in the diocese of York to hear confessions at an unknown date. He was replaced about 6 January 1352 by Robert de Popilton (BIA, Register 10, fol. 280r).

ITALY, Ambrose de: he was ordained p. on 20 December 1292 at Dorchester-on-Thames Abbey church (*Reg. Sutton*, vii, p. 36).

J.: on 20 March 1290 a licence was issued to to Brother J., lector of the Friars Minor of Doncaster, to absolve. The licence was renewed on 27 March of the same year (*Reg. Le Romeyn*, i, p. 97, no. 251).

JACSON (Jackson), John: he was a friar of York when he was ordained s. on

24 September 1502 at Blackfriars, York (BIA, Register 25, fol. 114r. Cf. Cross and Vickers, *MFN*, p. 440).

JERVANS, Francis: he was ordained a. on 20 December 1376 at Holy Trinity Priory, Micklegate (BIA, Register 12, fol. 126v).

JOBE, Jo[hn]: a friar of Scarborough dispensed to change his habit and hold a benefice on 20 June 1539 (Chambers, *Faculty Office Registers 1534–1549*, p. 187).

JOHN, Cornelius: he was a friar of Lincoln when he was ordained a. on 18 September 1507 in the chapel of St Mary Magdalene in Lincoln cathedral (LAO, Register 24, fol. 67v).

JOHN: he was custos of York on 18 February 1330 when he presented certain friars for licences in the diocese of Lincoln at the Old Temple in London (LAO, Register 5, fol. 402v).

JOHN: he was guardian of York when mentioned in the plea rolls of the Trinity term of 1379 (TNA, CP40/475, attorneys m. 3).

JOHNS, Walter: he was ordained s. at St Leonard's Hospital, York, on 20 September 1432 (BIA, Register 19, fol. 217r).

JOHNSON (Joonson), John: he was a friar of York when he was ordained a. on 19 September 1461 at Blackfriars, York, s. on 17 December 1463 at Austin Friars, York, and d. on 25 February 1464 at Whitefriars, York (BIA, Register 20, fols. 449r, 457r, 458r). He was at York on 26 February 1489 when William Cerff requested him to celebrate a trental of Masses for him (BIA, Probate Register 5, fols. 357v–58r).

JOHNSON (Jonson), Richard: he was a friar of York when he was ordained s. on 22 September 1442 at York Minster (BIA, Register 19, fol. 220v).

JOHNSON, Robert: he was a friar of York when he was ordained a. on 22 September 1492 at Whitefriars, York, s. on 22 December 1492 at Austin Friars, York, d. on 23 March 1493 at Greyfriars, York, and p. on 1 June 1493 at Blackfriars, York (BIA, Register 23, fols. 434r, 435v, 437r, 438v. Cf. Cross and Vickers, *MFN*, p. 438).

JOHNSON, Robert: he was a friar of York when he was ordained a. on 24 March 1520 at Greyfriars, York (BIA, Register 27, fol. 187r. Cf. Cross and Vickers, *MFN*, p. 445). He was a friar of Lincoln when he was ordained s. on 19 April 1522 in Lincoln cathedral and d. on 19 September 1523 at Liddington prebendal church (LAO, Register 26, fols. 4r, 7v).

JOHNSON, Thomas, senior: he was a friar of York when he was ordained a. on 28 February 1523 at Whitefriars, York, s. on 21 March 1523 at the same venue and d. on 30 May 1523 at Holy Trinity Priory, Micklegate, York (BIA, Register 27, fols. 198r, 198v, 200r). Either this friar or Thomas junior was at York at the Dissolution on 27 November 1538 (*Eighth Report of the Deputy Keeper of the Public Records*, p. 51). On 13 November 1544 Thomas Johnson was left 10s. by William Vavasour, then of St Mary, Bishophill Junior, to pray for his soul (*York Clergy Wills 1520–1600: II. City Clergy*, pp. 33–35; Cross and Vickers, *MFN*, pp. 445, 458).

JOHNSON (Jonson, Jonys, Jouson), Thomas, junior: he was a friar of York when he was ordained s. on 11 March 1536 at Greyfriars, York, d. on 1 April 1536 at Blackfriars, York (BIA, Register 28, fols. 194v, 196r), and p. on 15 April 1536 in the chapel of St Mary Magdalene in Lincoln cathedral (LAO, Register 26, fol. 52r). It is conceivable that this friar may be identified with Thomas Johnson, alias Bonaventure, a former Observant friar. At the suppression of the Observants he was erroneously said to have become an Austin Friar (*LPFD*, vii, p. 601, no. 1607). On 20 September 1534 Friars Jonys and Friar Massy, another Observant and a future rector of Rye, Sussex, visited Sir Edward Don at Horsenden, Buckinghamshire (*The Household Book (1510–1551) of Sir Edward Don: An Anglo-Welsh Knight and his Circle*, p. xlii (n. 72) and 281. He was assigned to friaries in the custody of York and may have been deemed a suitable candidate for ordination. Dr Vavasour sent him to Beverley, where he rejoiced in the Pilgrimage of Grace in October 1536 at the commons assembled outside the friary in Westwood (*LPFD*, xii, pt. 1, p. 183, no. 392. Cf. Cross and Vickers, *MFN*, pp. 446, 458).

JOHNSON, William: he was ordained d. on 17 December 1468 at Austin Friars, York, and p. on 25 February 1469 at Greyfriars, York (BIA, Register 22, fols. 197v, 198v). This friar may be identified with Sir William Johnson who was mentioned in the will of William Hoganson, a parishioner of St Peter, Eastgate, a suburb of Lincoln. Johnson's name is followed by a request for a trental of Masses from the four houses of friars in Lincoln in return for 12d. He also witnessed the will; his name was followed by that of the testator's curate (*Lincoln Wills, 1271–1532*, ii, p. 139).

JORDAYNS, Thomas: he was ordained p. on 14 June 1348 at St Mary's Abbey, York (BIA, Register 10A, fol. 25r).

JORZ, Simon: he was the lector at Boston on 10 August 1300 when he was licensed to hear confessions in the limitation of the friary at Boston in the diocese of Lincoln (Little, *Franciscan Papers, Lists, and Documents*, p. 237).

KATERALL, William: he was a friar of York when he was ordained a. on 26 May 1453 at Blackfriars, York (BIA, Register 20, fol. 415r).

KEGILL, John: he was employed by King Henry VI in negotiations with the Holy See regarding the election of a prior for the Cluniac Priory of Pontefract. Henry's letter of 26 June 1440 to Pope Eugene IV explained that the priory had been damaged by foreign priors and had more recently improved at the hands of an English prior. He sought papal approval for the free election of the next prior and commended his *nuncio*, John Kegill (*Bekynton's Correspondence*, i, pp. 121–22). It is not known when John reached the papal court in Florence. The elderly Cardinal Branda da Castiglione, the bishop of Piacenza, seems to have recommended (*ad relationem*) John to the pope. On 28 July 1441 Pope Eugene IV in Florence provided him to the diocese of *Philippopolis* void by the death of James outside the Roman court, during whose lifetime this pope specially reserved it. John was instructed that, as soon as he had had the present letters expedited, he should reside in his diocese and not exercise pontifical offices outside his city or diocese (*BF, ns*, i, p. 254, no. 529; Cenci, 'Vaticana Documenta', Part 3, p. 178). On 6 August 1441 the pope addressed two letters to John. *Cum nos pridem* issued a faculty for John to be consecrated by any Catholic bishop, who was assisted by two or three others. The principal consecrator was directed to receive and send to the pope John's oath of fealty. *Sincerae devotionis* acknowledged that John's diocese was *in partibus infidelium* and authorised him to exercise his episcopal ministry in the diocese of York (Cenci, *Supplementum ad Bullarium Franciscanum*, i, p. 442, nn. 912–13). On 20 December 1441 the pope, responding to petitions from John and Archbishop John Kempe, the newly created cardinal priest of St Balbina, acknowledged that the bishop elect had no hope of receiving anything from the episcopal *mensa* of his diocese *in partibus infidelium*. He was authorised to receive *in commendam*, even after he had been consecrated, and to hold for life a benefice, secular or regular (*BF, ns*, i, p. 266, no. 562; *CPL*, ix, pp. 225, 184–85, 180–81). Three days later, on 23 December, John was described as *episcopus Philippopolis*, when he made a payment of 10 florins *pro ballista* through the hand of Andrew Oles, the procurator of King Henry VI (Cenci, 'Vaticana Documenta', Part 3, p. 178).

Following his episcopal consecration, he returned to the north of England, where he became a suffragan bishop in the diocese of York from the spring of 1442 to the late summer of 1458. Initially John overlapped with his confrère, Bishop Warter, who died before the end of the decade. His first extant suffragan commission was on 27 March 1442. On 14 July 1442 he received a general commission for the exercise of his episcopal office in the diocese (BIA, Register 19, fols. 81v–82r). On 5 August 1446 he was commissioned to reconcile the cemetery of St Nicholas in Micklegate, York, from the shedding of blood (BIA, Register 19, fol. 208r). On 3 September 1444 he was licensed to reconcile the parochial cemetery at Dewsbury recently violated by bloodshed (BIA, Register 19, fol. 186r). On 14 April 1444 he was appointed rector of Holy Trinity, Goodramgate, York (BIA, Register 19, fol. 185v). On 8 April 1449 John was licensed to bless John Inkeley as abbot of Rievaulx. On 19 September 1449 he was commissioned to bless Richard Hilton as abbot of the monastery of St Agatha at Easby, and on 24 April 1450 he was commissioned to bless John Grene as abbot of the Premonstratensian monastery of St Mary at Welbeck (BIA, Register 19, fols. 420v, 421v–22r, 424rv). On 16 November 1452 Archbishop William Booth appointed Kegill to be one of the bishops who consecrated William Percy as bishop of Carlisle (BIA, Register 20, fol. 367r). On 2 February 1453 John owed £2 6s. 8d. to William Duffield, canon residentiary of York, Southwell and Beverley; the debt was described as difficult to recover (*TE*, iii, pp. 125–52, at 141; *Probate Inventories of the York Diocese, 1350–1500*, p. 601).

On 26 February 1454 the archbishop appointed William Lawrob, chaplain, to the parish of Holy Trinity, Goodramgate, which John had freely resigned On 14 September 1453 John was appointed as custodian or master of the Hospital of St John the Baptist at Ripon (BIA, Register 20, fols. 160v–61r). He received several commissions and ordained regularly in the 1440s and 1450s. Many of the ceremonies took place in the York Greyfriars. Along with Thomas Spofford, lately bishop of Hereford, Archbishop William Booth, Robert Nevill, bishop of Durham, and William Percy, bishop of Carlisle, he granted an indulgence of 40 days to those who devoutly read the Meditations on the Life of Christ attributed to Bonaventure (Lincoln Cathedral Chapter Library, MS.228 (B.6.6), fol. 1v; Cambridge University Library, MS. Mm. 5. 37, fol. 2r; Delehaye, 'Les lettres d'indulgence collectives', p. 323). The indulgence was granted at an unknown date between 1452 and 1456 (Thomson, *Lincoln*, p. 187).

His activities in the diocese of York ceased in the late summer of 1458. He had died before 20 July 1459, when Archbishop Booth appointed Richard Messing, a Carmelite friar and bishop of Dromore, to the Hospital of St John at Ripon (BIA, Register 20, fol. 49r. For additional references see BIA, Register 19, fols. 89v, 92r, 96v, 99v, 185r, 214v, 225r–26r, 239rv, 282v–87v, 287v–89Ar, 289Ar–91r, 291r–92r, 292r–93r, 293Ar–94r, 294rv, 295r–96r, 297r–99v, 300v–04r, 368r, 404v, 412, 424r, Register 20, fols. 5r, 30v, 191v–92r, 202v, 367v, 368r–69r, 378v, 396r, 418v–23r, 423v–24r, 424r–25r, 425r–26r, 426r–28v, 428r–30v, 431v–32v, 432v–34r, 434rv; Stephenson, 'Monumental

Brasses in the West Riding', p. 13; *The Fabric Rolls of York Minster*, pp. 238, 239, 240. Cf. Hamilton Thompson, 'The Register of the Archdeacons of Richmond, 1442–1477', part one, 1442–1465, pp. 84, 116–17; *The Archdeaconry of Richmond in the Eighteenth Century, Bishop Gastrell's 'notitia' – the Yorkshire Parishes 1714–1725*, pp. 50–51, no. 10, n. 17; Butler, 'Suffragan Bishops in the Medieval Diocese of York', pp. 49, 58).

KEKILL (Kekyll), John: he was ordained s. on 3 April 1400 at Blackfriars, Beverley, and p. on 20 December 1404 at All Saints, Cawood (*Reg. Scrope*, ii, pp. 55, 87, 131).

KEL (Kele, Kell), Robert: he was a friar of York when he was ordained d. on 23 December 1357 and p. on 21 September 1359; both ceremonies took place at Cawood manor chapel (BIA, Register 11, fols. 332r, 339r).

KELL, Stephen: he was ordained d. on 25 February 1363 at Bishopthorpe manor chapel (BIA, Register 11, fol. 352r).

KELLAW (Kelawe), John: he was ordained s. on 24 September 1345 in Durham cathedral and d. on 17 December 1345 in Auckland collegiate church. He was a friar of Hartlepool when ordained p. on 31 March 1347 in the collegiate church of Norton (Durham Registers: Hatfield, fols. 92r, 93r, 95v). He was licensed for the deaneries of Richmond and Catterick on 27 January 1349 (BIA, Register 10, fol. 278v). He went to Cambridge where he was 63rd master (Eccleston, p. 61) and was licensed for the diocese of Ely in February 1351 (CUL, EDR, G/1/1, De Lisle, fol. 90r). Later he returned to the diocese of York and was appointed a penitentiary in August 1351, being then a friar of Newcastle (BIA, Register 10, fol. 280r; *GFC*, pp. 187–88).

KELO (Kele, Kello), Robert de: he was a friar of Boston when he was ordained s. on 7 June 1354 at Liddington prebendal church (LAO, 9D, fol. 71v). He was guardian of that community when he was mentioned in the plea rolls of Trinity term 1379 (TNA, CP40/475, m. 173).

KEMPE, Richard: he was a friar of Boston when he was ordained a. on 12 June 1400 at Stow Park manor chapel (LAO, Register 13, fol. 92v). He was ordained s. on 10 March 1403 at York Minster, d. on 9 June 1403 at St Nicholas, Bawtry, and p. on 20 September 1404 at All Saints, Cawood (*Reg. Scrope*, ii, pp. 55, 87, 133).

KENINGTON, Reginald de: he was licensed to hear confessions in the diocese of York in 1300 (*Reg. Corbridge*, i, p. 24).

KERMYNGHOWE, Thomas de: he was licensed to hear confessions in the diocese of York at an unknown date. He was replaced by John de Saundeby about 6 January 1352 (BIA, Register 10, fol. 280).

KEY, William: he was a friar of York when he was ordained a. on 20 February 1535 in the lady chapel of York Minster, s. on 13 March 1535 at Blackfriars, York, d. on 11 March 1536 at Greyfriars, York, and p. on 1 April 1536 at Blackfriars, York (BIA, Register 28, fols. 189r, 191r, 195r, 196v. Cf. Cross and Vickers, *MFN*, p. 445).

KEYNESBUR', William de: he was ordained s. in 1267/68 at Selby Abbey (*Reg. Walter Giffard*, p. 190, no. 688).

KIDD (Kidde, Kydd), Robert: he was a friar of York when he was ordained a. on 21 March 1523 at Whitefriars, York (BIA, Register 27, fol. 198v). He was a friar of Lincoln when ordained s. on 19 September 1528 at Liddington prebendal church (LAO, Register 26, fol. 22r). He was at York at the Dissolution on 27 November 1538 (*Eighth Report of the Deputy Keeper of the Public Records*, p. 51. Cf. Cross and Vickers, *MFN,* pp. 454, 458).

KIGHELAY (Kiklay, Kyghlay), Roger: he was ordained a. and s. on 12 June 1367 and d. on 18 September 1367; both ceremonies took place at Bishopthorpe manor chapel (BIA, Register 11, fols. 366r, 367r).

KINGSBURY (Kyngesbury), Thomas: he was a friar of Oxford when he was ordained s. on 11 June 1351 at Boston parish church and d. on 22 September 1352 in Stow prebendal church (LAO, Register 9D, fols. 49r, 62v). He was described as *sacre theologie professor* when John Thoresby, archbishop of York, licensed him to hear confessions in the diocese in place of Robert Stanford, a deceased friar, at an unspecified date c.1369 (BIA, Register 11, fol. 397r). He became the 26th minister provincial in 1379 or 1380 and held the office for approximately a decade. Fr John Somer, a friar from the custody of Bristol, composed his *Kalendarium ad meridiem universitatis Oxoniae anno Domini 1380*. The preface states that he wrote for Joan of Kent, princess of Wales and duchess of Cornwall and countess of Chester and lady of Wake, the third wife of the Black Prince and the mother of the future king, Richard II. Somer wrote *ex precepto reverendi patris fratris Thome Kyngisburi ministrie Anglie* (*The Kalendarium of John Somer*, pp. 96–97). Kingsbury participated in the general chapter of Padua at Pentecost 1384 and on 4 June of that year he approved some conventions (Cenci, 'Bonifacio Lupi di Soragna e i Frati Minori', p. 106). Fr John Tewkesbury, also a friar from the custody of Bristol, gave a book called *Quatuor principalia Musice* (Oxford, Bodleian Library, Digby, MS.90) to the Oxford Greyfriars with the permission and agreement of the minister provincial in 1388 (*GFO*, pp. 60, 251; *BRUO*, p. 1857; Oxford, Bodleian Library, Digby, MS.90, flyleaf). On 18 September 1392 King Richard II recommended this friar to Pope Boniface IX for provision to the next vacant bishopric. During the early years of the Great Schism he persuaded the friars to support Pope Urban VI. He preached before King Richard II at Westminster on 7 June 1396, the second anniversary of his first wife, Anne of Bohemia, daughter of Emperor Charles IV, and was paid 40s. (TNA, E101/403/10, fol. 36rv). On 25 August 1396 he received 100s. in the will of Robert Morton of Bawtry, who requested burial in the lady chapel of the conventual church of Worksop and gave alms to the friary in Doncaster (*TE*, i, pp. 210–14, at 213). He was buried at Nottingham (*GFO*, pp. 250–51. Cf. *BRUO*, p. 1073).

KINGTON (Kyngton), John: he was mentioned on 24 February 1503 in the will of Robert Clifton, who had been collated to a stall at Wistow on 2 November 1479 and resigned it in favour of his brother, Gamaliel, before 15 July 1500. Robert requested burial in the church of St Mary at Clifton near his grandfather's tomb. John Kington, a professor of theology, witnessed the will and received £6 13s. 4d. to pray for the testator (*TE*, iv, p. 69n, BIA, Probate Register 6, fol. 25r). A friar and doctor of this name was associated with Oxford, Bodleian, Auct.4.Q.4.9, an *incunabula* copy of Scotus, *IV Sententiarum*, where his date of death is given as 1536. The book is heavily annotated (*MLGB, ii*, p. 106). A John Kynton, a Franciscan, was sometime the vice-commissary at Oxford University in the early sixteenth century. He had incepted in 1494 or 1495 and was mentioned in July 1508 and May 1513 (*Reg. Congreg., 1505–17*, i, pp. 346, 533, ii, p. 274).

KINGTON (Kinington), Reginald: on 19 June 1300 Archbishop Corbridge granted the petition of Henry de Lacy, earl of Lincoln, that Michael of Merton and Reginald of Kingston should hear the confessions of those who were accompanying the earl to fight in Scotland (*Reg. Corbridge*, i, pp. 23–24; *Historical Papers and Letters from the Northern Registers*, p. 143).

KIRKBY (Kirkeby), Henry de: he was licensed to hear confessions in place of William de Ferriby in the diocese of York at an unknown date (BIA, Register 11, fol. 396r).

KIRKBY (Kirkeby), John de: he was ordained a. and s. on 20 May 1307 at Dalston parish church (*Reg. Halton*, i, p. 279). He replaced a deceased friar and confessor in the diocese of York at an unknown date in the administration of Archbishop Thoresby (BIA, Register 10, fol. 279r). A John de Kirkeby was ordained p. in 1309 in St Paul's cathedral, London (*Reg. Reynolds*, p. 104).

KIRKBY (Kirbe, Kybe), John: he was a friar of York when he was ordained s. on 21 September 1426. He was ordained d. on 14 June 1427; both ceremonies were held at Blackfriars, York (BIA, Register 19, fols. 215r, 230r).

KIRKBY (Kirkeby), John: he was a friar of York when he was ordained a. on 19 September 1450 at Greyfriars, York, s. on 12 March 1457 at Whitefriars, York, d. on 11 June 1457 at Holy Trinity Priory, Micklegate, York, and p. on 24 September 1457 at Whitefriars, York (BIA, Register 19, fol. 295v, Register 20, fols. 428r, 430v, 431v).

KIRKBY, Robert: he was ordained s. on 17 December 1379 at York Minster and d. on 19 May 1380 in Stillingfleet parish church (BIA, Register 12, fols. 135v, 137r). A friar of this name was described as the cousin [*cognatus*] of John Barker, who requested burial in the parish church of St Mary, Thirsk, in his will of 12 November 1395. The testator left his cousin £4 to pray for him for the space of one year (BIA, Probate Register 1, fol. 89r). William Barker, a brother of John, was described as a native of Whitby and requested burial in the church of St Mary (*ibid.*, fol. 92rv).

KIRKBY (Kirkeby, Kykeby), Thomas de: he was ordained d. on 29 March 1343 at Greyfriars, Beverley. He was a friar of York when ordained p. on 18 September 1344 at St Mary's Abbey, York (BIA, Register 10A, fols. 3r, 8v).

KIRKBY (Kirkeby), Thomas: he was a friar of York when he was ordained a. on 20 September 1516 at Greyfriars, York, s. on 11 April 1517 in the lady chapel of York Minster, and d. on 19 September 1517 at Whitefriars, York. He was a friar of Beverley when he was ordained p. on 18 September 1518 at Bishopthorpe manor chapel (BIA, Register 27, fols. 173v, 177r, 178r, 182r. Cf. Cross and Vickers, *MFN*, p. 444).

KIRKBY, Kirkeby), Walter de: he was ordained a. on 23 September 1346 at St Oswald's, Elvet, near Durham (Durham Registers: Hatfield, fol. 94r), d. on 20 December 1348 at York Minster (BIA, Register 10A, fol. 26r) and p. on 7 March 1349 in the church of St Nicholas, Newcastle (Durham Registers: Hatfield, fol. 97r).

KIRKBY, William: he was a friar of Stamford when he was ordained a. on 19 December 1472 in All Saints, Stamford. He was a friar of Lincoln when he was ordained s. on 12 June 1473 in Lincoln cathedral. Two friars of this name, one of Lincoln and the other of Grantham, were ordained d. on 18 December 1473 in St

Peter-at-arches, Lincoln. A friar of this name at Grantham was ordained p. on 5 March 1474 at Buckden prebendal church (LAO, Register 21, fols. 136r, 139v, 141r, 142r).

KIRKHAM, John de: he was ordained a. on 27 May 1363 at Bishopthorpe manor chapel (BIA, Register 11, fol. 352v).

KIRKHAM (Kyrkeham, Kirkby), Thomas: he went to Oxford in 1511 and was there when he was ordained s. on 27 March 1512, d. on 12 March 1513 and p. on 11 March 1514 (Salisbury Registers: Audley 2nd series, in the Wiltshire County Record Office, County Hall, Trowbridge). After 12 years of study he took his B.Th. on 20 June 1523 and his D.Th. on 1 July 1527. His composition was reduced to £4 on account of his poverty. In November of the same year he was dispensed from the greater part of his Oxford regency as guardian of the Doncaster Greyfriars (*Reg. Univ. Oxon*, p. 118; *BRUO, 1501–40*, p. 336; *GFO*, pp. 282–83). The will of Thomas Strey of Doncaster on 14 November 1530 was proved on 30 December of that year, leaving 20s. to the community and giving the master doctor of the Greyfriars 26s. 8d. for the purchase of a coat. Thomas witnessed the will (*TE*, v, pp. 294–97). He served as a cursor of theology at London in 1531 (*GFL*, p. 66).

He had already shown himself as a zealous opponent of King Henry VIII's divorce. He was licensed to preach and hear confessions in the diocese of York on 24 July 1534 (BIA, Register 28, fol. 85v). He was the guardian of Doncaster when he disputed with John Bale, the prior of the Doncaster Whitefriars, in the pulpit. The archbishop of York intervened on 1 August 1534, setting up a commission, pointing out that he had commissioned this friar and John Bale to preach the Gospel for the instruction of the common people. He lamented that the two friars were insulting each other from the pulpit. The commission was requested to seek evidence and interview witnesses in order to make a report (BIA, Register 28, fol. 91rv). Thomas was the guardian and one of the ten friars of Doncaster who signed the deed of surrender on 20 November 1538 (*Eighth Report of the Deputy Keeper of the Public Records*, p. 19; *LPFD*, xiii, pt. 2, p. 364, no. 877). This former friar joined the reformers and was successively rector of Colchester in 1539 and then rector of St Martin's, Outwich, in the city of London, in 1548. He preached at St Paul's cathedral (Dickens, *Lollards and Protestants in the Diocese of York 1509–1558*, pp. 140–41; Erler, *Reading and Writing during the Dissolution: Monks, Friars and Nuns 1530–1558*, p. 45). Professor Richard Rex regarded him as a leading figure among the reformers. In 1550 he preached against transubstantiation. Five years later he was deprived of his benefice because of his marriage (Rex, 'The Friars in the English Reformation', in *The Beginnings of English Protestantism*, p. 54; *LPFD,* xiii, 2, p. 364; Cross and Vickers, *MFN*, pp. 447–48).

KIRKLESWORTH (Kirkeleswurth'), John: he was ordained p. on 31 May 1292 at Lincoln cathedral (*Reg. Sutton*, vii, p. 30).

KIRKSTALL (Kirkstale) Semannus (Seman): he was ordained a. on 22 September 1414 at Blackfriars, York (BIA, Register 18, fol. 39Gr).

KIRKTON (Kyrkton), William de: he was at York when he was ordained a. and s. on 3 April 1378 at Greyfriars, York (BIA, Register 12, fol. 132r).

KIRSOP, John: he was ordained a. on 1 March 1393 at St Michael-le-Belfrey, York, s. on 31 May 1393 at Holy Trinity Priory, Micklegate, and d. on 20 September 1393 at St Leonard's Hospital, York (BIA, Register 14, fols. 65v, 67r, 68r).

KNAPTON, William de: he was ordained p. on 7 June 1343 at Greyfriars, York (BIA, Register 10A, fol. 4v).

KNIGHT (Knyght), John: he was a friar of Lincoln when he was ordained s. on 20 September 1404 and d. on 14 March 1405; both ceremonies took place in Lincoln cathedral (LAO, Register 13, fols. 115v, 118v). He was a friar of York when he was ordained p. on 24 September 1407 at Blackfriars, York (BIA, Register 5A, fol. 325v; *Reg. Sede Vacante, York, 1405–08*, pp. 66, 76, 89).

KNOLL, Ralph: a *scolar in sacra theologia* licensed to hear confessions in the archdeaconry of Richmond on 10 September 1444 (BIA, Register 19, fol. 214v. Cf. Hamilton Thompson, 'The Register of the Archdeacons of Richmond, 1442–1477', part one, 1442–1465, p. 84).

KNOLLES, Roger: he was ordained s. on 16 June 1375 at Cawood manor chapel, d. on 22 September 1375 at Whitefriars, York, and p. on 22 December 1375 at Cawood manor chapel (BIA, Register 12, fols. 120v, 121v, 123r). He was a friar of Beverley in receipt of a taxable stipend in 1406 (TNA, E179/66/411; Jurkowski, 'Were Friars Paid Salaries? Evidence from Clerical Taxation Records', p. 136, n. 28).

KORTBY, John de: he was ordained s. on 19 December 1383 at All Saints, Cawood (BIA, Register 12, fol. 140v).

KYM, William: he was ordained a. on 23 May 1472 at Blackfriars, York, and s. on 18 September 1473 at Greyfriars, York (BIA, Register 22, fols. 215v, 222v).

KYME, Thomas: he was a friar of Boston when he was ordained s. on 25 March 1497 in the chapel of St Mary Magdalene, Lincoln cathedral, on 25 March 1497, and d. on 20 May 1497 in the prebendal church of Sleaford (LAO, Register 24, fols. 7r, 8v).

KYRKETON, Kyrketon, William de: he was a friar who was left 20s. in the will of Richard de Daunton, a citizen of York, on 4 November 1393 (BIA, Probate Register 1, fols. 63v–64r).

LAKE (Laake), John: he was a friar of Beverley when he was ordained a. on 20 September 1455 at Holy Trinity Priory, York. He was a friar of York when he was ordained s. on 24 September 1457 at Whitefriars, York, and d. on 27 May 1458 at Blackfriars York. He was a friar of Scarborough when ordained p. on 23 December 1458 at Austin Friars, York (BIA, Register 20, fols. 422r, 431r, 435r, 436v).

LAMBERD (Lambard), John: he was ordained s. on 22 September 1375 and d. on 20 December 1376; both ceremonies took place at Whitefriars, York (BIA, Register 12, fols. 121v, 127r).

LAMBERT, John: he was a friar of Boston when he was ordained s. on 8 April 1508 in the prebendal church of Liddington and d. on 22 April 1508 in the chapel of St Mary Magdalene in Lincoln cathedral (LAO, Register 24, fols. 70r, 71r). He was a friar of York when he was ordained p. on 2 June 1509 at Whitefriars, York (BIA, Register 26, fol. 103r. Cf. Cross and Vickers, *MFN*, p. 442). An Observant friar of this name was reported to have fled to Scotland by 1534 (*LPFD*, vii, p. 602, no. 1607).

LANCASTER, William: a friar of Doncaster who received the royal alms on 4 July 1336 (TNA, E101/387/9).

LANGE (Lang), Thomas: he was a friar of Oxford when he was ordained s. on 19 September 1489 at All Saints, Northampton (LAO, Register 22, fol. 33r). A Thomas Long, a friar of York, was ordained d. on 6 March 1490 at Holy Trinity Priory, Micklegate, York, and p. on 5 June 1490 at Blackfriars, York (BIA, Register 23, fol. 420v).

LANGFORD (Langfordia), Dionysius de: he was ordained p. on 19 September 1411 at St Michael-le-Belfrey, York (BIA, Register 18, fol. 39Cv).

LANGFORD, Richard: he was ordained d. on 5 June 1417 at All Saints, Cawood (BIA, Register 18, fol. 397v).

LANGHAM, John: he was ordained s. on 8 March 1365 and d. 30 May 1366; both ceremonies took place at Bishopthorpe manorial chapel (BIA, Register 11, fols. 359r, 363r).

LANGHAM, Roger: he was a friar of Lincoln when he was ordained a. on 18 September 1451 in St Margaret's in Lincoln cathedral close (LAO, Register 19, fols. 32v, 68v).

LANGLEY, John: one of the ten friars of Doncaster who signed the deed of surrender on 20 November 1538, perhaps a lay brother (*Eighth Report of the Deputy Keeper of the Public Records*, p. 19. Cf. Cross and Vickers, *MFN*, p. 447).

LANGLEY, Robert de: he was a friar of Richmond licensed to hear confessions in the diocese of York at the recommendation of Richard, custos of Newcastle, on 27 January 1349 (BIA, Register 10, fol. 278v).

LANGTHORP, Christopher: he was a friar of York when he was ordained a. on 20 September 1494 at Greyfriars, York, s. on 14 March 1495, and p. on 19 September 1495. The second and third ordinations took place at Whitefriars, York (BIA, Register 23, fols. 443r, 444v, 448r. Cf. Cross and Vickers, *MFN*, p. 438).

LANGTOFT, Richard de: he was ordained d. on 24 September 1362 at Bishopthorpe manor chapel (BIA, Register 11, fol. 350v).

LANSAM, Peter: he was a friar of Lincoln when he was ordained p. on 27 February 1496 in the chapel of St Mary Magdalene in Lincoln cathedral (LAO, Register 24, fol. 1v).

LASCELS (Lascells), William: he was a friar of York when he was ordained s. on 21 May 1345 in Thirsk parish church. He was ordained d. on 24 September 1345 in Ripon Minster and p. on 11 March 1346 at Whitefriars, York (BIA, Register 10A, fols. 11r, 13r, 14v).

LAUNDE, Peter: a friar of York mentioned in the plea rolls during the Trinity term of 1364 (TNA, CP40/418, m. 359d).

LAVANIA, Henry de: he was a friar of Boston when he was ordained a. on 12 June 1400 in the manor chapel of Little Stow (LAO, Register 13, fol. 92v).

LAWRENCE (Laurence, Lourence, Lowrans), Richard: he was a friar of York when he was ordained a. on 19 September 1405 at Greyfriars, York, s. on 21 May 1407 at Blackfriars, York, and d. on 17 December 1407 at Holy Trinity Priory, Micklegate, York (BIA, Register 5A, fols. 317v, 324v, 325v; *Reg. Sede Vacante, York, 1405–08*, pp. 66, 76, 89). He was ordained p. on 21 December 1409 at All Saints, Cawood (BIA, Register 18, fol. 391v).

LAYBURN (Laiburne, Layburne), Roger or Richard: Roger de Laiburne was ordained a. in the manor chapel of Stockton on 22 September 1341. Richard de Layburne was ordained s. on 21 September 1342 at Durham cathedral (*Reg. Pal. Dun*, iii, pp. 111, 119). Richard Layburn was ordained d. on 29 March 1343 at Greyfriars, Beverley (BIA, Register 10A, fol. 3r).

LAYNG (Laing), John: he was a friar of York when he was ordained d. on 14 June 1511 at Blackfriars, York, and p. on 20 September 1511 at Holy Trinity Priory, Micklegate, York (BIA, Register 26, fols. 114r, 115r; *Reg. Bainbridge*, p. 364. Cf. Cross and Vickers, *MFN*, p. 443).

LEAKE (Lek'), Peter de: he was ordained s. on 22 September 1291 at Grantham parish church (*Reg. Sutton*, vii, p. 18).

LEE, John: he was ordained p. on 17 December 1345 at Liddington prebendal church (LAO, Register 7B, fol. 3r).

LEEDS (Ledes), William: he was ordained a. on 9 March 1381 in St Mary's church at Beverley (BIA, Register 12, fol. 138v).

LEGARD, Richard: he was a friar at York when he was ordained s. on 5 June 1512 and d. on 21 May 1513. Both ceremonies took place at Blackfriars, York (BIA, Register 26, fols. 119r, 124v. Cf. Cross and Vickers, *MFN*, p. 443).

LEICESTER (Lester, Lecsetre, Lereston), John: he was a friar of York when he was ordained a. on 20 September 1505 at Bishopthorpe manor chapel, s. on 20 December 1505 at Austin Friars, York, d. on 7 March 1506 at Whitefriars, York, and p. on 28 March 1506 at Greyfriars, York (BIA, Register 25, fols. 130r, 131r, 132r, 133r. Cf. Cross and Vickers, *MFN*, p. 441).

LEICESTER (Leycestr'), Richard de: he was ordained d. on 31 May 1298 in Brampton prebendal church (*Reg. Sutton*, vii, p. 107). He was licensed for the diocese of Lincoln on 20 June 1318 (LAO, Register 3, fol. 390rv). By 18 November 1320 he had been transferred to the diocese of York (LAO, Register 5, fols. 265v–66r).

LEICESTER (Leycetour), Roger: he was ordained p. on 19 March 1401 at Blackfriars, York (BIA, Register 16, fol. 158v). The editor mistakenly identifies him as a Dominican (*Reg. Scrope*, ii, pp. 55, 90, 132).

LEKE (Leek), Richard: he was ordained s. on 21 December 1364 at Greyfriars, York, and d. on 7 June 1365 at Bishopthorpe manor chapel (BIA, Register 11, fols. 358v,

360v). He was guardian of Scarborough when he was mentioned in the plea rolls for Trinity term 1388 (TNA, CP40/510, m. 377).

LEMYNG (Leeming), John: he was the son of John Lemyng, cooper and parishioner of St Michael-le-Belfrey, York. He was a friar of York when he was ordained s. on 28 February 1428 at Whitefriars, York, and d. on 20 March 1428 at Greyfriars, York. He was ordained p. on 17 December 1429 at Austin Friars, York (BIA, Register 19, fols. 231v, 232r, 236r). He was a member of that community on 8 May 1443 when he received a piece of silver in his father's will (York, Dean and Chapter Library, MS.L 2/4, fol. 258r).

LETTON, Henry de: he was the guardian of York when he was mentioned in the plea rolls of the Trinity term of 1364 (TNA, CP40/417, m. 63d and CP40/418, m. 359d). His Christian name is given as John in the plea rolls during the Trinity term of 1365, when he was still the guardian (TNA, CP 40/420, m. 169d).

LEVERTON, Henry: he was ordained a. on 18 September 1400 at All Saints, Cawood, and s. on 18 December 1400 at the chapel of St Nicholas, Bawtry (*Reg. Scrope*, ii, pp. 55, 90, 131).

LEVISHAM (Levesham), John de: he was ordained s. on 16 June 1291 at Boston parish church (*Reg. Sutton*, vii, p. 14).

LEYLOND, Richard: he was a friar of Lichfield when he was ordained s. on 15 February 1421 and d. on 17 May 1421. He was at Coventry when he was ordained p. on 17 June 1424 (LRO, B/A/1/9, fols. 205v, 206r, 211r). On 10 September 1444 he was admitted to hear confessions in the archdeaconry of Richmond, when he was described as a *scolar in sacra theologia* (BIA, Register 19, fol. 214v. Cf. Hamilton Thompson, 'The Register of the Archdeacons of Richmond, 1442–1477', part one, 1442–1465, p. 84).

LEYS, John: he was licensed to hear confessions in the diocese of York on 7 May 1401 (*Reg. Scrope*, ii, p. 12, no. 737).

LEYTON, Ric[hard]: a master at the friary of Lincoln whose name was mentioned in a manuscript belonging to the friary in Lincoln – *Istum librum [...] a M. Ric' Leyton fratre conuentus Lincoll' pro iii li. xiii s. iiii d. [...]*. He may have been the lector. This inscription had been erased from Peterhouse Library, MS.89 (Thomson, *Peterhouse*, p. 49).

LEXMUND, Hermann: he was a friar of Lincoln when he was ordained s. on 27 February 1496 in the chapel of St Mary Magdalene in Lincoln cathedral. He was a friar of Leicester when he was ordained p. on 28 May 1496 in Buckden prebendal church (LAO, Register 24, fols. 1, 4v).

LIGHTSHAW (Lightshawe), Robert: he was ordained a. on 20 December 1432, s. on 7 March 1433, d. on 19 December 1433. He was a friar of York when he was ordained p. on 12 March 1435. The first and third ceremonies were at Austin Friars, York, and the second and fourth at the city's Greyfriars (BIA, Register 19, fols. 242v, 243v, 245v, 248r).

LILLY, William: he was a friar of York when he was ordained a. on 19 December 1450 at Austin Friars, York, and d. on 3 June 1452 at Whitefriars, York (BIA, Register 19, fols. 296v, 303v).

LINCOLN, Adam de: he was at Oxford between 1284 and 1286 (Glorieux, 'Le Manuscrit d'Assise, Bibl.comm.158: Date et mode de composition', pp. 289, 294). *Lincolniensis* is cited in Assisi, MS.196, fol. 42v (Pouillon, 'Le manuscrit d'Assise, Bibl. comm.196. Description', p. 341). He became a doctor of theology and the 24th regent master of the friars' school there about 1292 (Eccleston, p. 54). Assisi, Biblioteca commune, MS.158, quotes Adam, *respondit Lincol.* (Henquinet, 'Descriptio codicis 158 Assisii in Bibliotheca Communali', p. 216). Adam preached before the University of Oxford on 6 December 1292 and 2 February 1293. One of the incipits is *Domine, dilexi decorem domus tuae*, fols. 34v–36v, and the other *Statim veniet ad Templum* in New College Library, Oxford, MS.92, fol. 91v (Schneyer, *Repertorium*, i, p. 46; Little and Pelster, *Oxford Theology and Theologians*, pp. 92, 110, 162, 163, 178, 182, 184, 185, 189, 248, 249, 261; Thomson, *Worcester*, p. 145). In the early fourteenth century William of Nottingham cited him as an authority in Gonville and Caius College, MS.300/514, fol. 65r, his *Commentary on the Sentences* (Longpré, 'Le commentaire sur les Sentences de Guillaume de Nottingham, O.F.M.', pp. 232–33. Cf. Meier, 'Wilhelm von Nottingham (†1336), ein Zeuge für die Entwicklung der distinctio formalis an der Universität Oxford', pp. 256–57. He is named in Worcester MS.Q.99.

He was 15th minister provincial of England in succession to Hugh of Hartlepool in 1302/03 and held office until 1310. He wrote to the king about the arrest of Arthur of Hartlepool, an apostate friar of Richmond, who carried away items deposited at the friary for safekeeping. On 29 October 1304 King Edward I instructed the sheriff of Cumberland to return this friar who had been arrested to Richmond (*CCR, 1302–107*, p. 174). He wrote to the king again on 23 March 1310 regarding an apostate friar (TNA, Chancery Warrants, I, 1792, no. 15). He may have been released from office in the general chapter of Padua on 19 April 1310. On 21 February 1311 he was described as a doctor of theology at York when he was summoned to take part in the trial of the Templars in the Minster. Another letter was sent to him on 18 April 1311 (*Reg. Greenfield*, iv, pp. 358, 366, nn. 2342, 2352). On 1 July 1311 he and Thomas of Pontefract were named in the proceedings of the fifth day (*Reg. Greenfield*, iv, p. 368, no. 2352; *Records of the Northern Convocation*, pp. 34–35, 41, 59; *Councils and Synods with other documents relating to the English Church II. A.D. 1205–1313*, ii, pp. 1323, 1329, 1344). He died c.1334 and was buried at Lincoln, where miracles were associated with him: *jacet Lyncolnie qui fecit mirabila* (*Monumenta Franciscana*, i, p. 537; *Franciscan Papers, Lists, and Documents*, p. 195; Little and Pelster, *Oxford Theology and Theologians*, p. 92; Sharpe, *Handlist*, p. 17, no. 27).

LINCOLN', John de: he was a friar of London in the Michaelmas term of 1287 when he received 25 marks from the crown for the support of the friars of Oxford. He received £8 6s. 8d. for the support of the friars of Cambridge in the same term. He received the royal alms of 20 marks for two days for the support of the provincial chapter (TNA, E403/55, m. 1, courtesy of Dr Jens Röhrkasten). On 19 February 1290 he was given 20s. to purchase a habit. He was associated with Eleanor of Castile (BL, MS.Add.352954, fol. 6v; *The Court and Household of Eleanor of Castile in 1290*, p. 89).

LINCOLN (Lyncoln), John de: he was a friar of Lincoln when he was ordained s. on 19 September 1355 in Lincoln cathedral (LAO, Register 9D, fol. 77). He was ordained

d. on 4 March 1357 at Bishopthorpe manorial chapel and was at York when he was ordained p. on 21 December 1359 at Cawood manorial chapel (BIA, Register 11, fols. 329v, 339v).

LINCOLN, John de: he was a friar of Lincoln when he was ordained s. on 22 September 1358 in Sleaford prebendal church (LAO, Register 9D, fol. 89r).

LINCOLN (Lyncoln), John: he was a friar of York when he was ordained a. on 20 March 1428 at Greyfriars, York (BIA, Register 19, fol. 232r).

LINCOLN (Lincolnia), Richard de: he was a friar at Oxford at the time of his death, probably at the end of the thirteenth century. He notified his confessor, William de Hickling, of a vision of angels. The latter preached at Oxford in the 1290s. The two friars are mentioned in an *exemplum* contained in a fourteenth-century collection of sermons (St John's College Library, Cambridge, MS.255 [S.19], fol. 497r).

LINCOLN (Lincolnia), Richard de: probably a friar of London when he was left 3s. 4d. in the will of Robert de Pleseley, rector of Southfleet, in the diocese of Rochester, on 22 May 1368. The rector requested burial in St Martin-le-Grand, London (*Reg. Langham*, p. 356).

LINCOLN, Robert de: he was licensed to hear confessions in the diocese of York at an unknown date. He was replaced by Richard de Baryngton also at an unknown date in the administration of Archbishop Thoresby (BIA, Register 11, fol. 396r).

LINCOLN (Lincolnia), Stephen de: he gave a fourteenth-century copy of the works of St Augustine to the friars of Lincoln which is now Lincoln Cathedral Library, MS.208 (B.5.6). Folios 5r, 166v contain inscriptions: *de communitate fratrum minorum Lincolnie* at the head and *ex dono fratris Stephani de Lincolnia* at the foot (Thomson, *Lincoln*, pp. 168–69).

LINCOLN, Thomas: he was ordained s. on 18 September 1473 at Greyfriars, York (BIA, Register 22, fol. 222v).

LINCOLN, Walter de: Simon Gomer was excommunicated for assaulting this friar and priest of Scarborough. On 6 February 1303 the culprit was pardoned (*Reg. Corbridge*, i, p. 182, no. 507).

LINCOLN (Lincolnia), William de: he was ordained d. at Selby Abbey in 1267/68 (*Reg. Walter Giffard*, p. 189, no. 688).

LINCOLN (Lincolnia), William de: he was a friar of Lincoln when he was ordained d. on 15 March 1320 in Rochester cathedral (*Reg. Hethe*, i, p. 66, ii, p. 1128).

LINGISTON (Lungeston), Thomas de: he was a friar of Lincoln who was involved in the abduction of a nun from Broadholme Priory in 1350 (Power, *Medieval English Nunneries*, pp. 449–450; Logan, *Runaway Religious in Medieval England*, p. 89). On 10 February 1352 he received a royal pardon from Edward III (*CPR, 1350–1354*, p. 225).

LINWOD (Linwood), John: he was a friar of York when he was ordained d. on

21 September 1454 at Blackfriars, York (BIA, Register 20, fol. 418r). He was the guardian of an unspecified friary in the diocese of York on 10 July 1478 when Pope Sixtus IV described him as a professor of the *Sentences* of Peter Lombard. He was given a licence and a faculty for six years to hear the confessions of all the faithful, absolve them and impose a salutary penance (*BF, ns*, iii, p. 539, no. 1098; *CPL*, xiii, ii, p. 615). While the second of these texts asserts that he was the guardian of Beverley, Moorman maintains that he was the guardian of the friary at York rather than a friary within that diocese (*Medieval Franciscan Houses*, p. 527).

LOFFENHAM, John de: he was ordained d. on 26 May 1347 at Lincoln cathedral (LAO, Register 7B, fol. 14v).

LOFTHOUSE, William: he was a friar of York when he was ordained a. on 21 December 1504 at Austin Friars, York, s. on 17 May 1505 at Blackfriars, York, d. on 7 March 1506 at Whitefriars, York, and p. on 28 March 1506 at Greyfriars, York (BIA, Register 25, fols. 126r, 129r, 132r, 133r). He was at Richmond at the Dissolution on 19 January 1538 (*Eighth Report of the Deputy Keeper of the Public Records*, p. 38). Afterwards he became chaplain to St John's guild in Richmond. On its suppression in 1548 he received a pension of £5 6s. 8d. His will of 2 October 1560 requested burial in the porch of St John in Richmond, near his brother Sir Gabriel. He left to the high altar a cloth of red say with roses on it; the altar of St John was left a cloth with the image of St Lawrence. Among his very few other bequests he included 20s. for the poor of Richmond and 3s. 4d. to the repair of the bridges at both Catterick and Grinton (*Wills and Inventories illustrative of the history, manners, language, statistics, etc, of the Northern Counties of England*, p. 144; Aveling, *Northern Catholics*, p. 51; Cross and Vickers, *MFN*, pp. 441, 450).

LOK, Peter: he was a friar of York when he was ordained p. on 19 September 1439 at Greyfriars, York (BIA, Register 19, fol. 260v).

LONESDALE, Gilbert: he received the royal alms of 20s. 4d. for the friary at Boston on 22 May 1300 (*Liber quotidianus contrarotulatoris garderobae*, p. 36).

LONG, Thomas: he was a friar of York when he was ordained d. on 6 March 1490 at Holy Trinity Priory, Micklegate, York, and p. on 5 June 1490 at Blackfriars, York (BIA, Register 23, fols. 420v, 423r. Cf. Cross and Vickers, *MFN*, p. 437).

LONGESDON (Langesdon), Thomas de: he was ordained p. on 21 December 1342 in the parish church of St George, Doncaster (BIA, Register 10A, fol. 2v; *Reg. Kirkby*, i, p. 154, no. 733). He was a friar of York at Michaelmas 1351 when his name occurs in the plea rolls (TNA, CP40/367, m. 173d, attorneys 8).

LONGESTON, Henry de: he was ordained s. on 25 February 1363 and d. on 27 May 1363; both ceremonies occurred at Bishopthorpe monorial chapel (BIA, Register 11, fols. 351v, 353r).

LONGEVILE (Longevill, Longevull, Longeville), Gregory or George: a Gregory Longevile was ordained s. on 18 March 1363 in St Mary's at Oxford (LAO, Register 9D, fol. 111). He is probably to be identified with George Longevull or Longeville of London ordained d. on 16 February 1364 at St Thomas of Acon and p. on 21 September 1364 in St Paul's cathedral (*Reg. Sudbury*, ii, pp. 23, 28).

LOUND, John de: he was a friar of York when he was ordained p. on 18 September 1350 at Whitefriars, York (BIA, Register 10A, fol. 49v).

LOUND, Peter de: he was a friar of York when mentioned in the plea rolls of Trinity 1364 with Henry de Letton, the guardian of York (TNA, CP40/417, m. 63d).

LOUTH (Luda), Gilbert de: he was a friar of Grimsby licensed to hear confessions within the limitation of his convent on 10 August 1300 and again on 12 October 1300 (Little, *Franciscan Papers, Lists and Papers*, pp. 237, 238).

LOUTH (Luda), John de: he was a friar of York when he was ordained s. on 21 May 1345 at Thirsk parish church (BIA, Register 10A, fol. 11r). He was ordained p. on 26 May 1347 at Lincoln cathedral (LAO, Register 7B, fol. 15v).

LOUTH (Louthe, Lowth), William: he was ordained a. and s. on 5 March 1384 at St Michael-le-Belfrey, York (BIA, Register 12, fol. 141r).

LOVERSALE, William: he was a friar of Boston when he was ordained s. on 22 December 1352 and d. on 16 February 1353; both ceremonies were held at Stow prebendal church (LAO, Register 9D, fols. 63v, 65r).

LOWDHAM, John: he was ordained p. on 22 December 1403 in the chapel of St Nicholas, Bawtry (*Reg. Scrope*, ii, pp. 55, 91, 131).

LOWNES, John de: he was ordained s. on 10 June 1346 at Whitefriars, York (BIA, Register 10A, fol. 15v).

LUCY (Luscy), Anthony: he was ordained s. on 18 December 1344 in Durham cathedral and d. on 26 March 1345 in St Andrew's church, Aukland (*Reg. Kellaw*, iii, pp. 145, 151). He was ordained p. on 20 September 1348 in Skipton parish church (BIA, Register 10A, fol. 25v).

LUDFORD (Lucheford, Ludeford, Lufdeford), Adam de: he was a friar of Lincoln licensed for the *limitatio* of that friary on 10 August and 12 October 1300 (Little, *Franciscan Papers, Lists, and Documents*, pp. 237, 238). On 4 August 1317 King Edward II wrote from Nottingham to the guardian or whoever supplied his place at the Lincoln Greyfriars, commanding him to cause certain writings, charters, covenants, fines and other muniments regarding the inheritance of John, son and heir of Robert le Chaumberleyn, tenant in chief and a minor in the king's wardship, to be examined in the presence of Henry de Baiocis, kinsman of the heir, and of William of Ayremynne, to whom the king had committed the lands, or of William's deputy on his behalf, to be kept by him for the use of the heir, as shall seem best to Henry and William for his security. The king had been informed that these muniments came into the hands of Adam de Lucherford, a member of the Greyfriars of Lincoln from Philip de Lyndeseye, who held certain lands of the aforesaid inheritance. The king wished to provide for the heir's security because he was a minor, and because Philip had sided with the Scottish rebels (*CCR, 1313–1318*, p. 562). Adam was seemingly still a friar of Lincoln on 20 June 1318 when his name appears second in a long list of friars licensed as confessors by Bishop Dalderby; this prominent position may indicate that he was already occupying a post of some seniority in the community, perhaps as vicar or lector (LAO, Register 3, fol. 393r). On 7 December 1321 Bishop Burghersh reported that Adam, then the guardian of the Lincoln Greyfriars, went to the episcopal manor at Nettleham, a few miles north-east of the cathedral city, to present a letter from John Thurgutthorp, the custos of York, written on 20 November. The custos explained that the business of the order prevented him from travelling to meet the bishop and he presented a list of eight friars elected to hear confessions, in accordance with the terms of *Super cathedram*. Only one of the friars was licensed by the ordinary (LAO, Register 5, fols. 299v–300r). By 26 March 1322 Ludford had ceased to be the guardian when he and Robert de Wynthorp, a Dominican, were commissioned by Bishop Burghersh to hear the confessions of the Benedictine nuns of Stainfield, a few miles east of Lincoln. The bishop acknowledged the pastoral zeal of these two friars and their suitability for the office of hearing confessions (LAO, Register 5, fol. 306v). This friar is probably the Adam Lufdeford, priest and professed of Grimsby, whose death is recorded in BL, Cotton Charter xxx, 40, about 1334 (Little, '*Records, Franciscan Province*', pp. 144, 152).

LULLEY (Lullay), William: he was a friar of York when he was ordained a. on 22 September 1487 at Whitefriars, York, s. on 31 May 1488 at Blackfriars, York, d. on 4 April 1489 and p. on 26 February 1491. The last two ceremonies took place at Greyfriars, York (BIA, Register 23, fols. 408v, 413r, 416v, 425v. Cf. Cross and Vickers, *MFN*, p. 436).

LUNBURGH, Anselm: he was ordained p. on 28 May 1401 in Bishop Burton church, near Beverley (*Reg. Scrope*, ii, pp. 55, 91, 131; Walmsley, 'Some Dutch Franciscans in England during the Later Middle Ages', p. 248).

LYELL, John: he was a friar of Richmond when he was ordained d. on 19 June 1451, and at York when he was ordained p. on 24 February 1453. Both ceremonies took place at Blackfriars, York (BIA, Register 19, fol. 299v, Register 20, fol. 413v).

LYMBERGH (Lymbergh), Henry de: on 14 July 1317 he and his unnamed *socius* from York received royal alms for travelling to the king at Leicester on the business of their house (London, Society of Antiquaries, MS.121, fol. 2r). He was licensed in the diocese of Lincoln but replaced by Peter de Mora on 18 February 1330 (LAO, Register 5, fol. 402v).

LYMBY, Thomas: he was a friar of Boston when he was ordained s. on 20 September 1399 at Stow prebendal church (LAO, Register 13, fol. 88v).

LYNAM, John: he was at York when he was ordained a. on 22 February 1494, s. on 4 April 1495 at Holy Trinity Priory, Micklegate, York, d. on 27 February 1496 at Greyfriars, York, and p. on 17 December 1496. The first and last ordinations occurred at Whitefriars, York (BIA, Register 23, fols. 440r, 445r, 449v, 453r. Cf. Cross and Vickers, *MFN*, p. 438).

LYNATRE, John de: he was ordained p. on 7 June 1343 at Greyfriars, York (BIA, Register 10A, fol. 4v).

LYNDBY, Thomas: he was ordained d. on 18 September 1400 at All Saints, Cawood (*Reg. Scrope*, ii, pp. 55, 91, 131).

LYNDESAY (Lyndesay, Lindsay), John: he was a friar of York when he was ordained

a. on 25 May 1426 at Holy Trinity Priory, Micklegate, York. He was ordained s. on 21 May 1429 at Blackfriars, York (BIA, Register 19, fols. 227r, 234v).

LYNDRYK, John: he was ordained a. and s. on 31 May 1393 at the parish church of St Michael-le-Belfrey, York, d. on 20 September 1393 at St Leonard's Hospital, York, and p. on 13 June 1394 at St Mary's Abbey, York (BIA, Register 14, fols. 66v, 67r, 68r, 70r).

LYNDSAY (Lindsay), Richard: he was a friar of York when he was ordained a. on 27 May 1480 at Blackfriars, York (BIA, Register 5A, fol. 515r; BL, MS. Cotton Galba, E.X, fol. 133r). He was ordained s. on 22 September 1481 at Whitefriars, York. He was at Richmond when ordained d. on 13 March 1484 at Holy Trinity, Micklegate, York, and at York when he was ordained p. on 18 September 1484 at Whitefriars, York (Register 23, fols. 377v, 390v, 394r. Cf. Cross and Vickers, *MFN*, p. 435).

LYNESAY (Lindsay, Lonesay), Alan: he was ordained d. on 28 February 1366 at St Mary's, Bishophill Senior, York, and p. on 30 May 1366 at Bishopthorpe manor chapel (BIA, Register 11, fols. 362r, 363v).

LYNWOD, Matthew: he was ordained s. on 4 April 1416 and d. on 13 June 1416; both ceremonies took place in the prebendal chapel at Cawood (BIA, Register 18, fols. 39Hv, 39Ir).

LYNWOD (Lynwode, Lynwood), Thomas: he was ordained p. on 6 March 1479 at Austin Friars, York (BIA, Register 22, fol. 377r). On 12 November 1490 he was appointed to the convent of Oxford *de familia* under the obedience and correction of the prelates for the present time until the 1491 general chapter to be held in Assisi (*Regesta Ordinis Fratrum Minorum Conventualium*, 1 (1488–94), p. 165, no. 1343). He was afterwards janitor to the friars of London and confessor to the nuns of Barking. He died on 1 November 1506 and was buried in London (*GFL*, pp. 67, 99).

LYNWODE, Richard: he was a friar of York when he was ordained a. on 27 May 1469 at Blackfriars, York (BIA, Register 22, fol. 200v).

LYON (Leo, Lyonn), John: he was ordained a. on 8 June 1370 at Bishopthorpe manorial chapel, s. on 20 September 1371 at St Mary, Bishophill Senior, and d. on 18 December 1372 at Whitefriars, York (BIA, Register 11, fols. 378v, 384v, 390r). He was ordained p. on 16 June 1375 at Cawood manor chapel (BIA, Register 12, fol. 121r).

MABERGH, John: he was a friar of Beverley when he was ordained d. on 22 December 1358 at Cawood manorial chapel (BIA, Register 11, fol. 335v).

MABLETHORPE (Mablethorp, Malburthorpe), John de: he was ordained s. on 29 May 1344 in Darlington parish church (*Reg. Kellaw*, iii, p. 142), d. on 14 June 1348 at St Mary's Abbey, York, and p. on 20 September 1348 in Skipton parish church. His name occurs twice in the register as a priest (BIA, Register 10A, fol. 25rv). Either he or the next friar featured in the Cambridge account roll in 1363 (Harris, *Origin of the Leicester Codex*, pp. 23–25; *GFC*, p. 193). In 1368 he was guardian of London (*GFL*, p. 56) and entered into agreements regarding the donation of windows on the south side of the church (*Monum. Franciscana*, i, p. 521). A friar of this name was granted an annual payment of 40 marks from the royal exchequer from 9 May 1370 to celebrate Masses and pray for the soul of the late Queen Philippa, whose confessor he had been (*CPR*,

1367–1370, p. 432). Subsequent payments were made on 10 May 1371 *ad totam vitam* (TNA, 403/441, m. 24) and 24 November 1372 in two stages (TNA, 403/447, m. 9).

MABLETHORPE (Mablethorp), John de: he was licensed to hear confessions in the diocese of Lincoln, but was replaced about 5 October 1346 (LAO, Register 7, fol. 99r). A friar of this name was the guardian of York at Michaelmas 1351, when his name occurs in the plea rolls (TNA, CP40/367, m. 173d, attorneys 8).

MABLETHORPE (Malbirthorp), Thomas: he was ordained s. on 1 June 1398 at St Michael-le-Belfrey, York (BIA, Register 5A, fol. 255v; BL, MS. Cotton Galba, E.X, fol. 119v). He was a friar of Lincoln when he was ordained d. on 22 February 1399 in Stow prebendal church (LAO, Register 13, fol. 85r). He was ordained p. on 10 March 1403 at York Minster (*Reg. Scrope*, ii, pp. 55, 91, 131).

MABUL, John: he was ordained s. on 17 December 1345 at Liddington prebendal church (LAO, Register 7B, fol. 2r).

MAKEBLYTH (Makblith, Malebhy), John: he was a friar of Lichfield when he was ordained s. on 28 February 1450 at Lichfield cathedral (*Reg. Bothe*, p. 142, no. 330). He was at Nottingham when ordained d. on 30 May 1450 at St Margaret's church in the close of Lincoln cathedral (LAO, Register 19, fol. 16). He was at York when he was ordained p. on 23 September 1452 at Greyfriars, York (BIA, Register 19, fol. 304r). He was there in 1470 when he became a member of the guild of *Corpus Christi* (*Corpus Christi Guild*, p. 74). On 26 February 1489, William Cerff asked him to celebrate a trental of Masses for him (BIA, Probate Register 5, fols. 357v–58r). He remained there for many years and received 3s. 4d. on 9 January 1502 to pray for the soul of Jane Chamberleyn, a parishioner of St John the Baptist, Hungate, whose confessor he was (*TE*, iv, pp. 200–02).

MALENERE, Emerisus: he was ordained s. on 19 May 1380 in the parish church of Stillingfleet (BIA, Register 12, fol. 137r).

MALERBE (Malvyle), John: he was ordained d. on 20 December 1348 and at Beverley when ordained p. on 19 September 1349; the last two ceremonies took place at York Minster (BIA, Register 10A, fols. 26r, 34r).

MALERBE, Philip de: he was licensed to hear confessions in the diocese of Lincoln for one year on 10 March 1347 (LAO, Register 7, fol. 100r).

MALLOME (Mallom), William: he was a friar of York when he was ordained a. on 19 September 1450 and s. on 22 December 1453, both at Greyfriars, York. He was ordained d. on 21 December 1454 at Austin Friars, York, and p. on 11 June 1457 at Holy Trinity Priory, Micklegate, York (BIA, Register 19, fol. 295v, Register 20, fols. 416v, 419r, 430v).

MALTON, Benedict de: on 12 August 1314 he was appointed as confessor to the nuns of Moxby (*Reg. Greenfield*, iii, p. 85, no. 1326).

MALTON, John: he was ordained d. on 22 September 1397 at Holy Trinity Priory, Micklegate, York (*Reg. Waldby*, p. 45), and p. on 22 February 1399 at Cawood chapel (*Reg. Scrope*, ii, pp. 54, 91, 131).

MALTON, Richard de: he was a friar of Beverley when he was ordained a. on 19 December 1349 at St Michael-le-Belfrey, York (BIA, Register 10A, fol. 34v).

MALTON, William de: he was ordained s. on 20 December 1337 in Auckland manor chapel and p. on 21 September 1342 in Durham cathedral (*Reg. Kellaw*, iii, pp. 121, 190).

MALVYLE, John: he was ordained d. on 19 September 1349 at York Minster (BIA, Register 10A, fol. 33v).

MANGAYN, John: he was ordained p. on 22 May 1361 at York Minster (BIA, Register 11, fol. 345r).

MANLEY, John: he was a friar of Beverley when he was mentioned along with the guardian, William Whalley, in the plea rolls during the Michaelmas term of 1417 and the Trinity term of 1419 (TNA, CP40/627, m. 264 and CP40/633, m. 274).

MANSER, Thomas: a novice at York at the Dissolution on 27 November 1538 (*Eighth Report of the Deputy Keeper of the Public Records*, p. 51).

MAR, Thomas de: on 6 May 1294 he was signified for arrest. He was a lay brother at the friary in York. Roger Marston, minister of the friars in England, was at Shrewsbury when he announced that this friar had apostatised from the order and resumed secular dress (TNA, c.81/1792/14).

MARCHE (Marshe, March), John: he was ordained a. on 18 September 1400 at All Saints, Cawood (*Reg. Scrope*, ii, pp. 55, 92, 131) and d. on 5 June 1406 at Austin Friars, York, and was at York when he was ordained p. on 18 September 1406 at Blackfriars, York (BIA, Register 5A, fols. 322r, 323r; *Reg. Sede Vacante, York, 1405–08*, pp. 66, 77, 89).

MARDESLAY (Marthelay), John de: he incepted as a D.D. of Oxford before 1355, when he disputed with the Dominican, William Jordan, on the theology of the Immaculate Conception in the chapter house of York Minster. His letter to the cathedral chapter of York is dated 10 April 1355 and refers to him as *sacre pagine professor*, supplying details of the dispute, its venue and cause in question. Responding to comments about his manner of disputing, the cathedral chapter of York issued a letter of 10 April 1355 testifying to this friar's good conduct and courtesy (BL, Harley, MS.6971, fol. 113v; Marcett, *Uthred de Boldon, Fr William Jordan and Piers Plowman*, pp. 25–37; *Monumenta Franciscana*, i, p. 561; *GFO*, p. 242). In the context of this dispute he compiled a book and overcame his Dominican adversary (*Leland, De viris illustribus*, pp. 664–67, no. 456). In 1357–58 he took part with Roger Conway in answering the attacks of Richard Fitzralph, archbishop of Armagh, on the mendicant orders. In 1359–60 he was associated with Roger Conway and Hugh Bernardi, minister provincial of Ireland, in obtaining an authentic copy of Pope John XXII's bull, *Vas electionis*, from the papal curia (*BF*, vi, p. 319, no. 759). He is mentioned again on 10 January 1371 in connection with the chapter house and the dispute about the theology of the Immaculate Conception; the Carmelites and Dominicans were also mentioned (BL, Harley, MS.6971, fol. 127r). He preached before King Edward III at the feast of Pentecost, 21 May 1374. The king then invited him to the council at Westminster over which the archbishop of Canterbury and the Black Prince presided.

He attended with three other doctors and he was the spokesman of his order. He skilfully showed that Jesus Christ had no temporal dominion and did not grant it to the apostles. His case was based on scriptural texts, the doctors and the Church, and the example of holy men. He argued that the pope had no temporal dominion and pointed to the general denial of Pope Boniface VIII's claims in France and England. He stated, on the authority of St Thomas, that temporal power went back to the emperor Constantine, not to Christ. He swung clerical opinion away from the papalist viewpoint, which had been propounded by John Ourtiedum, a monk of Durham (*Eulogium Historiarum*, III, pp. 337–38; *GFO*, p. 242; Catto, 'An Alleged Great Council of 1374', p. 767). He was minister provincial in 1375–79 or 1380 (Cf. Workman, *John Wyclif*, i, pp. 228–29). He died at York in 1376 (Little, *Franciscan Papers, Lists, and Documents*, p. 197). Bale attributed a tractate *Super Mariae Conceptione* and *Questions* to him (*BRUO*, p. 1221).

MARISCO (Marsh), John de: he was ordained p. on 22 September 1296 in Lincoln cathedral (*Reg. Sutton*, vii, p. 85).

MARKHAM, John de: he was ordained a. on 10 June 1346 at Whitefriars, York (BIA, Register 10A, fol. 15r), s. on 23 September 1346 at Austin Friars, Stamford, and d. on 26 May 1347 at Lincoln cathedral (LAO, Register 7B, fols. 8r and 14v).

MARLAY, Richard: he was ordained d. on 5 June 1479 at Holy Trinity Priory, Micklegate, York (BIA, Register 22, fol. 379r).

MARLBURGH (Marlebergh), John de: he was ordained s. on 26 May 1358 at Greyfriars, York (BIA, Register 11, fol. 111v), and p. on 25 February 1363 in Lincoln cathedral (LAO, Register 9D, fol. 110r).

MARLEBERGH (Marlborough), William de: he was a friar of Doncaster when he was ordained a. on 21 September 1359 at Cawood manor chapel (BIA, Register 11, fol. 338v).

MARMADUKE: he was ordained s. on 26 February 1295 and d. on 19 May 1296. Both ceremonies took place in Lincoln cathedral (*Reg. Sutton*, vii, pp. 62, 79).

MARMYRTH, William: he was ordained d. on 20 February 1361 at Cawood manor chapel (BIA, Register 11, fol. 343v).

MARRICK (Marrik), William: he was a friar of York when he was ordained a. on 31 May 1488 at Blackfriars, York, s. on 18 September 1490, and d. on 7 April 1492. The second and third ordinations took place at Whitefriars, York (BIA, Register 23, fols. 412v, 423v, 431v. Cf. Cross and Vickers, *MFN*, pp. 436–37).

MARSHALL (Marshall), Richard: he was a friar of York when he was ordained a. on 13 March 1462 at Greyfriars, York, and p. on 26 May 1464 at Blackfriars, York (BIA, Register 20, fols. 450r, 460r).

MARSHALL, William: he was a friar of York when he was ordained s. on 18 December 1512 at Austin Friars, York, d. on 21 May 1513, and p. on 23 September 1514. The second and third ceremonies took place at Blackfriars, York (BIA, Register 26, fols. 121r, 124v, 150r). He was at York at the Dissolution on

27 November 1538 (*Eighth Report of the Deputy Keeper of the Public Records*, p. 51). In 1548 a priest of this name was ministering to a guild in the parish of Whitgift with a stipend of 70s. per year (*Chantries, Guilds, Hospitals*, ii, pp. 288–89; Cross and Vickers, *MFN*, pp. 444, 458).

MARTYN (Martin), Roger: he was ordained d. on 20 September 1371 at St Mary, Bishophill Senior (BIA, Register 11, fol. 384v) and p. on 17 March 1375 at Cawood manor chapel (BIA, Register 12, fol. 119v).

MARYKYN (Marikyn), John: he was a friar of York when he was ordained a. on 24 September 1407 at Blackfriars, York, and s. on 17 December 1407 at Holy Trinity Priory, Micklegate, York (BIA, Register 5A, fol. 325rv; *Reg. Sede Vacante, York, 1405–08*, pp. 66, 77, 89). He was ordained p. on 17 June 1413 at Greyfriars, York (BIA, Register 18, fol. 39Fv).

MASON, Miles: he was a friar of Richmond when he was ordained a. on 22 December 1509 at an unrecorded venue. He was a friar of York when he was ordained s. on 14 June 1511. He was back at Richmond when he was ordained p. on 5 June 1512. The second and third ceremonies took place at Blackfriars, York (BIA, Register 5A, Register 26, fols. 114r, 119v; *Reg. Bainbridge*, p. 363). He was at Richmond at the Dissolution in 1538 (*Eighth Report of the Deputy Keeper of the Public Records*, p. 38. Cf. Cross and Vickers, *MFN*, pp. 442, 449, 450).

MASON, Peter: he was a friar of York when he was ordained a. on 26 March 1502 at York Minster, s. on 10 June 1503 at Blackfriars, York, d. on 23 September 1503 at Greyfriars, York, and p. on 2 March 1504 at Whitefriars, York (BIA, Register 25, fols. 111v, 119r, 120r, 122v. Cf. Cross and Vickers, *MFN*, p. 440).

MASTE, John: he was a friar at York when he was ordained s. on 13 March 1462 at Greyfriars, York, and d. on 3 April 1462 at Blackfriars, York (BIA, Register 20, fols. 450v, 451r), and at Lichfield when ordained p. on 24 September 1463 in the diocese of Coventry and Lichfield (LRO, B/A/12, fol. 191v).

MASUARII, Robert: on 31 December 1424 the dean and chapter of York authorised this friar, a member of the province of France, and Lord John Ashton, a knight, to hear the confessions of his subjects who had perpetrated misdemeanours in the deanery of Preston in the archdeaconry of Richmond and to grant absolution and acquittances, even in cases reserved to the dean and chapter, except those concerning the violation of the liberties of the Minsters or collegiate churches of Beverley, Ripon and Southwell (BIA, Register 5A, fol. 394v; *Reg. Sede Vacante, York, 1423–26*, p. 47, no. 294).

MATLOT (Matlat), John: he was a friar of Doncaster when he was ordained a. on 22 September 1487 at Whitefriars, York (BIA, Register 23, fol. 408v. Cf. Cross and Vickers, *MFN*, p. 436). He was at Oxford when ordained d. on 19 September 1489 at All Saints, Northampton, and p. on 6 March 1490 in the chapel of St Mary Magdalene, Lincoln cathedral (LAO, Register 22, fols. 33r, 34v; *BRUO*, p. 1242).

MATTHEWS (Mathew), Alexander: he was ordained a. on 18 September 1479 at Whitefriars, York, s. on 18 December 1479 at Austin Friars, York, and d. on 26 February 1480 at Greyfriars, York (BIA, Register 22, fols. 380r, 381v, 382v).

MATTHEWS (Mathew), Cornelius: he was ordained p. on 17 June 1413 at Greyfriars, York (BIA, Register 18, fol. 39Fv).

MAUG, John: he was a friar of Boston when he was ordained d. on 13 March 1361 in Holbeach church (LAO, Register 9D, fol. 98v).

MAULEVERER (Maulinerer, Mallore), Peter: he was ordained a. on 20 September 1365 at Cawood manor chapel, s. on 21 March 1366 in Beverley Minster and d. on 18 September 1367 at Bishopthorpe manor chapel (BIA, Register 11, fols. 360v, 362v, 367r).

MAUTHORPE, William: he was ordained s. on 26 May 1347 at Lincoln cathedral (LAO, Register 7B, fol. 13r).

MAWLEY, John: he was a friar of York when he was ordained d. on 16 September 1391 at Holy Trinity Priory, Micklegate, York (BIA, Register 14, fol. 63r).

MAYNARD, Thomas: a friar of Beverley on 24 May 1300 when Edward I gave the friars there 38s. (*Liber quotidianus contrarotulatoris garderobae*, p. 37).

MELBOURNE (Melburn, Melborne), William de: he was ordained p. on 22 September 1296 in Lincoln cathedral (*Reg. Sutt*on, vii, p. 85).

MELBURN (Meburne), John de: he was ordained a. on 21 September 1341 in the manor chapel of Stockton, s. on 21 September 1342 in Durham cathedral and d. on 21 December 1342 in the manor chapel at Aukland (*Reg. Kellaw*, iii, pp. 112, 119, 124). He was ordained p. on 10 June 1346 at Whitefriars, York (BIA, Register 10A, fol. 16r).

MELTON, William: he was a friar of Colchester when he was ordained p. on 19 September 1405 (London Registers: Walden). A marginal note in the MS. identifies him as the friar, a celebrated preacher, who moved to [King's] Lynn about 1420. Margery Kempe was moved to tears by his sermons on the passion in the church of St James, a chapel-of-ease of St Margaret's at Lynn. She reports that people used to travel to hear him preach, following him from town to town. He refused to allow her to weep during his homilies. He came to be regarded as unsympathetic. She was consoled by the prediction that her reputation would recover, while his would diminish (*The Book of Margery Kempe*, pp. 148–69, at 321). One of his homilies on the Blessed Virgin appears in the model sermons assembled by Nicholas Philip (Fletcher, *Preaching, Politics and Poetry in Late-Medieval England*, pp. 45, 50–51). A friar of this name was described as *a most famous preacher of the word of God*. In his *suis diversis sermonibus* at York he recommended the *Corpus Christi* play to the people, affirming that it was good in itself and praiseworthy. However, he pointed out that some citizens and visitors to the city for the festival joined in revellings, drunkenness, clamour, singing and other improprieties. They paid little attention to the divine offices of the day, losing the benefit of the indulgences conceded by Pope Urban IV. He persuaded the people of the city that the play should be held on one day and the procession on another so the people might attend church and receive the indulgences. Persuaded by the friar, the city council won the assent of the people for the ordinance that thenceforth the solemn play of *Corpus Christi* should be played annually every year on Wednesday, the vigil of the feast, and the procession on the feast day itself. His preaching moved people to expel the prostitutes and procuresses from the city (*York*

Memorandum Book, ii, pp. 156–59). He was a D.Th. of Oxford by 1426. By the time that he preached in York he was a professor of theology. A letter from the University of Oxford to Duke Humphrey, king's counsel, of 1427, mentioned that Melton had travelled through the provinces preaching senseless things and in a great many places seditiously instructed the simple people in careless words (*Bekynton's Correspondence*, ii, p. 249). Little argues that these vows were introduced following the condemnations of William Russell on 12 October 1424 and 28 January 1425 for preaching against tithes (*GFO*, p. 259). On 25 February 1429 a papal bull ordered James, bishop of Adria, to relax the oaths which Melton had taken at Oxford and to release him from them (*BF*, vii, pp. 718–19, no. 1849; *CPL*, viii, p. 86; *Monumenta Franciscana*, ii, p. xxviii). He may have returned to Lynn in 1430 or 1431, when and where Nicholas Philip collected sermons under the name of Melton in his diary (Little, *Franciscan Papers, Lists, and Documents*, pp. 244–56). Homan states that there is no proof that all the references denote a single friar, but believes that such a chronology would fit (Homan, 'Old and New Evidence of the Career of William Melton, O.F.M.', pp. 25–33). Gonville and Caius College Library, Cambridge, MS.356/583, fol. 3r, states that a Friar Melton, OFM, preached in Bury on the feast of St Ethelreda on the Sunday before the feast of St Michael. Only one of the sermons from this notebook was expressly attributed to this friar; no subsequent authors are mentioned in the two-year cycle of sermons which runs throughout the year.

MERC (Merk), Eustace de: he was at Oxford in the time of Agnellus of Pisa and was guardian there for some time (*diu*); he was there in 1237–38 when he was unfairly disciplined by Wygerius, the third visitator, despite his reputation for integrity. He contributed an anecdote about the vocation of Lanfranc, archbishop of Canterbury. He was renowned for his abstinence and penitential exercises. Albert of Pisa obliged him to eat fish, commenting that too many friars had died because of their indiscretion. He was custos of York towards the end of his life, and died in a devout manner (Eccleston, pp. 40, 64, 84, 88–89; *BRUO*, p. 1262).

MERSTON, John de: he was ordained s. on 29 March 1343 at Greyfriars, Beverley. He was a friar of York when he was ordained d. on 18 September 1344 at St Mary's Abbey, York. He was ordained p. on 22 December 1347 at Greyfriars, Doncaster (BIA, Register 10A, fols. 3r, 8r, 20r).

MERTON, Michael de: on 19 June 1300 Archbishop Corbridge granted the petition of Henry de Lacy, earl of Lincoln, that Michael of Merton and Reginald of Kingston should hear the confessions of those who were accompanying the earl to fight in Scotland (*Reg. Corbridge*, i, pp. 23–24; *Historical Papers and Letters from the Northern Registers*, p. 143). A friar of this name was licensed to hear confessions in the diocese of Canterbury in c.1300–04 (*Reg. Winchelsey*, i, p. 394). On 15 January 1305 a papal indult was issued to Henry de Lacy to be accompanied by his Franciscan confessor, de Merton (Mercona), a friar who had full faculties except in reserved cases (*CPL*, ii, p. 7).

MESSYNGHAM (Massingham), Thomas de: he was a friar of Doncaster when he was ordained s. on 21 September 1359. He was ordained d. on 30 May 1360; both ceremonies took place at Cawood manor chapel (BIA, Register 11, fols. 338v, 341r).

METCALF, Henry: he was a friar of York when he was ordained a. on 17 March 1492, s. on 21 April 1492 at the lady altar in York Minster, d. on 21 September 1493 at Whitefriars, York, and p. on 15 March 1494. The first and last ordinations took place at Greyfriars, York (BIA, Register 23, fols. 430r, 432r, 439r, 441v. Cf. Cross and Vickers, *MFN*, p. 438).

METHAM, John de: he was ordained s. on 18 December 1344 at Whitefriars, York, d. on 17 December 1345 at Whitefriars, York, and p. on 14 June 1348 at St Mary's Abbey, York (BIA, Register 10A, fols. 8v, 13v, 25r).

MIDDELBURG (Midilburgh), Cornelius: he was ordained p. on 22 February 1399 at Cawood manor chapel (*Reg. Scrope*, ii, pp. 55, 93, 131; Walmsley, 'Some Dutch Franciscans in England during the Later Middle Ages', p. 257).

MIDDELBURG (Midelburgh), Lawrence: he was ordained p. on 17 December 1401 at St Mary's Abbey, York (*Reg. Scrope*, ii, pp. 55, 93, 131; Walmsley, 'Some Dutch Franciscans in England during the Later Middle Ages', p. 257).

MIDDELBURGH (Midelburg), Nicholas: he was ordained a. on 17 May 1410 and s. on 20 September 1410; both ceremonies took place at All Saints, Cawood (BIA, Register 18, fol. 392rv).

MIDDELBURGH (Midelburgh), William: he was a friar of Boston when he was ordained p. on 7 March 1422 at Liddington prebendal church (*Reg. Fleming*, ii, p. 82, no. 482).

MIDDLEHAM (Middilham, Midelham, Midlam), Henry: he was a friar of York when he was ordained a. on 19 September 1422 at Holy Trinity Priory, Micklegate, York, d. on 23 December 1424 at Whitefriars, York (BIA, Register 18, fol. 413v, Register 5A, fol. 394r; *Reg. Sede Vacante, York, 1423–26*, pp. 99, 113, 125). He was a friar of Lincoln when he was ordained p. on 2 June 1425 at Liddington prebendal church (*Reg. Fleming*, ii, p. 114, no. 522).

MIDDLEHAM (Midilham, Midelham), Thomas: he was a friar of York when he was ordained s. on 21 September 1426 at Blackfriars, York. He was ordained d. on 17 December 1429 at Austin Friars, York, and p. on 11 March 1430 at Greyfriars, York (BIA, Register 19, fols. 215r, 236rv).

MIDDLETON (Midelton), John de: he was ordained a. on 24 September 1351 at York Minster and s. on 17 December 1351 at Austin Friars, York (BIA, Register 10A, fols. 52v, 53v).

MIDDLETON (Midelton), Thomas: he was ordained a. on 13 June 1394 in St Mary's Abbey, York, and s. on 19 September 1394 at Austin Friars, York (BIA, Registers 14, fols. 69v, 70r). A friar of this name was at Reading when he was ordained p. on 23 December 1396 in the diocese of Salisbury (Salisbury Registers: Mitford, fol. 154r).

MIDELTON, Richard de: he was ordained d. on 18 September 1350 at Whitefriars, York, and p. on 2 June 1352 at St Mary's Abbey, York (BIA, Register 10A, fols. 49r, 55v). A friar of this name, probably at York, received five marks in the will of John de Burton, rector of Huggate, near York, on 6–7 May 1373 (York Minster, Dean and Chapter Library, MS.L 2/4, fol. 56v).

MIDILTON (Midelton), Robert de: he was ordained a. on 10 June 1346 at Whitefriars, York, and d. on 15 March 1348 at York Minster (BIA, Register 10A, fols. 15r, 21v).

MILINGTON (Milyngton), Robert de: he was ordained a. on 18 December 1344, s. on 12 March 1345, both at Whitefriars, York, and d. on 24 September 1345 at Ripon Minster (BIA, Register 10A, fols. 8v, 10r, 13r). He was ordained p. on 17 March 1347 at Burton parish church beside Lincoln (LAO, Register 7B, fol. 11v).

MILITIS, Nicholas: he was a friar of York when he was ordained s. on 18 December 1423 at York Minster (BIA, Register 5A, fol. 354v; *Reg. Sede Vacante, York, 1423–26*, pp. 99, 113, 125).

MILNER (Mylner), Wiliam: he was a friar of York when he was ordained a. on 21 March 1523 at Whitefriars, York (BIA, Register 27, fol. 198v. Cf. Cross and Vickers, *MFN*, p. 455).

MILTON, John: one of the friars of York who accompanied Thomas Richmond of York when he preached at the chapel of St Anne on Foss bridge on 26 June 1426. On 13 August of that year he attended the chapter house with Richmond and testified before the bishop of Durham to the content of the friar's vernacular sermon (*Convocation, York*, pp. 389–390; *Records of the Northern Convocation*, p. 151).

MIRESCUGH (Murscugh), John: John de Mirisco was ordained d. on 18 December 1378 in Hereford cathedral (*Reg. Gilbert*, p. 136). John Mirescugh, a friar of Preston, was licensed to hear confessions in 1400. On 26 June 1414 he was described as master and was left £4 by Lady Beatrice de Roos, the daughter of Ralph, the earl of Stafford, and widow of first Maurice, earl of Desmond, secondly, Thomas Lord Roos of Hamlake and Belvoir, and thirdly, Sir Richard Burley, knight (*TE*, i, pp. 375–79, at 376; Goldthorp, 'The Franciscans and Dominicans in Yorkshire', 284; *Women of the English Nobility and Gentry 1066–1500*, pp. 227–30).

MISERICORDE, Henry: a lay brother and first guardian of the friary at Lincoln about 1230 (Eccleston, p. 10).

MISTERTON, Thomas de: he was ordained p. on 4 March 1357 at Bishopthorpe manor chapel (BIA, Register 11, fol. 330r).

MITON, Robert: he was a friar of Lincoln when he was ordained s. on 25 March 1486 in Lincoln cathedral, d. on 20 May 1486 at Sleaford prebandal church and p. on 23 September 1486 in St Mary's priory at Huntingdon (LAO, Register 22, fols. 21v, 22rv).

MITTEFORD, Thomas: he was ordained a. on 19 September 1394 at Austin Friars, York (BIA, Register 14, fol. 70r).

MOISES (Moiser, Moyser), John: he was a friar at York when he was ordained a. on 21 December 1504 at Austin Friars, York. He was a friar of Richmond when he was ordained s. on 15 February 1505. He was back at York again when he was ordained d. on 8 March 1505 and p. on 17 May 1505. The third and fourth ordinations took place at Blackfriars, York (BIA, Register 25, fols. 126r, 127r, 128r, 129v). He was at Richmond at the Dissolution on 19 January 1538 (*Eighth Report of the Deputy Keeper of the Public Records*, p. 38. Cf. Cross and Vickers, *MFN*, pp. 441, 451).

MOLET (Molett, Molyet), John: he was a friar of York when he was ordained a. on 19 September 1489, s. on 17 March 1492 at Greyfriars, York, d. on 7 April 1492 and p. on 22 September 1492. The first, third and fourth ceremonies took place at Whitefriars, York (BIA, Register 23, fols. 418v, 430v, 431v, 434v. Cf. Cross and Vickers, *MFN*, p. 437).

MONKETON (Monkton), John: he was a friar of York when he was ordained p. on 22 September 1442 at York Minster (BIA, Register 19, fol. 220v).

MONTE, Gerard de: he was a friar of Lincoln when he was ordained a. on 15 March 1432 in the prebendal church of Sleaford and s. on 14 June 1432 at St Benedict's church, Lincoln (LAO, Register 17, fols. 205v, 207r).

MORA (More), Peter de: he was licensed to hear confessions in the diocese of Lincoln on 18 February 1330 *in loco* Henry de Lymbergh (LAO, Register 5, fol. 402v).

MORE (Mowe), Robert: he was at York when he was ordained a. on 23 December 1508 at Austin Friars, York, s. on 22 December 1509 at an unspecified venue, d. on 21 September 1510 at Holy Trinity Priory, Micklegate, York, and p. on 15 March 1511 at Whitefriars, York (BIA, Register 26, fols. 99r, 105r, 109v, 112r). He was there at the Dissolution on 27 November 1538 (*Eighth Report of the Deputy Keeper of the Public Records*, p. 51). In his will dated 13 November 1544 his former guardian, William Vavasour, gave him £9 6s. 8d. to celebrate for his soul for two years in the church of St Mary, Bishophill Junior (*York Clergy Wills 1520–1600: II. City Clergy*, pp. 33–35; Cross and Vickers, *MFN*, pp. 442, 458–59).

MORE, William de la: a friar of Beverley through whom King Edward I paid 34s. to the friars there on 21/23 July 1306 (TNA, E101/369/11, fol. 28v). He was licensed for the diocese of Lincoln on 20 June 1318; he was probably a friar of Lincoln (LAO, Register 3, fol. 390r). A William Mora of Bristol was licensed for the diocese of Bath and Wells in January 1323 (Bath and Wells Registers: Drokensford, fol. 195r).

MORPATH, Walter: he was a friar of York when he was ordained s. on 20 February 1445 at Greyfriars, York (BIA, Register 19, fol. 280v).

MORPATH (Morepath), William: he was a friar of Leicester when he was ordained a. on 23 February 1499 at St Mary de Pratis, Leicester. He was a friar of Boston when he was ordained s. on 30 March 1499 in Lincoln cathedral and d. on 25 May 1499 in Sleaford prebendal church (LAO, Register 24, fols. 15v, 17v, 18v). He was a friar of York when he was ordained p. on 21 September 1499 at Blackfriars, York (BIA, Register 23, fol. 465v. Cf. Cross and Vickers, *MFN*, p. 439).

MORTHELES, Peter de: on 19 January 1319 he was licensed to hear the confessions of the household of John of Brittany, earl of Richmond, during his time in the diocese of York (*Reg. Melton*, i, p. 3, no. 18).

MORTHING, William de: he was ordained p. on 14 June 1348 at St Mary's Abbey, York (BIA, Register 10A, fol. 25r).

MORTON (Moreton), John de: a native of Gainsborough, he was ordained s. on 18 December 1294 in Stow prebendal church, d. on 22 September 1296 in Lincoln cathedral and p. on 21 December 1297 in Louth prebendal church (*Reg. Sutton*, vii, pp. 60, 83, 101). He was the lector of the friary at Boston when, on 14 March 1319, he travelled to Buckden and presented letters from the minister provincial and the custos of York to Bishop Dalderby, who licensed him to hear confessions in the diocese of Lincoln until the provincial chapter in August of that year. He was described as the long-standing support of Bishop Dalderby (LAO, Register 3, fols. 411r–12r). He probably spent much of his religious life in the Lincolnshire houses in the custody. He received the royal alms on the occasion of the provincial chapter at Lincoln in 1326 (Little, *Franciscan Papers, Lists, and Documents*, p. 213). Together with Alan, vicar of Little Cawthorpe, he was licensed to hear the confessions of the Cistercian nuns of Legbourne, Lincolnshire, on 9 December 1339, even in cases reserved to the bishop or the vicar general (LAO, Register 5, fols. 154r, 518r; *Reg. Burghersh*, iii, p. 372, no. 4824).

MOSELAY, John: he was ordained s. on 28 May 1401 at Bishop Burton, d. on 17 December 1401 at St Mary's Abbey, York, and p. on 20 September 1404 at All Saints, Cawood (*Reg. Scrope*, ii, pp. 55, 94, 131).

MOSS (Mosse) John: he was a friar of York when he was ordained a. on 19 September 1450 (BIA, Register 19, fol. 295v). He was a friar of Lincoln when he was ordained s. on 18 September 1451 in St Margaret's in the close of Lincoln cathedral (LAO, Register 19, fols. 32v, 68r), and was back at York again when ordained d. on 18 December 1451. The first and third ceremonies took place at Greyfriars, York (BIA, Register 19, fol. 300v).

MOSS (Moser, Mosse), Robert: he was a friar of York when he was ordained a. on 18 December 1507 at Austin Friars, York, s. on 18 March 1508 at Greyfriars, York, and p. on 22 September 1509 at Holy Trinity Priory, Micklegate, York (BIA, Register 5A, fols. 582r, 587r, Register 26, fol. 103r. Cf. Cross and Vickers, *MFN*, p. 442).

MOWBRAY (Moubray, Mumbray), Thomas de: he was licensed to hear confessions in the diocese of Lincoln on 9 February 1332 (LAO, Register 5, fol. 455v). He was at Doncaster in 1332 when, together with the guardian and three other friars, he was sued by John de Malghum for false imprisonment. He probably held some office in the house at this time (*Notes on Religious Houses*, i, p. 37; TNA, CP40/292, m. 141, for the Michaelmas term). He was still there when his name occurs in the plea rolls of the Trinity term of 1333 (TNA, CP40/294, m. 272).

MOWTER (Moter, Mowtter), John: he was ordained a. on 27 March 1479 at Greyfriars, York, and s. on 5 June 1479 at Holy Trinity Priory, Micklegate, York (BIA, Register 22, fols. 377r, 379r). A friar of this name was dispensed to hold and receive a benefice on 11 April 1514 at his own petition (*CPL*, xx, p. 307, no. 431).

MUDFORD, William de: he was ordained s. on 20 September 1348 in Skipton parish church (BIA, Register 10A, fol. 25r).

MULTON, John: he was ordained a. on 20 December 1404 at All Saints, Cawood (*Reg. Scrope*, ii, pp. 55, 94, 131), s. on 6 March 1406 at Holy Trinity Priory, Micklegate, York. He was a friar of York when he was ordained p. on 24 September 1407 at Blackfriars, York (BIA, Register 5A, fols. 320r, 325v; *Reg. Sede Vacante, York, 1405–08*, pp. 66, 78, 89). It is improbable that this friar was associated with the *Magister* Multon admitted to the *Corpus Christi* guild at York in 1453 (*Corpus Christi Guild*, p. 54) and even less likely that he was the friar of this name, a doctor of sacred science, who was left a small piece of silver in the will of Eufemia, widow of John Langton of Farnley, near Leeds, on 26 August 1463. She requested burial in Leeds parish church beside her husband and left 6s. 8d. to each mendicant house of York (*TE*, ii, pp. 258–60).

MULTON, Richard de: he was presented to the bishop of Lincoln by the guardian of Lincoln in December 1321 for a licence but rejected (LAO, Register 3, fols. 299v–300). He was licensed in the diocese of York at an unknown date. On his death he was replaced by Arnalens Hiliest during the administration of Archbishop Thorsby (BIA, Register 11, fol. 396r).

MURO, John de: he was ordained d. on 29 March 1343 at Greyfriars, Beverley (BIA, Register 10A, fol. 3r).

MURO, William de: he was probably a friar of Lincoln when he was licensed to hear confessions in that diocese on 20 June 1318 (LAO, Register 3, fol. 390r).

MUSCHAM, Nicholas de: he was a friar of Beverley on 11 August 1318 when he was licensed to hear confessions in the diocese of York (BIA, Register 9, fol. 326v; *Reg. Melton*, vi, p. 17, no. 73). He was a priest at Beverley when he died c.1334 (Little, '*Records, Franciscan Province*', p. 151).

MUSKER (Muscar), Robert: he was ordained d. on 2 June 1352 at St Mary's Abbey, York (BIA, Register 10A, fol. 55r). A friar of this name was ordained p. on 22 December 1352 in the manor chapel at Esher (*Reg. Edington*, ii, p. 168, no. 838).

MUSTON, Robert: he was licensed in the diocese of York in place of Simon Badby, who had been appointed elsewhere (BIA, Register 11, fol. 397r).

NAGHENBY, John: he was ordained p. on 24 September 1362 at Bishopthorpe manor chapel (BIA, Register 11, fol. 350v).

NARENBY (Naunby, Navenby), John de: he was ordained s. on 22 December 1358, d. on 29 February 1360, and p. on 11 June 1362. The first two ceremonies took place at Cawood manor chapel and the third at Bishopthorpe manor chapel (BIA, Register 11, fols. 335v, 340r, 349v, 350r). A John Navenby was mentioned in the plea rolls with John de Staynton, guardian of Lincoln, in the Michaelmas term of 1375 (TNA, KB27/459, attorneys, m. 3).

NESEHAM, William: he was a friar and master of York on 1 December 1435 who received 6s. 8d. in the will of Richard Russell, merchant and parishioner of St John the Baptist at Hungate (*TE*, ii, pp. 52–57, 55).

NEUNLE, John de: a friar, probably belonging to the custody of York, who received papal permission to transfiliate to the Cistercian monastery of Louth Park on 13 September 1331 (*CPL*, ii, p. 366).

NEWARK, H. de: at the request of Master Peter de Ros and Master Robert de la Forde, on 14 March 1300 the goods of Archbishop Henry Newark were sequestered on account of something due to the dioceses and deposited in the local Greyfriars. The following day two friars, G., chamberlain of the friary, and H. de Newark, brought nine large and four small chests containing the late prelate's goods to the cathedral chapter house (*Fasti Eboracenses*, p. 353n, citing *Acta Capituli*, fol. 9v).

NEWARK, John de: he was licensed to hear confessions in the diocese at an unknown date. Following his death, he was replaced by Ralph de Hertilburgh on 17 October 1347 (BIA, Register 10, fol. 278r).

NEWARK (Newerk), Philip de: he was licensed to hear confessions in the diocese of York at an unknown date. He died and was replaced by Thomas Warr c.1360 (BIA, Register 11, fol. 397r).

NEWBOLD, William: he was assigned to the friary at York, but had connections in Lincolnshire. The will of Peter Dalton, canon and treasurer of Lincoln cathedral, on 1 February 1402 left William 40s. for prayers for his soul, *si vivat* (LAO, Register 13, fols. 50v–52v).

NEWBOTTLE (Newbotill), William de: he was the guardian of Hartlepool when he was licensed for the diocese of York on 2 October 1350 (BIA, Register 10, fol. 279v).

NEWBURGH, John: he was a friar of York when he was ordained s. on 10 March 1498 at Greyfriars, York (BIA, Register 23, fol. 458r. Cf. Cross and Vickers, *MFN*, p. 439).

NEWBURN, John: he was ordained d. on 5 June 1479 at Holy Trinity Priory, Micklegate, York. He was a friar of York when he was ordained p. on 27 May 1480 at Blackfriars, York (BIA, Register 22, fol. 379r, Register 5A, fol. 515v).

NEWLAND, Edmund: he was a friar of York when he was ordained a. on 24 September 1468 at Whitefriars, York (BIA, Register 22, fol. 196r).

NEWSON (Neusom), Richard: he was a friar of Beverley when he was ordained s. on 18 September 1417 at the prebendal chapel at Cawood (BIA, Register 18, fol. 398r). He was a friar of Lincoln when he was ordained p. on 1 June 1420 in St Katherine's priory outside Lincoln (*Reg. Fleming*, ii, p. 64, no. 471).

NEWTON (Neuton), John: he was ordained s. on 19 December 1388 at York Minster (BIA, Register 14, fol. 10v).

NEWTON, Robert de: he was a friar of York when he was ordained d. on 24 September 1496 at Austin Friars, York (BIA, Register 23, fol. 452r. Cf. Cross and Vickers, *MFN*, p. 438).

NEWTON (Neuton), Walter de: he was licensed to hear confessions in the diocese of York at an unknown date. After his death he was replaced by Adam de Acaster during the administration of Archbishop John Thoresby (BIA, Register 11, fol. 396r).

NEWTON, William de: he was ordained d. on 22 September 1369 at Bishopthorpe manor chapel and p. on 21 February 1372 at St Mary, Bishophill Senior (BIA, Register 11, fols. 375v, 387r).

NICHOLAS: he was guardian of Lincoln on 26 June 1289 when he wrote in support of the petition for the canonisation of Robert Grosseteste, bishop of Lincoln (Moorman, *Medieval Franciscan Houses*, p. 266, citing Lincoln MSS, Press II, 1, 20, Box 2a; Robson, 'Robert Grosseteste: his memory among the Greyfriars, his cult in Lincoln cathedral and the petition for his canonisation').

NICHOLSON, Peter: he was a friar of York when he was ordained d. on 24 May 1494 at Blackfriars, York, and p. on 20 September 1494 at Greyfriars, York (BIA, Register 23, fols. 442r, 443v. Cf. Cross and Vickers, *MFN*, p. 438).

NICHOLSON (Nycolson), Robert: a former friar of Lincoln who obtained his capacity on 8 October 1539 (Chambers, *Faculty Office Registers 1534–1549*, p. 195).

NOCTON (Nokton, Noktun), William: he was a friar of York when he was ordained a. on 1 June 1420, s. on 19 December 1422 and d. on 18 December 1423 at York Minster. The first two ceremonies took place at Cawood prebendal chapel (BIA, Register 18, fols. 406r, 414rv, Register 5A, fol. 354v; *Reg. Sede Vacante, York, 1423–26*, pp. 99, 114, 125). He was a friar of Stamford when he was ordained p. on 3 March 1425 at Liddington prebendal church (*Reg. Fleming*, ii, p. 104, no. 500).

NORBURY, Edmund de: he was a friar at Doncaster on 12 November 1299 when King Edward I paid 10s. to the friars there through him (TNA, E101/356/7; Goldthorpe, 'The Franciscans and Dominicans in Yorkshire', p. 298).

NORMAN, John: he was ordained a. on 13 March 1378 at Holy Trinity Priory, Micklegate, York, d. on 4 June 1379 at St Mary's Abbey, York, and p. on 17 December 1379 at York Minster (BIA, Register 12, fols. 131r, 134r, 136r).

NORMANTON, John de: he was a friar of Grantham when he was ordained s. on 7 June 1354 at Liddington prebendal church (LAO, Register 9D, fol. 71v). He was a friar of York when he was ordained p. on 26 May 1358 at Greyfriars, York (BIA, Register 11, fol. 334r).

NORTH, John: he was a friar of Doncaster when he was ordained a. on 30 March 1370 at Bishopthorpe manor chapel (BIA, Register 11, fol. 378v).

NORTH, William: he was ordained a. on 24 February 1369 at Bishopthorpe manor chapel. He was a friar of Beverley when ordained d. on 21 December 1370 at Whitefriars, York. He was ordained p. on 21 February 1372 at St Mary, Bishophill Senior (BIA, Register 11, fols. 372v, 380v, 387r).

NORTH DALTON, John de: he was ordained s. on 29 March 1343 at Greyfriars, Beverley. He was a friar of York when he was ordained d. on 18 September 1344 at St Mary's monastery in York (BIA, Register 10A, fols. 3r, 8r).

NORTHON (Norton), Henry de: he was ordained a. and s. on 26 May 1358 at Greyfriars, York (BIA, Register 11, fol. 333rv).

NORTHWALLE, Robert de: a friar of Doncaster, priest and professed. He died c.1304 (Little, '*Records, Franciscan Province*', p. 152).

NORTON, Peter de: he was ordained d. on 27 May 1290 at All Saints, Hertford (*Reg. Sutton*, vii, p. 2).

NORTON, Roger de: he was ordained d. on 3 April 1294 at Spaldwick and p. on 21 December 1297 in Louth prebendal church (*Reg. Sutton*, vii, pp. 51, 101). He was a priest and professed friar at Lincoln. He died c.1304 (Little, '*Records, Franciscan Province*', p. 153).

NORTON (Nortone), William: he was a friar of Worcester when he was ordained s. on 5 March 1383 at Bromyard and d. on 7 May 1385 at Ledbury (*Reg. Gilbert*, pp. 158, 165). Although this friar's roots were in the Midlands, he was transferred from the custody of Worcester to that of York. He was described as a friar of York on 19 December 1392, when he received a legacy of 3s.4d. in the will of Richard Bridesall, a citizen of York and parishioner of St John the Evangelist, North Street (*TE*, i, pp. 174–75). He may have moved to York for educational reasons. John Bale describes him as a friar of Coventry and a writer who flourished at the beginning of the fifteenth century. He spent most of his life at the Universities of Oxford and Cambridge. He edited the works of Nicholas de Lyra, the *Tabula super doctorem de Lyra*, which survives in seven manuscripts and one attested copy. In 1403 he was the scribe of a MS. which is now at Eton College Library, MS.108, part 2, fols.112r–85v (Bale, *Index*, pp. 139, 499, GFC, p. 197, Sharpe, *Handlist*, p. 795, no. 2133, *UCLC*, pp. 96, 740, *UCLO*, ii, pp. 965–66, 1255, nn.2, 6).

NOTTINGHAM (Notinham, Notyngham), John de: he was a friar of Nottingham when he was ordained s. on 20 February 1361 at Sawley prebendal church (*Reg. Stretton*, p. 162). He was ordained p. on 18 March 1363 in St Mary's church, Oxford (LAO, Register 9D, fol. 111v). He was licensed to hear confessions in the diocese of York at an unknown date. After his death he was replaced by Thomas Bidenham during the administration of Archbishop John Thoresby (BIA, Register 11, fol. 397r).

NOVELLA (Nevella, Nonella), James de: he was ordained a. on 4 April 1405 at All Saints, Cawood (*Reg. Scrope*, ii, pp. 95, 131) and s. on 19 December 1405 at Blackfriars, York (BIA, Register 5A, fol. 319r; *Reg. Sede Vacante, York, 1405–08*, pp. 66, 79, 89).

NUSSIA (Neuss), Hermann de: he was a friar of Boston when he was ordained d. on 6 June 1422 in Liddington prebendal church (LAO, Register 16, fol. 180v).

NUTEL, Peter: he was a friar of Beverley when he was ordained d. at an unspecified date in 1274 in the church of Blyth (*Reg. Walter Giffard*, p. 197, no. 697).

NYMME (Nym), William: he was ordained s. on 24 September 1474 at Blackfriars, York, and p. on 1 March 1477 at Austin Friars, York (BIA, Register 22, fols. 229v, 364v).

ó TIGERNAIG, Gilbert: the dean and chapter of Annaghdown elected this Irish friar as their bishop in 1306. His election and subsequent episcopate in Ireland were vigorously opposed by the archbishop of Tuam, who protested to Pope Clement V. The metropolitan refused to approve the election and argued that Annaghdown was no longer a diocese, claiming that it was no more than a parish church in his diocese. Gilbert then betook himself to the dean and chapter of the diocese of Armagh, where the archbishop had the process of election examined. Reginald Taff, vicar general of the diocese of Armagh, confirmed this election in the absence of Archbishop John Taff, and arranged for Gilbert to be consecrated (*Materials, Ireland*, pp. 83, 110–12). On 8 February 1308 the new king granted protection to Gilbert, who wished to remain in England for two years, and on 15 July 1308 he instructed John Wogan, justiciar of Ireland, to deliver the temporalities of the diocese to Gilbert. Although the dean and chapter of Annaghdown had held the election without licence from the crown and had not presented Gilbert for royal assent, the king excused this irregularity in consideration of a fine of £300 paid by Gilbert for himself and the dean and chapter (*CPR, 1307–1313*, pp. 99, 135). The next day the king pardoned Gilbert 410 of the 450 marks and returned the fine (*CFR, 1307–1319*, p. 27; *Materials, Ireland*, p. 83).

Gilbert served as suffragan in several dioceses in England, including Coventry and Lichfield from 1308 to 1312 (*Reg. Langton*, ii, pp. 50–70, 94–97, nn. 1299, 1300, 1301, 1309; *Reg. Norbury*, p. 243), Chichester in March 1309 (Eton College Archives, 56/56–57, and 57–58), Worcester from 1309 to 1318 (*The Liber Albus of the Priory of Worcester*, p. 33, no. 513; *The Liber Albus*, pp. 27, 41, 64, nn. 435, 609, 780; Cambridge University Library, MS.Ll.1.10, fol. i, verso; *Reg. Reynolds*, pp. 71, 72, 73; *Reg. Sede Vacante, Worcester, 1301– 1435*, p. 151), Salisbury in 1311 (*Reg. Gandavo*, ii, p. 901), Winchester in 1315 (*Reg. Woodlock*, p. 872) and Hereford in the same year (*Reg. Swinfield*, p. 499).

Gilbert's name first occurs in the Lincoln registers on 7 June 1308, when he received a licence to dedicate altars, fixed and portable, and to bless chalices and ecclesiastical ornaments while passing through the diocese on his way from Lichfield to London (LAO, Register 3, fol. 137r). On 28 October 1309 he granted an indulgence of 20 days to Richard and his wife (LAO, Register 3, fol. 168r). On 3 February 1312 he received suffragan commissions for the archdeaconries of Leicester and Oxford to dedicate churches and cemeteries and to reconcile them from the shedding of blood and sexual intercourse. Instructions were also given about payment. The commission was valid until 24 June 1312. Three days later the same commission was also extended to the archdeaconry of Northampton (LAO, Register 3, fols. 244v–45r, 256r). On 3 November 1312 the bishop of Lincoln ratified an indulgence of 20 days granted by Gilbert to all those who contributed to the construction or repair of the bridge at Cropredy (LAO, Register 3, fol. 264r). On 11 November 1312 Bishop John Dalderby ratified an indulgence granted by Gilbert to all those who made a contrite confession and for those who prayed for the souls of Robert de Cesterton of Banbury and Sir Roger Cyyne of King's Sutton and Johanne, his wife, whose bodies were interred in the prebendal cemetery of the church of Banbury, and the prebendal church of King's Sutton (LAO, Register 3, fol. 264v). On 7 January 1313 Bishop Dalderby again ratified an indulgence granted by Gilbert to all those who devoutly confessed and prayed for the souls of a certain Gilbert le Webstere whose body was interred in the cemetery of the church of St Mary at Stamford and for Matilda, his wife, whose body was buried in the cemetery of the church at Halughton (LAO, Register 3, fol. 267v). On 18 January 1322 the rector of Whitton was authorised to have his cemetery reconciled from the spilling of blood by Gilbert (LAO, Register 5, fol. 303v).

On 28 January 1313 Archbishop Greenfield commissioned Gilbert to reconcile the church and churchyard of Rotherham polluted by the shedding of blood (*Reg. Greenfield*, v, p. 115, no. 2569). On 16 September 1313 he authorised Gilbert to reconcile the churchyard of Preston, polluted by the shedding of blood (*Reg. Greenfield*, iv, p. 220, no. 2119); the same commission was also addressed to Thomas Kirkcudbright, bishop of Galloway. On 21 December 1313 Gilbert was authorised to ordain Robert de Holden, clerk of the household of the earl of Lancaster, Coventry and Lichfield diocese, to all minor orders, and on 27 December 1313 he was licensed to reconcile the churchyard of the chapel of Wentworth, polluted by the shedding of blood (*Reg. Greenfield*, v, p. 135, no. 2576). On 11 February 1314 Greenfield commissioned Gilbert to reconcile the parish church of Skipton in Craven from the shedding of blood, and on 17 September 1314 he licensed him to dedicate an altar lately built (*de novo constructum*) in the York Greyfriars (*Reg. Greenfield*, v, pp. 136, 141, nn. 2579, 2584). At York in 1314 he was commissioned to consecrate Burnham church which had been rebuilt. The commission took no effect, since the ordinary himself carried out the ceremony. On 27 August 1314 Gilbert was given protection for two years. The justiciary of Ireland in the king's name was empowered to receive fealty from Lawrence, the bishop elect of Elphin. Gilbert had informed the king that sickness presently prevented Lawrence from approaching the king to do fealty (*CPR, 1313–1317*, pp. 167, 182).

On 26 September 1321 King Edward II wrote to Pope John XXII on behalf of Gilbert (*Materials, Ireland*, pp. 110–12). On 21 April 1322 the king gave him simple protection for three years (*CPR, 1321–1324*, p. 100). Gilbert granted an indulgence of 40 days to William Fundu and Sarah his wife, and Felicity his daughter, who were buried in the church of Holy Apostles Sts Peter and Paul at Kynesbury. He also named St Francis, the confessor, as one of the saints on whose intercession he depended. The indulgence was granted on 12 September 1322 and his seal was attached to the grant issued at the monastery of Benedictine Nuns de Polesworth (BL, Cart. Cott. XV.15). Gilbert claimed that he was deprived of his see by Malachy, archbishop of Tuam. The archbishop's proctor reiterated the customary opposition to the diocese of Annaghdown. The pope committed this case to Peter, cardinal priest of St Stephen (*Materials, Ireland*, pp. 127, 217). On 16 December 1323 Pope John XXII ratified the appointment of James Ó Cethernaig to the bishopric of Annaghdown vacant by the death of Gilbert (*CPL*, ii, p. 238). On 8 November 1325 John XXII declared that Bishop Gilbert had protested that he had been deprived of his see by Malachy, archbishop of Tuam (*BF*, v, pp. 293–94, no. 592; *CPL*, ii, p. 248; *Jean XXII, Lettres Communes*, vi, pp. 363–37, no. 23747; Theiner, *Monumenta Hibernorum et Scotorum*, p. 231. On his seal see Armstrong, *Irish Seal Matrices and Seals*, p. 44; Smith, 'Suffragan Bishops in the Medieval Diocese of Lincoln', p. 23; Robson, 'Gilbert Ó Tigernaig, O.F.M., bishop of Annaghdown, c.1306–23'; Butler, 'Suffragan Bishops in the Medieval Diocese of York', pp. 52, 56).

OAKHAM (Okam, Okeham), Thomas de: he was ordained s. on 19 May 1296 in Lincoln cathedral, and d. on 21 December 1297 in Louth prebendal church (*Reg. Sutton*, vii, pp. 77, 101).

OCKHAM (Okham), John: he was a friar of Boston when he was ordained a. on 24 March 1425 at Liddington prebendal church (*Reg. Fleming*, ii, p. 105, no. 501). A friar of this name at London was ordained d. on 21 September 1426 at St Bartholomew's priory, London (London Registers: Gray; Davis, *London Clergy*, no. 9775, stating that he was ordained p. on that occasion).

OEM, Gerard: he was ordained d. on 2 June 1414 at St Michael-le-Belfrey, York (BIA, Register 18, fol. 39Gr).

OKDP, William: he was ordained s. on 4 June 1379 at St Mary's Abbey, York (BIA, Register 12, fol. 134r).

OKHAM, John: he was at Nottingham and a *scolaris in theologia* on 20 February 1460, when the archbishop of York appointed him as his penitentiary in the archdeaconry of Nottingham and licensed him to hear confessions in that archdeaconry (BIA, Register 20, fols. 89v–90r).

OLDENSELL, John: he was a friar of York when he was ordained s. on 28 February 1428 at Whitefriars, York. He was ordained d. on 21 May 1429 at Blackfriars, York (BIA, Register 19, fols. 231v, 235r).

OLIVER (Ollyffe, Olyffe), John: he was a friar of Lincoln when he was ordained a. on 27 March 1535 in Lincoln cathedral (LAO, Register 26, fol. 43r). He was one of the ten friars of Doncaster who signed the deed of surrender on 20 November 1538 (*Eighth Report of the Deputy Keeper of the Public Records*, p. 19). A cleric of this name was admitted to the rectory of Plumtree in Nottinghamshire in May 1552 and he subscribed to the articles of religion in 1571; he was still serving the parish in 1582. Another hypothesis is that the former friar may have become a school teacher in Hull. John Olyvver, schoolmaster of the grammar school at Kingston on Hull, made his will on 22 July 1554. After asking to be buried in the graveyard of Holy Trinity church, he left a hive of bees to Roger Webster's wife and all the rest of his possessions to his wife, Janet, and his son, Timothy (Institution Act Book, 1, fol. 200r; Institution Act Book, pt. III, fol. 123r; High Commission Act Book, 10, fol. 168rv; BIA, Probate Register 14, fol. 293r; Cross and Vickers, *MFN*, pp. 447–48).

ORDESLAY, Thomas de: he was ordained p. in December 1357 at Cawood manor chapel (BIA, Register 11, fol. 332r).

ORMESKIRK (Ormeskyrk), William de: he was ordained a. and s. on 26 May 1369 at Bishopthorpe manor chapel (BIA, Register 11, fols. 373v, 374r).

OSNEY, Edmund de: a friar of Lincoln through whom King Edward III paid the royal gift on 6 September 1329 (TNA, E.101/383/14).

OTTRINGHAM (Otryngham), Robert de, junior: Robert de Ottringham was described as senior (Nicholson, *Templars*, i, p. 184, ii, p. 192).

OTTRINGHAM (Otryngham), Robert de, senior: he recounted incidents at the preceptories of the Knights Templar at Ribston and Wetherby. The first occurred c.1290 and the second c.1303/4. In the first episode, Robert had lodged with the Templars, where one evening he heard that the grand commander of the Temple would not be attending the collation because he was preparing relics which he had brought from the Holy Land. In the depths of the night the friar heard a commotion and raised voices in the chapel. Through a keyhole he saw a huge fire or candlelight and witnessed proceedings. When, the following day, he enquired of a Templar about the saint who was being venerated in the chapel, the Templar looked stunned and enjoined him to leave the house and keep his silence. At the preceptory the friar had seen a filthy cross on the altar. The friar's exhortation to wash it was ignored. The second event was a display of disrespect towards the altar on the part of a Templar at Ribston. On that occasion the unnamed chaplain had reviled the Templars (Nicholson, *Templars*, i, pp. 184, 383, 396, 417, 427, ii, pp. 192, 437, 453, 476, 488).

OTTRINGHAM (Otryngham), Stephen: he was a friar at York when he was ordained p. on 21 December 1392 at Holy Trinity Priory, Micklegate, York (BIA, Register 14, fol. 65v).

OUNDEL (Oundal), John: he was ordained a. on 20 December 1376 at Holy Trinity Priory, Micklegate, York. He was a friar of York when he was ordained s. on 21 February 1377 at Whitefriars, York, and d. on 23 May 1377 at York Minster (BIA, Register 12, fols. 126v, 127r, 128v). He was the custos of York c.1408 (Oxford, Bodleian Library, MS.Arch. Selden B 23, fol. 56r).

OUSEGATE (Usegate), Thomas de: a friar of York accused of malpractice regarding property in Michaelmas 1298. The charge was later withdrawn (TNA, KB27/156, mem. 72; *Notes on Religious Houses*, i, pp. 243–44).

OVERTON, Geoffrey de: he was licensed in the diocese of Lincoln in January 1334 (LAO, Register 5, fol. 471r).

OWSELE, William: he was a friar at Beverley when he was ordained p. on 16 March 1437 at St Leonard's Hospital, York (BIA, Register 19, fol. 253v).

OXINFORD (Oxenford), Thomas: he was a friar at Lincoln when he was ordained d. on 24 September 1401 in the prebendal church of Stow (LAO, Register 13, fol. 95v). He was ordained p. on 10 March 1403 at York Minster (*Reg. Scrope*, ii, pp. 55, 96, 131).

OXON (Oxford), Thomas de: he was ordained s. on 10 June 1346 at Whitefriars, York (BIA, Register 10A, fol. 15v).

PAA (Pay), William: he was a friar of York when he was ordained d. on 21 December 1392 at Holy Trinity Priory, Micklegate, and when he was ordained p. on 13 June 1394 at St Mary's Abbey, York (BIA, Register 14, fols. 65v, 70r).

PALMER, Gilbert: he was a friar of Lincoln when he was ordained s. on 20 May 1486 in Sleaford prebendal church (LAO, Register 22, fol. 22r).

PALMER, Peter: he was a friar of Beverley when he was ordained d. on 24 September 1373 at St Mary, Bishophill Senior (BIA, Register 11, fol. 392v). He was ordained p. on 16 June 1375 at Cawood manor chapel (BIA, Register 12, fol. 121r).

PALMER, Richard: he was a friar of Lincoln when he was ordained s. on 23 December 1508 in the prebendal church of Liddington (LAO, Register 24, fol. 73r). He was a friar of York when he was ordained d. on 3 March 1509 at Greyfriars, York, and p. on 2 June 1509 at Whitefriars, York (BIA, Register 26, fols. 100r, 103r. Cf. Cross and Vickers, *MFN*, p. 442).

PAPPILWYCK, Edmund: he was a friar of York when he was ordained d. on 22 September 1492 at Whitefriars, York (BIA, Register 23, fol. 234v). A friar called Edward Papelwyk of Nottingham was ordained p. on 23 March 1493 at Liddington prebendal church (LAO, Register 22, fol. 48r. Cf. Cross and Vickers, *MFN*, p. 438).

PARDESHOME, Robert: he was ordained p. on 20 September 1348 at Skipton parish church (BIA, Register 10A, fol. 25v).

PARDESHOW (Pardeslawe, Pardishow, Pardisowe), Robert de: he was ordained a. on 18 December 1344 in Durham cathedral and s. at St Andrew's at Auckland on 26 March 1345 (*Reg. Kellaw*, iii, pp. 144, 151). He was at Richmond when ordained d. on 17 December 1345 (Durham Registers: Hatfield, fol. 93r). He was ordained p. on 10 June 1346 at Whitefriars, York (BIA, Register 10A, fol. 16r).

PARDESHOW (Pardisowe), William de: he was ordained s. on 18 December 1344 in Durham cathedral and d. on 26 March 1345 at St Andrew's church, Auckland (*Reg. Kellaw*, iii, pp. 145, 151).

PARISH (Parysch), Thomas de: he was ordained s. on 24 September 1351 in St Mary's at Oxford (LAO, Register 9D, fol. 53).

PARISH (Parisshe), Thomas: he was ordained s. on 14 March 1416 at Cawood prebendal church (BIA, Register 18, fol. 39Hr).

PARISH (Parysh), William: he was ordained s. on 27 May 1396 at St Mary, Bishophill Senior (BIA, Register 14, fol. 72v) and p. on 1 June 1398 at St Michael-le-Belfrey, York (BIA, Register 5A, fol. 256v).

PARISIUS (Paris), Stephen de: he was ordained d. on 12 June 1367 at Bishopthorpe manor chapel (BIA, Register 11, fol. 366v).

PARKE (Park), Anthony: he was a friar of York when he was ordained a. on 19 March 1519 at Greyfriars, York, s. on 24 March 1520 at Greyfriars, York, d. on 2 June 1520 at Blackfriars, York, and p. on 22 December 1520 at Whitefriars, York (BIA, Register 27, fols. 183r, 187r, 188r, 189r). He was at York at the Dissolution on 27 November 1538 (*Eighth Report of the Deputy Keeper of the Public Records*, pp. 445, 454. Cf. Cross and Vickers, *MFN*, pp. 445, 459).

PARKE (Park), Richard: he was a friar of York when he was ordained a. on 26 March 1502 in the lady chapel of York Minster, d. on 10 June 1503 at Blackfriars, York, and p. on 2 March 1504 at Whitefriars, York (BIA, Register 25, fols. 111v, 119v, 122v. Cf. Cross and Vickers, *MFN*, p. 440).

PASMER, Gilbert: he was a friar of York when he was ordained a. on 24 September 1485 at Rotherham parish church and d. on 9 June 1487 at Blackfriars, York. He was a friar of Doncaster when he was ordained p. on 22 September 1487 at Whitefriars, York (BIA, Register 23, fols. 398r, 408r, 409r. Cf. Cross and Vickers, *MFN*, p. 436).

PASSELAW (Pascelewe, Paslew, Passelewe), de Ledes, Robert: he was ordained a. on 7 June 1343 at Greyfriars, York, s. on 17 December 1345 at Whitefriars, York, and d. on 22 December 1347 at Greyfriars, Doncaster (BIA, Register 10A, fols. 3v, 13v, 20r).

PASSELAW (Paslew, Paslowe), John: he was ordained s. on 26 May 1358 at Greyfriars, York, d. on 22 September 1358 at Bishop Burton near Beverley (BIA, Register 11, fols. 333v, 334v), and p. on 25 February 1363 in Lincoln cathedral (LAO, Register 9D, fol. 110r).

PASSELAW (Passelewe), Ralph: son of Robert Passelewe of Leeds, he was ordained a. on 21 February 1377 at Whitefriars, York (BIA, Register 12, fol. 127r).

PASTELE, John: he was a friar of York when he was ordained a. on 4 March 1357 at Bishopthorpe manor chapel (BIA, Register 11, fol. 329v).

PASTON, William: he was a friar of Lincoln when he was ordained s. on 24 May 1404 in Liddington prebendal church, d. on 20 September 1404 and p. on 20 December 1404. The second and third ceremonies took place in Lincoln cathedral (LAO, Register 13, fols. 114v, 116r, 117v).

PATRINGTON, Adam de: on 12 October 1300 he was a friar of Lincoln licensed to hear confessions for that house (Little, *Franciscan Papers, Lists, and Documents*, p. 238). He seems to have been at the same friary when licensed again for the diocese of Lincoln on 20 June 1318 (LAO, Register 3, fol. 390rv).

PATRINGTON, John de: he was ordained s. on 19 September 1293 at Lincoln cathedral and d. on 18 December 1294 at Stow prebendal church (*Reg. Sutton*, vii, pp. 40, 61). He was licensed to hear confessions for the diocese of Lincoln on 20 June 1318 (LAO, Register 3, fol. 390rv).

PATRINGTON, Peter de: probably a friar of Lincoln on 20 June 1318 when he was licensed for the diocese of Lincoln (LAO, Register 5, fol. 390rv).

PATRINGTON, Thomas de: he was ordained p. on 21 December 1359 in Lincoln cathedral (LAO, Register 9D, fol. 94r).

PAULYN (Palin), Peter: he was ordained a. and s. on 18 September 1372 at Greyfriars, York (BIA, Register 11, fols. 388v, 389r). He was a friar of Nottingham when he was ordained d. on 20 December 1376, and at Lichfield when he was ordained p. on 14 March 1377 at Colwich prebendal church (*Reg. Stretton*, pp. 313, 321).

PAY, Thomas: he was a friar of York when he was ordained a. on 18 September 1445 at Austin Friars, York (BIA, Register 19, fol. 282r).

PAY, Thomas: a second friar of this name was at York when he was ordained a. on 17 December 1446 at Whitefriars, York, s. on 25 March 1447 at St Leonard's Hospital, York, and p. on 23 September 1452 at Greyfriars, York (BIA, Register 19, fols. 285v, 225v, 304r).

PAY, William: he was a friar of York when he was ordained d. on 21 December 1392 at Holy Trinity Priory, Micklegate. He was a friar of York when he was ordained p. on 13 June 1394 at St Mary's Abbey, York (BIA, Register 14, fols. 65v, 70r).

PEACOCK (Pecock, Peycocke), Gabriel: he was an Observant friar at Newark when he was ordained p. on 6 June 1517 at Austin Friars, York (BIA, Register 27, fol. 177v). He was the guardian of the Observant friary in Canterbury in 1532 (*GFCant*, p. 77). On 8 April 1534 there was an extensive account of a sermon which he had preached on Passion Sunday at the church of St Swithin, Winchester. His tone was conservative and he cited evidence for the Petrine supremacy. On the same day Henry Huttoft notified Thomas Cromwell that he had received a letter regarding the guardian of Southampton, who was preaching abroad (*LPFD*, vii, pp. 185–86, nn. 449, 450). On 12 April 1534 Huttoft and John Perchard, mayor of Southampton, wrote to Cromwell to recommend Peacock and his influence among the friars

(*LPFD*, vii, p. 194, nn. 472–73). He was the guardian at Southampton when he wrote to Thomas Cromwell on 16 July 1534, saying that he wished to avoid the royal displeasure and that of his official, that is, Cromwell (*LPFD*, vii, pp. 377–78, no. 982). After the suppression of the Observants, he was sent to Lincoln with two other members of the order (*LPFD*, vii, p. 601, no. 1607), where he stayed. He was there when he obtained his capacity on 8 October 1539 (Chambers, *Faculty Office Registers 1534–1549*, p. 195).

PEARSON (Perseson), Nicholas: he was a friar of York when he was ordained a. on 24 May 1483 at Blackfriars, York, d. on 19 September 1489 at Whitefriars, York, and p. on 19 December 1489 at Austin Friars, York (BIA, Register 23, fols. 387v, 418v, 419v. Cf. Cross and Vickers, *MFN*, p. 435).

PEARSON (Pereson), William: he was a friar of York when he was ordained a. on 18 December 1451, s. on 3 June 1452, and d. on 22 September 1453. The first and third ceremonies took place at Greyfriars, York, and the second was at the city's Whitefriars (BIA, Register 19, fols. 300v, 303r, Register 20, fol. 416r).

PELMELTON, William: he was a friar of York when he was ordained d. on 22 December 1442 at Austin Friars, York (BIA, Register 19, fol. 267v).

PENRETH (Pontenay), John: he was a friar of York when he was ordained s. on 26 May 1464 at Blackfriars, York (BIA, Register 20, fol. 459v).

PENRETH (Penrith, Perithe), William: he was an Observant friar of Newcastle when he was ordained d. on 14 June 1511 at Blackfriars, York (BIA, Register 26, fol. 114r; *Reg. Bainbridge*, p. 363), and p. on 26 March 1513 at St Paul's cathedral, when he was a friar of Greenwich; he was presented by Francis de Zufania (London, Guildhall Hall Library, MS.9531/9, fol. 165v). He presented Thomas Perpwaynt for ordination on 21 December 1521 (London Registers: Fitzjames). He was *magister iuvenum* at Richmond, Surrey, on 15 March 1522 when he presented more friars for ordination at St Paul's cathedral (Canterbury Registers: Warham, fol. 296v). After the suppression of the Observants he was sent to York (*LPFD*, vii, p. 601, no. 1607), where he remained until the surrender of the friary on 27 November 1538 (*Eighth Report of the Deputy Keeper of the Public Records*, p. 51). A friar of this name was awarded 26s. 8d. at the suppression (Goldthorp, 'The Franciscans and Dominicans in Yorkshire', p. 291, n. 3, citing TNA, Mins. Accounts, 29–30, Henry VIII, no. 197 (Yorkshire), Suppression Papers, III, fol. 93r. Cf. Cross and Vickers, *MFN*, p. 459).

PENTENAY (Penteneye), Thomas de: he was ordained p. on 21 December 1359 in Lincoln cathedral (LAO, Register 9D, fol. 94r).

PENTENAY (Pontenay), William de: he was ordained a. on 8 March 1365 at Bishopthorpe manor chapel, s. on 20 December 1365 at York Minster, d. on 21 March 1366 at St Mary, Bishophill Senior, when he was a friar of Beverley, and p. on 21 March 1366 (BIA, Register 11, fols. 359r, 361v, 362rv).

PENYLTON, John: he was a friar of York when he was ordained s. on 22 September 1442 at York Minster (BIA, Register 19, fol. 220v).

PENYSTON (Penylton), William: he was a friar of York when he was ordained a.

on 24 February 1442 and p. on 20 February 1445; both ceremonies were held at Greyfriars, York (BIA, Register 19, fols. 265v, 281r).

PEPIR (Pepre), William: he was a friar of York when he was ordained a. on 24 February 1442 and d. on February 1445, both at Greyfriars, York, and p. on 12 March 1446 at Whitefriars, York (BIA, Register 19, fols. 265v, 280v, 283v).

PERCY, Richard: he was licensed as a penitentiary in the archdeaconry of Lincoln for one year on 1 December 1339 *in loco* John de Thornton, whose licence had been revoked (*Reg. Burghersh*, iii, p. 372, no. 4821).

PERCY, Walter: he was a friar of Beverley, *sacre theologie professor*, when licensed to hear confessions in the diocese of York on 22 February 1349 and 5 March 1350 (BIA, Register 10, fols. 278v, 279r).

PERON, William: he was a friar of Beverley when he was ordained a. on 7 March 1433 at Greyfriars, York (BIA, Register 19, fol. 243r).

PETER (Petyr), John: he was a friar of Boston when he was ordained a. on 21 September 1482 at All Saints, Northampton. He was a friar of Stamford when ordained s. on 15 March 1483, d. on 20 September 1483, and p. on 3 April 1484. The last three ceremonies took place in St Mary *ad pontem*, Stamford (LAO, Register 22, fols. 9r, 10v, 12r, 14r).

PETERS (Petri), Cornelius: he was a friar of York when he was ordained d. on 2 March 1420 at Cawood prebendal chapel (BIA, Register 18, fol. 405r).

PETERS (Petri), John: he was ordained p. on 14 March 1405 at All Saints, Cawood (*Reg. Scrope*, ii, pp. 57, 97, 131).

PHILIPPE (Phillip), Robert: he was licensed to hear confessions in the diocese of York on 7 May 1401 (*Reg. Scrope*, ii, p. 12, no. 737). A Friar Robert Philip was custos of Bristol c.1408 (Oxford, Bodleian Library, MS.Arch.Selden, B.23, fol. 56r).

PICKERING (Pykeryng), John: he was a friar of York when ordained p. on 22 September 1442 at York Minster (BIA, Register 19, fol. 220v).

PICKERING (Pikering, Pykering), John: he was a friar of Grimsby when he was ordained a. on 6 March 1479 at Louth prebendal church (LAO, Register 21, fol. 165r). He was ordained s. on 27 March 1479 at Greyfriars, York, and d. on 18 December 1479 at Austin Friars, York (BIA, Register 22, fols. 377v, 381v). He was at Oxford when he was ordained p. in Wycombe parish church on 23 December 1480 (LAO, Register 22, fol. 2r).

PISA, Boniface de: this Tuscan friar was born out of wedlock. He was a man of some learning and had filled the office of lector, probably in his native province. After the death of Bishop Comita of Iglesias in 1324, Boniface was elected by the cathedral chapter, confirmed and consecrated. Pope John XXII, however, refused to ratify the election, explaining that provision was reserved to the Holy See and that Boniface was also disqualified on account of a defect of birth. The Dominican, Ange Portasole, replaced him in 1325 and held the diocese until 1330, in which year he was translated to the Tuscan diocese of Grosseto. Boniface went to Avignon where he explained his situation to the pope and remained on the fringes of the papal court; his name appears on several indulgences issued by groups of bishops, most of whom were residing in Avignon. On 10 September 1326 Raymond, patriarch of Jerusalem, and 18 other bishops, including Boniface, issued an indulgence in favour of the church of Santa María de Guadalupe (Linehan, 'The Beginnings of Santa María de Guadalupe and the Direction of the Fourteenth Century'). On 25 January 1328 Boniface was one of the bishops who granted an indulgence to Wombridge Priory (Cheney, 'Illuminated Collective Indulgences from Avignon', pp. 361–63). Some of the collective indulgences bore the names of two bishops of Iglesias, such as one granted on 20 April 1330 (Delehaye, 'Les lettres d'indulgence collectives', p. 295). On 13 May 1332 he was dispensed from illegitimacy (*Jean XXII, Lettres Communes*, xi, p. 194, no. 57213). On 3 June 1332 he was provided to the see of Corbavia in Croatia (*BF*, v, pp. 527–28, no. 981; *Jean XXII, Lettres Communes*, xi, p. 205, no. 57374). His work in Croatia has been described in brief (Zugai, 'Franjevci Konventualci Biskupi U Senjskoji i Krbavskoj ili Modruskoj Biskupi', pp. 63–64). As bishop of Corbavia, Boniface remained at the papal court and continued to add his name to collective indulgences. On 10 May 1334 he was one of the bishops who granted an indulgence to the monastery of Santa Chiara in Assisi (Bihl, 'Documenta Inedita Archivi protomonasterii Sanctae Clarae Assisii', p. 677). On 4 May 1335, as bishop of Corbavia, he was one of the prelates to grant an indulgence in favour of the church of St Michael Penkevel (Orme, 'Indulgences in Medieval Cornwall', pp. 155, 160).

By the later 1330s Boniface had settled in England, where he acted as a suffragan bishop in various dioceses, including Lincoln and York. On 12 December 1338 Adam Orleton, bishop of Winchester, granted him a licence to dedicate the conventual church of Bermondsey and to consecrate other altars within it. The ceremony apparently took place on 18 January 1338 ('Annales monasterii de Bermundesea, A.D. 1042–1432', *AM*, iii, pp. 421–87, 473). He held ordinations in the diocese of Durham between 28 March 1338 and 2 June 1341. A dimissorial letter for William, son of Gilbert de Wolveston, to be ordained subdeacon by Boniface on the Saturday of Pentecost week was issued (*Reg. Kellaw*, iii, pp. 106, 194–97, 203–07, 216). He was the recipient of a commission from Bishop Burghersh on 20 March 1338 permitting him to dedicate 20 portable altars in the diocese and to hear confessions (LAO, Register 5, fol. 558r). On 26 January 1339 he was given protection for one year during which he prosecuted the business of the king in England. The protection extended to the men and servants of his household (*homines et servientes de familia sua*), their harness, goods and possessions (TNA, C66/195, m. 38; *CPR, 1338–1340*, p. 198). On 28 March 1340 a note was made of a licence granted to Boniface to confirm children and adults, dedicate churches and altars, reconcile churchyards and churches polluted by bloodshed, consecrate chalices and patens, bless vestments and church ornaments and confer the first tonsure on suitable persons of the diocese and others with letters dimissory (*Reg. Melton*, iii, 184, no. 295). Radoslavus, OFM, became bishop of Corbavia c.1341 (*Hierarchia catholica*, I, 208. Cf. Smith, 'Suffragan Bishops in the Medieval Diocese of Lincoln', p. 24; Robson, 'Boniface of Pisa, O.Min., bishop of Iglesias and then Corbavia (†1341)'; Butler, 'Suffragan Bishops in the Medieval Diocese of York', pp. 50, 57).

PISTORIS, Conrad: he was a friar of York when he was ordained d. on 21 March 1450 at St Leonard's Hospital, York (BIA, Register 19, fol. 286v).

PLAUSWORTH (Planesworth), Hugh de: he was ordained p. on 2 June 1352 at St Mary's Abbey, York (BIA, Register 10A, fol. 55v). Hugh de Planesworth, a friar of Newcastle, was licensed to hear confessions in the diocese of Durham on 27 December 1362 (Durham Registers: Hatfield, fol. 43r).

PLESYNGTON, Richard: he was ordained p. on 17 December 1429 at Austin Friars, York (BIA, Register 19, fol. 236r).

PLUMMER (Plumer), William: he was ordained s. on 18 September 1479 and d. on 22 September 1481. He was a friar of York when ordained p. on 21 September 1482. All three ordinations took place at Whitefriars, York (BIA, Register 22, fol. 380r, Register 23, fols. 377v, 384r. Cf. Cross and Vickers, *MFN*, p. 437).

PLUMOUTH, William: he was a friar of York when he was ordained s. on 18 September 1491 at Whitefriars, York, d. on 7 April 1492 at Whitefriars, York, and p. on 16 June 1492 at Blackfriars, York (BIA, Register 23, fols. 428v, 431v, 433v).

P'MYNGHAM, Ludovicus: he was ordained p. on 22 September 1408 at Holy Trinity Priory, Micklegate, York (BIA, Register 18, fol. 39v).

POCKLINGTON (Pokelington), Thomas de: he was a friar of Lincoln when he was licensed to hear confessions for that house on 12 October 1300 (Little, *Franciscan Papers, Lists, and Documents*, p. 238).

POLOWE (Pollowe), Thomas: he was ordained p. on 18 September 1400 at All Saints, Cawood (*Reg. Scrope*, ii, pp. 55, 97, 131).

POMERIO, John de: he was a friar of York when he was ordained d. on 6 June 1444 at Blackfriars, York (BIA, Register 19, fol. 280r).

PONTEFRACT (Pontefract), Adam de: he was ordained s. in 1267/68 at Selby Abbey (*Reg. Walter Giffard*, p. 190, no. 688).

PONTEFRACT, Edmund de: he was ordained s. in Lent 1267/68 at Selby Abbey (*Reg. Walter Giffard*, p. 190, no. 688).

PONTEFRACT (Pomfret), Peter: he was a friar of York when he was ordained a. on 19 February 1407 at Blackfriars, York (BIA, Register 5A, 323v; *Reg. Sede Vacante, York, 1405–08*, pp. 66, 80, 89).

PONTEFRACT (Pontefracto), Ralph de: he was a friar of Lincoln when he was ordained s. on 25 March 1486 in Lincoln cathedral, d. on 14 April 1487 in the chapel of St Mary Magdalene in Lincoln cathedral, and p. on 22 September 1487 at All Saints, Northampton (LAO, Register 22, fols. 21v, 25r, 26).

PONTEFRACT, Simon de: he was ordained a. and s. on 26 May 1358 at Greyfriars, York, and p. on 23 December 1363 at St Mary's Abbey, York (BIA, Register 11, fols. 333rv, 355r).

PONTEFRACT (Pontefracto), Thomas de: he was a friar of Oxford on 26 July 1300 when the minister provincial nominated him for a licence to hear confessions in the archdeaconry of Lincoln. He was not among the friars licensed by the bishop (*GFO*, pp. 164–65; Little, *Franciscan Papers, Lists, and Documents*, p. 235). A cleric of this name in 1303 gave certain benefactions to Balliol College of which he was visitor (*The Oxford Deeds of Balliol College*, pp. 14–15, 118, 141; Jones, *Balliol College: A History, 1263–1939*, p. 23). He was the 35th regent master of the friars' school at Oxford about 1306. He and John de Claxton, guardian of Oxford, on 13 May 1306 approached King Edward I about business concerning William Gainsborough, bishop of Worcester, and received 15s. (TNA, E.101/369/11, fol. 32r; *BRUO*, p. 426). It is probable that these commissions were issued during his regency; some of his predecessors had carried out similar roles (Little and Pelster, *Oxford Theology and Theologians*, p. 272, n). On 21 June 1307 he and John de Claxton received expenses for going to Scotland to investigate the murder of John de Comyn in the friars' church of Dumfries (TNA, E101/368/27, fol. 38v). On 1 July 1311 he and Adam de Lincoln were named in the proceedings of the fifth day in the trial of the Templars at the provincial chapter of York (*Reg. Greenfield*, iv, p. 368, no. 2352; *The Records of the Northern Convocation, Councils and Synods with other documents relating to the English Church II. A.D. 1205–1313*, ii, p. 1344; *BRUO*, p. 1497).

PONTEFRACT (Pontefracto), William de: he was a friar of York accused of malpractice regarding property in Michaelmas 1298. The charge was later withdrawn (TNA, KB27/156, mem.72; *Notes on Religious Houses*, i, pp. 243–44).

PONTEFRACT (Pontefracto), William de: he was a friar of Boston when he was ordained s. on 21 December 1359 and at Northampton when ordained d. on 29 February 1360; both ceremonies took place in Lincoln cathedral (LAO, Register 9D, fols. 93v, 94v). He was ordained p. on 20 February 1361 at Cawood manor chapel (BIA, Register 11, fol. 343v). The will of Brian Stapleton, proved on 26 June 1394, left 20s. to a friar of this name (*TE*, i, pp. 198–201). A friar of this name was one of the doctors who examined the accusations against John Badby for heresy on 17 February 1409 in a synod of the southern province meeting at St Paul's cathedral, London (Wilkins, *Concilia*, iii, p. 326).

PONTENEY, William de: he was a friar of Beverley when he was ordained d. on 28 February 1366 at St Mary, Bishophill Senior (BIA, Register 11, fol. 362r).

POPLEY, Robert: he received 6s. 8d. from the will of Robert Halitreholme, rector of Bidenham, Bedfordshire, who drew up his will on 12 April 1525; it was proved on 14 April 1525. Popley was described as Halitreholme's spiritual son; the rector was probably his confessor. The references to Beverley may indicate that he was a member of the friary in the East Riding, where the will was written (*TE*, v, pp. 202–03).

POPPLETON, Robert de: this friar of York was licensed to hear confessions in the diocese of York about 6 January 1352 (BIA, Register 10, fol. 280r).

PORRET (Perrott, Porrott), John: he was a friar of York when he was ordained a. on 23 September 1503 and s. on 23 March 1504. Both ceremonies took place at Greyfriars, York (BIA, Register 25, fols. 120r, 122v; Cross and Vickers, *MFN*, p. 440). A friar of this name was at Hereford when ordained d. on 19 September 1506 in Hereford cathedral (*Reg. Mayew*, p. 246). He was at Oxford on 19 November 1511 when he obtained leave to enter the Library (*Reg. Cancelarii*, F, fol. 156v). After 16 years studying logic, philosophy and theology, on 26 April 1520 he supplicated to proceed to his bachelor's degree in theology and was admitted on 5 May. He was licensed for the doctorate in theology on 8 July 1527 (*Reg. Univ. Oxon*, p. 113). On 10 October

1527 he was dispensed from his regency as the guardian of Boston (*GFO*, pp. 277–78; *BRUO, 1501–40*, p. 442).

PORTEWS, Alexander: he was a friar of York when he was ordained a. on 19 September 1506 in Tadcaster parish church, s. on 29 May 1507 at Blackfriars, York, d. on 18 September 1507 at Whitefriars, York, and p. on 18 December 1507 at Austin Friars, York (BIA, Register 25, fols. 135r, 140v, Register 5A, fols. 580r, 584v. Cf. Cross and Vickers, *MFN*, p. 442, give Andrew as the Christian name).

POTYNDEN, J. de: between 9 and 19 January 1300 King Edward I sent 20s. to the friars of Doncaster by this friar (*Liber quotidianus contrarotulatoris garderobae*, p. 28).

POULE (Pole), William: he was a friar at Beverley when he was ordained a. on 18 September 1490 at Whitefriars, York. He was a friar of York when he was ordained s. on 24 September 1491, d. on 7 April 1492, and p. on 16 June 1492. The first three ordinations took place at Whitefriars, York, and the last at Blackfriars, York (BIA, Register 23, fols. 428v, 431v, 433v. Cf. Cross and Vickers, *MFN*, p. 437).

POULTNEY (Pulteneye), William de: he was ordained s. on 27 May 1290 at All Saints, Hertford, d. on 17 March 1291 at St Andrew's church, Northampton, and p. on 31 May 1292 at Lincoln cathedral (*Reg. Sutton*, vii, pp. 1, 12, 30).

POWER, Peter: he was ordained s. on 18 December 1400 in the chapel of St Nicholas, Bawtry (*Reg. Scrope*, ii, pp. 55, 98, 131).

POWME (Pome), James: he was a friar at York when he was ordained a. on 18 March 1458 at Greyfriars, York, and when he was ordained d. on 19 September 1461 at Blackfriars, York, and at York when he was ordained p. on 17 December 1463 at Austin Friars, York (BIA, Register 20, fols. 433r, 449r, 457v).

POWTER, John: he was ordained d. on 18 December 1479 at Austin Friars, York (BIA, Register 22, fol. 381v).

PRESTON, Henry: a former friar of Lincoln who received his capacity on 8 October 1539 (Chambers, *Faculty Office Registers 1534–1549*, p. 195).

PRESTON, Hugh de: he was ordained a. on 7 June 1343 at Greyfriars, York. He was at York when he was ordained s. on 21 May 1345 at Thirsk parish church. He was ordained d. on 10 June 1346 at Whitefriars, York (BIA, Registers 10A, fols. 3v, 11r, 16r).

PRESTON, John: he was a friar of Cambridge when he was ordained a. on 18 September 1456 at Barnwell Priory (CUL, EDR, G/1/5, fol. 203r; *GFC*, p. 202). He was at York when ordained s. on 24 September 1457 at Whitefriars, York, and d. on 18 March 1458 at Greyfriars, York (BIA, Register 20, fols. 431r, 434r). Along with the guardian of Lincoln, William Hikam, he was mentioned in the plea rolls in Trinity term of 1468. He was cited with the same guardian in the Trinity term of 1473, but they were not found. He was cited a third time with the same guardian in the Trinity term of 1481 and did not appear. In the Michaelmas term of 1483 he was cited alone, but did not appear (TNA, KB27/829, rex mm. 11d, 14d, KB27/848, rex m. 35, KB27/878, rex m. 12 and KB27/883, rex m. 23d).

PRESTON, William de: he was ordained a. on 26 May 1358 at Greyfriars, York; the register states that he was ordained s. on the same occasion, but this is undoubtedly an error. He was a friar of Grimsby when he was ordained s. on 21 December 1359 and at Northampton when ordained d. on 29 February 1360. The second and third ceremonies took place at Lincoln cathedral. He was ordained p. on 23 December 1363 at St Mary's Abbey, York (BIA, Register 11, fol. 333rv; LAO, Register 9D, fols. 93v, 94v; BIA, Register 11, fol. 355r).

PREVXCELLIS, John: he was a friar of York when he was ordained s. on 22 December 1442 at Austin Friars, York (BIA, Register 19, fol. 267v).

PRICIA, Christopher de: he was a friar of York when he was ordained p. on 15 March 1432 at Greyfriars, York (BIA, Register 19, fol. 241v).

PRINCE (Prynce), Robert: he was a friar of York when he was ordained a. on 26 March 1502 in the lady chapel of York Minster, s. on 23 March 1504 at Greyfriars, York, d. on 17 May 1505 at Blackfriars, York, and p. on 20 September 1505 at Bishopthorpe manor chapel (BIA, Register 25, fols. 111v, 122v, 129v, 130v. Cf. Cross and Vickers, *MFN*, p. 440).

PROCTOUR, John: he was the son of Robert Proctour, who, then aged 60, testified at Bolton Percy on 10 November 1382 that Margaret, daughter of John, son of John, son of John Chaumont, knight, was born in the town of Colton and baptised in the church of All Saints, Bolton Percy, on 11 October 1367. On that day his son, John, had entered the order at York (*Cal. Inquisitions*, xv (Richard II), p. 352, no. 893).

PSALLEY, Henry de: he was a friar of Lincoln when he was ordained p. on 22 December 1352 at Stow prebendal church (LAO, Register 9D, fol. 64v).

PUND, Robert: he was ordained d. on 25 February 1363 at Bishopthorpe manor chapel (BIA, Register 11, fol. 353r).

PURCHASE (Purchace, Purchas), John: he was ordained s. on 20 September 1343 at Whitefriars, York (BIA, Register 10A, fol. 5r). He held a licence to hear confessions in the diocese of York from an unknown date. After his death he was replaced by Hugh Bruggeford (BIA, Register 11, fol. 397r).

PWINY, William: he was a friar of York when he was ordained s. on 28 February 1461 at Blackfriars, York (BIA, Register 20, fol. 446v).

PYROT, Roger: he was ordained d. on 18 September 1294 at Dunstable parish church (*Reg. Sutton*, vii, p. 57).

QUADRYNG, John: he was ordained a. on 15 March 1399 at Cawood manor chapel (*Reg. Scrope*, ii, pp. 54, 98, 131).

QUENELL, Richard: he was ordained p. on 22 December 1369 at Bishopthorpe manor chapel (BIA, Register 11, fol. 376v).

QUERCU, Henry de: he was at York when he was ordained s. on 18 December 1423 and d. on 18 March 1424; both ceremonies took place at York Minster (BIA, Register 5A, fols. 354v, 356r; *Reg. Sede Vacante, York, 1423–26*, pp. 99, 115, 125).

QWALLAY, William: on 21 September 1418 he was left 10d. in the will of William Kelk, a soldier and lord of Barnetby, for the period of three years. He seems to have been a friar of Beverley at the time (BIA, Episcopal Register 18, fol. 372v).

QWITAKER (Whitaker), William: he was a friar of York when he was ordained p. on 19 December 1388 at York Minster (BIA, Register 14, fol. 11v).

RADFORD, Alexander: he was a friar of York when he was ordained p. on 5 June 1501 at Blackfriars, York (BIA, Register 25, fol. 109r. Cf. Cross and Vickers, *MFN*, p. 439).

RAND (Rande, Randy), John: he was a friar of York when he was ordained a. on 12 March 1513 at Whitefriars, York, s. on 23 September 1514 at Blackfriars, York, d. on 22 December 1515 at Greyfriars, York, and p. on 19 September 1517 at Whitefriars, York (BIA, Register 26, fols. 122v, 149r, Register 27, fols. 170v, 178v. Cf. Cross and Vickers, *MFN*, p. 444).

RANYER (Raymer), Robert: he was ordained a. on 24 May 1404, s. on 20 September 1404 and d. on 20 December 1404; the three ceremonies took place at All Saints chapel, Cawood (*Reg. Scrope*, ii, pp. 55, 99, 131).

RASYN (Rasen), John de: he was ordained d. on 26 May 1347 at Lincoln cathedral (LAO, Register 7B, fol. 14v) and p. on 14 June 1348 at Bardney Abbey (LAO, Register 9D, fol. 5r). A Friar John de Rasen was the guardian of the Grimsby Greyfriars when his name was mentioned in the plea rolls in the Hilary term of 1483 (TNA, CP40/488, m. 479, attorneys).

RASYN, John: he was ordained p. on 20 September 1404 at All Saints, Cawood (*Reg. Scrope*, ii, pp. 55, 99, 131).

RATCLIFF (Ratclyff, Ratcliff), John: he was a friar of Stamford when he was ordained a. on 23 September 1475 in St Mary *ad pontem*, Stamford (LAO, Register 21, fol. 150v). He was ordained d. on 6 March 1479 at Austin Friars, York (BIA, Register 22, fol. 376v).

RATFORD (Ratforde, Retford), John de: he was licensed to hear confessions in the archdeaconry of Lincoln on 1 March 1320 for one year (LAO, Register 5, fol. 149v). He was the 51st regent master at Oxford c.1328 (Eccleston, p. 56; *GFO*, p. 169; *BRUO*, p. 1548). He was licensed to hear confessions in the archdeaconry of Lincoln for one year from 1 March 1338 (*Reg. Burghersh*, iii, p. 354, no. 4645). He died before October 1346 when another friar called William Sturney replaced him (LAO, vii, fol. 99r). In three theological questions in MS. Bodley, Digby 216, fol. 40 the name 'Ratforde' is prefixed. They might equally be by Friar Thomas Ratford. Ratford is named in the margin of Città del Vaticano, Biblioteca Apostolica Vaticana, Vat. lat. 1110, fol. 24r, a copy of Adam Wodeham's *Commentary on the Sentences* (Pelzer, *Bibliothecae Apostolicae Vaticanae, Codices Vaticani Latini, II, pars prior, Codices 679–1134*, p. 729).

RATFORD (Retford, Ratford), Thomas de: he was the 63rd regent master at Oxford c.1340 (Eccleston, p. 57).

RATHEBY, John: he was a friar of York when he was ordained p. on 9 March 1381 at the parish church of St Mary, Beverley (BIA, Register 12, fol. 139v).

RAVENSER, William de: he was presented to the bishop of Lincoln by the guardian of Lincoln on 7 December 1321 and licensed (LAO, Register 3, fols. 299v–300).

RAVENSWATH, Alexander de: he was ordained s. in the prebendal chapel of Cawood on 10 June 1419 (BIA, Register 18, fol. 403r).

RAVERSER, Richard de: a friar, priest and professed, of York. He died c.1334 (Little, '*Records, Franciscan Province*', p. 151).

RAWLYN, Robert: he was ordained a. on 11 March 1475 at Greyfriars, York, and s. on 23 December 1475 at Holy Trinity Priory, Micklegate, York (BIA, Register 22, fols. 232v, 236v).

RAYN, William: he was a friar of York when he was ordained p. on 4 June 1463 at Whitefriars, York (BIA, Register 20, fol. 456r).

READING (Redyng), Robert de: he was ordained d. on 26 May 1347 at Lincoln cathedral (LAO, Register 7B, fol. 14v).

REDBURN, William: he was a friar of Lincoln when he was ordained s. on 19 September 1528 (LAO, Register 26, fol. 22r).

REMYE, Thomas: he was a friar of Boston when he was ordained d. on 8 April 1508 in Liddington prebendal church and p. on 22 April 1508 in the chapel of St Mary Magdalene in Lincoln cathedral (LAO, Register 24, fols. 70r, 71v).

RETFORD, Geoffrey de: he was guardian of York in Michaelmas 1298 when an action was brought against the convent by John de Burton (TNA, KB27/156, mem. 72; *Notes on Religious Houses*, i, pp. 242–43).

REVBY, Thomas de: he was ordained s. on 20 September 1348 in Skipton parish church (BIA, Register 10A, fol. 25r).

RICCALL (Rikall, Rykhall), John: he was a friar of York when he was ordained p. on 23 September 1396 at Holy Trinity Priory, Micklegate, York (BIA, Register 14, fol. 74r). On 18 September 1426 he was the guardian at York and vicar provincial when he appeared before the diocesan officials in connection with the retraction given by Thomas Richmond, another friar of York. There was a general procession to the priory of Holy Trinity at Micklegate, where Riccall preached. During the ceremonies Richmond recanted his error (*Convocation, York*, pp. 399–400; *The Records of the Northern Convocation*, pp. 166–68). On 25 March 1434 Petronilla Russell left 6s. 8d. to this friar, who was described as a master (BIA, Probate Register 3, fol. 425r). He was a friar and master of York on 1 December 1435 when he received 40s. in the will of Richard Russell, merchant, citizen of York and widower of Petronilla. He requested burial in the church of St John the Baptist at Hungate (*TE*, ii, pp. 52–57, 55).

RICCALL (Rikall), Thomas: he was ordained d. on 20 September 1410 in the prebendal chapel at Cawood and p. on 19 September 1411 at St Michael-le-Belfrey, York (BIA, Register 18, fols. 392v, 39Cv).

RICHARD, son of Henry: he was ordained p. on 18 September 1372 at Greyfriars, York (BIA, Register 11, fol. 389r).

RICHARD: he was guardian of Doncaster in 1479 when he issued letters of fraternity to Roger Alyn (TNA, Chanc.Misc. 15/6/13). In the same year he issued a similar letter in favour of John Denton and Christina, his wife (*Yorks. Deeds*, vi, pp. 59–60, no. 194).

RICHARDSON, John: he was a friar of Lincoln when he was ordained s. and d. on 16 March 1521 at Sleaford prebendal church and 30 March 1521 at Lincoln cathedral (LAO, Register 25, fols. 135r, 136r). A friar of this name signed the deed of surrender at London on 12 November 1538 (*GFL*, p. 222). A John Richardson, formerly of Greenwich, received his capacity on 20 October 1538 (Chambers, *Faculty Office Registers 1534–1549*, p. 152).

RICHARDSON, Thomas: he was a friar of York at the Dissolution on 27 November 1538 (*Eighth Report of the Deputy Keeper of the Public Records*, p. 51). In 1540 Thomas Richardson, who could have been the former friar of York, was a chantry priest in St Peter the Little, York (*Chantries, Guilds, Hospitals*, i, pp. 48–49). A Thomas Richardson witnessed wills as a curate of Harthill between 1543 and 1546. Another Thomas Richardson acquired the living of Melton in the diocese of York in October 1572. He may have been the same man as the cleric who became vicar of Sheriff Hutton in October 1573, which he held until his death in 1583. His will of 20 November 1583 requested burial in Sheriff Hutton church beside his brother, Richard Richardson, who had also been a clerk. He was not married and gave half his books to his nephew, William Harrison, on condition that his father kept him at learning, and the other half of his library to William Pickering. There is nothing in the will to associate him with the former friar (BIA, Caveat Book i, fol. 22r; Probate Register 13, fols. 1v, 288v, 466rv; *CPR, Elizabeth*, v, no. 2921, Institution Act Book, 3, fol. 35v; BIA, Register 31, fol. 93v; Cross and Vickers, *MFN*, p. 459).

RICHMOND (Richemond), John de: he was ordained p. on 30 May 1366 at Bishopthorpe manor chapel (BIA, Register 11, fol. 363v).

RICHMOND (Richemond, Richemund), Thomas de: he was ordained a. on 14 June 1348 at St Mary's Abbey, York, s. on 20 September 1348 at Skipton parish church and d. on 20 December 1348 at York Minster (BIA, Register 10A, fols. 23r, 25r, 26r).

RICHMOND (Richemond), Thomas de: he does not appear in the registers of ordination at Lincoln and York. It is probable that he joined the fraternity towards the end of the first decade of the fifteenth century and was ordained in the second. On 11 May 1420 a friar of this name received a bequest of 20s. from John Olney of Weston, Buckinghamshire, who asked for burial in the parish church of Weston and left money to the friars of Northampton and Bedford in return for prayers (*The Fifty Earliest English Wills in the court of Probate, London*, pp. 47–48). As a friar of York, he was invited to preach in a newly built chapel of St Anne on Foss bridge on the feast of St Anne, that is, on 26 July 1426; the occasion was attended by a large number of clergy and laity. His homily in the vernacular was deemed to have been contrary to the faith of the Church and critical of the clergy. The speed with which the ecclesiastical authorities acted betrays a deep anxiety about the content of the friar's teaching. Three days later he was summoned to the chapter house of York Minster in the presence of Master John Selow, vicar general, Bishop Warter and masters and canons. When the charges were read out, Richmond openly and publicly protested his good faith and his fidelity to the Church. The vicar general ordered him to appear on 2 August with an authentic text of his homily. The friar produced the text of his sermon, written in his own hand on a roll, and he swore on the Gospels that this was a copy of what he had preached. He was suspended from the office of preaching by Selow and he was commanded to appear at the archbishop's court on 12 August in the chapter house.

The bishops of Durham and Carlisle were present along with the abbot of St Mary's and diocesan officials. Richmond's text was found to contain certain erroneous articles and heresy on six points; first, he had taught that a priest guilty of mortal sin ceases to be a priest in God's sight; secondly, a civil judge who arrests such a priest is within his rights, committing no act of violence; thirdly, the priestly office in the Old Testament was fulfilled by sacrifice and incense and in the New Testament by the Eucharist; fourthly, where the Church fails to punish fornicators, the state should do it and bring them before the judge; fifthly, where the Church neglects to act against perjury, the secular power should take action; and sixthly, priests refusing to be properly imprisoned may be beaten by the secular powers and imprisoned. The friar's views on the question of Church and state rang alarm bells among the archbishop's senior officials. Richmond denied the charges which had been read out. He was accompanied by three confrères, John Milton, John Hamsthwayte and Thomas Waltham, who had been present at his homily. Examined by the bishop of Durham, the friars affirmed that they had heard Richmond make the claim that the priest in mortal sin forfeits his sacred office. They added that they did not wish to defend his errors. At that point Richmond acknowledged his errors and submitted himself to the Church's correction, giving an undertaking to appear before the metropolitan or his delegate on 2 September to make a recantation. On 9 September in the manor chapel at Cawood, Richmond appeared before diocesan officials and from the pulpit publicly confessed his errors. His suspension from the office of preaching was ratified. A day was assigned for the customary confession and recantation to be read in a church of York. This penitential deed was performed by John Riccall, the guardian of the local Greyfriars and vicar provincial. On 21 September there was a general procession to the priory of Holy Trinity and a sermon was delivered by Riccall. During the ceremonies Richmond confessed his error (*Convocation, York*, pp. 386–403; *The Records of the Northern Convocation*, pp. 146–72).

RICHMOND (Richemond), Thomas: he was admitted to the guild of *Corpus Christi* at York in 1431/32 (*Corpus Christi Guild*, p. 32). On 11 July 1454 Elizabeth de la Ryver of Brandesby, a widow who asked for burial in St Clement's, instructed her executors to provide a friar of this name with 'ane abitt of russet'. The friar was a master of theology (*TE*, ii, pp. 173–74; BIA, Probate Register 2, fol. 301r). On 25 February 1457 he was described as a master of theology when he received a papal dispensation to hold a benefice (*BF, ns*, ii, p. 134, no. 2, 56; *CPL*, xi, p. 145). He was appointed as rector of the parish of St Cuthbert, Peasholme, York, on 24 December 1457, at the presentation of the prior and convent of the Holy Trinity (BIA, Register 20, fol. 10v). He had probably resigned the parish by 16 August 1458, when he was appointed as the archbishop's penitentiary in the city and archdeaconry of York. He was a doctor of theology (BIA, Register 20, fols. 199r, 200r). A friar of this name was given six marks by the exchequer on 26 September 1424 along with John Waltham and John Bromwich (*CCR, 1429–1435*, p. 369).

RICHMOND (Richemond), William: he was a friar of York when he was ordained a. on 27 May 1469 at Blackfriars, York. He was ordained s. on 22 September 1470 at Greyfriars, York, d. on 21 December 1471 at Austin Friars, York, and p. on 28 March 1472 at York Minster. The register states that on the last occasion he was ordained d., but this is clearly an error for p. (BIA, Register 22, fols. 200v, 207r, 213r, 215r).

RICROFTE (Ricroft, Rycroft), William: he was ordained a. on 21 December 1471 at Austin Friars, York, s. on 18 February 1475 at Whitefriars, York, and d. on 11 March 1475 at Greyfriars, York (BIA, Register 22, fols. 212v, 232r, 233r).

RIGGETON (Rigton, Ryggeston), Adam de: he was ordained a. on 13 March 1350 at Beverley Minster, and s. on 18 December 1350 at Blackfriars, York. He was ordained d. on 12 March 1351. He was a friar at York when ordained p. on 11 June 1351 at St Mary's Abbey, York (BIA, Register 10A, fols. 44r, 50r, 51r, 52r).

RILLINGTON (Rillyngton), John: the son of Thomas de Rillington, he was a friar of York in 1330. On Tuesday 22 March 1351 Robert de Rillington, the son of Thomas Rillington, was aged 56, when he confirmed the proof of age of William, son and heir of William Latimer, knight, who had been born in the parish of Scampston, Yorkshire, on the Saturday before the feast of the Annunciation in the fourth year of Edward III, that is, 20 March 1330, and was baptised in the church of St Andrew at Rillington, which was in the parish of Scampston, by Master John de Lutton, chaplain. He testified that he had a brother named John, who had become a friar at York within a month of William's birth and that 21 years had elapsed since then (*Cal. Inquisitions*, ix (Edward III), pp. 452–53, no. 671; Goldthorp, 'The Franciscans and Dominicans in Yorkshire', p. 274n).

RIMSWELL (Rymeswell), Robert de: he was licensed to hear confessions in the diocese of York at an unknown date. He was replaced during the administration of Archbishop Thoresby (BIA, Register 11, fol. 396r).

RINAKRIS (Rinakrs, Rynaker), John de: he was a friar of York when he was ordained a. on 18 September 1350 at Whitefriars, York. He was ordained p. on 24 September 1351 in York Minster (BIA, Register 10A, fols. 49r, 53r).

RIPON (Riponia), John de: he was ordained d. on 20 December 1371 at St Mary, Bishophill Senior (BIA, Register 11, fol. 386r).

RIPON, Richard de: described as the lector of Ripon, he was licensed to hear confessions in the diocese of York on 2 October 1350 (BIA, Register 10, fol. 279v). His place in the register leaves no doubt about his Franciscan identity. Was he a theologian for the canons at Ripon? He may have been the lector at one of the *studia* in the custodies of York or Newcastle.

RIPON (Riponia), Roger de: he was ordained s. on 24 September 1345 at Ripon Minster (BIA, Register 10A, fol. 12v). He was a friar of Hartlepool when he was ordained d. on 17 December 1345 (Durham Registers: Hatfield, fol. 93r) and p. on 20 December 1348 at York Minster (BIA, Register 10A, fol. 26r).

RIPON (Rypon), Thomas: he was a friar of York when he was ordained a. on 18 September 1428 at York Minster. He was ordained s. on 24 September 1429 at Whitefriars, York, and d. on 22 September 1431 at Greyfriars, York (BIA, Register 19, fol. 216r, 235r, 240v). He was a friar of Lincoln when he was ordained p. on 24 September 1435 at Sempringham parish church (LAO, Register 17, fol. 221r).

ROBARDS (Robardes), William: he was a friar of York when ordained s. on 20 September 1505 at Bishopthorpe manor chapel, d. on 20 December 1505 at Austin Friars, York, and p. on 7 March 1506 at Whitefriars, York (BIA, Register 25, fols. 130r, 131r, 132r. Cf. Cross and Vickers, *MFN*, p. 441).

ROBERT: he resigned the vicarage of Horbling, Lincolnshire, to become a friar. His successor was instituted on 2 April 1278 (*Rot. Gravesend*, pp. 80, 286; Bennett, *Lincolnshire Parish Clergy c.1214–1968: A Biographical Register*, i, p. 256).

ROBINSON (Robynson), John: he was ordained a. on 8 June 1476 at Blackfriars, York (BIA, Register 22, fol. 239v).

ROBINSON (Robynson), John: he was a friar of York when he was ordained a. on 31 May 1488 at Blackfriars, York, s. on 4 April 1489 at Greyfriars, York, d. on 18 September 1490 at Whitefriars, York, and p. on 21 April 1492 at the lady altar of York Minster (BIA, Register 23, fols. 412v, 416r, 432v. Cf. Cross and Vickers, *MFN*, p. 437). He was at York and was the confessor of Thomas Roclyfe, gentleman, whose will was compiled on 1 January 1504. He received 6s. 8d. in the will (BIA, Probate Register 6, fol. 131rv).

ROBSON, Hugh: he was ordained s. on 23 December 1480 and d. on 17 March 1481. Both ceremonies took place at Austin Friars, York (BIA, Register 23, fols. 373r, 374r. Cf. Cross and Vickers, *MFN*, p. 435).

ROBTIS, Peter: he was ordained a. on 8 March 1516 at All Saints, Northampton (LAO, Register 25, fol. 117r).

ROERMOND (Rosamunda), Gerard de: he was ordained s. on 17 December 1429 at Austin Friars, York, and d. on 11 March 1430 at Greyfriars, York (BIA, Register 19, fols. 235v, 236v; Walmsley, 'Some Dutch Franciscans in England during the Later Middle Ages', p. 258).

ROKE (Rok), Richard: he was ordained a. on 18 September 1400 at All Saints, Cawood, s. on 28 May 1401 at Bishop Burton, and p. on 9 June 1403 in the chapel of St Nicholas at Bawtry (*Reg. Scrope*, ii, pp. 55, 100, 131).

ROPER, Robert: a former friar of Scarborough who received his capacity on 20 June 1539 (Chambers, *Faculty Office Registers 1534–1549*, p. 187).

ROSE, Richard: he was ordained p. on 24 September 1468 at Greyfriars, York (BIA, Register 22, fol. 193v).

ROSE, William: in the Michaelmas term of 1424 he was described as recently guardian of Lincoln when he was mentioned in the plea rolls along with the guardian of Coventry, Richard Hanbury (TNA, CP40/655, part 1, m. 51d).

ROSEBY (Roxby), William: he was a friar of York when he was ordained a. on 21 March 1523 and s. on 30 May 1523 at Holy Trinity Priory, Micklegate, York. He was at Scarborough when ordained p. on 10 June 1525 at Blackfriars, York (BIA, Register 27, fols. 198v, 200r, 207r. Cf. Cross and Vickers, *MFN*, p. 445).

ROTHERFELD, William de: he was a friar of Doncaster when he was ordained s. on 26 June 1350 at Austin Friars, York (BIA, Register 10A, fol. 48r).

ROTHERHAM (Roderam), John de: he was ordained d. in 1267/68 in Selby Abbey (*Reg. Walter Giffard*, p. 189, no. 688).

ROUCEBY, William: he was a friar of Lincoln when he was ordained d. on 1 April 1525 at All Saints, Northampton (LAO, Register 26, fol. 11r).

RUDFORTH, Alexander: he was a friar of York when he was ordained d. on 10 April 1501 at the lady altar of York Minster (BIA, Register 5A, fol. 532v, Cf. Cross and Vickers, *MFN*, p. 439).

RUSSELL (Russel), William: he was ordained s. on 17 December 1345 at Liddington prebendal church, d. on 10 June 1346 at Buckden prebendal church and p. on 17 March 1347 at Burton parish church, close to Lincoln (LAO, Register 7B, fols. 2r, 6v, 11v).

RUSSELL, William: he was ordained a. on 17 December 1401 at St Mary's Abbey, York, s. on 20 May 1402 in the chapel of All Saints, Cawood, d. on 23 September 1402 at Blackfriars, York, and p. on 9 June 1403 in the chapel of St Nicholas, Bawtry (*Reg. Scrope*, ii, pp. 55, 100, 131). He was the guardian of London on 16 May 1424 when he and Roger Filby received six marks from the crown (*CCR, 1422–1429*, p. 486). In 1425 he was the guardian of London when he gave £3 towards the tiling of the cloister roof (*GFL*, pp. 57–58, 171). He was still the guardian of that community in the Trinity and Michaelmas terms of 1424, when he was named along with John Holdich, recently guardian of Chichester, in the plea rolls (TNA, CP40/655, part 1, m. 236, CP40/653, m. 302). On 28 January 1425 he was still in office when he preached at St Paul's Cross and opined that the payment of personal tithes to clerks with cure of souls was not enjoined by divine law, and that they might be applied to works of mercy instead. He was still the guardian in the Easter and Trinity terms of 1425 (TNA, CP40/658, m. 120d, CP40/657, mm. attorneys 1d). On 18 May 1425 he was obliged to recant his errors. Later he defaulted on the penance which had been enjoined upon him. When cited, he refused to appear. He was then pronounced contumacious and was formally prosecuted by the clergy of the province of Canterbury before William Lynwood. The depositions of the witnesses concurred on the main facts, showing that Russell had drawn a distinction between praedial and personal tithes, admitting the former as sanctioned by God's law, but not the latter. On 28 May 1425 the sheriff of Sussex was ordered to arrest him and deliver him to the archbishop of Canterbury (*CPR, 1422–1429*, p. 300). On 13 July 1425 his opinion was condemned and he was pronounced a heretic. On 11 August 1425 Edmund Lacy, bishop of Exeter, published a letter of 13 July received from Archbishop Chichele on the conduct of this friar (*Reg. Lacy*, i, pp. 127–28). On 2 March 1426 Archbishop Chichele instructed John David, minister provincial, to ensure that the friars did not preach against the payment of personal tithes. On 24 April 1426 Winchelsea gave in and publicly repudiated Russell's views at St Paul's Cross. Russell's teaching on tithes was condemned by the University of Oxford. On 22 July 1426 the University of Cambridge censured the friar's views. Meanwhile Russell had sought help at the Roman curia. On 7 June 1426, however, Cardinal Branda da Castiglione, papal judge and procurator, recited the case against the friar and found against him. Russell had escaped back to England. Archbishop Chichele consulted convocation and it was decided that senior members of the London Greyfriars should be summoned to appear. Thomas Winchelsea was charged with maintaining a heretic. Russell's opinion was condemned and the Holy See ordered his imprisonment by the bishop of London until further orders were issued. Russell had already returned to England and had been received by his confrères in London. On 18 February 1427 William Lynwood prosecuted the friar at the request of Master Richard Collyng and recited the bull of Pope Martin V of 19 May 1426. On 21 March 1428 Russell publicly revoked his errors and on the same date the bishop of London was required to imprison him until the Holy See authorised his release (*Reg. Chichele*, iii, pp. 104–05, 108, 110, 118–38, 141–2, 147, 151–7, 175–7. Cf. 178–79, 181–2, 186, 193–4; Wilkins, *Concilia*, iii, pp. 438–62; Robinson, 'The Tithe-Heresy of Friar William Russell'; *BRUO*, pp. 1611–12). His writings are: *Super Porphyrii Universalia compendium, Commentarium in Aristotelis Predicamenta* (*GFO*, pp. 257–59).

RUSTON (Roston, Rustone), Thomas de: he was ordained a. on 3 March 1425 (*Reg. Sede Vacante, York, 1423–26*, pp. 99, 116, 125), s. on 21 May 1429 at Blackfriars, York, d. on 22 September 1431. He was at York when he was ordained p. on 15 March 1432; the first and third ceremonies took place at Greyfriars, York (BIA, Register 19, fols. 234v, 240v, 241v).

RYBY (Riby, Ryghy), John: he was a friar of York when he was ordained a. on 22 April 1424 at St Michael-le-Belfrey, York (BIA, Register 5A, fol. 368r; *Reg. Sede Vacante, York, 1423–26*, pp. 99, 116, 125), and s. on 21 September 1426 at Blackfriars, York (BIA, Register 19, fol. 215r). He was ordained d. on 14 June 1427 at Blackfriars, York (BIA, Register 19, fol. 230r).

RYE, William: he was at York at the Dissolution on 27 November 1538 (*Eighth Report of the Deputy Keeper of the Public Records*, p. 51).

RYHALL, Alan de: he was licensed to hear confessions in the diocese of Lincoln in August 1300 (LAO, Register 3, fol. 16v).

RYRSTON, Robert: he was ordained s. on 6 March 1406 at Holy Trinity Priory, Micklegate, York (BIA, Register 5A, fol. 320r; *Reg. Sede Vacante, York, 1405–08*, pp. 66, 81, 89).

RYSWARP, John de: he was ordained a. on 30 May 1366 at Bishopthorpe manor chapel, s. on 19 September 1366 at the same venue, d. on 19 December 1366 at St Leonard's Hospital chapel, York, and p. on 13 March 1367 at St Mary's, Bishophill Senior, York (BIA, Register 11, fols. 362v, 363v, 364v, 365v).

ST PAULO, Hugh de: he was guardian at York on 12 February 1333 when he acted as the sub-executrix for the provision of Peter de Credonio to the prebend of Stillington (*Reg. Melton*, v, pp. 134–35, no. 379). He was at Beverley when he received the royal alms of 8s. 8d. on 22 May 1336 (TNA, E101/387/9).

ST PAULO, John de: he was ordained s. on 20 February 1350 at Doncaster parish church and d. on 22 May 1350 at Blackfriars, York (BIA, Register 10A, fols. 42r, 47r).

SADLER, John: he was a friar of York when he was ordained a. on 4 April 1500 at Holy Trinity Priory, Micklegate, York, s. on 6 March 1501 at Greyfriars, York, d. on 24 September 1502, and p. on 10 June 1503. The third and fourth ordinations took place at Blackfriars, York (BIA, Register 23, fol. 467r, Register 5A, fol. 530v, Register 25, fols. 114v, 119v. Cf. Cross and Vickers, *MFN*, p. 439).

SALKELD, John: he was a friar of York when ordained d. on 22 December 1492 at Whitefriars, York (BIA, Register 23, fol. 454r).

SALKELD, Thomas de: he was ordained a. on 29 May 1344 in Darlington parish church (*Reg. Kellaw*, iii, p. 142), s. on 18 September 1344 at Carlisle cathedral (*Reg. Kirkby*, i, p. 160, no. 772), and d. on 18 December 1344 in Durham cathedral (*Reg. Kellaw*, iii, p. 146). He was a friar of York when he was ordained p. on 10 June 1346 at Whitefriars, York (BIA, Register 10A, fol. 16r). A friar of this name was consecrated as bishop of *Chrysopolis*. On 22 April 1355 he was given a mandate to receive the oath of fealty from Nicholas de Qwitrig, rector of Caldbeck in the diocese of Carlisle, and to forward it under seal to Pope Innocent VI. The rector had been appointed a papal chaplain (*CPL*, iii, p. 563). A suffragan commission was granted to Thomas on 11 July 1354 (BIA, Register 11, fol. 28v). On 2 August 1356 Archbishop Thoresby commissioned him to bless Robert of Beverley, the abbot elect of the Cistercian monastery of Meaux, Yorkshire (BIA, Register 11, fol. 194v). His name appears at York in 1357 (Smith, *Ecclesiastical Cause Papers at York: The Court of York 1301–1399*, p. 27). He brought several serious charges against the bishop of Durham, but King Edward III acquitted the latter on 10 March 1358 (Rymer, *Foedera*, iii, pars i, p. 389). On 17 January 1363 Thomas was appointed to the parish of Crossthwaite in the diocese of Carlisle, notwithstanding that he held the church of Clifton in the same diocese. On 17 February 1363 he was given a benefice to the value of £25 in the gift of the bishop of Carlisle. He was prepared to resign the parish of Clifton (*Calendar of entries in the Papal registers relating to Great Britain and Ireland. Petitions to the Pope, vol. 1, A.D. 1342–1419*, pp. 397, 402). W. Stubbs states that Archbishop Zouche awarded him an annual salary for consecrating altars and churches and confirming and that his salary in 1349 was 40 marks and five years later it was £20. No corroborative texts were cited (Stubbs, *Registrum Sacrum Anglicanum*, p. 196. Cf. Butler, 'Suffragan Bishops in the Medieval Diocese of York', p. 57).

SALLAY, Henry de: he was ordained a. on 12 March 1351 at Blackfriars, York, s. on 3 March 1352 at Austin Friars, York, and d. on 2 June 1352 at St Mary's Abbey, York (BIA, Register 10A, fols. 50v, 54r, 55r).

SALTLEETBY (Saltfletby), Thomas de: he was a friar of Boston when he was ordained s. on 24 March 1352 in Sleaford prebendal church (LAO, Register 9D, fol. 59r).

SAMPSON, Geoffrey: Christiana, widow of William of Long Bennington, bequeathed half a mark to the Greyfriars of Lincoln to be placed at the disposition of Friar Geoffrey Sampson, a friar of Lincoln, at an unspecified date in 1283 (*Lincoln Wills, 1271–1532*, i, p. 2).

SANBY, George: he was a friar of York when he was ordained d. on 18 September 1456 at Austin Friars, York (BIA, Register 20, fol. 426r).

SANCEM, William: he was licensed to hear confessions in the archdeaconry of Lincoln on 5 March 1338 (LAO, Register 5, fol. 150).

SANDALE, William de: he was ordained p. on 7 June 1343 at Greyfriars, York (BIA, Register 10A, fol. 4v).

SANDALL, John de: he was ordained d. on 30 May 1366 and p. on 3 June 1368; both ceremonies took place at Bishopthorpe manor chapel (BIA, Register 11, fols. 363r, 370r).

SAUCEMER, William: he was licensed to hear confessions in the archdeaconry of Lincoln for one year from 5 March 1338 (*Reg. Burghersh*, iii, p. 354, no. 4647).

SAUNDBY, John de: he was a friar of York when he was licensed in the diocese of York about 6 January 1352 (BIA, Register 10, fol. 280r).

SAUNDBY (Saundeby), Thomas de: he was the guardian of Doncaster in 1332 when he and several friars were accused of seizing and imprisoning John de Malghum (*Notes on Religious Houses*, i, p. 37; TNA, CP40/292, m. 141, Michaelmas term 1332). He was still in office when his name appears in the plea rolls of the Trinity term of 1333 (TNA, CP40/294, m. 272).

SAXONY (Saxonia), Christianus de: he was ordained p. on 22 May 1434 at Blackfriars, York (BIA, Register 19, fol. 247r).

SAXONY (Saxonia), Godfrey de: he was a friar of York when he was ordained d. on 6 June 1433 at St Katherine's Priory, Lincoln (LAO, Register 17, fol. 211r).

SAYTON, Thomas: he was a friar of York when he was ordained p. on 6 March 1406 at Holy Trinity Priory, Micklegate, York (BIA, Register 5A, fol. 320v; *Reg. Sede Vacante, York, 1405–08*, pp. 66, 81, 89).

SCALBY (Scalleby), Robert de: he was ordained d. in 1267/68 in Selby Abbey (*Reg. Walter Giffard*, p. 189, no. 688).

SCALDEFORD, Robert de: he was a friar of Lincoln when he was ordained s. on 18 December 1333 at an unspecified venue (*Reg. Kirkby*, i, p. 28, no. 152).

SCARBOROUGH (Scardburgh), John de: he was a friar of Lincoln on 4 May 1336 when he received alms of 12s. 4d. from King Edward III for the 37 friars there (TNA, E101/387/9). A friar of this name was at York when he was licensed to hear confessions in the diocese on 14 June 1350 (BIA, Register 10, fol. 279r).

SCARBOROUGH (Scarburgh), John: he was a friar of Boston when he was ordained a. and s. on 20 September 1404 and d. on 14 March 1405; both ceremonies took place in Lincoln cathedral (LAO, Register 13, fols. 115v, 118v). He was at York in 1415 when he, along with John Belacyse, guardian, and Friars Thomas Bury and William Dynlay and many others, was accused of seizing Joan, the wife of Henry Lescrop, a chivaler, at Faxfleet, abducting and detaining her and certain goods and chattels (*Notes on Religious Houses*, ii, p. 93).

SCARBOROUGH (Scardeburgh), John: he was a friar of York when he was ordained d. on 21 September 1454 at Blackfriars, York, and p. on 18 September 1456 at Austin Friars, York (BIA, Register 20, fols. 418r, 427r).

SCARBOROUGH (Scarburgh), William: he was a friar of York when he was ordained a. on 3 April 1462 at Blackfriars, York, s. on 17 April 1462 at York Minster, and d. on 4 June 1463 at Whitefriars, York (BIA, Register 20, fols. 451rv, 456r).

SCAWRAY, William: he was a friar of York when he was ordained d. on 7 March 1506 at Whitefriars, York (BIA, Register 25, fol. 132r. Cf. Cross and Vickers, *MFN*, p. 441).

SCHELBRUK (Scelbruk, Skelbrok, Skelbroke, Kelbruke), Richard de: he was ordained a. on 30 January 1350 at York Minster, s. on 22 May 1350 and d. on 26 June 1350 at Austin Friars, York (BIA, Register 10A, fols. 39r, 47r, 48v). He was guardian of Oxford when he was mentioned in the plea rolls during the Trinity term of 1367 (TNA, CP40/427, m. 386 d). On 3 February 1375 he was examined by Fr Odoric de Forli, a Dominican, for his licence in theology in the episcopal palace of Bologna. He was incorporated as a master (F. Ehrle, *I pìu antichi statuti della facoltà teologica di Bologna*, p. 104; Piana, *Chartularium Studii Bononiensis S. Francisci [saec. XIII–XVI]*, pp. 31, 93*. Cf. Pergamo, 'I Francescani alla facoltà teologica di Bologna (1364–1500)', p. 20).

SCOTT', William: the breviator, the bearer of the mortuary roll of John Hemingborough, prior of Durham (†1416), was received at Scarborough. This deceased friar's name was entered on the roll and prayers were solicited for him. It is probable that he had been a member of the community at Scarborough (*Obituary Roll, Durham*, p. 65, no. 46).

SELBY, Thomas: he was at York when he was ordained a. on 17 December 1496 at Whitefriars, York, and s. on 18 February 1497 at Greyfriars, York (BIA, Register 23, fols. 452v, 453v. Cf. Cross and Vickers, *MFN*, p. 438).

SELBY, Walter de: he was a friar of York when he was ordained d. on 22 September 1380 at Greyfriars, York (BIA, Register 12, fol. 137v).

SELBY (Seleby), William de: he was ordained p. at an unspecified location and date between September 1346 and September 1347 (BIA, Register 10A, fol. 18a).

SELBY, William: he was a friar of Boston when he was ordained s. on 16 March 1426 and d. on 25 May 1426; both ceremonies occurred in Boston parish church (*Reg. Fleming*, ii, pp. 121, 124, nn. 544, 546). He was ordained p. on 24 September 1429 at Blackfriars, York (BIA, Register 19, fol. 235v). On 4 November 1446 he was admitted to hear confessions in the diocese of York, having been presented by the minister provincial (BIA, Register 19, fol. 107v).

SEMPRINGHAM (Sempryngham), John: he was a friar of Bedford when ordained a. on 17 December 1496 at All Saints, Northampton, and s. on 18 February 1497 at Buckden prebendal church (LAO, Register 24, fols. 5v, 6v). He was a friar of York when he was ordained d. on 27 March 1501 at Whitefriars, York, and p. on 5 June 1501 at Blackfriars, York (BIA, Register 5A, 532r, Register 25, fol. 109r. Cf. Cross and Vickers, *MFN*, p. 439).

SEMTLOWIS, Thomas de: he was ordained a. on 15 March 1348 at Blackfriars, Northampton (LAO, Register 9D, fol. 1v).

SERGYUS (Sergius), Dedericus: he was a friar of York when ordained p. on 15 March 1432 at Greyfriars, York (BIA, Register 19, fol. 241v).

SETON, Thomas: he was ordained a. on 20 September 1404 at All Saints, Cawood (*Reg. Scrope*, ii, pp. 55, 102, 131). He was a friar of Lincoln when he was ordained s. on 20 December 1404 and d. on 14 March 1405, both at Lincoln cathedral (LAO, Register 13, fols. 117r, 118v).

SETON, William: he was at York when he was ordained a. on 24 February 1453 at Blackfriars, York (BIA, Register 20, fol. 412v). A friar of this name was admitted to the *Corpus Christi* guild at York in 1494 (*Corpus Christi Register*, p. 138).

SEUTHEY, William: he was ordained d. on 22 September 1358 at Bishop Burton manor chapel near Beverley (BIA, Register 11, fol. 334v).

SEYWYN (Streyn), Gilbert: he was ordained s. on 9 March 1476 at Greyfriars, York, and d. on 8 June 1476 at Blackfriars, York (BIA, Register 22, fols. 237r, 240r).

SHAPP, John: he was ordained s. on 3 April 1400 at Blackfriars, Beverley (*Reg. Scrope*, ii, pp. 55, 102, 131).

SHARNBROOK, John de: he was licensed to hear confessions in the diocese of Lincoln on 31 January 1334 (LAO, Register 5, fol. 471).

SHARP, Thomas: he was a friar of York when he was ordained s. on 21 May 1513 at Blackfriars, York (BIA, Register 26, fol. 124r. Cross and Vickers, *MFN*, p. 444).

SHAW, Richard: he was ordained d. on 27 March 1479 at Greyfriars, York (BIA, Register 22, fol. 377v).

SHEFFIELD, John de: he was licensed in the diocese of York, but replaced on 10 October 1348 (BIA, Register 10, fol. 278v).

SHEFFIELD (Shefeld), William de: he was a friar of Scarborough when he was ordained s. on 22 September 1369 at Bishopthorpe manor chapel (BIA, Register 11, fol. 375r).

SHERBURGH, Thomas: he was ordained s. on 22 March 1477 at Greyfriars, York (BIA, Register 22, fol. 365r).

SHERET, Thomas: he was ordained a. on 21 December 1476 and p. on 5 June 1479. Both ceremonies took place at Holy Trinity Priory, Micklegate, York (BIA, Register 22, fols. 363r, 379v).

SHERWYN, Henry: full details of the family of this friar emerge from the testamentary dispositions of his two brothers. Alice was the friar's mother and she had three sons, Henry, Robert and Thomas, and four daughters, Katherine, Cecilia, Joanne and Elizabeth, whose married name was Hertgill. Joanne subsequently married William Bukler, a tapiter of York. Joanne and her husband had three daughters, Elizabeth, Joanne and Helen. He left 5s. to the Greyfriars of York for a trental in his will of 20 March 1483 and asked for burial in St Helen's, Stonegate (BIA, Probate Register 5, fol. 45rv). Because Robert and Thomas requested burial in St Helen's in Stonegate at York this may have been the parish in which Henry grew up. Henry, who may have been the youngest son, was a friar at York when ordained a. on 18 March 1458 at Greyfriars, York, and d. on 28 February 1461 at Blackfriars (BIA, Register 20, fols. 433r, 446v). His progress in the study of theology in the local and custodial schools was noted by the custos and other officials, who sent him to the University of Cambridge shortly after his ordination to the priesthood. He was given a grace towards incepting in theology in 1472–73 so that he should preach thrice and respond *ad placitum*. In 1474–75 he was admitted to incept in theology and paid the *communa* and the following year he obtained his doctorate (Leathes, *Grace Book A*, pp. 96, 101, 103, 111). His case demonstrates that the friars continued to select suitable men for study in the universities in preparation for teaching positions in the custody.

Sherwyn may have returned to the custody immediately to take up the post of lector, perhaps in the custodial school where a succession of graduates from Oxford and Cambridge lectured. In 1481 he joined the select band of friars admitted to the guild of *Corpus Christi* (*Corpus Christi Register*, p. 109). He was still a member of that community on 6 November 1487 when John Carre, once lord mayor and a parishioner of St Sampson's, left him 20s. (*TE*, IV, pp. 26–30). On 24 July 1475 Robert, a pewderer and parishioner of St Helen, in Stonegate, York, drew up his will in which he requested burial in the ambulatory before the crucifix in his parish church of St Helen in Stonegate. Having made arrangements for his funeral and given an offering for the fabric of York Minster, he left 13s. 4d. to his brother, whom he described as a friar at York. Henry's mother was still alive and received half of Robert's best vases. His sister Katherine, a nun at Moxby, received 6s. 8d. Isabelle was Robert's widow. Henry was appointed as Robert's executor. In the event of his being absent, these duties should be undertaken by another friar of York, John Harwood (BIA, Probate Register 4, fol. 91r). Further details on the family are provided by the will of Thomas, a glazier of York, whose will was written on 2 October 1481. He, too, made offering for his funeral and for the fabric of York Minster. He left 3s. 4d. to his mother, 2s. to his sister, described as Lady Katherine, and a coffer to his brother, Master Henry, the friar, and 12d. to his sisters, Cecilia, Joanne Bukler and Elizabeth Hertgill. The testator's son was Matthew. Henry was appointed to supervise Thomas's will (BIA, Probate Register 5, fols. 112v–13r). He was asked to celebrate a trental of Masses for William Cerff, rector of Rowley in the East Riding, on 26 February 1489 (BIA, Probate Register 5, fols. 357v–58r). On 1 June 1491 he witnessed the will of Richard Baynbrig, parson of York Minster, who was buried at Greyfriars, York (York Minster, Dean and Chapter Library, MS.L 2/4, fol. 377r).

SHILTON, Robert: he was ordained a. on 24 September 1468 at Greyfriars, York (BIA, Register 22, fol. 193r).

SHILTON, William: he was a friar of York when he was ordained a. on 22 September 1442 at York Minster, s. on 22 December 1442 at Austin Friars, York, d. on 6 April 1443 at Whitefriars, York, and p. on 15 June 1443 at Blackfriars, York (BIA, Register 19, fols. 220v, 267v, 268v, 269v).

SHIPTON, Henry de: between 12 and 14 June 1300 King Edward I sent 57s. 4d. to the friars of York by this friar, a member of the community (*Liber quotidianus contrarotulatoris garderobae*, p. 39).

SHIRBORN, Thomas: he was a friar of York when he was ordained a. on 21 September 1510 at Holy Trinity Priory, Micklegate, York, and s. on 15 March 1511 at Whitefriars, York (Register 26, fols. 109r, 111r. Cf. Cross and Vickers, *MFN*, p. 443). He was at Oxford when he was ordained d. in March 1512 in the diocese of Salisbury (Salisbury Registers: Audley) and then at Grantham when he was ordained p. on 18 December 1512 at Buckden prebendal church (LAO, Register 24, fol. 90v).

SHIRBURN (Schireburn'), Stephen de: he was ordained s. on 22 March 1298 in Lincoln cathedral (*Reg. Sutton*, vii, p. 103).

SHIRBURN (Sherborne, Schirborn), Thomas de: he was a friar of Grimsby when he was ordained s. on 21 December 1359. He was a friar of Northampton when he was ordained d. on 29 February 1360; both ceremonies took place in Lincoln cathedral (LAO, Register 9D, fols. 93v, 94v). He was ordained p. on 23 December 1363 at St Mary's Abbey, York (BIA, Register 11, fol. 355r).

SHIRBURN (Schirburn), William: he was licensed in the diocese of Lincoln on 5 October 1346 (LAO, Register 7, fol. 99r).

SHIRBURN (Schirburne, Shireburn', Schireburn', Schyrbourne), William de: he was ordained p. on 17 March 1291 at St Andrew's, Northampton (*Reg. Sutton*, vii, p. 13). He was at Oxford on 26 July 1300 when he was presented for a licence to hear confessions in the archdeaconry of Oxford, but was rejected (Little, *Franciscan Papers, Lists, and Documents*, p. 235). He became 38th regent master at Oxford c.1312 (Eccleston, 55). He was already a master when his name was mentioned in connection with the inception of Henry Croy, a Dominican at Oxford (*Collectanea*, ii, p. 230, n. 5). He supported the Dominicans in their quarrel with the University of Oxford (*GFO*, p. 165). His *Quodlibeta*, a notable work in its day, was known to Leland (*Leland, De viris illustribus*, pp. 698–99, no. 496; Sharpe, *Handlist*, p. 809, no. 2176) and a copy was at the Augustinian Canons at Gisborne Priory (*The Libraries of the Augustinian Canons*, p. 31, no. 4). He is quoted in Gonville and Caius College Library MS.300/514; *BRUO*, p. 1691).

SHIRLOWE, John: he was a friar of York who received a pair of quartillets and 6s. 8d. in the will of George Darrell, a parishioner of Sessay, compiled on 3 October 1432. Darrell requested burial at the Greyfriars of York (*TE*, ii, pp. 27–28).

SIAM, Thomas: he was ordained s. on 15 March 1427 at Whitefriars, York. He was a friar of Beverley when ordained d. on 20 September 1427 at Holy Trinity Priory, Micklegate, York (BIA, Register 19, fols. 216r, 228v).

SIBSON (Sybson), John: he was a friar of York when he was ordained s. on 18 December 1423 at York Minster, d. on 22 April 1424 at St Michael-le-Belfrey, York, and p. on 14 June 1427 at Blackfriars, York (BIA, Register 5A, fols. 354v, 368v, Register 19, fol. 230r; *Reg. Sede Vacante, York, 1423–26*, pp. 99, 117, 125).

SIGHLESTHORNE, Adam de: he was a friar of York when he was ordained s. on 21 May 1345 in Thirsk parish church. He was ordained d. on 24 September 1345 in

Ripon Minster and p. on 20 December 1348 in York Minster (BIA, Register 10A, fols. 11r, 13r, 26r).

SILLOW (Syllow), John: on 13 February 1490 his supplication was recorded at the papal court. His personal history was recounted at some length and he was described as a scholar in the diocese of York. On 29 May 1490 the pope intervened on behalf of this friar who, under the care of his stepmother, at the age of 7 or under had been induced to enter the order and did so with childish levity. At 14 he tried to leave, but the friars would not allow it, and he was forced to make profession. About 1476 he fled and was considered as an apostate by the friars. Pope Innocent VIII cleared him of any taint of apostasy and ruled that profession had been made by virtue of force and fear (*BF, ns*, ii–iv, pp. 644, 690–91, nn. 1736, 1845; *CPL*, xiv, pp. 38–39).

SILVESTON, John: he was licensed to hear confessions in the diocese of York at an unknown date. He was replaced by John of Nottingham at another unknown date during the administration of Archbishop Thoresby (BIA, Register 11, fol. 397r).

SIMMONDS (Symonds, Symondeshened), John: he was ordained a. on 24 September 1373 in St Mary, Bishophill Senior, York (BIA, Register 11, fol. 392v).

SIMMONSIDE (Symondsyde), Robert: he was a friar of Scarborough when he was ordained a. on 13 June 1489 at Blackfriars, York. He was a friar of York when he was ordained s. on 18 September 1490 at Whitefriars, York. He was back at Scarborough when he was ordained d. on 26 February 1491 at Greyfriars, York and p. on 28 May 1491 at Holy Trinity Priory, Micklegate, York (BIA, Register 23, fols. 417v, 423v, 425v, 428r. Cf. Cross and Vickers, *MFN*, p. 437).

SIMMS (Symmys, Symys), William: he was a friar of York when he was ordained a. on 7 March 1506 at Whitefriars, York, s. on 18 December 1507 at Austin Friars, York, d. on 22 September 1509 at Holy Trinity Priory, Micklegate, York, and p. on 25 May 1510 at Blackfriars, York (BIA, Register 25, fol. 131v, Register 5A, fol. 582v, Register 26, fols. 103v, 108v. Cf. Cross and Vickers, *MFN*, pp. 441, 449). He was granted a licence to preach and hear confessions in the diocese of York on 24 July 1534 (BIA, Register 28, fol. 85v). He may have been at Doncaster on 30 June 1538, when he was left 3s. 4d. in the will of John Wheite of Ancres, who was buried at Sprotborurgh, near Doncaster (BIA, Probate Register 11, fol. 331r.).

SIMMS (Symyes), William: a novice and one of the ten friars of Doncaster who signed the deed of surrender on 20 November 1538 (*Eighth Report of the Deputy Keeper of the Public Records*, p. 19. Cf. Cross and Vickers, *MFN*, pp. 447, 449).

SIMON [no surname given]: in an inventory of the effects of Thomas de Dalby, archdeacon of Richmond, on 21 May 1400 this friar received a mantle (*TE*, iii, pp. 9–22, at 21; *Probate Inventories of the York Diocese, 1350–1500*, p. 506).

SIMPSON (Symson), Thomas: he was a friar of Lincoln when he was ordained s. on 16 March 1521 at Sleaford prebendal church, d. on 30 March 1521 in Lincoln cathedral (LAO, Register 25, fols. 135r, 136r), and p. on 21 September 1521 in the prebendal church at Buckden (LAO, Register 26, fol. 1v). Formerly of Lincoln, he received his capacity on 8 October 1539 (Chambers, *Faculty Office Registers 1534–1549*, p. 195).

SISSON (Sysson), Robert: he was a friar of York when he was ordained a. on 6 March 1479. He was ordained s. on 27 March 1479, and d. on 17 March 1481. He was a friar of York when he was ordained p. on 2 March 1482 at Austin Friars, York. The first, third and fourth ceremonies took place at Austin Friars, York; the second one was held at Greyfriars, York (BIA, Register 22, fols. 376r, 377v, Register 23, fols. 374r, 380v. Cf. Cross and Vickers, *MFN*, p. 435).

SKELLAWE (Skellaw), William de: he was ordained a. and. s. on 18 December 1372 at Whitefriars, York, and at Beverley when he was ordained d. on 24 September 1373 at St Mary, Bishophill Senior (BIA, Register 11, fols. 389v, 392v).

SKELTON, John: he was ordained d. on 22 September 1403 at Blackfriars, York (*Reg. Scrope*, ii, pp. 55, 103, 131).

SKESTELYNGH, William de: he was a friar licensed to hear confessions in the diocese of York in June 1350 (BIA, Register 10, fol. 279r).

SKIPTON, Richard: the son of Alice and John Skipton, a skinner, citizen of York and a parishioner of St Peter the Little. His father's will is not extant. His mother's will of 18 October 1437 states that her husband had predeceased her and been buried at Greyfriars in York. She requested burial beside him and her mortuary offering was left to the rector of her parish church, the Franciscan bishop of Dromore. Offerings were made towards the fabric of York Minster and her parish church. The only mendicants to benefit from her will were the Greyfriars. Alice asked Richard, her son, to administer the residue of her estate for the welfare of her soul. By choosing burial in Greyfriars Richard's parents ensured that their graves would be well tended and that there would be a perpetual remembrance of their souls in the community's necrology and its devotional exercises (BIA, Probate Register 3, fol. 506r).

SKIPWITH (Skypwyth), Thomas: he was ordained s. on 17 December 1345 at Liddington prebendal church (LAO, Register 7B, fol. 2r), d. on 15 March 1348 at York Minster, and p. on 14 June 1348 at St Mary's Abbey, York (BIA, Register 10A, fols. 21v, 25r).

SKIPWITH (Skypwith), Thomas: he was a friar of Beverley when he was ordained p. on 19 September 1349 at York Minster (BIA, Register 10A, fol. 34r).

SKIRB', William de: he was ordained s. on 21 December 1342 at St George's parish church in Doncaster (BIA, Register 10A, fol. 2v; *Reg. Kirkby*, i, p. 151, no. 733).

SKIRBECK (Skyrbek), Richard de: he was the guardian of Lincoln in the Michaelmas term of 1351 when he was mentioned in the plea rolls (TNA, CP40/367, mm. 173d, attorneys 8).

SKIRBECK (Skyrbek), Walter: he was ordained a. and s. on 5 March 1384 at the church of St Michael-le-Belfrey, York (BIA, Register 12, fol. 141r).

SKIRBECK (Skirbek, Skyrbek), William de: he was a friar of Boston when he was ordained s. on 22 December 1352. He was a friar of Lincoln when he was ordained d. on 19 May 1353; both ceremonies took place at the prebendal church of Stow (LAO, Register 9D, fols. 63v, 66v).

SLATER (Sclater, Sclatter), Thomas: he was a friar of York when he was ordained a. on 10 June 1503 at Blackfriars, York, and s. on 23 September 1503 at Greyfriars, York (BIA, Register 25, fols. 118v, 120r). He was a friar of Oxford when he was ordained d. on 8 March 1505 in the conventual church of Osney and d. on 18 March 1505 and p. on 18 March 1508 in Buckden prebendal church (LAO, Register 24, fols. 49r, 69v). He was admitted to the *Corpus Christi* guild at York in 1510 (*Corpus Christi Register*, p. 173). He went to Cambridge, where he took his B.D. in 1520 (*Grace Book B*, ii, p. 78; *Grace Book Γ*, p. 183). On 15 December 1524 John Marshall, a merchant of York and parishioner of St Mary at Castlegate, left him 10s. (*TE*, v, pp. 191–93). He was guardian of Scarborough. During a quarrel between the friars of the town and the chaplain of the parish in 1532 it was alleged that the friars had spent 20 marks belonging to the parish church. Slater was said to have been in the town for two years, as the previous guardian (Cause Papers, G 222; *GFC*, p. 208). On the grounds of age and education it is unlikely that the former friar can be identified with the priest of the same name, who was aged 57 in 1548. This priest was the incumbent of Sir Ralph Bulmer's chantry in St Michael-le-Belfrey, York, and was 'of honest qualities and condicions and not lerened' (*Chantries, Guilds, Hospitals*, ii, pp. 469–70; Cross and Vickers, *MFN*, pp. 440, 451, 452)

SLEAFORD (Sleford), John: he was a friar of York when he was ordained a. on 19 September 1450 at Greyfriars, York (BIA, Register 19, fol. 287v).

SLEDMER (Sledin), Robert: he was ordained s. on 19 December 1366 at St Leonard's Hospital, York, d. on 26 May 1369 at Bishopthorpe manor chapel, and p. on 20 December 1371 at St Mary, Bishophill Senior, York (BIA, Register 11, fols. 364v, 374r, 386r).

SLESTELING, William de: he was ordained p. on 20 September 1343 at Whitefriars, York (BIA, Register 10A, fol. 5r).

SMALES, Henry: he was ordained d. on 19 December 1478 at Holy Trinity Priory, Micklegate, York, and p. on 18 December 1479 at Austin Friars, York (BIA, Register 22, fols. 375r, 381v).

SMART, Thomas: he was a friar of Lincoln when he was ordained p. on 3 April 1507 in the chapel of St Mary Magdalene in Lincoln cathedral (LAO, Register 24, fol. 65v).

SMELT, Richard: he was a friar of York when he was ordained s. on 21 September 1482 at Whitefriars, York, d. on 21 December 1482 at Austin Friars, York, and p. on 18 September 1484 at Whitefriars, York (BIA, Register 23, fols. 383v, 384v, 394r. Cf. Cross and Vickers, *MFN*, p. 435). He was at York on 26 February 1489 when William Cerff requested him to celebrate a trental of Masses for him (BIA, Probate Register 5, fols. 357v–58r).

SMERT (Smerte), Thomas: he was a friar of Doncaster when he was ordained s. on 19 December 1506 at Austin Friars, York, and d. on 20 March 1507 at Greyfriars, York (BIA, Register 25, fols. 136r, 138r. Cf. Cross and Vickers, *MFN*, p. 442).

SMETHETON (Smeaton), Peter de: he was ordained p. on 18 December 1294 at Stow prebendal church (*Reg. Sutton*, vii, p. 61).

SMITH (Smyth), George: he was a friar of York when he was ordained p. on 7 April

1492 at Whitefriars, York (BIA, Register 23, fol. 431v. Cf. Cross and Vickers, *MFN*, p. 437).

SMITH (Smyth, Smythe), John: he was a friar of York when he was ordained a. on 14 March 1489 at Holy Trinity Priory, Micklegate, York, s. on 4 April 1489 at Greyfriars, York, d. on 18 September 1490 at Blackfriars, York, and p. on 28 May 1491 at Holy Trinity Priory (BIA, Register 23, fols. 415r, 416r, 423v, 428r. Cf. Cross and Vickers, *MFN*, 437). John Smith, a bachelor of theology at Oxford, supplicated on 30 June 1506 to incept in theology. This was granted on condition that he did so before 2 February 1507. He was a still a bachelor of theology on 27 November 1506, when he submitted another supplicat and this time he was granted a dispensation to do this before the feast of the Annunciation on conditon that appropriate suffrages were offered for the regent house. On 26 January 1507 he supplicated for permission to incept in theology. He had studied theology for four years as a bachelor. He was dispensed from the *depositiones* on 3 July 1507. On 20 November 1507 he obtained a dispensation to defer his sermon before the feast of the conversion of St Paul. On 28 June 1508 he was dispensed from his sermon (*Register of Congregations 1505–1517*, i, pp. 416, 430, 435, 443, 479, 492–93, 530). He was appointed an executor of the will of Nicholas Upton of Northolme by Wainfleet, Lincolnshire, on 9 January 1533 (*Lincoln Wills, 1532–1534*, pp. 92–93, no. 139). He was described as recently guardian of Lincoln when he was dispensed to hold a benefice with a change of habit on 8 October 1539 (Chambers, *Faculty Office Registers 1534–1549*, p. 195).

SMITH (Smyth), Richard: he was a friar of York when he was ordained p. on 6 April 1504 in the lady chapel of York Minster (BIA, Register 25, fol. 124r. Cf. Cross and Vickers, *MFN*, p. 441).

SMITH (Smythe), Roger: he was a friar of Beverley when he was ordained s. on 18 September 1518 and at York when ordained d. on 18 December 1518 at Austin Friars, York (BIA, Register 27, fols. 181v, 182v). He was formerly a friar of Scarborough on 20 June 1539 when he obtained his capacity (Chambers, *Faculty Office Registers 1534–1549*, p. 187. Cf. Cross and Vickers, *MFN*, pp. 444, 454).

SMITH (Smyth), Thomas: he was a friar of York when ordained a. on 23 September 1503, s. on 2 March 1504 at Whitefriars, York, and d. on 23 March 1504. The first and third ordinations took place at Greyfriars, York (BIA, Register 25, fols. 120r, 122r, 123r. Cf. Cross and Vickers, *MFN*, p. 440).

SMITH (Smyth), William: he was a friar of York when he was ordained p. on 18 December 1512 at Austin Friars, York (BIA, Register 26, fol. 121v. Cf. Cross and Vickers, *MFN*, p. 444).

SNAWDON, Peter: one of the ten friars of Doncaster who signed the deed of surrender on 20 November 1538 (*Eighth Report of the Deputy Keeper of the Public Records*, p. 19. Cf. Cross and Vickers, *MFN*, p. 447).

SNAWHALLE (Snawball, Snaweball), John: he was a friar of York when he was ordained a. on 19 September 1450 at Greyfriars, York, and s. on 26 May 1453 at Blackfriars, York (BIA Register 19, fol. 295v, Register 20, fol. 415r). A Friar Snawball was left 5s. to celebrate a trental of Masses for Henry Salvin (Salvane), who, on 15 September 1464, asked for burial in the York Greyfriars (*TE*, ii, pp. 263–64). A

Friar Snaweball was guardian of Doncaster in the Hilary term of 1492, when he was named in the plea rolls (TNA, CP40/919, m. 314). A John Snowball was a beneficiary of the will of Master William Ecopp, rector of Heslerton, on 6 September 1472 (*TE*, iii, pp. 199–200).

SNITHERTON, Thomas de: he was ordained a. at an unknown venue and date between September 1346 and September 1347 (BIA, Register 10A, fol. 18a).

SOFTLAW, William: he was the lector of York when he was licensed to hear confessions on 30 August 1398 (*Reg. Scrope*, ii, p. 12, no. 729).

SOUTHCOTE (Sthycote), Thomas: he was ordained a. on 22 March 1477 at Greyfriars, York (BIA, Register 22, fol. 365r).

SPALDING (Spaldyng), John: he was ordained s. on 18 September 1361 at Cawood manor chapel and d. on 27 May 1363 at Bishopthorpe manor chapel (BIA, Register 11, fols. 345r, 353r).

SPALDING, William de: he was ordained s. on 17 December 1345 at Liddington prebendal church, d. on 17 March 1347 in Burton parish church beside Lincoln and p. on 14 June 1348 at Bardney Abbey (LAO, Register 7B, fols. 2r, 11r, Register 9D, fol. 5r).

SPARHAM, John: he was a friar of Lincoln when he was ordained d. on 29 March 1483 in the church of St Peter-at-arches (LAO, Register 22, fol. 11).

SPARHONK (Sparhouk, Sparhawke), John: he was ordained a. on 26 February 1480 at Greyfriars, York. He was a friar of York when he was ordained s. on 22 February 1483 at Holy Trinity Priory, Micklegate, York, and p. on 20 September 1483 at Whitefriars, York (BIA, Register 22, fol. 382r, Register 23, fols. 385v, 389r). He was a friar of Lincoln on 5 May 1509 when he witnessed the will of Thomas Meryng, gentleman and a parishioner of St Swithin, Lincoln. Meryng had requested burial in the city's Greyfriars (*Lincoln Wills, 1271–1532*, i, p. 39). A former friar of this name was at Lincoln when he received his capacity on 8 October 1539 (Chambers, *Faculty Office Registers 1534–1549*, p. 195).

SPELLAN, Dionysius: he was ordained p. on 22 September 1408 at Holy Trinity Priory, Micklegate, York (BIA, Register 18, fol. 39v).

SPILSBY (Spillesby, Spilleby), John: he was ordained a. on 9 June 1403 in the chapel of St Nicholas, Bawtry, s. on 20 September 1404, d. on 20 December 1404, both at All Saints, Cawood (*Reg. Scrope*, ii, pp. 55, 105, 131), and p. on 5 June 1406 at Austin Friars, York (BIA, Register 5A, fol. 322v; *Reg. Sede Vacante, York, 1405–08*, pp. 66, 82, 89). On 25 February 1443 John Spilleby, a Franciscan, received 6s. 8d. in the will of Margaret Kirkham, a widow of York (BIA, Probate Register 2, fol. 61v).

SPRANGE, Henry: he was a friar of Lincoln when he was ordained d. on 15 March 1432 at Sleaford prebendal church (LAO, Register 17, fol. 206r).

SPRINGTHORPE (Spryngthorp), John: he was ordained a. and s. on 19 May 1380 at Stillingfleet parish church (BIA, Register 12, fols. 136v, 137r).

SPROTE, John: he was a friar of York when he was ordained p. on 20 December 1522 at Austin Friars, York (BIA, Register 27, fol. 197v. Cf. Cross and Vickers, *MFN*, p. 445).

SPROTTON, John de: he was licensed to hear confessions in the diocese of Lincoln on 31 January 1334 (LAO, Register 5, fol. 471r).

SPRYNGHYNG (Springing), John: he was a friar of York when he was ordained p. on 18 December 1507 at Austin Friars, York (BIA, Register 5A, fol. 584v).

STAG (Stage), John: he was a friar of York when he was ordained s. on 12 March 1446 and d. on 25 March 1447; both ceremonies were at St Leonard's Hospital, York (BIA, Register 19, fols. 225v, 283v).

STAINDROP, John de: he was licensed in the diocese of York, but replaced on 6 January 1352 (BIA, Register 10, fol. 280r).

STALYNBURGH, William de: he was a friar of Beverley when ordained a. on 21 December 1359. He was ordained d. on 19 December 1360; both ceremonies took place at Cawood manor chapel (BIA, Register 11, fols. 339r, 343r).

STAMFORD (Staunford), Hugh de: he was ordained s. on 31 May 1292 at Lincoln cathedral and d. on 24 September 1295 at Berkhamstead parish church (*Reg. Sutton*, vii, pp. 26, 69).

STANDBERGH, John de: he was ordained s. on 22 December 1380 at Greyfriars, York (BIA, Register 12, fol. 138r).

STANDISH, Oliver: a *scolar in sacra theologia* admitted to hear confessions in the archdeaconry of Richmond on 10 September 1444 (BIA, Register 19, fol. 214v. Cf. Hamilton Thompson, 'The Register of the Archdeacons of Richmond, 1442–1477', part one, 1442–1465, p. 84).

STANFORD (Staynford), John: he was a friar of York when he was ordained s. on 19 December 1405, d. on 27 March 1406, and p. on 18 September 1406 at Austin Friars, York; all three ceremonies took place at Blackfriars, York (BIA, Register 5A, fols. 319r, 321r, 323r; *Reg. Sede Vacanter, York, 1405–08*, pp. 66, 82, 89).

STANFORD, Robert: he was licensed in the diocese of York at an unknown date. After his death he was replaced by Thomas Kyngesbury. No date is given (BIA, Register 11, fol. 397r).

STANGROND, John: he was ordained d. on 17 December 1345 at Liddington prebendal church and p. on 17 March 1347 in Burton parish church close to Lincoln (LAO, Register 7B, fols. 2v, 11v).

STANLAKE, John: he was ordained p. on 22 December 1403 in the chapel of St Nicholas, Bawtry (*Reg. Scrope*, ii, pp. 55, 105, 131).

STANLAY (Stanley), Nicholas: he was ordained p. on 14 June 1348 at Bardney Abbey (LAO, Register 9D, fol. 5r).

STANTON, John de: he was the only son of Agnes and John de Stanton, parishioners of St Michael-le-Belfrey, which was adjacent to York Minster. His father was a clerk in the diocese of Ely and public notary in York and his connection with Ely may indicate that he or his ancestors hailed from Stanton, north-east of Bury St Edmunds. There was a Stanton to the north of York. Another John de Stanton, a cleric of York, was appointed as his executor. There was another friar of this name at York in the early fifteenth century. The public notary compiled the will of John senior on 15 September 1386 and requested burial in his parish church beside the body of Agnes, his wife. The customary offering was made to his parish church for his funeral and for forgotten tithes. Money was left to the parochial chaplain and arrangements were made for ten chaplains to celebrate Masses for him on the day of his burial. The sum of 30s. 8d. was set aside for his funeral expenses and for the gathering of his friends. The testator appointed John de Stanton, a clerk and his executor, to supervise the payment of alms to the poor in the year following his death. Another John de Stanton, the testator's son and a friar, was given a small book entitled *Florent Moralium*, a volume which addressed the theological virtues of faith, hope and charity. He received five marks in sterling to remember his father in his prayers. This may have been interpreted as a request for his father's name to be enrolled in the friary's martyrology; the testator's failure to solicit prayers for his deceased wife is a curious omission. In September 1386 there may have been some concerns about the friar's health because the testator inserted a clause which would be invoked in the event of his son predeceasing him (York Minster, Dean and Chapter Library, MS.L 2/4, fols. 87v–88r). It is probable that John was clothed in the habit of St Francis at the local friary and embarked upon his theological studies in the 1340s. He may have been associated with John de Staunton, a friar of York, ordained d. on 26 May 1358 at Greyfriars, York, and p. on 15 June 1359 (BIA, Register 11, fols. 333v, 338r). A John de Staynton was guardian of Lincoln when he was mentioned in the plea rolls in the Michaelmas term of 1375 and the Trinity term of the following year (TNA, KB27/459, attorneys, m. 3, and KB27/462, mm. 8d, 64d).

STANTON (Staynton), John: he was ordained d. on 23 September 1402 at Blackfriars, York, and p. on 9 June 1403 in the chapel of St Nicholas, Bawtry (*Reg. Scrope*, ii, pp. 55, 105, 131).

STAVELL, Nicholas de: he was ordained d. on 26 May 1347 at Lincoln cathedral (LAO, Register 7B, fol. 14v).

STAWRAY (Stawra, Staura), William: he was a friar of York when he was ordained a. on 26 March 1502 in the lady chapel of York Minster, s. on 20 September 1505 in Bishopthorpe manor chapel, York, and p. on 28 March 1506 at Greyfriars, York (BIA, Register 25, fols. 111v, 130r, 133r. Cf. Cross and Vickers, *MFN*, p. 440).

STAYNDORP (Staindrop), Robert de: he was the guardian of York when on 27 October 1322 Edward II gave him a safe-conduct, valid until Whitsunday, to go to Scotland on affairs concerning John of Brittany, earl of Richmond, who had been captured at Byland that month. Robert and another English friar were authorised to remain with the earl 'for his recreation and solace' (*CPR, 1321–1324*, p. 210).

STENETON, William de: he was ordained p. on 7 June 1343 at Greyfriars, York (BIA, Register 10A, fol. 4v).

STEVENSON, Hugh: he was a friar of Newcastle when he was ordained a. on

30 March 1499 in the chapel of the south aisle of Durham cathedral (*Reg. Fox*, p. 85). He was at York when ordained s. on 18 September 1501 at Greyfriars, York. He was a friar of Richmond when he was ordained d. on 18 December 1501 at Whitefriars, York. He was back at York again when he was ordained p. on 26 March 1502 in the lady chapel of York Minster (BIA, Register 25, fols. 109v, 111r, 112r. Cf. Cross and Vickers, *MFN*, p. 440).

STEVENSON, William: he was a friar of York when he was ordained a. on 18 December 1512 at Austin Friars, York, and d. on 2 June 1515 at Blackfriars, York (BIA, Register 26, fol. 121r, Register 27, fol. 169r. Cf. Cross and Vickers, *MFN*, p. 444).

STIXWALD, William: he was a friar of York on 18 September 1426 when he witnessed the public revocation by Thomas Richmond (*Convocation, York*, pp. 399–400; *Records of Northern Convocation*, p. 167).

STOCKWITH (Stockwyth, Stokwyt), Thomas: he was ordained a. on 22 December 1403 in the chapel of St Nicholas, Bawtry, s. on 20 September 1404, d. on 20 December 1404, both at All Saints, Cawood (*Reg. Scrope*, ii, pp. 55, 106, 131), and p. on 5 June 1406 at Austin Friars, York (BIA, Register 5A, fol. 322v; *Reg. Sede Vacante, York, 1405–08*, pp. 66, 82, 89). He was at Beverley on 28 February 1424 when he was granted 40s. by King Henry VI (*CCR, 1422–1429*, p. 486).

STOKDALE (Stokdall), Richard: he was a friar of Beverley when he was ordained a. on 10 March 1498 at Greyfriars, York, and s. on 22 September 1498 at Austin Friars, York. He was a friar of York when he was ordained d. on 23 February 1499 at Holy Trinity Priory, Micklegate, York, and p. on 16 March 1499 at Whitefriars, York (BIA, Register 23, fols. 458r, 461r, 462r, 463r. Cf. Cross and Vickers, *MFN*, p. 439).

STOKESLAY, William de: he was a friar of Beverley when ordained d. on 22 December 1358 at Cawood manor chapel. He was ordained p. on 18 December 1361 at York Minster (BIA, Register 11, fols. 335v, 347r).

STOKTON, Walter de: he received the royal alms of 35s. 4d. for the friary of Lincoln on 24 May 1300 (*Liber quotidianus contrarotulatoris garderobae*, p. 37). He received the royal alms of 44s. for three days for a second time for that friary on 7 January 1305 (BL, MS.Add. 35292, fol. 64v).

STONE, John de: he was ordained s. on 24 September 1351 in York Minster and d. on 2 June 1352 at St Mary's Abbey, York (BIA, Register 10A, fols. 52v, 55r).

STRANGLAND, William: he was a friar of York when he was ordained s. on 26 May 1464 at Blackfriars, York (BIA, Register 20, fol. 459v).

STRANTON, John: he was ordained p. on 17 December 1412 at Greyfriars, York (BIA, Register 18, fol. 395v).

STRASBOURG (Argentina), John Heinrici de: he was at York when ordained d. on 25 March 1447 at St Leonard's Hospital, York (BIA, Register 19, fol. 225v). He was at Oxford for some years and supplicated for the B.Th. on 20 October 1449. On 22 July 1456 he obtained a dispensation to hold a benefice when he was a chaplain and continual commensal of Queen Margaret (*CPL*, xi, p. 118). He became rector of Bix, Oxfordshire, in 1457, but left the next year to become rector of Whitchurch (1457–62). In 1460 he was rector of St Olaf's, Chester (Jones, *The Church in Chester 1300–1540*, p. 178). On 30 November 1459 he obtained a further dispensation to hold another benefice (*CPL*, xi, p. 562; *BF, ns*, ii, pp. 102, 370; *BRUO*, p. 45).

STRATFORTH, Edmund: he was a friar of York when he was ordained a. on 23 September 1503 at Greyfriars, York, and s. on 6 April 1504 in the lady chapel of York Minster (BIA, Register 25, fols. 120r, 123v. Cf. Cross and Vickers, *MFN*, p. 440).

STRATHERN (Stakedern), Roger de: he was ordained p. on 23 September 1290 at St Leonard's church in Stamford (*Reg. Sutton*, vii, p. 7).

STRELLEY, Thomas: he was ordained p. on 5 June 1417 at the prebendal chapel of Cawood (BIA, Register 18, fol. 397v).

STRETTON, John: he was a friar of York when he was ordained a. on 23 May 1377 at York Minster. He was ordained s. on 12 June 1378 at Greyfriars, York (BIA, Register 12, fols. 128r, 132v). He was at Stafford when ordained d. on 18 December 1378 and at Lichfield when ordained p. on 9 March 1381 in the diocese of Coventry and Lichfield. Both ceremonies took place at Colwich prebendal church (*Reg. Stretton*, pp. 342, 360).

STURMY (Sturme, Stormy, Sturrne, Sturyne), John: he was ordained a. on 7 June 1343 at Greyfriars, York, s. on 18 December 1344 at Whitefriars, York, and d. at an unspecified location and date between 23 September 1346 and 22 September 1347 (BIA, Register 10A, fols. 3v, 8v, 18A).

STURMY, William: he was licensed in the diocese of Lincoln in October 1346 in place of John de Retford who had died (LAO, Register 7, fol. 99r). He was licensed in the diocese of York on 17 October 1347 in place of the deceased Roger of Chester (BIA, Register 10, fol. 278r).

STYNETON, William de: he was licensed to hear confessions and to preach in the diocese of York on 11 March 1349 (BIA, Register 10, fol. 278v).

SUDBURY, John de: he was a friar of York when he was ordained a. on 19 September 1377 at St Mary's Abbey, York (BIA, Register 12, fol. 129r).

SUTELL (Sotyll), Nicholas: he was a friar of York when he was ordained s. on 6 March 1490 at Holy Trinity Priory, Micklegate, York, d. on 18 September 1490 at Whitefriars, York, and p. on 26 February 1491 at Greyfriars, York (BIA, Register 23, fols. 420v, 423v, 425v. Cf. Cross and Vickers, *MFN*, p. 437).

SUTTERTON (Suterton), Thomas de: he was ordained d. on 19 September 1293 at Lincoln cathedral and p. on 18 September 1294 at Dunstable (*Reg. Sutton*, vii, pp. 42, 58). He was probably a friar of Grimsby when licensed to hear confessions in the diocese of Lincoln on 20 June 1318 (LAO, Register 3, fol. 380rv). He was licensed again in January 1334 (LAO, Register 5, fol. 471r).

SUTTON, Geoffrey: he was ordained p. in Lincoln cathedral on 26 May 1347 (LAO, Register 7B, fol. 15v).

SUTTON, John de: he was ordained a. on 12 March 1351 at Blackfriars, York, and s. on 24 September 1351 in York Minster (BIA, Register 10A, fols. 50v, 52v).

SUTTON, Robert de: a friar of York, priest and professed. He died c.1327 (Little, '*Records, Franciscan Province*', p. 148).

SUTTON, William de: he was ordained a. on 21 December 1364 at Greyfriars, York. He was at Doncaster when he was ordained s. on 3 June 1368 at Bishopthorpe manor chapel (BIA, Register 11, fols. 358r, 369v).

SWABY, John de: he was ordained s. on 18 December 1294 at Stow prebendal church, d. on 19 May 1296 at Lincoln cathedral, and p. on 21 December 1297 at Louth prebendal church (*Reg. Sutton*, vii, pp. 60, 79, 101).

SWALE, Robert: he was ordained p. on 17 December 1429 at Austin Friars, York (BIA, Register 19, fol. 236r).

SWALMAN, Martin: he was a friar of York when he was ordained s. on 24 March 1425 at St Michael-le-Belfrey, York (BIA, Register 5A, fol. 402v; *Reg. Sede Vacante, York, 1423–26*, pp. 99, 118, 125).

SWAN (Swanne), William: he was a friar of York when ordained a. on 7 June 1460 at Whitefriars, York, and s. on 28 February 1461 at Blackfriars, York. He was at Doncaster when ordained d. on 19 September 1461 at Blackfriars, York (BIA, Register 20, fols. 444r, 446v, 449r).

SWELLOLEGH, Wiliam de: he was ordained p. on 21 February 1377 at Whitefriars, York (BIA, Register 12, fol. 127v).

SWILLINGTON (Swillyngton), John: he was a friar of York when he was ordained d. on 26 May 1453 at Blackfriars, York. He was described as an Austin Friar of York when he was ordained p. on 22 September 1453 at Greyfriars, York (BIA, Register 20, fols. 415r, 416r).

SWYNBORN (Gwynborne, Swinburn, Swynborne), William: he was a friar of York when ordained a. on 18 February 1497 at Greyfriars, York, s. on 19 December 1500 at Austin Friars, York, d. on 6 March 1501 at Greyfriars, York, and p. on 5 June 1501 at Blackfriars, York (BIA, Register 23, fol. 453v, Register 5A, fols. 529v, 531r, Register 25, fol. 109r). Afterwards he was at Cambridge where he took his B.D. in 1514–15 and his D.D. in 1516–17 (Venn, *Alumni Cantabrigienses*, pt.1, iv, p. 193). He was the guardian of Cambridge in 1527–28 (*Grace Book B*, ii, pp. 36, 51, 54, 143, *Grace Book Γ*, pp. 128, 236; *GFC*, p. 214). On 6 July 1534 Friar George Browne, who was visiting the northern friaries for the government, sent this friar to London for examination on suspicion of having written 'divers libels' against King Henry VIII, particularly against his 'just matrimony'. Browne's judgement that the friar could not have written such works, since he was 'poorly booked and poorly learned', was contradicted by the observation of the Gilbertine sub-prior of Watton after the Pilgrimage of Grace; the sub-prior's statement is bolstered by the friar's academic achievements at Cambridge (*LPFD*, vii, p. 363, no. 953 XII, pt. 1, 98–100, no. 201; Cross and Vickers, *MFN*, pp. 438, 447).

SWYNESHEDE, John: he was ordained d. on 20 September 1399 in the prebendal church of Sherburn in Elmet (*Reg. Scrope*, ii, pp. 55, 107, 131).

TACHAN, Thomas de: he was a friar of Grimsby when he was ordained d. on 21 December 1359 in Lincoln cathedral (LAO, Register 9D, fol. 93v).

TADCASTER, Thomas de: a friar of Boston who was licensed to hear confessions in the diocese of Lincoln within the *limitatio* of that house on 10 August 1300 and again on 12 October 1300 (Little, *Franciscan Papers, Lists, and Documents*, pp. 237, 238). A Thomas de Tademinstre, a Franciscan, was described as prior of the community in Lincoln, when his view on the 'Templars' vices was cited by Roger de Ware, a Dominican, in 1310/11. The editor interprets this as an error for Tadcaster (*Proceedings against Templars*, i, p. 197, ii, pp. 213–14, n. 168). He was a friar of Grimsby at his death c.1327 (Little, '*Records, Franciscan Province*', p. 150).

TALBOT, John: he was ordained s. on 19 December 1383 at All Saints, Cawood (BIA, Register 12, fol. 140v).

TALBOT, William: he was ordained a. on 18 September 1406 at Blackfriars, York (BIA, Register 5A, fol. 322v; *Reg. Sede Vacante, York, 1405–08*, pp. 66, 83, 89). A friar of an unspecified order was ordained s. on 6 June 1411 at Spalding Priory (Canterbury Registers: Arundel, ii, fol. 88v). This entry might be merged with the one below, although the lapse of time is unusually long.

TALBOT, William: he was a friar of York when he was ordained d. on 23 September 1413 in the diocese of Salisbury (*Reg. Hallum*, p. 180).

TAMWORTH, Robert: he was ordained s. on 17 December 1351. He was a friar of Boston when he was ordained d. on 3 March 1352; both ceremonies took place in Sleaford prebendal church (LAO, Register 9D, fols. 55r, 57v).

TANFELD, John: he was a friar of Boston when he was ordained s. on 20 September 1421 at Sleaford prebendal church and d. on 7 March 1422 in the prebendal church of Liddington (*Reg. Fleming*, ii, pp. 77, 82, nn. 480, 482).

TATEWIC (Tatwyk), William de: a note on the flyleaf of Peterhouse Library, Cambridge, MS.89, a copy of the *Moralia in Job*, states that William de Tatewic commissioned this copy of Gregory the Great's *Moralia in Job* with the help of friends, and that he had indexed it himself (fols. 253–85). In 1299, presumably as soon as the book was completed, Hugh of Hartlepool, minister provincial, permitted William to assign it to the Lincoln Greyfriars after the death of Thomas Whapelad, who had been been given the use of it during his lifetime: *iste Liber pertinet ad communitatem fratrum minorum Lincolnia post decessum fratris Thome de quappelod' per assignacionem fratris Willelmi de Tatewic. de Licencia fratris hugonis de hertelpoll' provincialis ministri Anno domini. m.cc. xcix. quem dictus frater W. scribi fecit et de amicorum suorum elemosinis pro scriptura satisfieri procuravit et nichilhominus manu sua a principio ad finem diligenter correxit et notablia specili in marginibus titulavit et per decursum alphabeti in separatis quaternis pro modum tabule designavit et ideo quicumque huius libri 'usum' habuerit tanquam gratus laboribus fructuosis orare dignetur pro anima predicti fratris. W. et orent pro eo omnes sancti. Amen* (Robinson, *Catalogue of Dated and Datable Manuscripts c.737–1600 in Cambridge Libraries*, i, p. 83; Parkes, 'Layout and Presentation of the Text', p. 72, n. 118; *BRUO*, pp. 2029–30). He was a friar of Lincoln when he was licensed to hear confessions for that house on 12 October 1300 (Little, *Franciscan Papers, Lists, and Documents*, p. 238).

TAUNTON, John: he was ordained d. on 17 March 1397 at Greyfriars, York (BIA, Register 5A, fol. 230r; BL, MS. Cotton Galba, E.X, fol. 130v). He was a friar of Boston when he was ordained p. on 22 February 1399 at Stow prebendal church (LAO, Register 13, fol. 85v).

TAYLOR (Tailyor), Simon: he was a friar of York when ordained a. on 19 September 1489 at Whitefriars, York, s. on 18 September 1490 at Whitefriars, York, d. on 18 December 1490 at Austin Friars, York, and p. on 26 February 1491 at Greyfriars, York (BIA, Register 23, fols. 418v, 423v, 424v 425v. Cf. Cross and Vickers, *MFN*, p. 437).

TAYLOR (Taylyor), Thomas: a novice at York at the Dissolution on 27 November 1538 (*Eighth Report of the Deputy Keeper of the Public Records*, p. 51). A Thomas Taylor, clerk, and five others, all from Langton upon Swale in Yorkshire, were pardoned on 25 April 1570 for their participation in the rebellion of the earls. This man might have been the former friar (Cf. Cross and Vickers, *MFN*, p. 460).

TEBALD, William: he was a friar of York when he was ordained d. on 8 March 1438 at Whitefriars, York (BIA, Register 19, fol. 256v).

TELE (Tile), John: he was ordained s. on 7 March 1433 at Greyfriars, York, d. on 28 March 1433 at St Michael-le-Belfrey, York, and at Beverley when he was ordained p. on 16 March 1437 at St Leonard's Hospital, York (BIA, Register 19, fols. 243v, 244r, 253r).

TELLER, John: he was ordained p. on 21 December 1342 at St George's parish church in Doncaster (BIA, Register 10A, fol. 2v; *Reg. Kirkby*, i, p. 154, no. 733).

TEMPEST, Richard: he was ordained p. on 19 September 1383 at St Mary, Bishophill Senior, York (BIA, Register 14, fol. 140r).

TERBOKE (Terbok'), Richard: on 26 January 1415 the bishop was at Sleaford when he licensed this friar to preach and hear confessions in the diocese of Lincoln, in accordance with the constitution *Super Cathedram* (*Reg. Repingdon*, iii, p. 39, no. 49).

TERRINGTON (Teryngton), Thomas: he was a friar of Beverley when he was ordained a. on 22 September 1487 at Whitefriars, York. He was a friar at York when he was ordained s. on 14 March 1489 at Holy Trinity Priory, Micklegate, York, and at Scarborough when ordained d. on 13 June 1489 at Blackfriars, York. He returned to York and was there when ordained p. on 27 March 1490 at Greyfriars, York (BIA, Register 23, fols. 408v, 415v, 418r, 421v. Cf. Cross and Vickers, *MFN*, p. 436).

THELBY, William de: he was ordained a. on 13 March 1350 at Beverley Minster (BIA, Register 10A, fol. 44r).

THETILTHORP (Thethilthorp), John: he was ordained s. on 21 December 1398, d. on 22 February 1399, both in Cawood church, and p. on 17 December 1401 at St Mary's Abbey, York (*Reg. Scrope*, ii, pp. 38–9, 108, 131).

THIRWALL, John: he was ordained p. on 15 March 1348 at York Minster (BIA, Register 10A, fol. 21v).

THOERN, Robert: he was ordained p. on 16 June 1375 at Cawood manor chapel (BIA, Register 12, fol. 121r).

THOMAS LE PORTER: a friar of York in Michaelmas 1298 when named in a dispute regarding property in the city (TNA, KB27/156, mem. 72; *Notes on Religious Houses*, i, pp. 243–44).

THOMAS LE QUERUR: a friar of York in Michaelmas 1298 when named in a dispute regarding property in the city (TNA, KB27/156, mem. 72; *Notes on Religious Houses*, i, pp. 243–44).

THOMLINSON (Thomlynson), William: he was a friar of York when he was ordained d. on 24 September 1513 at Holy Trinity Priory, Micklegate, York (BIA, Register 26, fol. 125r. Cf. Cross and Vickers, *MFN*, p. 444).

THOMSON (Thompson), Thomas: he was a friar of York when he was ordained a. on 23 September 1503 at Greyfriars, York, s. on 23 March 1504 at the same venue, and d. on 6 April 1504 in the lady chapel of York Minster (BIA, Register 25, fols. 120r, 122v, 123v). In 1534 he supplicated for his B.D. at Oxford, having studied there and at Cambridge for 15 years (*GFO*, p. 290; *GFC*, p. 216). He was the guardian at Beverley when the friary was suppressed early in 1539 (Goldthorp, 'The Franciscans and Dominicans in Yorkshire', p. 320, citing TNA, Mins. Accts. 30–31, Henry VIII, Yorks, no. 166). The popularity of his surname complicates the search for him among priests active in the diocese beyond the Dissolution. The 70-year-old 'unlerned' incumbent of the Tempest chantry in Giggleswick church, North Yorkshire, in 1548 is an unlikely candidate (*Chantries, Guilds, Hospitals*, ii, p. 409). A more plausible one is the royal chaplain named Thomas Tompson, who was presented to Cherry Burton church in the East Riding on 31 January 1541, which he held until his death in 1556. Another candidate is the Thomas Tomson who was admitted to the vicarage of Humbleton in East Yorkshire in December 1540, making his will on 2 July 1561. He earmarked 40s. for the local poor and bequeathed his farmhold to his kinsman, Robert Deyne, and most of his goods and farming stock to his sister, Agnes, and other close relatives. He left six of his best books to be chained in the chancel of his parish church and gave the remainder to John Newton the younger and Brian Bray. His books were valued at £3 6s. 8d. and his total estate at £69 10s.10d., £58 8s. clear. The appointment to Humbleton might have suited the former guardian of the friary in the East Riding, despite the 57 years between his ordination to the priesthood and his will (Chancery Court Act Book 8, fol. 111r, Caveat Book 1, fol. 28r, Chanc. Wills, 1561. Cf. Cross and Vickers, *MFN*, p. 440, 446).

THORESBY (Thorisby), William de: he was a friar at Boston when he was ordained s. on 7 June 1354 at Liddington prebendal church. He was ordained p. on 21 December 1359 at Lincoln cathedral (LAO, Register 9D, fols. 71v, 94r).

THORNELL, Henry de: he received 6d. in the will of Richard Warter, a carpenter and parishioner of All Saints, Peasholme-in-the-Marsh, on 21 November 1397 (BIA, Probate Register 2, fol. 9rv).

THORNTON (Thorton), John de: he was the 46th regent master at Oxford c.1323

(Eccleston, p. 56; *GFO*, p. 168; *BRUO*, p. 1867). John of Reading, the 45th regent master at Oxford c.1323, cites the opinion of his predecessor in his questions on the *Sentences* in Florence, MS. Biblioteca Nazionale, Conv.Soppr D.IV.95, fols. 128r, 136r. Cf. Percan, *Teologia come scienza pratica secondo Giovanni di Reading*, p. 113*; and Longpré, 'Jean de Reading et le B. Jean Duns Scot', p. 107). On 24 March 1338 he was licensed to hear confessions in the archdeaconry of Lincoln for one year. He was replaced by Richard Percy on 1 December 1339 (*Reg. Burghersh*, iii, pp. 357, 372, nn. 4668, 4821).

THORNTON, John: he was a friar of Oxford when he was ordained a. on 21 March 1450 at St Fridewide's Priory, Oxford (LAO, Register 19, fol. 11v). A friar of this name was at York when he was ordained d. on 5 March 1463 at Blackfriars, York, and p. on 4 June 1463 at Whitefriars, York (BIA, Register 20, fols. 454r, 456r; *BRUO*, p. 1867).

THORNTON, Robert: he was ordained p. on 18 September 1473 at Greyfriars, York (BIA, Register 22, fol. 223r).

THORNTON, Thomas de: he was a friar of Boston licensed to hear confessions within the limitation of that house on 10 August 1300 and 12 October 1300 (Little, *Franciscan Papers, Lists, and Documents*, pp. 237–38).

THORP, Edward de: he was ordained s. on 11 June 1351 in St Mary's Abbey, York (BIA, Regster 10A, fol. 52r).

THORP, Geoffrey de: he was ordained a. on 7 June 1343 at Greyfriars, York, s. on 18 December 1344 at Whitefriars, York, d. on 24 September 1345 in Ripon Minster (BIA, Register 10A, fols. 3v, 8v, 13r), and p. on 26 May 1347 at Lincoln cathedral (LAO, Register 7B, fol. 15v).

THORP', John: on 6 March 1322 he was the custos of York when he received the royal alms from the king, the queen and their children for the general chapter due to meet that summer at Assisi. The general chapter was, in fact, held at Perugia (TNA, E 403/196, m. 6, E403/197, mem. 5).

THORP, John de: he was ordained s. on 19 December 1366 at St Leonard's Hospital, York, d. on 13 March 1367 and p. on 21 February 1372; the second and third ceremonies took place at St Mary's, Bishophill Senior, York (BIA, Register 11, fols. 364v, 365r, 387r).

THORP, Reginald de: he was ordained s. on 22 September 1291 at Grantham (*Reg. Sutton*, vii, p. 18).

THREWIT, Thomas: he was ordained s. on 24 September 1468 at Greyfriars, York, and p. on 23 May 1472 at Blackfriars, York (BIA, Register 22, fols. 193r, 216r).

THURGENTHORPE, John de: he was the guardian of the friary at York in 1316 when he received money from the crown for the repair of a wall built in 1291 (J. Raine, *York*, p. 70; Goldthorp, 'The Franciscans and Dominicans in Yorkshire', p. 319; Richardson, 'The Mendicant Friars of Medieval York', p. 67). He was still the guardian on 26 May 1318 when he received 10 marks towards the cost of the friary's wall (Society of Antiquaries, MS.121, fol. 3r). He was custos of York on 20 November

1321 when he wrote to the bishop of Lincoln, recommending certain friars for a licence to hear confessions (LAO, Register 5, fols. 299v–300).

THURLOWE (Thurlawe), John: he was ordained a. on 3 April 1378 at Greyfriars, York (BIA, Register 12, fol. 132r). He was the brother of Mariota Hawkynsawe, a widow who was buried in the cloister of St Clement's in the suburbs of York. Her will of 16 February 1437 begins with bequests to the prioress, sub-prioress and the Benedictine nuns of St Clement. The next beneficiaries were the Greyfriars, the only mendicant community to be named in the will. The sum of 40d. was bequeathed to each community of Greyfriars in Yorkshire. The friary in York was mentioned by name and received various household items, including linen sheets. This entry is followed immediately by a bequest to her brother, a friar, who received a pair of linen sheets, a piece of silver and a chalice. The chalice might be taken as confirmation of his status as a priest. The friar also witnessed her will (BIA, Probate Register 3, fol. 483v). He received 6s. 8d. from Agnes Stapilton, a widow, who was buried in Blackfriars, York, on 27 March 1448 (*North Country Wills*, i, pp. 48–49).

THWENG, William: he was a friar at Doncaster when he was ordained a. on 21 May 1440 at Blackfriars, York, and s. on 23 September 1441 at Bishopthorpe manor chapel, York. He was a friar of York when he was ordained d. on 24 February 1442 at Greyfriars, York, and p. on 26 May 1442 at Blackfriars, York (BIA, Register 19, fols. 220r, 262r, 266r, 267r).

THWKYLL (Thurkyll), Thomas: he was a friar of Lincoln when he was ordained s. on 20 September 1404 and d. on 20 December 1404; both ceremonies were held in Lincoln cathedral (LAO, Register 13, fols. 115v, 117r). He was a friar of York when he was ordained p. on 6 March 1406 at Holy Trinity Priory, Micklegate, York (BIA, Register 5A, fol. 320v; *Reg. Sede Vacante, York, 1405–08*, pp. 66, 83, 89).

TICKHILL (Tikill, Tykehill'), John de: he was ordained s. on 19 March 1295 at Stow prebendal church, d. on 22 September 1296 at Lincoln cathedral, and p. on 21 December 1297 in Louth prebendal church (*Reg. Sutton*, vii, pp. 65, 83, 101).

TICKHILL (Tykhull), Richard de: he was a friar of York who was accused of malpractice regarding property in 1298. The charge was later withdrawn (TNA, KB27/156, mem. 72; *Notes on Religious Houses*, i, pp. 243–44).

TICKHILL (Tykhill), William de: he was licensed to hear confessions in the parish of St Peter, Ingoldmells, Lincolnshire, for one year from 8 April 1338 (*Reg. Burghersh*, iii, p. 357, no. 4673).

TILTON, Robert de: he was a friar of Stamford when he was ordained d. on 26 May 1358 at Newstead Priory (LAO, Register 9D, fol. 88v). He was a friar of Nottingham when he was ordained p. on 18 September 1361 at Heywood manor chapel (*Reg. Stretton*, p. 168). He was licensed in the diocese of York at an unknown date. He was replaced by William Baldock during the administration of Archbishop Thoresby (BIA, Register 11, fol. 397r).

TINK, Richard: he was a friar of York when he was ordained p. on 19 December 1388 at York Minster (BIA, Register 14, fol. 11v).

TODDE (Toode), Richard: he was a friar of Oxford when he was ordained d. on 18 June 1519 at Liddington prebendal church (LAO, Register 25, fol. 130r). He was licensed to preach and hear confessions in the diocese of York on 24 July 1535 (BIA, Register 28, fol. 85v). He was probably at Lincoln at the surrender of the friary and was in the cathedral city when he received his capacity on 8 October 1539 (Chambers, *Faculty Office Registers 1534–1549*, p. 195).

TODDE, Robert: he was a friar of Richmond when he was ordained a. on 18 September 1434 in the parish church of St Oswald, Durham, *per litteras gardiani sui debite presentatus* (*Reg. Langley*, iv, p. 131). He was a friar of York when he was ordained d. on 8 March 1438 at Whitefriars, York. He was back at Richmond when he was ordained p. on 7 June 1438 at Blackfriars, York (BIA, Register 19, fols. 256v, 257v).

TOFT (Toftes, Tofts), Ralph de: he was the 14th regent master at Oxford c.1285 (Eccleston, p. 53; *GFO*, p. 157). After his university teaching, he returned to the custody and was active in Lincolnshire, particularly in the service of Bishop Sutton, who appointed him as his penitentiary. Walter of Lowthorpe was provided to the church of Greetham, Lincolnshire, and was instituted at Edlesborough, Buckinghamshire, on 6 June 1289 in the presence of this friar and a canon of Lincoln (*Reg. Sutton*, i, p. 120). On 20 June 1290 a note was made of absolution granted by this friar, the bishop's penitentiary, to Hugh le Warenner, servant of Lady Avis de Grele. Excommunication had been pronounced because the servant had assaulted Walter of Great Casterton, close to Stamford, and stabbed him in the thigh. Although Walter had been provocative and had struck the first blow, Hugh was instructed to make three penitential processions around the church at Great Casterton; the dean of Rutland was to be made responsible for seeing that this was undertaken (*Reg. Sutton*, iii, pp. 13–14). A note was made on 30 August 1290 of the absolution granted by this friar, the bishop's penitentiary, from the sentence of excommunication imposed on Richard Bishop of Fulstow, Lincolnshire, which he had incurred by consenting to the forcible removal of a fugitive seeking sanctuary in Fulstow churchyard. The penitent was to receive five beatings on five Sundays in that aforesaid churchyard and the parish priest was ordered to ensure that the penance was carried out (*Reg. Sutton*, iii, pp. 39–40). He was at North Scarle, Lincolnshire, on 11 April 1291, when he heard a reading of the bishop's appeal to the pope against the action of the official of the archbishop of Canterbury; John of Yarwell, another friar, was present (*Reg. Sutton*, iii, pp. 86–90). On 14 May 1291 an announcement was made of the public penance imposed by Ralph, the bishop's penitentiary, upon John of Craven, servant of the Benedictine nuns of Stainfield, for using a stick to strike the head of a certain woman in the churchyard at Stainfield. The culprit was ordered to go in three penitential processions from the gate of the churchyard to the altar of the parish church of Stainfield on three Sundays, offering a twopenny candle on each occasion. A private penance was also imposed upon him (*Reg. Sutton*, iii, p. 100). At the command of the bishop, Ralph represented the abbot of Waltham, when John of Fotherby was ordained deacon to the title of that monastery in Boston parish church on 16 June 1291 (*Reg. Sutton*, vii, p. 16). He was at Stow Park when he was one of several witnesses to the last will and testament of the bishop on 18 May 1291; Bishop Sutton had drawn up the document the previous day (*Sutton*, iii, pp. 103–04). He was in the bishop's chamber on 30 December 1291, when he joined three canons of Lincoln to witness the appointment of Master Jocelyn of Kirmington to the archdeaconry of Stow (*Reg. Sutton*, viii, pp. 205–06).

TOLVEY (Toly, Tolby), William: he was a friar of York when he was ordained a. on

19 February 1407 and s. on 12 March 1407; both ceremonies took place at Blackfriars, York (BIA, Register 5A, fols. 323v, 324r; *Reg. Sede Vacante, York, 1405–08*, pp. 66, 83, 89).

TONERNSIS, Peter: he was ordained s. on 20 September 1432 at St Leonard's Hospital, York (BIA, Register 19, fol. 217r).

TOUMBY (Tumby), Philip de: on 4 December 1335 he was appointed as confessor to the Cistercian house of Nun Appleton (BIA, Register 9, fol. 251r). On 21 November 1347 he received 40s. in the will of John de Har, a native of York, buried in the cemetery of St Dunstan's, Fleet Street, London (BIA, Register 10, fol. 320r).

TOURES (Tours, Towro), John de: he was ordained d. on 23 September 1363 and p. on 12 June 1367; both ceremonies took place at Bishopthorpe manor chapel (BIA, Register 11, fols. 354r, 366v).

TOYNTON, Simon: he was a friar of York when he was ordained a. on 20 February 1445 at Greyfriars, York (BIA, Register 19, fol. 280v). He was a friar of Lincoln when he was ordained s. on 20 December 1449 and d. on 30 May 1450; the two ceremonies were held in St Margaret's in the close of Lincoln cathedral (LAO, Register 19, fols. 7r, 16r). He was back at York when he was ordained p. on 19 December 1450 at Austin Friars, York (BIA, Register 19, fol. 296r).

TOYNTON (Tynton'), Thomas de: he was ordained s. on 22 September 1291 at Grantham, d. on 19 September 1293 in Lincoln cathedral, and p. on 18 September 1294 at Dunstable (*Reg. Sutton*, vii, pp. 18, 42, 58). He was a friar of Boston on 14 March 1319 when he was licensed to hear confessions in the diocese of Lincoln until the next provincial chapter (LAO, Register 3, fols. 411v–12r).

TREVERENSIS, Peter: he was ordained d. on 20 December 1432 at Austin Friars, York (BIA, Register 19, fol. 243r).

TREVERIS, Wynandus de: he was ordained p. on 11 March 1419 at Cawood prebendal chapel (BIA, Register 18, fol. 402v).

TREVERS, Richard: he was licensed to hear confessions in the diocese of Lincoln on 15 August 1442 (LAO, Register 15, fol. 40r). He was a B.Th. by December 1454 (*GFO*, p. 262).

TREW, Thomas: he was a friar of Lincoln when he was ordained s. on 16 March 1521 at Sleaford prebendal church, d. on 30 March 1521 in Lincoln cathedral and p. on 21 September 1521 (LAO, Register 25, fols. 135r, 136r, Register 26, fol. 1v).

TRIKENHAM (Tregumham), Robert de: a woman gave him evidence about murders perpetrated by the Templars. He had passed this information to Nicholas de Chinon, a friar who testified at the trial of the Templars in 1310 (*Proceedings against Templars*, i, pp. 185, 381, 399, ii, pp. xxxiii, 194, 435, 456).

TROLLOP (Trolhop), Richard: he was at Hartlepool when he was ordained a. on 22 September 1436 in Durham cathedral (*Reg. Langley*, iv, p. 201). He was a friar of York when he was ordained d. on 24 February 1442 at Greyfriars, York, and p. on 22 September 1442 at York Minster (BIA, Register 19, fols. 220v, 266r).

TRUMPINGTON (Trumpyngton), Giles de: he was a friar of York on 14 July 1324 when he received the royal alms for the provincial chapter to be held at York that summer (TNA, E403/209, mem. 9).

TRYKINGHAM (Trikyngham), Ralph de: a friar of Doncaster to whom King Edward I sent a gift for the friars there in November 1299; the amount is illegible (TNA, E101/358/20, fol. 8). He was still there when the same monarch sent them alms on 29 November 1300 (BL, Add.MS.7966, fol. 25v).

TULKUTH (Tulcuth), Robert de: he was ordained a. on 20 September 1348 at Skipton parish church and s. on 6 June 1349 at Blackfriars, York (BIA, Register 10A, fols. 25r, 29v).

TUMBY, William de: he was ordained s. on 31 May 1292 and d. on 19 September 1293; both ceremonies took place at Lincoln cathedral. He was ordained p. on 18 December at Stow prebendal church (*Reg. Sutton*, vii, pp. 26, 42, 61).

TUNCHLEY, Philip: a friar who received 40s. in the will of John de Hay of York on 21 November 1347 (BIA, Register 10, fol. 320r).

TURBINGTHORPE, John de: on 17 November 1299 King Edward I gave the friars of York 52s. for three days' food through this friar (TNA, E101/356/7; Goldthorp, 'The Franciscans and Dominicans in Yorkshire', p. 274).

TURRIBUS, Nicholas de: John Le Romeyn, archbishop of York, commissioned his official on 27 January 1293 to receive the resignation of Nicholas, rector of the church of Kirkheaton, who was entering the Franciscan order (*Reg. Le Romeyn*, i, p. 123, no. 338), a parish to which he had been appointed as a subdeacon on 13 August 1282 (*Reg. Wickwane*, p. 45, no. 151).

TWENG' (Twenge), William: a friar of York accused of malpractice regarding property in 1298. The charge was later withdrawn (TNA, KB27/156, mem. 72; *Notes on Religious Houses*, i, pp. 243–44).

TYKESON, John: he was ordained p. on 19 September 1394 at Austin Friars, York (BIA, Register 14, fol. 70v).

TYREL, John: a friar of York accused of malpractice regarding property in Michaelmas 1298. The charge was later withdrawn (TNA, KB27/156, mem. 72; *Notes on Religious Houses*, i, pp. 243–44).

UGYWYE, Thomas: he was a friar of York when he was ordained d. on 21 September 1454 at Blackfriars, York (BIA, Register 20, fol. 418r).

UPSALE (Upsall, Upsaly), Thomas de: he was ordained a. on 20 September 1365 at Cawood manor chapel, s. on 21 March 1366 at Beverley Minster and d. on 3 June 1368 at Bishopthorpe manor chapel (BIA, Register 11, fols. 360v, 362v, 370r).

UTRECHT (Traiecto), John de: he was a friar of Doncaster when he was ordained d. on 11 March 1419 at Cawood prebendal chapel (BIA, Register 18, fol. 402r; Walmsley, 'Some Dutch Franciscans in England during the Later Middle Ages', p. 259).

UTRECHT (Traiecto), John de: he was ordained d. on 17 December 1429 at Austin Friars, York, and p. on 26 May 1431 at Blackfriars, York (BIA, Register 19, fols. 236r, 240r; Walmsley, 'Some Dutch Franciscans in England during the Later Middle Ages', p. 259).

UTY (Hute), John: he was a friar of York when he was ordained a. on 18 February 1497 at Greyfriars, York, d. on 22 December 1498 at Rotherham parish church and p. on 25 May 1499 at Blackfriars, York (BIA, Register 23, fols. 453v, 461v, 464v. Cf. Cross and Vickers, *MFN*, pp. 438–39, where two friars are listed).

VASYN, John de: he was ordained s. on 10 June 1346 at Whitefriars, York (BIA, Register 10A, fol. 15v).

VAVASOUR (Vavasor, Vavasur, Vanisor, Vavysur), William: he was a member of a gentry family from Copmanthorpe, near York (Cross, 'Monastic Learning and Libraries in Sixteenth-Century Yorkshire', p. 259). He was the younger son of Richard and Isabella Vavasour (*Corpus Christi Guild*, pp. 129, 176, n. z). He was probably born about 1460 and admitted to the order about 1475. He was a friar of York when he was ordained a. on 13 March 1484 at Holy Trinity Priory, Micklegate, York, s. on 18 December 1484 at Austin Friars, York, and d. on 22 September 1487 at Whitefriars, York (BIA, Register 23, fols. 390r, 394v, 409r). After his diaconal ordination he was probably sent to Stamford, where he was ordained p. on 22 March 1488 at the town's church of St Mary *ad pontem* (LAO, Register 22, fol. 28r).

By 1490 he was at Oxford convent, where he transcribed two manuscripts: First, Oxford, Corpus Christi College Library. MS.227, Antonii Andreae *tractatus de tribus principiis naturalibus*, folios 49–120v. The second part of the manuscript was transcribed by Vavasour: *exceptus de dictis doctoris subtilis eiusdem ordinis scriptus per me fratrem Wyllelmum studentem Oxonie anno incarnacionis Dominice 1419* [*sic*]. The manuscript was transcribed in 1491. At the end of Scotus's commentary on Aristotle's *Meteora* is a further note by Vavasour: *expliciunt questiones tertii libri metheororum secundum doctorem subtilem ordinis minorum, ac scripte per manum fratris Wyllelmi Vavysur, eiusdem ordinis, anno Dominice incarnacionis 1491. Amen* (Thomson, *Corpus Christi*, Oxford, pp. 113–14; Thomson, *Catalogue of Medieval Manuscripts of Latin Commentaries on Aristotle in British Libraries*, pp. 265–66). This manuscript was acquired by the Elizabethan bookseller, John Dee, who seems to have purchased it at York on 24 November 1559 (Cf. *John Dee's Library Catalogue*, pp. 127–28). Secondly, MS.228, a volume which contains texts on logic. The third item, *De fallaciis*, folios 8–13v, concludes with the words: *expliciunt fallacie per manum fratris Wyllelmi Vavysur.* The seventh text in the manuscript contains the following note at the conclusion of the *Quaestiones de anima*, folios 52–61: *Amen quod frater Wyllelmus Vavysur. Expliciunt questiones de anima valde perutiles anno Domini 1490.* The two volumes transcribed by Vavasour were acquired by Dee. Vavasour took his D.D. in 1500 (*Fasti Oxonienses, or, Annals of the University of Oxford, by Anthony à Wood*, i, p. 5) and was guardian of Oxford about this time. The general chapter of 1504 appointed him as the regent at Oxford (*Regesta Ordinis Fratrum Minorum Conventualium, 2 (1504–1506)*, p. 12, no. 43). The absence of his name from the *Register of Congregations 1505–1517* suggests that his time in the University of Oxford had come to an end. By then he may have returned to his own custody.

Vavasour was admitted to the guild of *Corpus Christi* of York, in 1512, when he was described as master (*Corpus Christi Guild*, p. 176). He was a beneficiary of the wills of some members of the guild of *Corpus Christi*. On 15 December 1524 John

Marshall, merchant, citizen of York and parishioner of St Mary, Castlegate, appointed him as an executor and gave him five marks and a gilt spoon to pray for him and those to whom he was bound. Vavasour was named as an executor of the will (*TE*, v, pp. 191–93; BIA, Probate Register 9, fol. 357v). On 12 June 1529 he witnessed the will of Thomas Threpland, vicar of Christ Church, King's Square, York (*York Clergy Wills 1520–1600: II City Clergy*, ii, pp. 9–10). He is mentioned in Thomas Cromwell's list of learned persons living outside Oxford in 1531 in connection with the king's divorce (*LPFD*, v, p. 6, no. 6, xviii). He seems to have exercised some of the powers of the custos. He assigned Thomas Johnson, alias Bonaventure, to the friary at Beverley at some point between 1534 and 1536 (*LPFD*, xii, pt. ii, p. 183, no. 392). It was alleged by the executors of the will of Dame Elizabeth Metham, a widow, that she had entrusted £32. 19s. to Vavasour, a doctor of divinity and guardian of the York Greyfriars, and that he had not used it in accordance with her wishes. Vavasour explained in some detail that on 21 April 1534 the money had been deposited in the sacristy of the Greyfriars. Sums of money had been withdrawn from the box and delivered to Walter Bradeford and to two masons working on her tomb. Money had also been used to make a donation to the four houses of friars in York and some poor people (*Monastic Chancery Proceedings (Yorkshire)*, pp. 161–62, no. 166). On 23 July 1535 John Besby (Beisbey), a parishioner of St Michael, Spurriergate, and an alderman, asked for burial in the friars' church at York between the altar of the resurrection and the grave of Sir Brian Roclif. He gave 5s. to Vavasour, the guardian, for his burial and asked his wife Margaret to consult the friar about her duties as an executor. The friar was a supervisor of Besby's will; he received an additional 10s. for his labour (BIA, Probate Register 11, fols. 147r–48r). On 11 August 1537, John Burton, a parishioner of St Martin-le-Grand, York, gave him 5s. to pray for his soul and to act as the supervisor of his will (BIA, Probate Register 11, fol. 249r). In 1538 he was listed as one of the doctors of theology in the English province (*LPFD*, xiii, pt. 2, p. 508, no. 1211).

On 27 November 1538 he was the last guardian of York who signed the deed of surrender in the chapter house (*Eighth Report of the Deputy Keeper of the Public Records*, p. 51). He was granted a pension of £5 per year (*LPFD*, xiii, pt. 2, pp. 381–82, no. 917). This was unusual for mendicants (Cross, 'The Dissolution of the Monasteries in Sixteenth-Century York', p. 160). He made his will on 13 November 1544, asking to be buried in the south aisle of St Mary, Bishophill Junior, York, where he requested a trental of Masses to be said for his soul. He bestowed 30s. upon the poor of the parish and 10s. upon prisoners in York castle in addition to other charitable bequests. Thomas Johnson, a former friar of York, received 10s. to pray for him. Robert Moore, another former member of that community, was given £9 6s. 8d. to celebrate for two years at St Peter's altar, where he wished to be buried. In addition to many legacies to the Vavasour family of Copmanthorpe he donated 6s. 8d. and his furred gown to the anchoress of Bishophill. He left his servant, John Hogeson, a trotting nag to take him to school in addition to two pairs of hose, a doublet and the bed in which he slept. He set aside 26 books, which he did not name, for various priests in York, reserving the remainder of his library for the former friar, Ralph Clayton, together with his desks and all things belonging to them. He appointed Clayton and Thomas Vavisour his executors. After his death his goods were valued at £79 17s. and his will was proved on 16 January 1545 (*BRUO*, p. 1943; BIA, Register 27, folios. 164v–65r; *York Clergy Wills 1520–1600: II City Clergy*, pp. 33–35; Cross and Vickers, *MFN*, pp. 436, 454, 455). His collection of books was larger than the library of Archbishop Melton. Professor Cross believes that Vavasour probably took the friary's books with him (Cross, 'York Clergy and their Books in the Early Sixteenth Century', p. 347).

VEER, Robert: he was guardian of Scarborough on 31 March 1479 when he was licensed to hear confessions in the diocese of York (BIA, Register 22, fol. 316r).

VEERT, John: he was a friar of York when he was ordained d. on 24 March 1425 at St Michael-le-Belfrey, York (BIA, Register 5A, fol. 402v; *Sede Vacante, York, 1423–26*, p. 120).

VENDUR, John: he was ordained s. on 12 June 1367 and d. on 3 June 1368; both ceremonies took place at Bishopthorpe manor chapel (BIA, Register 11, fols. 366r, 370r).

VERNEY, John: Bishop Repingdon issued a licence on 8 November 1416 permitting this friar to hear the confessions of the household of Mary Bohun, the queen mother, while she was in the diocese of Lincoln (*Reg. Repingdon*, iii, p. 149, no. 283).

VIZENIA, William de: he was a friar of York when he was ordained a. on 24 February 1453 at Blackfriars, York (BIA, Register 20, fol. 412v).

WADSWORTH (Wadworth), Richard: he was a friar of York when he was ordained a. on 25 May 1510 at Blackfriars, York, s. on 21 September 1510 at Holy Trinity Priory, Micklegate, York, d. on 21 December 1510 at Austin Friars, York, and p. on 15 March 1511 at Whitefriars, York (BIA, Register 26, fols. 108r, 109r, 110v, 112r. Cf. Cross and Vickers, *MFN*, p. 443).

WADSWORTH (Waddesworth, Wardeworth), William: he was a friar of Grimsby when he was ordained p. on 19 December 1355 in Stow prebendal church (LAO, Register 9D, fol. 78r). He was mentioned in the plea rolls with John of Staynton, guardian of Lincoln, in the Michaelmas term of 1375 and the Trinity term of the next year (TNA, KB27/459, attorneys, m. 3 and KB27/462, mm. 8d, 64d).

WAGASE, William: he was ordained p. on 8 June 1476 at Blackfriars, York (BIA, Register 22, fol. 240r).

WAINFLEET (Wayneflet), John de: he was ordained d. on 12 June 1367 and p. on 3 June 1368; both ceremonies took place ar Bishopthorpe manor chapel (BIA, Register 11, fols. 366v, 370r).

WAKEFIELD (Wakefeld), John de: he was ordained a. on 27 May 1363 at Bishopthorpe manor chapel, near York (BIA, Register 11, fol. 352v).

WAKEFIELD (Wakefeld), John de: he was ordained d. on 19 December 1383 at All Saints, Cawood (BIA, Register 12, fol. 140v). On 6 November 1400 a friar of this name was mentioned in the will of Thomas de Syke, senior, and tapiter of York, who was buried in the cemetery of St Mary's, Bishophill Senior. John de Wakefield of the local Greyfriars was given four marks to pray for Syke, his deceased wife, and the souls of all the faithful departed for the space of a year. In the event of this friar being unable to fulfil these request, the testator wished that William de Doncaster should celebrate these suffrages (BIA, Probate Register 3, fol. 49v).

WAKEFIELD (Wakefield), William de: he was ordained a. and s. on 26 May 1369 in the Bishopthorpe manor chapel, near York (BIA, Register 11, fols. 373v, 374r).

WALAYS (Wales), Roger: he was ordained s. on 17 December 1362 at St Leonard's Hospital, York, d. on 21 December 1364 at Greyfriars, York, and p. on 18 December 1367 at Bishopthorpe manor chapel (BIA, Register 11, fols. 351r, 358v, 368r).

WALCOT (Walcotes, Walcote, Walkote), John de: he was ordained s. on 9 March 1381 at St Mary's church, Beverley (BIA, Register 12, fol. 139r). On 7 October 1414 at Verona Pope John XXIII provided him to the diocese of Nisch in Bulgaria and authorised him to be consecrated by any Catholic archbishop and to exercise his office outside his diocese (*BF*, vii, p. 487, no. 1349, n. 3). He served as suffragan to the archbishop of York in 1414 and 1419. He held an ordination at Cawood prebendal church on 11 March 1419 (BIA, Register 18, fols. 401v–02r). He ordained five acolytes at a date between 21 December 1420 and 14 February 1421 (BIA, Register 18, fol. 407v).

WALDINGFELD, Adam de: he was ordained d. on 10 June 1346 at Whitefriars, York (BIA, Register 10A, fol. 16r).

WALKER, William: he was a friar of York when he was ordained s. on 24 March 1509 at Blackfriars, York, d. on 2 June 1509 at Whitefriars, York, and p. on 22 September 1509 at Holy Trinity Priory, Micklegate, York (BIA, Register 26, fols. 101r, 103r, 104r. Cf. Cross and Vickers, *MFN*, p. 442). He proceeded to Oxford where, after 14 years of study, he supplicated for his B.D. on 3 June 1527 (*Reg. Univ. Oxon*, p. 147; *GFO*, p. 284; *BRUO, 1501–40*, p. 602). On 20 July 1538 he was dispensed to become a secular priest (Chambers, *Faculty Office Registers 1534–1549*, p. 143).

WALSOKEN (Waldokim, Walsokim, Walsokyn), John: he was ordained s. on 21 December 1471 at Austin Friars, York, and p. on 19 September 1472 at Holy Trinity Priory, Micklegate, York (BIA, Register 22, fols. 213r, 217v). As one *de soluto genitus et soluta* he sought a dispensation to be promoted to various offices in the order. His supplication was heard on 7 April 1490 (*BF, ns*, ii–iv, p. 672, no. 1797; *Supplic. Apost. Penit.*, ii, pp. 417–18, no. 3314).

WALTER, William de: he was the son of John. He was ordained a. on 22 December 1431 at Austin Friars, York (BIA, Register 19, fol. 240v).

WALTHAM, John: on 26 September 1424 he, along with Thomas Richmond and John Bromwich, was mentioned in relation to a payment (*CCR, 1429–1435*, p. 369).

WALTHAM, Robert: he was guardian at Grimsby in 1446 when he brought an action against Richard Bridlington, a confrère, for trespass (Gillett, *A History of Grimsby*, p. 76).

WALTHAM, Thomas: he was a friar of Lincoln when he was ordained p. on 18 March 1424 at the prebendal church of Liddington (*Reg. Fleming*, ii, p. 99, no. 495). He was one of three friars of York who accompanied Thomas Richmond of York when he preached at the chapel of St Anne on Foss bridge on 26 June 1426. On 13 August of that year he attended the chapter house with Richmond and testified before the bishop of Durham to the content of his confrère's sermon in the vernacular (*Records of Convocation, XIII: York, 1313–1461*, pp. 389–90; *Records of the Northern Convocation*, p. 151; Wilkins, *Concilia*, iii, p. 488). On 1 February 1460 a friar of this name, aged 60, requested a licence to eat meat, eggs and dairy produce at times when they are prohibited, on the grounds of his frailty (*Supplic. Apost. Penit.*, i, p. 220, no. 1032).

WALTHAM, William: he was a friar of Northampton when he was ordained s. on 6 March 1512 in Buckden prebendal church and d. on 27 March 1512 in the prebendal church of Liddington. He was a friar of Lincoln when ordained p. on 10 April 1512 in Lincoln cathedral (LAO, Register 24, fols. 86v, 87v, 88).

WALTON, John de: he was a friar of Leicester when he was ordained s. on 20 December 1343 in the diocese of Coventry and Lichfield (LRO, B/1/1, fol. 194r). He was a friar of Beverley when he was ordained d. on 18 December 1344 at Whitefriars, York. He was ordained p. at an unspecified place and date between September 1346 and September 1347 (BIA, Register 10A, fols. 9r, 18a). He was at Beverley when he was licensed to hear confessions in the diocese of York on 14 June 1350 (*ibid.*, fol. 279r).

WARD, Elias: he was ordained d. on 22 September 1397 at Holy Trinity Priory, Micklegate, York (*Reg. Waldby*, p. 45), and p. on 12 June 1400 in Bishop Burton church. In the second of these entries he is recorded as having been ordained deacon, which is probably an error for priest (*Reg. Scrope*, ii, pp. 55, 112, 131).

WARD (Warde), Geoffrey: he was ordained s. on 11 March 1346 at Whitefriars, York (BIA, Register 10A, fol. 14r).

WARD (Warde), Henry: a friar, cleric and professed, of Lincoln. He died c.1327 (Little, '*Records, Franciscan Province*', p. 150).

WARD (Warde), Thomas: he was a friar of York when he was ordained a. on 8 March 1460 at Greyfriars, York, and p. on 20 December 1466 at Austin Friars, York (BIA, Register 20, fol. 441v, Register 22, fol. 184v). He was described as the deputy of the guardian on 1 January 1504 by Thomas Roclyfe, gentleman of York (BIA, Probate Register 6, fol. 131rv).

WARD (Warde), William: he was a friar of York when he was ordained a. on 4 March 1452, s. on 26 May 1453, d. on 22 December 1453, and p. on 21 December 1454. The first, third and fourth ceremonies took place at Austin Friars and the second at Blackfriars, York (BIA, Register 19, fol. 301r, Register 20, fols. 415r, 416v, 419r).

WARMESBY, Hugh de: he was a friar of Doncaster on 16 November 1348 when he was authorised to act as confessor to Margery, widow of Sir Hugh de Hastings, a knight, and her family for one year (BIA, Register 10, fol. 278v; *Fasti Eboracenses*, p. 444n; Goldthorp, 'The Franciscans and Dominicans in Yorkshire', p. 299).

WARMSWORTH (Warmesworth), Nicholas de: probably a friar of Doncaster when, on 28 May 1348, Nicholas de Launeyr, rector of the church of Briseley in the diocese of Norwich, asked for burial in the Doncaster Greyfriars. Nicholas received 13s. 4d. (BIA, Register 10, fol. 326r).

WARR', Richard de: he received the royal alms of 32s. for three days for the community at Beverley on 25 November 1299 (*Liber quotidianus contrarotulatoris garderobae*, p. 25).

WARTER (Wartre), Nicholas: he was ordained a. on 14 March 1394 at All Saints, Pavement, York, and d. on 19 September 1394 at Austin Friars, York (BIA, Register 14, fols. 69r, 70r). On 17 March 1419 he was provided to the see of Dromore by Pope Martin V at Florence; the see was vacant through the death of John (*BF*, vii, pp. 518–19, no. 1409; *CPL*, vii, p. 132). On 5 May of that year he was at the papal court in Florence, where he paid 33 gold florins (Cenci, 'Documenta Vaticana', Part 2, p. 74). He acted as suffragan in the diocese of York throughout his life as a bishop and assisted Archbishops Bowett and Kempe between 15 February 1421 and 24 September 1445. He carried out the vast majority of the ordinations between 15 February 1421 and 22 May 1445; many of these ceremonies were held at the Greyfriars of York. About March 1421 Nicholas informed Pope Martin V of the wars that impeded his ministry in Ulster. On 18 June 1421, the pope gave him permission to accept a benefice (BIA, Register 18, fols. 197v–98r). On 2 December 1422 he was appointed as vicar of the parish of All Saints at Skeckling in Holderness (BIA, Register 18, fol. 198r). On 23 February 1424 he was appointed as rector of the parish of Holtby in the diocese of York and inducted on the same day (BIA, Register 5A, fols. 361–62r). On 30 January 1431 he was instituted as rector of St Peter the Little in York and on the same day he was inducted by the archdeacon of York (BIA, Register 19, fol. 355r). Nicholas was mentioned as rector of that parish on 14 January 1435 (BIA, Register 19, fol. 384r). At an unknown date he became rector of St Mary at Castlegate, York, which he held until his death.

Nicholas was admitted to the guild of *Corpus Christi* at York in 1429/30 (*Corpus Christi Guild*, p. 28). Following Archbishop Bowet's death on 20 October 1423, Nicholas received numerous *sede vacante* commissions. On 17 May 1424 he was authorised to dedicate the Premonstratensian church of Blessed Angela near Richmond and an area for their cemetery (*The Fabric Rolls of York Minster*, pp. 237–38). On 26 June 1424 he was commissioned to dedicate the church of St Helen on-the walls, York, along with its cemetery (*The Fabric Rolls of York Minster*, p. 237; BIA, Register 5A, fol. 376r). On 26 June 1424 he was authorised to reconcile the cemetery in South Kirkeby (BIA, Register 5A, fol. 376r). On 22 July 1441 he was licensed to consecrate and dedicate the chapel and churchyard of St Michael at Bempton, in the parish of Bridlington (*The Fabric Rolls of York Minster*, p. 238). He acted as executor in the will of Simon Wenteslawe, rector of St Mary at Cowlam in the East Riding. The will was drawn up on 20 March 1439 and proved on 23 March 1439 (BIA, Probate Register 3, fols. 563–64r). On 26 March 1435 he was commissioned to bless Thomas Passelew as abbot of the Cistercian monastery of Fountains (BIA, Register 18, fol. 392v). On 31 May 1436 he was commissioned to bless John Brompton as abbot of the Cistercian monastery of Jervaulx (BIA, Register 18, fol. 392v). On 11 May 1437 he was commissioned to bless Hugh Ellerton as abbot of the Benedictine monastery of Sts Peter and Hilda at Whitby (BIA, Register 18, fols. 391rv). The new abbot's profession of obedience to the metropolitan confirmed that he had received blessing from Nicholas.

On 30 January 1448 Warter drew up his will. Describing himself as the rector of the church of St Mary at Castlegate, York, he was manifestly in poor health and commended his soul to God, the Virgin Mary, St Francis and all the Saints, asking for burial in the Franciscan church at York. His funeral seems to have been planned for his parish church. Small sums of money were left to members of his household and friends at York. Money was left to York Minster, the guilds of St Christopher and *Corpus Christi*, of which he had been a member, and the guild of St James at Warter. His will was proved on 1 April 1448 (BIA, Probate Register, 2, fols. 268v–69r. For additional references see: BIA, Register 18, fols. 197v–98r, 257rv, 407v–16v; *Reg. Sede Vacante, York, 1423–26*, pp. vii, xi, 2, 13, 53, 55–56, 89–91, 93, 133–34, 153, 172–74,

192–93, 218, 223, 293, 313, 330, 335, 349–50, 353, 373, 399, 491, 494, 496–97, 524–25, 526, 562, 579, 589–90, 600, 609; Register 19, fols. 28v–29r, 215r–16r, 227v–28r, 228r–36r, 306v; *Fasti Parochiales*, iv, p. 58; Butler, 'Suffragan Bishops in the Medieval Diocese of York', pp. 53, 58; Robson, 'Nicholas Warter, the Franciscan Bishop of Dromore (c.1372–1448)'.

WARTER (Wartre), Richard: he was the son of Adam Warter, a citizen and spurrier of York. His mother's name remains unknown and she had died by 1430. He and his sister, Agnes, were parishioners of St Martin-le-Grand, Coney Street, in York. Agnes married Walter Graystok, another parishioner of St Martin's, to whom she bore a son, John. Adam's will, written on 31 March 1430 and proved on 14 May of that year, requested burial in the parish's cemetery. St Martin's parish was near the Greyfriars and on the same side of the river. Adam followed his trade as a spurrier in the county town; the adjacent parish was St Michael, Spurriergate. It remains unclear whether Adam's origins lay in the East Riding or in York. His parents may have migrated from Warter to the prosperous centre of York in the aftermath of the Black Death. Adam left 5s. for the fabric of his parish church and 3s. 4d. to the fabric of York Minster. The chaplain of his parish church was given 12d. The only mendicant community mentioned in Adam's will was the Greyfriars to which he left 3s. 4d. and the more handsome sum of 40s. to his son, Richard, described as a member of that fraternity. The bequest was not tied to a request for Masses because his son was not yet a priest. Richard was probably a friar at York when he was ordained a. on 21 May 1429, s. on 22 September 1431 and d. on 7 March 1433. All three ceremonies were conducted by the suffragan, Bishop Warter, his confrère, and the last two took place at Greyfriars, York (BIA, Register 19, fols. 234v, 240r, 243v). Along with his brother-in-law and John Arksay, another spurrier, Richard was an executor of his father's will. When probate was granted, Richard was appointed as administrator. The fact that Richard was named before Agnes in the will may indicate that he was the older of the two (BIA, Probate Register 2, fol. 669v). Nothing further is known of Richard's ministry as a friar and priest. He was not mentioned in the will of his brother-in-law on 18 March 1473 and may have been dead by that date. Graystok, described as a cellarer, requested prayers for his deceased wives and left 30s. 4d. to Thomas Graystok, chaplain, and his son, and 20s. to Joanna Tesedale, his daughter. He nominated Canon John Graystok, his son, as one of his executors and left him 13s. 4d. (BIA, Probate Register 4, fol. 188rv). This friar may be associated with the Frater Richard Waretyr who was admitted to the *Corpus Christi* guild of York in 1453 (*Corpus Christi Guild*, p. 52).

WARTON, Richard: he was a friar of Doncaster when he was ordained d. on 19 September 1461 at Blackfriars, York. He was a friar of York when he was ordained p. on 19 December 1461 at Austin Friars, York (BIA, Register 20, fols. 449r, 450r).

WARWICK (Warewyk), John de: he was licensed to hear confessions in the diocese of Lincoln on 31 January 1334 (LAO, Register 5, fol. 471r).

WARYNER, William: he was a friar of York when he was ordained s. on 26 May 1453 at Blackfriars, York (BIA, Register 20, fol. 415r).

WATKINSON (Watkynson), Gregory: a novice at York at the Dissolution on 27 November 1538 (*Eighth Report of the Deputy Keeper of the Public Records*, p. 51).

WATSON, Christopher: he was a friar of York when he was ordained a. on 26 March

1502 in the lady chapel of York Minster and d. on 10 June 1503 at Blackfriars, York (BIA, Register 25, fols. 111v, 119v. Cf. Cross and Vickers, *MFN*, p. 440).

WATSON, Hugh: he was a friar of York when he was ordained d. on 18 September 1507 at Whitefriars, York (BIA, Register 5A, fol. 580r).

WATSON, John: he was a friar of York when he was ordained a. on 17 June 1508 at Blackfriars, York, s. on 24 March 1509 at Blackfriars, York, and d. on 2 June 1509 at Whitefriars, York. He was a friar of Richmond when he was ordained p. on 22 December 1509 at an unrecorded venue (BIA, Register 5A, fol. 597r, Register 26, fols. 101r, 103r, 105v. Cf. Cross and Vickers, *MFN*, p. 442).

WATSON, Richard: he was a friar of York when he was ordained a. on 13 March 1535 at Blackfriars, York, s. on 11 March 1536 at Greyfriars, York, d. on 1 April 1536 at Blackfriars, York, and p. on 24 February 1537 at Austin Friars, York (BIA, Register 28, fols. 190v, 195r, 196r, 197v). He was at York at the Dissolution on 27 November 1538 (*Eighth Report of the Deputy Keeper of the Public Records*, p. 51. Cf. Cross and Vickers, *MFN*, pp. 445, 460).

WATSON, William: he was a friar of Richmond when he was ordained a. on 27 March 1501 in the parish church of Barnard castle (*Reg. Fox*, p. 152). He was a friar of York when he was ordained s. on 18 September 1501 at Greyfriars, York. He was at Richmond when he was ordained d. on 18 December 1501 at Whitefriars, York, and p. on 21 May 1502 in a chapel beside the walls of St Mary's Abbey, York (BIA, Register 25, fols. 109v, 111r, 113v. Cf. Cross and Vickers, *MFN*, p. 441). A William Watson of Stamford received his capacity on 12 December 1538 (Chambers, *Faculty Office Registers 1534–1549*, p. 168).

WAYNEMAN, John: he was a friar of York when he was ordained s. on 21 September 1504 at Greyfriars, York, d. on 20 September 1505 in Bishopthorpe manor chapel, York, and p. on 20 December 1505 at Austin Friars, York (BIA, Register 25, fols. 125v, 130r, 131v. Cf. Cross and Vickers, *MFN*, p. 441). He may have been a native of the Doncaster area and was at the local friary on 6 June 1527 when his twice widowed sister, Agnes Kellome, compiled her will, requesting burial in the parish church of St George at Doncaster. In the event of her son, William, dying without issue, her two houses were to pass to John, her brother, for the support of the friary. The residue of her estate was to be disposed of in alms on the Fridays before the feast of All Saints. She left 10s. to her curate, Sir John Drinkale, who was appointed as an executor along with her son, William Blenkynsope (BIA, Probate Register 9, fol. 376r).

WEDERAL (Wederhale), John de: this friar, who may have been on a preaching tour in North Yorkshire, rehearsed the conversation that took place at the table of Alan Malcake at Lockton in Blackmore, on the North Yorkshire moors. One of Malcake's former employees had worked for the Knights Templar at the preceptory of Foulbridge and gave evidence about Robert de Rygate (Bayset, Raygat), formerly commander of the Templars in Coupmanthorpe in 1297, who had died before 1308. The knight told those working on the farm that he regretted giving himself to the devil and falling from grace. Wederal added that he heard the confession of Richard of Hales, the commander of the preceptor of Foulbridge. He gave his evidence to Bishop Burghersh (*Proceedings against the Templars*, i, pp. 185, 200, 381, ii, pp. 193, 218, 435).

WELBURN, John: he was a friar of Beverley when he was ordained a. on 20 December 1449 at Austin Friars, York. He was at York when he was ordained s. on 18 December 1451 at Greyfriars, York (BIA, Register 19, fols. 293Ar, 300v).

WELLESWYK, Roger de: he was licensed to hear cofessions in the diocese of Lincoln for the household of John de Mowbray c.1310 (LAO, Register 3, fol. 460r).

WELLIA, John de: he was licensed to hear confessions in the diocese of Lincoln on 9 February 1332 (LAO, Register 24, fol. 455v).

WELLINGTON (Wellyngton), Roger de: he was licensed to hear confessions in the diocese of Lincoln on 9 February 1332 (LAO, Register 5, fol. 455v).

WELLS (Welles), John: he was a friar of Lincoln when he was ordained a. on 24 May 1404 in the prebendal church of Liddington, s. on 20 December 1404 and d. on 14 March 1405; the second and third ceremonies took place in Lincoln cathedral (LAO, Register 13, fols. 114r, 117r, 118v).

WELLS (Welles, Wellys), Robert: he was licensed to hear confessions in the diocese of Coventry and Lichfield on 8 August 1453, being presented by Thomas Radnor, minister provincial. He was a friar at Coventry when licensed again on 20 December 1459 (LRO, B/A/1/11, fol. 44v, B/A/1/12, fol. 125r). On 14 July 1473 Pope Sixtus IV provided him to the diocese of Achonry and letters were sent concurrently to the archbishop of Tuam, the chapter and clergy of the city and King Edward IV (*BF, ns*, iii, pp. 191–92, no. 475; *CPL*, xiii, i, p. 331). On 24 July of that year at his own petition and that of King Edward IV, Robert was granted permission to have, after consecration, and retain for life *in commendam* the said church with two benefices and resign or exchange them as he pleased (*BF, ns*, iii, p. 192, no. 478; *CPL*, xiii, i, p. 332). He was admitted to the confraternity of the English hospice in Rome on 29 December 1474. He was chaplain of the hospice in 1474 and auditor in 1475 (Newns, 'The Hospice of St Thomas and the English Crown 1474–1538', p. 188, n. 2). He was an auditor of the hospital (Kenny, 'The Hospice of St Thomas and the English Crown 1474–1538', 266). He was consecrated on 4 June 1475 in the hospice chapel by Benedict, OSB, archbishop of Mytilenen, Francis de Sanctis, OFM, and bishop of Scutaren. in Albania, and Orlando, bishop of Antheraden. (Cenci, 'Documenta Vaticana', Part 6, p. 392). On 8 May 1475 he paid tax of 17 florins and 43s. for his diocese (Brady, *The succession in England, Scotland and Ireland A.D. 1400 to 1875*, ii, p. 185).

On 22 November 1475 he was appointed as vicar of the parish of Wybunbury in the archdeaconry of Chester. On 12 February 1478 he exchanged this parish for that of Colwich (LRO, B/A/1/12, fol. 110r, B/A/1/12, fol. 111v). At Lichfield on 12 February 1478 Master Thomas Reynolds, the vicar general, admitted Robert as vicar of the prebendal church of Colwich in the archdeaconry of Stafford (LRO, B/A/1/12, fol. 50v). On 31 January 1478 the vicar general admitted him as rector of Waters Upton in the archdeaconry of Shrewsbury on the resignation of the last rector at the presentation of the monastery of St Peter at Shrewsbury (LRO, B/A/1/12, fol. 90r). He had freely resigned the parish by 21 July 1483, when his successor was appointed (LRO, B/A/1/12, fol. 91v). Before 3 November 1486 he had freely resigned the parish of Colwich (LRO, B/A/1/12, fol. 91v; *ibid.*, fol. 54r). He carried out the majority of the ordinations in the diocese from 23 December 1475 to 24 September 1491. On 22 March 1481 a dispensation was granted to Richard Swyndilhirst of Mitton for having received the order of acolyte and other minor orders from Robert, bishop of Achonry, at Preston (*Reg. Rotherham*, p. 188, no. 1524). Most of the ceremonies were held in Lichfield cathedral, but some of the special ceremonies took place in the Franciscan church at Lichfield. He received a *sede vacante* commission in the diocese of Coventry and Lichfield on 22 May 1491 to administer an oath of perpetual chastity to Cecily, widow of Sir Thomas Gerard, knight, late of the parish of Winwick, Lancashire, and to invest her with the veil, ring and mantle, which customarily signify this state. Robert celebrated most of the ordinations in the diocese of Coventry and Lichfield between 23 December 1475 and 18 September 1490 (*Reg. Morton*, ii, p. 5, no. 21. Cf. Butler, 'Suffragan Bishops in the Medieval Diocese of York', pp. 51, 53, 59).

WELLS (Welles), Thomas: he was a friar of York when he was ordained a. on 22 September 1436 at Greyfriars, York (BIA, Register 19, fol. 217v).

WELLYS (Wells, Willis), Thomas: he was ordained a. on 11 March 1475 at Greyfriars, York, s. on 23 September 1475 at Whitefriars, York, and d. on 23 December 1475 at Holy Trinity Priory, Micklegate, York (BIA, Register 22, fols. 232v, 235v, 236v).

WELTON, Stephen: he was a friar of York when he was ordained p. on 21 December 1443 at Austin Friars, York (BIA, Register 19, fol. 222r).

WELWICK (Wellewyk'), Walter de: he was ordained d. on 3 April 1294 at Spaldwick parish church and p. on 22 December 1296 at the priory of St James at Huntingdon (*Reg. Sutton*, vii, pp. 51, 89).

WENT, John: he was licensed as a confessor in the diocese of York in place of John de Busse at an unspecified date in the administration of Archbishop Thoresby (BIA, Register 11, fol. 396r). A friar of the same name received five marks in the will of John Sayvell of Elland. The undated will was proved on 23 September 1399. Half a mark was also left to William de Fenton, who is not expressley described as a Franciscan (BIA, Register 16, fol. 170r).

WERKILL, William: he was ordained d. on 12 June 1462 at Whitefriars, York (BIA, Register 20, fol. 452r).

WERMESWORTH, Hugh de: he was a friar of Lincoln when he was ordained p. on 15 June 1359 at Liddington prebendal church (LAO, Register 9D, fol. 92r).

WERMESWORTH, Nicholas de: he was a friar of Doncaster who received the royal alms for that friary on 15 July 1336 (BL, MS. Cotton Nero, C.VIII, fol. 205r; Goldthorp, 'The Franciscans and Dominicans in Yorkshire', p. 299).

WERMESWORTH (Warmesworth), William: he was ordained a. on 22 September 1369 at Bishopthorpe manor chapel, s. on 20 September 1371 at St Mary, Bishophill Senior, York, d. on 18 September 1372 at Greyfriars, York (BIA, Register 11, fols. 375r, 384v, 389r), and p. on 22 December 1375 at Cawood manor chapel (BIA, Register 12, fol. 123r).

WEST, John: he was a friar of Lincoln when he was ordained p. on 29 March 1354 at Daventry priory (LAO, Register 9D, fol. 71r).

WEST, Thomas: he was a friar of York when he was ordained s. on 22 September

1487 at Whitefriars, York, d. on 14 March 1489 at Holy Trinity Priory, Micklegate, York, and p. on 18 September 1490 at Whitefriars, York (BIA, Register 23, fols. 408v, 415v, 424r. Cf. Cross and Vickers, *MFN*, p. 436). He was at York when he was admitted to the *Corpus Christi* guild in 1497 (*Corpus Christi Guild*, p. 145).

WESTFALIA (Wesalia), John de: he was ordained d. on 17 December 1429 at Austin Friars, York (BIA, Register 19, fol. 236r).

WESTON, Henry: he was ordained a. and s. on 27 May 1396 at St Mary, Bishophill Senior, York (BIA, Register 14, fol. 72rv), d. on 17 March 1397 at Greyfriars, York (BIA, Register 5A, fol. 230r; BL, MS. Cotton Galba, MS.E.X, fol. 130v). He was a friar of Lincoln when he was ordained p. on 21 December 1398 at Torksey Priory (LAO, Register 13, fol. 84r).

WESTON, Roger de: he was ordained p. on 21 December 1342 in St George's parish church at Doncaster (BIA, Register 10A, fol. 2v; *Reg. Kirkby*, i, p. 154, no. 733).

WESTON, William de: he was ordained a. on 11 June 1373 at Whitefriars, York (BIA, Register 11, fol. 391r). On 23 December 1398 he had papal permssion to choose his confessor (*CPL*, v, p. 216).

WETWANG (Wetewang'), Laurence de: he was the guardian of Scarborough on 27 August 1293 when he was authorised to absolve a Scarborough man from a vow made 36 years earlier to go to Compostella (*Reg. Le Romeyn*, i, pp. 229–30, no. 656; *CPL*, i, p. 521). He was at Beverley on 4 April 1318 when he was commissioned to hear the confessions of the prioress and convent of the Cistercian nunnery at Swine in the East Riding (*Reg. Melton*, vi, p. 7, no. 36; BIA, Register 9, fol. 323v).

WHALLEY (Wallay, Whallay), William: he was ordained a. on 19 September 1394 at Austin Friars, York, and s. on 6 March 1395 at Holy Trinity Priory, Micklegate. At his diaconal ordination he was described as a Dominican on 5 June 1395 at St Mary, Bishophill Senior, York (BIA, Register 14, fols. 70rv, 72r). He was the warden of Beverley during the Michaelmas term of 1417 and the Trinity term of 1419, when he was named in the plea rolls (TNA, CP40/627, m. 264 and CP40/633, m. 274).

WHAPLODE, John de: he was probably a friar of Boston when he was licensed to hear confessions in the diocese of Lincoln on 20 June 1318 (LAO, Register 3, fol. 390rv). He was probably the J. de Cappelade, friar of Boston, who died c.1327 (Little, '*Records, Franciscan Province*', p. 150).

WHAPLODE (Quappelad), John de: he was a friar of Grimsby on 26 February 1348 when he was licensed to hear confessions in the archdeaconry of Lincoln *infra limitacionem* [*sic*] of the friary for a year (LAO, Register 9C, fol. 43r).

WHAPLODE (Waplod), John: he was ordained a. and s. on 27 May 1396 at St Mary, Bishophill Senior, York (BIA, Register 14, fol. 72rv)

WHAPLODE (Capelode), Robert de: he was ordained d. at Selby Abbey in 1267/68 (*Reg. Walter Giffard*, p. 189, no. 688).

WHAPLODE, Robert de, senior: a friar presented to the bishop of Lincoln for a licence to hear confessions on 7 December 1321, but rejected (LAO, Register 5, fols. 299v–300r).

WHAPLODE, Robert de, junior: a friar, junior in profession to the friar of the same name and described as senior on 7 December 1321 (LAO, Register 5, fols. 299v–300r).

WHAPLODE (Capelad, Quappelade, Whapelad), Thomas de: he preached at Oxford on 26 December 1292 (Little and Pelster, *Oxford Theology and Theologians*, pp. 162, 178, 184). There is a *reportatio* of a sermon in Worcester Cathedral Library, MS.Q.46, fols. 98–100v, *Stephanus plenus gratia et fortitudine* (Thomson, *Worcester*, p. 145). He was at Oxford on 21 June 1297 when King Edward I sent £16 13s. 4d. to the friars of Oxford by him (BL, Add.MS.7965, fol. 9r). A note on the flyleaf of Cambridge, Peterhouse Library, MS.89 states that William de Tatewic had this copy of Gregory the Great's *Moralia in Job* written with money provided by his friends. In 1299 William of Hartlepool, the minister provincial, allowed him to assign the volume to the Greyfriars of Lincoln after the death of Thomas Whapelad who was permitted to use it during his lifetime. Readers of the volume were requested to pray for the repose of William's soul (Robinson, *Catalogue of Dated and Datable Manuscripts c.737–1600 in Cambridge Libraries*, i, p. 83; *BRUO*, pp. 2029–30). A friar of this name was guardian of London on 19 January 1303 and died soon after (*CPR, 1301–1307*, p. 108; *GFL*, pp. 54–55). See Tatewic, William.

WHAPLODE (Quappelade), William de: he was ordained s. on 22 September 1291 at Grantham prebendal church, d. on 19 September 1293 at Lincoln cathedral, and p. on 18 September 1294 at Dunstable parish church (*Reg. Sutton*, vii, pp. 18, 42, 58).

WHAPLODE (Qwaplode), William: he was ordained s. on 1 June 1398 in St Michael-le-Belfrey, York (BIA, Register 5A, fol. 255v; BL, MS. Cotton Galba, E.X., fol. 119v). He was a friar of Lincoln when he was ordained d. on 22 February 1399 in Stow prebendal church (LAO, Register 13, fol. 85r).

WHATTON, William de: he was ordained s. on 26 May 1347 at Lincoln cathedral (LAO, Register 7B, fol. 13r).

WHELPDALE (Qwelpdall, Whelpedale), William: he was a friar of York when he was ordained a. on 26 May 1464, s. on 8 June 1465, d. on 31 May 1466 and p. on 20 December 1466. The first two ceremonies took place at Blackfriars, York, and the third and fourth in the city's Greyfriars and Whitefriars (BIA, Register 20, fol. 459v, Register 5A, fol. 506v, Register 22, fols. 183r, 184v). On 23 October 1483 he was guardian at Beverley when he was licensed to preach with Friar William Lator (BIA, Register 23, fol. 42v, Reg. Rotherham, p. 39, no. 304).

WHICOPP (Whicop), John de: he was ordained p. on 17 December 1351 at Austin Friars, York (BIA, Register 10A, fol. 54r).

WHITBY (Wyteby), Andrew de: he was a friar of Beverley when he was ordained p. in 1274 (*Reg. Walter Giffard*, p. 198, no. 697).

WHITBY (Wyteby), John de: he was ordained s. on 3 April 1294 at Spaldwick parish church and d. on 22 September 1296 at Lincoln cathedral (*Reg. Sutton*, vii, pp. 51, 83). He was probably a friar of Lincoln when he was licensed to hear confessions in the diocese of Lincoln on 20 June 1318 (LAO, Register 3, fol. 390rv). He was a friar of Grimsby whose death was reported c.1327 (Little, '*Records, Franciscan Province*', p. 150).

WHITBY (Whyteby), John de: he was a friar of Scarborough when he was ordained d. on 11 June 1351 at St Mary's Abbey, York (BIA, Register 10A, fol. 52r).

WHITE (Wyght), William: he was ordained d. on 24 May 1404 at All Saints, Cawood (*Reg. Scrope*, ii, pp. 55, 116, 131).

WHITE, William: he was a friar of York when he was ordained a. on 23 March 1504 at Greyfriars, York, s. on 19 December 1506 at Austin Friars, York, and d. on 27 February 1507 at Whitefriars, York (BIA, Register 25, fols. 122v, 136v, 137v. Cf. Cross and Vickers, *MFN*, p. 441). He was the limiter at Beverley when he received 12d. in the will of Edward Morton of Little Wassand in Holderness on 8 March 1527 (BIA, Probate Register 9, fol. 375r). He was at Lincoln on 8 October 1539 when he obtained his capacity (Chambers, *Faculty Office Registers 1534–1549*, p. 195).

WHITEHILL (Wythill), Hugh: he was ordained p. on 17 December 1345 at Liddington prebendal church (LAO, Register 7B, fol. 3r).

WHITEMORE, William: he was ordained p. on 15 June 1359 at Cawood manor chapel (BIA, Register 11, fol. 338r).

WHITFIELD (Qwitfeld), John: he was ordained d. on 13 June 1416 in the prebendal chapel at Cawood (BIA, Register 18, fol. 39Ir).

WHITGIFT (Whitgifte, Whitgyft, Qwedgyft), Richard: he was ordained a. on 5 June 1406 at the Austin Friars, York. He was at York when he was ordained s. on 19 February 1407 at Blackfriars, York, d. on 21 December 1409 and p. on 17 May 1410. The third and fourth ceremonies took place at All Saints, Cawood (BIA, Register 5A, fols. 321v, 323v, Register 18, fols. 391v, 392v; *Reg. Sede Vacante York, 1405–08*, pp. 66, 85, 89).

WHITLEY (Whitlay), Thomas: he was a friar of York when he was ordained a. on 14 March 1500 and s. on 4 April 1500; both ceremonies took place at Greyfriars, York. He was ordained d. on 18 April 1500 at the lady altar of York Minster, and p. on 13 June 1500 at Blackfriars, York (BIA, Register 23, fols. 466v, 467v, 468r, Register 5A, fol. 528r. Cf. Cross and Vickers, *MFN*, p. 439). He was at York on 9 September 1510 when he witnessed the will of Sir Henry Ughtred, a knight of Kexby (*Yorks. Deeds*, ii, p. 124, no. 337).

WHITTINGBURGH (Whittyngburgh), John de: he was ordained p. on 22 December 1375 at Cawood manor chapel (BIA, Register 12, fol. 123r).

WICKHAM (Wikeham, Wikham, Wycam), John: he was a friar of York when he was ordained a. on 23 September 1503 and s. on 23 March 1504; both ceremonies took place at Greyfriars, York. He was ordained d. on 20 September 1505 in Bishopthorpe manor chapel, York, and p. on 20 December 1505 at Austin Friars, York (BIA, Register 25, fols. 120r, 122v, 130r, 131r). He received 4d. to celebrate Mass for John Besby (Beisbey), alderman of York, whose will was compiled on 23 July 1535 (BIA, Probate Register 11, fol. 148r). He was at York at the Dissolution on 27 November 1538 (*Eighth Report of the Deputy Keeper of the Public Records*, p. 51). Within weeks of the suppression he was assisting at *obits* in St Michael's, Spurriergate, York, between 1538 and 1543, dying shortly afterwards (*Churchwardens' Accounts of St Michael, Spurriergate*, pp. 10*, 198, 223–24, 250–51, 261. Cf. Cross and Vickers, *MFN*, pp. 441, 460).

WIEGHTE, Hugh: formerly a friar of Lincoln who obtained his capacity on 8 October 1539 (Chambers, *Faculty Office Registers 1534–1549*, p. 195).

WIGTON (Wygton), Richard: he was a friar of York when he was ordained s. on 29 May 1507 at Blackfriars, York, d. on 18 September 1507 at Whitefriars, York, and p. on 18 December 1507 at Austin Friars, York (BIA, Register 25, fol. 140v, Register 5A, fols. 580r, 584v. Cf. Cross and Vickers, *MFN*, p. 442).

WILDEST (Wyldest), Robert: he was a friar of York when he was ordained s. on 16 March 1499 at Whitefriars, York, and d. on 30 March 1499 (BIA, Register 23, fol. 463r, bis). He was a friar of Lincoln when he was ordained p. on 25 May 1499 at Sleaford prebendal church (LAO, Register 24, fol. 18v).

WILHAM, John de: he was a friar of York when he was ordained p. on 23 September 1363 at Bishopthorpe manor chapel (BIA, Register 11 fol. 354r).

WILLI, Cornelius: he was ordained d. on 17 December 1412 at Greyfriars, York (BIA, Register 18, fol. 395v).

WILLIAM: at Michaelmas 1368 he was the guardian of Lincoln when he was named in the plea rolls with William de Dalton (TNA, CP40/432, m. 14d, 475). The same two friars were mentioned in Trinity term of the next year (TNA, CP40/434, m. 262d).

WILLIAM: he was the guardian of York when he was named in the plea rolls of Easter 1383 (TNA, CP40/489, m. 489).

WILLIAM: he was guardian of York in 1508 when he granted letters of fraternity to Master Thomas Berkeley (*Descriptive catalogue of the charters and muniments in the possession of the Rt. Hon. Lord Fitzhardinge at Berkeley Castle*, p. 201, no. 671).

WILLIAMSON, John: a former friar of Scarborough who obtained his capacity on 20 June 1539 (Chambers, *Faculty Office Registers 1534–1549*, p. 187. Cf. Cross and Vickers, *MFN*, p. 454).

WILLINGHAM (Wilingeham), Alexander de: he was a friar of Beverley when he was ordained p. in 1274 (*Reg. Walter Giffard*, p. 198, no. 697).

WILLOUGHBY (Wylugbi), John de: he was a friar of Lincoln through whom King Edward I paid £4 4s. to the friars there in February 1300/01 (BL, Add.MS.7966a, fol. 27r).

WILLOUGHBY (Wylughby), Richard de: he was probably a friar of Grimsby when he was licensed to hear confessions in the diocese of Lincoln on 20 June 1318 (LAO, Register 3, fol. 390r).

WILLOUGHBY (Wylughby), Thomas de: he was a friar of York when he was ordained p. on 26 May 1358 at Greyfriars, York (BIA, Register 11, fol. 334r).

WILSON (Wylson), John, senior: he was a friar of York when ordained a. on 21 September 1510 at Holy Trinity Priory, Micklegate, York, s. on 18 December 1512 at Austin Friars, York, d. on 21 May 1513 and p. on 23 September 1514. The last two ceremonies took place at Blackfriars, York (BIA, Register 26, fols. 109r, 121r, 124v, 150r, Register 5A, fol. 622v). He was one of the ten friars of Doncaster who signed the deed of surrender on 20 November 1538 (*Eighth Report of the Deputy Keeper of the Public Records*, p. 19). In 1548 a John Wilson was one of the four priests serving Southil's chantry in Wakefield parish church (*Chantries, Guilds, Hospitals*, ii, pp. 306–07). This cleric was still living at Wakefield when he made his will on 24 October 1575 and requested burial in Wakefield churchyard, setting aside 10s. to be distributed in bread to the poor on the day of his burial. After making some bequests to relatives, he gave the residue of his goods to his executors to be disposed on behalf of the poor and in works of charity (BIA, Probate Register 20, fol. 19r). If this testator is to be identified with the former friar of either Doncaster or York, he must have been born about 1490 (cf. Cross and Vickers, *MFN*, pp. 443, 447, 449).

WILSON, John, junior: he was a friar of Lincoln when he was ordained s. on 15 April 1536 in the chapel of St Mary Magdalene, Lincoln cathedral, and d on 10 June 1536 in the prebendal church at Buckden (LAO, Register 26, fol. 52rv). He was one of the six friars of Grimsby to sign the deed of surrender at the Dissolution on 9 October 1538 (*Eighth Report of the Deputy Keeper of the Public Records*, p. 22).

WILSON, Richard: in the defamation case of 1532 this friar of Scarborough was alleged to have called Henry Dykonson, chaplain in the parish church, a 'false priest, lewd priest, naughty priest, drunken priest', adding for good measure, that he was the 'falsest priest that ever came to Scarborough'. By 1544 a priest of this name had secured the rectory of Roxby in Lincolnshire. A cleric of this name resigned the vicarage of Walkington in March 1590 (Cause Papers, G 222; *LPFD*, p. xix, n. 610 (74); Institution Act Book 3, fol. 224v. Cf. Cross and Vickers, *MFN*, p. 454).

WILSON, William: he was a friar of Oxford when he was ordained s. on 19 September 1489 at All Saints, Northampton. He was a friar of Stamford when he was ordained d. on 27 March 1490 at Liddington prebendal church, and at Lincoln when he was ordained p. on 11 April 1490 in the chapel of St Mary Magdalene in Lincoln cathedral (LAO, Register 22, fols. 33r, 35r, 36r; *BRUO*, p. 2052).

WILSON, William: he was a friar of York when he was ordained a. on 20 February 1524 at Whitefriars, York (BIA, Register 27, fol. 200v. Cf. Cross and Vickers, *MFN*, p. 445).

WILTON (Wylton), John de: while he was a student at Oxford he was chosen to accompany William Gainsborough to the general chapter of Assisi in 1295. On 1 March 1295 the king gave the two friars a letter of credence and explained that they were expediting business on his behalf (*CCR, 1288–1296*, p. 440). On 1 September 1295 John received 20s from the crown to be passed to William Gainsborough (TNA, E36/202, fol. 44v). Courtenay suggests that he was at Paris in June 1303, when he supported Pope Boniface VIII rather than King Philip the Fair (Courtenay, 'Early Scotists at Paris: A Reconsideration', p. 226, n. 112). Bale claims that he lectured at Paris (cf. *GFO*, p. 166). He was the 40th regent master at Oxford and in that capacity he was one of the 12 regent masters who condemned certain theological propositions in 1314 (Eccleston, p. 55; *BRUO*, p. 2053; *Munimenta Academica or documents illustrative of academical life and studies at Oxford*, i, p. 101). John of Reading cites him in his *Commentary on the Sentences* (Longpré, 'Jean de Reading et le B. Jean Duns Scot', p. 103).

WINTERSHAM (Witringham, Wyntresham), Thomas de: he submitted written testimony regarding a visit to the Knights Templar at the preceptory of Temple Bruer, between Lincoln and Boston, on Christmas day about 1302/03 in the company of another friar, Simon of Geuertodes; the two friars made certain observations about the Knights' liturgical practices (Nicholson, *Templars*, i, pp. 185, 387, ii, xxxi, pp. 193–94, 442).

WINTRINGHAM (Wyntryngham), James: he was a friar of Boston when he was ordained s. in the chapel of St Mary Magdalene, Lincoln cathedral, on 25 March 1497 (LAO, Register 24, fol. 7r). He was a friar of York when he was ordained p. on 23 September 1497 at Whitefriars, York (BIA, Register 23, fol. 457r. Cf. Cross and Vickers, *MFN*, p. 439, where they give the Christian name of John).

WINTRINGHAM (Wyntringham), Robert de: he was ordained s. on 23 September 1290 at St Leonard's in Stamford, d. on 31 May 1292 at Lincoln cathedral, and p. on 19 September 1293 also in the cathedral (*Reg. Sutton*, vii, pp. 4, 28, 44). He was licensed in the diocese of York to hear the confessions of the Cistercian nuns of Nun Appleton on 17 October 1300 (*Reg. Corbridge*, i, p. 34, no. 94). He was still at York on 12 April 1318 when he was licensed as a confessor to the same nunnery (BIA, Register 9, fol. 155r). He and a Dominican were appointed to hear the confessions of the Benedictine nuns of Wilberfoss on 13 June 1318 (*Reg. Melton*, vi, p. 11, no. 59). He was licensed in the diocese of Lincoln on 20 June 1318, probably as a friar of Lincoln (LAO, Register 3, fol. 390rv).

WIRKESALE, William de: he was ordained p. on 14 June 1348 at St Mary's Abbey, York (BIA, Register 10A, fol. 25r).

WISBECH (Wysebeche), John de: he was licensed in the diocese of York in place of Alexander de Wisebech at an unknown date (BIA, Register 11, fol. 396r).

WISBECH (Wisebech), Reginald de: he was a friar of Boston when he was ordained s. on 16 March 1359 in Liddington prebendal church. He was at Grimsby when he was ordained d. on 21 December 1359. He was a friar of Northampton when he was ordained p. on 29 February 1360; the second and third ceremonies were held in Lincoln cathedral (LAO, Register 9D, fols. 91r, 93v, 95r).

WISTHORN (Wisthoring), John de: he was ordained d. on 29 May 1344 in the parish church of Newark (BIA, Register 10A, fol. 7r) and p. on 17 December 1345 at Liddington prebendal church (LAO, Register 7B, fol. 3r).

WITTENHAM (Wytenham), John de: he was ordained p. on 22 September 1358 at Bishop Burton manor chapel near Beverley (BIA, Register 11, fol. 335r).

WITTON (Wyton), Thomas de: he was ordained p. on 23 September 1368 at Bishopthorpe manor chapel (BIA, Register 11, fol. 371r).

WODEHALLE, John de la: on 19 August 1286 the Franciscans in the diocese of

York were empowered to absolve persons excommunicated for laying violent hands on clerks. This friar was singled out for special mention (*Reg. Le Romeyn*, i, p. 189, no. 541).

WODEROVE (Woderoue), William de: he was ordained p. on 21 March 1360 in Durham cathedral (Durham Registers: Hatfield, fol. 103r). He may be identified with William Woderove, guardian of Doncaster in the Trinity term of 1379, when he was mentioned in the plea rolls (TNA, CP40/474, m. 260, CP40/475, m. 77).

WOLFE (Wolf), Roger: he was a friar of Beverley when he was ordained p. on 20 December 1449 at Austin Friars, York (BIA, Register 19, fol. 293Ar).

WOLLOR, Thomas: he was the lector at York on 30 August 1398 when he was licensed as a confessor in the diocese (*Reg. Scrope*, ii, p. 12, no. 729).

WOLSTONE (Wolston), Henry: he was a friar of York when he was ordained a. on 25 February 1464 at Whitefriars, York, at Beverley when he was ordained s. on 17 March 1464 at Greyfriars, York, and at York when he was ordained d. on 26 May 1464 at Blackfriars, York (BIA, Register 20, fols. 457v, 458v, 460r).

WORMELE (Wormeley), Robert de: he was a friar of Boston when he was ordained p. on 19 December 1355 at Stow prebendal church (LAO, Register 9D, fol. 78r).

WORP (Worpe), John: he was a friar of York when he was ordained s. on 3 June 1452 at Whitefriars, York, d. on 23 September 1452 at Greyfriars, York, and p. on 23 December 1452 at Austin Friars, York (BIA, Register 19, fols. 303r, 304r, Register 20, fol. 412v).

WOTTON, John: he was a friar of Boston when he was ordained a. on 24 March 1425 at Liddington parish church (*Reg. Fleming*, ii, p. 105, no. 501). He was a friar of Doncaster when he was licensed to hear the confessions of the nuns of Hampole on 10 September 1426 (BIA, Register 19, fol. 28r).

WOTTON, Thomas de: he was ordained d. on 20 September 1365 in Cawood manor chapel (BIA, Register 11, fol. 361r).

WRAA, John: he was a friar of York when he was ordained a. on 19 September 1461 at Blackfriars, York (BIA, Register 20, fol. 449r).

WRIGHT (Wight), Hugh: he was a friar of Lincoln when he was ordained a. on 30 March 1532, s. on 12 April 1533, d. on 4 April 1534 in the lady chapel of Lincoln cathedral, and p. on 19 September 1534 at Liddington prebendal church. The first two ordinatons were celebrated in Lincoln cathedral. Prior to his diaconal ordination he was examined by the chancellor of the diocese and the prior of St Katherine's in Lincoln, and on the fourth by Robert King, the suffragan bishop of *Reonensis* (LAO, Register 26, fols. 30r, 33v, 39r, 41r).

WYKYNBY, William: he was a friar of York when he was ordained s. on 23 May 1377 at York Minster (BIA, Register 12, fol. 128v).

WYNDER, Richard: a friar of Scarborough who obtained his capacity on 20 June

1539 (Chambers, *Faculty Office Registers 1534–1549*, p. 187. Cf. Cross and Vickers, *MFN*, p. 454).

WYNDILL, Edward: he was a friar of York when he was ordained a. on 24 March 1509 at Blackfriars, York, s. on 25 May 1510 at Blackfriars, York, d. on 21 September 1510 at Holy Trinity Priory, Micklegate, York, and p. on 21 December 1510 at Austin Friars, York (BIA, Register 26, fols. 101r, 108r, 109r, 110v. Cf. Cross and Vickers, *MFN*, p. 443).

WYNK (Wink), Peter: he was a friar of York when he was ordained a. on 24 September 1468 at Whitefriars, York, s. on 27 May 1469 at Blackfriars, York, and d. on 22 September 1470 at Greyfriars, York. He was ordained p. on 21 December 1471 at Austin Friars, York (BIA, Register 22, fols. 196r, 201r, 207v, 213r).

WYRKESWORTH (Werkesworth, Wirkesworth, Wyrkesworth), John de: he was a friar of York when he was ordained a. on 24 April 1350 at Greyfriars, York. He was ordained d. on 18 December 1350 at Blackfriars, York, and p. on 12 March 1351 also at Blackfriars, York (BIA, Register 10A, fols. 45v, 50r, 51r).

WYSEMALE, Michael: he was a friar of York when he was ordained p. on 20 September 1483 at Whitefriars, York (BIA, Register 23, fol. 389r. Cf. Cross and Vickers, *MFN*, p. 435).

YARM (Jarom, Yarom), John de: he was ordained s. on 29 March 1343 at Greyfriars, Beverley (BIA, Register 10A, fol. 3r). He was ordained d. on 20 December 1343 in Durham cathedral and p. on 29 May 1344 in Darlington parish church (*Reg. Kellaw*, iii, pp. 134, 143).

YARWELL (Jarewell), Richard de: on the deposition of Peter of Thurlby (*Rot. Gravesend*, p. 77), he was elected as prior of the Augustinian Canons of Nocton Park, Lincolnshire (1277–86). His name as prior occurs between Michaelmas 1277 and Michaelmas 1278 (TNA, E159/51, m. 19d). He resigned to become a friar before 10 May 1286 (*Reg. Sutton*, i, pp. 83–85; *Heads*, ii, p. 433).

YARWELLE (Yarwell), Walter de: a priest and novice at York. He died c.1327 (Little, '*Records, Franciscan Province*', p. 150).

YNGLEBY (Ingelby, Yngilby), Thomas: he was a friar of Lincoln when he was ordained a. on 20 March 1451 at St Margaret's in the close of Lincoln cathedral (LAO, Register 19, fol. 29v). A friar of this name, a priest and scholar in the diocese of Lincoln, sought a dispensation from illegitimacy on 19 March 1461; his parents were both unmarried (*Supplic. Apost. Penit.*, i, p. 233, no. 1104). Parkinson describes him as a professor of divinity (*Collectanea Anglo-minoritica*, p. 206). He was provided to the diocese of Maghera on 20 April 1471 and on 23 April 1471 he was consecrated in the church of the English Hospital by Peter, *episcopus Othanensis*, James, *episcopus S.Angeli de Lombardis*, and Anthony, *episcopus Assolicensis* (Brady, *The succession in England, Scotland and Ireland A.D. 1400 to 1875*, i, p. 323). He held the diocese until his death in the summer of 1499. His name does not occur in *Materials, Ireland*.

He acted as suffragan at Lincoln between 1472 and 1496 (LAO, Register 21, fols. 136rv, 140v, 143v, 145v, 147v, 148v, 150v, 156v, 157v, 159, 160v–61v, 162v–64, 165,

166, 167, 168–69, 170–71, Register 22, fols. 1r, 2r, 3r, 4rv, 6v, 7, 8rv, 9v, 10v–11v, 12v–13v, 14v, 15r, 16r–17r, 18r–19v, 20v, 21r, 22r–23v, 24v–26v, 27v, 46rv, 49rv, 50v–51v, 52v, 53v, 54, Register 24, fol. 4r). On 1 February 1475 he is described as living in the diocese of Lincoln when Sixtus IV appointed him and the bishops of Winchester and Bangor to arbitrate in a matrimonial case (*CPL*, xiii, i, pp. 398–99). On 24 February 1477 Thomas, described as the king's clerk and bishop of Maghera, was presented to the parish church of Sutton Bonington, Nottinghamshire, in the diocese of York. He resigned the parish and on 22 April 1480 his successor was appointed (*CPR, 1476–1485*, pp. 16, 189). He was admitted to the guild of *Corpus Christi* at Boston in 1479 (BL, Harley, MS.4795, fol. 48r). He was also suffragan at London. On 23 April 1487 he and William of Dromore were commissioned to reconsecrate the Franciscan church of Scarborough polluted by the violent effusion of blood (*Reg. Rotherham*, p. 219, no. 1752). He held ordinations in the diocese of London on 19 March 1491 and 2 April 1491 (GHL, MS.9531/8, fols. 22v–23r). He was appointed vicar of South-Weld in the archdeaconry of Essex on 8 October 1498 (GHL, MS.9531, viii, fol. 44r). He had died by 30 October 1499 when his successor was appointed (GHL, MS.9531/8, fol. 50v). Stubbs maintains that he died shortly before 8 July 1499 (Stubbs, *Registrum Sacrum Anglicanum*, p. 209). Newcourt claims that the parish of South-Weld, in the archdeaconry of Essex, was filled on 30 October 1499, and that the bishop had been appointed as vicar on 8 October 1498 (Newcourt, ii, p. 645; Smith, 'Suffragan Bishops in the Medieval Diocese of Lincoln', p. 26; Butler, 'Suffragan Bishops in the Medieval Diocese of York', p. 59).

YODALE, John: he was a friar of Doncaster when he was ordained s. on 19 December 1506 at Austin Friars, York, and d. on 20 March 1507 at Greyfriars, York. He was at York when ordained p. on 23 December 1508 at Austin Friars, York (BIA, Register 25, fols. 136r, 138r, Register 26, fol. 100r. Cf. Cross and Vickers, *MFN*, p. 442).

YONKE, John: he was a friar of Lincoln when he was ordained p. on 12 April 1533 in Lincoln cathedral (LAO, Register 26, fol. 34r).

YOUNG (Yong), John: he was a friar of Doncaster when he was ordained s. on 2 March 1420. He was at York when ordained d. on 1 June 1420. Both ceremonies took place at Cawood prebendal chapel (BIA, Register 18, fols. 405r, 406r).

YOUNG (Yonge), John: he was a friar of Lincoln when he was ordained s. on 12 June 1473 in Lincoln cathedral. He was at Bedford when he was ordained d. on 24 September 1474 at Towcester parish church (LAO, Register 21, fols. 139v, 145r).

YOUNG (Yonge), John: he was a friar of York when ordained a. on 18 September 1484 at Whitefriars, York (BIA, Register 23, fol. 393v. Cf. Cross and Vickers, *MFN*, p. 436).

YORK (Ebor), Adam de: one of two friars whom the minister general sent to lecture at Lyon (Eccleston, p. 49). He was described as a native of the county town (*Leland, De viris illustribus*, pp. 454–55, no. 248).

YORK, Alan de: on 3 September 1300 he received the royal alms of £10 for the provincial chapter at Stamford (BL, MS.Add.7966A, fol. 28r).

YORK (Ebor), Henry de: he was ordained s. on 19 September 1293 in Lincoln cathedral and d. on 18 December 1294 at Stow prebendal church (*Reg. Sutton*, vii, pp. 40, 61).

YORK (Ebor), John de: a friar of Lincoln licensed to hear confessions within the *limitatio* of Lincoln on 10 August and again on 12 October 1300 (Little, *Franciscan Papers, Lists, and Documents*, pp. 237, 238).

YORK (Ebor), John de: he was a friar of Boston on 13 November 1347 when he was licensed to hear confessions *infra limitacionem* [*sic*] of the friary for one year (LAO, Register 9C, fol. 40r).

YORK (Ebor), John de: he was ordained d. on 22 September 1414 at Blackfriars, York (BIA, Register 18, fol. 396v).

YORK (Ebor), Robert de: he was ordained d. in 1267/68 at Selby Abbey (*Reg. Walter Giffard*, p. 189, no. 608). A friar of this name was cited as witness in the trial of the Knights Templar in 1310/11. He testified that about 1290 he had been approached by an unnamed Templar after confession who asked what would happen if he denied God (Nicholson, *Templars*, i, pp. 184–85, 381, ii, 193, 435, 474).

YORK, Thomas de: he probably entered the order c.1230/35 at York. He was first mentioned as a very dear friar in Adam Marsh's letter of January 1245 when he was in possession of the chapters of the first philosophy, the *Liber de philosophia prima* (*Letters of Adam Marsh*, pp. 516–17). Thomas was described as Grosseteste's most obedient servant, *subiectissimo reverentie vestre famulo* (*ibid.*, pp. 170–71). William of Nottingham, minister provincial, solicited Adam Marsh's advice about Thomas, a friar of bright genius, accomplished learning and well-governed integrity, in 1250/51. Adam's advice was that Thomas should be commanded to apply himself to the study of the Scriptures, to hear the doctors' lectures and to examine their writings; he should not be burdened with the office of teaching and should be groomed as the next regent master at Oxford (*ibid.*, pp. 480–81). Thomas was of sufficient stature in the English province by 1251 to be consulted about James Erlandson, bishop of Roskilde, and his application for English friars to minister in Denmark (*ibid.*, pp. 22–25). In 1252 Adam received a letter from Grosseteste regarding the Crusaders' reverses in the Holy Land and took the opportunity to recommend the business of the monastery of Grace Dieu at Belton. Adam refers to Thomas as the prelate's most obedient servant, who was energetic, discreet and well disposed and fired by heaven with a burning ardour for all things pertaining to the salvation of souls (*ibid.*, pp. 64–65). An undated letter from Adam Marsh to Grosseteste repeats this commendation and remarks that he had written to Thomas about the business of Grace Dieu (*ibid.*, pp. 170–71). Adam Marsh refers to consulting Thomas along with John de Kent, the papal *nuncio*, the guardian of Oxford and Richard Rufus of Cornwall about a communication from the minister general to Richard Rufus (*ibid.*, pp. 438–39).

In February 1253 the University of Oxford approved Thomas's appointment as the fourth Franciscan regent master on account of his distinguished conduct, his intellectual gifts and his proven learning, although some objected that he was not a master of arts (*ibid.*, pp. 450–51). In the absence of Adam Marsh, Peter Manners, a Dominican regent master in theology, presided over Thomas's inception (*ibid.*, pp. 468–69). Thomas joined John, custos of Oxford, and Adam Marsh in writing to the minister provincial (*ibid.*, pp. 454–55). Similarly, he was one of the friars of Oxford who wrote an undated letter to the custos of Worcester (*ibid.*, pp. 474–75). Three of Adam Marsh's letters were addressed to Thomas (*ibid.*, pp. 538–43). The middle one alludes to Thomas's kindness to the father of John of Beverley, a friar (*GFO*, pp. 140–41), and the third at Cambridge about three years later (*GFC*, p. 225; *BRUC*, p. 666).

Thomas's sermon on the passion is at Trinity College Library, Cambridge, MS.B.15.38 (Reilly, 'A sermon of Thomas of York on the passion'). He is credited with a Commentary on Ecclesiastes (*Leland, De viris illustribus*, pp. 458–59, no. 254). His *Manus quae contra Omnipotentem* was written against William of St Amour about 1256 (Thomas of York, '*Manus, que contra Omnipotentem tenditur*', *Bettelorden und Weltgeistlichkeit an der Universität Paris: Texte und Untersuchungen zum literarischen Armuts- und Exemtionsstreit des 13. Jahrhunderts (1255–1272)*). Pelster ('Thomas von York, O.F.M., als Verfasser des Traktats Manus quae contra Omnipotentem tenditur', pp. 3–22, at 15–19) argues that Thomas wrote this in Paris, a conclusion also reached by Denifle and Longpré. He was the only English friar to enter the first phase of the mendicant controversy at the University of Paris. A copy of Thomas's polemical treatise was at Merton College Library in 1483 (*UCLO*, ii, 956, no. 40). Fr Longpré maintains that Thomas's *Sapientiale* was written between 1250 and 1256 (Longpré, 'Fr. Thomas d'York, O.F.M. La première Somme métaphysique du XIIIe siècle'; Sharp, *Franciscan Philosophy at Oxford*, pp. 49–112. Cf. Longpré, Thomas d'York et Matthieu d'Aquasparta, Textes inédits sur le problème de la création', pp. 269–308). More recent scholarship shows that he was working on this text until his death c.1260. Dr F. Retucci quotes Biblioteca Apostolica Vaticana, Vat. Lat 4301, fol. 194vb: *explicit liber septimus quem non complevit morte preventus* (Retucci, 'The *Sapientiale* of Thomas of York, OFM: The Fortunes and Misfortunes of a Critical Edition', pp. 140, 142). She adds that about 70 years after Thomas's death the *Sapientiale* was reproduced verbatim by Berthold of Moosburg, the principal lector of the Dominican studium at Cologne, in his *Expositio super elementationem theologicam Procli*, although he did cite him as *Magister Thomas Anglicus minor* in a table of doctors of theology on whose work he had drawn (*Berthold von Moosburg, Expositio super Elementationem theologicam Procli*, VI, 1, 3–4). Berthold reproduces parallel passages (Retucci, 'The *Sapientiale* of Thomas of York, OFM: The Fortunes and Misfortunes of a Critical Edition', pp. 135–40). Book one, chapters 27–29, of the *Sapientiale* have been transcribed by Professor Retucci ('Tomasso di York, Eustrazio e la dottrina delle idee di Platone', pp. 89–110). She is currently preparing a critical edition of the *Sapientiale* that is found in three thirteenth-century manuscripts (Città del Vaticano, Biblioteca Apostolica Vaticana, Vat.lat.4301 and 6771, and Florence, Biblioteca Nazionale, Conv.Soppr.A.VI.437). Thomas's partial commentary on *Liber XXIV philosophorum*, which was incorporated into the *Sapientiale*, has been edited by Professor Françoise Hudry (*Liber viginti quattuor philosophorum*; *BRUO*, pp. 2139–40; Sharpe, *Handlist*, p. 696, no. 1865; Little, 'The Franciscan School at Oxford in the Thirteenth Century', pp. 839–41). Prior to his death Thomas returned to his native city of York (*Leland, De viris illustribus*, pp. 458–59, no. 254). He died about 1260.

YORK (Ebor), Thomas de: he was ordained d. on 29 March 1343 at Greyfriars, Beverley (BIA, Register 10A, fol. 3r). A friar of this name received £4 in silver in the will of Eva de Crome, widow of John de Crome, citizen of York and merchant, on 5 May 1395 (BIA, Probate Register 1, fol. 96v).

YORK, William: styled as a *solemnis bachelarius* who entered the order with Adam Rufus at Oxford on 25 January 1229 or 1230 (Eccleston, p. 16). He is probably to be identified with an Oxonian master of that name who witnessed the institution of

Thomas de Longa Villa as prior of St Andrew's, Northampton, on 10 June 1228 (*Rot. Welles*, ii, pp. 144–45; *GFO*, p. 179; *BRUO*, p. 2140).

YORK (Ebor), William de: he was ordained p. on 17 December 1345 at Whitefriars, York (BIA, Register 10A, fol. 13v).

YOZATE, Peter de: he was a friar of Boston when he was ordained d. on 20 September 1404 in Lincoln cathedral (LAO, Register 13, fol. 116r).

YPRIS, Peter de: he was ordained d. on 1 March 1393 in the parish church of St Michael-le-Belfrey, York (BIA, Register 14, fol. 66r).

YRETON, Hugh de: he was licensed to hear confessions in the diocese of York on 29 October 1351 (BIA, Register 10A, fol. 280r).

YRNAM, John: he was a friar of York on 18 September 1426 when he witnessed the public revocation by Thomas Richmond (*Convocation, York*, pp. 399–400; *Records of the Northern Convocation*, p. 167).

ZETON, John: he was a friar of York when he was ordained p. on 20 September 1438 at Greyfriars, York (BIA, Register 19, fol. 258r).

Select bibliography

Primary sources

Adam de Wodeham, Lectura Secunda in librum primum Sententiarum, ed. R. Wood and G. Gál, 3 vols (The Franciscan Institute, St. Bonaventure University, New York, 1990).

The Anonimalle Chronicle 1307 to 1334: From Brotherton Collection MS 29, ed. W.R. Childs and J. Taylor, YAS, RS, CXLVII (1991).

Anonymus, Directio Periodici, 'Compendium Chronicarum Fratrum Minorum scriptum a Patre Mariano de Florentia', *AFH*, II (1909), pp. 92–107, 305–18, 457–72, 626–41.

The Archdeaconry of Richmond in the Eighteenth Century, Bishop Gastrell's 'notitia' – the Yorkshire Parishes 1714–1725, ed. L.A.S. Butler, YAS, RS, CXLVI (1990).

Archivio Sartori: documenti di storia e arte francescana, ed. G. Luisetto, 4 vols (Padua, 1983–89).

Ball, R.M., *Thomas Gascoigne, Libraries and Scholarship*, Cambridge Bibliographical Society, XIV (Cambridge, 2006).

Baskerville, G., 'Married Clergy and Pensioned Religious in Norwich Diocese, 1555', *EHR*, XLVIII (1933), pp. 43–64, 199–228.

Bede Ecclesiastical History of the English People, ed. B. Colgrave and R.A.B. Mynors, OMT (Oxford, 1969).

'Bernardi de Bessa, Liber de laudibus beati Francisci', *FF*, pp. 1253–96.

Berthold von Moosburg, Expositio super Elementationem theologicam Procli, Corpus Philosophorum Teutonicorum Medii Aevi, ed. K. Flasch et al., 8 vols (Hamburg, 1984–2014).

'Bettelorden und Weltgeistlichkeit an der Universität Paris: Texte und Untersuchungen zum literarischen armuts-und exemtionsstreit des 13' in Jahrhunderts (1255–1272)', ed. M. Bierbaum, Franziskanische Studien, II (Münster, 1920), pp. 37–168.

Beverley Town Documents, ed. A.F. Leach, Selden Society, XIV (London, 1900).

Bihl, M., 'Ordinationes a Benedicto XII pro Fratribus Minoribus promulgatae per bullam 28 Novembris 1336', *AFH*, XXX (1937), pp. 309–85.

Bihl, M., 'Raymundus Gaufridi, Minister generalis, Parisiis 9 iunii 1292 confirmat conventionem initam inter Provincias Austriae et Alemaniae Superioris de terminis eleemosynarum conquirendarum in confiniis', *AFH*, XXXVI (1943), pp. 98–102.

Bihl, M., 'Statuta provincialia provinciarum Aquitaniae et Franciae (saec. XIII–XIV)', *AFH*, VII (1914), pp. 466–501.

The Book of Margery Kempe, ed. S.B. Meech with notes by H.E. Allen, Early English Texts Society (Oxford, 1940).

Bougerol, J.G., 'Sermons de maîtres franciscains du XIII siècle', *AFH*, LXXXI (1988), pp. 17–49.

Brady, W.M., *The succession in England, Scotland and Ireland A.D. 1400 to 1875: with appointments to monasteries and extracts from consistorial acts taken from MSS in public and private libraries in Rome, Florence, Bologna; Ravenna and Paris*, 3 vols (Rome, 1876–77).

Brigg, W., 'Testamenta Leodiensia', *Miscellanea*, PThS, II (1891), pp. 98–110, 205–14.

Brigg, W., 'Testamenta Leodiensia', *Miscellanea*, PThS, IV (1895), pp. 1–16, 139–47.

Brown, W., 'Old Wills from Harpham (preserved at Scampston)', *The Transactions of the East Riding Antiquarian Society*, XXI (1915), pp. 70–79.

Bughetti, B., 'Tabulae Capitulares Provinciae Tusciae O.M. (saec. XIV–XVIII)', *AFH*, X (1917), pp. 413–97.

Burton, J.E., 'Archbishop William Melton's Visitations of St Mary's Abbey and St Clement's Priory, York, 1317–1324', *The Church in Medieval York, Records edited in honour of Professor Barrie Dobson*, ed. D.M. Smith, BTC, XXIV (York, 1999), pp. 29–49.

Butler, L.A.S., *The Archdeaconry of Richmond in the Eighteenth Century, Bishop Gastrell's 'notitia' – the Yorkshire Parishes 1714–1725*, YAS, RS, CXLVI (1990).

Butler, L.A.S., 'Suffragan Bishops in the Medieval Diocese of York', *NH*, XXXVII (2000), pp. 49–60.

Calamandrei, J., 'Constitutiones Fratrum Minorum Observantium Provinciae Thusciae ann.1507 et 1523', *AFH*, VIII (1915), pp. 189–225.

Calendar of entries in the Papal registers relating to Great Britain and Ireland. Petitions to the Pope, ed. W.H. Bliss (London, 1896).

Callebaut, A., 'Acta Capituli Generalis Mediolani celebrati an.1285', *AFH*, XXII (1929), pp. 273–91.

The Calverley Charters presented to the British Museum by Sir Walter Calverley Trevelyan, baronet, vol. 1, ed. W.P. Baildon and S. Margerison, PThS, VI (1904).

Canterbury Professions, ed. M. Richter, CYS, LXVII (1973).

Cartularium abbathiae de Whiteby, ordinis S. Benedicti, fundatae anno MLXXVIII, ed. J.C. Atkinson, 2 vols, SS, LXIX, LXXII (1879, 1881).

Castleford's Chronicle or The Boke of Brut, ed. C.D. Eckhardt, 2 vols, Early English Text Society, original series, CCCV, CCCVI (Oxford, 1996).

Catto, J.I. and L.R. Mooney, 'The Chronicle of John Somer, OFM', *Chronology, Conquest and Conflict in Medieval England*, Camden Miscellany, XXXIV, CS, Fifth Series, X (Cambridge, 1997), pp. 197–285.

Cenci, C., 'Antonio da Pereto, Ministro generale O.F.M. e i Capitoli generali di Roma (1411) e di Mantova (1418)', *AFH*, LV (1962), pp. 468–500.

Cenci, C., 'Bonifacio Lupi di Soragna e i Frati Minori', *AFH*, LVII (1964), pp. 90–109.

Cenci, C., 'Constitutiones Provinciales Provinciae Umbriae anno 1316', *AFH*, LVI (1963), pp. 12–39.

Cenci, C., '*Fra Francesco da Lendinara e la storia della Provincia di S.Antonio tra la fine del s. XIV e l'inizio del s.XV*', *AFH*, LV (1962), pp. 103–92.

Cenci, C, 'Ordinazioni dei capitoli provinciali umbri dal 1300 al 1305', *CF*, 55 (1985), pp. 5–31.

Cenci, C., *Supplementum ad Bullarium Franciscanum continens litteras Romanorum pontificum annorum 1378–1484 pro tribus S.P.N. Francisci ulterius obtentas*, 2 vols (Grottaferrata, Rome, 2002–03).

Chambers, D.S, *Faculty Office Registers 1534–1549: A Calendar of the first two Registers of the Archbishop of Canterbury's Faculty Office edited with an Introduction and Index* (Oxford, 1966).

Chartularium Studii Bononiensis S. Francisci [saec. XIII–XVI], ed. C. Piana, AF, XI (Florence, 1970).

Chronica monasterii de Melsa, a fundatione usque ad annum 1396, auctore Thoma de Burton, abbate. Accedit continuatio ad annum 1406 a monacho quodam ipsius domus, ed. E.A. Bond, 3 vols, RS, XLIII (London, 1866–68).

A chronicle of England during the reigns of the Tudors, from A.D.1485 to 1559, by Charles Wriothesley, Windsor herald, ed. W.D. Hamilton, 2 vols, CS, New Series, XI, XX (London, 1875–77).

The Chronicle of Pierre de Langtoft, in French verse, from the earliest period to the death of King Edward I, ed. T. Wright, 2 vols, RS, XLVII (London, 1866–68).

The chronicle of St Mary's Abbey, York from Bodley MS. 39, ed. H.H.E. Craster and M.E. Thornton, SS, CXLVIII (1934).

The chronicle of Walter of Guisborough previously edited as the chronicle of Walter of Hemingford or Heminburgh, ed. H. Rothwell, CS, 3rd series, LXXXIX (London, 1957).

Chronicles of the reigns of Edward I. and Edward II., ed. W. Stubbs, 2 vols, RS, LXXVI (London, 1882–83).

Chronicon abbatie de Parco Lude, ed. E. Venables, Lincolnshire Record Society, I (Horncastle, 1891).

Chronicon de Lanercost M.CC.I.–M.CCC.XLVI., ed. J. Stevenson (Edinburgh, 1839).

Chroniques de J. Froissart, ed. S. Luce et al., 16 vols, Société de l'histoire de France, CXLVII, CXLVIII, CLIV, CLIX, CLXIX, CLXXX, CLXXXVIII, CCXXXVII, CCXXXVIII, CCLXIX, CCLXXXII, CCXCIV, CCCCXXV (Paris, 1869–1975).

Churchill, I.J., *Kent Records: Calendar of Institutions by the Chapter of Canterbury Sede Vacante*, Kent Archaeological Society, VIII (1923), pp. 147–51.

Churchwardens' Accounts of St Michael, Spurriergate, York, 1518–1548, ed. C.C. Webb, 2 vols, BTC, XX (York, 1997).

Clark, E.K., 'The Foundation of Kirkstall Abbey', *Miscellanea*, PThS, IV (1895), pp. 169–208.

Clarke, M.V. and N. Denholm-Young, 'The Kirkstall Chronicle, 1355–1400', *Bulletin of the John Rylands Library*, XV (1931), pp. 100–37.

Cook, R.B., 'Wills of Leeds and District (Leeds, Aberford, Adel, Arthington, Allerton Bywater, Altofts, Ardsley, Austhorpe)', *Miscellanea*, PThS, XXII (1915), pp. 85–102.

Cook, R.B., 'Wills of Leeds and District (Bardsey, Batley, Birstall, Bramham, Calverley, Castleford, Collingham, Featherstone, Fenton, Fryston, Garforth, Guiseley)', *Miscellanea*, PThS, XXII (1915), pp. 235–64.

Cotton, C., 'Notes on the Documents in the Cathedral Library at Canterbury relating to the Grey Friars', *Collectanea Franciscana*, ed. A.G. Little, C.L. Kingsford et al., BSFS, V, X (Manchester, 1922), ii, pp. 1–9.

Councils and Synods with other documents relating to the English Church II. A.D. 1205–1313, ed. F.M. Powicke and C.R. Cheney, 2 vols (Oxford, 1964).

The Court and Household of Eleanor of Castile in 1290, ed. J.C. Parsons, PIMS, Studies and Texts, XXXVII (Toronto, 1977).

Cresi, D., 'Statistica dell'Ordine Minoritico all'anno 1282', *AFH*, LVI (1963), pp. 157–62.

Cross, M.C., *York Clergy Wills 1520–1600: II. City Clergy*, BTC, XV (York, 1989).

Cruickshank, J.L., *Headingley-cum-Burley c.1540–c.1784*, PThS, 2nd series, XXII (2012).

Davis, V., *Clergy in London in the late Middle Ages: a register of clergy ordained in the diocese of London based on episcopal ordination lists 1361–1539* (London, 2000).

De conformitate vitae Beati Francisci ad vitam Domini Iesu auctore Fr. Bartholomaeo de Pisa, Analecta Franciscana, IV (Florence, 1906).

Delehaye, H., 'Les lettres d'indulgence collectives', *Analecta Bollandiana*, XLVI (1928), pp. 287–343.

Descriptive catalogue of the charters and muniments in the possession of the Rt. Hon. Lord Fitzhardinge at Berkeley Castle, ed. I.H. Jeayes (Bristol, 1892).

Dobson, R.B., *York City Chamberlains' Account Rolls 1396–1500*, SS, CXCII (1980).

Documents Illustrating the Crisis of 1298–98 in England, ed. M. Prestwich, CS, 4th series, 24 (London, 1980).

The Ecclesiastical History of Orderic Vitalis, ed. M. Chibnall, 6 vols, OMT (Oxford, (1969–80).

Edward I and the Throne of Scotland 1290–1296: an edition of the record sources for the Great Cause, ed. E.L.G. Stones and G.G. Simpson, 2 vols (Oxford, 1978).

Eighth Report of the Deputy Keeper of the Public Records, Appendix II (London, 1847).

An English Chronicle of the reigns of Richard II., Henry IV., Henry V. and Henry VI. Written before the year 1471, ed. J.S. Davies, CS, Old Series, LXIV (London, 1856).

English Episcopal Acta 29, Durham 1241–1283, ed. P.M. Hoskin (Oxford, 2005).

Eulogium (Historiarum sive temporis): Chronicon ab orbe condito usque ad annum Domini M. CCC. LXVI., a monacho quodam Malmesburiensi exaratum, ed. F.S. Haydon, 3 vols, RS, IX (London, 1858–63).

The fabric rolls of York Minster; with an appendix of illustrative documents, ed. J. Raine, junior, SS, XXXV (1859).

Fasciculi zizaniorum magistri Johannis Wyclif cum tritico. Ascribed to Thomas Netter of Walden, provincial of the Carmelite order in England and confessor to King Henry the Fifth, ed. W. Waddington Shirley, RS, V (London, 1858).

Fasciculus morum, ed. S. Wenzel (Pennsylvania, c.1989).

Fasti Dunelmenses. A record of the beneficed clergy of the diocese of Durham down to the dissolution of the monastic and collegiate churches, ed. D.S. Boutflower, SS, CXXXIX (1926).

Fasti Oxonienses, or, Annals of the University of Oxford, by Anthony à Wood, ed. P. Bliss, 2 vols (London, 1815–20).

Fasti Parochiales, ed. A. Hamilton Thompson, C.T. Clay, N.K. Gurney and N.A.H. Lawrence, 4 vols, YAS, LXXXV, CVII, CXXIX, CXXXIII (1933–71).

Feet of Fines of the Tudor Period, anonymous, 4 vols, YAS, RS, II, V, VII, VIII (1887–90).

The Fifty Earliest English Wills in the court of Probate, London, ed. F.J. Furnivall, Early English Texts Society, LXV (London, 1882).

Fratris Thomae vulgo dicti de Eccleston Tractatus de adventu Fratrum Minorum in Angliam, ed. A.G. Little (Manchester, 1951).

Fussenegger, G., 'Definitiones Capituli generalis Argentinae celebrati anno 1282', *AFH*, XXVI (1933), pp. 127–40.

'Gesta Dunelmensia, A.D. M.CCC', ed. R.K. Richardson, *Camden Miscellany*, 3rd series, XIII (London, 1924), pp. 1–58.

Gieben, S., Servus of Sint Anthonis [Gieben], 'Preaching in the Thirteenth Century. A Note on Ms. Gonville and Caius 439', *CF*, XXXII (1962), pp. 310–324.

Gieben, S., 'Robert Grosseteste on Preaching, with the Edition of the Sermon "Ex rerum initiatarum" on Redemption', *CF*, XXXVII (1967), pp. 100–41.

Gieben, S., 'Robert Grosseteste at the Papal Curia, Lyons 1250. Edition of the Documents', *CF*, XLI (1971), pp. 340–93.

Grace Book A, ed. S.M. Leathes, Cambridge Antiquarian Society, Luard Memorial Series, I (Cambridge, 1897).

Grace Book B, ed. M. Bateson, 2 vols, Cambridge Antiquarian Society, Luard Memorial Series, II and III (Cambridge, 1903, 1905).

Grace Book Γ, ed. W.G. Searle & J.W. Clark (Cambridge, 1908).

Gransden, A., *Historical Writing in England*, 2 vols (London, 1974–82).

Hamilton Thompson, A., 'The Registers of the Archdeaconry of Richmond, 1361–1442', *YAJ*, XXV (1918–20), pp. 129–268.

Hamilton Thompson, A., 'The Registers of the Archdeacons of Richmond, 1442–1477, part one, 1442–1477', *YAJ*, XXX (1930–31), pp. 1–132.

Hamilton Thompson, A., 'The Registers of the Archdeacons of Richmond, 1442–1477, part two, 1465–1477', *YAJ*, XXXII (1934–36), pp. 111–45.

Handbook of British Chronology, ed. E.B. Fryde, D.E. Greenway, S. Porter and I. Roy, Royal Historical Society, Guides and Handbooks, 3rd edn (London, 1986).

Henquinet, F.M., 'Descriptio codicis 158 Assisii in Bibliotheca Communali', *AFH*, XXIV (1931), pp. 91–254.

Heresy Trials in the Diocese of Norwich 1428–1431, ed. N.P. Tanner, CS, 4th series, XX (London, 1977).

Hierarchia catholica medii et recentioris aevi: sive Summorum pontificum, S.R.E. cardinalium, ecclesiarum antistitum series: e documentis tabularii praesertim Vaticani collecta, digesta, ed. C. Eubel, 8 vols (Regensburg, 1913).

Historia Selebiensis Monasterii, The History of the Monastery of Selby, ed. J.E. Burton, OMT (Oxford, 2013).

The Historians of the Church of York and its Archbishops, ed. J. Raine, 3 vols, RS, LXXI (London, 1879–94).

Historical Papers and Letters from the Northern Registers, ed. J. Raine, RS, LXI (London, 1873).

Hoskin, P.M., 'The Accounts of the Medieval Paternoster Gild of York', *NH*, XLIV (2007), pp. 7–33.

The Household Book of Queen Isabella of England for the fifth regnal year of Edward II, 8 July 1311 to 7 July 1312, ed. F.D. Blackley and G. Hermansen, The University of Alberta Classical and Historical Studies, I (Alberta, Canada, 1971).

The Household Book (1510–1551) of Sir Edward Don: An Anglo-Welsh Knight and his Circle, ed. R.A. Griffiths, Buckinghamshire Record Society Publications, XXXIII (Amersham, 2004).

Hughes, B., *De Numeris Misticis by John Pecham. A Critical Edition*, *AFH*, LXXVIII (1985), pp. 3–28, 333–83.

I testamenti dei cardinali dei duecento, ed. A.P. Bagliani, Miscellanea della società Romana di storia patria, XXV (Rome, 1980).

The Itinerary of John Leland in or about the years 1535–1543, ed. L. Toulmin Smith, 5 vols (London, 1906–10).

James, M.R., 'The Anlaby Chartulary', *YAJ*, XXXI (1932–34), pp. 337–47.

James, M.R., *The Western Manuscripts in the Library of Trinity College, Cambridge: A Descriptive Catalogue*, 4 vols (Cambridge, 1900–04).

Jeayes, I.H., *Description of Documents Contained in the White Vellum Book of the Scarborough Corporation* (Scarborough, 1914).

John Dee's Library Catalogue, ed. J. Roberts and A.G. Watson (London, 1990).

John Duns Scotus, The Report of the Paris Lecture, Reportatio IV-A, 2 parts, ed. O.V. Bychkov and R. Trent Pomplun (St Bonaventure, New York, 2016).

John of Gaunt's Register (1371–1375), ed. S. Armitage-Smith, 2 vols, CS, 3rd series, XX–XXI (London, 1911).

John Pecham, Tractatus de perspectiva, ed. S.F. Brown, Franciscan Institute Publications, XVIII (St Bonaventure, New York, 1972).

The Kalendarium of John Somer, ed. L.R. Mooney, Chaucer Library Series (Athens, GA, 1998).

Kingsford, C.L, 'Additional Material for the History of the Grey Friars, London', *Collectanea Franciscana*, ed. C.L. Kingsford, A.G. Little, M.R. James and H.M. Bannister, 2 vols, BSFS, V, X (Aberdeen and Manchester, 1915, 1922), ii, pp. 61–149.

Kingsford, C.L., 'Defensio Fratrum Mendicantium', *Fratris Johannis Pecham quondam archiepiscopi Cantuariensis Tractatus tres de Paupertate*, ed. Kingsford, A.G.Little, F. Tocco, BSFS, II (Aberdeen, 1910), pp. 148–98.

The Kirkstall Abbey Chronicles, ed. J. Taylor, PThS, XLII (1952).

Knighton's Chronicle 1337–1396, ed. G.H. Martin, OMT (Oxford, 1995).

The Letters of Adam Marsh, ed. C.H. Lawrence, 2 vols, OMT (Oxford, 2006–10).

Liber quotidianus contrarotulatoris garderobae. Anno regni regis Edwardi primi vicesimo octavo regni regis Edwardi primi vicesimo octavo. A.D.MCCXCIX & MCCC. Ex codice MS. in bibliotheca sua asservato typis edidit Soc. Antiq. Londinensis, ed. J. Topham (London, 1787).

Liber S.Marie de Calchou, Registrum cartarum abbacie Tironensis de Kelso, 1113–1567, ed. C. Innes, 2 vols (Edinburgh, 1846).

Liber viginti quattuor philosophorum, ed. F. Hudry, CCCM, 143a (Turnhout, 1997).

The Libraries of the Cistercians, Gilbertines and Premonstratensians, ed. D.N. Bell, CBMLC, III (London, 1992).

Literae Cantuarienses. The letter books of the monastery of Christ Church, Canterbury, ed. J. Brigstocke Sheppard, 3 vols, RS, LXXXV (London, 1887–89).

Little, A.G., '*Records of the Franciscan Province of England*', *Collectanea Franciscana*, I, ed. Little, M.R. James and J.M. Bannister, BSFS, V (Aberdeen 1914), pp. 141–53.

Little, A.G., 'Two Sermons of Fr. Raymond Gaufredi, Minister General, Preached at Oxford in 1291', *CF*, IV (1934), pp. 161–74.

Longpré, E., 'Le commentaire sur les Sentences de Guillaume de Nottingham, O.F.M.', *AFH*, XXII (1929), pp. 232–33.

Longpré, E., 'Fr. Thomas d'York, O.F.M. La première Somme métaphysique du XIIIe siècle', *AFH*, XIX (1926), pp. 875–930.

Longpré, E., 'Thomas d'York et Matthieu d'Aquasparta, Textes inédits sur le problème de la création', *Archives d'histoire doctrinale et littéraire du moyen âge*, I (1926), pp. 269–308.

Lumb, G.D., 'Testamenta Leodiensia, 1514–1521', *Miscellanea*, PThS, IX (1899), pp. 81–96.

Lumb, G.D., 'Testamenta Leodiensia, 1521–1526', *Miscellanea*, PThS, IX (1899), pp. 161–92.

Lumb, G.D., 'Testamenta Leodiensia, 1526–1531', *Miscellanea*, PThS, IX (1899), pp. 246–77.

Lumb, G.D., 'Testamenta Leodiensia, 1531 to 1534', *Miscellanea*, PThS, XI (1904), pp. 37–68.

Lumb, G.D., 'Testamenta Leodiensia, 1534 to 1537', *Miscellanea*, PThS, XI (1904), pp. 289–320.

Lumb, G.D., 'Testamenta Leodiensia, 1537–1559', *Miscellanea*, PThS, XV (1909), pp. 10–25.

Magistri Petri Lombardi Parisiensis episcopi Sententiae in IV Libris distinctae, ed. I.C. Brady, 2 vols, SB, IV, V (Grottaferrata, 1971–81).

The Manuscripts of Lincoln, Bury St. Edmund's, and Great Grimsby Corporations: and of the Deans and Chapters of Worcester and Lichfield, Historical Manuscripts Commission, Fourteenth Report, Appendix, Part VIII, XXXVII (London, 1895).

The Medieval Lindsey Marsh: Select Documents, ed. A.E.B. Owen, LRS, LXXXV (1996).

Memorials of the Abbey of St. Mary of Fountains, ed. J.R. Walbran and J. Raine, 3 vols, SS, XLII, LXVII, CXXX (1863–1918).

Memorials of Beverley Minster: The Chapter Act Book of the Collegiate Church of S. John of Beverley, A.D. 1286–1347, ed. A.F. Leach, 2 vols, SS, XCVIII, CVIII (1898–1903).

Memorials of the church of Ss. Peter and Wilfrid, Ripon, ed. J.T. Fowler, SS, LXXIV, LXXVIII, LXXXI, CXV, 4 vols (1882–1908).

Monastic Chancery Proceedings (Yorkshire), ed. J.S. Purvis, YAS, RS, LXXXVIII (1934).

Monumenta de Insula Manniae: or, A collection of national documents relating to the Isle of Man, ed. J.R. Oliver, 3 vols, Manx Society, IV, VII, IX (Isle of Man, 1860–62).

Mooney, L.R., *The Index of Middle English Prose. Handlist 11:Manuscripts in the Library of Trinity College, Cambridge* (Woodbridge, 1995).

Munimenta Academica or documents illustrative of academical life and studies at Oxford, ed. H. Anstey, 2 vols, RS, L (London, 1868).

Murray Jones, P., 'Mediating Collective Experience: The *Tabula Medicine* (1416–1425) as a Handbook for Medical Practice', *Between Text and Patient: The Medical Enterprise in Medieval and Early Modern Europe*, ed. F.E. Glaze and B.K. Nance, Micrologus' library, 39 (Florence, 2011), pp. 279–307

Nicolini, U., 'Le tavole dei capitoli provinciali dell'Umbria del 1408 e del 1431', *AFH*, LIX (1966), pp. 301–22.

Oliger, L., 'Liber exemplorum Fratrum Minorum saeculi XIII (excerpta e cod. Ottob. Lat.522', *Antonianum* II (1927), pp. 203–76.

Original Papal Documents in England and Wales from the Accession of Pope Innocent III to the Death of Pope Benedict XI (1198–1304), ed. J. Sayers (Oxford, 1999).

The Oxford Deeds of Balliol College, ed. H.E. Salter, OHS, LXIV (1913).

Placitorum in domo capitulari Westmonasteriensi asservatorum abbreviatio. temporibus regum Ric. I, Johann. Henr. III, Edw. I., Edw. II, ed. W. Illingworth, Record Commission (London, 1811).

Pouillon, D.H., 'Le manuscrit d'Assise, Bibl.comm.196. Description', *RTAM*, XII (1940), pp. 329–58.

Poulson, G., *Beverlac; or, The antiquities and history of the town of Beverley, in the county of York; and of the provostry and collegiate establishment of St. Johns; with a minute description of the present minster and the church of St. Mary and other ancient and modern edifices*, 2 vols (London, 1829).

Pergamo, B., 'I Francescani alla facoltà teologica di Bologna (1364–1500)', *AFH*, XXVII (1934), pp. 3–61.

Petrus Lombardus Sententiae, ed. I.C. Brady, SB, IVab,V, 3 vols (Florence, 1971–81).

Priory of Coldingham. The correspondence, inventories, account rolls, and law proceedings, of the priory of Coldingham, ed. J. Raine, SS, XII (1841).

Probate Inventories of the York Diocese, 1350–1500, trans. P.M. Stell, The Archaeology of York, Historical Sources for York Archaeology after AD1100 2/3 (Dorset, 2006).

The Proceedings Against the Templars in the British Isles, ed. H.J. Nicholson, 2 vols (Aldershot, 2011).

Purvis, J.S., 'Four Antiquarian Notes', *YAJ*, XLII (1967–70), pp. 52–53.

Purvis, J.S., 'A Selection of Monastic Rentals and Dissolution Papers', *Miscellanea*, III, YAS, RS, LXXX (1931), pp. 1–148.

Records of Antony Bek, Bishop and Patriarch, 1283–1311, ed. C.M. Fraser, SS, CLXII (1953).

Records of Convocation, XIII: York, 1313–1461, ed. G. Bray (Woodbridge, 2006).

The Records of the Northern Convocation, ed. G.W. Kitchin, SS, CXIII (1907).

Records of the parliament holdfen at Westminster on the twenty-eighth day of February, in the thirty-third year of the reign of King Edward the First, A.D. 1305, ed. F.W. Maitland, RS, XCVIII (London, 1893).

Regesta Ordinis Fratrum Minorum Conventualium, 2 (1504–1506), ed. G. Parisciani, Fonti e Studi Antoniania, VII (Padua, 1998).

Les Registres de Nicolas III (1277–1280) recueil des bulles de ce pape publiées ou analysées d'après les manuscrits originaux des Archives du Vatican, ed. M.J. Gay, Bibliothèque des écoles françaises d'Athènes et de Rome, 2e serie, XIV (Paris, 1898–1938).

Registrum Anglie de libris doctorum et auctorum veterum, ed. R.A.B. Mynors, R.H. Rouse and M.A. Rouse, CBMLC, II (London, 1991).

Reilly, J.P., Jr, 'A Sermon of Thomas of York on the Passion', *FS*, XXIV (1964), pp. 205–22.

Report on the Manuscripts of the Corporation of Beverley, Historical Manuscripts Commission, LIV (London, 1900).
Rutledge, P., 'The Will of Oliver Wyth, 1291', *A Miscellany*, Norfolk Record Society, LVI (1991), pp. 9–30.
Rymer, T., *Foedera, Conventiones, Literae et cujuscunque generis Acta Publica inter reges Angliae, et alios quosvis imperatores, reges, pontifices, principes, vel communitates*, 2nd edn, 4 vols (London, 1816–69), OP, 1.25–30
The St Albans Chronicle, The Chronica maiora of Thomas of Walsingham, I, 1376–1422, ed. J. Taylor, W.R. Childs and L. Watkiss, 2 vols, OMT (Oxford, 2003–11).
Schlageter, J., 'Die Chronica des Bruders Jordan von Giano. Einführung und kritische Edition nach den bisher bekannten Handschriften', *AFH*, CIV (2011), pp. 3–63.
Sede Vacante Wills: A Calendar of Wills proved before the Commissary of the Prior and Chapter Christ's Church, Canterbury, during vacancies in the primacy, ed. C.E. Woodruff, Kent Archaeological Society, Records Branch, III (1914).
Sir Thomas Gray Scalacronica 1272–1363, ed. A. King, SS, CCIX (2005).
A subsidy collected in the diocese of Lincoln in 1526, ed. H.R. Salter (Oxford, 1909).
Trevelyan, G.M., 'An account of the rising of 1381', *EHR*, XIII (1898), pp. 509–22.
Venn, J. and J.A., *Alumni Cantabrigienses: a biographical list of all known students, graduates and holders of office at the University of Cambridge, from the earliest times to 1900: Part one. From the earliest times to 1751*, 4 vols (Cambridge, 1922–27).
Vita Edwardi secundi: The Life of Edward the second, ed. W.R. Childs, OMT (Oxford, 2005).
Les vrayes Chroniques de Messire Jehan le Bel, ed. M.L. Polain, 2 vols, Académie Royale de Belgique (Brussels, 1863).
Walter Chatton, Lectura super Sententias, Liber I, distinctiones 1–17, ed. J.C. Wey and G.J. Etzkorn, 3 vols, PIMS, Studies and Texts, CLVI, CLVIII, CLXIV (Toronto, 2007–09).
Walter Chatton, Reportatio super Sententias, Libri III–IV, ed. J.C. Wey and G.J. Etzkorn, 2 vols, PIMS, Studies and Texts, CXLVIII, CXLIX (Toronto, 2004–05).
Walter Map, De nugis Curialium: Courtiers' Trifles, ed. M.R. James, C.N.L. Brooke and R.A.B. Mynors, OMT (Oxford, 1983).
Weiland, L., ed., *Continuationes chronici Martini Oppaviensis, iii, Continuationes Anglicae Fratrum Minorum*, in *Monumenta Germaniae historica*, scriptorum, XXIV, ed. G.H. Pertz (Hannover, 1879), pp. 253–59.
The Westminster Chronicle, 1381–1394, ed. L.C. Hector and B.F. Harvey, OMT (Oxford, 1982).
'Wills of Leeds and District (Leeds, Aberford, Adel, Arthington, Allerton Bywater, Altofts, Ardsley, Austhorpe)', ed. R.B. Cook, *Miscellanea*, PThs, XXII (1915), pp. 85–102, 235–64.
Women of the English Nobility and Gentry 1066–1500, ed. and trans. J. Ward, Manchester Medieval Sources series (Manchester, 1995).
Workman, H.B., *John Wyclif*, 2 vols (Oxford, 1926).
Young, C.G., 'Notices Concerning Religious Houses in Yorkshire, with the Names of their Founders, and of Persons Buried Therein', *Collectanea Topographica et Genealogica*, ed. F. Madden et al., 8 vols (London, 1834–43), iv, pp. 73–79, 128–33.
Yorkshire Monasteries. Suppression Papers, ed. J.W. Clay, YAS, RS, XLVIII (1912).

Secondary sources

Aveling, J.C.H., *Northern Catholics* (London, 1966).
Baskerville, G., *English Monks and the Suppression of the Monasteries* (London, 1937).

Bennett, N., 'Pastors and Masters: The Beneficed Clergy of North-East Lincolnshire, 1290–1340', *The Foundations of Medieval English Ecclesiastical History: Studies Presented to David Smith*, ed. P. Hoskin, C.N.L. Brooke and R.B. Dobson, Studies in the History of Medieval Religion, XXVII (Woodbridge, 2005), pp. 40–62.

Bennett, S. and Bennett, N., *An Historical Atlas of Lincolnshire* (Hull, 1993).

Beverley Minster: An Illustrated History, ed. R.E. Horrox (Beverley, 2000).

Bihl, M., 'Documenta Inedita Archivi protomonasterii Sanctae Clarae Assisii', *AFH*, V (1912), pp. 291–98, 663–97.

Binns, J., *The History of Scarborough from the Earliest Times to the Year 2000* (Pickering, 2001).

Bourdua, L., '*Master* Plans of Devotion or Daily Pragmatism? The Dedication and Use of Chapels and Conventual Spaces by the Friars and the Laity at the Santo 1263–1310', *Il Santo: Rivista Francescana di storia dottrina arte*, LI (2011), pp. 491–510.

Boyle, L., 'Notes on the Education of the *Fratres communes* in the Dominican Order in the Thirteenth Century', *Xenia Medii Aevi Historiam Illustrantia oblata Thomae Kaeppeli O.P.*, ed. R. Creytens and P. Künzle, 2 vols, Storia e Letteratura raccolta di Studi e Testi, CXLI, CXLII (Rome, 1978), i, pp. 249–67.

Brodrick, G.C., *Memorials of Merton College with biographical notices of the wardens and fellows*, OHS, IV (Oxford, 1885).

Bruzelius, C., '*The Dead Come to Town: Preaching, Burying and Building in the Mendicant Orders*': *The Year 1300 and the Creation of a New European Architecture*, ed. A. Gajewski and Z. Opacic (Turnhout, 2007), pp. 203–24.

Bruzelius, C., *Preaching, Building, and Burying: Friars in the Medieval City* (New Haven, 2014).

Bryce, W.M., *The Scottish Grey Friars*, 2 vols (Edinburgh, 1909).

Burton, J., *Monasticon Eboracense: and the Ecclesiastical History of Yorkshire* (York, 1758).

Burton, J.E., *The Monastic Order in Yorkshire 1069–1215*, Cambridge Studies in Medieval Life and Thought, 4th series, XL (Cambridge, 1999).

Burton, J.E., *The Religious Orders in the East Riding of Yorkshire in the Twelfth Century*, East Yorkshire Local History Society, XLVII (Beverley, 1989).

Catto, J.I., 'An Alleged Great Council of 1374', *EHR*, LXXXII (1967), pp. 764–71.

Catto, J.I., 'Franciscan Learning in England 1450–1540', *The Religious Orders in Pre-Reformation England*, ed. J.G. Clark, Studies in the History of Medieval Religion, XVIII (Woodbridge, 2002), pp. 97–104.

Cheney, C.R., 'Illuminated Collective Indulgences from Avignon', *Palaeographica, Diplomatica et Archivistica: Studi in onore di Giulio Battelli*, II, Storia e Letteratura raccolta di Studi e Testi, CXL (Rome, 1979), pp. 353–73.

The Church in Medieval York, Records Edited in Honour of Professor Barrie Dobson, ed. D.M. Smith, BTC, XXIV (York, 1999).

Cole, R.E.G., 'The Priory of Broadholme', *Associated Architectural Societies' Reports and Papers*, XXVIIII (1905–06), pp. 66–67.

Colish, M.L., *Peter Lombard*, Brill's Studies in Intellectual History, XLI–XLII, 2 vols (Leiden, 1994).

Collectanea, Oxford, ed. C.R.L. Fletcher, E. Burrows et al., 4 vols, OHS, V, XVI, XXXII, XLVII (Oxford, 1885–1905).

Collectanea Anglo-minoritica: or, A collection of the antiquities of the English Franciscans, or Friers minors, commonly call'd Gray friers: in two part: with an appendix concerning the English nuns of the Order of Saint Clare, ed. A. Parkinson (London, 1726).

Collier, C.V., 'Documents at Scampston', *The Transactions of the East Riding Antiquarian Society*, XXI (1915), pp. 25–69.

Courtenay, W.J., 'Academic Formation and Careers of Mendicant Friars. A Regional

Approach', *Studio e Studia: Le scuole degli ordini mendicanti tra il XIII e XIV secolo: Atti del XXIX Convegno internazionale, Assisi, 11–13 ottobre 2001* (Spoleto, 2002), pp. 199–217.

Courtenay, W.J., 'Between Pope and King: The Parisian Letters of Adhesion of 1303', *Speculum*, LXXI (1996), pp. 576–605.

Courtenay, W.J., 'Early Scotists at Paris. A Reconsideration', *FS*, LXIX (2011), pp. 175–229.

Courtenay, W.J., 'The Instructional Programme of the Mendicant Convents at Paris in the Early Fourteenth Century', *The Medieval Church: Universities, Heresy, and the Religious Life. Essays in Honour of Gordon Leff*, ed. P. Biller and R.B. Dobson (Woodbridge, 1999), pp. 77–92.

Courtenay, W.J., 'Nicholas of Assisi and Vatican MS. Chigi B.V.66', *Scriptorium*, XXXVI (1982), pp. 260–63.

Courtenay, W.J., *Schools and Scholars in Fourteenth-Century England* (Princeton, 1987).

Courtenay, W.J., 'Scotus at Paris: Some Reconsiderations', *Archa Verbi, Subsidia 4, The Opera Theologica of John Duns Scotus: Proceedings of 'The Quadruple Congress' on John Duns Scotus*, ii, ed. R. Cross (Franciscan Institute Publications, New York, 2012), pp. 1–19.

Courtenay, W.J., 'Some Notes on Robert of Halifax, O.F.M.', *FS*, XXXIII (1973), pp. 135–42.

Cross, M.C., 'The Dissolution of the Monasteries in Sixteenth-Century York', in *YAJ*, LXXX (2008), pp. 153–66.

Cross, M.C., *The End of Medieval Monasticism in the East Riding of Yorkshire*, East Yorkshire Local History Society, XLVII (Beverley, 1993).

Cross, M.C., 'The End of Medieval Monasticism in the North Riding', *YAJ*, LXXVIII (2006), pp. 145–57.

Cross, M.C., 'Monastic Learning and Libraries in Sixteenth-Century Yorkshire', *Humanism and Reform: The Church in Europe, England and Scotland, 1400–1643*, ed. J. Kirk, Studies in Church History, Subsidia, VIII (Oxford, 1991), pp. 255–69.

Cross, M.C., 'Monasticism and Society in the Diocese of York 1520–1540', *Transactions of the Royal Historical Society*, 5th series, XXXVIII (1988), pp. 131–45.

Cross, M.C., 'Origins and University Connections of Yorkshire Religious, 1480–1540', *The Medieval Church: Universities, Heresy, and the Religious life: Essays in Honour of Gordon Leff*, ed. P. Biller and R.B. Dobson (Woodbridge, 1999), pp. 271–91.

Cross, M.C., 'York Clergy and their Books in the Early Sixteenth Century', *The Church and Learning in Late Medieval Society: Studies in Honour of Professor R.B. Dobson*, ed. C. Barron and J. Stratford, Harlaxton Medieval Studies, XI (Donington, 2002), pp. 344–54.

Crouch, D.J.F., *Piety, Fraternity and Power: Religious Gilds in Late Medieval Yorkshire, 1389–1547* (York, 2000).

Daniell, C., 'Early Medieval York', *The History of York: From Earliest Times to the Year 2000*, ed. P. Nuttgens (York, 2001), pp. 73–99.

Davis, V., 'Mendicants in London in the Reign of Richard II', *The London Journal*, XXV (2000), pp. 1–12.

Debenham, L.S., 'Scarborough's Water Supply', *Transactions of the Scarborough and District Archaeological Society*, XV, 1972, pp. 1–32.

Dickens, A. G., *Lollards and Protestants in the Diocese of York, 1509–1558* (London, 1959).

Dobson, R.B., 'Contrasting Chronicles: Historical Writing at York and Durham in the Later Middle Ages', *Church and Chronicles in the Middle Ages: Essays Presented to John Taylor*, ed. I. Wood and G.A. Loud (London, 1991), pp. 201–18.

Dobson, R.B., 'Later Medieval York', *The History of York: From Earliest Times to the Year 2000*, ed. P. Nuttgens (York, 2001), pp. 100–40.

Dobson, R.B., 'Mendicant Ideal and Practice in Late Medieval York', *Archaeological Papers from York Presented to M.W. Barley*, ed. P.V. Addyman and V.E. Black (York, 1984), pp. 109–22.

Dobson, R.B., 'Yorkshire Towns in the Late Fourteenth Century', *Miscellany*, PThS, LIX (1983), pp. 1–21.

Doucet, V, 'Bibliografia', *AFH*, XXVII (1934), pp. 274–280.

Drake, F., *Eboracum or the history and antiquities of the city of York from the original to the present times, together with the history of the cathedral church and the lives of archbishops of that see* (London, 1736).

Dyer, A., 'Ranking Lists of English Medieval Towns', *The Cambridge Urban History of Britain, I, 600–1540*, ed. D.M. Palliser (Cambridge, 2000), pp. 747–70.

Edwards, R., 'Themes and Personalities in *Sentence* Commentaries at Oxford in the 1330s', *Mediaeval Commentaries on the Sentences of Peter Lombard, volume 1, Current Research*, ed. G.R. Evans (Leiden, 2002), pp. 379–93.

Ehrle, F., *I più antichi Statuti della Facoltà teologica dell'Università di Bologna*, Universitatis Bonon., Monumenta, I (Bologna, 1932).

Emden, A.B., *A Survey of Dominicans in England Based on the Ordination Lists in Episcopal Registers (1268 to 1538)*, Institutum Historicum FF. Praedicatorum Romae ad S. Sabinae, Dissertationes Historicae, XVIII (Rome, 1967).

Erler, M.C., *Reading and Writing during the Dissolution: Monks, Friars and Nuns 1530–1558* (Cambridge, 2013).

F. Nicholai Triveti, de ordine Frat. Praedicatorum, Annales sex regum Angliae, ed. T. Hog (London, 1845).

Fairbank, F.R., 'The House of Grey Friars, Doncaster', *YAJ*, XII (1892–93), pp. 481–86.

The Foundation History of the Abbeys of Byland and Jervaulx, ed. J.E. Burton, BTS, XXXV (York, 2006).

The Foundations of Medieval English Ecclesiastical History: Studies Presented to David Smith, ed. P. Hoskin, C.N.L. Brooke and R.B. Dobson, Studies in the History of Medieval Religion, XXVII (Woodbridge, 2005).

Fr. Rogeri Bacon Opera quaedam hactenus inedita, ed. J.S. Brewer, RS, XV (London, 1859).

Fuller, T., *History of the University of Cambridge*, ed. J. Nichols (London, 1840).

Garrett, C.H., *The Marian Exiles: A Study in the Origins of Elizabethan Puritanism* (Cambridge, 1938).

Garrod, H.W., *Injunctions of Archbishop Kilwardby 1276* (Oxford, 1929).

Gibbons, A., *Early Lincoln Wills* (Lincoln, 1888).

Gillett, E., *A History of Grimsby* (Oxford, 1970).

Glorieux, P., 'Jean de Saint-Germain maître de Paris et copiste de Worcester', *Mélanges Auguste Pelzer Études d'histoire littéraire et doctrinale de la Scolastique médiévale offertes à Monseigneur Auguste Pelzer à l'occasion de son soixante-dixième anniversiare*, Université de Louvain recueil de travaux d'histoire et de philologie, 3me série, XXVI fascicule (Louvain, 1947), pp. 513–29.

Glorieux, P., 'Mâitres franciscains régents à Paris. Mise au point', *RTAM*, XVIII (1951), pp. 324–32.

Glorieux, P., 'Le Manuscrit d'Assise, Bibl.comm.158: Date et mode de composition', *RTAM*, VIII (1936), pp. 282–95.

Goldberg, P.J.P., *Medieval England: A Social History 1250–1550* (London, 2004).

Goldberg, P.J.P., *Women, Work, and Life Cycle in a Medieval Economy: Women in York and Yorkshire c.1300–1520* (Oxford, 1992).

Goldthorp, L.M., 'The Franciscans and Dominicans in Yorkshire', *YAJ*, XXXII (1934–36), pp. 264–320, 365–428.

Greatrex, J., *Biographical Register of the English Cathedral Priories of the Province of Canterbury c.1066–1540* (Oxford, 1997).

Greatrex, J., *The English Benedictine Cathedral Priories: Rule and Practice c.1270–c.1420* (Oxford, 2011).

Henquinet, F.M., 'Descriptio codicis 158 Assisii in Bibliotheca Communali', *AFH*, XXIV (1931), pp. 91–108, 215–54.

Hey, D., *A History of Yorkshire 'County of Broad Acres'* (Lancaster, 2005).

Hill, F., *Medieval Lincoln* (Cambridge, 1948).

Homan, R.L., 'Old and New Evidence of the Career of William Melton, O.F.M.', *FS*, XLIX (1989), pp. 25–33.

Horrox, R.E., 'The Borough and Liberties of Beverley', *VCH, Beverley*, pp. 1–62.

Horrox, R.E., 'The Later Medieval Minster', *Beverley Minster: An Illustrated History*, ed. Horrox (Beverley, 2000), pp. 37–49.

Hughes, J., *Pastors and Visionaries: Religion and Secular Life in Late Medieval Yorkshire* (Woodbridge, 1988).

Hunt, R.W., 'Manuscripts Containing the Indexing Symbols of Robert Grosseteste', *Bodleian Library Record*, IV (1953–54), pp. 241–55.

James, M.R., 'The Anlaby Chartulary', *YAJ*, XXXI (1932–34), pp. 337–47.

Jennings, B., *The Grey Friars of Richmond* (Richmond, 1958).

The Jewish Communities of Medieval England: The Collected Essays of R.B. Dobson, ed. H. Birkett (York, 2010).

John Le Neve, Fasti Ecclesiae Anglicanae 1066–1300, III. Lincoln, ed. D.E. Greenway (London, 1977).

John Le Neve, Fasti Ecclesiae Anglicanae 1300–1541, Northern Province, ed. B. Jones (London, 1963).

John Le Neve, Fasti Ecclesiae Anglicanae 1066–1300, VI. York, ed. D.E. Greenway (London, 1999).

Jones, D., *The Church in Chester 1300–1540* (Manchester, 1957).

Jones, J., *Balliol College: A History, 1263–1939* (Oxford, 1988, 1999).

Jurkowski, M., 'Were Friars Paid Salaries? Evidence from Clerical Taxation Records', *The Fifteenth Century XIII: Exploring the Evidence: Commemoration, Administration and the Economy*, ed. L. Clark (Woodbridge, 2014), pp. 131–45.

Kane, B., 'Return of the Native: Franciscan Education and Astrological Practice in the Medieval North of England', *Franciscan Organisation in the Mendicant Context: Formal and Informal Structures of the Friars' Lives and Ministry in the Middle Ages*, ed. M.J.P. Robson and J. Röhrkasten, Vita Regularis, XLIV (Münster, 2010), pp. 281–306.

Kehnel, A., 'The Narrative Tradition of the Medieval Franciscan Friars on the British Isles. Introduction to the Sources', *FS*, LXIII (2005), pp. 461–530.

Kenny, A., 'From Hospice to College 1559–1579', *The English Hospice in Rome*, The Venerabile, XXI (Exeter, 1962), pp. 218–73.

Kermode, J., *Medieval Merchants: York, Beverley and Hull in the Later Middle Ages*, Cambridge Studies in Medieval Life and Thought, fourth series, XXXVIII (Cambridge, 1998).

Kingsford, H.S., 'The Seals of the Franciscans', *Franciscan History and Legend in English Medieval Art*, ed. A.G. Little, BSFS, XIX (Manchester, 1937), pp. 81–100.

Kissane, A., *Civic Community in Late Medieval Lincoln: Urban Society and Economy in the Age of the Black Death, 1289–1409* (Woodbridge, 2017).

Knowles, D.M., *Saints and Sinners: Twenty-Five Medieval Portraits* (Cambridge, 1962).

Lawrence, C.H., *The Friars: The Impact of the Early Mendicant Movement on Western Society*, The Medieval World (London, 1994).

Leach, A.F., *Early Yorkshire Schools*, 2 vols, YAS, RS, XXVII, XXXIII (1899–1903).

Leadman, A.D.H., 'The insurrection and death of Archbishop Scroope, and the Battle of Bramham Moor ', *YAJ*, XI (1890–91), pp. 189–99.

Lechner, J., 'Beiträge zum mittelalterlichen Franziskanerschrifttum, vornehmlich der Oxforder Schule des 13./14. Jahrhunderts, auf Grund einer Florentiner Wilhelm von Ware-Hs', *Franziskanische Studien*, XIX (1932), pp. 99–127.

Lee, J.S., 'Piped Water Supplies Managed by Civic Bodies in Medieval English Towns', *Urban History*, XLI (2014), pp. 369–93.

Linehan, P., 'The Beginnings of Santa María de Guadalupe and the Direction of the Fourteenth Century', *JEH*, XXXVI (1985), pp. 208–304.

Little, A.G., 'The Authorship of the Lanercost Chronicle', *EHR*, XXXI (1916), pp. 269–79 and XXXII (1917), pp. 48–49.

Little, A.G., 'Chronicles of the Mendicant Friars', *Franciscan Essays*, 2 vols, ed. P. Sabatier, F.C. Burkitt, H.E. Goad and A.G. Little (Manchester, 1912–32), ii, pp. 85–103.

Little, A.G., *Franciscan Papers, Lists, and Documents*, Manchester University Press, CCLXXXIV, Historical Series, LXXXI (Manchester, 1943).

Little, A.G., 'The Franciscan School at Oxford in the Thirteenth Century', *AFH*, XIX (1926), pp. 803–74.

Little, A.G., 'The Friars v. the University of Cambridge', *EHR*, L (1935), pp. 686–96.

Little, A.G., 'The Grey Friars of Beverley', *VCH, Yorkshire*, iii, pp. 264–66.

Little, A.G., 'The Grey Friars of Boston', *VCH, Lincolnshire*, ii, pp. 215–16.

Little, A.G., 'The Grey Friars of Doncaster', *VCH, Yorkshire*, iii, pp. 266–67.

Little, A.G., 'The Grey Friars of Grimsby', *VCH, Lincolnshire*, ii, p. 219.

Little, A.G., 'The Grey Friars of Lincoln', *VCH, Lincolnshire*, ii, pp. 222–24.

Little, A.G., *Grey Friars in Oxford*, OHS, XX (Oxford, 1892).

Little, A.G., 'The Grey Friars, Scarborough', *VCH, Yorkshire*, iii, pp. 274–76.

Little, A.G. 'The Grey Friars of York', *VCH, Yorkshire*, iii, pp. 287–91.

Little, A.G., *Studies in English Franciscan History being the Ford Lectures delivered in the University of Oxford in 1916* (Manchester, 1917).

Little, A.G. and F. Pelster, *Oxford Theology and Theologians c.A.D. 1282–1302*, OHS, XCVI (Oxford, 1934).

Logan, F.D., *Runaway Religious in Medieval England, c. 1240–1540* (Cambridge, 1996).

Logan, F.D., *University Education of the Parochial Clergy in Medieval England: The Lincoln Diocese, c. 1300–c. 1350*, PIMS, Studies and Texts, CLXXXVIII (Toronto, 2014).

Longpré, E., 'Fr. Thomas d'York, O.F.M. La première Somme métaphysique du XIIIe siècle', *AFH*, XIX (1926), pp. 875–930.

Longpré, E., 'Jean de Reading et le B. Jean Duns Scot', *La France Franciscaine*, VII (1924), pp. 99–109.

Longpré, E., 'Maîtres franciscains de Paris: Guillaume de la Mare, O.F.M. (XIIIe s)', *La France Franciscaine*, IV (1921), pp. 288–302, and V (1922), pp. 289–306.

Longpré, E., 'Philip de Bridlington O.F.M. et le Bx. Duns Scot', *AFH*, XXII (1929), pp. 587–88.

Marcett, M.E., *Uthred de Boldon, Fr William Jordan and Piers Plowman* (New York, 1939).

Martin, A.R., 'The Greyfriars of Lincoln', *Archaeological Journal*, 2nd series, XCII (1936), pp. 42–63.

Meier, L., 'Wilhelm von Nottingham (†1336), ein Zeuge für die Entwicklung der distinctio formalis an der Universität Oxford', *Philosophia Perennis*, I, Festgabe Josef Geyser, Zum 60. Geburtstag (Regensburg, 1930), pp. 249–66.

Miller, E., 'Medieval York: The 12th and 13th Centuries', *VCH, Yorkshire: The City of York*, pp. 25–116.

Moorman, J.R.H., 'The Foreign Element among the English Franciscans', *EHR*, LXII (1947), pp. 289–303.

Moorman, J.R.H., *Medieval Franciscan Houses*, Franciscan Institute Publications, IV (St Bonaventure, New York, 1984).

Nessi, S., 'S.Chiara da Montefalco e il Francescanesimo', *MF*, LXIX (1969), pp. 369–408.

Newcourt, R., *Repertorium Ecclesiasticum Parochiale Londinense*, 2 vols (London, 1708–10).

Newns, B., 'The Hospice of St Thomas and the English Crown 1474–1538', *The English Hospice in Rome: The Venerabile*, XXI (1962), pp. 145–92.

Offler, H.S., 'A Note of the Northern Franciscan Chronicle', *Nottingham Medieval Studies*, XXVIII (1984), pp. 45–59.

Orme, N.I., *Education and Society in Medieval and Renaissance England* (London, 1989).

Orme, N.I., *English Schools in the Middle Ages* (London, 1973).

Orme, N.I., 'Indulgences in Medieval Cornwall', *Journal of the Royal Institution of Cornwall*, ns, ii (i) (1992), pp. 149–70.

Owen, D.M., *Church and Society in Medieval Lincolnshire*, History of Lincolnshire, V (Lincoln, 1971).

Palmer, C.F.R., 'The Friars Preachers, or Black Friars of Beverley', *YAJ*, VII (1881–82), pp. 32–43.

Palliser, D., 'The Early Medieval Minster', *Beverley Minster: an illustrated history*, ed. R. Horrox (Beverly, 2000), pp. 23–35.

Parkes, M.B., 'Layout and Presentation of the Text', *The Cambridge History of the Book in Britain, volume 2, 1100–1400*, ed. N.J. Morgan and R.M. Thomson (Cambridge, 2008), pp. 55–74.

Péano, P., 'Jacques de'Tolomei de Sienne, O.F.M. (1323–1390): éléments de biographie', *AFH*, LXVIII (1975), pp. 273–97.

Pearce, E.H., *The Monks of Westminster being a register of the brethren of the convent from the time of the confessor to the dissolution with lists of the obedientiaries and an introduction* (Cambridge, 1916).

Pearson, T., *The Archaeology of Medieval Scarborough: Excavation and Research 1987–2004*, Scarborough Archaeological and Historical Society, Research Report, XII (York, 2005).

Pellegrini, L., *Insediamenti Francescani nell'Italia del Duecento*, Storia e richerche, nuova serie (Rome, 1984).

Pelster, F., 'Thomas von York, O.F.M., als Verfasser des Traktats Manus quae contra Omnipotentem tenditur', *AFH*, XV (1922), pp. 3–22.

Pelzer, A., *Bibliothecae Apostolicae Vaticanae, Codices Vaticani Latini, II, pars prior, Codices Vaticani Latini, II, pars prior, Codices 679–1134* (Rome, 1931).

Percan, J., *Teologia come scienza pratica secondo Giovanni di Reading*, SB, XXVI (Grottaferrata, 1986).

Piana, C., 'Promozioni di religiosi francescani agli Ordini sacri a Bologna (an' 1349–1508), *AFH*, LVII (1964), pp. 3–89.

Piana, C. and C. Cenci, *Promozioni agli ordini sacri a Bologna e alle dignità ecclesiastiche nel Veneto nei secoli XIV–XV*, SB, III (Florence, 1968).

Pouillon, D.H., 'Le manuscrit d'Assise, Bibl.comm.196. Description', *RTAM*, XII (1940), pp. 329–58,

Power, E, *Medieval English Nunneries c.1275–1535* (Cambridge, 1922).

Raine, A., *Medieval York: A Topographical Survey Based on Original Sources* (London, 1955).

Raine, J., *York*, Historic Towns Series (London, 1893).

Retucci, F., 'The *Sapientiale* of Thomas of York, OFM: The Fortunes and Misfortunes of a Critical Edition', *Bulletin de Philosophie Médiévale*, LII (2010), pp. 133–55.

Retucci, F., 'Tomasso di York, Eustrazio e la dottrina delle idee di Platone', *Per perscrutationem philosophicam Neue Perspektiven der mittelalterlichen Forshung*, ed. A. Beccarisi, R. Imbach and P. Porro, Corpus Philosophorum Teutonicorum medii aevi, Beiheft, IV (Hamburg, 2008), pp. 79–110.

Rex, R., 'The Friars in the English Reformation', *The Beginnings of English Protestantism*, ed. P. Marshall and A. Ryrie (Cambridge, 2002), pp. 38–59.

Richard Scrope: Archbishop, Rebel, Martyr, ed. P.J.P. Goldberg (Donington, 2007).

Richardson, H., 'The Mendicant Friars of Medieval York', *Annual Report of the Council of the Yorkshire Philosophical Society, for 1965* (1952–65), pp. 40–73.

Rimington, F.C., with a foreword by Maurice F. Beresford, *The Deserted Medieval Village of Hatterborard, near Scarborough*, Scarborough and District Archaeological Society, Research Report, 2 (Scarborough, 1961).

Robinson, C.A., 'The Tithe-Heresy of Friar William Russell', *Albion*, 8 (1976), pp. 1–16.

Robinson, P.R., *Catalogue of Dated and Datable Manuscripts c.737–1600 in Cambridge Libraries*, 2 vols (Cambridge, 1988).

Robson, M.J.P., 'Benefactors of the Greyfriars in York Alms from Testators, 1530–1538', *NH*, XXXVIII (2001), pp. 221–39.

Robson, M.J.P., 'A Biographical Register of the English Province of the Greyfriars: A Sample from the Custody of York', *The Franciscan Order in the Medieval English Province and Beyond*, ed. Robson and P. Zutshi, Church, Faith and Culture in the Medieval West (Amsterdam, 2018), pp. 67–92.

Robson, M.J.P., 'The Birth-Place of Blessed John Duns Scotus: Thomas Gascoigne, a Hitherto Unnoticed Witness', *MF*, CIII (2003), pp. 703–18.

Robson, M.J.P., 'Boniface of Pisa, O.Min., bishop of Iglesias and then Corbavia (†1341)', in *Biblioteca Francescana Sarda*, VII (1997), pp. 219–44.

Robson, M.J.P., 'Franciscan Bachelors and Masters of Theology in the Custody of York (1250–1350)', *Revue d'histoire ecclésiastique,* CXI (2016), pp. 5–33.

Robson, M.J.P., 'The Franciscan Custody of York in the Thirteenth Century', *The Friars in Medieval Britain, Proceedings of the 2007 Harlaxton Symposium*, ed. N. Rogers, Harlaxton Medieval Studies, XIX (Donington, 2010), pp. 1–24.

Robson, M.J.P., 'The Franciscans in the Custody of York: Evidence Drawn from Chronicles and Annals', *Self-Representation of Medieval Religious Communities: The British Isles in Context*, ed. A. Müller and K. Stöber, Vita Regularis, XL (Münster, 2009), pp. 341–68.

Robson, M.J.P., *The Franciscans in the Medieval Custody of York,* Borthwick Institute of Historical Research, University of York, Borthwick Papers, XCIII (York, 1997).

Robson, M.J.P., 'The Grey Friars in York, c.1450–1530', *The Religious Orders in Pre-Reformation England*, ed. J.G. Clark, Studies in the History of Medieval Religion, XVIII (Woodbridge, 2002), pp. 109–19.

Robson, M.J.P., 'The Greyfriars' Itinerant Ministry inside their *Limitatio*: Evidence from the Custody of York, c.1230–1539', *Canterbury Studies in Franciscan History*, I, ed. M.J.P. Robson and J. Röhrkasten (Canterbury, 2008), pp. 9–49.

Robson, M.J.P., 'The Greyfriars of Lincoln, c.1230–1330: The Establishment of the Friary and the Friars' Ministry and Life in the City and its Environs', *Franciscan Organisation in the Mendicant Context: Formal and Informal Structures of the Friars' Lives and Ministry in the Middle Ages*, ed. M.J.P. Robson and J. Röhrkasten, Vita Regularis, XLIV (Münster, 2010), pp. 119–37.

Robson, M.J.P., 'Hugh, the exiled bishop of Byblos (c.1245/50–1325)', in *Il Santo, rivista antoniana di storia dottrina arte*, XXXV (1995), pp. 479–501.

Robson, M.J.P., 'Nicholas Warter, the Franciscan Bishop of Dromore (c.1372–1448)', *Collectanea Hibernica*, XLII (2000), pp. 7–26.

Robson, M.J.P., 'Peter of Bologna (c.1260–1332) Franciscan Bishop of Corbavia', *CF*, LXIII (1993), pp. 7–35.

Robson, M.J.P., 'A Prosopographical Study of the Greyfriars of York, ca.1230–1538', *Medieval Prosopography*, XXII (2001), pp. 1–29.

Robson, M.J.P., 'Robert Grosseteste and the Greyfriars in the Diocese of Lincoln', *Robert Grosseteste and the Beginnings of a British Theological Tradition,* ed. M. O'Carroll, Bibliotheca Seraphico-Capuccina, LXIX (Rome, 2003), pp. 289–317.

Robson, M.J.P., 'Robert Grosseteste: his memory among the Greyfriars, his cult in Lincoln cathedral and the petition for his canonisation', in *Miscellanea Francescana*, CIV (2004), pp. 306–23.

Robson, M.J.P., 'William de Calverley (c.1275–1319), a Notable Franciscan Friar', *Miscellany*, PThS, The Leeds Historical Society, 2nd series, XX (2010), pp. 1–11.

Robson, M.J.P., 'William Duffield, bishop of Ascalon', *The Oxford Dictionary of National Biography*, www.oxforddnb.com (from 8 October 2009).

Robson, M.J.P., 'York, Dean and Chapter Library, MS.Add.770, a Franciscan Volume Once Owned by Ralph Thoresby', *Miscellany*, PThS, 2nd series, XX (2010), pp. 23–39.

Roest, B., *A History of Franciscan Education (c. 1210–1517)*, Education and Society in the Middle Ages and Renaissance, XI (Leiden, 2000).

Roest, B., 'The Role of Lectors in the Religious Formation of Franciscan Friars, Nuns and Tertiaries', *Studio e Studia: Le scuole degli ordini mendicanti tra XIII e XIV secolo, Atti del XXIX Convegno internazionale, Assisi, 11–13 ottobre 2001* (Spoleto, 2002), pp. 83–115.

Rollason, L., 'Medieval Mortuary Rolls: Prayers for the Dead and Travel in Medieval England', *NH*, XLVIII (2011), pp. 187–223.

Rosemann, P.W., *Peter Lombard*, Great Medieval Thinkers (Oxford, 2002).

Sayles, G.O., *The Functions of the Medieval Parliament of England* (London, 1988).

Şenocak, N., *The Poor and the Perfect: The Rise of Learning in the Franciscan Order, 1209–1310* (Ithaca, 2012).

Sharp, D.E., *Franciscan Philosophy at Oxford*, BSFS, XVI (London, 1930).

Sheehan, M., 'A List of Thirteenth-Century English Wills', *The Genealogist's Magazine*, XIII (1961), pp. 259–65.

Sheehan, M.W., 'The Religious Orders 1220–1370', *The History of the University of Oxford, vol. I, The Early Oxford Schools*, ed. J.I. Catto (Oxford, 1984), pp. 193–223.

Smith, D.M., 'Alexander Hamilton Thompson', *Some Historians of Lincolnshire*, Occasional Papers in Lincolnshire History and Archaeology, IX (1982), pp. 61–66.

Smith, D.M., *Cause Papers at York: The Court of York 1301–1399*, BTC, XIV (York, 1988).

Smith, D.M., *Guide to Bishops' Registers of England and Wales: A Survey from the Middle Ages to the Abolition of Episcopacy in 1646*, Royal Historical Society, Guides and Handbooks, XI (London, 1981).

Smith, D.M., 'A Reconstruction of the Lost Register of the Vicars-General of Archbishop Thoresby of York', part 1, *Borthwick Institute Bulletin*, III, no. 1 (1983), pp. 29–61.

Smith, D.M., 'A Reconstruction of the Lost Register of the Vicars-General of Archbishop Thoresby of York', part 2, *Borthwick Institute Bulletin*, III, no. 2 (1984), pp. 102–13.

Smith, D.M., 'A Reconstruction of the York *Sede Vacante* Register, 1352–3', *Borthwick Institute Bulletin*, I (1976), pp. 75–90.

Smith, D.M., 'Suffragan Bishops in the Medieval Diocese of Lincoln', *Lincolnshire History and Archaeology*, XVII (1982), pp. 17–27.

Stella, P.T., '"Res generabilis simplex est": il radicalismo antilemorfico di Tomasso Barneby e di Giacomo di Carseto nella recensione di Pieto Tomás (Thomae)', *Salesianum*, XXXVIII (1976), pp. 775–806.

Stephenson, M., 'Monumental Brasses in the West Riding', *YAJ*, XV (1900), pp. 1–60.

Storey, R.L., *Thomas Langley and the Bishopric of Durham 1406–1437* (London, 1961).

Stubbs, W., *Registrum Sacrum Anglicanum* (Oxford, 1897).

Tanner, T., *Notitia Monastica; or, an account of all the abbies, priories, and houses of friers formerly in England and Wales, and also of all the colleges and hospitals founded before A.D.MDXL* (Cambridge, 1787).

Taylor, J., *English Historical Literature in the Fourteenth Century* (Oxford, 1987).

Taylor, J., 'Fourteenth-Century Chronicle Writing in the Diocese of York', *Proceedings of the Leeds Philosophical and Literary Society* (Literary and Historical Section), VIII, part 1 (1956), pp. 51–61.

Taylor, J., *Medieval Historical Writing in Yorkshire*, St Anthony's Hall Publications, XIX (York, 1961).

Thomson, R.M., *Catalogue of Medieval Manuscripts of Latin Commentaries on Aristotle in British Libraries* (Turnhout, 2011).

Traver, A.G., 'Thomas of York's Role in the Conflict between Mendicants and Seculars at Paris', *FS*, LVII (1999), pp. 179–202.

Vickers, N., 'The Social Class of Yorkshire Medieval Nuns', *YAJ*, LXVII (1995), pp. 127–32.

Walker, J.W., 'The Burghs of Cambridgeshire and Yorkshire and the Watertons of Lincolnshire and Yorkshire', *YAJ*, XXX (1930–31), pp. 311–419.

Walmsley, C., 'Some Dutch Franciscans in England during the Later Middle Ages', *Tijdschrift voor Taal en Letteren*, XXVII (1939), pp. 242–60.

Watt, J.A., *The Church and the Two Nations in Medieval Ireland*, Cambridge Studies in Medieval Life and Thought, 3rd series, III (Cambridge, 1970).

Watt, J.A., 'The Papacy and Ireland in the Fifteenth Century', *The Church, Politics and Patronage in the Fifteenth Century*, ed. R.B. Dobson (Gloucester, 1984), pp. 133–45.

Webster, L.E. and J. Cherry, 'Medieval Britain in 1975', *Medieval Archaeology*, XX (1976), pp. 158–201.

Werronen, S., *Religion, Time and Memorial Culture in Late Medieval Ripon*, Royal Historical Society, Studies in History, new series (Woodbridge, 2017).

Whitfield, D.W., 'Conflicts of Personality and Principle: The Political and Religious Crisis in the English Franciscan Province, 1400–1409', *FS*, XVII (1957), pp. 321–62.

Wilford, J., 'Lincoln Greyfriars: Retrospect and Prospect', *Lincoln Archaeology*, VI (1993–94), pp. 38–40.

Wilkinson, L.J., *Women in Thirteenth-Century Lincolnshire*, Royal Historical Society, Studies in History, new series (Woodbridge, 2007).

Wilson, J.M., *The Worcester Liber Albus: Glimpses of Life in a Great Benedictine Monastery in the Fourteenth Century* (London, 1920).

Wordsworth, C., 'On Some Pardons or Indulgences Preserved in Yorkshire, 1412–1527', *YAJ*, XVI (1902), pp. 369–423.

York Civic Ordinances, 1301, ed. M. Prestwich, Borthwick Institute of Historical Research, University of York, Borthwick Papers, XLIX (York, 1976).

Index